MW00807489

GENEALOGY

OF THE

BALCH FAMILIES

IN

AMERICA

BY

GALUSHA B. BALCH, M. D.,

YONKERS, N. Y.

EBEN PUTNAM,
SALEM, MASSACHUSETTS,
PUBLISHER.

1897.

PREFACE.

The making of genealogies is as old as the history of Adam. With it, Moses begins the history of his race. The reverence for ancestry, the love of kindred, and the care of offspring are inherent in human nature and fostered by civilization. Though the love of parents and children leads the affections in divergent lines, yet some subtle connection seems to make them one. With development of either they both increase, and our debt of gratitude to noble ancestry inspires us to repay it in fuller measure to our children and contribute our proper share in the progress of the race.

The guiding power of surrounding conditions in selecting and fixing the peculiarities of animal species, is alike potent in imparting race types to man. The great mass of recently emigrated population has sprung from a past in which slavish obedience under monarchial rule has stifled every tendency to independent progressive thought. They have been taught no ambition beyond material prosperity, and have failed to learn the lesson of self-government on which our country must depend for its honorable perpetuity. Far different have been the influences at work alone those lines that run to the early English pioneers. To them America's golden allurements were political and religious freedom. These were the ambitions of the people from which they came ; then the Puritans revolted against the tyranny and licentiousness of the Stuarts, and England was preparing the civil war which resulted in the dethronement and beheading of Charles I.

Having been nurtured with these tendencies, they crossed the mysterious ocean when the paths were as yet untried when the goal itself was unknown, and America held out but the opportunities to grow the fruits of liberty. The wild freedom of a new country was poison to the unaccustomed. From it Weston's men were forced to flee; and even to those who had acquired a taste, it at first brought many evils; but they were evils whose final correction came by continued freedom.

Thus reared with an ardent love of liberty, John Balch left Old England for the New, and with this bias he and his associates and their descendants helped to lay deeply and well the foundations of our Nation. It should therefore be a matter of proper pride to know that the family line dates back to a sturdy, liberty-loving ancestry and passed through generations of industry, thrift and New England hardihood, calculated to produce a self-reliant capable manhood. For the most part the families have led quiet uneventful lives. They have lived long and left small estates, but for their descendants they have given that best dower of all, a constitution free from inherited diseases, a far better factor for happiness and usefulness than inherited wealth.

The earliest efforts, so far as known, in the preparation of a genealogy of the Balch family was made about a century ago by Benjamin Balch, of Essex Co., Massachusetts. Seven hundred words comprised all that he recorded. Next followed some additions to this by Dr. William F. Balch, and the whole was published in the New England Historical and Genealogical Register for July, 1855. A few years later David M. Balch took up the subject and worked at it, until about 1876. In this he was assisted by Frank W. Balch, and together they explored the early records in Essex county, and vicinity, and collected considerable material. In 1884, I commenced a search for records of direct ancestors. The work proved a fascinating one and quickly led into all the other family branches.

Genealogical investigation is beset with many difficulties, and some of the solutions have been reached in curious and unexpected ways. In several instances, slight clues concerning members of the family would be found which baffled every effort at systematic investigation, but whose records were traced through unexpected channels. One of these was 63 Josiah[5], another was 357 Cyrus[7] and a third was 882 Samuel Williams[7].

After the record of the latter had gone into type two of his daughters, both over eighty years of age, were found to be living within a few minutes' ride of the office of the writer's son. From them it was ascertained that their father was United States Minister at Rio Janeiro, Brazil, in the early part of this century. There are a few puzzles, similar to the above which have as yet resisted solution. They belong to the Maryland family and are appended as "broken families."

Acknowledgments are due and are hereby made to William Lincoln Balch, of Boston, for his contributions of the chapters on Name, Arms, and English records; to David M. Balch, and Frank W. Balch, for kindly placing their manuscript notes at my service; to Augustus A. Galloupe, of Beverly, who, though no relative of the family, has given valuable assistance, and to all the members of the family, both of the North and South, who have so kindly aided me in the preparation of this work.

GALUSHA B. BALCH, M. D.

THE NAME.

The task of tracing the descent of any of the millions of families inhabiting this planet is not, under the most favorable circumstances, an easy one, but is beset at every step with various difficulties. The present inquiry into the origin and history of the Balch family, while simplified by the peculiarity of the name and the comparatively small number who have borne it, is, at the same time, rendered more difficult by those very conditions, especially as few of the name have ever achieved more than local distinction, though they have always been respected in the localities where they have lived.

John Balch [the first in America] came from Somerset, England, to Massachusetts, in 1623. With this central fact the Balch genealogy in America begins, and its branches have been traced out down to the present day. But to go even one step backward from that point has not been so easy, and it must be confessed at the outset that the missing links between the Balches who came to America and those who remained in the old country have not been found.

The search, however, has brought to light the names of many Balches in England and much information in regard to them which cannot fail to be of interest to all who bear the name in this country, for there can be little or no doubt that they were all related to each other in the same way that the American Balches are related.

The subject of the origin of the name of Balch opens an ample field for philological discussion, which has not been covered to any extent, for the reasons already indicated. It seems tolerably certain that the name is of Teutonic derivation, and as an English patronym, therefore, might have come in with the Saxons, about A. D. 500.

Mark Antony Lower, one of the first to write analytically on the subject of British surnames, says in his "Patronymica Britannica," that the name is an abbreviation of Balchin, a very old Teutonic personal name—in old German Baldechin. In his "Essay on Family Nomenclature," however, he says that Balchin, in the middle and western counties of England means an unfledged bird.

Robert Ferguson, in "English Surnames and their place in the Teutonic Family," after supposing a relation between the name of the great Italian poet, Dante Alighieri, and the English name Alger, observes: "Other of the Italian poets have names more certainly Teutonic, as Alamanni, Baldacchini," etc. "These correspond with the old German names Alaman, Baldechin, etc., and with our Allman, Balchin," etc. Further on, in speaking of names derived from mental and moral qualities, he says, "Thus we have Bold and its patronymic Balding—Ball, the patronymic Ballinger, the diminutive Balchin, Baldock, etc."

How far the imagination enters into comparative philology is seen when it is observed that another writer on " English Surnames," Charles Wareing Bardsley, while not taking cognizance of Balchin at all, derives Ballinger from boulanger, a baker, and Bald and Ball not from bold, but from the very prosaic characteristic of baldness of the cranium !

William F. Balch [1100] devoted considerable time in the early fifties to an investigation of the origin of the family, and he mentions in a paper published in the New England Historical and Genealogical Register for July, 1855, that he found the name of " Balchman of Bodeherstegate " on the roll of " Battle Abbey " [A. D. 1066]. The name of Balchi, he also says, is to be found in " Doomsday Book," the great survey of England, which was made by order of William the Conqueror, in 1086, and to have been recorded therein the bearer of the name must have been of at least Thane's rank. He also states that a John Balch was Sheriff of Somerset in 1392, and, starting with that name, he constructs a pedigree ending with John Balch who came to America in 1623.

Now all these assumptions can be shown to be erroneous, and though it is only just to say that they were not put forth as being absolutely correct, it seems proper to call attention to them, as they are in print [in the Historical and Genealogical Register,] and copies of the false pedigree are in existence in possession of members of the family and might prove misleading.

In the first place, the document, usually called the " Roll of Battle Abbey " was a list of those Normans who took part in the conquest of England, and of course one would not look there for a Saxon name. The list referred to in the article in question was really of the names of residents of the settlement which sprang up around the Abbey while it was building, to commemorate the battle of Hastings, composed of those brought there from surrounding counties for that purpose, together with the amount of tax, or the kind of service, which they were to render for their houses and lands, which they held under feudal tenure. These persons were, of course, the Saxon inhabitants, but the name, No. 104 on the list, which the compiler mistook for "Balchman" of Bode-herstegate was really "Blacheman" and he was no more likely to have been an ancestor of a Balch than No. 26, "Blacheni, the cowherd."

The "John Balch" who, he says, was sheriff of Somerset in 1392, was, by a similar error in the eyesight, really John Bache, probably of Dorset, as those two counties had but one sheriff before 1566.

That disposes of the foundation of the pedigree, and as for the second step it is certain that no George Balch, between the years 1362 and 1420, was "the founder of St. Andries, the seat of the family in Somersetshire," as that estate, which is one of the best known in the county, did not come into the possession of a Balch until long after John Balch had come to America.

The earliest mention of a Balch in Somerset records, which is at present known, occurs in a tax list compiled in the first year of the reign of Edward III, 1327, and it is remarkable that at that early date it takes the simple form of Balch, while in the meantime it has, at different periods, and in individual instances, lapsed into such odd orthography as Balche, Balsh, Balshe, Baulch, Bawlch, etc.

But in 1327 at least two persons in Somerset were taxed under that name. "Willelmo Balch, xii d., "Purye" [perhaps Puriton Hundred] and "Roberto Balch, i i j S., v. d.," in "Manerium de Wryngton" [manor of Wryngton]. There also appears on the same roll the name Balth, Blatche, Borliche, Barlich, Balrich, Bolde and Bald— any or all of whom might have been Balches, since other and far more common names, such as Baker, Brown and Smith, appear with almost as peculiar variations.

It would be strange indeed, at a time when the English

language was not yet crystalized, when only "clerks" and priests could write, and official documents were drawn up in a medley of Latin, Norman-French and Anglo-Saxon, if such a name had escaped variation. One can well imagine the queer twists that spelling would take, when the Norman tax gatherer attempted to set down the name of a "Zummerzet" rustic as given to him with a broad west country accent.

Barlich and Barliche would certainly not be improbable metamorphoses under such circumstances, and, indeed, the fact that these forms have not survived would seem to be evidence that they were merely clerical errors. Some of the forms which we know the name to have assumed at later dates were evidently phonetic, and point to the probability that the "a" in Balch had a very broad sound, much broader than it has at present as pronounced in this country.

It is of interest in this connection to remark that some of the name in London pronounce the "a" sharp, as in "bat," and also to note that, out of the more than four million people in the British metropolis, there are but six of the name of Balch registered in the Post Office Directory of London of a recent date—both "court" and "commercial" divisions included— while there are an equal number of Balchins, one Baulch, one Balck and one Baldach.

It thus appears that Balchin remains a surname in England today, and seems, like Balch, to be a shortening of the earlier form—Baldechin. It has been spelled Balchen, Ballchen and Balchan. In 1744 Admiral Sir John Ballchen was lost in his ship, the Victory, off Alderney.

Baldachin is defined by Johnson's Cyclopedia—and the definition is retained by our modern American dictionaries— as "The canopy carried over the Host in processions. The term is derived from Baldach, a corruption of Bagdad, the early seat of the manufacture [of the stuff of which the canopy was made] and was originally applied to the canopy carried over an Oriental prince."

It has been objected to by a scholarly member of the Balch

family that the deduction of Baldach from Bagdad is unten-
able on philological grounds, and he remarks that " the old
Persian city Balkh bears exactly our family name." But
whether Balkh or Baldach furnished the root of the word, it
appears to have come from the Orient. The Teutons came
from the East, their language, culminating in modern German, had many Oriental affinities, and it is not too improbable
to suppose that the Teuton who took, or more likely had bestowed upon him, the name of Baldechin, might have been
one of the bearers of a princely or ecclesiastical
canopy.

The stuff of which these canopies, and priestly vestments,
generally, was made, was a very rich fabric of silk and gold
embroidery, and in old English records the word is variously
found written baudekin, bawdekin and even bodkyn and
bodkin, certainly as wide a departure from baldachin in orthography as is Balch.

THE COAT OF ARMS.

Though perhaps not really germane to the subject, it seems
interesting to note that in the reign of Edward IV, the
baudekin reserved by sumptuary law for the use of royalty
was woven of blue and gold stripes, which happen to be the
chief colors of the Balch coat of arms. Those colors, with
the red in which the " bend " crossing the shield is embla-
zoned, are esteemed as among the most noble in heraldry, and
the simplicity of the coat itself would seem to be an evidence
of antiquity. There is nothing however, to show that it was
granted at a very early date. It appears in the visitation of
Somerset in 1623, the very year in which John Balch came
to America.

The visitation of the counties by the King's stewards and
officers-at-arms, under special warrants of the sovereign, for
the purpose of collecting and recording the pedigrees and
arms of the nobility and gentry resident therein, is of very

ancient date, and the genealogies and arms thus collected are well known by the name of " Visitations." These records are preserved in the College of Arms, London, from the year 1523 to 1686.

There were visitations of Somerset in 1531, the 22d year of the reign of Henry VIII.; by Benolte, Clarencieux King-of-Arms, in 1573, the 15th year of Elizabeth; by Brooke, Clarencieux, by his deputies, Henry St. George, Richmond herald, and Sampson Lennard, Bluemantle pursuivant, in 1623 by the last mentioned, and in 1672, 23d year of Charles II., and the last visitation, made by Bysshe, Clarencieux.

The arms of Balche, of Horton, as illustrated in the frontispiece to this volume, and accompanied by a pedigree which forms the basis of the sketch of early English Balches, which follows, are thus described in the Visitation of 1623:

" Barry of six, Or and Azure ; on a bend, engrailed, Gules, three spear heads, Argent."

No crest is described with this shield.

Sir Bernard Burke, the English authority, in his " General Armory of England, Scotland and Wales," edition of 1883, describes the arms of Balche of Horton as above, and adds: " Balche [Virginia, Maryland and Philadelphia, North America], the same arms. Crest, out of a ducal coronet, Or, a demi-griffin, ppr.

Mottoes — Ubi libertas, ibi patria [Where liberty is there is my country]. " Not laws of man, but laws of God."

Another motto which has been attached to the arms, as used by the Philadelphia branch, is, " Coeur et Courage font l'ouvrage,"—Heart and courage do the work.

It has been stated that some of the southern Balches, being allied to the Macgregors, use their crest, a lion's head proper, crowned with an antique crown.

. Culleton, a London heraldic engraver, gives the Balch

arms as already described, and the motto as being, "Fait
Devoyr," "Do your duty."

E. de Vermont, in his "American Heraldry," copies
Burke.

Daniel Balch, of Newburyport, Mass., in his will, dated
March 9, 1789, left to his eldest son, Daniel, Jr., "my coat
of arms." That he inherited his copy from his father, Rev.
William, or his grandfather, Freeborn, or that John brought
it with him to America, in 1623, is a matter of mere conjec-
ture. To a copy in the possession of a descendant of Daniel
is attached the note: "The above are the arms of Balche
of Horton, in the county of Somerset, as they appear recorded
to that family in the Herald's visitation of that county, made
in 1623. Albert W. Woods, Herald." As Sir Albert W.
Woods is at present (1896) Garter King of Arms of the
Heralds' College, it is evident that this copy it comparatively
recent.

The crest and motto found with a copy of the Balch arms,
published by a descendant of Daniel—William F.—in the
New England Historical and Genealogical Register, in 1855,
have been a puzzle. The crest is a mailed arm and gaunt-
letted hand, grasping broken spears or javelins. The Latin

motto accompanying this crest—"Usus a
Punctum"—seems to refer to the spears,
but, with its grammatical incorrectness,
leaves a doubt whether it was meant to
convey the admonition to "use to the
point," or the boast that the spears had
been so used, as their broken condition
would suggest. Nothing is known in the
history of the family in England to justify
such a warlike blazon.

A variation of the coat of arms, in which the spear heads
are replaced by golden disks, or "bezants," a word derived
from Byzantium, the ancient Constantinople, and applied to
gold coins of that country, appears in the church of St.

Mary, in the parish of Poorstock, in Dorset. In the chancel is this escutcheon: "Barry of six, Or and Azure; on a bend, indented, Gules, three Bezants." Under it, "Scutum Gulielmi Balch, obiit 89 die of Januarii, anno Dom., 1681." The shield of this William Balch is thus nearly the same as the one already described, except that the "bend" has serrated, instead of scalloped edges—which might have been merely the result of imperfect workmanship or imperfect description—and the silver spear heads are changed to golden disks. The peculiarity of the inscription, in giving the date of the bearer's decease as the 89th of January, may, perhaps, be accounted for by an attempt to reconcile the "old style" and "new style" of chronology, between which there was then a difference of ten days.

As to the crests and helmet used by the American Balches there appears to be no old authority. The helmet used by William F. Balch in the Historical and Genealogical Register is that belonging to royalty, so it must be wrong. The helmet should be that of an esquire.

EARLY HOME OF THE FAMILY IN SOMERSETSHIRE.

John Balch, the earliest ancestor in America of the New England branch, the first of his name to come to the New World, was undoubtedly a member of a family once numerous and well known in Somerset. He is said, in Felt's "Annals of Salem" and in Hubbard's History of New England, to have come "from near Bridgwater," which is in the very heart of Somersetshire, and one of its largest and most ancient towns. It is doubtful if he ever resided there, and a recent search of the well preserved parchment records of the church of St. Mary Magdalen, from the year 1575 to a date later than that of his emigration to Massachusetts, failed to reveal any mention of the baptism, marriage or burial of a Balch. The name, however, appears in Bridgwater at a later date, and may still be traced upon the worn memorial stones with which the church aisles are flagged.

Benjamin Balch, who left a brief genealogical manuscript of the family more than a century ago, said that, according to family tradition, John Balch came from Horton.   At all events, it is extremely probable that he was a member,—and as is shown by his becoming a pioneer in the westward migration of his countrymen beyond the sea, doubtless one of the younger and dowerless cadets—of an old family in one of the most ancient corners of Saxon England.

Somerset, the English home of the Balches, bears upon almost every square mile of its topography, on every page of its history, and in all its wealth of legends, quaint nomenclature and curious customs, traces of the tidal wave of conquest that surged over it in early days, and, retreating, left upon the land their indelible impress.

Briton, Gaul, Roman, Saxon, Dane and Norman in turn possessed and made for themselves a home of the fair southwest of England, and left behind them the tokens of their prowess, language, laws, religion and civilization.

While the Britons, who may be regarded as the aboriginal inhabitants, were in possession, the Belgæ, a warlike people of Celtic origin, from Gaul, descended upon the country about 350 years before the Christian era, and overran that portion which is now known as Somerset, Dorset and Devon, together with parts of Cornwall, Wiltshire, Hampshire, Sussex and Middlesex.   They gained such a foothold that the portion which they held was formally divided off from that retained by the British by an immense trench and earthwork, 80 miles long, called Wansdyke, portions of which still remain running across the country to the Bristol channel.   When they were securely in possession they were joined by a large accession of their countrymen, under Divitiacus, King of Soissons, in France, who came over about B. C. 68.

Then came the Romans, about A. D. 40, who drove out the Cangii, a posthumous tribe of the Belgæ, and retained possession for 400 years, leaving everywhere fortifications, roads, temples, baths and other substantial evidences of their occupation.

About half a century later the Saxons came upon the scene, landing on the shores of Hampshire under the leaders Cerdic and Cynric, in A. D. 495, and spreading slowly through Hampshire, Dorset, and Somerset, for some years, if not generations, stopping at the rivers Parret [ancient Pedred] and Upper Axe, which were an understood boundary between the Saxon English and British races.

Then the Danes invaded the country, keeping it for generations in a state of seige, until they were finally conquered and expelled, and the Saxon heptarchy grew and strengthened, only to fall into the hands of the Norman Conqueror, A. D., 1066.

The neighborhood in which we know that Balches have dwelt for more than 500 years, and very likely for a thousand, is intimately connected with the legendary history of the British hero, King Arthur, and the Saxon hero, Alfred the Great.

Cadbury Castle, the site of an ancient stronghold, is said to be the far famed Camelot or Camalet, which was one of the stations of the famous Round Table of King Arthur, the other principal places where it was set up being Winchester and Hampshire and Caerleon, in Monmouthshire, the latter county being formerly in Wales.

At Glastonbury Abbey, according to ancient writers, was the tomb of King Arthur, where he was buried after his last and fatal battle.

Of all the Arthurian legends the most widely known is, perhaps, that of the Holy Grail, which has figured largely in modern literature, art and drama, and with Glastonbury Abbey is connected the legend of the Holy Grail and Holy Thorn. This remarkable story is to the effect that Joseph of Arimathea, the wealthy man who offered his own tomb as a sepulchre for Jesus of Nazareth, with his own hands washed and prepared the body for burial. Afterward, at the command of the angel Gabriel, he left country, home and kindred, to preach the gospel to the heathen of distant lands. Joseph took with him on his mission the Holy Grail, that miraculous chalice, made of a single precious stone, brought from heaven by angels, from which Christ drank at the last supper, and in which the Arimathean caught and saved the last drops of His blood as he came from the cross. In another vessel were the blood and water which he preserved when he washed the body of his lord, and he also carried with him as a staff a piece of thorn tree from the Holy Land.

Combwich, in Somerset, on the river Parret, was the landing place in Britain of Joseph of Arimathea, according to this legend, and when he reached Glastonbury he planted his staff in the ground and established there the first Christian church. The thorn took root and flourished, and, in proof of its origin, blossomed miraculously at Christmas ever after. This legend is thus narrated in some curious old verse.

"The good saint Arimathean Joseph, borne by the Parret's tide
To Combwich, o'er the Mendips; at length he came to Glaston's Hide;
'Here I'll build a wattle church' He planted a Christian staff.
'Twas Christmas now—at Xmas time the staff with blossoms laugh;
A miracle—a miracle—a miracle it turned to be
That Christian churches from that time should cover the whole country.
The staff was a thorn brought from the Holy Land—'tis known.
The Christian churches throughout England—from its branches they
    have grown."

"Even as late as James II.'s time" says a Bridgwater antiquary, "the blossoms were esteemed such curiosities by people of all nations that Bristol merchants made a traffic of them and exported them to foreign parts."

The flowering of the miraculous thorn tree is noted in the Gentleman's Magazine, for 1753. People were then under some embarassment as to dates, owing to the change made in the calendar from Old to New style; "A vast number visited the noted thorn on Christmas day, new style, but there was no bloom. So they watched till January 5, the Christmas

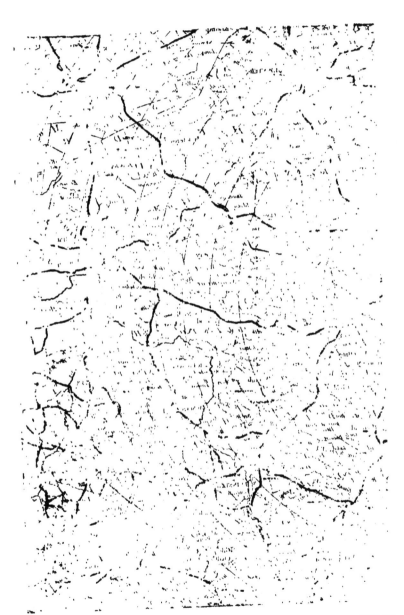

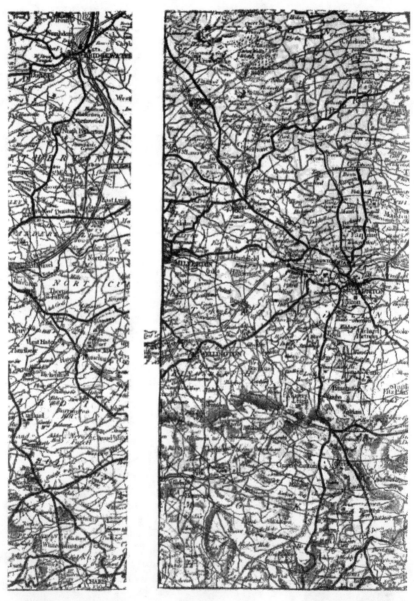

SOMERSETSHIRE. (FROM THE   MAP OF A PART OF S(

day of old style, when, true to tradition, it bloomed once more."

Another interesting legend of Glastonbury Abbey is that its first abbot was St. Patrick, A. D. 583, who was succeeded by St. Benignus or Benedict, a pupil of St. Patrick, who was also his successor in the archiepiscopal see of Armagh, Ireland, A. D. 601. The 27th abbot, according to this legendary history, was the famous St. Dunstan, afterwards primate of England, who had a personal encounter with the Evil One and put him to flight by seizing him by the nose with a pair of tongs.

In the Saxon era Somerset was a central part of the important Kingdom of Wessex [West Seaxe] other Kingdoms of the heptarchy being Essex [East Seaxe] Sussex [South Seaxe] and Middle Seaxe. It was in the Isle of Æthelingey [isle of Nobles] now known as Athelney, at the junction of the rivers Tone, from which comes the name of Tonetown— [Taunton] and Parret, in the parish of Lyng, about seven miles from Bridgwater, that tradition says that in 879 the great Aelfred was sheltered from the Danes by the herdsman Denwulf, whose goodwife has passed into history from having scolded the King for neglecting to watch the cakes by the fire while she fed the pigs. When later, by strategy, Alfred surrounded and totally defeated the Danes at Ætheldune, now Edington, seizing the Danish banner with its magically wrought raven, it was at Aller church, near Langport, that Guthrum, the vanquished Danish chieftain, allowed himself to be baptized Edelstane, Alfred standing as sponsor.

Cannington, which is mentioned in the English chronological notes as being, among other places, a locality in which "Nicholas Balche, de Horton, generosus" (that is, well or nobly born), owned property, was the birthplace of the "fair Rosamond" Clifford. Cannington was once the abode of the Cangii, a tribe of the Belgæ, and the legions of the Emperor Claudius are said to have passed that way at the time of the second Roman invasion.

The river Parret, which, the earlier legend tells us, bore
Joseph of Arimathea to Combwich, and which a later, if not
more veracious tradition says bore John Balch to the ocean,
on his way to America, flows completely across Somerset,
through a rich and fertile country.

Running in the same general direction as the Parret, a few
miles to the westward, are the Quantock hills, which rise at
their highest point to about 1200 feet, and enjoy a local reputation for picturesque beauty.

The Quantocks are truly picturesque, and where they ter-
minate, near the Bristol channel, are located East and West
Quantoxhead, names which are to be found in connection
with the manor of St. Audries, the seat for many years of a
branch of the Balch family, and that from which the southern branch in this country claims its descent.

A "History and Antiquities of the County of Somerset"
was published by the Rev. John Collinson, vicar of Long
Ashton, in 1791, to which Robert Everard Balch, Esq., and
George Balch, Esq., of St. Audries, were subscribers, and in
its pages the estate is thus described:

"St. Audries, or West Quantockshead, lies eastward from
St. Decumans, close under the steep western head of Quantock, sheltered from the east and northeast winds, with the
sea within a mile to the north and northwest, and a very rich
and beautiful country to the south and west.

"This manor was given by the Conqueror to Sir William
de Mohun, and is thus recorded in the survey [Doomsday
Book]: William himself holds Cantocheve. Elnod held it
in the time of King Edward, gelded for three hides and a
half. The arable is eight carucates. In demesne are three
carucates, and seven servants and ten villanes, and four cot-
tagers, with six ploughs. There are sixteen acres of meadow
and fifty acres of wood. Pasture one mile long and one mile
broad. It was worth three pounds, now four pounds.

"It was held in the time of King John by William de
Punchardon, of Dunster Castle. It then passed into the

family of Malet, and continued in that family, in a regular descent, until the time of Henry VIII. In the time of Charles I. Arthur Malet sold it to Thomas Malet, who died in 1664, leaving two sons, Sir John and Sir Michael. Sir John's grandson, William, was the last of the family that possessed St. Audries. The manor now [1791] belongs to Robert Everard Balch, Esq., who has an elegant little seat.

"The church is dedicated to St. Ethelred, or Aldred, from whom the parish received one of its appellations, of which that now used is a flagrant corruption."

In 1886 it was the residence of Rev. Elias Webb, and in 1878 of Sir A. Hood.

Some brief explanation of the old Saxon terms used in describing the above estate will form a fitting conclusion to this chapter. As regards the measures of land recorded in Doomsday Book, Sir H. Ellis says: "The truth seems to be that a hide, a yardland, a knight's fee, etc., etc., contained no certain number of acres, but varied in different places," but it has been described to be "as much as was sufficient to the cultivation of one plough."

"The carucate, which is also to be interpreted the plough land, was as much arable land as could be managed with one plough and the beasts belonging thereto in a year, pasture and houses for the householder, and cattle belonging to it," and it appears that "the hide was the measure of land in the Confessor's reign, the carucate [Latin, caruca, a team], that to which it was reduced by the Conqueror's new standard."

The hide is generally supposed to have been equal to 120 acres, though Sir R. W. Eyton, in "Doomsday Studies, an Analysis and Digest of the Somerset Survey," says that the Somerset hide was 299 2-3 acres. "Glaston's Hide," referred to in the verses relating the legend of Joseph of Arimathea, is that division of the country called "Glaston Twelve Hides," and was therefore anciently a description of the locality by measurement. Money mentioned in Domesday records is generally estimated as at thirty times its present value, so that the revenue of St. Audries, in the Conqueror's time, £4, was equivalent to at least $600. The term "hundred," to designate a division of an English county, had this origin, as defined by Blackstone: Ten families of freeholders made up a town or tithing, so ten tithings composed a superior division called a hundred, as consisting of ten times ten families.

SOME PRE-AMERICAN BALCHES.

The earliest glimpse we have of the Balch family in Somerset is afforded in a tax roll of that shire made in 1327, the first year of Edward III., the hero of Crecy, the father of the Black Prince, who there began his brilliant military career. It was toward the end of his reign that law pleadings in English were first permitted. The tax roll in which the Balches are inscribed is in Latin and is thus headed: "Collecta XX ^{me} domino Edwardo tercio, post conquestem Regi Anglie concesse facta, per Johannem de Clyvedon et Johannem de Erle, anno domini Regis primo."

The list includes all those in the county, worth 10 shillings or more, and among them are Willelmo Balch, Thrubbewelle, iiii s., Willelmo Balch, Purye, xii d., Roberto Balch, Manerium de Wryngton, iii s., and others.

A gap of 168 years intervenes before we find the next mention of a Balch. In May, 1495, three years after the discovery of America by Columbus, Richard Balch died in Farnham, Surrey. He made his will in Latin on the 12th of that month, and it was proved in the prerogative court of Canterbury on the 27th. He directs his body to be buried in the ancient chapel of the blessed virgin Mary, within the parish church of St. Andrew of Farnham, next the body of his father. He leaves to Matilda, relict of William Balche, a tenement in which she is living for the term of her life, and after her death to Nicholas Balche, son of the said William and Matilda. Other legatees are his wife Isabella, his daughter Florence [wife of Henry] Quynby, and John and Margaret Balch, children of

William Balch before mentioned. In this document the name is spelled both with and without the " e."

There is nothing to connect the interesting family group thus faintly outlined with any earlier or later Balches in the West of England.

It will be observed that this was in the days when England was still Catholic, the authority of the Roman Pontiff was acknowledged, and ecclesiastical institutions were liberally endowed with lands.

In the declaration of the rental and possessions of the chantries, colleges and free chapels in the county of Somerset, [Land Revenue Records, vol. 97], is the numeration of those in the deanery of Crewkerne, was included, in 1528, the chantry of St. Katherine, within the parish church at Ilminster, founded by John Wadham, " esquire." There was no monastic establishment at Ilminster, but the manor belonged to the abbey of Muchelney. The manor of Ilminster [the church on the river Ile] with the whole place, was given by Ina, King of the West Saxons, to the abbey of Muchelney, founded by King Athelstan in 939.

In 1528 its lands and possessions were "leased to farm for divers years and given for the fee or stipend of three chaplains or priests [John Rippe, Thomas Thorne and William Webbe] celebrating in the Ilminster parish church.

Among the tenants of these lands were a John and George Balche. The lease from the abbot reads in part as follows:

" All those messuages, lands, tenements, meadow pasture and feed, with their appurtenances, in the tithing of Winterhaye, in the parish of Ilminster, called Modies tenement, by John Sherbourne, abbot, formerly of the monastery of Muchelney aforesaid, and the convent of the same place, leased to farm to Henry Dawbeny, Kt., lord de Dawbeny, Thomas Speke, Hugh Paulet, Nicholas Wadham, Jr., esquire, John Pool, Thomas Michell, John Battyn, clerk, John Bonvyle, *John Balche*, *George Balche*, John Chyke, his son, Thomas Hawker, John Barfote, John Radbere, clerk, by deed of the same abbot and convent, given in their chapter house, under the seal of the convent aforesaid, the third day of November, 1528."

This John and George may have been, and probably were sons of the William Balche who figures next in our chronology as being "of Higham," Somerset, who died on the 20th of March, 1533, and as appears by the "inquisitio post mortem" taken at Wells in Somerset on the 8th of November, 1534, in the 25th year of the reign of Henry VIII. [the year in which popery was abolished in England], was a person who had acquired a large amount of landed property in the county. He was regarded as the founder of a family, and his name heads the family tree recorded in the Somerset visitation of 1623.

The inquisitio post mortem, or escheat, was instituted to enquire, at the death of any man of fortune, the value of his estate, the tenure by which it was holden, and who was the heir, and of what age, thereby to ascertain the value of the "premier seizin," or the "wardship and livery" accruing to the King thereupon. The court of wards and liveries, which was instituted in the reign of Henry VIII., was abolished, with other feudal customs, on the restoration of Charles II. Some idea of the contempt into which the practice had fallen may perhaps be gathered from the fact that the word cheat is derived from escheat.

The inquisition into the affairs of William Balche of Higham—which may have been the locality now known as High Ham—and which was conducted with a view, if possible, of putting money into the coffers of the bluff King Hal, by Thomas Horner as escheator, states that William, at the time of his death was "Seized of 200 acres of pasture, 100 acres of Arable and 40 acres of meadow and 30 acres of woodland, with the appurtenances, etc., in East Coker, etc., held of Sir William Courtenaye, Knight, as of his manor of East Coker, and the said William Balche died so seized; after whose death the said pasture and land and meadow and wood, with the

appurtenances, etc., descend to John Balche, as son and heir
of the said William.   And the said William was seized of one
messuage, 20 acres of land, meadow and pasture, with its
appurtenances, in Witencomb, in the said county of Somerset,
etc., held of Robert Pike, as of his manor of Pykkeseighe, etc.,
also of the moiety of a messuage, 20 acres pasture, with its
appurtenances, in Aldon, and 20 acres in Fydington, next
Stokegursey, etc., held of Sir William Tarrant, as of his manor
of Fydington, etc., all of which descended to John Balche, as
above.   The jurors found the said William Balche died 20
March, 24th of Henry VIII., and John Balche is the son and
heir of the said William, and is 36 years of age and more."

Two years later, April 1, 1536, this John Balche in turn
made his will, though he did not die until 1552.   He and his
descendants are described as being of " Horton," a hamlet, a
mile and a half west of Ilminster church.   To his daughters,
Anne, Alice and Agnes, he bequeathed £10 each upon their
majority.   It appears from another source—the visitation of
Somerset of 1531—that he had an elder daughter, Joan, who
had probably received her portion upon her marriage with
Robert Hyett, of Street.   Agnes wedded Christopher Bourman [Bowerman or Boreman] of Wells.   His son John received a legacy of £10.   His sons Thomas and Anthony are
mentioned, and to George, his son and heir, is bequeathed his
bay gelding in Donyett Park.   There is also a bequest to
St. Andrews church at Wells.   Hugh Balche, another son, is
not mentioned in the will, but the residue of the estate is
given to Isabell, the widow, who is made executrix, with John
Walys and William Balche overseers.

This William may have been a brother, a son of William of
Higham, and he is an interesting personage if he was, as
would appear, the William Bawlche of West Chinnock, husbandman, who died in 1611, for he must have been at the
time of his decease a centenarian.

Sir Nicholas Wadham, of Muryfelde [Merrifield] Knight,
left by his will, which was proved in 1542 and directed his

burial to be at Ilminster, the sum of £3, 6 shillings and 8
pence, besides their wages, to each of his servants, Roger
Fontleroy, *John Balche*, William Bevyn and Anthony
Bolleyn. That they were esteemed and trusted is shown by
the fact that two of them were among the executors of the
will, and it is to be remembered, in judging of the value of
the properties mentioned in those ancient documents, that the
sums named had many times the purchasing power of the
money of these latter days.

It is possible that this John Balche was the son of that
name mentioned in the will of John Balche, and it may have
been this same John who, ten years later, in 1549, the third
year of the pious young King Edward VI., was made one of
the trustees of the noted Ilminster free grammar school,
which, upon the dissolution of the chantries, an act of reformation which took place in 1547, was endowed with the lands
formerly dedicated to their support. The possessions of the
chantries passed to the crown, and those of the four connected with Ilminster church were purchased of the King by
Giles Kaleway, of Stroud, in Dorset, and William Leonard, a
merchant, of Taunton, Somerset, and by them conveyed to
Humphrey Walrond, of Sea, in the parish of Ilminster, commonly called the founder of the school, and Henry Greenfield,
for the consideration of £126. They "tendering the virtuous education of youth in literature, and godly learning,
whereby the same youth, so brought up might the better
know their duty as well to God as the King's majesty, and for
divers other honest and godly considerations," assigned over
all the premises acquired, including "Mody's tenement," before referred to, in May, 1549, to John Balche, gentleman, and
others to the number of eighteen, for the purpose of choosing
a proper school master. Humphrey Walrond was the precep-
tor chosen, and a house called the Cross house was appointed
for his use.

George Balche, of Ilminster, gentleman, was the next representative of this well-to-do family at Horton. Born

about 1524, he died June 23, 1569. His will was dated June 21 of that year, and proved August 6th by Nicholas, his eldest son. In it he directs that he be buried in the southern aisle of the church at Broadway. This village, a few miles from Ilminster, took its name from its situation, being originally a few huts built on each side of a broad path cut through the woods of the forests of Neroche. This forest was named from a very ancient Roman encampment, called Roche castle, on the edge of Blackdown hill.

Bequests are made in George's will to his wife Margery, his daughter Katherine, to whom he left £60, and his sons Nicholas, George and John. His brother Hugh is mentioned. His widow Margery Bery, daughter of Bery, of Bery Nabor, Devonshire, was his third wife, and the mother of his youngest child, Walter of Tavistock, Devon, who left two children, George and William. His second wife, named Katherine, was probably the mother of the Katherine to whom he left £60, while his first wife, Jane, daughter of Nicholas Ashford, of Ashford, Devon, was the mother of his eldest son and heir, Nicholas, and of George, John and Maximilian, the three last named dying without issue [obiit sine prole] as they are marked on the genealogical chart of the visitation of 1623.

George had lands in Horton, East Coker, Martock and Cannington as appears by the inquisitio post mortem taken at Yeovil, October 29, 1569, the 11th year of Queen Elizabeth, Stephen Brent being the escheator. Nicholas, the heir, was not yet 18 years of age at the time of his father's death.

It was about this period in history that desperate attempts were made by the adherents of the church of Rome to bring England again under the domination of the papacy, and the country was for a long time threatened with a Spanish invasion. Elizabeth came to the throne in November, 1558, and for thirty years from that time, until the great Armada was finally repulsed and scattered in July, 1588, the whole south of England was in a constant state of watchfulness and

preparation. During that time the English militia system
was first organized and developed.

In September, 1560, two years after Elizabeth's accession,
the "mowster mayster" [muster master] of the county of
Somerset, George Broughton, with a commission consisting
of seven Knights and eleven esquires, returned a most quaint-
ly spelled and worded "certyffycathe unto the quenes ma^{tie}
and here honorable counsell, of all syche abell men and ar-
mures as ys within the countey afforsayde," by which it appears that the total strength of the militia in the county was
close on to 7000 men. The account from which this
extract is taken "The Preparations in Somerset
Against the Armada," by Emanuel Green, states that
there were twenty-one "captaynes" of the "abell" men
of Somerset, and that "each captain had 300 men, except
William Balche, who had 200 only, the total available being
about 6,939."

No place in this genealogy of the Balches, of Horton, can
be assigned to this particular Captain William Balch. The
company of "byllmen," which he commanded was credited
to the hundred of Mark and Bempstone, on the northern
edge of the county. William, the farmer of West Chinnock,
on the southern edge of the county some 25 miles away, was
then about 60 years of age. Nicholas had a cousin William,
the son of his uncle Hugh, but he was then a mere infant, if
indeed he was yet born.

Twenty-three years later, however, Nicholas, then 31 years
old, and just about a year married, was among those gentlemen of the county whose means rendered them liable to furnish and equip a "light horseman" for the service.

On the 30th of September, 1583, the commissioners for
Somerset certified that, according to their orders of the 26th
of August, they had reviewed the demi-lances and light
horsemen, and found them in readiness, according to their
certificate, and such as since the last certificate had died or
gone away were replaced. Where men were wanting to

serve on the horses, time was given to the first of November
to supply them.

Under the head of the hundred of Abdick, in which Horton is situated, they note that "Nicholas Balche, gent.
made defalte and hath daye given him to furnish one l. h. as
aforesaid."

In the hundred of Somertom, on the same date, Thomas
Balche was one of two light horsemen furnished by James
Hodges. It is possible that Thomas was cousin of Nicholas.
Three years afterwards, March 14, 1586, in a return of "the
names of those persons charged to find horses in the west
part of Somerset," Nicholas was again set down to furnish
one light horseman.

In the same year two other Balches, also possibly cousins
of Nicholas, for he had cousins of their names, were included
among "The names of the CCC Shott and Pyckes, trayned
by Sir John Stawell, Knight, at Bridgewater, the VIIIth of
October in the XXVIIIth year of her ma^{ties} Raigne, anno
Dom. 1586." These were William Balche, corporal of "shott,"
in the hundred of Langport, Muchelney and Pitney, and
John Balch of the "pyckes" of North Curry.

After all this drilling and training for thirty years, the
men of Somerset were not destined to strike a blow. The
Spaniards never succeeded in landing, and when, in 1588, the
great Armada finally appeared in English waters, it was
chased up the channel so far out to sea that it could not be
seen from the Dorset coast, and no beacon was fired. Still,
as the enemy was known to have passed, the militia of the
counties moved with him toward London. Following the
pre-arranged plan, 3000 men from Dorset marched into
Hampshire to protect Plymouth, and a similar number from
Somerset were sent into Dorset. From Dover to Gravesend
every man was astir, but, except as a prisoner, no enemy was
allowed to land.

During all these stirring years, Nicholas Balche—described
in the inquisition taken after his death as "generosus," that

is, well born, of good extraction—was apparently leading a quiet and prosperous life. In him the fortunes of the family seem to have culminated. At about the age of 29 he married Sarah, the daughter of Robert May, of Charterhouse Hidon, near Chedder, in Somerset, then deceased, who probably brought him large landed property in addition to that inherited from his father and grandfather. A deed in Latin, executed by him in 1582, soon after his marriage, under the name Nicholas Balche de Horton, for the benefit of his wife and children, makes mention of houses and lands, in Ilminster, East Coker, Martock, Cannington and Fidington. At his death George Balche of Horton, 23 years of age, also described as " generosus " was his eldest son and heir.

It was this George, who, in 1623, being then 39 years of age, subscribed to the genealogy and coat of arms recorded in the " visitation " of that year. He was then a bachelor, and there is no evidence that he ever married, but reason to suppose that he was single to the day of his death at the age of 74, in 1658.

During his long life Elizabeth had died, James had reigned, Charles met his unhappy fate, Cromwell ruled, and the restoration of Charles II., in 1660, was near at hand.

George Balche was loyal to the King, and his property was sequestered by the victorious Puritans, " for his delinquency that he adhered to the forces raised against the Parliament," and on January 11, 1648, he was constrained, much against his will, perhaps, to make a petition in which he, " Humbly prayeth to be admitted to a favorable composition for his said delinquency." Nearly a year elapsed, and then, December, 23, 1648, some of his friends petitioned in his behalf, but with what success does not appear. It would seem very likely, however, that these efforts were fruitless, and that much of his large estate was alienated, and that, perhaps, little remained to be administered upon by his niece, Dorothy Warre, his executrix, when he died ten years later. With him and his brother Nicholas, who died a month earlier, the fortunes of this branch apparently ended.

Pedigree of Balch of County Somerset.

(Buried in the Chapel of the Blessed Virgin Mary, in the church of St. Andrew of Farnham.)

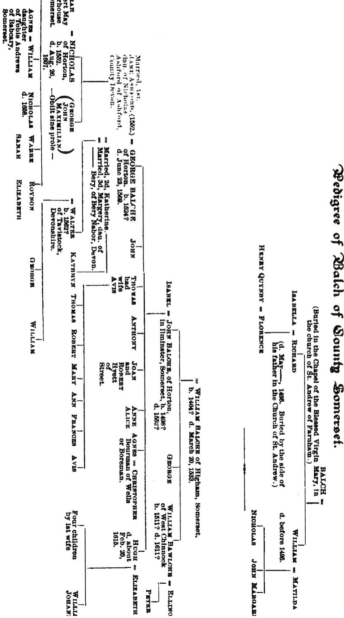

BALCH =

WILLIAM = MATILDA

ISABELLA = RICHARD
(d. May——, 1495. Buried by the side of his father in the Church of St. Andrew.)

d. before 1495.

HENRY QUINBY = FLORENCE

NICHOLAS   JOHN   MARGARET

WILLIAM BALCH of Higham, Somerset, b. 1464? d. March 20, 1533.

ISABEL = JOHN BALCH, of Horton, in Ilminster, Somerset, b. 1498? d. 1562?

= WILLIAM BALCHE of Horton, b. 1494? d. March 20, 1533.

GEORGE   WILLIAM BAWLCHE of West Chinnock b. 1517? d. 1611?   ELLINOR

HUGH = ELIZABETH d. about Feb. 20, 1613.

WILLIAM   JOHAN

PETER

ANNE   AGNES = CHRISTOPHER
Alice   Bourman of Wells of Boreman.

THOMAS   ANTHONY   JOAN and ROBERT Hyett of Street.

Four children by 1st wife

Married, 1st, JANE ASHFORD, (1592.) dau. of Nicholas Ashford of Ashford, County Devon.

GEORGE BALCHE of Horton, b. 1524? d. June 23, 1568.

JOHN

Married, 2d, Katherine.
Married, 3d, Margret, dau. of Bery, of Bery Nabor, Devon.

WALTER b. 1552? of Tavistock, Devonshire.

KATHRYN   THOMAS   ROBERT   MARY   ANN   FRANCES   AVIS

d. of Robert May of Charterhouse Hidon, Somerset.

NICHOLAS of Horton, b. 1552. d. Aug. 26, 1637.

GEORGE
JOHN
MAXIMILIAN
—Obiit sine prole —

SARAH = WILLIAM of Horton, b. 1552, d. Aug. 26, 1637.

GEORGE of Horton, b. 1594, d. 1654. Aet. 74?

AGNES = WILLIAM daughter of Toble Andrews of Babcary, Somerset.

NICHOLAS WARRE d. 1668.

ROYNON   GEORGE   WILLIAM

SARAH   ELIZABETH

It was during the lifetime of this George, and in the year in which he subscribed to the Balch genealogy and arms, apparently as the recognized head of the family, that John Balch, five years his senior, went to America. John may have been a grandson of the first George Balch of Horton, and a son of either Thomas, Robert or William, but no evidence of such a descent is found, except a family tradition that John Balch was of Horton.

Much interesting data remains, relating to the English Balches of a later date, but not sufficiently connected to form a narrative. It is to be hoped that some one of them of the present day, with the facilities which the examination and publication of ancient documents now afford more abundantly than ever before, may undertake the task of compiling a family history which shall show exactly the relationship of all the Balches of Southern England.

For a number of years a branch of the family owned the manor of St. Audries, previously alluded to, and the " Gentlemen's Magazine" of March, 1814, contains this notice.

"Died, at St. Audries, George Balch, Esq., last male descendant of an ancient family.

BALCH CHRONOLOGICAL NOTES.

1327. Willelmo Balch, "Purye," Roberto Balch, "Manerium de Wryng-
ton," Mathaeo Palch, Porlock, Roberto Borliche, "Pockyngtone,"
Johanne Balth, Stapletone, Rogero Barlich, "Wollavingtone,"
Willelmo Baltche, Chiltone, and others, who may have been
Balches, were taxed, 1st year of Edward III.

14— Assumed date of birth of Richard Balch's father.

14— Assumed date of birth of William Balche of Higham. [High Ham?]

1495. May. Death of Richard Balch of Farnham, Surrey. Will proved
in the Prerogative Court of Canterbury. [21Vox.]

1498? Birth of John Balch, son of William of Higham.

1511? Birth of William Bawlche of West Chinnock. [Son of William of
Higham.]

1524? Probable date of birth of George Balche of Horton.

1528. Mody's tenement leased to John Balche, George Balche and others.

1533. March 20, Death of William Balche of Higham, leaving large estate
as per Inquisitio post mortem taken at Wells, Nov. 8, 1534.

1536. April 1, John Balch of Horton made a will, mentioning son and
heir George, sons John, Thomas and Anthony, and daughters
Anne, Alice and Agnes. Probably an elder dau. Joan. [24
Powell.]

1539. Nov. 25, Sir Nicholas Wadham, Knt., of Merrifield, Som., made a
will, proved Jan. 30, 1542, leaving £3, 6sh., 8d., to " my servant
John Balche."

1549. May 18, [3d Edw. VI.] John Balch, gent., and others, trustees of
Ilminster grammar school. [Collinson's History of Somerset.]
[Somerset and Dorset Notes and Queries.]

1552. John Balch died. Buried at Ilminster. Wife Isabel, extx., William Balch and John Walys, overseers. [24 Powell.]

1552? Probable date of birth of Nicholas Balche, son of George.

1560. September. William Balche [Hundred of Mark and Bemstone] a
captain of forces raised for defence against the Armada. [" The
preparations in Somerset against the Armada "—Emanuel
Green.]

1569. June 28, George Balche of Horton dies. To be buried in south
aisle of Broadway church. Held lands in Horton, East Coker,
Martock and Cannington, as per Inquisitio taken at Yeovil, Oct.
29, 1569.

1570? About this time Jane, daughter of Edward Baishe of Kintsbury,
Devon, was wife of William Handcock of Combe Martin. [Ped.
in Visitation of Devon, 1564.]

About this time Joan, daughter of John Balch of Horton, was wife of Robert Hyett of Street. [Visitations of Somerset, 1531 and 1573.]

About this time Agnes Balche was wife of Christopher Bourman of Wells. [Visitations, etc., 1531 and 1573.]

About this time Alice Radbard, of Aller, was wife of ——— Balch. [Idem.]

Probable date of marriage of Nicholas Balche of Horton, age 29.

April 22. Deed of marriage settlement between Nicholas Balche of Horton, and John and Dorothy, son and widow of Robert May, of Charterhouse Hydon [near Chedder] on behalf of his wife Sarah May.

Sept. 30. Nicholas Balche [Hundred of Abdick] was noted as failing to furnish a light horseman as required. ["Armada, etc."]

Sept. 30. Thomas Balch [Hund. of Somerton] was one of two light horsemen furnished by James Hodges, gent. [Idem.]

Probable date of birth of George Balche of Horton.

March 14. Nicholas Balche [Abdycke] "to furnish one light horseman." ["Armada."]

Oct. 4. William Balche, a corporal in Sir John Stawell's band. [Hundred of Langport, Muchelney and Pytney.] [Idem.]

Oct. 4. John Balch. [Hund. North Curry.] "Pyckes." [Id.]

April 18. Will of Thomas Balche of Cote in Martock. Wife Avis, sons, Thomas and Robert; daughters, Mary, Ann, Frances and Avis. Hugh Balche a witness. [51 Dixey.]

Oct. 20? Will of Thomas Balche of North Curry. To be buried there. Son John. [Adopted children named Miller?] Will proved July 17, 1600.

April 10. Will of Mary Lottisham of Godmanston, Dorset, widow. "My sister, Joan Balch." [46 Montague.]

Aug. 26. Nicholas Balche of Horton died. His wife Sarah was living and held possession of lands in Ilminster, East Coker, Cannington, Martock and Fiddington. Son George, heir, age 23. [Inquisition taken at Bridgwater, Sept. 17, 1607.] Had son William as shown by pedigree in Somerset Visitation, 1623, and, from other data, probably son Nicholas, and daughters Sarah and Elizabeth.

Dec. 7. Will of William Bawlche, of West Chinnock, husbandman.

May 27. Will proved. It made bequest to wife Ellinor, son Peter and to Azarius Bawlche and Johane, daughter of Hugh B.

Feb. 17. Nuncupative will of Hughe Balche, of Ilminster, gent. Wife Elizabeth, son William and five children by former wife.

March 21. Will of Oliver Lottishan of Fordington in Babcary, gent. "My kinswomen Sarah and Elizabeth Balch."

Thomas Hodges died leaving as heir to property in Shepton Mallet, his cousin Rebecca Hodges, then 12 years old, who in

1639 was wife of "a certain John Balch." [Fine Roll, 14th
Charles I., part 26.]

1623. George Balche, of Horton was a bachelor, 39 years old. [Visi.]

1623. Carolus Balch, gent., of Stockgumber, was cited to appear at the
Visitation of that year, and the note made against his name.
"Sarvant to the E. of Pemb. and will be at Ilchester or London."

1629. Will of William Balch of Beere in High Ham. Dated Nov. 9,
proved 1630, Aug. 3. To be buried at High Ham. All to son
Samuel.

1648. Jan. 11-13. George Balche, of Horton, gent., petitioned that he be
admitted to composition for his delinquency in adhering to the
forces raised against the Parliament. Lands in Huister [?] Coker
and other places sequestrated.

1648. Will of Thomas Balch, Vicar of Dulverton. Proved by widow
. Elizabeth, Sept. 11. Daughter, Ellinor; sons, Francis, John.
Thomas and Robert; brothers, Robert and John. [130 Essex
and Taunton Reg.]

THE NEW ENGLAND FAMILY.

FIRST GENERATION.

1.   **John Balch,**[1] heads the family which is now scattered across the United States and along the Pacific coast.   While it has been possible to learn with much accuracy his own history since he landed in September, 1623, all efforts to trace him and his ancestry prior to his settling in America have met with but slight success.   But it is known that he came from Somerset county, England, and early family tradition says from Horton.

He came with a colony in charge of Captain Robert Gorges, son of Sir Fernando, who had a grant of a large tract of land which he wished to colonize.   They landed at Wessegusset, now known as Weymouth, Massachusetts.   It is learned from British archives that Capt. Gorges was commissioned Governor of New England.

Concerning this place prior to his landing some interesting facts deserve attention.   Palfrey tells us in his history that early in the year 1621 Mr. Weston of London sent over two vessels, the Charity and the Swan, with some fifty men, to settle a plantation for him in the Massachusetts Bay.   Concerning them Bradford of the Plymouth Colony received warning from Cushing and Pierce, in England, that they were base in condition and unfit for an honest man's company.   These men located at Wessegusset, and stole vegetables from the gardens of the Plymouth Colony.   During their second winter their condition became desperate, and, under the leadership of their chief man, Saunders, they took food by force from the Indians. The Plymouth Colony remonstrated in the strongest terms against this robbery, and because of it the Indians formed a plot to exterminate not only Weston's company, but the Pilgrims as well. This would have probably succeeded, if the Plymouth Colony had not been warned by a friendly Indian. In the spring of 1628 the settlement was abandoned by Weston's people.

Next came the Gorges company, of which John Balch was a member, to the deserted settlement, in the fall of 1623. This was the first direct from Great Britain to form a nucleus for a permanent settlement in New England. The Plymouth Colony and the Weston company were indeed earlier, but the former came by way of Holland, and the latter dispersed.

Independence of religious thought and a disposition from the first to break away from the Church of England characterized the Gorges company. An Episcopal clergyman named Morrell, who came with them, finding no opportunity to exercise his ecclesiastical authority, returned to England. The vessel, that brought them over, shortly afterward sailed with passengers to the Virginia Colony, while Capt. Gorges made an exploration to the north, and soon returned to England. After he left, the settlers were joined by some disaffected and expelled members of the Plymouth Colony, among whom was the Rev. John Lyford and Roger Conant.

About this time English capitalists formed the Dorchester Company, with these settlers as its agents and employees. The object was to carry on a fishery, and in 1624 the colony removed to Cape Ann for this purpose. They had about two hundred servants. An attempt had been made the year before to establish a plantation at Cape Ann, with Thomas Gardner as overseer, with small success. Roger Conant, who was described as "a religious, sober, and prudent gentleman," was appointed Governor of the Dorchester Company, and Lyford was the minister of the place.

Cattle were received from England in 1625. The fishing business not succeeding, most of the servants were returned to England, and the colonists determined to change their vocation from fishing to agriculture. The location at Cape Ann was ill adapted to the new occupation, and in September, 1626, they removed with their families, stores and cattle, to the Sagamoreship of Naumkeag, a densely wooded peninsula, where the Boston & Maine R. R. now crosses onto the bridge over the harbor from Salem to Beverly. These first settlers were:

Roger Conant,	John Woodbury,	John Balch,
Peter Palfrey,	Rev. John Lyford,	Thomas Gardner,
William Allen,	Thomas Gray,	Richard Norman, Sr.
Richard Norman, Jr.	Walter Knight,	John Tilley,

Capt. William Trask, and others.

Some were married and had children, and there were in all between twenty-five and thirty souls. The rock on which this noble band of pioneers stepped ashore at Naumkeag can be seen from the cars as they cross Beverly harbor. It is known as Forefathers' Rock.

Here was a tribe of Indians, much reduced in numbers by pestilence and wars, who gladly received the settlers for the protection they might afford.

In the following year Lyford, who seems to have had a restless disposition, planned to remove the colony to Virginia, but Rev. John White, a Puritan, known as the patriarch of Dorchester, learning of the contemplated move, wrote a letter from England on behalf of the Dorchester merchants who had organized the company, which deterred most of the settlers from leaving. In it he exhorted Conant not to desert the business, and faithfully promised him that if he, with John Woodbury, John Balch and Peter Palfrey, whom he knew to be honest and prudent men, would stay at Naumkeag, he would provide a patent for them. White was unable to keep his promise. It was evidently on these four men that the projectors of the colony relied for the energy

and intelligence requisite for the success of their enterprise.
The four came to be known as "the Old Planters." None
of them or their descendants are known to have been among
the persecutors of the Baptists, the Quakers, or the Witches,
but, on the contrary, a descendant of Woodbury kept a horse
saddled and a lantern lighted to aid any accused of witchcraft to escape, and a grandson of John Balch dared to sign
a remonstrance against their persecution.

Carpenters among the settlers at Naumkeag built a frame
house for Conant, and assisted the others in the construction
of snug huts, so that they were enabled to pass the winter in
comfort. For two years they thus prospered, attended to
their cattle, and raised maize and hunted in common with
their Indian friends. Their various doings are set forth at
length in the papers by Geo. D. Phippen, in the Historical
Collections of the Essex Institute, Vol. I.

In the meantime the Dorchester Company in England sold
their interest in the colony to the Massachusetts Bay Company.
The description of the Bay Colony's grant shows how meagre
the geographical knowledge of America was at that time, for
its bounds are given as three miles north of the Merrimack,
three miles south of the Charles, and running west from the
Atlantic to the South seas.

John Endicott was sent over as governor of this new company. On September 6, 1628, he landed at Naumkeag with
his Puritanical band, and then it was that Conant's party
learned of the change in their governors. Although the
original settlers desired accessions to their colonies, they were
not pleased with the followers of Endicott, for they quickly
perceived in them that stern religious intolerance which was
so soon to develop into the cruel persecutions that have
stained the pages of New England history.

The winter's stores were inadequate for the double colony.
The sad scenes of the Pilgrims' first winter at Plymouth were
repeated at Naumkeag, and many died before spring.

Early in the following summer many more settlers ar-

rived, abundant supplies were received from England, and
the colony was firmly established. The differences between
the adventurers (as the first settlers were often called) and
the Puritanical followers of Endicott were amicably adjusted,
and to commemorate the event, the town was incorporated in
July 1629, and named Salem, the Hebrew word for peaceful.

John Balch and about eighteen others, being members of
the church, were made freemen, May 18, 1631, that is, given
the right to vote and hold office. This is the first date on
which freemen were made in America. Early in the year
1635 the Massachusetts Bay Company gave to the several
towns within its grant the right to give grants of land. The
town of Salem, in order to exercise this right, at once appointed five overseers and layers out of land for its precinct,
and one of these was John Balch. His name frequently appears in this capacity upon the records. On November 25,
1635, the town granted a thousand acres in what was then
known as the Bass River District, to be divided between
Roger Conant, John Woodbury, John Balch, Capt. Trask
and Peter Palfrey. They divided it to suit themselves. This
land was located between the head of Bass river and Wenham pond. It afterwards became known as the "Old Planters' grant," and was included in the town of Beverly, incorporated in 1668.

John Balch, in 1638, built a two story frame house upon his
land, in which he spent the remainder of his life. In it his
son Benjamin² and Benjamin's grandson 23 Benjamin⁴ lived
and reared their families. From this last Benjamin it passed
to his daughter 78 Deborah⁵ [Balch] Dodge in which family
and name the house has continued to the present time. The
Balch house, although subjected to some changes, is still standing in a good state of preservation. Roger Conant and John
Woodbury also built houses near by, but Conant's is now
entirely obliterated, and only the cellar hole remains to mark
the sight of the one reared by Woodbury.

The first thirteen executive rulers of Salem were chosen

January 26, 1636-7, and in June following the number was twelve selectmen. The name of John Balch appears in both lists. Both his name and that of his wife Margary are in the list of the first members of the first church in Salem. The organization of this church was completed August 6, 1629, and was the first Congregational church completely formed and organized in America. The Plymouth church was the first, but it was formed and organized at Leyden, in Holland, during the temporary sojourn of the Pilgrims there, on their way to this country. So large a part of it was transferred, that it was considered the church to the new colony in America.

John Balch was twice married, Margary was the given name of his first wife. There is no record of her parentage or the date of their marriage, but it is not improbable that theirs may have been the first and perhaps only marriage in the Naumkeag settlement.

To them were born three sons.

2* BENJAMIN,²   b. Winter of 1628 and 9;   d. after Jan. 31, 1714-15.
3* JOHN,²   b. about 1630;   d. June 16, 1662.
4* FREEBORN,²   b. about 1631;   d. about 1658.

His second wife Agnes or Annis [Patch] gave him no children.

John¹ died at his estate on Bass river, in May, 1648. His will was duly made and filed among the Essex County records, where it now is. A printed copy and a fac simile are appended. The inventory of John Balch's estate rendered by Benjamin Balch, February 2, 1648-9, amounted to 220£ s.13. d.4.

THE WILL OF JOHN BALCH.

The last will & testamt of John Balch, of Salem, bearing Date the 15th day of May, 1648.

I, John Balch sick in bodie but in pfect memorrie doe make this my last willj & testamt in manner & forme following my debts paid & funeral expences discharged those goods God hath gyven me it is my will to dispose of them as Followeth. Imprimis I gyve unto Annis Balch my loving wife the Room nev-lie Built wth twelve Akers of land of woh 4 akers to be in tilt and

4 Akers of medowe with some pt of the barne to lay in her fruits & halfe of the great fruit trees for & during the life of said Annis.

Itm I gyve Vnto my said wife my best bed wth all Convenient furniture there vnto belonging & one fourth pt of all my household goods except the rest of my bedding & also 2 Cowes by name Reddie & Cherie & one yearling heaffer. Further my will is that soe long as my said wife shall live my said sonnes shall sowe or plant 2 Akers of aforesaid 4 akers for my said wife for the term of 7 years and after that our sonne Beniamin shall doe all him sefe.

Item I gyve & bequeth to beniamin Balch my eldest sonne one half of my farm to him and his heirs for ever as alsoe two yoke of oxen 1 Cowe one third of my young Cattle & of the mare Colt with one fourth pt of my household goods & halfe of the great fruit trees & after the decease of my said wife my will is that the said Beniamin shall have them all with those he hath planted himself.

Item my will is that all my Corne growing upon the ground shall be equallie Divided into 4 equall pts among my wife & children.

Item I gyve vnto John Balch my second sonne one fourth of my farme and one yoke of oxen one third of my young Cattle & mare Colt one fourth of my household goods & half of the young aple trees undispost of and one cow.

Item I gyve to ffree born Balch my youngest sonne one fourth pt of my ffarme one yoke of oxen & one Cow I bred up for him one third of the young Cattell & one third of the mare & one fourth of my household goods & half the young Aple trees betwixt him & his brother John equallie to be divided & further my last will & testament & my loving friends John Proctor & william Woodberrie shall be overseers of the same in witness hereof I have herevnto put my hand the day & year above written. JOHN BALCH.

Witness:
 PETER NICHOLAS PATCH,
 PALFREY JEFFERIE MASSEY.

Agnes the second wife of John Balch[1], left a will which was declared illegal. In Nov. 1657, her stepson Benjamin Balch[2] brought into court a statement signed by several of his neighbors that all her estate was not sufficient to satisfy his demands upon it.

BILL OF EXPENSES FOR LAST SICKNESS AND FUNERAL OF AGNES BALCH.

Nouember 25, 1657.

	£	s.	d.
a bill of charges in hir sickness and death by tendance for two years and better 3s. per weake and is fifteen pound twellfe shillins	15	12	00
for my time for coming to town to Mr. Emri and other ocations	1	00	00
at hir buriell for ofen and caks and drinks 40s.	2	00	00
	18	12	00

The above menchened carg is in the sickness and death of Ane Balch by me.   BENIAMIN BALCH.

The amount of Agnes' estate as per inventory was 9£ 11s. 00d.

2. Benjamin,[2] eldest son of 1 John[1] and Margary Balch was born in the Sagamoreship of Naumkeag during the severe and trying winter of 1628 and 9 which followed the arrival of Endicott. *Benjamin Balch*, The evidence which conclusively fixes his birth in this winter was collected by David M. Balch and published in the *Salem Gazette* on May 10, 1878, and in Balch Leaflets, Nos. 1-8. Twenty-two years after the death of Benjamin's third son John[3] the tradition of the family was committed to writing, that Benjamin[2] was the first born male child in the Massachusetts Bay Colony. Since it was in September, 1628, that the Naumkeag settlers learned that they were the Massachusetts Bay Colony, and the name of the place was changed to Salem in the following July, the tradition is interpreted as indicating that Benjamin's birth was between these dates. April 10, 1706, he gives his age in a sworn deposition as about 77. This places his birth prior to April, 1629, and fixing it in the winter above mentioned. The word male presented in the tradition seems to hint that a female was born in the Colony before him.

Claims conflicting with the tradition that Benjamin[2] was the first born have been held by the descendents of others, and it will therefore be important to notice them in passing.

After the place took the name of Salem, Roger Conant, Jr. was born, and when ten years old was granted 20 acres of land as the "first born child in Salem." He died in 1672. This left John Massey entitled to describe himself as the oldest planter living in Salem who was born there. He was, however, as several depositions show, two years younger than Benjamin Balch[3] who lived in Beverly.

Benjamin[2] received at his father's death half of the farm and sundry other goods. From his brother John[2] he purchased his share in the old homestead on Bass River, and in 1658 secured possession of his brother Freeborn's[2] share in his father's estate. He lived in the old home from its building when he was nine years old, and in it all of his children were born.

His independence of the rigid puritanical notions of the times appears in several instances. For entertaining and giving a night's lodging to a stranger on foot, he was arrested and fined, and he left the baptism of his children to their own desires.

Previous to Benjamin's last marriage he gave part of his farm to three of his sons, and after his last wife's death he deeded the home lot for a maintainance in his old age to his grandson Benjamin[4]. He executed other deeds to his sons, and the last of these which has been found was given January 81, 1714-15, and shows that he completed his 86th year. He left no will as most of his property was disposed of while living. The date of his death is not known.

Benjamin[2] was married first about 1650, to Sarah, the eldest daughter of Thomas Gardner, the overseer of the first Cape Ann Plantation. They had the following children, of which the ten eldest were baptized April 10, 1670.

5[⦁]	SAMUEL,[3]	b.	May — 1651;	d. Oct. 14, 1723.
6[⦁]	BENJAMIN,[3]	b.	1653;	d. Spring of 1698.
7[⦁]	JOHN,[3]	b.	1654;	d. Nov. 19, 1788.
8[⦁]	JOSEPH,[3]	b.	1658;	d. Sept. 16, 1675.
9[⦁]	FREEBORN,[3]	b.	Aug. 9, 1660;	d. June 11, 1729.
10[⦁]	SARAH,[3]	b.	1661;	d. prior to 1717.
11[⦁]	ABIGAIL,[3]	b.	1668;	d. Apr. 30, 1706.
12[⦁]	RUTH,[3]	b.	1665;	d.
13[⦁]	MARY,[3]	b.	1667;	d. Mch. 12, 1787.
14	JONATHAN,[3]	bapt. Apr. 10,1670;	probably d. y.	
15	DAVID,[3]	b.	July 9, 1671;	d. u. m. Apr. 17, 1690.

Benjamin's wife Sarah died April 5, 1686, and February 5, 1689, he married Abigail, widow of Matthew Clarke, of Marblehead. She died in January, 1690, aged 55 years. His third and last marriage was to Grace Mallet. The ceremony was performed on March 15, 1691-2 by Simeon Bradstreet, Esq. To Benjamin and Grace were born two daughters.

16ᵃ DEBORAH,³ b. June 6, 1698.   d. May 5, 1717.
17ᵃ LYDIA,³ b. Aug. 28, 1695.

His wife Grace probably died before 1704, since he signed a deed alone in that year.

3. John,² son of 1 John¹ and Margary Balch, was born at Salem, Mass., about 1630. He was drowned by the upsetting of a skiff in a storm when crossing the ferry between Salem and Beverly, June 16, 1662. He married Mary, daughter of Roger Conant. They had only one child.

18 MARY,³ died young.

John's widow married William Dodge, " ye yonger." The inventory of his estate is given in a quaint old document which is here copied entire.

JOHN BALCH, ESTATE.

Court at Ipswich, March term, 1662. Administration granted to Mary, relick, Salem, June. Inventory returned re. Ipswich 31, March 1663 No. 30. Whereas there was administration granted to Mary Balch of the estate of her late husband John Balch, & the court at Salem the 4th, month 1662 did divide the estate between the said Mary Balch & Mary the daughter of the s'd John Balch : now the said daughter being dead, by the consent of parties it is ordered that Benjamin Balch shall after the end of seven years next coming, enjoy all the lands that did belong to the said John Balch, being 50 acres in all more or less, only the said Mary to enjoy all the improved land, upland and meadow, during the said term of seven years the rest to be in his possesion.

An Inventory of all such goods and lands as John Balch of Salem deceased was possessed of, made the 19th, of the first month 1662, and prized by us subscribed

	£.	s.	d.
Imprimis his house with 5 akres of Land adjoining	35	0	0
Item. the quarter part of his Fathers farm about 50 akers	50	0	0
Item, two akers and half of meadow in the old planters marsh	12	0	0
Item, A Mare and Colt	15	0	0
Item, A Cow	4	10	0
Item, A fether bed and bolster, a rugg, blanket & purtenances & bed stead	10	10	0
Item, Another bead and beadstead with the appertenances	6	10	0
Item, Some other small bedding	2	0	0
Item, The platters and porringers &c.	5	0	0
Item, A kettell, two skillets a warmingpan and skimmer,	1	12	0
" A small iron pot small kettle and old iron	0	8	0
" 2 chests a Cupboard, and boxes	2	0	0
" A little table and four Chairs,	0	16	0
" His wearing apparell	10	0	0
" Two Cushings and some sea garments	1	03	0
" pillowpies, Sheets, napkins &c.	6	10	0
" A friing pan, a Bellows and smoothing iron	0	08	0
" Two Hats	1	00	0
" There is also an eight part of a Ketch but there is still owing for prised	26	00	0
Total	189	17	0

	£	s.	d.	
This is owing unto Lott Conant of Marblehead the sum of	26	00	00	{ Roger Conant
more in the debts	4	00	00	{ Samuel Corning
£	30	00	00	

The above Inventory is allowed of in Court at Salem 25th, 4th, mo. 1662.   Attest.

HILLYARD VERENS.

4. **Freeborn,**[2] son of 1 John[1] and Margary Balch, was born in Salem, Mass., about 1631. He was probably named to commemorate the event of his father being made a freeman that year. Family tradition says that he went to England and died there about 1657. His estate in Salem was purchased in 1658 by his brother Benjamin, from Walter Price, a shopkeeper of that place, who was his executor and administrator. [Essex Reg. Deeds, Vol. 1, p. 82, Jan. 20, 1659.]

It is probable that at the time of his death Freeborn was in debt to, or in Price's employ, and it may be assumed that he was a mariner and was lost at sea. His brother Benjamin purchased his inheritance from Price, and paid for it £20 and 2¼ acres in the "Old Planters Marsh." The deed shows that Freeborn's death was uncertain, for it recites, "alwaise Provided y[t] if the above sd. Freeborne Balch appears to be alive, then this bargain to be voyd." On May 26, 1660, Price gave his receipt for the money and the land was deeded, and it is to be presumed that then, either because Freeborn had not appeared for two years, or on account of information of his death, that his estate was settled up.

"The Old Planters Marsh" referred to was located on the peninsula where they first landed, in the present city of Salem.

THIRD GENERATION.

5. Samuel,[3] eldest son of 2 Benjamin[2] and Sarah (Gardner) Balch, was born in the old homestead, at the head of Bass river, in May, 1651, and died October 14, 1723. He was married, October 27, 1675, to Martha, daughter of John and Martha (Gould) Newmarch, of Ipswich, Mass. She died July 7, 1720, aged 67 years. They had seven sons and three daughters, all born in Beverly.

20° MARTHA,[4] b. Sept. 13, 1676.
21° SAMUEL,[4] b. May 16, 1678; d. 1754.
22° JOSEPH,[4] b. Apr. 26, 1680; d. Dec. 9, 1732.
23° BENJAMIN,[4] b. Mch. 29, 1682; d. Jan. 8, 1749-50.
24° JOHN[4] (twin), b. Mch. 29, 1682, d. 1756.
25° PHEBE,[4] b. Apr. 1, 1684; d.
26° PETER,[4] b. May 6, 1685; d. Dec. 27, 1755.
27° CORNELIUS,[4] b. May 1, 1687; d. 1730.
28 ABIGAIL,[4] b. May 24, 1689; d. Sept. 26, 1711.
29 THOMAS,[4] b. Apr. 1, 1692; d. Aug. 15, 1699.

He married again, November 23, 1721, the widow, Martha Butman. She died in 1745, without issue.

When nineteen years of age he was baptized, at his own desire, and united with the First church of Beverly, of which he afterwards became a deacon. He was chosen town clerk of Beverly, and took the oath of office, June 27, 1693. This office he held for seven years. He was several times chosen a representative of the town, and was evidently honored and respected by his neighbors as a man of integrity and ability.

By a conveyance recorded April 25, 1692, his father deeded

(14)

to him one-half of a 40 acre lot, which was bounded easterly with Samuel's own land, west with country road, north by the Raiments, southerly with Peter Woodbury. It is evident from this and other deeds that he was quite a land owner near Wenham pond.

His will, dated November 30, 1722, making his son John sole executor, was probated at Ipswich, October 28, 1723. [Reg. Essex Prob., Vol. 18, p. 359.]

6. Benjamin,[3] son of 2 Benjamin[2] and Sarah (Gardner) Balch, was born in the old homestead, about 1658, and baptized at his own desire, April 10, 1670. He died in Beverly in the spring of 1698.

He was married October 11, 1674, to Elizabeth, daughter of John and Elizabeth Woodbury, and granddaughter of the old planter, John, and his wife, Agnes Woodbury. She was born Aug. 15, 1654, and died a short time after her husband. Their children were:

30* ANN,[4] b. about 1675; d. Aug. 23, 1726.
31* JOSEPH,[4] b. Sept. 26, 1677; d. Aug. 14, 1712.
32* EBENEZER,[4] b. June 6, 1680.
33* ABIGAIL,[4] b. May 17, 1682.
34   ELIZABETH,[4] b. July 6, 1688; d. y.
35   RUTH,[4] b. Aug. 29, 1691.

He received 25 acres from his father, by a deed dated February 25, 1688-9. This land is bounded north by a birch tree on the way from Beverly to Ephrim Herrick's, south by country road to Wenham, and east by Jno. Raymond, Jr. The deed also conveyed one acre of meadow in Wenham. [Essex Deeds, Vol. 21, p. 20.]

From the Essex County records it appears that his oldest surviving son Joseph was appointed executor June 27, 1698. These records note that Benjamin[3] was a Mariner.

7. John,[3] son of 2 Benjamin[2] and Sarah (Gardner) Balch, was born at the old homestead about 1654, and died at Beverly, November 19, 1738. No record of his birth has been found, but several depositions among the County Court papers give his

age at various times and thus enables the year of his birth
to be determined. One of these is as follows. "The deposition of John Balch (son to Benjamin Balch), age 16 years or
thereabouts that he saw Wm. Barnes, Mr. Thorndik's man
coming out of Goodin Lambert's house at yᵉ window on yᵉ
last day of yᵉ weeke wch was before yᵉ Generall trayning
when they trayned at Beverly. Taken upon oath 28, & 9 mo·
1670." It was the custom in those days at stated times known
as training days to gather together all the militia of the County at one town or another to be drilled.

He was married to Hannah Veren, December 23, 1674. She
was the granddaughter of Philip Veren of New Sarum (Salisbury), a roper by trade, who came over in the James from
Southampton, and arrived in Boston in 1635, bringing his wife
Dorcas and ~~four~~ sons, Philip, Hilliard, Nathaniel and Joshua.

Philip Veren Jr. was admitted to Salem Church, January
3, 1640-41. He was a wheelwright by trade, and his wife's
name was Joanna. Their children were: Bethrib, bapt. Nov.
14, 1641; Dorcas, bapt. April 16, 1643; Philip, bapt. March
28, 1644-5; *Hannah*, b. 1655; Adoniram; Mary, b. Aug. 10,
1659; and Deliverance.

John³ and Hannah Balch lived to celebrate their 64th wedding day. The farm on which all their wedded life was spent
was a portion of the old Planters' grant. Part of it came from
his father by a conveyance recorded April 25, 1692, which
recites, "Benjamin Balch yeoman of Beverly to son John, etc.
half my 40 acres where he now dwelleth, his portion to be next
the Country road, and the land to be eaqually divided between
my two sons Samuel and John."

Unto John and Hannah, were born 14 children.

36* REBECCA,⁴ b. about 1675.
37* HANNAH,⁴ b. about 1676.
38   JOHN,⁴ b. Nov. 1677; d. April 27, 1679.
39* JOHN,⁴ b. about 1679; d. about 1723.
40* ISRAEL,⁴ b. Sept. 3, 1681; d. 1753.
41* SARAH,⁴ b. March 20, 1682-3.
42   JOSHUA,⁴ b. 1684; d. y.
43   JOANNA,⁴ b. 1686; d. y.

Map of ancient Beverly, 17th Century.
Drawn by SAMUEL W. BALCH.

44 RUTH⁴, b. Oct. 6, 1687; d. y.
45* JOSHUA⁴, b. Nov. 5, 1688; d.
46* CALEB⁴, b. Oct. 14, 1689; d. summer of 1775.
47* DAVID⁴, b. Oct. 1, 1691; d. Sept. 25, 1769.
48 JOANNA⁴, bapt. Nov. 20, 1692; d. y.
49 ROGER⁴, b. July 14, 1693; d. y.

He a was carpenter or "housewright," and also a farmer.
He was admitted to full communion, in the first parish church
of Beverly, June 2, 1680.   March 23, 1686-7, his wife Hannah was also admitted to full communion.   On May 19, 1680,
He was made a freeman.   He held the following offices :
March 15, 1682-3, Surveyor of highways ; March 15, 1685-6,
Tythingman ; Dec. 9, 1690, Grand Juryman ; 1693, Tythingman ; 1694, Sergeant ; 1694, Constable ; 1695 to 1699, Selectman ; 1700, Ensign ; 1705, Lieutenant ; 1711, Representative.

Just a month before his death, his long will was drawn up
and signed.   His son Caleb was named as sole executor.   It
notes minutely the provisions for the widow; and among
other privileges it specifies "also yᵉ Liberty of Gathering so
many Beans in yᵉ field as she may have occasion of for her
own use both for summer and winter" [It seems Beverly did
not neglect her staple even in those early days]. "Twenty
bushels of Good Indian Corn five bushels of Malt.   Two hundred Pounds of Beef Out of which Quarter of yᵉ Beast She
Pleaseth to have it.   Two Barrell of Cyder, with Apples Sufficient for her use, and fifteen pounds of flax from yᵉ Swingle."
"To keep for her use both Summer and Winter Two Cows &
four sheep" "yᵉ Service of my Indian Woman Called Quando
& yᵉ Privelege of a Horse to Ride upon for her necessary occasions."

The will mentions sons Caleb, Joshua, Israel, David, grandson Andrew son of John deceased, daughters Sarah Richardson, Hannah Leach, and grandchildren of his daughter Rebecca
Dodge, deceased.

Among other things the inventory mentions, 1 Negro man
value £95, and 1 Old Indian Woman £18.   He died Nov.
19, 1738, and his wife soon followed March 7, 1738-9.   His

estate was proved Dec. 11, 1788, but his widow was too feeble
to attend the court.

8.   Joseph,[3] son of 2 Benjamin[2] and Sarah [Gardner]Balch,
was born in the old homestead in 1658.   He was a soldier in
Capt. Lathrop's company and was slain at the famous Indian
battle of Bloody Brook, September 18, 1675, in King Phillip's
war.   Palfrey's History gives an account of the battle.

Deerfield was abandoned, before the inhabitants had secured
their harvest.   "From Hadley, twenty miles distant, the headquarters of the troops, a party was dispatched to finish thresh-
ing the grain and bring it in.   Eighteen wagons, with their
teamsters, were convoyed by a company of ninety picked
men, led by Capt. Lathrop."

On their return after securing the crop they were surprised
at a small stream in the township of Deerfield.   Here as they
were crossing, a large force of Indians suddenly fell upon
them and slew all but seven or eight of the company.   The
stream was named Bloody Brook from this disaster.

9.   Freeborn,[3] son of 2 Benjamin[2] and Sarah [Gardner]
Balch, was born in the old homestead at Beverly, August 9,
1660, the year following the incorporation of the town.   He died
in Beverly, June 12, 1729.   His death was probably quite
sudden, for his long will was drawn up and signed the day
that he died.   His grave-
stone stands on a hill in the   *Freeborn Balch,*
cemetery   near   Wenham
Lake with those of his mother-in-law, Sarah Fairfield, and
his two children, Skipper and Sarah.

Freeborn was a farmer, and lived on a portion of his father's
estate in North Beverly, on the East shore of Wenham Lake.
His thrifty husbandry reared the finest apple orchard in the
county, which he willed, together with his cider mill and
cider house, to his son William.   He married first, late in the
Autumn of 1682, the widow Mirriam Bachelder.   She was
born in January, 1657-8, and was the daughter of Robert
Moulton, Jr., and his wife Abigail [Goode?].   She first mar-

ried Joseph, son of John Bachelder, October 8, 1677. By him she had two children, Joseph, b. July 18, 1678, and Abigail. Bachelder was a mariner, and died or was lost at sea, probably late in 1681. There is no record of her marriage with Freeborn, but as she signs her name as a witness to a deed dated November 18, 1682, "Mirriam Bachelder" their marriage must have been subsequent to that time. There is no record of Mirriam's death which probably occurred in 1688.

Mirriam Moulton was a granddaughter of Robert Moulton, who came to this country in 1629, with six ship-builders, of whom he was chief. The first fishing and trading boats built in Salem were built by him and his men. He died in April, 1655, leaving a son Robert and daughter Dorothy. Robert Moulton, Jr., married Abigail Croad, a niece of Emanual Downing, by whom he had eight children, Robert, Abigail, Samuel, Hannah, John, Joseph, Mirriam, and Mary. He died in September, 1665.

Freeborn and Mirriam had three children.

50* MIRRIAM,[4] b. Aug. 2, 1683; d. 1748.
51* FREEBORN,[4] b. Nov. 25, 1685; d. March, 1770.
52* BENJAMIN,[4] b. April 17, 1688; d. Jan. 28, 1741-2.

The Essex County Court Records give the marriage of Freeborn Balch and Mallis, February 20, 1688-9. She must have died soon after for no other record is to be found.

Freeborn's third marriage was on April 30, 1690, to Elizabeth Fairfield, daughter of Walter Fairfield, and his wife Sarah [Skipperway] of Wenham. She was born August 9, 1666, and died January 31, 1736-7.

They had seven children.

53* SKIPPER,[4] b. July, 25, 1692; d. Sept. 13, 1714, unm.
54² ELIZABETH,[4] b. 1696; d. May 1, 1718.
55 SARAH,[4] b. 1698; d. Sept. 30, 1714, unm.
56* ABIGAIL,[4] b. 1700; d.
57* TABITHA,[4] b. 1702; d.
58* WILLIAM,[4] b. Sept. 30, 1704; d. Jan., 1791-2.
59* MARY,[4] b. June 5, 1707; d. Oct. 10, 1788.

10. **Sarah**,[3] daughter of 2 Benjamin² and Sarah [Gardner] Balch, was born about 1661, and died prior to 1717. She

was married, December 20, 1680, to James Patch, son of
James and Hannah Patch. He was born in Salem, June 21,
1655, and died at Ipswich in February, 1732-3. In June,
1717, he married again, this time to Mary Thorne, who was
the daughter of Bernard Thorne, and widow of David
Thorne.

Sarah and James Patch had five children: James, d. unm.
in 1714; John, b. 1699, d. May 30, 1775; Mary; Bertha, m.
Samuel Whipple, June 20, 1726; Hannah, m. Nathaniel
Potter in Oct., 1710.

11. **Abigail,**[3] daughter of 2 Benjamin[2] and Sarah [Gard-
ner] Balch, was born in 1663, and died April 30, 1706. She
was married February 8, 1680-81, to Cornelius Larcum.
Their children were: Jonathan, b. Mar. 8, 1690-91; Cornelius,
b. Feb. 15, 1697-8; Benjamin, b. Feb. 6, 1699-1700; David, b.
Oct. 28, 1701.

On March 28, 1707, the year after Abigail's death, Larcum
married Margaret Low. He died June 9, 1747, aged 94
years, and Margaret died, Dec. 10, 1756, aged 85 years.

12. **Ruth,**[3] daughter of 2 Benjamin[2] and Sarah [Gardner]
Balch, was born at Beverly, Mass., about 1665, and was
baptized April 10, 1670. She was married to Joseph Drinker,
who was born at Exeter, England, March 31, 1653. He
emigrated to America, in July, 1655, with his father and
mother, Philip and Elizabeth Drinker, in the ship Abigail,
Robert Hackwell, master. They resided at Beverly, where
Joseph and Ruth were married. A deed signed by her Oct.
15, 1731, shows that then she was a widow, and living in
Boston.

They had three sons:* Joseph, d. in 1742; m. July 9, 1708,

DRINKER.

*CHILDREN OF JOSEPH[4] AND MARY [JANEY] DRINKER.

HENRY DRINKER, b. about 1709; d. 1746; m. Mary Gottier of Burlington, N. J., Nov. 26, 1731. Four sons.

JOSEPH DRINKER, m. Sarah Grice, one daughter.

JOHN DRINKER, d. Mar. 13, 1787; m. Susanna Allen, had three sons
who left no descendants.

Mary Janney, from Cheshire, Eng. ; she d. Mar. 17, 1764, aged 83 years. Edward, b. Dec. 24, 1680 ; d. in Philadelphia, Pa., Nov. 19, 1782, aged 101 years. John, lost at sea, unm.

13. **Mary,**[3] daughter of 2 Benjamin[2] and Sarah [Gardner] Balch, was born about 1667, and died March 12, 1737. She married Nathaniel Stone, March 26, 1689. He was the son of Nathaniel and Remember [Corning] Stone, and was born Sept. 15, 1663, and died February 28, 1741. Mary and Nathaniel had ten children : Sarah, b. 1690 ; Josiah, b. 1692 ; Nathaniel, b. 1693, d. y. ; Nathaniel, b. 1694 ; Benjamin, b. 1696 ; Ruth, b. 1699 ; Hannah, b. 1702 ; Phebe, b, 1703 ; David, b. 1706 ; Abigail, b. 1708.

16. **Deborah,**[3] daughter of 2 Benjamin[2] and his third wife, Grace [Mallet] Balch, was born June 6, 1693, at Beverly, Mass., and died at Rochester, Mass., May 5, 1717.

CHILDREN OF HENRY[6] AND MARY [GOTTIER] DRINKER.

JOHN DRINKER, b. 1733; d. July 27, 1800; m. Rachel Renier, Feb. 27, 1756. Four children and numerous descendants.

HENRY DRINKER, b. Feb. 21, 1733-4; d. June 26, 1809; m. Elizabeth Sandwith, Jan. 13, 1761. Five children.

DANIEL DRINKER, b. 1735; d. Nov. 25, 1815; m. first Elizabeth Hart, 1760; m. second Hannah Prior, Apr. 6, 1796.

JOSEPH DRINKER, d. Aug. 22, 1809; m. Hannah Hart 1760. Three children.

CHILDREN OF HENRY[6] AND ELIZABETH [SANDWITH] DRINKER.

SARAH S. DRINKER, b. Oct. 23, 1761; d. Sept. 25, 1807; m. May 15, 1787, to Jacob Downing.

ANN DRINKER, b. Jan. 11, 1764; d. Feb. 14, 1830; m. May 17, 1791, to John S. Ryrin.

WILLIAM DRINKER, b. Jan. 28, 1767; d. u. m., 1821.

HENRY S. DRINKER, b. Oct. 23, 1770; d. July 3, 1824; m. Dec. 11, 1794, to Hannah Smith. Six children.

MARY DRINKER, b. Mar. 14, 1774; d. May 2, 1856; m. Aug 8, 1796, to Samuel Rhoady.

CHILDREN OF HENRY S.[7] AND HANNAH [SMITH] DRINKER.

WILLIAM DRINKER, b. Oct. 14, 1795; d. 1836; m. Elizabeth Rodman. No children.

ESTHER DRINKER, b. Nov. 5, 1798; d. Aug., 1856; m. Jan. 28, 1841, to I. P. Pleasants.

ELIZABETH DRINKER, b. Dec. 11, 1801; d. July 11, 1874; m. July 5, 1829, to Samuel C. Paxton.

SALLY DRINKER, b. May. 9, 1803; d. Jan 3, 1877; m. Apr. 3, 1828, to James C. Biddle.

HENRY DRINKER, b. Aug. 11, 1804; d. Feb. 5, 1868; m. June 5, 1845, to Frances Morton.

SANDWITH DRINKER, b. Nov. 19, 1808; d. Jan. 18, 1857; m. Mch. 17, 1840, to Susanna B. Shober.

She was married February 8, 1710-11, to William Raymond, Jr., a brother of Daniel, who married Abigail Balch, and Paul, who married Tabitha Balch, daughters of Deborah's brother Freeborn Balch.

It appears that they removed to Rochester, Mass., as Raymond was clerk of that town, 1738-1787, and held various other town offices. He was a member of the Congregational Church. Their children were : William Raymond, b. Beverly, Feb. 7, 1711-12; Benjamin Raymond, b. Rochester, Dec. 4, 1714 ; Daniel Raymond, b. Rochester, March 27, 1717.

Wm. Raymond married, 2d, Tabitha Edwards, by whom he had several other children. He lived at " Raymond's Landing," which was afterwards set off to Wareham.

17. Lydia,[3] daughter of 2 Benjamin[2] and Grace [Mallet] Balch, was born in Beverly, August 28, 1695.

She married Samuel Bowles, and lived at Rochester, Mass. A deed, executed November 18, 1743, in which she joins with her husband, Samuel Bowles, of Rochester, in Plymouth county, is a conveyance to a sheep pasture in Beverly, which is referred to as a common right unto the heirs of Benjamin Balch, senior, deceased (our honored father). This deed is in the possession of Wm. F. Abbot, of Worcester, Massachusetts.

FOURTH GENERATION.

20. Martha,[4] daughter of 5 Samuel[3] and Martha [Newmarch] Balch, was born in Beverly, Sept. 13, 1676, and married about 1698 to Thomas Hovey, of Ipswich [now Topsfield]. Nothing further is known concerning her.

21. Samuel,[4] eldest son of 5 Samuel[3] and Martha [Newmarch] Balch, was born in Beverly, May 16, 1678, and died in the same town in 1754. He married first, September 23, 1702, Eleanor, daughter of William and Martha Cleves. She died Dec. 12, 1708, aged 30 years. Three children were born in Beverly.

60 MARTHA,[5] b. Aug. 14, 1703; d. March 5, 1703-4.
61 THOMAS,[5] b. Aug. 15, 1705; d. unm. abroad in 1728.
62 SAMUEL,[5] b. June 1,1707; drowned in Exeter river Oct. 12,1728, unm.

He married second, Sept. 3, 1710, Mary, widow of Jonathan Baker, of Salem. Their children were as follows:

63* JOSIAH,[5] bapt. Oct. 28, 1711.
64   EBENEZER,[5] bapt. Jan. 24, 1713-14; d. May 15, 1714.
65* MARTHA,[5] bapt. Oct. 30, 1715.
66* NATHANIEL,[5] born Oct. 13, 1717.

He was a deacon in the church in Beverly, a mariner, and later in life a farmer.

22. Joseph,[4] son of 5 Samuel[3] and Martha [Newmarch] Balch, was born in Beverly, April 26, 1680, and drowned December 9, 1732. He married in Boston, October 23, 1712, Mary, daughter of Timothy and Deborah Osgood, of Andover. She was born February 11, 1690, and died in Boston Oct. 22, 1752. They had six children, all born in Boston.

67* JOSEPH,[5] b. Jan. 13, 1714-15; d. unm. Aug. 20, 1738.
68* MARY,[5] b. March 4, 1716-17.
69* DEBORAH,[5] b. Sept. 8, 1719.
70* EBENEZER,[5] b. May 14, 1723; d. April 28, 1808.

71* TIMOTHY,[5] b. May 28, 1725; d. April 11, 1776.
72* SARAH,[5] b. April 13, 1728.

Joseph was a sea captain, and resided in Boston. The following account of his death is an extract of a letter printed in
the *Boston News Letter*, January 25, 1732-3, from Mr. David
Linzey, mate of brigantine "Robert," and is dated at St.
Christophers, December 13, 1732, via Rhode Island:

"Sir, this comes to acquaint you of the dismal misfortune
that has hapened, Viz., the loss of Captain Balch. He was
knocked overboard with the gaft seventeen days after we left
Boston, about 5 o'clock in the afternoon, in lat. 17° 8' N. We
reckoned ourselves four leagues to the east'd of the Island
of Antigua." Antigua is one of the Caribbean islands, belonging to Great Britain.

23. Benjamin,[4] son of 5 Samuel[3] and Martha [New-
march] Balch, was born in Beverly, March 29, 1682, and died
January 8, 1749-50. He was married June 27, 1705, to Mary
Leech, daughter of John and Mary Leech, and granddaughter of John and Sarah [Conant] Leech of Wenham. They
had seven children, all born in Beverly.

73   MARTHA,[5] b. Dec. 9, 1706; d. y.
74*   MERCY[5], b. Feb. 4, 1708-9.
75   MARTHA,[5] b. Feb. 2, 1712-13; d. Aug. 18, 1714.
76*   MARY,   } twins b. Jan. 9, 1715-16.
77*   MARTHA,[5] }
78*   DEBORAH,[5] b. Aug. 20, 1720.
79   BENJAMIN,[5] b. Sept. 22, 1725; d. Aug. 4, 1736.

Benjamin was a farmer and a deacon in the church. He
lived with his grandfather (2) Benjamin,[3] on the old homestead. This appears from a deed of gift, dated January 4,
1703-4, as follows: "Benjamin Balch, to grandson, Benj.
Balch, Jr., who dwell with me for good will," etc., "conveyes
dwelling house, barn, orchard, upland, salt marsh, 6 acres, 7
acres more, 10 acres to mill, 25 acres beyond to geo. Trow's
on the south, after my decease." The will of Benjamin [23],
dated Sept. 4, 1749, is in the Essex County Probate Records.

24. John,[4] son of 5 Samuel[3] and Martha [Newmarch]

Balch, was born in Beverly, March 29, 1682, a twin of Benjamin[4]. He died probably in December, 1756, in Beverly, and his will was probated at Ipswich, January 3, 1757. He was married first, December 24, 1708, to Mary, daughter of John and Rachel Tuck. She was born in 1682, and died February 20, 1741-2. John and Mary had five daughters. He was a farmer in Beverly.

80 RACHEL,[5] }
81 MARY,[5] } Twins, bapt. May 6, 1711; both died May 12, 1711.
82* ABIGAIL,[5] b. Oct. 5, 1712.
83 SARAH,[5] bapt. April 15, 1716; d. y.
84* DEBORAH,[5] b. Dec. 19, 1717.

John married second, December 25, 1743, Eunice, the widow of Samuel Kimball, of Bradford. She died in 1770, without issue.

25. Phebe,[4] daughter of 5 Samuel[3] and Martha [Newmarch] Balch, was born in Beverly, April 1, 1684. She married Samuel Chapman, and removed to Greenland, N. H. Nothing more is known of her.

26. Peter,[4] son of 5 Samuel[3] and Martha [Newmarch] Balch, was born in Beverly, May 6, 1685, and died in Framingham, December 27, 1755, of a cancer of the hand. He married Elizabeth Dwight of Medfield, Mass., a daughter of Timothy Dwight. The ceremony was performed by Mr. Joseph Baxter. Peter Balch was a deacon in the church in Medfield, and on removing to Framingham was made a deacon in the church there. In 1744 he was elected selectman of Framingham. He was a cordwainer by trade. His will, recorded in the Middlesex County Records, shows that he left a slave, Flora, and children. Temple's History of Framingham mentions a slave negro child name Phebe sold by Elizabeth Balch, August 18, 1767. Children of Peter and Elizabeth:

85 MARY,[5] b. 1726; d. 1730.
86* ELIZABETH,[5] b. 1729; d.
87 TIMOTHY,[5] b. 1732; d. Feb. 7, 1740-41.
88* SARAH,[5] b. 1734; d.

27. Cornelius,[4] son of 5 Samuel[3] and Martha [New-march] Balch, was born in Beverly, May 1, 1687, and died after 1730, at which time he was living in Topsfield. He was a cooper by trade. In 1711 he married Mary Shaw. They had two children.

89 MARY,[5] b. Feb. 22, 1714-15; bapt. Mar 6, 1714-15; d. in childhood.
90* CORNELIUS,[5] bapt. Jan. 1717-18; d. Dec. 20, 1749.

Cornelius' widow married Feb. 5, 1753, Dr. Mical Dwinell, of Topsfield. Two entries in the Topsfield Church Records conclude their history: "Died, September 19, 1770, Mical Dwinell, an aged man, who died suddenly." "Died April 14, 1774, widow Mary Dwinell, who died suddenly, a very aged woman, upwards of 90 years."

30. Ann,[4] daughter of 6 Benjamin[3] and Elizabeth [Woodbury] Balch, was born in Beverly about 1675, and died August 23, 1726. She married first a Mr. Rich and probably had no children, as none are recorded. She married second Nathaniel Wallis, April 20, 1698. He died in 1762 at a very advanced age. His ancestry is appended to the record of 18 Mary.[3] Among their children were the following: Margaret, b. Nov. 11, 1699, who married December 26, 1725, David Ellenwood, whose first wife was 96 Joanna,[5] daughter of 39 John Balch,[4] Jr., and had five children. Nathaniel, b. Nov. 11, 1700. Anna, who married Richard Wittredge. Josiah, bapt. Aug. 26, 1711. Mary, bapt. June 20, 1714, who married Benj. Rayment.

31. Joseph,[4] son of 6 Benjamin[3] and Elizabeth [Woodbury] Balch, was born in Beverly, September 26, 1677, and died August 14, 1712. His gravestone still stands in Beverly's old church yard. On March 21, 1696-7, he was published to Sarah Hart of Salem, who was a daughter of Jonathan Hart, and his wife Lydia [Neal] and grand-daughter of John Neal of Salem. Joseph was a weaver by occupation. His widow

married, December 25, 1716, William Mellowes [now spelled
Mellus], a farmer of Scituate, and moved there with her
children.   Joseph was appointed administrator of his father's
estate, as already noted under 6 Benjamin.[3]   The children
of Joseph and Sarah were the following :

91* BENJAMIN,[5] bapt. Oct. 18, 1702; d. 1753.
92* ELIZABETH,[5] b. Dec. 11, 1704.
93* LYDIA,[5] b. Apr. 7, 1707.
94* SARAH,[5] b. Dec. 1, 1709.
95* JOSEPH,[5] bapt. June 22, 1712.

32. Ebenezer,[4] second son of 6 Benjamin[3] and Elizabeth [Woodbury] Balch, was born in Beverly, June 6, 1680.
He is the first male in the family whose descendants, other
than a daughter, if there were any, it has not been possible
to find and trace for this genealogy.   The following from
Essex Land Records, Vol. 28, p. 212, is all that is certainly
known concerning him.   "May 7, 1714, Ebenezer Balch,
sayler, with wife Ann, for 250 deeds 6½ acres of land in
Beverly to people of ¦the precinct, and bounded on one side
by land of my uncle Samuel Balch."   They probably had a
daughter Ann who married in 1731, one James Butler, of
Boston.

33. Abigail,[4] daughter of 6 Benjamin[3] and Elizabeth
[Woodbury] Balch, was born in Beverly, May 17, 1682.
She was married in 1705 to Edward Rainsford, a weaver.

36. Rebecca,[4] daughter of 7 John[3] and Hannah [Veren]
Balch, was born in Beverly about 1675, and baptized July 25,
1680.   She died September 24, 1704.   She was married
November 28, 1695, to Joseph Dodge, of Beverly, the ceremony being performed by the Rev. John Hall.   Joseph
Dodge was a descendant of Richard Dodge, who with his
brother William, came over from England prior to 1638.
Richard, in his will dated September 14, 1670, mentions his
wife Edith, sons Richard, Samuel, John, Edward and Joseph,
daughter Mary Herrick, and daughter Sarah.   Joseph married Sarah Eaton, February 21, 1671-2.   A son, Joseph,

was born to them about 1675.   Rebecca and Joseph had six children living and mentioned in the will of their grandfather 7 John Balch[3] in 1738.

37. **Hannah,**[4] daughter of 7 John[3] and Hannah [Veren] Balch, was born in Beverly, about 1676, and was baptized, with her sister Rebecca, July 25, 1680.   The date of her death is not known, but in April, 1739, she was a widow, and living at Ashford, Ct.   She received her share of her father's estate from her brother Caleb, who was executor. Her marriage to Richard Leach, of Wenham, was performed by Rev. Thomas Blower, March 7, 1703-4.   Leach died at Wenham in June, 1719.   He descended from Lawrence and Elizabeth Leach, who came to America with their children. One of their sons was Capt. Richard Leach, b. 1618.   His son John married Sarah Conant, in 1643.   Their son John, by his wife Mary, had a son Richard, and a daughter Mary, who married 22 Benjamin Balch.

Richard and Hannah [Balch] Leach had the following children, all born at Wenham: John, b. May 12, 1705, m. Feb. 1, 1727-8, by Rev. Robert Ward, to Lydia Machintyre, of Ipswich, Mass.; Hannah, b. May 28, 1707 ; Deborah, b. May 21, 1708, m. March 3, 1724-5, to Nehemiah Wood, of Ipswich; Mary, b. June 17, 1710 ; Richard, b. July 11, 1711, m. Rebecca Bugbee; Ebenezer and Ruth, twins, b. June 10, 1714 ; Sarah, b. Aug. 17, 1715 ; Abigail, b. June 4, 1718, m. June 4, 1739, James Agard, of Windham.

Of the above children Richard and Ebenezer, and possibly some of the others, removed to Ashford, Windham county, Connecticut, and Richard removed later to Torrington, Connecticut.   In the history of that town some of his family are mentioned.   Among his descendants was the director of the mint, under President Benjamin Harrison.

39. **John,**[4] son of 7 John[3] and Hannah [Veren] Balch, was born about 1679, in Beverly, and died about 1723.   He was married in October, 1700, to Elizabeth, daughter of Richard Ober.   She

died in 1731. John was a mariner, and lived in Beverly.
John and Elizabeth had two children.

96* JOANNA,⁴ b. April 30, 1702; d. May 23, 1725.
97* ANDREW,⁵ b. Feb. 27, 1706-7; d.

40. Israel,⁴ son of 7 John³ and Hannah [Veren] Balch,
was born in Beverly, Sept. 3, 1681, and died in 1758. He
was married first, about 1707, to Ruth, daughter of Edward
and Mary Dodge. She was born Aug. 15, 1685, and died
January 9, 1727. She was the mother of all of Israel's children, nine in number.

98* JONATHAN,⁵ b. April 19, 1709.
99* RUTH,⁵ b. July 3, 1711.
100* JOHN,⁵ b. May 4, 1713; d. 1788.
101* ROGER,⁵ b. June 24, 1715; d. 1744.
102* REBECCA,⁵ b. April 10, 1717.
103* JOSHUA,⁵ b. May 17, 1719; d. March 1, 1804.
104 ISRAEL,⁵ b. Feb. 4, 1720-21; d. y.
105* VEREN,⁵ b. May 22, 1724; d. 1797.
106* HANNAH,⁵ b. Jan. 1, 1726-7; d. unm.

Israel married second, Aug. 28, 1727, Ann Coe of Wenham. She died in 1770. "The Sabbath in Puritan New
England," by Alice Morse Earle, tells of a Bay Psalm Book
published in 1709, which Israel undoubtedly owned. With
the characteristic indifference of our New England forefathers for tiresome repetition, or possibly with their disdain
of novelty, he had inscribed on every blank page of the
book :

> "Israel Balch, His Book.
> God give him Grace therein to look,
> And when the Bell for him doth toal
> May God have mearcy on his Sole."

What the diction lacked in variety is quite made up, however, in spelling, which was was painstakingly different on
each page.

41. Sarah,⁴ daughter of 7 John³ and Hannah [Veren]
Balch, was born in Beverly, March 20, 1682-3. She was living in 1739, and received her share of her father's estate from
her brother Caleb Balch, his executor. Richard Richardson

and Sarah Balch were married by Eben Pemberton, March 3, 1711-12, according to the Boston records. These give the following children of Richard and Sarah: John, b. Aug. 29, 1713, d. Sept. 17, 1713; Sarah, b. July 16, 1714; John, b. Oct. 11, 1716.

45. Joshua,[4] son of 7 John[3] and Hannah [Veren] Balch, was born in Beverly, Nov. 5, 1688. November 11, 1725, he married Rebecca Brown of Boston. The ceremony was performed by Rev. Thomas Foxcraft, pastor of the First Church, Boston. By her he had two children and possibly more, but beyond the record of the birth of these two nothing has been learned regarding Joshua and his family.

107   REBECCA,[5] b. in Boston, Sept. 19, 1727.
108   CALEB,[5] b. in Boston, Oct. 2, 1729.

46. Caleb,[4] son of 7 John[3] and Hannah [Veren] Balch, was born in Beverly, October 14, 1689, and died in the same town in the summer of 1775. He always resided upon his father's farm in North Beverly, which he inherited.

He was first married February 21, 1739-40, to Jerusha Porter of Salem, who was the mother of his five children.

109*   HANNAH,[5] b. May 8, 1741.
110   JERUSHA,[5] b. June 19, 1743, d. y.
111   SARAH,[5] b. Apr. 27, 1745, d. unm. in 1775.
112*   CALEB,[5] b. June 7, 1747, d. Jan. 19, 1820.
113*   ANN,[5] b. Dec. 31, 1748.

Caleb,[4] married second, October 7, 1753, Mary Felton, of Danvers, who outlived him. She was born in March, 1721-2.

47. David,[4] son of 7 John[3] and Hannah [Veren] Balch, was born in Beverly, Oct. 1, 1691, and died in Topsfield, September 25, 1769. He was married April 29, 1713, to Hannah, daughter of Thomas and Sarah [Wallis] Perkins. She was born February 10, 1692-3, and died in Topsfield, January 1, 1747-8. They had three sons.

114* DAVID,⁵ b. Apr. 26, 1715, d. Apr. 17, 1787.
115* JOHN,⁵ b. Nov. 2, 1716, d. Dec. 31, 1774.
116* JOSHUA,⁵ b. July 17, 1720, d. 1766.

David had no children by his second wife Ester Dwinell, whom he married November 14, 1752. She was born May 1, 1720, and died January 13, 1815-16. She was a daughter of Thomas and Mary [Perkins] Dwinell of Topsfield.

50. Mirriam,⁴ daughter of 9 Freeborn³ and Mirriam [Moulton] Balch, was born at Beverly, August 2, 1683, and died at Wenham in 1743. She was married first, February 22, 1704-5, to Richard, son of Joseph and Elizabeth [Hutton] Fowler, of Wenham. December 17, 1707, the Fowler Genealogy states that Richard received from his father land in Wenham upon his marriage with Mirriam. They lived at Wenham, and Fowler died in that town, January 24, 1717-18. They had six children, all born at Wenham : Elizabeth, b. Feb. 19, 1705-6, m. Thomas Perkins, of Ipswich, Feb. 8, 1830-31; Abigail, b. Jan. 4, 1706-7, m. Josiah White, Aug. 19, 1729; Mirriam, b. April 28, 1712, d. y.; Martha, b. June 1, 1714, d. previous to 1743, unm.; Mirriam, b. April 25, 1715, d. previous to 1743, unm.; Joseph, b. Aug. 3, 1717, m. Elizabeth Perkins.

Mirriam married second, Ezikiel Day, of Nutfield, by whom she is not known to have had children. Of her children only Joseph and Elizabeth survived her and shared her estate.

51. Freeborn,⁴ son of 9 Freeborn³ and Mirriam [Moulton] Balch, was born in Beverly, November 25, 1685, and died in that town in March, 1770, aged 85 years. He was married first in Boston, June 19, 1712, to Susanna Woliston. The ceremony was solemnized by Rev. Cotton Mather. Susanna was living in 1732, but there is no record of her death. The issue of this marriage was seven children, all born in Boston.

117* FREEBORN,⁵ b. Feb. 5, 1712-13; d. 1786.
118* SUSANNA,⁵ b. Feb. 11, 1714-15; d. after 1773.
119* ABIGAIL,⁵ b. March 9, 1717-18; d. prior to 1773.
120 MIRRIAM,⁵ b. March 18, 1718-19; d. unm. prior to 1773.

121   JOHN,⁵ b. Sept. 8, 1722; d. y.
122   EBENEZER,⁵ b. Jan. 16, 1723-4; d. y.
123   ELIZABETH,⁵ b. March 2, 1725-6; d. y.

He was married second, January 23, 1736-7, to Mary Hubbard, who died in 1753, without issue. His third wife, Mrs. Sarah Dodge, was married to him November 5, 1758. She died before him, without issue, and at the time of his death only two of his children were living. He was a cordwainer by trade, and lived in Boston some fifteen years. Upon the death of his father, in 1729, he removed to Beverly, and thereafter resided on his portion of the inheritance.

52. Benjamin,⁴ son of 9 Freeborn³ and Mirriam [Moulton] Balch, was born in Beverly, April 17, 1688. He was married in Cambridge, Massachusetts, January 4, 1710-11, to Mary, daughter of Solomon, and his wife, Hepziba [Dunn] Prentice.

There are records of but two children.

124* THOMAS,⁵ b. Oct. 17, 1711; d. June 8, 1774.
125* MARY,⁵ b. June 4, 1714; d. April 29, 1782.

Benjamin was a blacksmith, and lived in Charlestown, Massachusetts. After his father's death he returned with his family to the house built by his father, near Wenham line, and lived in it with his brother Freeborn. The following is taken from the Essex county records: March 3, 1730-31, Benjamin Balch, of Beverly, and Mary, his wife, for £143, sell to John Conant his part of house, barn, cyder mill, &c., "according to yᵉ division made with my brother, Freeborn Balch, of the estate of our father, Freeborn, deceased."

A gravestone still standing in the old Cambridge cemetery, opposite the college, is inscribed as follows: "Here lyes Buried yᵉ Body of Mrs. Mary Balch, wife to Mr. Benjamin Balch, who Departed this life Jan. 28, Anno Dom., 1741-2, in the 64th year of her age." She was born January 4, 1678-9.

53. Skipper,⁴ son of 9 Freeborn³ and Elizabeth [Fairfield] Balch, was born in Beverly, July 25, 1692, and died in

1714 as shown by the following, copied from his tombstone near Wenham Lake.

" Here lyes buried the body of Mr. Skipper Balch who departed this life the 13 September, 1714 in ye 28d year of his age."

Between the graves of Skipper and that of his father is another which reads; " Here lyes buried the body of Mrs. Sarah Balch who departed this life ye 30 September, 1714 in ye 15^6 year of her age."

The monogram "15^6" means 15 to 16. The three stones are still well preserved. The title Mr. was applied, according to the custom then prevailing, to captains and mates of vessels, military captains, eminent merchants, schoolmasters, doctors, magistrates, clergymen, persons who had received a degree at college, and freemen. It appears also that not only the wives but the daughters as well of such men, even when unmarried, were given the title Mrs. Sarah Balch was given this title because her father was a man of quality and not on account of marriage.

54. **Elizabeth,**[4] daughter of 9 Freeborn[3] and Elizabeth [Fairfield] Balch, was born in Beverly about 1696, and died May 1, 1718. She was married April 20, 1715, to John Elliot, born May 16, 1693 and died April, 1751, by whom she had two sons. Skipper, b. Jan. 1, 1715-16; John, b. Mar. 10, 1717-18.

Both sons were living in 1764, Skipper in Newburyport, and John in New Hampshire.

56. **Abigail,**[4] daughter of 9 Freeborn[3] and Elizabeth [Fairfield] Balch, was born in Beverly, about 1700. She was published to Daniel* Raymond, Dec. 5, 1713, and was subse-

---

*William Raymond b. 1639, m. Hannah, dau. of Edward Bishop, b. Apr. 12, 1646. Edward Bishop's second wife, Bridget, was the first sufferer in the Salem Witchcraft delusion. His son William, m. Mary, youngest dau. of John and Elizabeth Kettle, and was killed Jan., 1701, by a falling tree in Beverly woods. Mary died shortly after. Their children were cared for by their uncles Edward Raymond and James Kettle. The children of William and Mary [Kettle] Raymond, are as follows: Mary, b. May 16, 1688, d. Jan. 20, 1688-9. William, b. Feb. 11, 1689-90, m. Feb. 8, 1710-11, Deborah (16) Balch.[3] Daniel, b. Nov. 25, 1691, m. Mar. 11, 1713-14, Abigail (56) Balch.[4] Paul, b. Jan. 22, 1694-5, m. Feb. 28, 1716-17, Tabitha (57) Balch.[4]

quently married to him March 11, 1713-14. Raymond removed to Marblehead, Mass., and lived there from 1715 to
about 1730. Thence he moved to Beverly, and shortly after
to Concord, Mass. He died in 1745, aged about 59 years,
while in the expedition against Canada. His eldest son
whose name is not known, also died while on this expedition. The following children of Daniel and Abigail (Balch)
Raymond were born at Concord, Massachusetts. Abigail
Raymond, b. Mch. 1, 1730-31; Paul, b. Apr. 5, 1733; Elizabeth, b. Dec. 25, 1735; Mary, b. Mch. 8, 1737-8; Freeborn B.,
b. Feb. 20, 1739-40.

57. **Tabitha,**[4] daughter of 9 Freeborn[3] and Elizabeth
[Fairfield] Balch, was born in Beverly about 1702. She
married Feb. 28, 1716-17, Paul Raymond, a brother of her
sister's husband, Daniel. Paul was born Jan. 22, 1694-5.
The baptism of five of their children is recorded in Salem.
They sold their property on Main street Jan. 27, 1730-31, and
removed to Bedford, Middlesex Co., where he died in 1759.
Their three youngest children were born at Bedford. Elizabeth, bapt. Apr. 9, 1721. Mary, bapt. Mar. 3, 1722-3.
William, bapt. Aug. 1, 1725; b. July 30, 1725. Edward,
bapt. Dec. 17, 1727; d. y. Paul, bapt. May 17, 1730; d. y.
Paul, born May 12, 1732; m. 1775, Abigail Jones. Tabitha,
b. Sept. 19, 1743. Lucy, b. Aug. 5, 1737. Nathan, b. Feb.
28, 1739-40.

58. **William,**[4] son of 9 Freeborn[3] and Elizabeth [Fair-
field] Balch, was born in Beverly, Sept. 30, 1704, and died in
Bradford [name changed to Groveland, Feb. 20, 1850] Jan.
12, 1791-2. He married, March
12, 1727-8, Rebecca Stone,
only child of Daniel and
Hannah [Woodbury] Stone.
She was born March 23, 1709-10, and died July 2, 1749.
William and Rebecca had seven children, all born in Bradford.

126* REBECCA,[5] b. Aug. 9, 1729; d. May 6, 1790.
127* WILLIAM,[5] b. July 15, 1730; d. May 6, 1806.
128* HANNAH,[5] b. May 25, 1732; d. July, 1755.
129* SARAH,[5] b. Dec. 16, 1733; d. Dec. 1753.
130* DANIEL,[5] b. Mar. 14, 1734-5; d. Nov. 30, 1790.
131* NATHANIEL,[5] b. Jan. 17, 1737-8; d. Oct. 26, 1802.
132* BENJAMIN,[5] b. Apr. 4, 1743; d. Oct. 16, 1828.

Rev. William Balch married, second, Abigail Blodgett, no issue. She died April 10th, 1793, aged 88 years, William Balch graduated from Harvard in 1724, then he studied Theology, and was settled over the just organized parish of East Bradford, June 7, 1727, and held the place for nearly 65 years. He is said to have possessed strong powers of mind, was mild and conciliatory in manner, and universally beloved by his flock. He was a man of great learning.

"Rev. Mr. Chipman, of Beverly, his old pastor, with Rev. Mr. Wiggleworth, published a controversial pamphlet directed against Rev. Mr. Balch, whom they accused of Arminianism. In reply to Chipman, he says: "It is the grief of my Soul to see the Bible so much neglected and other books so much made the standard. I cannot help miserably bewailing the state of the reformed churches who stick where they were left by the Reformation."

He was very fond of agriculture. Beside his homestead farm, in part presented him by the parish, he inherited from his father, Freeborn, a good estate in North Beverly, on which there was an apple orchard of six acres; moreover, his wife Rebecca inherited a considerable estate from her father. The fruit from his orchard was considered the best in Essex county, and his cider bore the best price in the market. They called it "Arminian cider." His large landed property should have made him quite independent of the meagre salary paid country ministers in those days, which made life with many of them a struggle for existence.

59. Mary,[4] daughter of 9 Freeborn[3] and Elizabeth [Fairfield] Balch, was born in Beverly, June 5, 1707, and died in Amesbury, Mass., Oct. 10, 1788. She was married Dec. 12,

1727, to Rev. Paine Wingate, of Amesbury, who died in
Amesbury, Feb. 19, 1786. He was the son of Col. Joshua
and Mary [Lunt] Wingate, of Hampton. They had twelve
children: Mary, b. Dec. 17, 1728, d. March 12, 1800, m.
Ephrim Elliot ; Elizabeth, b. Sept. 6, 1730, d. Nov. 5, 1815,
m. Bartlett; Paine, b. Aug. 10, 1732, d. in infancy; Sarah,
b. Nov. 12, 1734, d. October, 1736 ; Sarah, b. April, 1737,
d. September, 1825, m. Samuel Bradley, d. in Amesbury;
Paine, b. May 14, 1739, d. March 7, 1838, m. Eunice Pickering; was a S. Court Judge of N. H., U. S. Senator, or Representative during Washington's first term, 1789 to 1793, at
the same time her cousin, Col. Tim. Pickering, was Secretary
of War and Secretary of State ; for some years he was the
oldest graduate of Harvard, graduating in 1759 ; John, b.
July 4, 1741, d. in infancy ; John, b. June 25, 1743, d. July
26, 1819 ; William, b. July 3, 1745, d. Nov. 3, 1821, m. Mehitable Bradley ; Joshua, b. March 3, 1746, d. Oct. 11, 1844,
m. Hannah Carr; Abigail, b. March 27, 1749, d. Aug. 28,
1807, m. —— Ingalls ; Joseph, b. July 17, 1751, d. Aug. 2,
1824, m. Judith Carr.

Rev. Paine Wingate graduated from Harvard College in
1723.

FIFTH GENERATION.

63. Josiah,[5] son of 21 Samuel[4] and Mary [Baker] Balch, was born in Beverly, Mass., and was baptized October 28, 1711. He married in 1735, Patience, daughter of Joseph Chamberlain, one of the first settlers of Oxford, Mass., from which place he had moved to Keekamooching, in the town of Dudley. Patience probably died before 1755, as she is not named in a deed signed in that year by her husband, and recorded in the Essex records, vol. 116, p. 166. In this deed he is designated as Josiah Balch, house-wright, of Douglas, Worcester county. It appears that after leaving Beverly he located in Thompson, Connecticut, and from there moved into Worcester county. In 1744, with his brother-in-law, Ebenezer Chamberlain, he bought 320 acres of land from the state. It was in the wilderness, on one of those bits of land known as gores, which in the crude surveys of early times were sometimes left unsurveyed between the boundary lines of towns which were intended to join. This territory was called the South Gore, but being near Douglas, Josiah became known as Josiah of Douglas. In the partition of the purchase he took the south part, near the Connecticut line, where he probably died. In 1759 he deeded his farm to his son. The South Gore was subsequently taken into the town of Oxford.

Josiah and Patience had but two children, both born on their farm in the South Gore.

133 MARY,[6] b. July 27, 1737.
134* SAMUEL,[6] b. June 25, 1739; d. Feb. 11, 1816.

The connecting of Josiah with his descendants now living was one of the difficult problems in the preparation of this genealogy. For a long time it was not possible to trace him beyond his giving of a deed in 1755, and there was no evidence of his marriage. Inquiry of the town clerk of Douglas and the county clerk of Worcester elicited no information concerning him. However, the name Josiah appearing again, 60 years later, in a family living at Athens, Vermont, led to suspicions of family ties, which it seemed impossible to complete. These suspicions were strengthened, because the Christian name Josiah occurred in only these two instances in the genealogy. The family in Athens traced its ancestry back to a grandfather Samuel, but knew not the name of his father. Assistance to complete the chain came curiously through chance inquiry of the writer, concerning an old resident of Yonkers, who formerly lived in Oxford, adjoining Douglas, Massachusetts. This led to communication with Mr. George F. Daniels, a resident of Oxford, who was engaged on a history of his town. He was able and willing to supply the information needed to complete the broken chain.

65. **Martha,**[5] daughter of 21 Samuel[4] and Mary [Baker] Balch, was born in Beverly, Massachusetts, October 80, 1715. She was married October 3, 1735, to Nathaniel Raymond. He was born April 1, 1712. Their children were all born at Beverly. Hannah Raymond, b. May 1, 1786; m. John Porter, Jr., of Danvers, July 22, 1755; they removed to Lyman, Me. John Raymond, b. June 5, 1738. Sarah Raymond, b. Oct. 3, 1740; m. Ebenezer Porter, Nov. 20, 1760; they lived at Danvers. Samuel Raymond, b. July 7, 1743. Martha Raymond, b. Feb. 13, 1744-5; d. Sept. 26, 1805; m. John Low, May 14, 1767; they lived at Lyman, Me. Nathaniel Raymond, b. May 8, 1749, a sailor; m. Phœbe Dodge of Amherst, now Mt. Vernon, N. H.; they had six children. Nathan Raymond, bapt. May 29, 1757; m. Mehitable Green; they had five children.

66. **Nathaniel,**[5] son of 21 Samuel[4] and Mary [Baker] Balch, was born in Beverly, October 13, 1717. He married Joanna Dodge. They were published March 4, 1737-8. About 1744 they removed from Beverly to Haverhill, Mass., and

some dozen years later to Wakefield, N. H. They had eleven children. The first three were born in Beverly, the others in Haverhill. Nathaniel was admitted to full communion in the Haverhill church, June 1, 1746,* by dismission from the Second church of Beverly. Wakefield, N. H., was incorporated in 1774. The town was settled under the name of Easton, in 1767. Nathaniel Balch was the first deputy in the Provincial Congress of New Hampshire, from Wakefield, being elected in 1775. A deed, on record in Exeter, from John Horn to Nathaniel Balch, dated 1773, shows that he lived on Witch-trot road, between John Horn and Eliphelet Quimby. Nathaniel was a prominent man in the church and town. He moved from Wakefield over the line into Maine, and the Balch mills in Acton took their name from him. Nathaniel and Joanna had the following children:

135 BENJAMIN,⁵ b. March 3, 1738-9; d. March 11, 1739.
136 LYDIA,⁵ b. May 10, 1740.
137 MARY,⁵ b. Feb. 4, 1741-2.
138* JOANNA,⁵ b. Dec. 18, 1744.
139 BETTY,⁵ b. Jan. 11, 1746-7.
140 ABIGAIL,⁵ b. Sept. 9, 1748.
141 SARAH,⁵ b. July 30, 1749.
142* ANNA,⁵ b. July 22, 1751.
143* NATHANIEL,⁵ b. Sept. 18, 1753;* d. April, 1795.
144* HEPZIBAH,⁵ b. Jan. 18, 1755; d. 1816.
145 MARTHA,⁵ b. May 2, 1756.

67. **Joseph,⁵** son of 22 Joseph⁴ and Mary [Osgood] Balch, was born in Boston, Jan. 13, 1714-5, and died unmarried in New London, Ct., Aug. 20, 1788.

68. **Mary,⁵** daughter of 22 Joseph⁴ and Mary [Osgood] Balch, was born in Boston, March 4, 1716-17. She married

---

*[At the time of Nathaniel's baptism question was raised in the Haverhill Church regarding the Orthodox belief of Mr. Balch. It was proven that he did not regard all parts of the bible equally, that he denied the doctrine of original sin, of eternal damnation, and that Christ was God. His position was substantially that of the Unitarians to-day. The church found that his opinion in all the points but two could not prohibit his partaking of communion with them. Of these two, the identity of Christ with God was debated and twice postponed without action, but upon the question of the "eternal torments of Hell" he was suspended from the church. But, it was voted that his children might be baptized. This was in 1753, long before the Liberal Unitarian movement came to the surface, and shows him to have been a remarkable man for his time.—See Balch Leaflets, Vol. I. E. P.]

James Dodge, of Boston, September 16, 1736. Nothing more
is known of her.

69. Deborah,[5] daughter of 22 Joseph[4] and Mary [Osgood]
Balch, was born in Boston, Sept. 16, 1719. She married
James Robbins. Nothing more is known of her.

70. Ebenezer,[5] son of 22 Joseph[4] and Mary [Osgood]
Balch, was born in Boston, Mass., May 14, 1723, and died in
Hartford, Conn., April 28, 1808.
He was married twice, his first *Eben ⁓. Balch*
wife was Miss Sarah Belden,
daughter of Capt. Jonathan Belden, of Wethersfield, Conn.
The marriage ceremony was solemnized by the Rev. James
Lockwood, at Wethersfield, on June 28, 1750. Sarah died
April 3, 1756 in the 29th year of her age. Their three
children born in Hartford, were the following:

146* Sarah,[6] b. Apr. 1, 1751; d. Mar. 4, 1823.
147* Mary,[6] b. Nov. 17, 1752; d. Sept. 16, 1852.
148* Jonathan Belden,[6] b. Nov. 14, 1754; d. Feb. 16, 1825.

Ebenezer married for his second wife, Miss Lois Belden, a
cousin of his first wife, and daughter of Ezra Belden, of
Wethersfield. The ceremony was solemnized by the Rev.
Elnathan Whitman, November 29, 1756. She died May 27,
1798. Their seven children were born in Wethersfield.

149 Lois,[6] b. Feb. 27, 1758; d. Aug. 15, 1760.
150* Joseph,[6] b. Feb. 16, 1760; d. Dec. 5, 1855.
151* Lois,[6] b. Dec. 20, 1761; d.   1852.
152* Lucy,[6] b. Dec. 21, 1763; d. July 17, 1854.
153* Ebenezer,[6] b. Aug. 30, 1766; d. Dec. 31, 1848.
154* Timothy,[6] b. Oct. 26, 1768; d. Nov. 22, 1844.
155* William,[6] b. May 17, 1778; d. Mar. 31, 1857.

This family was remarkable for their great longevity, for the
average ages of Ebenezer and the nine children that grew to
maturity was nearly 84 years. Two were between 70 and 75
years; two between 75 and 80; two between 80 and 85; two
between 90 and 95; and two between 95 and 100.

Ebenezer was a goldsmith and clock-maker by occupation.
When he came to his majority, he left his home in Boston and
went to Hartford, but removed to Wethersfield 12 April,

1756. A letter written by him to his mother and now in the possession of Rev. Manning B. Balch, of DeSoto, Wis., shows his deep religious sentiment and his love for his mother. There was no regular mail service between Boston and Hartford in those days, their letters being carried by chance travellers. From this letter it would appear that his mother married a second husband. In the Town Clerk's office in Hartford, Vol. 9, p. 46 is a record of a deed from Ebenezer Balch, to James Cadwell of a tract of land and buildings in the city of Hartford near Great Bridge. The sum paid was 3000 pounds in money of the old Tenor Bill of Credit; it is dated Nov. 19, 1755, 29th y. of the reign of George the 2nd. A fragment of a diary kept by Ebenezer Balch is now in possession of his descendant, John Watson Case, and has been printed in Balch Leaflets, Vol. I.

71. **Timothy,**[5] son of 22 Joseph[4] and Mary [Osgood] Balch, was born in Boston, May 28, 1725, and died in Newport, R. I., Apr. 11, 1776. He married Nov. 29, 1757, Sarah, daughter of Capt. Joseph Rogers of Newport. She was born October 18, 1735, and died July 24, 1811. They had six children all born in Newport:

156 SARAH,[6] b. Sept. 20, 1759; d. Sept. 9, 1765.
157 MARY,[6] b. Feb. 9, 1762; d. unm. Jan. 5, 1831.
158 JOSEPH,[6] b. Sept. 16, 1764; d. Sept. 16, 1765.
159* JOSEPH,[6] b. Oct. 25, 1766; d. July 20, 1845.
160 TIMOTHY,[6] b. July 5, 1769; d. unm. Oct. 29, 1822.
161* JOHN ROGERS,[6] b. May 18, 1772; d. Apr. 2, 1848.

72. **Sarah,**[5] daughter of 22 Joseph[4] and Mary [Osgood] Balch, was born in Boston, April 13, 1728. She married Capt. John Malcom.

74. **Mercy,**[5] daughter of 28 Benjamin[4] and Mary [Leech] Balch, was born in Beverly, February 4, 1708-9. She married John Lovett, Jr., in 1729. They had five children. Ann Lovett, b. July 19, 1731; Mary, b. Sept. 3, 1733; Thomas, b. Sept. 17, 1735; Benj. Balch, b. Dec. 13, 1737, was in the French and Indian War; John, b. Dec. 21, 1739; Peter, b. June 26, 1741; Simon, b. May 28, 1743.

76. Mary,[5] daughter of 23 Benjamin[4] and Mary [Leech] Balch, was born in Beverly, January 9, 1715-6. She was married at Ipswich, Mass., May 9, 1734, by Symonds Epps, Esq., to Mihill Woodbury, who died in England, in 1755. Their three children were born in Beverly. Myhil Woodbury, b. Oct. 8, 1734, d. Aug. 29, 1738; Myhil Woodbury, b. Oct. 25, 1739, d. Jan. 14, 1741; Mara Woodbury, b. Oct. 5, 1741.

Mara Woodbury married Richard Butman, at Beverly, March 16, 1761, and they had nine children, as follows: Richard Butman, b. Mar. 6, 1762; Myhil, b. Jan. 26, 1764; Mary, b. Feb. 3, 1766; Hannah, b. Apr. 30, 1767, m. Issachar Thissell, Feb. 5, 1785; Benjamin, bapt. Nov. 6, 1768, d. y.; Benjamin, b. Oct. 22, 1769; Samuel, b. Sept. 3, 1771; Thomas, b. June 13, 1774; and Joanna, b. Mar. 16, 1776.

Mihil Woodbury was a lineal descendant of William Woodbury, a brother of the "Old Planter" John Woodbury. William settled in a beautiful location on the north shore of Beverly harbor, now Beverly Farms, three miles east of the home of his brother John, at the head of Bass River.

77. Martha,[5] daughter of 23 Benjamin[4] and · Mary [Leech] Balch was a twin sister of Mary. She was married June 5, 1735, to William Trask. Their children were: Martha Trask, b. 1737; William, b. 1740, d. y.; Deborah, b. 1744; William, b. 1747, d. y.; Osman, b. 1749; William, b. 1751; Barnabas, b. 1754; Mercy, b. 1757.

78. Deborah,[5] daughter of 23 Benjamin[4] and Mary [Leech] Balch was born in Beverly, Aug. 20, 1720. She was married April 13, 1743 to Jonathan Dodge.[4] They had five children born in Beverly. Previous to 1759, they removed from Beverly to Ipswich. Cornelius Dodge, b. Jan. 7, 1744; Benjamin, b. Jan. 17, 1745, d. y.; Miall, b. Mar. 20, 1748; Benj. Balch, b. June 8, 1753; Abner, bapt. Mar. 30, 1753.

Cornelius Dodge, eldest son of Deborah[5] and Jonathan Dodge inherited the John Balch homestead. He had four children, Azor, Jessie, Seth and Bethia. Azor, the eldest son of Cornelius, married Elizabeth Foster and had ten children. Azor, Benjamin Balch, Joshua Foster, Joseph, Bethiah, Lydia, Elizabeth, Joanna, Mary and Caroline.

Joshua Foster Dodge inherited the old homestead with about eight acres of land. He married Mary Porter and had two children, Martha and Adie Frances. She has outlived him and two additional husbands. Her daughter Martha died young, and her second daughter, Adie Frances married Charles Herrick, and now owns the old homestead.

82. **Abigail**,[5] daughter of 24 John[4] and Mary [Tuck] Balch, was born in Beverly, October 5, 1712. She was married May 11, 1731 to Nathaniel Brown of Salem. Record exists of the birth of but one child, Mary, who was bapt. Sept. 24, 1732.

84. **Deborah**,[5] daughter of 24 John[4] and Mary [Tuck] Balch, was born in Beverly, December 19, 1717. She was married July 13, 1738, to William Dodge, Jr. They had ten children born in Beverly. Mary Dodge, b. 1739; William, b. 1741; Samuel, b. 1743, d. y.; Huldah, b. 1745; Samuel, b. 1748; Martha, b. 1750; John, b. 1753; Thomas, b. 1755; Cornelius, b. 1758; Sarah, b. 1761.

86. **Elizabeth**,[5] daughter of 26 Peter[4] and Elizabeth [Dwight] Balch, was born in Medfield, Mass., in 1729. She was married in Framingham, Mass., Sept. 22, 1748, to Daniel Adams.

88. **Sarah**,[5] daughter of 26 Peter[4] and Elizabeth [Dwight] Balch, was born in Medfield, Mass., in 1734. She was married in Framingham, to John Pike, of that town. Nothing further regarding the families of these two daughters of Peter[4] has been found.

90. **Cornelius**,[5] only son of 27 Cornelius[4] and Mary [Shaw] Balch, was born in Boxford, Mass., and was bapt. in Jan. 17, 1717-18, and died in Topsfield, Mass., Dec. 20, 1749. He was married in Boxford, January 24, 1739-40 to Martha, daughter of Joseph and Martha Robinson, of Topsfield. She

was born July 16, 1720, and died in Topsfield, June 11th, 1815, aged 94 years, 10 months, and 24 days. Their five children were born in Topsfield.

162* MARY,⁶ b. Feb. 15, 1741.
163* MARTHA,⁶ b. Apr. 9, 1743; d. Apr. 6, 1822.
164 JOSEPH,⁶ b. April 14, 1745; d. Jan. 25, 1750.
165 ELIZABETH,⁶ b. Feb. 22, 1747; d. Sept. 7, 1749.
166 CORNELIUS,⁶ b. Dec. 23, 1748; d. Sept. 22, 1749.

The gravestones of Cornelius, and his three children still stand in the old graveyard, at Topsfield and are among the oldest legible.

Martha [Robinson] Balch, married again, April 16, 1752, to John Cree, by whom she had three children. Asa Cree, b. Feb. 10, 1755. Elizabeth, b. July 24, 1757. Cornelius, b. Sept. 9, 1759.

91. Benjamin,⁵ son of 31 Joseph⁴ and Sarah [Hart] Balch was baptized Oct. 18, 1702, grew up in Scituate, where he had removed with his mother upon her second marriage, and practised his father's trade of a weaver. He seems, however, to have subsequently changed his occupation for that of a sailor, as he is mentioned as a "marriner" in 1733, just after his removal to Boston. Drew's History of Scituate, states that he resided in Scituate for several years "near the North Meeting House, 50 rods south."
He died in 1758.
September 8, 1726, he married Nazareth, daughter of Judge John, and Deborah [Loring] Cushing. She was born Sept. 11, 1703. [Judge Cushing was descended from Peter Cushing of Hingham, Norfolk Co., Eng., whose son Theophilus, b. 1579, settled in Hingham, Mass., in 1663, and Nazareth was a cousin of the Margaret Cushing who married May 30, 1717, Admiral Wm. Fletcher, b. in Sussex, Eng., March, 1668, whose daughter Mary, b. June 20, 1780, married (170) Nathaniel⁶ Balch.]
The children of Benjamin, and Nazareth were at least six in number.

167* Deborah,[6] b. 1727.
168* Hart,[6] b. 1731; d. about 1751.
169* Benjamin,[6] b. March 4, 1732-3; d.
170* Nathaniel,[6] b. May 7, 1735; d. Sept. 18, 1808.
171 John,[6] b. May 16, 1737; d. y. baptized as Joseph.
172* Joseph,[6] b. Feb. 10, 1738-9; d. Sept. 1, 1826.
173 Elizabeth,[6] bapt. July 25, 1742.

The five last children were baptized at the New South Church, Boston, as children of Benjamin and Nazareth Balch.

92. Elizabeth,[5] daughter of 81 Joseph[4] and Sarah [Hart] Balch, was born in Beverly, Dec. 11, 1704. She was married February 25, 1727-8, to Alexander Thorpe.

93. Lydia,[5] daughter of 81 Joseph[4] and Sarah [Hart] Balch, was born in Beverly, April 7, 1707. She was married January 28, 1723, to Israel Cowen.

94. Sarah,[5] daughter of 81 Joseph[4] and Sarah [Hart] Balch, was born in Beverly. She was married December 7, 1732 to David Cole, son of Ambrose Cole of Cohassett. He was born in 1704. They had five children.

Lydia Cole, b. 1733, William, b. 1735, David, b. 1737, Elizabeth Cole, b. 1739, Abigail, b. 1743.

95. Joseph,[5] son of 81 Joseph[4] and Sarah [Hart] Balch, was born in Beverly, and baptized June 22, 1712. Whether he ever married and had children has not been learned. In October, 1733, he was a cooper and living in Plymouth, Mass. In the list of persons who settled in Machias, in 1765, as given in the "Historical Sketch of Machias, Maine, Memorial of the Centennial anniversary of that town May 20, 1863," is the name Joseph Balch, does it mean him?

96. Joanna,[5] daughter of 89 John[4] and Elizabeth [Ober] Balch, was born in Beverly, April 30, 1702, and died May 28, 1725. She was married Dec. 23, 1719 to David, son of Benjamin and Mary Ellengwood, a mariner. He was born August 17, 1699. The issue was three children. David, b. Oct. 17, 1720, d. Oct. 30, 1720 ; David, b. Sept. 17, 1721 ; Joanna, b. Oct. 29, 1722, d. Jan. 25, 1824.

Ellengwood married second, Margaret Wallis, who was born Nov. 1, 1699. She was a daughter of Nathaniel and 80 Ann[4] [Balch] Wallis. They were married Dec. 26, 1725, and had five children.

97. Andrew,[5] son of 39 John[4] and Elizabeth [Ober] Balch, was born in Beverly, Feb. 27, 1706-7. His death occurred near Keene, New Hampshire, but its date is not known. He was married first Jan. 1, 1728-9, to Bethiah Lovett, by whom he had at least five children. Bethiah died Sept 15, 1745, aged 37 years. Their children, born in Beverly, were as follows :

174   ELIZABETH,[6] b. Apr. 6, 1733, d. May 16, 1736.
175* JOHN,[6] b. Oct. 12, 1735, d. Apr. 30, 1808.
176   ANDREW,[6] bap. Dec. 23, 1738, d. 1738.
177* CALEB,[6] b. Oct. 16, 1740.
178   JOANNA,[6] b. Sept. 9, 1744.

Andrew was married to Ruth Woodbury, January 21, 1745-6. Only one son seems to have been the issue of this second marriage, and the tradition in the family says he was born at Dedham, Mass.

179* BENJAMIN,[6] born 1747 or 8.

Daniel F. Secomb's History of Amherst, N. H. states that in June, 1785, Andrew was a landholder in that town. He was at Keene, N. H., in 1773, when he signed the Alarm list.

Andrew, with his sons Benjamin and John signed the following pledge of the Committee of Safety dated at Keene, N. H., Mar. 14, 1776.

" We the subscribers do hereby solemnly engage, and promise, that we will to the utmost of our powers at the Risque of our Lives and Fortunes, with Arms oppose the Hostile Proceedings of the British Fleets and Armies against the United American Colonies."

98. Jonathan,[5] son of 40 Israel[4] and Ruth [Dodge] Balch, was born in Beverly, April 17, 1709.

He was married Nov. 18, 1733, to Esther, daughter of William Hall, of Mansfield, Ct. She was born in Mansfield,

Oct. 22, 1713. They had one child mentioned in Weaver's History of Ancient Windham, Ct.

180ᵉ RUTH.⁶

99. Ruth,⁵ daughter of 40 Israel⁴ and Ruth [Dodge] Balch was born in Beverly, July 3, 1711.

She was married first, Sept. 23, 1731 to Ebenezer Meacham, by whom she had four children. James Meacham, bapt. Oct. 20, 1734 ; Ruth, bapt. May 9, 1736, d. y.; Ruth, bapt. May 21, 1738 ; Anna, bapt. Apr. 24, 1743.

Meacham died in 1748, and Ruth married April 27, 1757, Nathaniel Bragg, of Wenham. There is no record of any children by this marriage.

100. John,⁵ son of 40 Israel⁴ and Ruth [Dodge] Balch, was born in Beverly, Mass., May 4, 1718. He died about 1788. He married Elizabeth, daughter of William Hall, of Mansfield, Conn., Nov. 9, 1736, a sister of his brother Jonathan's wife. They had one child.

181ᵉ JOHN,⁶ b. about 1737.

101. Roger,⁵ son of 40 Israel⁴ and Ruth [Dodge] Balch was born in Beverly, June 24, 1715, and died about 1744. He was married in Charlestown, Mass., Feb. 23, 1742, by the Rev. Mr. Hall, to Ann, daughter of Jonathan and Katherine [Waters] Kettell. She was born May 14, 1721. Roger was a mariner, their only child.

182ᵉ JONATHAN,⁶ b. Nov. 26, 1743, d. in 1812.

Roger's widow was married Aug. 18, 1748, to Shippie Townsend, of Boston, and removed there with her son. Shippie Townsend was the son of David and Mable Townsend, of Charlestown, born Nov. 27, 1722. His first wife was Mehitable Whittemore of Charlestown, b. 1717. She died March 10, 1746-7. He died of yellow fever, Aug. 31, 1798.

102. Rebecca,⁵ daughter of 40 Israel⁴ and Ruth [Dodge] Balch, was born in Beverly, April 10, 1717. She was married January 7, 1746-7, to Joseph Hull. Two of their children were baptized in the Second Church of Beverly. Rebecca Hull, bapt. May 1, 1748 ; Mary Hull, bapt. Feb. 4, 1749-50.

103. Joshua,[5] son of 40 Israel[4] and Ruth [Dodge]
Balch, was born in Beverly, May 17, 1719, and died in
North Beverly, March 5, 1804. He was married first, November 28, 1743, to Joanna Williams, who died in December, 1767. They had nine children, all born in Beverly.

183* JOANNA,[6] b. Sept. 15, 1744; d.
184   SARAH,[6] b. April 13, 1746; d. unm. after 1804.
185* RUTH,[6] b. Sept. 15, 1748; d.
186* JOSHUA,[6] b. Nov. 28, 1750; d. about 1778 or 9.
187* ISRAEL,[6] b. April 1, 1753; d. 1827.
188   MARY,[6] b. May 20, 1755; d.
189   WILLIAM,[6] b. May 1, 1757; d.
190* HANNAH,[6] b. Dec. 26, 1760; d.
191* ISAAC,[6] b. Dec. 27, 1766; d. March 6, 1842.

Joshua married second, October, 1769, Patience Pitman of
Marblehead, by whom he had three children. She was born
in 1740, and died in August, 1824.

192   JOHN,[6] b. March 17, 1771; d. y.
193* BETSEY,[6] b. Feb. 10, 1772; d. Oct. 13, 1863.
194   JOHN,[6] b. Nov. 2, 1777; d. y.

105. Veren,[5] son of 40 Israel[4] and Ruth [Dodge] Balch,
was born in Beverly, May 22, 1724, and died in Connecticut
about 1797. He was married September 26, 1750, to Sarah,
daughter of Henry Taylor, of Mansfield, Connecticut. They
resided in Mansfield, where their children were all born.

195* ISRAEL,[6] b. Jan. 26, 1751.
196   A son b. July 27, 1752, d. same day.
197* HENRY,[6] b. July 2, 1753.
198   SARAH,[6] b. May 4, 1757.
199* MARY,[6] b. May 26, 1760.
200   JOSEPH,[6] b. Apr. 8, 1763, d. Aug. 8, 1764.
201* HANNAH,[6] b. Oct. 8, 1765.
202   LYDIA,[6] b. Oct. 10, 1768.

106. Hannah,[5] daughter of 40 Israel[4] and Ruth [Dodge]
Balch, was born in Beverly, January 1, 1726-7. After her
father's death she lived with her aged stepmother. She never
married, was living in Beverly in 1805, aged 78 years.

109. Hannah,[5] daughter of 46 Caleb[4] and Jerusha [Por-
ter] Balch, was born in Beverly, May 8, 1741. She married
John Raymond, of North Beverly, Aug. 28, 1760.

112. **Caleb,**[5] son of 46 Caleb[4] and Jerusha [Porter] Balch, was born at Beverly, Massachusetts, June 7, 1747, and died at Windham, N. H., January 19, 1820. He was married in February, 1780, to Miss Mary Saunders, who died at Windham, August 28, 1843, aged 88 years ; "Caleb went to Windham, N. H. about 1784 and bought a farm. He had a respectable property, but lost much of it by becoming security for his brother-in-law, James Saunders, of Salem, N. H." Caleb and Mary [Saunders] Balch had eight children.

203   CALEB,[6] b. May, 1781, in Beverly, d. Sept. 17, 1799, at Windham.
      "He slid down the side of a barn head foremost between the boards and the hay and was smothered."
204* POLLY,[6] b. Jan. 16, 1783, in Beverly, d. Apr. 5, 1869.
205* WILLIAM,[6] b. Aug. 31, 1786, at Windham, d. June 24, 1830.
206   JOHN,[6] b. 1789, at Windham, d. July 19, 1790.
207* JERUSHA,[6] b. Jan. 26, 1791, at Windham, d. Oct. 8, 1874.
208   SAMUEL P.,[6] b. 1793 at Windham, d. Feb. 27, 1798.
209   ROXANA,[6] b. Apr. 25, 1797, at Windham, d. Dec. 17, 1816.
210   PORTER,[6] d. y. at Windham.

113. **Ann,**[5] daughter of 46 Caleb[4] and Jerusha [Porter] Balch, was born in Beverly, December 31, 1748. She married Lot Conant, of Beverly, June 20, 1780.

114. **David,**[5] son of 47 David[4] and Hannah [Perkins] Balch, was born in Topsfield, April 25, 1715, and died April 17, 1787. He married his cousin Hannah, daughter of Samuel and Margaret [Tower] Perkins, November 21, 1752. She was born June 17, 1720, and died September 14, 1807. David and Hannah had eight children, all born in Topsfield.

211* DAVID,[6] b. Aug. 19, 1753; d. July 22, 1812.
212* SAMUEL,[6] b. Feb. 7, 1755; d. June, 1840.
213   ISRAEL,[6] b. April 3, 1756; d. unm. Nov. 23, 1777, at Halifax, N. S.
214   THOMAS,[6] b. Jan. 22, 1759; d. Apr. 1, 1759.
215* THOMAS,[6] b. Mar. 29, 1761; d. Mar. 10, 1830.
216   RICHARD,[6] b. Dec. 23, 1762; d. unm. Jan. 4, 1770.
217   WILLIAM,[6] b. May 26, 1764; d. unm. Feb. 26, 1776.
218   JOSHUA,[6] b. June 6, 1769, d. unm. Nov. 11, 1839.

115. **John,**[5] son of 47 David[4] and Hannah [Perkins] Balch, was born in Topsfield, November 2, 1716, and died December 31, 1774. He was married June 17, 1740, to Rebecca

Smith, daughter of Samuel and Rebecca [Curtis] Smith.
She died March 1, 1794, aged 80 years.

John[5] was a tanner and currier, and acquired a large estate
by that business. He left each of his five sons a good farm
in Topsfield. The house which he built in 1774, is now
owned and occupied by his great-grandson 974, Benj. J.
Balch.[8]

219* DAVID,[6] b. Jan. 4, 1740-41; d. July 31, 1801.
220* JOHN,[6] b. Mar. 26, 1742; d. July 25, 1798.
221* SAMUEL,[6] b. Mar. 20, 1743-4; d. unm. 1820.
222* ROBERT,[6] bapt. July 28, 1745; d. Aug. 3, 1830.
223* HANNAH,[6] bapt. Mar. 29, 1747; d.
224* CORNELIUS,[6] b. Nov. 26, 1749; d. May 21, 1795.
225   WILLIAM,[6] b. 1752; d. unm. Mar. 22, 1764.
226* ROGER,[6] b. May 26, 1755; d. Jan. 8, 1842.
227* REBECCA,[6] b. Mar. 27, 1758; d.

116. Joshua,[5] son of 47 David[4] and Hannah [Perkins]
Balch, was born in Topsfield, July 17, 1720, and died in 1766.
He was married August 25, 1748, to Sarah Town. They
resided in Boxford, Mass., where Joshua died, and their two
children were born.

228* JOSHUA,[6] bapt. July 2, 1749; d. about 1777.
229* ARCHELAUS,[6] bapt. Oct. 14, 1750; d. about 1777.

117. Freeborn,[5] eldest son of 51 Freeborn[4] and Susanna
[Wolliston] Balch, was born in Boston, February 5, 1712-13,
and died in Brad-
ford, Mass., 1786.
He was married
about 1760 to the widow Platt, whose maiden name was Mary
Perkins. By her first husband she had two children. She
died August 7, 1808, at the home of her son, Wesley Perkins
Balch, in Haverhill, Mass.

Freeborn lived upon his father's estate in North Beverly,
and his seven children were born in that town. He removed
to Bradford, Mass., May 12, 1779,* from Haverhill.

---

*He had been in Bradford with his family in 1771 as per warning in
Court files, but the date of his beginning a permanent residence there
appears on the Town records as above. (E. P.)

280 MARY,⁵ b. July 25, 1761; d.
281* MEHITABLE,⁵ b. March 3, 1763; d. Jan 5, 1853.
282* BENJAMIN,⁵ b. Jan. 10, 1705; d. 1852.
233* WESLEY PERKINS,⁵ b. Aug. 14, 1766; d. Apr. 27, 1827.
284* ABIGAIL,⁵ b. Aug. 19, 1768; d. 1842.
285* EUNICE,⁵ b. Apr. 14, 1771; d. Mar. 21, 1855.
286* JOHN,⁵ b. July 18, 1772; d. 1849.

118. Susanna,⁵ eldest daughter of 51 Freeborn⁴ and Susanna [Wolliston] Balch, was born in Boston, February 11, 1714-15. She married Richard Kimball of Wenham, they were published February 6, 1737. The date of her death is not known, but she was living in 1773.

119. Abigail,⁵ second daughter of 51 Freeborn⁴ and Susanna [Wolliston] Balch, was born in Boston, March 9, 1717-18, the date of her death is not known, but it was prior to 1773. She was married to Israel Porter, of Wenham, to whom she was published September 27, 1741. Porter dying, she married a second time to Francis Symonds, of Topsfield, they were published February 21, 1748.

124. Thomas,⁵ son of 52 Benjamin⁴ and Mary [Prentice] Balch, was born in Charlestown, Mass., Oct. 17, 1711, and died at South Dedham, January 8, 1774. He married Mary Sumner, daughter of Edward and Eliza [Clapp] Sumner of Roxbury, Mass., October 11, 1737. She was born October 9, 1717, and died March 31, 1798. She was aunt to Gov. Increase Sumner, of Roxbury.

237* THOMAS,⁵ b. August 31, 1738; d. unm. Sept. 29, 1756.
238* MARY,⁵ b. Nov. 16, 1740; d. Nov. 3, 1815.
239* BENJAMIN,⁵ b. Feb. 12, 1743; d. May 4, 1816.
240* ELIZABETH,⁵ b. Sept. 2, 1746; d. Sept. 15, 1820.
241* LUCY,⁵ b. Jan. 10, 1748; d. Mar. 17, 1776.
242* IRENE,⁵ b. Feb. 6, 1753; d. July, 1815.
243* HANNAH,⁵ b. Dec. 10, 1755; d. Apr. 17, 1839.
244* THOMAS,⁵ b. Feb. 21, 1761; d. 1780.

Thomas⁵ graduated from Harvard College in 1733, then studied theology, and was ordained at South Dedham, June 30, 1736, one week after the church was organized. In 1744 he was appointed by the Committee of War to accompany the expedition against Cape Breton as Chaplain. The following account by him, of the expedition, is taken from the records of the South Parish of Dedham.

" Having an Inclination and being desired by the Committee of War to attend the Army as one of the Chaplains in the Expedition against Cape Breton, I accordingly obtained consent of my People on March 11, 1744-5 and on the 13, took my leave of my family and People. Arrived in Safety & Health at Canso on the 2d of April. Sailed from Canso to Cape Breton on April 29, entered the Chappeaurouge Bay the next morning, and soon after went on Shoar. The seige of Louesborg continued until June 17. On which Day we entered and took possession of that Strong & important place, upon Terms of Capitulation. Sailed from Louisborg for New England, July 11, arrived in Safety at Boston on the 27 of 3d month, 1745, Laus Deo."

Rev. Thomas Balch was a man of great learning, and was classed among the principal literati of New England.

Mrs. Mary [Sumner] Balch died in the family of her son-in-law, Rev. Jabez Chickering, in South Dedham.

125. Mary,[5] daughter of 52 Benjamin[4] and Mary [Prentice] Balch, was born in Charlestown, Mass., June 4, 1714, and died in New Ipswich, N. H., in the family of her son Aaron, April 29, 1782. She was married in Cambridge, Mass., April 19, 1738, to Isaac Brown, he was born in 1711, and died October 6, 1759. He was a very active business man. He settled in Waltham Plain as a merchant and inn keeper. Their children were :

> MARY, b. Mar. 17, 1738-9, d. Nov. 18, 1740.
> ISAAC, b. Apr. 14, 1740, d. Nov. 16, 1740.
> MARY, b. Aug. 22, 1741, d. Oct. 7, 1742.
> ELIZABETH, b. Mar. 3, 1742-3, d. y.
> EUNICE, b. Oct. 10, 1744, d. Sept. 9, 1818. She was married Nov. 29, 1764, to Rev. Stephen Farrar, who was born Sept. 8, 1738, and graduated from Harvard in 1755. He was ordained at New Ipswich, N. H., in 1760, and died June 23, 1808. They had the following 13 children: *Eunice*, b. 1765; *Stephen*, b. 1766; *Eunice*, b. 1768; *James*, b. 1769; *Isaac Brown*, b. 1771; *Samuel*, b. 1772; *Prentice*,

b. 1773; *Polly*, b. 1775; *Moses*, b. 1777; *Lydia*, b. 1778; *Caleb*, b. 1780; *Nancy*, b. 1782; and *Ephraim Hartwell*, b. 1783. Their grandchildren numbered seventy-nine.

ISAAC, b. June 24, 1746, d. 1752.

MOSES, b. April 6, 1748, d. June 15, 1820. He was fitted for College by his uncle, Rev. Thomas Balch, of Dedham. He graduated at Harvard in 1768. After teaching school in Framingham, Lexington and Lincoln, he settled in Beverly as a merchant, in the autumn of 1772. He was very zealous in the cause of American Liberty, raised a Company, in July, 1775, under a Commission from Jos. Warner, Pres. of Prov. Cong., and in Jan., 1776, joined the American Army as Capt. in Glover's Regt. 14th Continentals with a commission signed by John Hancock, Pres. of Congress. He was in the Battle of Trenton. On the expiration of his term of enlistment in 1777, he returned to Beverly, and resumed business with Israel Thorndike. He retired in 1800 with an ample fortune. His constitution was vigorous and his life active and useful. He was a member of the State Legislature, and a Presidential Elector in 1808. He was dignified, and courteous in manner, he united integrity and benevolence; was exemplary in all social and domestic relations; and a generous contributor to public and private charities and associations. Quincy's History of Harvard College, notices Mr. Brown among beneficiaries of that institution. He is also referred to in Stone's History of Beverly. He married first, Oct. 16, 1774, Elizabeth Trask, daughter of Osmeyer Trask, of Beverly, she died leaving no children July 7, 1788. On May 3, 1789, he married second, Mary Bridge, who outlived him. She died Feb. 21, 1842. Their children were, *Charles*, b. May 14, 1793; *George*, b. Nov. 27, 1794, d. July 25, 1796; *George*, b. Nov. 24, 1799, d. Aug. 1848.

MARY, b. Dec. 29, 1749, d. Nov. 30, 1824. Mary Brown was married June 1, 1769, to Ephraim Hartwell, Jr. They settled in New Ipswich, N. H. Hartwell was a merchant, and magistrate. One child, *Mary*, was born to them Aug. 24, 1770, she married March 6, 1791, Col. Caleb Bellows, of Walpole, N. H.

SARAH, b. Oct. 6, 1751, d.

AARON, b. Sept. 16, 1752, d. Nov. 14, 1811. He was a merchant in Boston, afterwards of New Ipswich, N. H. He married 1st, Elizabeth Stowell, who was the mother of all his children, she d. Aug. 4, 1797. He married 2d, Thesta Dana, daughter of Hon. Sam'l Dana, of Brighton. Aaron had nine children as follows: *Aaron*, b. Jan. 15,

1774, d. June 12, 1843; *Mary*, b. Nov. 27, 1777, d. Nov. 8, 1830; *Betsey*, b. Dec. 1779, d. Jan. 29, 1822; *Isaac*, b. Sept. 1782, d. Sept. 27, 1827; *Samuel*, b. Aug. 20, 1785, d. Sept. 18, 1812; *Sarah*, b. July 6, 1788, d. Aug. 21, 1790; *Lucy*, b. April 9, 1792; *Sarah*, b. 1794, and a son unnamed.

126. Rebecca,[5] daughter of 58 Rev. William[4] and Rebecca [Stone] Balch was born in Bradford, Mass. (now Groveland), August 9, 1729, and died in East Bradford, May 6, 1790. She was married Nov. 1, 1750, to Bradstreet, son of Abraham and Elizabeth Parker, who was born July 28, 1729, and died April 8, 1809. Their names stand side by side in the baptismal record for 1729. They passed their lives in E. Bradford on the farm still owned by their descendants. They had twelve children all born in East Bradford. Benjamin Parker, b. April 8, 1751, d. June 16, 1753; Rebecca, b. Dec. 8, 1752, d. Mar. 17, 1830; Phineas, b. Sept. 6, 1754, d. Mar. 30, 1811; Moses, b. April 20, 1756, d. July 8, 1837; Hannah, b. Nov. 9, 1757, d. Sept. 13, 1783; Benjamin, b. Nov. 11, 1759, d. May 12, 1845; Abigail, b. July 19, 1763, d. Dec. 19, 1824; Nathan, b. July 8, 1765, d. Aug. 22, 1765; Mary, b. Dec. 8, 1767, d. Jan. 5, 1839; Bradstreet, b. July 26, 1770, d. Sept. 6, 1798; William Balch, b. Apr. 27, 1772, d. May 1, 1844; Betsey, b. Apr. 20, 1775, d. Mar., 1861.

127. William,[5] son of 58 Rev. William[4] and Rebecca [Stone] Balch, was born in East Bradford, July 15, 1730, and died May 6, 1806. He married Rebecca Bailey, daughter of Jonathan Bailey, Nov. 15, 1759. She was born July 28, 1736, and died April 23, 1827. William was a deacon in the church at East Bradford, and Selectman in 1779. He was a farmer, and passed his life on the homestead farm in E. Bradford, where he died. They had eleven children all born in E. Bradford.

245   REBECCA,[6] b. June 30, 1760, d. Sept. 5, 1762.
246   WILLIAM,[6] b. Oct. 5, 1761, d. Sept. 17, 1762.
247*   REBECCA,[6] b. July 6, 1763.
248*   SARAH,[6] b. Aug. 26, 1765, d. Oct. 2, 1838.
249*   WILLIAM,[6] b. July 9, 1767, d. unm. July 9, 1862.
250*   JONATHAN,[6] b. June 15, 1769, d. April 4, 1838.

251 PERCIS,⁶ b. May 24, 1771, d. June 14, 1771.
252 CLARISSA,⁶ b. Sept. 3, 1772, d. unm. Dec. 14, 1827.
253ᵃ BENJAMIN,⁶ b. Nov. 9, 1774, d. summer of 1860.
254ᵃ MARY,⁶ b. Dec. 3, 1776, d. July 9, 1847.
255 TABITHA,⁶ b. Sept. 30, 1779, d. unm. Mar. 21, 1888.

128. Hannah,⁵ daughter of 58 Rev. William⁴ and Rebecca [Stone] Balch, was born in Bradford, May 25, 1732, and died July 17, 1755. She was married April 7, 1752, to Ezekiel Hale of West Newbury and was Hale's third wife. They had one child, Sarah Hale, who married Moses Pillsbury, by whom she had two children, Hannah and Oliver.

129. Sarah,⁵ daughter of 58 Rev. William⁴ and Rebecca [Stone] Balch, was born in Bradford, December 16, 1733, and died in Dec., 1753, in her 20th year. She married December 26, 1751, Orlando Sargent of Amesbury. They had one child, Abigail Sargent, who married James Bailey.

130. Daniel,⁵ son of 58 Rev. William⁴ and Rebecca [Stone] Balch, was born in Bradford, March 14, 1734-5, and died in Newburyport, Mass., Nov. 30, 1790. He was twice married, first to Miss Hannah Clemens, Aug. 19, 1756, who was the mother of all his children. He married second, March 24, 1784, Miss Judith Thurston, who was born in Newbury, a suburb of Newburyport. She died June 9, 1825. He was a watchmaker by trade, and lived in Newburyport, Mass. In his will dated March 9, 1789, he leaves to his eldest son Daniel, his "Coat of Arms." As his children Hannah and William are not mentioned, it is presumed that they died without issue.

256 HANNAH,⁶ b. 1758, d. unm. 1781.
257ᵃ DANIEL,⁶ b. Mar. 1, 1761, d. Oct. 13, 1835.
258 WILLIAM,⁶ b. d. y.
259ᵃ THOMAS HUTCHINS,⁶ b. July 7, 1771, d. June 28, 1817.

131. Nathaniel,⁵ son of 58 Rev. William⁴ and Rebecca [Stone] Balch, was born in Bradford, Jan. 17, 1737-8, and died in Newburyport, Oct. 26, 1802. He married first, Joanna, daughter of John and Abigail [Bailey] Day, of Bradford. She died Sept. 18, 1800, aged sixty years. They had sixteen children.

260 NATHANIEL,⁵ b. 1760, d. Sept. 6, 1761.
261* JOHN,⁵ b. Jan. 12, 1761, d. Dec. 29, 1836.
262* ABIGAIL,⁵ b. Nov. 12, 1762, d. Nov. 13, 1802.
263* NATHANIEL,⁵ b. Aug. 9, 1764, d. 1793.
264* HANNAH,⁵ b. June 11, 1766, d. July 17, 1833.
265* SAMUEL,⁵ b. Jan. 25, 1768, d. May 26, 1850.
266 JOSEPH,⁵ b. Mar. 1771, d. Aug. 27, 1774.
267 MEHITABLE,⁵ b. 1772, d. Jan. 24, 1773.
268* BETSEY,⁵ b. July 10, 1774, d. July 16, 1836.
269 MEHITABLE,⁵ b. Sept. 22, 1776, d. Feb. 22, 1778.
270 JOSEPH,⁵ b. Dec. 28, 1777, d. Jan. 10, 1778.
271* LUCY,⁵ b. Feb. 21, 1779, d. 1854.
272 PAMELA,⁵ b. Aug. 23, 1780, d. unm.
373 ALICE,⁵ d. unm. of Yellow fever, Sept. 14, 1800.
274 JOANNA,⁵ d. unm. of Yellow fever, Sept. 14, 1800.

Nathaniel,⁵ married second, July 22, 1802, the widow Sarah Coffin. He was constable at Bradford in 1779. By trade he was a cooper, lived upon a farm in Bradford until about 1800, when he removed to Newburyport. He was buried in the old cemetery near the Mall in Newburyport. His wife Sarah died January 26, 1804.

132. **Benjamin,**⁵ son of 58 Rev. William⁴ and Rebecca [Stone] Balch, was born in Bradford, April 4, 1748, and died Oct. 16, 1823. He married September 7, 1786, Hannah, daughter of Andrew, and Mary [Ronchon] Sigourney. She was born in April, 1754, and died December 15, 1838. When Benjamin married her she was the widow of Capt. John Patten of Biddeford, Me. Patten was shipwrecked, and drowned at Marshfield, January 11, 1783. Hannah was aunt to Charles Sigourney, husband of Mrs. Lydia H. Sigourney, the poet.

Benjamin and Hannah were an eccentric couple. They were both buried in the cemetery back of the Episcopal Church, on High street, in Newburyport. They had no children.

134. **Samuel,**[6] son of 63 Josiah[5] and Patience [Chamberlain] Balch, was born on his father's farm, in Oxford, Mass., June 25, 1739, and died in Athens, Vt., February 11, 1816. He married Miss Susan Aldrich. She died March 11, 1821, aged 78 years. They had ten children ; the seven eldest were born in Oxford, and the three youngest in Guilford, Vt.

275* Susanna,[7] b. May 23, 1762.
276* Olive,[7] b. May 4, 1764; d. March 1, 1826.
277* Samuel,[7] b. March 23, 1767; d. about 1847.
278* Josiah,[7] b. Dec. 25, 1769; d. Apr. 29, 1843.
279 Patience,[7] b. May 4, 1772; d.
280* Elizabeth,[7] b. Oct. 23, 1775; d.
281* Nathaniel,[7] b. Dec. 3, 1779; d. Dec. 25, 1857.
282 John,[7] d. aged 18 years.
283* Coben,[7] b. d.
284* Abigail,[7] b. March 30, 1786, d. March 30, 1858.

About 1778 Samuel emigrated with his family from Oxford, Mass., to Guilford, Vermont. In 1797 he paid a thousand dollars for one hundred acres of land situated in the southern portion of Athens, Vt., and it is probable that about this date he removed from Guilford to Athens.

138. **Joanna,**[6] daughter of 66 Nathaniel[5] and Joanna [Dodge] Balch, was born at Haverhill, Mass., December 18, 1744. She was married, December 31, 1769, to Enoch Chase, at Dover, N. H.

142. **Anna,**[6] daughter of 66 Nathaniel[5] and Joanna[Dodge] Balch, was born at Haverhill, Mass., July 22, 1751. She was married at Dover, N. H., March 9, 1769, to Paul Harford.

143. **Nathaniel,**[6] only son of 66 Nathaniel[5] and Joanna [Dodge] Balch, was born at Haverhill, Mass., September 18,

1753, and died at Wakefield, N. H., in April, 1795. His death was caused by the falling of a tree. He married Lydia, daughter of Jonathan and Deborah [Wentworth] Twombley. Deborah was the daughter of Ebenezer and Sarah [Roberk] Wentworth. Nathaniel lived in Wakefield, N. H., and his eight children were born in that town.

285* SAMUEL,[7] b. 1779; d.
286* JOSEPH,[t] b. March 7, 1781; d. Dec. 14, 1846.
287* DEBORAH,[7] b. Dec. 28, 1782; d. Sept. 25, 1863.
289* NANCY,[7] b. Dec. 8, 1784; d.
290 SALLY,[7] b.; m. Asa Abbott, no children; d.
291 BETSEY,[7] b.; m. Simon Brown, of China, Me.
292* FREDERICK B.,[7] b. May 13, 1790; d. Sept. 29, 1861.
293* ABIGAIL,[7] b. July 23, 1795; d. July 18, 1868.

Nathaniel signs a petition of Freeholders for a repeal of the " Lumber Act," addressed to the Legislature, dated at Wakefield, August, 1785. Vol. XIII. New Hampshire Town Papers, p. 590.

He enlisted as a private in Capt. Jeremiah Gilman's company, 18 July, 1777, and was discharged 30 September, 1777.

144. Hepzibah,[6] daughter of 66 Nathaniel[5] and Joanna [Dodge] Balch, was born at Haverhill, Mass., January 18, 1755, and died at Wakefield, N. H., in 1816. She married Tobias Hanson. They lived in Wakefield, and their children, all born in that town, were as follows :

TOBIAS, married Miss S. Adams. For a time they lived in Salem, Massachusetts, then they returned to Wakefield, and lastly removed to North Conway, New Hampshire, where he died, at the age of 93 years. They had five children: *Tobias Adams* and *Joseph*, both of whom lived in Salem, Massachusetts, and were men of large property and families; *John* and *Samuel* were merchants in Boston; *Susan A.* married A. G. Hoyt, a distinguished artist, who painted a portrait of Daniel Webster, now hanging in the State House at Concord, New Hampshire; Anna H. Hoyt, a daughter of Susan and A. G. Hoyt, married Prof. Horace Bumstead, of the Atlanta University, Georgia.

ISAAC, married and lived in Wakefield, N. H.

BARTLETT, married and left a large family, a son lives in Minneapolis, Minn.

JACKSON.

JOHN, married and left a family in Wakefield, N. H.

JOSEPH, left children.

SUSAN, married Joseph Pike, a lineal descendant of Robert Pike, the Puritan, and one of the few men of his time who dared stand up and boldly defend the Salem witches. They had two children, *Joseph Hanson Pike*; Joseph left a widow and three daughters, who were living at Wakefield in 1886. *Dolly Pike* was born in 1802, and died Sept. 17, 1886. Her son, Joseph P. Gilman, has furnished the records of Hepzibah Balch.

ROSE, married Robert Pike, a brother of Joseph, and left many descendants.

HANNAH, married a Mr. Wiggins, and left a daughter living in Dover, N. H., and grandchildren living in Wakefield.

LYDIA, married a southern gentleman, and has descendants.

NANCY, married a Mr. Edgerly, and has descendants.

146. **Sarah,**[6] daughter of 70 Ebenezer[5] and Sarah [Belden] Balch, was born at Hartford, Ct., April 1, 1751, and died at Wethersfield, Ct., March 4, 1823. She was married November 12, 1772, to Elijah, son of Joseph Wells, of Wethersfield. Elijah Wells was born February 27, 1751, and died at Wethersfield, Ct., December 28, 1796. Mr Wells was a farmer by occupation. He was a soldier in the American army during the Revolution, and among the many battles in which he participated were those of Bunker Hill, and Trenton. From exposure and hardships in the service his constitution was broken, and he died at the age of 45 years, leaving a family of eight children. Sarah, b. Aug. 2, 1773; d. Mar. 11, 1823. Elijah, b. Feb. 27, 1775; d. Sept. 18, 1830. Mary, b. Apr. 25, 1777; d. Sept., 1854. Patty, b. June 26, 1779; d. Nov. 18, 1855. Esther, b. July 24, 1781; d. July 11, 1818. Hannah, b. Oct. 2, 1783; d. Oct. 28, 1857. George, b. Aug. 26, 1786; d. Nov. 21, 1861. Henry, b. May 13, 1789; d. Jan. 19, 1858.

147. **Mary,**[6] daughter of 70 Ebenezer[5] and Sarah [Belden] Balch, was born at Hartford, Ct., November 17, 1752, and died at Wethersfield, Ct., September 16, 1852. She had lived nearly a century, and was bright and active to the last. At her death the church bell in Wethersfield tolled one

hundred times. Through all her long life her place at church was seldom vacant. In 1784 she married Daniel Ayrault, a son of Capt. Nicholas, and grandson of Dr. Nicholas Ayrault, a French Huguenot. Daniel Ayrault was born in 1736, and died at Wethersfield, March 8, 1807. They had but two children. Mary, b. May, 1785; d. Feb., 1854, married Edward Shepard; their son, Daniel Ayrault Shepard, was living in Cleveland, Ohio, in 1884. Daniel, b. Oct. 1786; d. Nov. 11, 1862, left descendants in the female line.

148. Jonathan Belden,[6] son of 70 Ebenezer[5] and Sarah [Belden] Balch, was born at Hartford, Connecticut, November 14, 1754, and died at West Hartford, Connecticut, February 16, 1825. He was married, December 6, 1766, at Wethersfield, Connecticut, to Hopeful, eldest daughter of Samuel Hurlburt. Six children were born to them on their farm in Hartford, where they always lived.

294° SARAH,[7] b. 1777; d. Oct. 5, 1807.
295 CLARISSA,[7] b. Nov. 21, 1779; d. unm. Sept. 20, 1796.
296° MARY,[7] b. Sept. 24, 1782; d. Oct. 18, 1845.
297° FLORA,[7] b. Apr. 24, 1785; d. Dec. 10, 1831.
298° JONATHAN,[7] b. Dec. 14, 1788; d. July 19, 1867.
299° BELA,[7] b. Feb. 6, 1792; d. May 6, 1852.

He married for his second wife Elenor Whitman, January 18, 1815, and she died at West Hartford, March 8, 1832, without issue. The Connecticut Records show that he served six days in Capt. Chester's Company from Wethersfield, and the Lexington Alarm list shows that he enlisted May 11, 1775, in the second Regt., 9th Company, as a private and was discharged in December of the same year.

150. Joseph[6], son of 70 Ebenezer[5] and his second wife Lois [Belden] Balch, was born at Hartford Ct., February 16, 1760, and died at Johnstown, N. Y., December 5, 1855. During the revolutionary war he served as a drummer boy. He was a thorough Christian and gentleman. His memory was retentive and he was always abreast of the times. His faculties he retained to the last.

In 1794 he settled at Williamstown, Mass., and followed the occupation of a silversmith, and clock-maker, a business he had learned from his father. In 1810 he removed to Johnstown, N. Y., where death came to him while in his accostomed seat in church, Bible in hand, following the scripture reading by his pastor. He was buried with military honors.

In 1786 he married Miss Mary Watson by whom he had seven children. Miss Watson was born March 6, 1765, and died February 11, 1844.

300 JOSEPH,[7] b. May 26, 1787. He went to Mexico or South America in 1817, and was never heard from.
301* JUSTIN,[7] b. Dec. 28, 1788; d. July 31, 1826.
302* SARAH MARIA,[7] b. Nov. 6, 1790; d. June 10, 1879.
303 AURELIA,[7] b. May 19, 1793; d. Sept. 17, 1794.
304* GUSTAVUS,[7] b. May 19, 1795; d. 1877.
305* CORNELIA,[7] b. Nov. 8, 1797; d. Jan. 19, 1863.
306* VISTUS,[7] b. Feb. 18, 1799; d. Oct. 25, 1884.

151. Lois,[6] daughter of 70 Ebenezer[5] and Lois [Belden] Balch, was born at Hartford, Connecticut, December 20, 1761, and died in 1852, at Cleveland, Ohio, and was buried at Atwater in that state. She married Oliver, son of Joseph, and Sarah Talcott. They lived at Southwick, Mass., until after all their children were born. In 1819 they moved to Cleveland, Ohio. Mr. Talcott was born at Glastonbury, Ct., November 29, 1759, and died at Atwater, Ohio, in 1830. Lois and Oliver had five children, all born at Southwick, Mass. Joseph, b. Feb. 12, 1789; d. at Atwater, Ohio, 1858; Sally, b., d. at Atwater, Ohio; Mary, b., d. at Brooklyn, N. Y.; Emily, b., d. at Atwater, Ohio; William, b., d. Wisconsin.

152. Lucy,[6] daughter of 70 Ebenezer[5] and Lois [Belden] Balch, was born at Hartford, Connecticut, December 21, 1768, and died at Hartford, Connecticut, July 17, 1854, and was buried at Wethersfield. She was married in 1788 to Wait Goodrich, a sea captain, and to them were born three children.

LUCY, b. 1789, d. Feb. 8, 1873. She married Fontaine Raphael, in May, 1811. He was born in 1761 and died Nov. 6, 1840.

They had three children. *Marie Louise Angelique Raphel*, b. Dec. 2, 1811, d. Feb. 5, 1852, and married a Mr. Brown; *Joseph D'Ortique Raphel*, b. Aug. 4, 1813, d. Nov. 19, 1857; *Adelaid Josephine Raphel*, b. Apr. 3, 1818, d. Jan. 16, 1858.

GROVE, d. in New York city in 1833. He married Laura Talcott, who died in New York city in 1834. He was a gold-beater by occupation. They had two daughters.

EMILY, d. y.

153. **Ebenezer,**[6] son of 70 Ebenezer[5] and Lois [Belden] Balch, was born in Hartford, Connecticut, August 30, 1766, and died at Plattsburgh, New York, December 31, 1846. About 1790 he married Sarah, daughter of James and Abigail [King] Burchard,* of Becket, Mass. She was born in June,

---

*BURCHARD GENEALOGY.

1 Thomas Burchard, b. in Roxbury, Eng., 1595, wife Mary, b. 1597, one son and five daughters, b. in England, came to America in the ship "True Love," landed at Boston late in 1636, and settled at Saybrook, Ct.

John, only son of Thomas and Mary Burchard, b. in England, 1628, d. in Lebanon, Ct., 1702. He married first, July 22, 1653, Charity Ann Andrews. His second wife was Jane Lee [relict of Samuel Hyde]. John was the father of fourteen children; six died in infancy.

Samuel, b. July, 1663; James, b. July, 1665; Abigail, b. November, 1667, m. John Calkins, Oct. 23, 1690; Thomas, b. January, 1669, settled in Norwich, Ct.; John, b. February, 1671, settled in Lebanon, Ct.; Joseph, b. February, 1673, settled in Lebanon; Mary, b. June, 1679, settled in Lebanon; Daniel, b. November, 1680, settled in Lebanon. John Burchard, as he spelled his name, was a man of considerable celebrity.

James, second son of John above, married Elizabeth Beckwith, March 17, 1697. They lived in Norwich, Ct., and had ten children: Elizabeth, b. September, 1697; James, b. May, 1699, d. June 12, 1782, in Becket, Mass.; Sarah, b. July, 1701, d. y.; Mathew, b. December, 1702; John, b. April, 1704, great-grandfather of the late President Rutherford Burchard Hayes; Phebe, b. October, 1705; Sarah, b. October, 1707; Jonah, b. October, 1709; Rebecca, b. October, 1717; Daniel, b. October, 1718.

James, eldest son of James and Elizabeth, married Deborah ——; she died in 1768. In 1775 he settled in Becket, then town No. 4, Berkshire county, Mass. For several years he was town clerk. He had but one son, James, b. 1730, d. July, 1820, in Becket.

James, only son of James and Deborah, married Abigail, daughter of David and Lydia King; she d. June 6, 1794, aged 63 years. They resided in Becket, and their seven children were born in that town: Lydia, b. 1757; Deborah, b. 1760; Abigail, b, 1762; Phebe, b. 1764; James, b. Aug. 17, 1766; Sarah, b. 1768, d. Oct. 23, 1852, married Ebenezer Balch; Betsey, b. June, 1772, m. Walter Cook, of Richmond, Mass.

1768, and died at Plattsburgh, N. Y., October 28, 1852. In 1891 the remains of Ebenezer and Sarah, his wife, were removed to the Riverside cemetery at Plattsburgh, and interred by the side of their son, Alvah Burchard, and the monument upon the lot was suitably inscribed. They had six children.

307* EBENEZER,⁷ b. June 22, 1792; d. Feb. 19, 1861.
308* SARAH,⁷ b. April 19, 1794; d. Sept. 15, 1871.
309* ALVAH BURCHARD,⁷ b. April 18, 1796; d. March 5, 1871.
310* BETSEY,⁷ b. July 22, 1798; d. Aug. 3, 1866.
311 CLARISSA,⁷ b. April 20, 1801; d. May 3, 1822; m. Thomas Thorn.
312* HORATIO JAMES.⁷ b. July 22, 1806; d. Jan. 17, 1846.

Ebenezer learned the trade of goldsmith and clock-maker with his father, but did not follow the trade. In 1800 he moved with his family, which consisted of his wife and four children, to Plattsburgh, N. Y., and soon after purchased two tracts of land, together containing 240 acres, and situated four miles west from the village, and bordering on the north side of the Saracac river. Immediately upon his occupancy of the tract of land he built a log house. In 1806 he built a frame barn, and in 1812 he built a two-story frame house, which for those days was considered very fine. All the nails used in its construction were made by him. There were no machine-made nails in those days. In this house he and his wife both died. For several years he was engaged in shipping timber to Quebec, Canada, by rafts, and by reason of this venture he became financially embarrassed, and sold his farm to his sons, Ebenezer and Alvah Burchard. He was a man of intelligence, uprightness of character, and honor. Both he and his wife were members of the First Presbyterian Church of Plattsburgh. He helped to build the church edifice in 1806. It was a historical structure in connection with the battle of Plattsburgh, September 11, 1814. In 1867 it burned down, and from it started the great fire of Plattsburgh.

Ebenezer was a member of a militia company called the "Silver Grays," and as such participated in the battle of

Plattsburgh. His character is well summed up in the text of
the sermon preached at his funeral. It was Psalms XXXVII.,
37: "Mark the perfect man, and behold the upright: for the
end of that man is peace."

154. Timothy,[6] son of 70 Ebenezer[5] and Lois [Belden]
Balch, was born at Hartford, Ct., October 26, 1768, and died
at Plattsburg, N. Y., November 22, 1842. He married Ann,
daughter of John and Ann [Skinner] Whitman. She was
born at Hartford, Ct., May 23, 1775, and died at Plattsburgh,
N. Y., April 11, 1848. About 1802 he located on a farm a
short distance to the north east of the farm belonging to his
brother Ebenezer. He and his wife were members of the
first Presbyterian church in Plattsburgh.

313* BETSEY,[7] b. May 4, 1794; d. June 26, 1864.
314* CHESTER,[7] b. July 26, 1796; d. June 3, 1875.
315 LUCY,[7] b. Mar. 12, 1799; d. s. p., Mar. 19, 1840, m. John Smith.
316 ELIZA,[7] b. Dec. 1, 1801; d. Aug. 8, 1828.
317* HENRY,[7] b. Nov. 24, 1803; d. June, 1875.
318* EMILY,[7] b. Mar. 29, 1807, d. 1893.
319 MARIETTA,[7] b. Nov. 15, 1809, d. Apr. 4, 1840.
320 JONATHAN W.[7] b. Apr. 5, 1811; d. unm. May 11, 1888.
321* WILLIAM SKINNER,[7] b. Oct. 22, 1813.

155. William,[6] son of 70 Ebenezer[5] and Lois [Belden]
Balch, was born at Hartford, Ct., May 17, 1778, and died in
that city, March 31, 1857. He married Miss Ann Smith,
May 13, 1801, who was born at Berlin, Connecticut, in 1776,
and died at Hartford, in February, 1858. William was a
carpenter and resided at West Hartford, Connecticut. The
six children of William and Ann [Smith] Balch were born
at West Hartford.

322 WILLIAM,[7] b. Apr. 25; 1802; d. unm. Jan. 4, 1822.
323 SYLVESTER,[7] b. Aug. 23, 1804; d. s. p., Nov. 28, 1877, m. Lucy
     Warren.
324* HENRY,[7] b. Oct. 10, 1806; d. Apr. 18, 1874.
325 EDWARD,[7] b. July 27, 1809; m. Mary Ann Corning of Hartford,
     Ct. Two children, d. y.
326* THOMAS,[7] b. Feb. 19, 1811; d. Feb., 1891.
327* ALONZO,[7] b, Apr. 12, 1814; d. May 26, 1885.

159. **Joseph,**[6] son of 71 Timothy[5] and Sarah [Rogers] Balch, was born at Newport, R. I., October 25, 1766, and died at Providence, R. I., July 20, 1845. He married Miss Martha Grise, December 20, 1792, at Providence. She was born at Boston, Mass., August 16, 1762, and by her Joseph had two children, both born at Providence.

328   CALEB G.[7] b. ; d. unm.
329* SARAH R.,[7] b.

161. **John Rogers,**[6] son of 71 Timothy[5] and Sarah [Rogers] Balch was born at Newport, R. I., May 18, 1772, and died at Providence, Rhode Island, April 2, 1848. He married Miss Saphira Packard, November 27, 1800. He engaged in mercantile and banking pursuits, and lived at Providence, R. I., where his three children were born.

330   JAMES ROGERS,[7] b. 1802; d. without issue, Sept. 28, 1828.
331* SOPHIA PACKARD,[7] b. May 9, 1805.
332* JOHN ROGERS,[7] b. Aug. 27, 1808; d. Oct. 25, 1886.

162. **Mary,**[6] daughter of 90 Cornelius[5] and Martha [Robinson] Balch, was born at Topsfield, Massachusetts, February 15, 1741. She was married February 15, 1761, to David Howlet. They were living at Keene, N. H., in 1815. They had three children. Cornelius, b. in 1761. Molly, b. in 1768. Martha, b. 1767.

163. **Martha,**[6] daughter of 90 Cornelius[5] and Martha [Robinson] Balch, was born at Topsfield, Mass., April 9, 1743, and died at Ridge, New Hampshire, April 6, 1822. She was married at Topsfield, October 81, 1769, to Jeremiah Towne, Jr. He died at Ridge, June 10, 1880, aged 82 years. They had two children, both born at Topsfield. Polly Towne, m. Thomas Tarbell; Cornelius Towne, b. Feb. 13, 1772; married, in 1791, to Hannah, daughter of Michael Chaplain, of Ridge, N. H. In 1804 Cornelius Towne moved with his family to Dublin, N. H. Their four eldest children were born at Ridge, and their youngest at Dublin. They were as follows: John, b. in 1792; Rebecca, b. in 1794; Moses, b. in 1796; Cornelius, b. in 1803; Elijah, b. in 1807.

167. Deborah,[6] daughter of 91 Benjamin[5] and Nazareth [Cushing] Balch, was born at Scituate, Massachusetts, in 1727. She married John, son of Capt. Alexander Forsyth.

168. Hart,[6] son of 91 Benjamin[5] and Nazareth [Cushing] Balch, was born at Scituate, Massachusetts, in 1731, and was lost at sea, on a voyage to the West Indies, in 1751, being at the time captain of the vessel. He was married early in 1750 to a Miss Bourne (?) who was a niece or cousin to Gen. Joseph Warren. She married for her second husband a British officer, and went to live in Halifax, Nova Scotia. It was reported that she left property to her son, which he never received. Hart Balch had by his wife a posthumous son.

333* HART,[7] b. Nov. 9, 1751; d. Feb. 15, 1846.

169. Benjamin,[6] son of 91 Benjamin[5] and Nazareth [Cushing] Balch, was born at Boston, Mass., March 4, 1732-3, and was baptized at the New South Church. The rolls of the French and Indian war show that he was a lieutenant in Captain Abel Keen's company, Colonel Joseph Thatcher's regiment, and that he was 23 years of age, by occupation a cooper, born at Boston, and residing at Scituate, that he entered the service February 18, 1756, and served until December 5, 1756. This company of men was raised for the expedition against Crown Point. From the same rolls it appears that he re-entered the service March 23, 1757, as second lieutenant, to go on an expedition to Fort William Henry, under the command of Colonel Frye, and was at its capitulation, August 9, 1757. It is not known whether or not he was killed in the massacre that followed. The Plymouth County Probate Records show that his estate was administered upon before the close of the year.

170. Nathaniel,[6] son of 91 Benjamin[5] and Nazareth [Cushing] Balch, was born at Boston, Massachusetts, May 7, 1735. He died in Boston, September 18, 1808. He was married, May 26, 1763, to Mary, daughter of Capt. William Fletcher, one of the officers in the Louisburg expedition. She died in Boston, October 7, 1797. They had five children, all born in Boston.

334* NATHANIEL,[7] b. Feb. 26, 1764; d. June 10, 1831.
335* WILLIAM,[7] b. July 11, 1765; d. Nov. 4, 1791.
336 MARGARET,[7] b. May 17, 1767; m. 1789, Samuel Whitewell.
337 MARY,[7] b. May 15, 1769; m. Dec. 17, 1789, Benjamin Morgan
         Stillman.
338* SARAH,[7] b. Dec. 5, 1774.

Nathaniel was a hatter, and carried on his business at No. 72 Cornhill, now Washington street, where he also resided. Under the title of " An Old Gentleman's Recollections," in Harper's Magazine for May, 1877, is the following reference to Nathaniel and his neighbors: "We had a medley of eccentric tradesmen in Boston in 1788, who were a compound of flat simplicity in manners and acute cleverness in conversation, shrewd, perhaps somewhat cunning, often witty, always smart and intelligent. Such was Copley, my tailor; Billings, of the same trade ; but, above all, Balch, the hatter. His shop was the principal lounge, even of the first people in the town. Governor Hancock, when the gout permitted, resorted to this grand rendezvous, and there exchanged jokes with Balch and his company, or, as sometimes happened, discussed grave political subjects, and tout em badinant settled the leading principles of his administration."

According to family tradition, Governor Hancock one day said to Balch, " Come up and see a Savage I have locked in my garret." He complied, and found that the Governor was protecting a portrait painter named Savage from arrest for debt. Savage was engaged on a portrait of the Governor, and at the request of Hancock, also made one of Balch. The latter is now in the possession of Nathaniel's great-grandson, William L. Balch, of Boston.

172. Joseph,[6] son of 91 Benjamin[5] and Nazareth [Cushing] Balch was born at Boston, Feb. 10, 1738-9, and died at West Cambridge, September 1, 1826. He was captain of a company in Colonel Thomas Craft's artillery regiment. As such he is referred to in the records of the Massachusetts Archives, Vol. 38, from January, 1776 to December, 1777. The orderly book of the regiment preserved in the Essex Institute

also refers to him.   He was married August 25, 1760, to
Abigail Audebert, who was baptized December 30, 1739, and
died at Billerica, Massachusetts, January 7, 1802.   She was a
granddaughter of William Palfrey, sail maker, of Milk Street,
Boston, to whom Joseph Balch was apprenticed.   Abigail was
one of the children of Mr. Palfrey's daughter Lydia, and
Philip Audebert, Jr., son of a French Huguenot.   Philip and
Lydia died young, and Abigail's grandfather Palfrey, was
appointed her guardian in 1752.   She grew up in his family,
together with Joseph Balch.   They had nine children.

339   JOSEPH,⁷ b. Feb. 18, 1761; d. Feb. 23, 1761.
340   LYDIA,⁷ b. Jan. 11, 1764; d. Aug. 15, 1764.
341   ABIGAIL,⁷ b. Mar. 18, 1765; d. Aug. 26, 1795, s. p.
342   LYDIA,⁷ b. Jan. 15, 1768; d. Oct. 9, 1768.
343*   JOSEPH,⁷ b. Sept. 15, 1769; d. Sept. 11, 1798.
344   BENJAMIN,⁷ b. Mar. 13, 1772; d. Aug. 2, 1773.
345   BENJAMIN,⁷ b. Aug. 10, 1774; d. Aug. 12, 1774.
346   LYDIA JARVIS,⁷ b. Mar. 24, 1777; d. Nov. 23, 1777.
347*   ELIZABETH,⁷ b. April 9, 1779; d. Jan. 29, 1859.

175.   John,⁶ son of 97 Andrew⁵ and Bethiah [Lovett] Balch,
was born at Beverly, Mass., October 12, 1735, and died at
Keene, N. H., April 30, 1808.   The records at Keene, N. H.,
show that his first wife was named Mary, but do not give her
maiden name.   They had two sons born at Keene.

348*   JOHN,⁷ b. Dec. 10, 1757; d. Mar. 15, 1824.
349*   TIMOTHY,⁷ b. about 1760; d.

John married for his second wife Safrona, by whom he had
six more children, all of them born at Keene.

350   ANDREW,⁷ b.   ; d. Sept. 11, 1767.
351   RUTH,⁷ b. Nov. 26, 1767; d.
352*   MARY,⁷ b. Feb. 10, 1770; d. Oct. 14, 1838.
353   SAFRONA,⁷ b. Feb. 14, 1773; d.
354   ANNA,⁷ b. Dec. 10, 1775; d. Sept. 10, 1777.
355   ANNA,⁷ b. Feb. 15, 1778; d. Sept. 1, 1799.

In 1759, John enlisted in Captain Bayley's company for the
French and Indian war.   In 1776, he was one of the petition-
ers to the New Hampshire legislature, remonstrating against
inoculation with small pox virus.   It appears that the belief
was then current, that small pox would be more managable if

given by inoculation than if contracted in the usual way. It was therefore the custom to perform such inoculations when the spread of the disease was feared. This was twenty years before the discovery of cow-pox vaccination by Jenner. Revolutionary war rolls of New Hampshire, John Balch enlisted as a private May 1, 1777, and served for three years in Captain William Ellis' company, third New Hampshire. John was a member of the foot company of Keene, in 1778. He declared himself on the side of the colonies by signing the pledge above given in the account of his father Andrew.

177. **Caleb,**[6] son of 97 Andrew[5] and Bethiah [Lovett] Balch, was born at Beverly, Mass., October 16, 1740, and died about 1794. He married Elizabeth M. and to them were born five children, all at Keene, N. H., as shown by the records of that town.

356 JOANNA,[7] b. Aug. 21, 1763; d.
357* CYRUS,[7] b. July 14, 1765, d. about 1805.
358* AMOS,[7] b. July 28, 1767; d.
359* CALEB,[7] b. Mar. 9, 1770; d.
360 BETHIAH,[7] b. July 15, 1772; m. at Westmoreland, Sept. 25, 1787, Josiah Leach; d.

After the birth of Bethiah, Caleb moved to Westmoreland, N. H., and may have had more children. The roll of Captain Ephraim Stone's company for the year 1780, contains Caleb's name and shows that he was paid 589 pounds, 16 shillings. The roll also states that his son Cyrus received 621 pounds, and one shilling. Caleb served in the Eighth company of Colonel Reed's regiment, New Hampshire Volunteers, Jacob Hinds was the Captain and Isaac Street, Lieutenant. This regiment was at the battle of Bunker Hill. Hind's company was called out on various occasions for short terms of service. It consisted of 65 men. After the fight at Bunker Hill, it was credited with 39 men fit for duty.

179. **Benjamin,**[6] son of 97 Andrew[5] and Ruth [Woodbury] Balch, was born at Beverly, Mass., in 1747, or 1748. When about 21 years of age he married Miss Elizabeth Blake, by whom he had seven children. Elizabeth died in 1785.

361   OLIVE,[7] b. Mar. 17, 1769; d. Oct. 21, 1773.
362* THANKFUL,[7] b. Apr. 23, 1772; d. 1856.
363* ABNER,[7] b. March 5, 1774; d.
364   ELIZABETH,[7] b. June 21, 1775; m. Jonah Edson; d.
365* ESTHER,[7] b. Oct. 13, 1778; d. Feb. 20, 1830.
366* OLIVE,[7] b. Aug. 25, 1780; d. after 1860.
367* BENJAMIN,[7] b. July 23, 1783; d. Sept. 27, 1829.

Benjamin was married second at Keene, to Miss Julia Ellis.
by whom he had six children.

368* SYLVANUS,[7] b. Oct. 11, 1786; d. after 1870.
369* CYNTHIA,[7] b. May 14, 1788; d. 1841.
370* ADIN,[7] b. Jan. 22, 1790; d. Apr. 2, 1859.
371* WILLIAM,[7] b. June 16, 1791; d. Jan. 6, 1868.
372* JAMES,[7] b. Nov. 3, 1794; d. 1885.
373   JULIA,[7] b. July 16, 1796; m. Nathan Rice. Two children; d.

About 1800, Benjamin left Keene, and went to Lunenburg,
Vermont, bought a tract of forest land, and built a log cabin
and barn. The following winter he moved his family, the
only conveyance being a long sled drawn by a yoke of oxen.
Upon the sled they piled all their household goods, wife and
babies. The older boys followed with two cows and two pigs.
These pioneers knew well the meaning of hard work and scanty
fare. By trade, Benjamin was a wooden bottle maker. The
New Hampshire town papers show that Benjamin signed the
petition against inoculation with small pox, described above
in the account of his brother John. He owned a pew in the
meeting house at Keene. He was a member of the foot company of Keene in 1778, and signed with his father as one of
the Committee of Safety in 1776. He was generally known
as Lieutenant Benjamin Balch. He enlisted as a private in
Capt. David Howlet's Co., January 29, 1777, and was discharged July 11, 1777.

180. Ruth,[6] daughter of 98 Jonathan[5] and Esther [Hall]
Balch, was born at Mansfield, Ct. She was married Novem-
ber 4, 1772 to Elijah Abee, who was born at Ashford, Ct.,
July 7, 1753. The issue of this marriage was one child, born
December 15, 1773, it died the next day.
Elijah Abee always lived at Mansfield near 421 Thomas

Balch[7] whose father 197 Henry,[6] was a cousin of Ruth [Balch]. Abee's property all went to Thomas.[7]

181. John,[5] son 100 John[5] and Elizabeth [Hall] Balch. He was probably born about 1737 in or near Mansfield, Connecticut and died there. About 1758, he married the widow Bigsby, who by her first husband had two sons Orran and Benjamin. John had at least four sons.

374* JOHN,[7] b. Sept. 2, 1759; died Nov. 10, 1845.
375* WILLIAM,[7] b. ; m. Oct. 26, 1786; d.
376* ISRAEL,[7] b. ; d.
377* BAZALAEL,[7] b. ; d. Feb. 23, 1817.

Family tradition says that John[6] was married twice but does not give the name of his second wife.

182. Jonathan,[6] son of 101 Roger[5] and Ann [Kettell] Balch, was born at Charlestown, Mass., Nov. 26, 1743, and died at Roxbury, Mass., about 1812. He was married December 5, 1771, to Abigail Williams, of Roxbury. She died in that town in November, 1815. They had eleven children, all born at Boston.

378 ABIGAIL,[7] b. Sept. 23, 1772; d. y.
379* JONATHAN,[7] b. Apr. 7, 1774; d. summer of 1803.
380 NABBY,[7] b. Mar. 14, 1776; d. y.
381 KATY,[7] b. Jan. 31, 1778; m. Nehemiah W. Skilling, a merchant of Dorchester, Mass.; d.
382* SAMUEL WILLIAMS,[7] b. Mar. 14, 1780; d.
383 SALLY,[7] b. Apr. 4, 1782; d. y.
384 DAVID,[7] b. May 14, 1784; d.
385* ALEXANDER,[7] b. Mar. 9, 1786; d. July 5, 1812.
386 SALLY,[7] b. Dec. 17, 1787; d. y.
387 NABBY,[7] b. June 1, 1789; d. unm.
388 ANN,[7] b. Mar. 3, 1793; d. unm. over 90 years of age.

Jonathan[6] was brought up in Boston by his step-father, Shippie Townsend, and followed his trade of block and pump making. By it he gathered a fair fortune. He was the owner of Balch's wharf with the flats adjoining, now beneath the pavements of Fulton and Commercial streets, and much real estate in Ann and Cross streets. He purchased the Increase Sumner estate in Roxbury where he passed the latter years of his life and on which he died.

183. **Joanna,**[6] daughter of 303 Joshua[5] and Joanna [Williams] Balch was born at North Beverly, Mass., September 11, 1744. She was married December 22, 1795 to Abner Pittee, and removed to Francestown, N. H. where she died April 22, 1832.

185. **Ruth,**[6] daughter of 103 Joshua[5] and Joanna [Williams] Balch was born at North Beverly, September 15, 1748, and was believed to be living in 1826. She was married to Robert Baker, April 2, 1767.

186. **Joshua,**[6] son of 103 Joshua[5] and Joanna [Williams] Balch was born at North Beverly, Mass., Nov. 28, 1750, and died at Francestown, N. H., December 31, 1780. He married Rebecca, daughter of James Hopkins, of Londonderry, N. H. She was Joshua's second wife and by her he had one son.

389* JOSHUA,[7] b. June 9, 1778; d. April 23, 1833.

Joshua's first wife, whose name has not been ascertained, died at Francestown, September 16, 1777. She bore at least three children, as shown by the Francestown records, all of whom died young.

187. **Israel,**[6] son of 103 Joshua[5] and Joanna [Williams] Balch was born at North Beverly, Mass., April 1, 1753, and died suddenly at Francestown, New Hampshire, in 1827. His home in Francestown, was on the Lyndborough addition on what was known as Balch Hill. He was a mason by trade. He married Miss Hannah Kimball, of Beverly, on February 2, 1772. They had five children all born at Francestown.

390* ISRAEL,[7] b. June 29, 1773; d. May 3, 1847.
391* HANNAH,[7] b. March 23, 1775; d.
392* SALLY,[7] b. Oct. 18, 1778; d.
393* POLLY,[7] b. Nov. 4, 1780; d.
394* JOHN,[7] b. Oct. 1, 1782; d.

Israel married for a second wife the widow Mary Fletcher, of Greenfield, New Hampshire, by whom he had six children, all born at Francestown.

395* JOANNA,[7] b. Jan. 20, 1786; d. Mar. 10, 1813.
396* VARION,[7] b. May 6, 1789; d. June 12, 1834.
397* PAMELA,[7] b. Nov. 7, 1791; d. Jan. 24, 1833.

398* WILLIAM,[7] b. Nov. 8, 1793; d. Jan. 19, 1877.
399 RUTH,[7] b. Sept. 10, 1796; m. Isaac Jones; d.
400 BETSEY,[7] b. Oct. 2, 1797; d.

In the year 1792 the Lyndborough addition was transferred from Greenfield to Francestown.

190. Hannah,[6] daughter of 103 Joshua[5] and Joanna [Williams] Balch was born at Beverly, Dec. 26, 1760. She was married January 1, 1793, to Robert Edwards, of Beverly, a fisherman.

191. Isaac,[6] son of 103 Joshua[5] and Joanna [Williams] Balch, was born at North Beverly, Dec. 27, 1766 and died at Lyme, New Hampshire, March 6, 1842. He was a mason by trade. He married Miss Olive Grant, and moved to Lyme, in 1790. His wife Olive died in 1797, leaving three children, all born at Lyme.

401 OLIVE,[7] b. July 7, 1791; d.
402* ISAAC,[7] b. Sept. 29, 1793; d. Dec. 27, 1873.
403 JOANNA,[7] b. May 3, 1796; m. and had a large family at Francestown, N. H.; d.

Isaac[6] was married second to Elizabeth Bell, by whom he had six children all born at Lyme. Elizabeth died March 13, 1860.

404* BETSEY,[7] b. Jan. 16, 1799; d. Mar. 24, 1873.
405 PAMELA,[7] b. Oct. 12, 1800; d. 1806.
406* ALBERT,[7] b. Sept. 6, 1802; d.
407* THEODORE,[7] b. Oct. 4, 1804; d.
408* JOHN,[7] b. June 18, 1809; d. 1846.
409 TRUMAN,[7] b. June 4, 1814; d. 1821.

193. Betsey,[6] daughter of 103 Joshua[5] and Patience [Pitman] Balch was born at Beverly, February 10, 1772 and died in the same town October 13, 1863. She was married to Joseph Grant who was born in Beverly April 28, 1774 and died in the same town, February 2, 1840.

They always lived in Beverly and their seven children were born there. Sally D., b. Apr. 27, 1795, d. Feb. 29, 1836, m. Stephen Dodge; Joseph, b. May 5, 1802, d. Jan. 29, 1881, m. Mary Farnes; John Balch, b. Sept. 6, 1806, d. Aug. 1830, m. Rebecca Harris; William H., b. Aug. 20, 1808, m. Mary Ann

Pousland ; Elizabeth, b. Sept. 1, 1810, d. April 8, 1836 ; m.
William Holt; Joshua Balch, b. Oct. 19, 1812, d. Apr. 1888,
m. Mary Lawrence ; Benjamin D., b. Aug. 15, 1815, m. Abigail Wood.

The above records were copied from the family Bible in
the possession of William H. Grant, upon the old homestead
of John Balch². Of Betsey [Balch] Grant it is said that she
knit hose for soldiers in the Revolution, in the war of
1812-14, and in the war of the Rebellion.

195. Israel,⁶ son of 105 Veren⁵ and Sarah [Taylor]
Balch, was born in Mansfield, Ct., January 26, 1751 and died
in Mansfield. He was married in February, 1771, to Sarah,
daughter of John Arnold. The record of the birth of their
three eldest children is in Mansfield. He served in the Revolution, first, Sept. 2, to Nov. 2, 1776, Captain Sargent's Co.,
second, July 8, 1780 to December 8, 1780 in 4th Connecticut
Regiment.

410* LUCINDA,⁷ b. Apr. 3, 1772; d.
411* ARNOLD,⁷ b. Feb. 8, 1775; d. Oct. 10, 1848.
412* ROGER,⁷ b. May 17, 1779; d. Feb. 12, 1831.
413* POLLY,⁷ b. Apr. 10, 1785; d. Jan. 11, 1844.
414* CHESTER,⁷ b. 1788; d. May 15 1847.
415* SYLVESTER,⁷ b.   ; d. 1848.

197. Henry,⁶ son of 105 Veren⁵ and Sarah[Taylor] Balch,
was born in Mansfield, Connecticut, July 2, 1753, and died
in the same town. He was married March 4, 1783, to Elizabeth Kimball of Colchester, Connecticut, by whom he had
seven children, all born in Mansfield.

416 HANNAH,⁷ b. Jan. 5, 1784; d.
417* HENRY TAYLOR,⁷ b. Nov. 28, 1785, d. Jan. 29, 1869.
418 JOSEPH,⁷ b. Mar. 10, 1788; d.
419* JOHN,⁷ b. May 10, 1791; d.
420 ELIZABETH,⁷ b,'Jan. 5, 1792; d.
421* THOMAS,⁷ b. Nov. 6, 1794; d.
422 MOLLIE BIBBINS,⁷ b. July 20, 1797; d.

199. Mary,⁶ daughter of 105 Veren⁵ and Sarah [Taylor]
Balch, was born in Mansfield, Ct., May 26, 1760. She married Nathaniel Bassett, and had two children, Sarah, b. Dec.
18, 1783 ; Nathaniel, b. Sept. 12, 1785.

201. **Hannah,**[6] daughter of 105 Veren[5] and Sarah [Taylor]Balch, was born at Mansfield,Connecticut, October 8, 1765. In 1785 she was married to Seth Jennings, who was born in 1760. They were early settlers in Killawog, N. Y., where Mr. Jennings died. They had eight children, Alfred, Rufus, Betsey, Harry, Patty, Lenda, Seth, and an infant unnamed.

204. **Polly,**[6] daughter of 112 Caleb[5] and Mary[Saunders] Balch, was born at Beverly, Mass., January 16, 1783, and died April 5, 1869, at Windham, N. H. She married Phineas Gordon as his second wife. They lived and died upon the old homestead in Windham, and had no issue. Gordon died Sept. 7, 1863, aged 93 years.

205. **William,**[6] son of 112 Caleb[5] and Mary [Saunders] Balch, was born at Windham, New Hampshire, August 31, 1786, and died in the same town June 24, 1830. He married a Miss Ayers of Salem, N. H. They had no children. William was a soldier in the war of 1812-14.

207. **Jerusha,**[6] daughter of 112 Caleb[5] and Mary [Saunders] Balch, was born at Windham, New Hampshire, January 26, 1791 and died in the same town October 8, 1874. She married John Kelly of Derry, New Hampshire, and after his death returned to the old homestead where she spent the remainder of her life. She had no children.

211. **David,**[6] son of 114 David[5] and Hannah [Perkins] Balch, was born in Topsfield, Mass., August 19, 1753, and died in the same town July 22, 1812. He was married April 21, 1782 to Betty Burnham of Dumbarton, New Hampshire, who was born June 6, 1763. They had one son.

423* DAVID BURNHAM,[7] b. June 29, 1784; d. June 27, 1860.

Betty died Oct. 14, 1784, and David was married again March 19, 1786 to Sarah Peabody, daughter of Jacob and Sarah [Potter] Peabody, of Topsfield. She was born June 6, 1769, and died March 2, 1845. They had three sons and two daughters.

424* ISRAEL,[7] b. Sept. 14, 1788; d. July 7, 1858.
425* POLLY,[7] b. Mar. 7, 1792; d. Jan. 7, 1859.
426   ABRAHAM,[7] b. Nov. 15, 1794; d. unm. Jan. 25, 1872.
427   DANIEL PERKINS,[7] b. July 23, 1797; d. at sea. unm. Nov. 1, 1828.
428* SALLY,[7] b. June 19, 1800.

David was a soldier in the Revolution and was at the battle of Bunker Hill. He was of a mechanical turn of mind and owned a foot lathe on which his son Israel learned to do turning. David was a self taught man. His monument stands in the Topsfield graveyard.

212 Samuel,[6] son of David[5] and Hannah [Perkins] Balch, was born in Topsfield, Feb. 7, 1755 and died in June, 1840.

The date of his marriage is unknown, his wife's first name was Molly. They lived in Amesbury, where he was a school-teacher. He graduated at Harvard in 1782. They had three children.

429* BENJAMIN B.[7] b.
430   HANNAH,[7] b.   ; m. William Lowell, and had three children: *William B.*, *Polly A.*, *Hannah E.*, and a grandson, William J. Lowell.
431* ANN,[7] b.   ; m. Henry Shoop and had two children: *William H.* and *Ann M.*

Samuel's will was probated June, 1840, and Mollie's will was probated in Dec., 1841.

215. Thomas,[6] son of David[5] and Hannah [Perkins] Balch, was born in Topsfield, March 29, 1761 and died March 10, 1830.

He was married June 14, 1761 to his cousin Dolly, daughter of Samuel and Dorothy Perkins. She died June 22, 1819, aged 59 years, 8 months and 12 days. No children survived them and they probably had none.

Thomas left his property to his nephews, 429 Benj. B., son of his brother, Samuel, and to William H., son of 428 David Burnham Balch.

219. David,[6] son of 115 John[5] and Rebecca [Smith] Balch, was born in Topsfield, January 4, 1740-41, and died in Keene, N. H., July 31, 1801. He was married Nov. 12, 1761, to Esther Esty, daughter of Aaron and Esther [Richards] Esty, of Topsfield. She was born in 1741. David was a soldier in the French and Indian War of 1758. They resided in Topsfield until about 1789 when they removed to Keene.

432 ESTHER,[7] b.
433* WILLIAM,[7] b.
434* LYDIA,[7] b. 1765; d. Apr. 18, 1834.
435* DAVID,[7] b. Sept. 1, 1771; d. Sept. 8, 1835.
436 DANIEL,[7] b. Mar. 6, 1783; d.s. p., 1827; m. Mary Clark, March 6, 1788, lived in Danvers, Mass.

220. John,[6] son of 115 John[5] and Rebecca [Smith] Balch, was born in Topsfield, March 26, 1742, and died in the same town, July 25, 1798. He was married October 30, 1767, to Sarah, daughter of Thomas, and Sarah [Wade] Baker of Topsfield. She was born May 24, 1743, and died January 16, 1831. They had one son and four daughters.

437 SARAH,[7] b. Jan. 18, 1770; m. Nov. 4, 1790, Roger Elliot, of Middleton, Mass.
438* MEHITABLE,[7] } twins, b. June 26, 1772. { Nov. 22, 1798, John m.
439 MARTHA,[7] Elliot, of Middleton, Mass.
440* JOHN,[7] b. Aug. 17, 1776; d. Oct. 24, 1837.
441 REBECCA,[7] b. Aug. 17, 1780; d. Sept. 8, 1802; m. Nov. 26, 1801 John Cummings.

221. Samuel,[6] son of 115 John[5] and Rebecca [Smith] Balch, was born in Topsfield, March 20, 1743-4, and died about 1820, aged 76, unmarried. His mind fell into a disordered state several years before his father's death, and the other sons were directed by their father's will to provide for him out of his share of the estate.

222. Robert,[6] son of 115 John[5] and Rebecca [Smith] Balch, was bapt. in Topsfield, July 28, 1745, and died at New Boston, N. H., August 3, 1830. He was married November 28, 1769, to Sarah, daughter of Deacon Solomon Dodge. She was born June, 1752, and died March 16, 1822.

Robert,[6] was a farmer and lived in Topsfield, until 1791, when he removed with his family to New Boston, N. H.

442* HANNAH,[7] b. Aug. 18, 1770; d. Mar. 20, 1867.
443* ROBERT,[7] b. Feb. 19, 1772; d. Mar. 4, 1842.
444* SOLOMON,[7] b. Oct. 20, 1773; d. Oct. 22, 1854.
445 SARAH,[7] b. June 2, 1775; d. Oct. 11, 1776.
446* MOSES,[7] b. Oct. 7, 1777; d. May 7, 1813.
447* JOHN,[7] b. June 25, 1779; d. June 20, 1822.
448 SARAH,[7] b. Mar. 20, 1781; d. June, 1856; m. John Cram of
      Weare, N. H., they had two sons, and four daughters.
449* DILLEY,[7] b. May 6, 1784; d. Oct. 19, 1864.
450* BETSEY,[7] b. Apr. 2, 1786; d. Nov. 10, 1813.
451* NANCY,[7] b. June 10, 1789; d. Jan. 30, 1850.
452* ALLEN,[7] b. July 19, 1791; d. Aug. 28, 1881.
453* WILLIAM,[7] b. July 20, 1793; d. Aug. 27, 1885.
454* REBECCA,[7] b. Dec. 19, 1796; d. Sept. 22, 1876.

223. Hannah,[6] daughter of [115] John[5] and Rebecca
[Smith] Balch, was born in Topsfield, March 29, 1747. She
was published to Israel Kenny, May 5, 1765. Nothing more
has been found regarding her.

224. Cornelius,[6] son of [115] John[5] and Rebecca
[Smith] Balch, was born in Topsfield, November 26, 1749,
and died in the same town, May 21, 1795. He was married
April 4, 1771 to Mehitable, daughter of Jacob and Kezia
[Gould] Dwinell of Topsfield. She survived him and was
married second to Amos Nelson of Rowley, November 7,
1799. She was born April 30, 1748, and died in 1844.
Three children were born to Cornelius and Mehitable, in
Topsfield.

455* ABIGAIL,[7] bapt. Dec. 22, 1771.
456 RICHARD,[7] bapt. May 15, 1774; d. Nov. 28, 1776.
457* MEHITABLE,[7] born Feb. 1778; d. Oct. 4, 1815.

226. Roger,[6] son of [115] John[5] and Rebecca [Smith]
Balch, was born in Topsfield, May 26, 1755 and died January 8, 1842. He was a soldier in the Revolution. He was
married May 14, 1782 to Sarah, daughter of Moses and
Hannah [Frye] Perley, of Boxford, Mass.

458* PERLEY,[7] b. Aug. 5, 1783; d. May 2, 1858.
459 MOODY,[7] b. Feb. 3, 1794; d. unm. Nov. 10, 1851.

227. Rebecca,[6] daughter of [115] John[5] and Rebecca
[Smith] Balch, was born in Topsfield, March 27, 1758. She
was married March 23, 1783 to Silas Dole of Rowley, Mass.

228. Joshua,[6] son of [116] Joshua[5] and Sarah [Tower] Balch, was born in Topsfield, July 22, 1749 and died in Bradford, where he then lived. He was married September 22, 1772 to Hannah Woodman, of Bradford, by whom he had three children.

460 JOSHUA,[7] b. Dec. 12, 1772; d. Oct. 1773.
461 JOSHUA,[7] bapt. Aug. 1, 1774; d. Nov. 10, 1774.
462 A child, b. 1776, d. without name.

Joshua was a blacksmith by trade. His widow administered upon his estate. She married James Greenough in March, 1785.

229. Archelaus,[6] son of [116] Joshua[5] and Sarah [Tower] Balch, was born in Boxford, Mass., September 29, 1750 and died about 1777. He was a blacksmith by trade, and lived in Boxford. He never married.

231. Mehitable,[6] daughter of 117 Freeborn[5] and Mary [Perkins] Balch, was born at North Beverly, Mass., March 8, 1763, and died at Hopkinton, New Hampshire, January 5, 1853. She was married October 16, 1781, to William Palmer, of Bradford, Mass. He was born December 10, 1763 and died August 20, 1851. They resided at Hopkinton, and had eleven children.

SAMUEL, b. Oct. 29, 1772; d.

POLLY, b. Mar. 5, 1784; d.

MEHITABLE BALCH, b. Dec. 7, 1785; d. March 7, 1874. She married Steven Parker, of Groveland, Mass. He died Aug. 22, 1861, aged 78 years. They had four children:—*Alfred*, b. at Groveland, Mar. 2, 1808; d. July 10, 1876, m. Adeline Parker, of Groveland, May 28, 1846, but had no issue; *Malinda*, b. Nov. 15, 1810; d. Dec. 1, 1889; *Mehitable Balch*, b. Apr. 26, 1815; d. Nov. 8, 1881; *Abigail Palmer*, b. Apr. 29, 1818, m. George Atwood, of Groveland, Sept. 29, 1846, who died at Groveland, Jan. 2, 1854, aged 35 years, leaving one daughter, Abbie Frances Atwood, b. Sept. 24, 1851, at Groveland, m. Edward M. Stacy, of Haverhill, Mass., but had no issue.

ABIGAIL, b. Dec. 30, 1786; d.

WILLIAM, b. Jan. 17, 1790; d. y.

WILLIAM, b. July 13, 1794; d. y.

MOSES, b. Sept. 14, 1796.

MARY, b. July 27, 1798.

EBENEZER, b. Feb. 12, 1801.

AARON, b. May 19, 1805.
WILLIAM, b. Sept. 17, 1807.

232. Benjamin,[6] son of 117 Freeborn[5] and Mary [Perkins] Balch, was born in North Beverly, Jan. 10, 1765, and died in Bradford, in 1852. He was married March 29, 1792 to Susan, daughter of Daniel Muliken and widow of Caleb Norton. She died Aug. 15, 1847, aged 78 years. Benjamin was a farmer and miller and resided at Bradford. Benjamin and Susan had six children.

464* BENJAMIN,[7] b. July 21, 1793; d. 1842.
465 BETSEY,[7] b. Mar. 25, 1794; d. 1796.
466* DANIEL,[7] b. Mar. 21, 1797; d. Aug. 21, 1875.
467* WILLIAM H.[7] b. Oct. 21, 1798; d. Feb. 14, 1835.
468* SOPHRONIA,[7] b. Oct. 6, 1801; d. Dec. 13, 1858.
469 CHARLES,[7] b. Apr. 17, 1810; m. Abigail Daggett, lived at Canton, Mass., no issue.

233. Wesley Perkins,[6] son of 117 Freeborn[5] and Mary [Perkins] Balch, was born in North Beverly, August 14, 1766, and died in Haverhill, April 27, 1827. His first wife was Margaret Lord, of Ipswich. She died at Haverhill, September 10, 1807. For a time they resided in Bradford, where their eldest daughter, Margaret, was born; about 1797 they removed to Haverhill, where he kept a country store, and was one of the earliest shoe manufacturers in Haverhill. They had seven children.

470* MARGARET,[7] b. July 24, 1796; d. Jan. 4, 1872.
471* WESLEY,[7] b. Mar. 25, 1798; d. July 5, 1853.
472* JOHN,[7] b. Jan. 7, 1800; d. May 28, 1868.
473 MATILDA,[7] b. Oct. 29, 1801; d. Oct. 8, 1802.
474 MATILDA,[7] b. Feb. 1, 1804; d. unm. Jan. 6, 1849, in Thomastown, Me. of consumption.
475 JACOB,[7] b. Nov. 25, 1806; d. in infancy.
476* SOPHIA,[7] b. Sept. 5, 1807; d. Mar. 22, 1855.

Wesley P. married for his second wife Miss Susan Osborn, on November 8, 1808; she was born in Boston in 1772, and died February 28, 1844. Three children was the issue of this marriage.

477 SUSAN BOARDMAN,[7] b. Aug. 29, 1809; d. Oct. 23, 1809.
478* SUSAN OSBORN,[7] b. June 11, 1811; d. Dec. 5, 1878.
479 MARY BOARDMAN,[7] b. Mar. 7, 1813; d. July 27, 1816.

234. Abigail,[6] daughter of 117 Freeborn[5] and Mary [Perkins] Balch, was born at Beverly, Aug. 19, 1768, and died at Blackville, New Brunswick, August 7, 1842. She was married January 22, 1789, at her father's residence in Haverhill, Mass., to James Christie, who died about 1793. Christie was a Loyalist during the Revolution, and found it unpleasant to remain in the United States after peace was declared and therefore removed to New Brunswick. They had two sons.

> JAMES, b. Oct. 22, 1789; d. Sept. 24, 1893. He m. Sarah Humpherys of St. John, New Brunswick, and had four children: —*Margaret*, m. William Selden, and had four children, Helen, Serah, Nancy and James Wesley; *James*, m. Sarah Coughlan, and had three children; *Mary*, d. unm.; *T. Wesley*, m. Catherine Bryant.

> WESLEY, b. Oct. 4, 1792; m. Sarah Weaver, and had seven children:—*Thomas, Abagail, George, Sarah, Mary Ann, Barbary* and *Wesley*.

Abigail,[6] was married second, October 25, 1795, to British Nathaniel Underhill, who was born in New York, June 22, 1778, and died at Blackville, New Brunswick, October 9, 1850. His father was a Loyalist, and found it unpleasant to remain in the United States, so in 1783 he removed with his family to Mangerville, St. Johns, New Brunswick. In 1806 he removed to Blackville. Abigail and nearly all of her descendants were Episcopalians. They had five children, born at Mangerville, and one, the youngest, born at Blackville, as follows:

> WILLIAM TRYAN, b. Aug. 28, 1796; d. Feb. 24, 1814.

> NOAH BISHOP, b. Aug. 8, 1798; died Aug. 6, 1850, at Blackville. m. in 1828, Miss Catherine Meehan, who was b. in 1813; d. May 22, 1881. Their children were *Mary*, d. unm. aged 22; *Catherine*, d. y.; *John*, b. 1829; d. 1887; m. Ann Fisher, who d. 1876; had twelve children.

> BRITISH NATHANIEL 2d, b. June 26, 1800; d. Oct. 1, 1883; m. Mary Kennedy of York County, N. B., April 18, 1822. She d. Sept. 23, 1883. They had nine children. *William Tryon*, b. March 8, 1823; m. Euphemia Smith, July 18, 1850. Issue, nine children. *British Nathaniel 3d*, b. Jan. 31, 1827; d. Feb. 23, 1892; m. Mary Colwell, Oct. 16, 1857. They had six children; *Abigail*, b. April 5, 1829; m. a Mr. Johnson; no issue; *Thomas Ward*, b. April 15, 1831; m. Lives in California, has one son;

James Wesley, b. May 16, 1833; m. Cynthia Colwell. Issue six children. *Susan*, b. Aug. 31, 1835; m. Chas. Mitchell. No issue. *Mary Jane*, b. Oct. 22, 1839; m. James Fisher. No issue. *Sarah Hannah*, b. June 11, 1843, unm.; *Eliza Rebecca*, b. Jan. 27, 1848; m. No issue.

THOMAS WARD, b. May 17, 1808; d. Dec. 2, 1873, at Blackville; m. April 5, 1827, to Mary, daughter of John Sutherland. She was born July 23, 1809; d. May 30, 1894, at Blackville. They always lived upon the old homestead at Blackville; their children were *Thomas Ward*, m. Abigail Colwell. They had seven children. *Mary Ann*, b. May 4, 1829; m. Oct. 16, 1856, to John Flett, of Nelson, N. B. He was born Feb. 1, 1822; d. July 2, 1889. They had seven children; Thomas Ward, Geo. Edward Albert, Charles Frederick, Mary Jane, Susan Grace, John Addison, William James. *William Tryon*, b. March 22, 1832; m. July 27, 1856, Abigail Coughlan. Five children: Charles Inkerman, b. June 10, 1857, d. May 7, 1864; Elizabeth Alena, b. Oct. 7, 1858; d. Nov. 3, 1858; William Willett, b. Nov. 29, 1860; Charlotte Elizabeth, b. April 4, 1864; Jacob David, b. Dec. 2, 1866, d. y. *British Nathaniel Tarlton*, b. Oct. 13, 1834; m. Aug. 9, 1865, Grace Mitchell. She was born Aug. 5, 1842; d. March 24, 1874. Issue, four children; Anna Mary, Grace Mable, Bessie Louisa and Alice Janet. *Susan Abigail*, b. March, 1838; d. Dec. 19, 1879; m. James M. Crawford. Five children; Albert, Mary, Charles, James, and Tryan Albert. *John Albert*, b. Nov. 27, 1841; m. Elizabeth Smith. Five children; Cruden Alexander, Beverly Addison, Blanche Susan, Mary Eliza and John Albert. *Hannah Moore*, b. Sept. 27, 1843; m. James W. Coughlin, ten children. *Alfredine Ernesta*, b. October 24, 1845; d. Nov. 21, 1872; m. Louisa A. E. Mitchell. One child, Alfred Ernest. *Arthur Averitt*, b. Oct. 22, 1848, d. Jan. 8, 1893; *James Hudson*, b. July 4, 1852; m. Elizabeth I. Smith. Issue, nine children.

MARY, b. June 1, 1805; d. Jan. 16, 1855; m. Thomas Coughlan, of Prince Edward's Island. Issue, nine children, two d. y. *Thomas, William, Nathaniel, David, James W., Benjamin, Mary.*

BENJAMIN NELSON, b. July 1, 1809; d. May 10, 1852; m. Mary Armstrong, Aug. 25, 1844. Three children, two d. y.; son, *British Nathaniel*, m. Annie Hoolarin. Have five children; Kenneth, Joseph, Benjamin, John and Myrtle.

235. Eunice,[6] daughter of 117 Freeborn[5] and Mary [Perkins] Balch, was born at Beverly, Mass., April 4, 1771, and died at Haverhill, Mass., March 21, 1855. About the year 1794 she was married to William, son of William and

Lydia [Paxton] Harmon. He was born at Braintree, Mass., December 1, 1760, and died at Haverhill, May 16, 1857. They had ten children, all of whom were born at Peterboro, N. H., except the eldest, who was born at Braintree, and the youngest, who was born at Bradford, Mass. In 1797 William Harmon, with his wife and one child, removed from Braintree to Peterboro, where he bought a large farm, upon which they continued to live until February, 1815, when he removed with his family to Bradford. In the fall of 1820 they moved to Haverhill, where they spent the remainder of their days. William and Eunice were Baptists. Their children were:

WILLIAM WESLEY, b. Jan. 7, 1797; d. Jan. 17, 1881, at Edwards, N. Y.; m. Feb. 25, 1823, Miss Harriet Viall, of Edwards. She was b. Nov. 8, 1805, and died in 1886. They had seven children, all born at Edwards. *Eunice*, b. Mar. 16, 1824; d. in Mich.; m. Sardine S. Van Ornum, of Edwards, Sept., 1843. *Susan Viall*, b. Dec. 7, 1826; m. Chauncy C. Gibbons, of Russell, N. Y., Jan. 1, 1855. *Paul Osgood*, b. June 21, 1829; d. Apr. 25, 1864, at Edwards; m. Mary Titus, of Edwards, Mch. 22, 1853. *Altha*, b. July 28, 1830; d. Feb. 10, 1884, at Pitcairn, N. Y.; m. John W. Laidlaw, of Hartford, N. Y., Jan. 1, 1851. *Adoniram Judson*, b. Aug. 8, 1832; d. y. *Sophronia*, b. Jan. 26, 1834; m. Ai Laidlaw, of Hermon, N. Y., Dec. 11, 1857. *Wesley Porter*, b. Oct. 13, 1838; m. Nancy Laidlaw, of Herman, N. Y., Sept. 4, 1860.

MARY BALCH, b. 1798; d. y.

DAVID PORTER, b. Mch. 11, 1800; d. Nov. 11, 1869, at Haverhill, Mass.; m. Almira, daughter of Moses Sargent, who was born at Candia, N. H. Her grandfather, who was also named Moses, was a soldier in the Revolution. She was b. at Candia, Jan. 18, 1802, and died July 13, 1875, at Haverhill. David P. and Almira Harmon had five children, all b. at Haverhill. *Henry Porter, Jr.*, b. June 11, 1835; d. Jan. 15, 1855, at Haverhill. *Walter Scott*, b. May 10, 1837; served in the Union army in the war of the rebellion; was wounded at South Mountain. *George Keeley*, b. July 2, 1840; m. at Brooklyn, N. Y., in March, 1868, to Cornelia Willis [Vogt] Douglas. She was born June 17, 1841, and was the widow of James Douglas, of Brooklyn, and had two children, Cornelia Maria and Hugh Henry. George K. and Cornelia W. had four children, all b. in Brooklyn: David Porter, 3d, b. July 28, 1869; d. March 30, 1875. Louisa Livingston, b. Sept. 10, 1871; d. Oct. 17, 1872. George Howard, b. Aug. 17, 1873. Annie Olivia Vogt, b. Feb. 22, 1876. George Keeley served in the war of the rebellion. *Mary Frances*, b. Jan. 4, 1842; m. W. J. Flanders, of Plaistow, N. H., June 17, 1868. He was born in Plaistow in 1842. *Edward Willard*, b. Aug. 16, 1843.

HERBERT SUMNER, b. June 5, 1801; d. May 10, 1852.

LYDIA PORTER, b. May 4, 1802; d. Oct. 11, 1869, unm., at Newburyport.

EUNICE BALCH, b. April 19, 1804; d. May 30, 1888, unm., at Haverhill.

BENJAMIN BALCH, b. at Peterboro, N. H., Sept. 1, 1806; d. Jan. 24, 1874, at Edwards, N. Y. He was married at East Haverhill, Mass., Nov. 30, 1830, to Eliza White, daughter of Dea. Humphrey and Rebecca Chase. She was born Oct. 11, 1806, at Plaistow, N.H., and died July 3, 1844, at Haverhill. They had five children. *Charles Porter*, b. Dec. 6, 1831, at Bradford, Mass., d. in 1865 at Haverhill; m. Louise G. Witherell, of North Falmouth, Mass., Oct. 30, 1855. They had two children, Julius, d. y.; Julia, d. y. *Ann Eliza*, b. Dec. 1, 1833, at Haverhill; m. about 1852, Charles, son of Rufus Kimball, of Bradford. They had three children, Annie, Florence, and Charles. *William Henry*, b. Aug. 5, 1836, at East Haverhill; m. about 1876, at Edwards, N. Y., Mary Rice, a widow. *Abbie Sweetzer*, b. July 24, 1839, at East Haverhill; m. at Bradford, June 30, 1860, James M. Witherell, of North Falmouth, Mass. They had two children, Lizzie and Horace. *Almira Porter*, b. Aug. 19, 1841; m. George W. Clark, of Portsmouth, N. H., and had one daughter, Mira. After the death of Benjamin's wife he moved to Edwards, and there, November 11, 1857, he was married to Mary, daughter of Abner and Elizabeth Rice, of Edwards. They had seven children. *Daniel Wesley*, b. Aug. 10, 1858; *Mary Louise*, b. Nov. 1, 1859; *Ebenezer Porter*, b. Jan. 15, 1861; *Nellie May*, b. May 15, 1864; *Eunice Balch*, b. Dec. 23, 1866; *Sarah Adelaide*, b. Oct. 23, 1869; *Eva St. Clair*, b. Sept. 28, 1871, d. May 24, 1873.

EBENEZER LORD, b. March 11, 1808; d. April 26, 1878, at Edwards, N. Y.; m. Sept. 26, 1830, Phila Viall, b. April 15, 1813, at Russell, N. Y. They had two children, *James*, b. Oct. 13, 1832, at Edwards, N. Y.; m. April 30, 1859, to Louise Johnson. *Charles Viall*, b. April 19, 1836, at Edwards, N. Y.; m. Jan. 1, 1861, to Mariette Maltby, of Russell, N. Y.

GEORGE OSGOOD, b. Jan. 27, 1809; d. Dec. 1, 1881, at Haverhill, Mass.; m. Dec. 5, 1855, Margaret Osborne, of Dover, N. H., b. April 11, 1833.

NANCY MARIA, b. Feb. 11, 1811; d. Dec. 9, 1892, at Yellow Medicine, Minn. She was married at Haverhill, April 5, 1846, to Josiah W. C. Pike, of Newburyport, Mass. He was b. Nov.

20, 1807, and died at East Douglas, Mass., Aug. 29, 1880.
They had four children: *Althea Maria*, b. March 11,
1848; m. at Weston, Vt., Aug. 19, 1868, Gamaliel L. Jones, of
Hubbardtown, Vt. and they had five children; *Eva St. Clair*,
b. Sept. 18, 1853; m. at Holland, Mass., Sept. 21, 1875,
Francis F. Young, of East Douglas, Mass.; *Sarah Adelaide*,
b. April 10, 1855; d. Jan. 1, 1868; *daughter*, d. unnamed.
JAMES, b. Sept. 9, 1818; d. Sept. 7, 1888, at Edwards, N. Y.; m.
Caroline A., daughter of Francis and Betty Butters, Dec. 29,
1841. Seven children: *Caroline B.*, b. Jan. 25, 1843; d. y.
James William, b. July 1, 1844, at Haverhill; m. Jan. 18,
1870, Cordelia A. Shaw, daughter of Elijah and Abigail Shaw,
of Edwards, b. July 24, 1846, d. Feb. 18, 1885. Five children:
Viola Abigail, b. July 28, 1872; Frank Henry, b. Sept. 26,
1874; Florence Grace, b. Sept. 12, 1877, d. Sept. 10, 1882;
Eugene Blaine, b. Dec. 14, 1879; James Merriman, b. May 4,
1882. *Carrie A.*, b. Aug. 2, 1847; d. y.; *Elizabeth Porter*, b.
Feb. 18, 1849; *Charles Luther*, b. Oct. 5, 1850; m. Nov. 27,
1879, Alice B., daughter of Henry and James Thompson, b.
Jan. 1, 1863; d. Nov. 7, 1887; *Julia A.*, b. Sept. 3, 1852, d. y.;
Ellsworth Scott, b. March 16, 1861, d. y.

236. John,[6] son of 117 Freeborn[5] and Mary [Per-
kins] Balch, was born in Beverly, July 18, 1772, and died
in 1849, at Medfield, Mass. He was married July 22, 1792,
to Phebe, daughter of William and Lydia [Faxon] Harmon,
of Braintree, Mass. She was born June 7, 1772, and died
in 1861. They had nine children. John was a farmer, and
lived in Medfield.

480* WESLEY PERKINS,[7] b. Sept. 2, 1794; d. Sept. 24, 1856.
481* PHEBE,[7] b. April 18, 1797; d.
482 ENOCH H.,[7] b. May 7, 1799; d. unm. 1825; buried in Medfield.
483* JOHN,[7] b. May 1, 1801; d. 1869.
484* BENJAMIN,[7] b. Jan. 11, 1804; d. April 28, 1888.
485* EBENEZER H.,[7] b. Jan. 28, 1806; d. 1878.
486 MARY BATTELLE,[7] b. June 27, 1807; d. 1840; m. George Davis.
487 LYDIA H.,[7] b. March 18, 1808; m. 1831, Orin Nichols of Lowell.
488 BETHSHEBA ELLEN,[7] b. Nov. 17, 1812; d. 1876; m. George Mason; ch., George and Harry, both d. unm.

237. Thomas,[6] son of 124 Thomas[5] and Mary [Sum-
ner] Balch, was born at Dedham, Mass., August 81, 1738.
He was in the French and Indian war, and died at Albany,
N. Y., September 29, 1756, from disease contracted while on
an expedition to Crown Point.

238. Mary,[6] daughter of 124 Thomas[5] and Mary [Sumner] Balch, was born at Dedham, November 16, 1740, and died November 8, 1815. She was married by her father to Rev. Manasseh Cutler, D. D., LL.D., of Hamilton, October 8, 1766. Their children were as follows:

> EPHRAIM, b. at Edgertown, Mass., April 13, 1767. He remained in Killingly, Ct., until the death of his grandfather, Hezekiah; married April 8, 1787, Leah Atwood, of K.; removed to Marietta, Ohio, in 1795; appointed Judge of Court of Common Pleas by Gov. St. Clair; was Representative of Territorial Government in 1801-2.
>
> JERVASE, b. at Edgertown, Sept. 17, 1768; d. at Evansville, Ind., Jan. 25, 1844. Went with first party under Gen. Putnam which made the first settlement in the U. S. northwest of the Ohio river; was an officer in the U. S. army, married, and had three sons and several daughters.
>
> MARY, b. at Dedham, May 3, 1771; married Dr. Joseph Torrey, of Beverly. Prof. Torrey, of Burlington, Vt., was a descendant.
>
> CHARLES, b. at Haverhill, March 26, 1773; d. at Ames, Athens county, O., in 1802; graduated at Harvard.
>
> LAVINIA, b. Aug. 6, 1775; married, and lived in Salem and Danvers; left no children.
>
> TEMPLE, b. April 10, 1778; d. same year.
>
> ELIZABETH, b. in Hamilton, July 4, 1779; married Mr. Fitch Pool, of Danvers, and lived in Peabody. A descendant, Mr. Fitch Pool, was Librarian in the Peabody Institute.
>
> TEMPLE, b. in Hamilton, Feb. 24, 1782; d. Nov. 5, 1857; always lived in Hamilton.

Rev. Manasseh Cutler was a man of high abilities and reputation. He was born at Killingly, Conn., May 3, 1742. [His grandfather was John Cutler, who removed to Killingly from Lexington, Mass., about 1700. His father was Hezekiah, born in 1706; married in 1730, Susan Clarke; died 1793, aged 87 years.] He graduated at Yale in 1765; married Mary Balch, 1766; then engaged in business at Nantucket. Studied law, afterwards theology, with his father-in-law; was ordained at Ipswich Hamlet [now Hamilton], Sept. 11, 1771. He served one year as chaplain in the Revolutionary war, and afterwards as surgeon. He gave great attention to botany, and soon became noted for his scientific attainments. In January, 1781, he was elected a member of the

American Academy of Arts and Sciences ; many communications from him are printed in their volumes ; was also a member of the leading scientific societies of this country and in Europe. In 1791 he received the honorary degree of LL. D. from Yale. He, in connection with Gen. Rufus Putnam, who has been called the "Father of the Northwest," was very active in promoting emigration to the west, secured the grant from Congress of a large tract of land in Ohio, and won for himself the title of Prince of Lobbyists. [See Harper's Monthly for September, 1885.]

In 1800 he was elected to Congress, and served two terms as Representative. He died at Hamilton, July 28, 1823, in his 82d year.

239. Benjamin,⁶ son of 124 Thomas⁵ and Mary [Sumner] Balch, was born at Dedham, Mass., February 12, 1743. He was graduated from Harvard College in 1763. He studied theology with his father, and evidently commenced preaching quite early, for while occupying a pulpit at Machias, Maine, one of his auditors, a pretty Irish girl, caught his eye and fancy, and in 1764 they were married.

This young woman was Miss Joanna O'Brien. She was born at Scarboro, Maine, and died at Barrington, N. H., September 1, 1820. Her brothers Jeremiah, John and Joseph, were all noted privateersmen, during the Revolution.

Rev. Benjamin returned to Dedham, with his wife, soon after their marriage, and he there temporarily occupied a pulpit. He then made a contract with the congregation of Mendon, South Precinct, and was settled over that church.

Benjamin remained as the pastor of the Mendon church for five years, when some differences arose regarding his salary, and he left them quite abruptly, and sold his property to a Quaker. This was almost an unpardonable sin in the eyes of the people.

In 1772 he established his home at New Mills, a part of Danvers, Mass., now known as Danversport, and here his family lived for eleven years. He was settled over no church but filled supplies in the vicinity, when not away in the service of the Army or Navy.

Benjamin Balch was admitted to Jordan Lodge of F. and A. M. of Danvers.

As Lieutenant of a Danvers Company, Capt. Edmund Putnam, commander, he marched with it to Lexington, April 19, 1775, and participated in the battle on that day.

He served in turn as Chaplain in Colonel Ephrim Doolittle's Regiment; the Frigate Boston, Captain McNeil, and other vessels.

In 1781 he was with the Frigate Alliance, Captain John Barry, when she conveyed the U. S. Ambassador to France. This vessel was in a severe engagement with a British ship and brig, which they captured off Halifax. The fierceness of the battle so excited the chaplain that he seized a musket and fought with such ardor that his exploits earned for him the sobriquet of " The Fighting Parson."

Benjamin's son Thomas was with him in the Alliance, and served as powder monkey. After the batttle he met his son with great joy and exclaimed, "What, Tom, are you alive!"

In August, 1784, he was settled over the church at Barrington, N. H., where he preached over thirty years, greatly beloved by his people. The Barrington records show that he performed the ceremony at nearly all the weddings in the vicinity.

Death came to him suddenly, on May 4, 1815. But a few days before, old age had led him to preach his farewell sermon and bring his thirty years pastorate to a close. He fell dead while walking through the town. He was burried in the woods about 40 rods to the northwest of his home, where he for so many years had lived. Tradition says that his faithful little dog refused to forsake him even in death, and died upon his grave.

Benjamin and Joanna had twelve children. The two eldest were born at Dedham, the next two at Mendon, the next five at Danvers, and three at Barrington.

489* Thomas,⁷ b. Oct. 2, 1765; d. Jan. 16, 1840.
490* Benjamin,⁷ b. Jan. 5, 1768; d. Apr. 10, 1809.
491* Mary,⁷ b. June 11, 1770; d. Aug. 30, 1855.
492* John,⁷ b. Sept. 4, 1772; d. Aug. 5, 1843.
493* William,⁷ b. Jan. 17, 1775; d. Aug 31, 1842.
494* George Washington,⁷ } twins, b. Oct.16,1777; { d. June 21, 1826.
495* Horatio Gates,⁷   { d. 1850.
496* Joanna,⁷ b. July 3, 1780; d. in 1866.
497* Martha,⁷ b. Jan. 19, 1783, d. Feb. 1866.
498* Jeremiah O.,⁷ b. July 31, 1785; d. Nov. 4, 1875.
499   Hannah,⁷ b. July 20, 1791; m. Mr. Church; d.
500   Joseph,⁷ b. Nov. 7, 1794; d. June 22, 1797.

240. Elizabeth,⁶ daughter of 124 Thomas⁵ and Mary [Sumner] Balch, was born at South Dedham, September 2, 1746, and died in that town, September 15, 1820. She married Jonathan Dean, of South Dedham, May 8, 1766. She left many descendants in South Dedham. Samuel Holmes, b. May 7, 1767; Francis, b. Mar. 24, 1769; Ebenezer, b. May 17, 1772, d. Oct. 23, 1854; Balch, b. Mar. 7, 1775; Mary.

241. Lucy,⁶ daughter of 124 Thomas⁵ and Mary (Sumner) Balch, was born at Dedham, January 10, 1748, and died March 17, 1776.

She married Rev. Moses Everett, of Dorchester, Mass., November 24, 1774. No issue. Everett was an uncle of Hon. Edward Everett.

242. Irene,⁶ daughter of 124 Thomas⁵ and Mary [Sumner] Balch, was born at Dedham, February 6, 1753, and died in July, 1815. She married Dr. Elijah Hewins, of Sharon, Mass., Dec. 10, 1797.

243. Hannah,⁶ daughter of 124 Thomas⁵ and Mary [Sumner] Balch, was born December 10, 1755, at Dedham. She died April 17, 1839. She married Rev. Jabez Chickering [who was her father's successor at South Dedham], April 22, 1777. Chickering was born at Dover, Mass., November 4, 1753, and died March 12, 1812. He graduated from Harvard University in 1774, and was ordained at South Dedham, July 8, 1776, and continued to be pastor of that church to the date of his death. Their children were as follows :

LUCY, b. March 12, 1778; d. unm. July 5, 1796.

JOSEPH, b. April 30, 1780; d. Jan. 27, 1844. Graduated from Harvard University 1799; was a clergyman; settled in Woburn, Mass., 1804, and in Phillipston, 1822.

JABEZ, b. Aug. 28, 1782; d. Oct. 20, 1826. Graduated at Harvard University 1804; was a lawyer; lived in South Dedham and in Monroe, Mich., where he died.

ELIZABETH, b. June 28, 1785; married Rev. Samuel Gay, of Hubbardston, Mass.

THOMAS BALCH, b. April 24, 1788; d. June, 1817; married Susan Swift; lived in Louisville, Ky., where he died.

HANNAH, b. Aug. 8, 1802; married, Feb. 2, 1826, John Kingsbury Briggs, M. D.; married second, Samuel Fletcher, a lawyer, Feb. 13, 1847.

244. Thomas,[6] son of 124 Thomas[5] and Mary [Sumner] Balch, was born at Dedham, Feb. 21, 1761; was a soldier in the Revolution, and died unmarried in 1780.

247. Rebecca,[6] daughter of 127 William[5] and Rebecca. [Bailey] Balch, was born at Bradford, July 29, 1763. She married, Nov. 26, 1786, Niles Tilden, a ship's carpenter, from Marshfield, Mass. Her grandfather, Rev. Wm. Balch, officiated. They lived in Bradford until their children were born, then in Salem awhile, then in Methuen, where she died. Niles married Rhoda Little, of Marshfield; resided in Methuen on a farm; removed to New Bedford, where he was a cigar manufacturer. Lucretia, d. y. Convers, d. aged 30 years, married Mary Chamberlain; lived in Salem; had children.

248. Sarah,[6] daughter of 127 William[5] and Rebecca [Bailey] Balch, was born at Bradford, August 26, 1765, and died October 2, 1838. She was married March 10, 1789, to Deacon Daniel Stickney, of Bradford. He was a son of Capt. Thomas and Sarah [Tenney] Stickney. He died May 8, 1840. They had six children: Benjamin, b. July 14, 1790; d. July 21, 1790. Leonard, b. September, 1791; d. Jan. 10, 1795. Daniel, b. July, 1793; d. Jan. 2, 1795. Sarah, b. March, 1796; d. unm. Sept. 28, 1817. Daniel Balch, b. July 21, 1798; d. in Groveland; married Ann, daughter of Samuel L. Parker, Mary, b. July 22, 1800; d. Feb. 2, 1874;

married her second cousin, William, son of Samuel and Betty [Balch] Savary.

249. William,[6] son of 127 William[5] and Rebecca [Bailey] Balch, was born at Bradford, July 9, 1767, and died July 9, 1862. He never married. He owned and occupied the old homestead of his ancestors at Groveland, formerly Bradford, and willed it to his nephew 505 Thomas Hutchinson[7] Balch.

250. Jonathan,[6] son of 127 William[5] and Rebecca [Bailey] Balch, was born at East Bradford, June 18, 1769, and died April 4, 1838, upon the place where his uncle Nathaniel once lived. He was married three times, first, August 13, 1796, to Abigail, daughter of Deacon Phineas and Susan [Stickney] Carlton, of Bradford. She was born November 1, 1773, and died August 4, 1802. The fruits of this marriage were three children:

501* PHINEAS CARLTON,[7] b. June 20, 1797; d. Jan. 24, 1880.
502* LEONARD,[7] b. Sept. 18, 1799; d. Aug. 9, 1871.
503* WILLIAM,[7] b. May 7, 1802; d. Oct. 25, 1841.

Jonathan married second, November 29, 1803, Mehitable, a sister to his first wife. She was born October 16, 1769, and died Sept. 20, 1830, at Bradford. They had five children:

504 URIAH,[7] b. Oct. 7, 1805; d. unm. Nov. 23, 1832.
505* THOMAS HUTCHINSON,[7] b. March 20, 1807.
506* JONATHAN,[7] b. Oct. 5, 1808; d. Nov. 15, 1892.
507 BAILEY,[7]
508 ABIGAIL,[7] } twins, b. Jan. 17, 1811; both d. y.

Jonathan married third, April 3, 1832, Mrs. Betsey [Clay] Danforth. She was born February 2, 1774, and died July, 1850. She was the widow of Eliphalet Danforth.

253. Benjamin,[6] son of 127 William[5] and Rebecca [Bailey] Balch, was born at Bradford, November 9, 1774, and died June 6, 1860. He was a watchmaker by trade. On the 13th day of July, 1796, he moved from Bradford to Salem, where he afterwards lived. He was married Dec. 4, 1800, to Lois, daughter of Moses H. Phippen. She died in 1863, aged 81 years. Benjamin learned his trade with his cousin Daniel, of Newburyport. Benjamin and Lois had ten children:

509* Louisa,[7] b. July 12, 1802; d. 1887.
510* Benjamin,[7] b. Jan. 25, 1804; d. Nov. 5, 1863.
511* James,[7] b. Feb. 21, 1806; d. November, 1846.
512* William,[7] b. Feb. 1, 1808; d. 187–.
513* Moses Phippin,[7] b. Jan. 28, 1810.
514* Clarissa,[7] b. June 22, 1812; d. 1842.
515 George,[7] b. March 30, 1814; d. April 25, 1814.
516 Lucy Ann,[7] b. Aug. 25, 1815; d. unm. Aug. 26, 1835.
517 Caroline,[7] b. Oct. 12, 1818; d. unm. Sept. 13, 1878.
518* Henry Freeborn,[7] b. Nov. 24, 1820.

254. **Mary**, or Polly,[6] daughter of 127 William[5] and Rebecca [Bailey] Balch, was born at Bradford, December 8,
1776, and died July 9, 1847. She was married April 19,
1798, to Nathaniel, son of Nathaniel and Abigail [Savory]
Wallingford, of East Bradford. Charles, d. y. Rebecca, b.
April 6, 1801; married Osgood George, son of Eliphalet and
Susan [Nichols] Boynton, of Haverhill, a shoe manufacturer. Sophia, b. 1804; d. unm. 1856. Clarissa, b. 1811; d.
unm. June 15, 1880. Charles, b. Dec. 8, 1812; d. Sept. 26,
1885; married Elizabeth H., daughter of Moses H. and Polly
[Hale] Palmer; they had four children, Byron, Mary,
Thomas and Fanny.

257. **Daniel**,[6] son of 130 Daniel[5] and Hannah [Clemens]
Balch, was born at Newburyport, March 1, 1761, and died at
the same town, October 13, 1835. He followed the occupation of his father, a watchmaker, at Newburyport. He was
a man of strong common sense, just and honest, quite irasci-
ble, and when aroused apt to use expressions more forcible
than polite. He was a Federalist, and very vituperative of
Andrew Jackson. Pecuniarily he was in moderate circumstances, and dependent on his trade. He had a comfortable
home, with considerable land, on which he raised hay and
vegetables. He was a great lover of tulips, the border of the
middle path of his garden back of his house was gay with
them in their season. Among them were the Dutch tulips,
which he esteemed as rare.

He was of an inventive mind. From the upper story of
his house, attached to clockwork, he suspended a cord with

a weight attached, so that when wound up it would turn the spit on which was the turkey or goose to roast.

He attended the Unitarian Church, but was not a communicant, and, in fact, was skeptically inclined, finding the origin of the universe and the destiny of man subjects too vast and mysterious to cope with.

He married first, November 27, 1783, Miss Lucy Hodge, daughter of Charles Hodge. She was born at Newburyport, April 6, 1760, and died December 27, 1797. The issue of this marriage was six children:

519* HANNAH,[7] b. Oct. 14, 1784; d. March 20, 1828.
520* ELIZABETH,[7] b. March 18, 1786; d. Oct. 17, 1873.
521* CHARLES HODGE,[7] b. Oct. 29, 1787; d. Nov. 18, 1852.
522* DANIEL,[7] b. June 16, 1790; d. Nov. 17, 1858.
523 WILLIAM,[7] b. May 12, 1793; d. June 18, 1794.
524* WILLIAM,[7] b. July 20, 1795; d. June 26, 1886.

Daniel married second, December 2, 1798, Martha Tarbox, by whom he had two sons. She died August 16, 1802.

525* JOHN THEODORIC,[7] b. Oct. 18, 1799; d. Feb. 24, 1847.
526 GEORGE,[7] b. March 31, 1802; d. Oct. 9, 1802.

Daniel married third, July 10, 1804, Mrs. Elizabeth Murray. She died November 16, 1819, aged 45 years. No issue.

259. Thomas Hutchinson,[6] son of 130 Daniel[5] and Hannah [Clemens] Balch, was born at Newburyport, July 7, 1771, and died in that town, June 28, 1817. He followed the occupation of his father, a watchmaker. He married Mrs. Agnes [Ware] Sloan, December 8, 1796. She was born in 1767, and died October 24, 1802. They resided in Newburyport, and all their children were born and died in that town, except Nancy, the youngest, who died in the Worcester Insane Asylum.

527 MARY SIGOURNY,[7] b. Feb. 29, 1798; d. unm. Sept. 29, 1808.
528 HANNAH,[7] b. Aug. 16, 1799; d. unm. Sept. 6, 1817.
529 AGNES,[7] b. May 20, 1801; d. unm. April 1, 1825.
530 NANCY,[7] b. Oct. 17, 1802; d. unm. Dec. 30, 1868.

Thomas H. married second, Mrs. Ann [Hodge] Hovey, July 26, 1808. She was born in 1769, and died April 14, 1818. No issue.

261. John,[6] son of 131 Nathaniel[5] and Joanna [Day] Balch, was born January 12, 1761, at East Bradford, Mass., and died at Newburyport, December 26, 1836. He and his wife were buried in the old cemetery near the Mall in Newburyport. He was a merchant, doing business on Merrimac street, in Newburyport. He was married March 1, 1783, to Eunice, daughter of Joseph and Sarah [Moses] Bartlett, of Newburyport. She was born April 30, 1763, and died August 7, 1828. Thirteen children was the issue of John and Sarah. Their five eldest were born in East Bradford. John moved to Newburyport in 1791, and the rest of his children were born in that town.

531　JOHN,[7] d. y.
532*　JOSEPH,[7] b. Dec. 5, 1785; d. Dec. 10, 1849.
533*　EUNICE,[7] b. Aug. 7, 1787.
534*　HANNAH,[7] b. Jan. 3, 1789.
535*　SARAH,[7] b. Dec. 21, 1790; d. Feb. 8, 1893.
536*　SOPHRONIA,[7] b. Feb. 14, 1793; d. June 24, 1872.
537　NATHANIEL,[7] b. March 17, 1794; d. July 2, 1795.
538*　LYDIA PILLSBURY,[7] b. March 1, 1797; d. Oct. 2, 1870.
539　LUCY,[7] b. July 28, 1798; d. Aug. 26, 1800.
540*　MARY,[7] b. April 17, 1800.
541*　LUCY,[7] b. Oct. 11, 1801; d. July 20, 1885.
542*　JOHN,[7] b. April 14, 1803; d.
543*　BENJAMIN,[7] b. April 16, 1805; d. Sept. 4, 1880.

262. Abigail,[6] daughter of 131 Nathaniel[5] and Joanna [Day] Balch, was born at East Bradford, November 12, 1762, and died November 13, 1802. She was married, September 16, 1782, to Dr. Seth Jewett, son of Jeremiah and Elizabeth [Choate] Jewett, of Rowley, Mass. He was born in 1756, and died at Newburyport, March 15, 1802. He practiced medicine in Rowley, until 1798, when he moved to Newburyport. They had five children.

> SOPHIA, b. Aug. 1, 1783; married Walter, son of Jeremiah Todd, of Rowley. He was a trader in Newburyport. Their children: *Seth*, married Ann Giles, and lives in Washington, D. C.: two children, Ellen and Seth Giles. *Sophia*. *William*, who married Eliza Giles, had two children, Esther and Thomas. *Mary*, who married George Sweetser, of Newburyport, child, Caroline Sweetser.

Commonwealth of Massachusetts.

OFFICE OF THE SECRETARY.

REVOLUTIONARY WAR SERVICE

—— OF ——

JOHN BALCH.

JOHN BALCH: Appears with rank of Private on Muster and Pay Roll of Capt. Stephen Jenkins' Co., Col. Jacob Gerrish's (Suffolk and Essex Co.) Regt.—Enlisted October 14, 1779.—Discharged November 22, 1779.—Time of service, 1 month, 20 days.—Detached to reinforce army under Gen. Washington by Resolve of October 9, 1779.

Vol. 20; p. 118.

Boston, June 14, 1897.

I certify the foregoing to be a true abstract from the Record Index to the Revolutionary War Archives deposited in this office.

Witness the seal of the Commonwealth.

Seal
Commonwealth
of
Massachusetts.

WM. M. OLIN, Secretary.

JOHN BALCH.
(261)
A soldier in the Revolution, 1779.

ABIGAIL, b. July 5, 1785; married Daniel Smith, an apothecary, of Newburyport.

WILLIAM, b. in 1787; d. y.

SETH, b. in 1793; d. y.

NATHANIEL, b. June 8, 1795; married Ann, daughter of James Prince, of Newburyport. They lived in Washington, D. C. Their children: *Laura, Ann, Corinna, Sebastin, Sidney,* and *Augustine.*

263. Nathaniel,[6] son of 131 Nathaniel[5] and Joanna [Day] Balch, was born in East Bradford, August 9, 1764, and died at Newburyport, October 19, 1793. He was married at Bradford, October 2, 1790, to Lucy Russell. She died September 24, 1847, aged 79 years. They had no issue. Nathaniel was a trader in Newburyport. His estate was administered by his brother John. Lucy, his widow, married Capt. Edward Kimball, of Newburyport, Nov. 80, 1796. They removed to Wenham.

264. Hannah,[6] daughter of 131 Nathaniel[5] and Joanna [Day] Balch, was born at East Bradford, June 4, 1766, and died July 17, 1831. She was married October 11, 1788, to Lieut. Silas Hopkinson, son of Ens. Samuel and Betty [Palmer] Hopkinson, her grandfather, Rev. Wm. Balch, officiating. He died June 29, 1828, aged 64 years. They resided in East Bradford, in the south half of the William Savory house. He was a cabinet-maker. Their five children were born in that town.

WILLIAM, b. July 9, 1790; married first, Maria, daughter of Simeon and Hannah [Bractley] Atwood, and second, Adeline, daughter of Richard Morse. She died Sept. 23, 1884, aged 82 years. William's children were: *William L.,* d. y.; *Hannah B.,* d. y.; *Jane K.,* unm.; *Wm. L., Jr.,* m. Cynthia G. Morse; *Benjamin B., Nathaniel G., Moses A., George P., Daniel P.,* and *Harriet A.*

URIAH, b. Sept. 28, 1791; married first, Judith Latham, and second, Lucy Chase, of West Newbury. Uriah's children were: *Hannah, Ann M., George W., Adeline C.* and *Joseph H.*

HANNAH, b. in 1794; d. Feb. 24, 1808.

ABIGAIL, b. June 28, 1796; married William, son of Samuel and Ann [Greenough] Parker, of Bradford. Their children were: *Julia A., William H., Henry T., Eustis P.,* d. y., *Alden B.* and *Catherine L.*

IRA, b. April 23, 1796; was a tanner and currier, and later was a farmer; was a deacon in the church. Married Julia, daughter of Daniel Poor, of Georgetown. Their children were: *Dophne*, d. y.; *Henry*, d. y.; *Julia P.*; *Silas H.*, and *Martha*, twins, d. y.; *Charles H.*; *Henry*, d. y.; *Daniel W.*, d. 1852, aged 15 years; *Mary A.*, who was clerk in the P. O., for her brother Charles H., who was p. m. in Groveland until removed by the Democratic administration in 1885.

265. **Samuel,**[6] son of 131 Nathaniel[5] and Joanna [Day] Balch, was born at East Bradford, January 25, 1768, and died in Georgetown, Mass., March 26, 1850. He was married first, May 5, 1794, to Betsey, daughter of William and Mary [Gage] Savary, of East Bradford. She was born June 24, 1774, and died at Portsmouth, N. H., September 15, 1800. They had three children, all born in Portsmouth.

544   BETSEY,[7] b. March 2, 1795; d. July 14, 1798.
545   NATHANIEL,[7] d. y.
546*   WILLIAM SAVARY,[7] b. Dec. 15, 1799; d. Jan. 22, 1871.

Samuel married second, in 1801, Hannah, daughter of Michael Widden, of Portsmouth. She was born in that town in 1773, and died in the same town, in February, 1817. She was the mother of five children, all born in Portsmouth.

547   SETH JEWETT,[7] b. March 7, 1802; d. unm. Nov. 10, 1820.
548*   MARY ELIZABETH,[7] b. June 1, 1804; d. Dec. 12, 1851.
549*   MEHITABLE MELCHER,[7] b. Aug. 10, 1806; d. Aug. 20, 1873.
550*   NATHANIEL,[7] b. Sept. 9, 1808; d. June 3, 1876.
551   GEORGE,[7] b. Jan. 25, 1810; d. unm. 1834.

Samuel married third, July 6, 1821, Abigail, daughter of Jacob and Catherine [Hall] Bartlett, of Deering, N. H. She died at Georgetown, Mass., May 29, 1849. Their three children were born in Portsmouth, N. H.

552*   EUNICE,[7] b. Aug. 23, 1822; d. Sept. 12, 1860.
553   JOHN,[7] b. March 15, 1824; d. October, 1824.
554*   SAMUEL,[7] b. Sept. 28, 1825.

268. **Betsey,**[6] daughter of 131 Nathaniel[5] and Joanna [Day] Balch, was born in East Bradford, July 10, 1774, and died July 16, 1838. She was married, May 7, 1793, to Stephen, son of Joseph Greely, of Haverhill, Mass. He died April 16, 1830. He was a boot and shoe dealer. They had seven children.

BENJAMIN, b. Dec. 11, 1793; married a Miss Sarah Knight; no issue.

NATHANIEL, b. Nov. 11, 1795; was drowned July 12, 1820; was called Captain Nathaniel Greely; married Nancy Swett, of Newburyport; one son, Nathaniel [posthumous], b. September, 1820, married first, Alice, daughter of Enoch Hall, two children; m. second, Elizabeth Bayley, of Amesbury, who d. 1891; children d. y.

JOHN, b. June 19, 1798; d. April 3, 1799.

ALICE, b. Nov. 14, 1800; d. y.

MARY ANN, b. Nov. 19, 1804; d. unm. in 1880.

JOHN BALCH, b. July 20, 1802; married Clarissa, daughter of William and Mehitable [Dole] Jewett, of Byfield. He lived in Newburyport, except three years that he lived in Haverhill. He was a boot and shoe manufacturer. He was known as Captain John B. Greely, having been a captain in the Mass. Militia, and as such commanded an escort to Lafayette in 1824. By his wife Clarissa he had seven children. *Steven*, b. 1823; d. unm. 1844. *John Augustus*, b. July 31, 1825; married Charlotte M., daughter of Jonathan and Mary [Hunton] Rundett, of North Hampton; b. in Nottingham, N. H., June 9, 1827; they live in Newburyport, and have had seven children, four d. y.; *William Henry*, b. 1827; d. Aug. 12, 1831. *Elizabeth Ann*, b. Aug. 21, 1829; married Lucius E. Hallock, of New York, merchant; four sons, one d. unm. *Mary Ann*, b. 1831; d. y. *William Henry*, b. in Haverhill, Dec. 25, 1833; married Eliza Ann Jones, of Salisbury; was a mason; resided at Newburyport; d. about 1859; all issue d. y. *James Henry*, b. about 1835; d. y.

Captain John Balch Greely's first wife died, and he married, in 1843, Miss Fanny Dunn, daughter of Deacon Samuel and Eleaner [Neal] Cobb, of Bartlett, N. H. She was born April 20, 1819. They had two children: Adolphus Washington,[*] b. March 27, 1844. Mary Ellen, b. 1846, d. 1850. Adolphus W., the celebrated Arctic explorer, was the first private soldier of the volunteer army to reach the grade of general in the regular army. He enlisted in 1861, in the 19th Mass., was brevet major U. S. Vols. in 1865, and is now a brigadier-general. The Lady Franklin Bay Expedition commanded by Gen. Greely reached the highest point north ever attained, i.e., 83°, 24'. This was in 1881 to 1884. During the war Gen. Greely was thrice wounded. He is now stationed in

[*]He was married June 20, 1878, to Henrietta Hudson Cruger, daughter of Thomas L. Nesmith. She was born Oct. 7, 1849. Their children are: Antoinette, b. 1879; Adola and ——, twins, b. 1881; John Nesmith, b. 1885; Rose Ishbel, b. 1887; Adolphus W., b. 1889; Gertrude Gale, b. 1891.

Washington in connection with the weather service. Mrs.
Sarah K. Bolton's "Famous Explorers," contains an excellent biographical notice of Gen. Greely.
ELIZABETH, b. July 30, 1810; d. Aug. 6, 1810.

271. Lucy,[6] daughter of 131 Nathaniel[5] and Joanna
[Day] Balch, was born at East Bradford, February 21, 1779,
and died in New York city in 1854. She was married, in
1799, to Samuel Perley, of Newburyport. They moved to
Harrisburg, Penn., where he died. His widow then moved
to New York city with her children. Lucy, married Capt.
Joseph Livermore, of Eastport, Me.; he died at sea of yellow
fever; three children, Amanda, Caroline, and John R. Samuel was a printer in Washington, D. C., and died there in
1881; his wife died in 1875, leaving two sons and three
daughters. Eustice, d. unm. Charles, born in Newburyport,
died in New York city, June 15, 1885; he was a ship machinist, married, and had twelve children; of these were
three pairs of twins.

275. Susanna,[7] daughter of 134 Samuel[6] and Susan [Aldrich] Balch, was born at Oxford, Mass., May 28, 1762. She married William Hoyt, and soon after they moved to St. Johnsbury, Vt., where they lived and both died. They had thirteen children, all were born in St. Johnsbury. Among them were the following :

> JOSEPH, d. in Jay, Vt.
>
> JOSIAH, d. in St. Johnsbury, Vt.
>
> HIRAM, b. Apr. 27, 1800, m. Eliza, daughter of Clark W. McKeige of Boston, Aug. 28, 1826. Hiram Hoyt was a physician and lived at Syracuse, N. Y., and died there Feb. 28, 1866. Son, *Dr. Elmere Hoyt,* d. in Syracuse in 1891.
>
> DAVID, m. Julia May. He was a physician ; lived and died at Palmyra, N. Y.
>
> NATHANIEL, d. at St. Johnsbury, Vt.

The eldest daughter of Susanna and William Hoyt, m. Mr. Higgins of St. Johnsbury, Vt. Another daughter m. John Guild, and lived in New York state.

276. Olive,[7] daughter of 134 Samuel[6] and Susan [Aldrich] Balch, was born at Oxford, Mass., May 4, 1764, and died at West Winfield, N. Y., March 1, 1826. She was married July 8, 1786, to Joel, son of Samuel and Ruth [Nims] Guild. He was born at Leyden, Mass., Feb. 1, 1764, and died at West Winfield. Joel Guild was a farmer. About 1794 he moved with his family from Leyden, Mass., to Paris, N. Y. They had six children ; the three eldest were born at Leyden, and the three youngest at Paris.

> JOEL, b. 1787; d. March 28, 1857.
>
> DANIEL, b. Dec. 11, 1790; d. June 16, 1853; m. Jan. 1, 1818, Rhoda Parmalee. She was b. 1798, d. at Paris, Mich. For a time after his marriage he lived at Frankfort, N. Y., then

moved to Michigan. *Isaac Phillips*, b. May 5, 1820; *Mary T.*,
b. Feb. 23, 1822; *Irene Amanda*, b. Nov. 11, 1823; *Olive E.*,
b. Sept. 10, 1825; *H. Newton*, b. Dec. 14, 1827; *Olive Cornelia*,
b. Nov. 11, 1829, at Frankfort, N. Y., and m. Jan. 5, 1864, to
Charles C. Comstock, of Grand Rapids, Michigan, who was
born March 5, 1818, in Sullivan, N. H.; *Sarah Elenor*, b. Sept.
5, 1831; *Chester Newton*, b. Sept. 25, 1833; *Harriet M.*, b.
December, 1836; *Richmond Daniel*, b. June 5, 1839.

LORENDA, b. March 3, 1793; d. Aug. 20, 1844.
EDWARD, b. Dec. 12, 1795; d. Sept. 13, 1871.
JOHN, b. Sept. 8, 1797; d. April 20, 1840.
OLIVE, b. Aug. 29, 1800; d. Feb. 20, 1862.

277. Samuel,[7] son of 184 Samuel[6] and Susan [Aldrich]
Balch, was born at Oxford, Mass., March 23, 1767, and died
at Frankfort, N. Y., about 1847. He was about 80 years of
age at his death, and was buried in Norwich Corners cemetery. He married Miss Mercy Atwood, of Douglass, Mass.
She died at Athens, Vt. They had eight children.

555* JOSEPH,[8] b.   ; d. 1828.
556* JOHN,[8] b. Oct. 29, 1796; d. Aug. 4, 1847.
557* DELIA,[8] b. 1800; d.
558* EBENEZER,[8] b. 1802; d. 1868.
559* ADELINE,[8] b. April 15, 1804.
560* OLIVE,[8] b. March 2, 1806; d. about 1876.
561* ABIGAIL,[8] b. Jan. 4, 1791; d. Jan. 8, 1853.
562* MERCY,[8] b. March 2, 1812; d.

278. Josiah,[7] son of 134 Samuel[6] and Susan [Aldrich]
Balch, was born at Oxford, Mass., December 25, 1770, and
died April 29, 1848. He was twice married, first to Sarah
Kimball, December 6, 1795. She was born May 6, 1776, and
died November 6, 1804. They had three children.

563   EDWARD,[8] b. Dec. 17, 1796; d.
564* CHARLOTTE,[8] b. Dec. 27, 1798; d.
565   JOHN,[8] b. July 6, 1802; d.

Josiah was married second, January 14, 1807, to Miss
Mercy Sterns. She was born June 12, 1781, and died November 9, 1856. Josiah and Mercy had four children.

566* SARAH,[8] b. March 11, 1808; d. Nov. 23, 1834.
567* PHILANDER,[8] b. May 21, 1812; d. May 30, 1885.
568   AVARINTHA,[9] b. July 6, 1814; d. Aug. 13, 1823.
569* LEONARD,[8] b. Dec. 3, 1816; d.

280. **Elizabeth**,[7] daughter of 134 Samuel[6] and Susan [Aldrich] Balch, was born in Kingley, Conn., October 23, 1775. She married Luther Chickering, of St. Johnsbury, and lived and died in that town. They had four sons and four daughters. One daughter, Angeline, married her cousin, James Towle.

281. **Nathaniel**,[7] son of 134 Samuel[6] and Susan [Aldrich] Balch, was born in Oxford, Worcester county, Mass., December 3, 1779, and died in Kalamazoo, Mich., December 25, 1857. On the 19th of September, 1805, he married Sally, daughter of Nathaniel and Sally [Wilson] Bennet. Bennet was a native of New Jersey. She was born in Rockingham, Vt., August 20, 1781, and died January 28, 1876, in Kalamazoo. Their children were all born in Athens, Vt.

570* MARY WILSON,[8] b. Aug. 31, 1806; d. Dec. 15, 1875.
571* NATHANIEL ALDRICH,[8] b. Jan. 22, 1808; d. Feb. 1, 1894.
572* SARAH CHAMBERLAIN,[8] b. Jan. 15, 1810; d. Nov. 26, 1841.
573* DREXA WEBB,[8] b. Dec. 25, 1811; d. June 18, 1887.
574* SAMUEL RAYMOND,[8] b. March 22, 1813; d. Aug. 2, 1890.
575* LOVINA CUMMINS,[8] b. Dec. 30, 1815; d. Sept., 1895.
576* ROYAL TYLER,[8] b. Dec. 17, 1817; d. Sept. 12, 1884.
577* SYBIL MAYNARD,[8] b. Nov. 22, 1819; d. March 31, 1891.
578* AMAZIAH ROBINSON,[8] b. Dec. 18, 1821; d. May 29, 1872.
579* ABAD CHICKERING,[8] b. Nov. 30, 1823.
580* CONFUCIUS ICILIOUS,[8] b. March 26, 1826.
581 OMAR W.,[8] b. Feb. 3, 1828; d. July 2, 1831.

Nathaniel Balch was a man of medium stature, but strongly built. In his early days, like most New England boys, he enjoyed wrestling, and was somewhat of a champion in that sport. He was an industrious, temperate, Christian man, retiring in disposition, but of a quick temper. He held the office of selectman for the town of Athens in the years 1831-32 and in 1842-43. He and all his sons were Democrats. He was a lover of education, and gave to his children all the advantages for its acquisition that his circumstances would permit. He removed from Athens to Kalamazoo in 1850, and since all of his children had found homes in the then far West, he lived with his son, Royal T., near Kalamazoo, until his death.

The children all inherited their father's Christian and temperance principles, and only one of this large family ever used tobacco in any form. All of them lived to grow up save the youngest, who died of scarlet fever in his third year. As a family they were strong and robust, imbibing into their very natures the ruggedness of their native mountains, and dearly they loved to recall their feats of strength and daring adventures, together with the merry makings incident to early New England life, as apple parings and husking bees.

283. Coben,[7] son of 134 Samuel[6] and Susan [Aldrich] Balch, was born at Guilford, Vt. He married Miss Patty Patch. They lived in Athens, Vt., and all their children were born in that town. About 1830 he moved to Lyden, Vermont, where he lived several years; then he moved to Chester, Vt., where his wife died, and he married a second, and then moved to Kalamazoo, Mich. They had nine children.

582   SAMUEL,[8] b. Nov. 27, 1805; d.
583*   COBEN,[8] b. May 2, 1807; d. Feb. 2, 1863.
584*   BARNABAS DODGE,[8] b. May 9, 1809; d. Nov. 30, 1872.
585   MARTHA,[8] b. April 2, 1811; d. unm.
586   JOHN,[8] b. Jan. 5, 1813; d. unm.
587   ELIZABETH P.,[8] b. Dec. 9, 1815; d. unm. July 8, 1891.
588*   SARAH,[8] b. March 26, 1817; d. July 8, 1891.
589   SANFORD,[8] b. Aug. 7, 1819; d. unm.
590*   LUTHER CHICKERING,[8] b. Feb. 1, 1826; d. May 7, 1883.

284. Abigail,[7] daughter of 134 Samuel[6] and Susan [Aldrich] Balch, was born at Guilford, Vt., March 30, 1786, and died at Victory, Vt., March 30, 1868, exactly 82 years of age. She married William Towle, of Fisherville, N. H. He died at Victory, Vt., January 22, 1850, aged 76 years. They lived in Windham, Vt., and their five children were born in that town.

     JAMES, b. Sept. 4, 1806; d. at Victory, Aug. 10, 1881. He married his cousin, Angelina Chickering, daughter of Luther and Betsey [Balch] Chickering, of Danville, Vt. She was born May 14, 1806, and died March 18, 1869. They had four

children: *John*, b. June 29, 1829; committed suicide March
4, 1849. *Rozana*, b. Jan. 4, 1834; m. Wm. Brooks, and lived
in Danville. *James*, b. Dec. 8, 1838; m. Harriet L. Town, in
Victory, June 2, 1870; their children were: Lillian E., b.
Feb. 26, 1871, d. Feb. 26, 1872; Alma E., born Jan. 21, 1873;
George E., b. June 29, 1874; and Charles E., b. Oct. 5, 1876;
the three eldest were born in Victory, the youngest in Lyndon, Vt.; Alma E. m. Fritz Norris in St. Johnsbury, Vt.,
April 22, 1887, resides at North Concord, Vt. *Royal*, b. Oct.
10, 1843, unm., lived at South Victory, Vt.

MIRRIAM, b. in Windham, Vt.; d. at Victory about 1865, aged 58
years. She married Warren Harrington, of Claremont, New
Hampshire; lived at Victory; no issue.

CAROLINE, b. in Windham, Vt.; m. Lyman Lawrence, of Newport, Vt., and was living in that town in November, 1889.
P. O. address, South Troy, Vt. Issue, two daughters.

ANGELINA, b. 1809; m. Jonathan Lawrence, a brother to her
sister Caroline's husband. They lived in various places.
She d. at Stanstead, Quebec, Oct. 17, 1888, aged 78 years.
She had two sons, both dead, and two daughters, both liv-
ing; one, Mrs. Sylvia Higgins, is living at Smith's Mills,
Quebec.

JOHN, b. April 22, 1815, in Townsend, Vt., and is now, Dec. 1,
1889, living at Victory, Vt. A farmer and machinist. On
the 14th of September, 1840, he married Pamelia, daughter
of Benjamin and Jerusha Brown. She was born at Stan-
stead, Nov. 4, 1819, and died at Victory, March 13, 1888.
The issue of John and Pamelia was two children: *William
Henry*, b. April 2, 1842, in Victory; m. Sept. 8, 1862, Emily
B., daughter of Ruben and Lydia Emerson. She was b. at
Whelock, Vt., June 20, 1842; they have four children, all b.
at Victory. Gertrude Estelle, b. July 15, 1864; m. Alex
Vachan, Dec. 24, 1883. Bertrand Edwin, b. July 5, 1866; m.
Louisa G. Graves, in West Concord, July 10, 1886; Lydia
Aurelia, b. April 20, 1872; Anna Blossom, b. Jan. 24,
1881. *Mary Ann*, b. Oct. 1, 1851, at Victory; m. Feb. 16,
1869, Joseph G., son of Joseph and Sarah Goddard; he was
b. at Bermuda Isle, March 1, 1841; they have five children:
Harley Elmer, b. Jan. 9, 1870; Cora Elsie, b. July 31, 1871,
m. Edgar O. Hayes, in West Concord, Vt., Dec. 26, 1887; b.
at Stowe, Vt., Nov. 5, 1866, issue, one son, b. Oct. 10, 1888;
Mary Ella, b. Sept. 23, 1876; Georgie May, b. May 1, 1882;
Harry Albert, b. July 8, 1888.

285. Samuel,[7] son of 143 Nathaniel[6] and Lydia [Towm-
bly] Balch, was born in Wakefield, N. H., about 1779. He
was married in Salem, Mass., August 27, 1819, to Eunice

Moses. The ceremony was performed by the Rev. Wm. Bailey.
They had one son and two daughters.

591   LYDIA,⁸ d. unm.
592* FREDERICK,⁸ b. in Salem, Sept. 8, 1817; d. Mar. 15, 1896.
593* MATILDA,⁸ b. about 1820; died April 19, 1875.

286. Joseph,⁷ son of 143 Nathaniel⁶ and Lydia [Towm-
bly] Balch, was born in Wakefield, N. H., March 7, 1781,
and died in Lancaster, N. H., December 14, 1846. He married Miss Eliza Legro, daughter of Dr. Legro, of Lancaster,
N. H. She was born Nov. 19, 1790, and died July 5, 1845.
Eleven children was the issue of this marriage.

594* ALMIRA,⁸ b. Dec. 19, 1811; d. Dec. 22, 1879.
595   JAMES H.,⁸ b. April 11, 1813; d. unm.; was a sailor.
596* AMOS,⁸ b. Nov. 1, 1815; d. July 5, 1884.
597* SAMUEL B.,⁸ b. July 11, 1817.
598   REUBEN,⁸ b. Jan. 20, 1819; d. May 16, 1820.
599   MARTHA,⁸ b. Oct. 21, 1820; d. Aug. 30, 1821.
600* JOSEPH H.,⁸ b. March 7, 1822; d. Dec. 2, 1869.
601* FREDERICK B.,⁸ b. Feb. 16, 1825.
602   JOHN L.,⁸ b. Oct. 20, 1826; d. unm. Sept. 3, 1873.
603* CHARLES W.,⁸ b. Feb. 6, 1829.
604* ELIZA A.,⁸ b. Feb. 24, 1832.

287. Deborah,⁷ daughter of 143 Nathaniel⁶ and Lydia
[Towmbly] Balch, was born at Wakefield, N. H., December
28, 1782, and died Sept. 25, 1863. She was married October
25, 1808, to Samuel Jones, he was born Nov. 25, 1780, and died
October 22, 1849. They lived in Gardner, Maine. Their children were as follows:

> JAMES HAYES, b. Oct. 25, 1809; d. in Newton, Mass., Jan. 12,
> 1872; married Miss Lucy Hurd; was a furniture merchant in
> New Orleans, La., and lived there during the war.
> JOSEPH, b. Nov. 7, 1811; d. Dec. 27, 1815.
> JOSHUA, b. July 14, 1814; d. May 20, 1888; married Miss Susan
> Trask; lived in Cincinnati, Ohio.
> FREDERICK B., b. April 18, 1816; d. May 20, 1816.
> BETSEY H., b. April 4, 1817; married, Nov. 26, 1835, to Henry T.
> Franklin. He was born Jan. 17, 1813. They were living in
> Elizabethport, N. J., in 1889.
> LYDIA B., b. Dec. 11, 1819; unm., living at Randolph, Me., in
> 1888.
> JOSEPH, b. June 16, 1823. He left his home and was never
> heard from afterwards. He left his watch hanging in his

room; in fact, he took nothing with him. His family thought
he was murdered, his disappearance was so sudden, complete, and unaccountable.

NANCY L., b. June 5, 1821; unm., living at Randolph, Me., in
1888.

EMELINE F., b. May 22, 1828; d. April 11, 1879; married, Oct. 13,
1847, Charles Morris Webber, a sea captain. He was born
May 29, 1820, and died of yellow fever at Maricabo, July 15,
1857.

289. Nancy,[7] daughter of 148 Nathaniel[6] and Lydia
[Towmbly] Balch, was born in Wakefield, N. H., December
8, 1784. She was married in April, 1806, to Douglas Spaulding, of Lancaster. He was born July 13, 1784. They lived
in Lancaster, where their eight children were born.

FREDERICK BALCH, b. Dec. 9, 1806; d. Dec. 8, 1850; married
Sally Derby, and had eight children. After his death widow
and children went West.

SOPHRONIA WILLARD, b. July 8, 1808; d. June 30, 1876; m. Isaac
N. Cotton, March 23, 1834. He was b. March 16, 1808; d.
Aug. 12, 1858. Their children: *George D.*, b. March 16,
1835; *Phebe A.*, b. May 17, 1837; *Delphia*, b.; *Isaac F.*, b.
April 25, 1843; *Sumner S.*, b. Dec. 23, 1850.

LYDIA HARMONY, b. April 1, 1810; m. Ezra Derby, Dec. 8, 1829;
he was b. Sept. 16, 1801; they had eight children: *Moses W.*,
John N., *Olive J.*, *Cynthia M.*, *William F.*, *Harriet, Alfred*,
and *Mary*.

PHEBE DUSTIN, b. May 5, 1812; m. Zenas Snow, of Lunenburg,
Vt.

DANIEL NATHANIEL, b. Dec. 9, 1813; m. first, Caroline Lovejoy,
July 5, 1840; she was b. April 10, 1826; m. second, Jane Winters, April 5, 1860; she was born April 20, 1831.

CATHERINE CHARLOTTE, b. Aug. 23, 1818; m. Prescott Lovejoy,
at Lancaster, N. H., Dec. 7, 1840. Their children were:
Lorin D., b. Feb. 28, 1841; *Austin S.*, b. Sept. 26, 1842.

MARTHA JANE, b. Oct. 17, 1820; d. Aug. 13, 1839.

WILLIAM FRANKLIN, b. Aug. 6, 1822; d. June 3, 1876.

292. Frederick Bell,[7] son of 148 Nathaniel[6] and Lydia
[Towmbly] Balch, was born in Wakefield, N. H., May 13,
1790, and died at Alexandria, N. Y., Sept. 29, 1861. He
was married November 20, 1815, to Harriet, daughter of
Samuel and Thankful [Knapp] Benedict. She was born in
Litchfield, Ct., July 2, 1796, and died at Hingham, Wis.,
August 7, 1861. Frederick B. was a cooper and farmer.

He resided at Alexandria, N. Y. They had four children, the two eldest were born at Alexandria, the other two at Batavia, New York.

605* ELVIRA,[8] b. Oct. 10, 1817.
606* EMELINE,[8] b. May 10, 1819.
607 HARRIET CELESTE,[8] b. Oct.17,1822;unm.lives at Alexandria,N.Y.
608* FREDERICK A., b. Aug. 21, 1824.

293. Abigail,[7] daughter of 143 Nathaniel[6] and Lydia [Towmbly] Balch, was born in Wakefield, July 23, 1795, and died at Great Falls, N. H., July 18, 1868. She married a Mr. Pray. They lived at Great Falls. They had three children ; Issac, m. had one daughter, Lydia ; Lydia ; Kate J. m. a Mr. Smith, and lives at Ashton, R. I.

294. Sarah,[7] daughter of 148 Jonathan Belden[6] and Hopeful [Hurlburt] Balch, was born at Hartford, Connecticut, in 1777, and died at Bristol, Maine, October 5, 1807. She was married September 17, 1801, to Rev. Jonathan Belden, of Hallowell, Maine. They had three children, all died young. Josiah, Louisa, and Jonathan. Mr. Belden graduated at Yale College, studied theology and became a Congregational clergyman, for many years he preached at Hallowell.

296. Mary,[7] daughter of 148 Jonathan Belden[6] and Hopeful [Hurlburt] Balch, was born at West Hartford, Ct., September 24, 1782, and died at the same city, October 18, 1845: She married Stephen Page of Kensington, N. H. He was born April 19, 1780, and died April 18, 1860. They were married on October 13, 1805, and had eleven children.

    ADDISON BALCH, d.
    STEPHEN BENSON, living in Cleveland, Ohio, in 1886.
    SAMUEL WIRE, living in Cleveland, Ohio.
    BELDEN BLOOMFIELD, living in Cleveland, Ohio.
    JONATHAN BELDEN, living in Hartford, Ct., in 1886.
    MARY, d. y.
    MARY, unm., living in Hartford, Ct., in 1888.
    WILLIAM HENRY, d.
    JONATHAN NEWTON, d.
    JULIA, d.

297. Flora,[7] daughter of 148 Jonathan Belden[6] and Hopeful [Hurlburt] Balch, was born at West Hartford, Ct.,

April 24, 1785, and died Dec. 10, 1881. She was married
February 20, 1810, to Austin Wells, who was born at Wethersfield, Ct., December 28, 1778, and died at Rosevelt, Oswego County, N. Y., May 20, 1850. They had six children.

> FLORA MARIA, b. Nov. 13, 1813.
> LUCY A., b. Oct. 4, 1815; m. a Mr. Allen, and resides at Wil-
> loughby, Ohio.
> SARAH E., b. Mar. 20, 1819.
> JONATHAN B., b. Apr. 26, 1821.
> MARY S., b. Mar. 19, 1824.
> HARRIET S., b. Feb. 22, 1826.

298. Jonathan,[7] son of 148 Jonathan Belden[6] and Hopeful [Hurlburt] Balch, was born at West Hartford, December
14, 1788, and died at Harwinton, July 19, 1867. He was
married June 9, 1813 to Minerva, daughter of James Brace,
(known as Esquire Brace) of Harwinton. She was born at
Harwinton, December 20, 1791, and died April 20, 1864.
Jonathan was a farmer. In 1819 he moved with his family
from Hartford to Harwinton where he continued to reside the
remainder of his life. For sixteen years he was a deacon of the
Congregational Church. The issue of Jonathan and Minerva
was seven children, the three eldest were born at West Hartford, the others at Harwinton.

> 609   SARAH MINERVA,[8] b. Feb. 18, 1815; d. Oct. 15, 1817.
> 610   JAMES BRACE,[8] b. Dec. 15, 1816; d. Jan. 27, 1817.
> 611   SARAH MINERVA,[8] b. Apr. 6, 1818; d. Aug. 1, 1826.
> 612* HENRY BRACE,[8] b. May 13, 1820; d. Mar. 19, 1886.
> 613* JONATHAN BELDEN,[8] b. Oct. 26, 1822.
> 614* JAMES SHELTON,[8] b. Apr. 21, 1825.
> 615   MARIA MINERVA,[8] b. Jan. 14, 1828; d. Oct. 14, 1851.

299. Bela,[7] son of 148 Jonathan Belden[6] and Hopeful
[Hurlburt] Balch, was born at West Hartford, Ct., February
6, 1792, and died in the same town, May 6, 1852. He was
twice married; first to Fannie E. Yale, June 21, 1820, who
died July 23, 1824, aged 24 years; and second, on October 5,
1825 to Miss Abigail Wheat, who was born December 16,
1791.
The children by his first wife were as follows :

616   FANNIE M.,[8] b. Nov., 1821; d. Jan. 19, 1825.
617   LORENZO D.,[5] b. 1823; d. Jan. 3, 1825.

There were also two children by his second wife:

618   LORENZO YALE,[8] b. July 16, 1826; d. Feb. 1, 1828.
619   GEORGE WHEAT,[8] b. Apr. 18, 1831; d. y.

301. Justin,[7] son of 150 Joseph[6] and Mary [Watson]
Balch, was born in Williamstown, Mass., December 28, 1788,
and died at Albany, N. Y., July 31, 1826. Justin was a tea
merchant and importer; he made a voyage to China.

In 1823 he married Miss Maria Veder, and by her he had
one daughter.

620*   ALIDA.[8]

302. Sarah Maria,[7] daughter of 150 Joseph[6] and Mary
[Watson] Balch, was born at Williamstown, Mass., November 6, 1790, and died at Johnstown, N. Y., June 10, 1879.
She married Belam, son of Allen Case, October 11, 1822.
Mr. Case was born in Kingsboro, N. Y., he was a farmer and
lived in Johnstown, where he died December 7, 1879, aged
86 years. They had seven sons and one daughter.

> SARAH MARIA, b. Oct. 18, 1823. She married Mathew LaRue
> Perrine Yale, Sept. 20, 1849. Mr. Yale was a merchant in N.
> Y. City; he died in Philadelphia, Pa., Oct. 21, 1876, aged 53
> years, he was buried in Johnstown. They had one child,
> *Arthur Wells Yale*, b. Feb. 14, 1856; d. unm. Feb. 11, 1876.
> Sarah M. [Case] married for her second husband, Rev. Robert
> A. Hill, Aug. 1, 1878. They reside at Pittsburg, Penn. No
> issue.
>
> JOSEPH WATSON, b. Dec. 18, 1825, married Miss Margaret Miller
> Dec. 29, 1859. They had one child, *Millee Laure*, b. July 7,
> 1861.
>
> CHARLES EDWIN, b. Mar. 27, 1829, married Miss Ann Earle, of
> Bergan, N. J. in Jan., 1861. They reside at Minneapolis, Minn.,
> and have two children, *Earle Case* and *Mona Belden*.
>
> CHESTER HINMAN, b. Mar. 27, 1831; resides at Johnstown, un-
> married.

304. Gustavus,[7] son of 150 Joseph[6] and Mary [Watson]
Balch, was born at Williamstown, Mass., May 19, 1795, and
died at Johnstown, in 1877. He married first, Mary Ann
Van Sickles; second wife, Elizabeth Potter. He had one son.

621*   JOSEPH,[8]

305. Cornelia,[7] daughter of 150 Joseph[6] and Mary
[Watson] Balch, was born in Williamstown, Mass., November 8, 1797, and died at Shopiere, Wis., January 19, 1863.
She was married to Jacob F. Dockstader, of Mohawk, N. Y.,
June 21, 1820. He was born April 7, 1796, and died at
Shopiere, Wis., November 22, 1867. Cornelia, her husband,
and children were all Congregationalists. She had ten children, and fifty-one grand-children. All of her children were
born at Mohawk, N. Y.

> MARIA, b. Apr. 5, 1821; married Jacob Dunn, resided at Grundy
> Center, Grundy Co., Iowa. They had ten children, two died
> in infancy.
>
> SARAH ANN, b. June 17, 1823; married Alfred T. Turner, June 1,
> 1851. Turner was born Mar. 25, 1819. They resided at Storm
> Lake, Buena Vista Co., Iowa. They had seven children,
> two died young.
>
> JOSEPH, b. June 24, 1825; married Sarah Chamberlin, resides at
> Shopiere, Wis., had four children, one died in infancy.
>
> JACOB VISTUS, b. Sept. 8, 1827; d. Aug. 14, 1836.
>
> HEZEKIAH, b. Nov. 21, 1829; d. Dec. 8, 1865; married Elizabeth
> Merry, of Shopiere, Wis., issue three children, one died young.
>
> CORNELIA, b. July 1, 1832; married Johnson Dole, resided at
> Shopiere, Wis., issue five children.
>
> CATHERINE A., b. May 25, 1834; married Dennis Jacobs, resides
> at Flandreau, Dakota, issue one child.
>
> CAROLINE E., b. May 25, 1834, twin of Catherine A., married
> Wm. Gardner, resides at Emerald Gore, Rock Co., Wis. They
> had eleven children, two d. y.
>
> JACOB VISTUS, b. Feb. 6, 1836; married Frances Allen, resides at
> Chetfield, Minn., two children, one d. y.
>
> FREDERICK G., b. Jan. 6, 1841; married Anna Merry, resides at
> Frederick, Dakota, two children, one d. y.

306. Vistus,[7] son of 150 Joseph[6] and Mary [Watson]
Balch, was born at Williamstown, Mass., February 18, 1799,
and died at Johnstown, N. Y., October 25, 1884. Vistus
was a quiet and unostentatious man, a
good citizen, and exemplary Christian, *D. Balch*
whom to know was to honor and respect.
By profession he was an engraver, and much of his time during the prime of life was spent in New York, devoted to his
chosen vocation, in which he became proficient. Many large

and beautiful steel engravings bear his imprint, but his work was generally confined to bank bills. For many years he was an elder in the Presbyterian church.

He was married three times. His first wife was Miss Rachel Buel Wells, daughter of John and Rachel [Buel] Wells, of Litchfield, Ct. They were married in February, 1828. She was born at Lanesboro, Mass., February 9, 1802, and died at Utica, N. Y., January 10, 1837. She was a lineal descendant of Rev. Benjamin Woolsey, of Desoris, L. I. They had no issue. He married for his second wife the widow of Dr. Saunders of Boston. His third wife was Margaret Dockstader, of Sharon, N. Y. She died Jan. 31, 1886. They had one son.

622ᵉ WILLIAM VISTUS,⁸ b. Dec. 17, 1849.

307. **Ebenezer,**⁷ son of 153 Ebenezer⁶ and Sarah [Burchard] Balch, was born at Wethersfield, Conn., June 22, 1792. When about eight years of age his father moved to Plattsburgh, N. Y. Here, with his father, he worked in clearing land and upon the farm *Ebenezer Balch.* until about twenty-two years of age, when he went to Pittsfield, Mass., and entered the office of Dr. James M. Brewster, and with him studied medicine. He settled as a physician in Sandisfield, Mass. The Springfield Union of March 7, 1879, says of him : " Ebenezer Balch was a man of strong individuality, some eccentricity, and much medical reading and skill, whom the Berkshire Medical College faculty pronounced equal to any in the county."

Ebenezer married Ann, daughter of Parson Stores, of Sandisfield. She was about twenty-one years his senior. She died May 22, 1851, and the Doctor died February 19, 1861. They were both buried in Sandisfield. They had no issue.

308. **Sarah,**⁷ daughter of 153 Ebenezer⁶ and Sarah [Burchard] Balch, was born at Wethersfield, Ct., April 19, 1794, and died at Schuyler Falls, N. Y., September 15, 1871. She

was married to Elijah Weston, of Schuyler Falls, November 15, 1825. She was Weston's third wife. They lived upon a farm in Schuyler Falls, and had three children, two of whom died in infancy.

> LAURA ELIZABETH, b. Sept. 12, 1830; d. at Vineland, N. J., Aug. 2, 1876; m. George Sutherland, of Schuyler Falls, July 2, 1857. They resided at Vineland, N. J. No issue.

309. **Alvah Burchard,**[7] son of 153 Ebenezer[6] and Sarah [Burchard] Balch, was born at Becket, Mass., April 18, 1796, and died at Plattsburgh, N. Y., March 5, 1871. He married Mary, daughter of Charles and Lovica (Jones) McArthur, March 15, 1821. She was born at St. Andrews, Canada, April 11, 1801, and died September 21, 1873. They both were buried in the Riverside Cemetery at Plattsburgh, N. Y. Alvah B. was a soldier in the war of 1812-14. He followed the occupation of a farmer, although he learned the carpenter's trade. He was a man of remarkable character, although of most quiet, unassuming manners. His tastes were of high intellectual order; his disposition mild and peaceful in the extreme. Nothing ever ruffled his temper. Although he talked very little on religious subjects, his life was eminently "an epistle known and read of all men." He lived on the earth as though not of it, yet faithfully attending to all the small details of daily life, and when the sudden summons came was in entire readiness to meet his Master. Early in life he joined the Masonic lodge at Plattsburgh, and always lived a consistent Mason. His life was spent upon the farm his father settled. Both he and his wife were members of the First Presbyterian Church of Plattsburgh.

Their issue was five children, two dying in infancy unnamed.

623* ALBERT VISTUS,[8] b. July 21, 1828.
624* CLARISSA,[8] b. Feb. 1, 1831; d. May 8, 1880.
625* GALUSHA BURCHARD,[8] b. Feb. 6, 1839.

310. Betsey,[7] daughter of 153 Ebenezer[6] and Sarah [Burchard] Balch, was born July 22, 1798, and died at Mondovi, Wis., August 3, 1866. She married Marenus Hilliard in 1814. Hilliard was a farmer, and lived in the town of Schuyler Falls, N. Y., where all their children were born. After the death of her husband she went to Wisconsin to reside with her son Obed. Betsey was the mother of thirteen children, five of whom died in infancy.

SAMANTHA A., b. March 4, 1816; m. Geo. Rosman, of Schuyler Falls, N. Y., in 1834; resides at Mondovi, Wis.

EBENEZER B., b. Oct. 27, 1817; m. Pache Milks, in 1846; resides at Warren, Ill.

LANSON H., b. July 18, 1819; m. Cecilia Myers, in 1845; resides at Elizabeth, Ill.

OREN D., b. Sept. 20, 1821; m. Julia Soper, in 1849; resides at Schuyler Falls, N. Y.; has three children.

ACHSA C., b. March 19, 1827; m. Henry Adams, in 1861; resides at Mondovi, Wis.; has five children.

ALLEN D., b. June 14, 1829; m. Augusta Battles, of Palmyra, N. Y.; they have five children.

OBED W., b. April 15, 1832; m. in October, 1865; resides at Mondovi, Wis.; has three children.

BRONSON, b. July 4, 1834; m. Eveline Soper, a sister of his brother Oren's wife. They live at Centre Point, Iowa, and have one child.

312. Horatio James,[7] youngest son of 153 Ebenezer[6] and Sarah [Burchard] Balch, was born at Plattsburgh, N. Y., July 22, 1806, and died in Knox county, Ind., January 17, 1846. He received a good common school education, was an excellent penman, and was ingenious in wood working. He married Sophronia Allaird, by whom he had ten children.

626 SARAH MARANDA,[8] b. ; m. A. J. Wheeler; lived at Hazleton, Ind.

627ª BETSEY SELINA,[8] b. Nov. 21, 1830.

628 ELVIRA CHRISTIAN,[8] b.   ; d. unm. previous to 1855.

629 MARY ELIZA,[8] b.   ; d. unm. previous to 1855.

630 LUCINDIA JANE,[8] b.   ; d. previous to 1875.

631 CHARLES HENRY,[8] b.   ; d., without issue, previous to 1875.

632ª ABIGAIL MELISSA,[8] b. Jan. 12, 1840.

633 NANCY SAMANTHA,[8] b.   ; d. previous to 1875.

634 JAMES HORATIO,[8] b.   ; d. unm. previous to 1855.

635 LEMUEL EBENEZER,[8] b.   ; d. without issue previous to 1875.

313. Betsey,[7] daughter of 154 Timothy[6] and Ann

[Whitman] Balch, was born at Hartford, Ct., May 4, 1794, and died at Malone, N. Y., June 26, 1864. She married first Jonathan Wood, of Plattsburgh. Wood became insane and committed suicide. She was married a second time, September 8, 1827, to Rev. Ashbel Parmelee, D. D., of Malone, N. Y. She was Dr. Parmelee's third wife. The following tribute to her memory is from the pen of her stepson, Hon. Ashbel B. Parmelee, of Malone, N. Y.: " She was a woman of great worth, devoted to her husband, and a fit partner in all his domestic and Christian labors. She never had any children of her own, but the large circle of her husband's, whom she adopted while still in their juvenile years, cherish her memory with the kindest and warmest regard." Dr. Parmelee was a remarkable man. He was the pioneer of Presbyterianism in northern New York. His biography is given in the History of Franklin County, N. Y.

314. Chester,[7] son of 154 Timothy[6] and Ann [Whitman] Balch, was born at Williamstown, Mass., July 26, 1796, and died at Plattsburgh, June 3, 1875. He was married first, September 10, 1821, to Miss Lucy Smedley, who was born at Williamstown, Mass., January 8, 1800, and died at Plattsburgh, May 21, 1842. He was a farmer, and resided about four miles out from the village of Plattsburgh, on the old military turnpike between Plattsburgh and Malone, N. Y. For more than thirty years he was a ruling elder in the First Presbyterian Church of Plattsburgh. He was a man of the old puritanical stamp. The children of Chester and Lucy were nine in number, all born at Plattsburgh.

636* CAROLINE E.,[8] b. Nov. 12, 1822; d. June 8, 1842.
637 MARY W.,[8] b. Feb. 24, 1825; d. unm. Oct. 15, 1846.
638 CELESTIA E.,[8] b. March 1, 1827; d. unm. April 1, 1842.
639* LOESA M.,[8] b. Aug. 18, 1829.
640 ELIZA A.,[8] b. Jan. 31, 1832; d. unm. April 24, 1847.
641 LUCY S.,[8] b. April 13, 1834; d. Feb. 1, 1839.
642* JOHN TIMOTHY,[8] b. Oct. 21, 1836.
643* LUCY SMEDLEY,[8] b. Feb. 9, 1839; d. July 30, 1868.
644 DELIA M.,[8] b. April 27, 1842; d. May 11, 1842.

Chester married for his second wife Mrs. Delia [Wood-

ward] Horton, widow of Harry Horton, of Malone, N. Y.,
October 4, 1842. She was born July 28, 1798, and died September 4, 1858. She was aunt to Vice-President William A.
Wheeler. They had no issue.

In 1864 Chester married for his third wife a Miss Ransom,
of Mooers, Clinton county, N. Y. No issue.

317. Henry,[7] son of 154 Timothy[6] and Ann [Whitman]
Balch, was born at Plattsburgh, N. Y., November 24, 1803,
and died in the same house in which he was born, in June,
1875. He married Miss Fannie Baker, of Plattsburgh. He
was a farmer, living upon the old homestead and was a quiet
and unostentatious citizen. They had two children.

645ᵉ HENRY,[8] b. about 1842.
646 MARYETT,[8] b. about 1844; d. unm. in 1874.

318. Emily,[7] daughter of 154 Timothy[6] and Ann [Whitman] Balch, was born at Plattsburgh, N. Y., March 29, 1807,
and died in 1893. She married James W. Banker, of Plattsburgh, in 1829. He was born September 27, 1803, and died
in Illinois, January 7, 1887. Banker was a farmer, and
lived in Plattsburgh, where their eight children were born.
About 1852 they moved to Wisconsin with their family.

> SEYMOUR W., b. March 29, 1830; living in Omaha, Neb. Married
> Miss Ellen Lassell, and had four children, *Florence, Lizzie,
> Janey,* and *Harvey,* all born in Wisconsin.
> ANNA P., b. June 12, 1830; d. at Mineral Point, Wis.; m. Luther
> J. Lassell.
> WILLIAM H., b. Jan. 4, 1835; m. Maria Mallet, and lives in Amboy, Illinois. They have one child, *Frank.*
> ELIZA MAY, b. July 14, 1839; m. Rev. O. G. May, and lives in
> California. They have six children: *Frank, Grace, Gertrude,
> William, Lucy,* and *Robert.*
> RICHARD R., b. Oct. 3, 1841; m. Mary Maloy. They live at
> Omaha, Neb. Issue, one child, *Emily M.*
> JAMES E., b. June 23, 1844; m. Aurora Sternes. They live at
> York, Neb., and have four children: *Bertha, Walter, Edna,*
> and *Arthur.*
> ELEANOR L., b. Sept. 11, 1847; d. April 3, 1878; m. Maurie Shafer
> Frye. They lived at Alton, Ill. Issue, four children:
> *Glenbee, Freddie, Harlic,* and *Charlie.*
> EMILY E., b. Nov. 30, 1850; m. James W. Holmes, of Amboy,
> Illinois.

WM. SKINNER BALCH.

321. **William Skinner,**[7] youngest son of 154 Timothy[6] and Ann [Whitman] Balch, was born at Plattsburgh, N. Y., October 22, 1813, and died December 8, 1895. William S. left his home in Plattsburgh in 1828, and went to live with his uncle Whitman, in Williamstown, Mass., in whose store he clerked it for five years. In the spring of 1842 he removed to Saratoga, N. Y., and began hotel keeping. For some eighteen years he kept the old Columbian, which was burned in 1861. For several years after the burning of the hotel he was a passenger conductor on the R. & S. R. R. In 1882 he left the railroad. During the summer of 1884 he kept the Wentworth Hotel at Round Lake, and from 1889 until his death he kept the Balch House at Saratoga Springs. The House is continued by his widow. He was a prominent member of the Methodist Church, and the hotels of which he was proprietor were kept on strict temperance principles. He married first Miss Caroline M. Martin, an adopted daughter of Hon. Manning Brown, of Williamstown. She died in 1858. They had two sons.

647* MANNING B.,[8] b. Sept. 23, 1836.
648* EDWARD N.,[8] b. March 2, 1841; d. Jan. 1, 1863.

William Skinner married second, November 30, 1858, Miss Vesta A., daughter of Ephrim Child, of Saratoga. They had three children.

649* CARRIE V.,[8] b. June 24, 1860.
650 NELLIE W.,[8] b. Feb. 21, 1865.
651 LILLIE,[8] b. March 29, 1868; d. Feb. 8, 1869.

324. **Henry,**[7] son of 155 William[6] and Ann [Smith] Balch, was born at West Hartford, Ct., October 10, 1806, and died at Sandisfield, Mass., April 18, 1874. He was a carpenter and farmer. He was honest, sober, and industrious, and a man highly respected in the community in which he lived. He was married January 12, 1834, to Miss Martha A., daughter of Pitt Fuller, of Windsor, Ct. She was born December 10, 1810, and died at Sandisfield, Mass., May 9, 1879. They

were both buried at Sandisfield. They had three children, born at Sandisfield.

652* JANE LOUISA,[8] b. Sept. 18, 1838.
653* CORNELIA ANN,[8] b. Nov. 19, 1845.
654* EDWARD HENRY,[8] b. April 23, 1852.

326. Thomas,[7] son of 155 William[6] and Ann [Smith] Balch, was born at West Hartford, Ct., February 19, 1811, and died February, 1891, at Hartford. He was a carpenter. He married Delia Parsons, who was born at Colebrook, Ct., November 8, 1818, and is now living. They were married November 8, 1836. They had five children, all born at Hartford.

655* ALONZO W.,[8] b. Sept. 16, 1837.
656* FREDERICK A.,[8] b. Aug. 22, 1839.
657* MARGARET S.,[8] b. Oct. 12, 1842.
658* ALFRED P.,[8] b. Aug. 19, 1844.
659* DELIA F.,[8] b. Oct. 7, 1848.

327. Alonzo,[7] son of 155 William[6] and Ann [Smith] Balch, was born at West Hartford, Ct., April 12, 1814, and died at Hartford, Ct., May 26, 1885. One week before his death he had a stroke of paralysis, and did not speak afterwards. Two days before he was stricken down he was planning to go to New Mexico. He was a carpenter. When a young man he went to South Carolina, and thence to Galveston, Texas. He was married May 12, 1847, to Eliza Jane McLane, who was born at Greenfield, S. C., June 29, 1832, and died at Galveston, Texas, January 18, 1881. No issue.

329. Sarah R.,[7] daughter of 159 Joseph[6] and Martha [Grise] Balch, was born at Providence, R. I. She was married at Providence, October 7, 1816, to John Miller, a journalist, and connected with the Providence Journal. Their issue was two children, born at Providence: John, d. y.; Sarah, married Elias Smith, of Brooklyn, N. Y.

331. Sophia Packard,[7] only daughter of 161 John Rogers[6] and Saphira [Packard] Balch, was born at Providence, R. I., May 9, 1805. She is now living in Providence. On September 8, 1824, she was married to Ebenezer, son of

Joseph Kelly. He was born at Warren, R. I., and died at Providence, on December 2, 1852. Their ten children were all born at Providence.

> Sophia Balch, b. Aug. 14, 1825; d. May 11, 1840.
> Mary Elizabeth, b. Aug. 12, 1827; d. July 16, 1843.
> Ann Frances, b. June 24, 1830; d. Sept. 6, 1832.
> Eben Augustus, b. April 9, 1833.
> John Henry, b. Aug. 5, 1835; d. Feb. 27, 1836.
> Emily Ann, b. March 31, 1837.
> Aujaneth Eddy, b. July 21, 1839; d. Sept. 14, 1842.
> Benjamin Eddy, b. Feb. 10, 1842; d. May 3, 1863.
> John Balch, b. July 2, 1844.
> Louisa Balch, b. Nov. 9, 1846; d. May 27, 1876.

332. John **Rogers**,[7] son of 161 John Rogers[6] and Saphira [Packard] Balch, was born at Providence, R. I., August 27, 1808, and died in that city, very suddenly, October 25, 1886. He married Elizabeth C., daughter of Isaiah and Mary [Collins] Lawton, of Newport, R. I. She died October 12, 1879, in her sixty-ninth year. Their issue was three children, born in Providence.

> 660° Ellen Elizabeth,[8] b. May 9, 1833.
> 661° Collins Lawton,[8] b. July 6, 1834.
> 662 John Lawton,[8] d. y.

John Rogers attended the public and private schools of Providence until he was fourteen years old, when he entered the house of Cook & Brown, cotton merchants, Providence, R. I. He remained with this firm twenty-three years, until its dissolution, in 1845. He then entered the employ of the Providence and Worcester R. R. Company, in which he remained to the day of his death. May 17, 1847, he was made assistant treasurer of the road, under Isaac Brown, treasurer. May 19, 1851, he was appointed treasurer, which position he held to the time of his death. Since 1851 all the records of the treasurer of the railroad company have been kept in his handwriting. During his period of service, covering in all

about forty years, he exhibited an unusual sound judgment
in the transaction of the business of the road, and his long
experience rendered his knowledge of railroad matters very
important. He invariably declined political office and public
duties, because of his preference for the duties of his railroad position. In early life he took an active interest in politics. He was a Whig, and later a Republican. In 1827 he
joined the First Light Infantry Company, and at the time of
his death was a member of the Infantry Veteran Association.

The following tribute was paid to him by the Providence
Journal of October 26, 1885 :

" It is rare indeed that an official is able to retain so oner-
ous and responsible a position as treasurer of an important
railroad corporation for forty years, as did Mr. John R. Balch
for the Providence and Worcester railroad, and the testimony
to his ability and integrity is an irrefragible one. As a modest, worthy and honorable citizen, Mr. Balch will be widely
mourned, as well as an official."

333. Hart,[7] only child of 168 Hart[6] and —— [Bourne]
Balch, was born at Newbury, Mass., Nov. 9, 1751, and died
at Andover, Vt., Feb. 15, 1846. He was a posthumous child.
His mother married a British officer and went to Halifax, N.
S. Hart lived with his aunt, in whose house he was born,
until bound out an apprentice to a shoe maker. The aunt was
Deborah, his father's sister, and wife of Captain John Forsyth.
He was married first in 1772 to Miss Priscilla Holt, by whom
he had three children.

663* Nathan,[8] b. Aug. 29, 1773; d.
664* Joel,[8] b. Feb. 6, 1774 ; d. Oct. 27, 1845.
665 Deborah,[8] b.   ; d. Aug. 14, 1777.

Hart's first wife died and he married for his second Dorcas
Somers, daughter of Isaac and Abigail S. Somers, by whom
he had eight more children.

666* Deborah,[8] b. Nov. 13, 1780.
667 Hart,[8] b. Sept. 27, 1784; d. unm. winter of 1810.
668* Asa,[8] b. May 12, 1786; d. in 1872.
669* Francis S.,[8] b. Sept. 2, 1788; d. Aug. 25, 1857.

670* Eb,[8] b. Feb. 10, 1794; d. Jan. 5, 1854.
671* Sally,[8] b. Oct. 7, 1795; d. June 15, 1874.
672* James Parker,[8] b. Dec. 4, 1797; d. Apr. 2, 1857.
673* Jacob Abbot,[8] b. July 9, 1800; d. Aug. 27, 1881.

Hart[7] was evidently a man of strong individuality, and some eccentricity. The following from the pen of his grandson, the late Rev. William Stevens Balch of Elgin, Ill., shows very much of the character of both.

" I have never strayed far from the plain path of present duty to search the records of ancestry for grace or glory to adorn my own name. I did once ask my grandfather, when grown to manhood, and he over ninety, about our ancestors, whether we were English, Scotch, Irish, Dutch, Greek, Hebrew or heathen. The old gentleman roused up and said rather seriously, 'What is it to you? we have only our own conduct to answer for.' That is very true, I replied, still, it is a satisfaction to know something of one's forefathers. The old gentleman replied, 'I have good reasons to desire no such thing. I have always thought it a disgrace and not an honor, to accept property or houses gained by others, not by myself. I never danced in borrowed pumps.' Then straightening himself into a dignified attitude he consented to gratify his grandson's request. 'I was born in the Old Bay State, town of Newbury. When a child I lived with my mother at my aunt's. I never saw my father. I was told he was a sea captain, and was lost with all his crew on a voyage to the West Indies. Whether so or not I never knew. That was no fault of mine. Yes, my mother left me when young, was married, I was told, and went to live in Nova Scotia, the home of the Tories. I have been told she died there and left me several hundred dollars. I never saw them,—just as well. When fourteen I was bound an apprentice to a shoemaker.' " The records at Keene, show that Hart had several real estate transactions in that town and Dublin, N. H.

Hart enlisted into Captain William Walker's company, Colonel Reed's regiment, April 23, 1775, and was discharged August 9, 1775. He enlisted again into Captain Gilmour's

company, June 29, 1777, and served one year and ten months.
When he enlisted in 1777, he was described as age 26 years,
height, 6 feet. He re-enlisted as a private in the First New
Hampshire, April 24, 1781, for three years, from Dublin,
N. H.

334. Nathaniel,[7] son of 170 Nathaniel[6] and Mary
[Fletcher] Balch, was born in Providence, R. I., February
26, 1764, and died in Boston, Mass., June 10, 1831. On
December 17, 1789, he was married to Miss Mary Stillman, and
at the same time Mr. Benjamin Stillman was married to Miss
Mary Balch, his sister. The officiating clergyman at this
double wedding was Rev. Dr. Samuel Stillman, father of two
of the young people concerned. Nathaniel and Mary had
five children.

674* MARIA S.,[8] b. Mch. 20, 1790; d.
675* WILLIAM,[8] b. Mch. 11, 1792; was lost at sea, after 1826.
676* NATHANIEL,[8] b. Feb. 13, 1794; d. unm. before 1850.
677* HARRIET,[8] b. Nov. 14, 1795.
678* BENJAMIN STILLMAN,[8] b. July 9, 1797; d. after 1850.

Mary, the wife of Nathaniel Balch, Jr., was born July 20,
1766, and died November 8, 1800.

Captain Nathaniel Balch celebrated the 4th day of July,
1818, by taking to himself for his second wife, Susan, daughter
of Captain William and Susannah [Foster] Young. She was
born in Boston, August 9, 1782. They had two sons.

679* EDWARD LAWRENCE,[8] b. May 31, 1816; d. Nov. 21, 1869.
680* WILLIAM YOUNG,[8] b. March 10, 1819; d. Dec. 17, 1882.

Both of these sons were born in Boston and baptized at the
Old South Church, by Rev. Dr. Wisner, their mother having
united with that church in February, 1811. She was a constant attendant of the services at the "Old South" for more
than half a century up to the second Sunday before her
death, which occurred December 26, 1864. Her funeral took
place from the Old South Chapel, in Spring Lane, her en-
tombment being one of the last permitted in the "Granary"
burying ground on Tremont street.

Nathaniel Balch, Jr., was commissioned by "His Excel-

Nath Balch

lency, Arthur St. Clair, Esq., President of the Congress of the United States of America," on October 20, 1786, to the rank of "Ensign in the second regiment in the army of the United States," the same regiment in which his younger brother William served.

Nathaniel resigned his commission, and in 1796 he was engaged in mercantile pursuits in Boston.

President John Adams commissioned him "Captain in the 15th regiment of infantry, in the service of the United States, to take rank from January 10, 1799." In the summer and fall of that year he was on recruiting service in the Province of Maine. On Wednesday, January 15, 1800, funeral honors were paid by the troops stationed at Oxford, Massachusetts, to the memory of their illustrious leader, General George Washington. Captain Nathaniel Balch was one of the pall-bearers. [History of Oxford.]

335. William,[7] son of 170 Nathaniel[6] and Mary [Fletcher] Balch, was born at Boston, July 11, 1765. He never married. When about 25 years of age he received a commission, signed by George Washington, then President of the United States, dated March 4, 1791, as ensign in the 2d regiment, in the service of the United States. With Capt. Samuel Newman and many others of Boston, he was killed in the battle with the Indians, near Miami Village, Ohio, Nov. 4, 1791, commonly called "St. Clair's defeat," being then a lieutenant.

338. Sarah,[7] daughter of 170 Nathaniel[6] and Mary [Fletcher] Balch, was born at Boston, December 5, 1774. She married Thomas Hughes, January 31, 1805. They had five children, as follows: Thomas Hughes, b. Nov. 16, 1805; Sarah, b. Sept. 8, 1808; George, b. Jan. 1, 1811; Mary, b. Aug. 30, 1812; Henry, b. May 29, 1816.

343. Joseph,[7] son of 172 Joseph[6] and Abigail [Audebert] Balch, was born in Boston, September 15, 1769, and died of yellow fever, September 11, 1798. Yellow fever was at that time epidemic in Boston where he died. He

was a sailmaker in Boston. He was married on the 5th of
October, 1794, to Hannah, eldest daughter of Dr. John and
Hannah [Raymar] Pope of Boston. She was born August 18,
1772, and died June 22, 1811. They had three children.

681* JOSEPH,⁸ b. July 16, 1796; d. July 16, 1872.
682 HANNAH POPE,⁸ b. Feb. 23, 1798; d. May 24, 1808.
683* ABIGAIL BRIGHT,⁸ b. Apr. 1, 1799; d.

347. **Elizabeth,**⁷ daughter of 172 Joseph⁶ and Abigail
[Audebert] Balch, was born at Boston, April 9, 1779, and
died January 29, 1759. She was married to Jonathan March
Dexter, June 19, 1808, at Billerica, Mass.

Mr. Dexter was born March 24, 1775 at Haverhill, and
died March 26, 1861 in the city of New York. Elizabeth and
Jonathan M. Dexter were buried in Greenwood Cemetery,
L. I. They had five children, the two eldest were born at
Billerica, the others at West Cambridge.

GEORGE, b. June 16, 1809; d. at Geneva, Switzerland, July 16,
    1872; m. Dec. 1, 1845 to Mary Elizabeth Phelps.
MARY ELIZABETH, b. Aug. 19, 1811; unm.
HENRY, b. Mar. 14, 1813; m. Oct. 11, 1858, Lucretia Marguand
    Perry. He was living in New York, May 1, 1892.
ABBA MARIA WELLINGTON, b. Apr. 10, 1816; d. at West Cam-
    bridge, July 5, 1819.
ABBA MARIA WELLINGTON, b. July 19, 1820; d. at Westport,
    Conn., Sept. 18, 1878; m. Dec. 29, 1852 to James Henry
    Peffers.

348. **John,**⁷ son of 175 John⁶ and Mary [——]Balch,
was born at Keene, N. H., December 10, 1757 and died in
the same town March 15, 1824. He was married in 1778 to
Lucy, daughter of Daniel and Abigail Snow. She was born
in 1762, and died July 5, 1831. John always lived in Keene,
and both he and his wife were buried in that town. They
had five children, all born at Keene.

684* HANNAH,⁸ b. Apr. 4, 1781; d. July 27, 1866.
685* LUCINDA,⁸ b. Mch. 23, 1783; d. Aug. 7, 1848.
686* NABBY,⁸ b. Mch. 28, 1785; d. Aug. 17, 1830.
687* ANDREW,⁸ b. May 2, 1787; d. May 26, 1845.
688* EZRA,⁸ b. 1798; d. Apr. 26, 1828.
689 ROSALIND,⁸ b. 1801; d. Aug. 23, 1824, unm.

John was a farmer, and the records in the Register's office at Keene show that he owned, and lived upon the farm that his grandfather located and cleared. When Lieut. Andrew Balch located at Keene, the country about was a wilderness, abounding with wild beasts. He built his house in a forest. One night John greased his boots and slicked up and went to a party. While on his way home wolves scented him or rather his boots, and gave chase. He ran for his life, and heard them snapping at his heels as he escaped through the house door. He inherited a walking stick that is now in the possession of his grandson John Edwin Balch of Wilson, Winona Co., Minn. Family tradition says it was the property of John,[1] the old planter. The cane is of hickory three feet long, has the appearance of having been varnished, and has an ivory head about one inch deep and the size of a silver half dollar.

When but fifteen years of age he was enrolled as one of the "foot company" of Keene. The Revolutionary War Rolls show that he enlisted in Capt. John Gregg's Co. as private in 1777, age 19. In the same year he served 26 days in Col. Sam'l Ashley's regt. The New Hampshire town papers, Vol. XXI. p. 319 show that John Balch's contract as Post Rider was made on the 27th day of July, 1781. His route was from Portsmouth on Saturday morning, thence to Conway, Plymouth and Haverhill, thence down the Connecticut river to Charlestown and Keene, and back to Portsmouth in fourteen days.

349. **Timothy,**[7] son of 175 John[6] and Mary [———] Balch, was born at Keene, N. H., about 1760. He died at Orwell, Oswego Co., N. Y., and was buried at Richland, N. Y. About 1788 he married Hannah Damon, of Manchester, Vt. who died at Orwell, N. Y., November 12, 1857. They had three sons and three daughters, all born at Manchester.

690* TIMOTHY,[8] b. Dec. 10, 1789; d. Aug. 10, 1843.
691* JOHN,[8] b. Feb. 14, 1792; d. Mch. 10, 1882.
692* SUSAN,[8] b. Aug. 22, 1794; d. June 2, 1880.
693* ANNA,[8] b. Aug. 27, 1798; d. Sept. 21, 1840.

694* DANIEL,⁶ b. July 29, 1800; d. May 25, 1874.
695* POLLY,⁶ b. Oct. 31, 1803; d. Sept. 18, 1893.

New Hampshire Town Papers. Vol. XII, page 320 show that on June 10, 1785, Timothy Balch was appointed Post-Rider, and carried the mail between Portsmouth, N. H. and Brattleboro, Vt. This was the first mail route in the state of Vermont. He moved with his family to Orwell, Oswego Co., N. Y. all that section of the state in those early days was called the Black River country. Here in that then wild country Timothy took up land and cleared a farm on which he lived the remainder of his life.

352. Mary,⁷ daughter of 175 John⁶ and his second wife Safrona [———] Balch, was born at Keene, New Hampshire, February 10, 1770 and died at New Ipswich, New Hampshire, October 14, 1838. She was married November 5, 1807 to Joel Pond, son of Daniel. He was born March 19, 1756, and died at Keene, February 23, 1821. They lived at Keene, and had one child.

357. Cyrus,⁷ son of 177 Caleb⁶ and Elizabeth M. [———] Balch, was born at Keene, N. H., July 14, 1765; and died about 1805. He was married about 1782 to Judith Stone. The records of the town of Westford, Vt. show that their six eldest children were born in that town, so they must have gone to live there soon after their marriage. Their four youngest children were born in the town of Enosburgh, Vt.

696 LUCINDIA,⁸ b. Oct. 13, 1783; d.
697 CAROLINE,⁸ b. Oct. 20, 1785; d.
698* EBENEZER,⁸ b. Sept. 16, 1787; d. 1849.
699* MARY,⁸ b. Aug. 20, 1791; d. Mch. 25, 1862.
700 JOHN,⁸ b. Jan. 21, 1793; d. Jan. 22, 1793.
701* JOHN,⁸ b. Jan. 29, 1794; d. Aug. 21, 1834.
702* SIMEON,⁸ b. 1796; d.
703* ENOS,⁸ b. 1797; d. 1872.
704* CYRUS,⁸ b. Apr., 1799; d. Aug. 7, 1878.
705* ELMIRA,⁸ b. 1801; d. Sept. 4, 1838.
706* ELI STONE,⁸ b. Feb. 13, 1803; d. Dec. 24, 1861.

The Town Papers of N. H. Vol. XII, p. 312 show by Capt.

Ephraim Stone's return of his company, that Cyrus Balch was a member, and received 621 lbs., 1 shilling. These returns were made in 1782 and show service during the Revolution, up to and including the year 1780. The records show a deed from him to Amos Balch for seventy-five pounds of one hundred acres of land.

The name of Cyrus Balch is not found upon the records of Westford later than Feb. 21, 1795.* Soon after this date he moved to the township of Enosburgh, Vt., where he took up land and cleared a farm, and he, with his family, were the first to winter in that town, 1796-97. His land was in the west part of the town, then and now called Balch Hill.

The information for this genealogy concerning Cyrus and his children were obtained with great difficulty. A number of families, scattered from Vermont to Dakota, and having common traditions, were found in various ways. None of them knew the name of their grandfather, or were able to tell where he lived. One of these traditions was that an uncle named Enos was the first child born in Enosburgh, Vermont. Another was that another uncle, named John, was drowned in Lake Champlain, and a third that their grandfather was killed while felling a tree. He was cutting into a tree against which another had lodged in falling. The tree he was chopping suddenly split and kicked back. It struck him under the chin and broke his neck. It was not possible to learn anything from the town clerk of Enosburgh, but the Vermont Gazette gave the name of the owner of the Balch farm. A letter directed to him fell into the hands of his executor, Benjamin Hoyt, who also was familiar with the tradition of the peculiar way in which the owner of Balch hill met his death, and was able from an old deed to fix the Christian name as Cyrus.

---

*The search of the manuscript records of the town of Westford, Vt., were made by Mrs. Clara Allen (Morgan) Cooley, of that town, a granddaughter of Cyrus.

358. Amos,[7] son of 177 Caleb[6] and Elizabeth [————]
Balch, was born at Keene, N. H., July 28, 1767. The first
marriage recorded upon the town records of Westford, Vt.,
is Amos Balch and Betsey Jarvis, married December 10, 1792.
They had children, as shown by the records.

707 SUSANNA,[8] b.   ; d. April 27, 1795, at Westford, Vt.
708 NATHAN,[8] b. Aug. 10, 1795; d.

The above mentioned records show that Amos Balch bought
and sold five different parcels of land between the dates July
31, 1792, and February 21, 1795. He went to Enosburgh in
1796, as appears by the Vermont Gazetteer, but he probably
returned to Westford, as his name appears as a witness to a
deed in 1799.

The above is all we know regarding this family, and is entirely from records.

359. Caleb,[7] son of 177 Caleb[6] and Elizabeth [————]
Balch, was born at Keene, N. H., March 9, 1770. He was
married April 3, 1812, to Patience Nye. The Westford town-
records show realestate transactions by him in 1812. From
these records it also appears that on January 5, 1793, he witnessed a deed as Caleb Balch, Jr., and on January 24, 1795,
he witnessed a deed as Caleb Balch, having dropped the Jr.
This would indicate that his father died between 1792 and
1795.

362. Thankful,[7] daughter of 179 Benjamin[6] and Elizabeth [Blake] Balch, was born at Keene, N. H., April 23,
1772, and died at Lunenburg, Vt., in 1856. She was married
to Azariah Snow, a brother to her sister's husband, John
Snow. They moved to Lunenburg, Vt., where they continued
to reside, and both died and were buried in that town. Mr.
Snow was one of the most influential men in that vicinity,
both in church and business. They were both members of
the Baptist denomination, of which he was for a long time a
deacon.

Mrs. Snow was an unusually energetic and truly good
woman, living to the age of 84 years. The last ten years of

her life she was entirely blind. They had five sons and one daughter, all born at Lunenburg : John, George, Daniel, Benjamin, Abigail, and Abner.

363. **Abner**,[7] son of 179 Benjamin[6] and Elizabeth [Blake] Balch, was born at Keene, N. H., March 5, 1774. He married first Miss Lydia P., daughter of Zeno and Lydia Alden. She was born in Stratford, Ct. They had nine children :

709   Aldin,[8] b.   ; d.
710   Albert,[8] b.   ; d. y.
711   Albert,[8] b.   ; d. y.
712* Abner,[8] b. January 1, 1804; d. Nov. 12, 1888.
713* Eliza,[8] b.   ; d. Dec. 6, 1828.
714* Lydia,[8] b.   ; d.
715* Alfred,[8] b. Jan. 8, 1806; d. April 11, 1892.
716* Almira A.,[8] b. Aug. 5, 1811.
717* Albert,[8] b. 1813; killed, railroad accident, 1846.

Abner[7] married for his second wife a Miss Latham, by whom he had one child.

718   Amanda,[8] b.   ; d. y.

Abner lived for a time at Bethel, Vt., where he owned and operated a fulling mill. Then he moved to Stratford, Vt.; then to St. Johnsbury, Vt. He was also engaged in farming. He was accounted an expert in the use of the ax, and was also celebrated as a high jumper.

Abner and his wives were buried at East St. Johnsbury, Vt.

365. **Esther**,[7] daughter of 179 Benjamin[6] and Elizabeth [Blake] Balch, was born at Keene, October 13, 1778, and died in the same town, February 20, 1880. She married John Snow, of Keene. Mr. Snow was a deacon in the Baptist church. Their ten children were born in Keene.

Perley Blake, b. Dec. 31, 1799; d. in Ills.
Laura, b.   ; d. in Keene.
Esther, b.   ; died in Keene.
Sylvia, b. 1806; d. in Westmoreland, N. H., Sept. 30, 1891.
Channey, b.   ; d. in Sugar Grove, Ills.
John, b.   ; d. in Springfield, Mo.
Joseph, b. Apr., 1819; d.
Cynthia, b.   ; d. at Keene.
George, b.   ; d. y.
Forbes, b.   ; d. y.

366. Olive,[7] daughter of 179 Benjamin[6] and Elizabeth [Blake] Balch, was born at Keene, N. H., August 25, 1780, and lived to be over 80 years of age.   She married Erastus Lane of Lunenburg, Vt., and had three children: Erastus, Sylvanus, and William.

367. Benjamin,[7] son of 179 Benjamin[6] and Elizabeth [Blake] Balch, was born at Keene, N. H., July 23, 1783, and died at Union, N. Y., September 27, 1829.   About 1808 he married Sarah, daughter of Matthew Stanley.   Matthew Stanley's lineage traces back to the Plantagenets. Sarah was born at St. Johnsbury, Vt., May 23, 1789, and died at Union, N. Y., December 11, 1863.   They had ten children.

719* SARAH STANLEY,[8] b. Nov. 27, 1809.
720 LUCY,[8] b. Jan. 8, 1811; d. Jan. 15, 1818.
721* BENJAMIN,[8] b. June 13, 1812; d.
722* MATTHEW STANLEY,[8] b. Aug. 4, 1813; d. Oct. 20, 1844.
723 BETSEY,[8] b. Mar. 19, 1815; d. unm. at Union, N.Y., Dec. 19, 1863.
724 MARY,[8] b. Oct. 14, 1817; d. unm. Feb. 22, 1836.
725* JAMES BRITTON,[8] b. June 22, 1819.
726* LUCY H.,[8] b. Feb. 12, 1821.
727* BENJAMIN FRANKLIN,[8] b. Dec. 8, 1822; d.
728* LYDIA M.,[8] b. Dec. 24, 1827.

368. Sylvanus,[7] son of 179 Benjamin[6] and Julia [Ellis] Balch, was born at Keene, N. H., October 11, 1786.   He married Catherine Wetherby, of Concord, Vt., by whom he had five children, two of whom died in infancy.

729* LAURA OLIVE,[8] b. June 24, 1820; d. May 24, 1873.
730* JOHN WETHERBY,[8] b. May 20, 1824.
731* SAMUEL ALBERT,[8] b. June 11, 1828; d. May 14, 1895.

Sylvanus lived at home and worked for his father, in Lunenburg, until he was 20 years of age, when he was given his time, which was to be his portion.   In a short time, with energy and perseverance he was the owner of a good farm. He first located at Concord, Vt., where he married.   In 1828 he moved with his family to Littleton, N. H., where he engaged in business, first, as clothier and farming.   Afterwards he became quite an extensive land owner.   In 1836, his wife died, and in 1837 he married Lydia Pratt of Oxford,

N. H. In 1870 he removed to St. Johnsbury, Vt. There were no children by the second marriage.

369. Cynthia,[7] daughter of 179 Benjamin[6] and Julia [Ellis] Balch, was born at Keene, N. H., May 14, 1788, and died at Lunenburg, aged 53 years. She married Stephen Smith of Lunenburg, and had nine children, the three eldest died in infancy. Benjamin, d. at 50; Julia, d. at 16; Cynthia; Ester; Henry, d. at 24; and Leander.

370. Adin,[7] son of 179 Benjamin[6] and Julia [Ellis] Balch, was born at Keene, N. H., January 22, 1790, and died at Lunenburg, Vt., April 2, 1859. He was a farmer by occupation, and a man of high moral and religious principles. He was married October 12, 1810, to Miss Martha Gee of Lunenburg. She was born June 16, 1793, and died at Lunenberg, January 31, 1880. They had 12 children, all born at Lunenburg, Vt., who were all noted for their musical talents.

732* SELINDA,[8] b. Feb. 1, 1812.
733 EDWARD,[8] b. Sept. 11, 1813; d. Jan. 14, 1814.
734* JAMES,[8] b. Feb. 23, 1816; d. Feb. 27, 1894.
735* EDWARD A.,[8] b. June 16, 1817.
736* WILLIAM,[8] b. May 1, 1819; d. Sept. 6, 1842.
737* MARTHA,[8] b. Apr. 17, 1821.
738* CAROLINE MATILDA,[8] b. Apr. 21, 1824; d. June 2, 1885.
739* RACHEL,[8] b. May 23, 1826.
740* ELIZABETH H.,[8] b. Jan. 6, 1828; d. Aug. 19, 1878.
741* GEORGE SHERMAN,[8] b. Sept. 16, 1833.
742* ISAAC A.,[8] b. Sept. 10, 1836.
743* LOUISA E.,[8] b. Mar. 16, 1838.

371. William,[7] son of 179 Benjamin[6] and Julia [Ellis] Balch, was born at Keene, N. H., June 16, 1791, and died January 6, 1868, at Lunenburg, Vt. He was a farmer and lived in the town of Lunenburg. He was married September 18, 1819, to Lucy Howland, of Lunenburg. She was born February 26, 1797, and died February 19, 1844. They had nine children, all born at Lunenburg.

744 GEORGE,[8] b. Jan. 3, 1820; d. y.
745 ELIZA,[8] b.   ; d. y.
746* LURA,[8] b. Sept. 1, 1822· d. Oct. 17, 1893.

747   NEWELL,⁸ b.   ; d. y.
748   NEWELL,⁸ b. May 27, 1825; d. June 15, 1889, unm.
749   LUCY,⁸ b. Jan., 1828; d. Mar. 1, 1852; m. Mackwith Smith. Had
        one son, d. y.
750   ALDIN,⁸ b. Feb. 22, 1830; unm.
751* ELECTA,⁸ b. Apr. 28, 1832; d. Mar. 13, 1888.
752   LEAFY,⁸ b. July 22, 1835; d. Nov. 20, 1879.

372. James,⁷ son of 179 Benjamin⁶ and Julia [Ellis]
Balch, was born at Keene, N. H., November 3, 1794, and died
at Davenport, Iowa, in 1885.   In July or August, 1820, he
married Miss Nancy Moore, of Lancaster, N. H., and to them
were born two sons.

753* GEORGE,⁸ b. Aug. 5, 1821; d. Jan. 2, 1880.
754* STEPHEN MOORE,⁸ b. Feb. 12, 1826; d. Dec. 20, 1876.

For several years following his marriage, James lived at St.
Johnsbury, Vt., then he moved to Lancaster, N. H., where
his wife died in 1864.   In 1865 he went to Davenport, Iowa,
to live with his son, and after his son's death he lived with
his widow until his death.   James was a genial, kind hearted
man and always had a good word for every acquaintance.
He was an earnest Christian and a member of the Congregational church.

374. John,⁷ son of 181 John⁶ and [——] Balch, was
born September 2, 1759, and died at Marcellus, New York,
November 10, 1845, and was buried at Amber, N. Y.   He
was married April 6, 1785, to Miss Lucy, daughter of William
Bowen, of Lebanon, Connecticut.   She was born July 20,
1761, and died at Marcellus, November 10, 1849.   Their ten
children were all born in Connecticut.

755* SUSAN,⁸ b. Feb. 8, 1786; d.
756* ANNA,⁸ b. Oct. 4, 1787; d.
757   EUNICE,⁸ b. July 17, 1789; d. at Onondaga, N. Y., unm.
758* LUCY,⁸ b. Nov. 20, 1791; d. Oct. 10, 1861, at Norvell, Mich.
759* JOHN,⁸ b. Dec. 20, 1793; d. Oct. 10, 1868, at Norvell, Mich.
760* IRA,⁸ b. May 20, 1796; d. Aug. 29, 1861, at Sodus, N. Y.
761   LYDIA,⁸ b. Aug. 8, 1799; d. at Onondaga, N. Y., unm.
762ᶜ CALISTA,⁸ } twins, b. Aug. 12, 1801; d.
763* CELINDA,⁸ }
764* DAVID,⁸ b. July 2, 1804.

John was a house joiner by occupation. In the month of January, 1809, he moved with his family, from Connecticut to Marcellus, N. Y., which was then called moving West. All their furniture, with the mother and small children, were packed into a one horse sleigh, and so part of the family walking and part riding, they made the journey to their new home. The military records of Connecticut show that John Balch, Jr., enlisted from Mansfield, into the First Connecticut Line. Benjamin Throop, Captain, Jedediah Huntington, Colonel. This regiment was raised from and after January 1, 1777, and took the field in the spring of that year. He joined April 26, 1777 and was discharged April 26, 1780. He was a pensioner and resided in New York state. The Pension Department records show that his application was made in April, 1818, and that he was in the battle at Stony Point, N. Y.

375. **William,**[7] son of 181 John[6] and [————] Balch, was born at Mansfield, Connecticut and died at Halls Corners, Onondaga Co., N. Y. He was married October 26, 1786, to Elizabeth, daughter of Josiah Hall, of Mansfield, Conn. They had eight children, the three eldest were born in Mansfield, the others at Onondaga, N. Y.

765* STEPHEN,[8] b. Nov. 29, 1787; d. Dec. 22, 1874.
767   BETSEY,[8] b. Oct. 27, 1789, m. a Mr. Hall and lived at Dowagiac, Mich. d.
768   ORIGIN,[8] b. June 15, 1794; d. Dec. 24, 1828.
769* PHEBE,[8] b. June 26, 1796; d. 1875.
770   NELSON,[8] b. Dec. 13, 1799; d. Sept. 10, 1828, unm.
771   FANNY,[8] b. Dec. 2, 1801; d. Dec. 27, 1830.
772   ALMIRA,[8] b. June 15, 1805; d. Sept. 22, 1831, m. Mr. Jackson and lived at Marcellus, N. Y.
773   MATILDA,[8] b. Nov. 2, 1807; d. Jan. 10, 1831.

376. **Israel,**[7] son of John[6] and [————] Balch was married in 1792. The dates of his birth and death have not been ascertained. His wife's first name was Sarah. They had three children, all born in Mansfield, Connecticut.

774* MARVIN,[8] b. Mch. 1, 1793; d.
775   RHODA,[8] b. Jan. 3, 1795; m. Mr. Ford, of Lebanon, Ct.
776   LUCIA,[8] b. Nov. 4, 1796; m. Mr. Thayer.

By the Military Records of Connecticut it is shown that Israel enlisted into the 4th Ct. July 8, 1780, and was discharged Dec. 14, 1780, also that he enlisted Sept. 7, 1776, in to Capt. Sergeant's Co., Major Backus' Regiment Light Horse, and was discharged from the same Nov. 2, 1776.

377. **Bazalael,**[7] son of 181 John[6] and [————] Balch, died at Mansfield, Ct., Feb. 23, 1817. Feb. 23, 1786, he married Miss Ruth Davis, of Mansfield, Ct., and to them were born nine children.

777 AHIMAAZ,[8] b. July 4, 1787; d. unm. Jan. 11, 1804.
778* ANN,[8] b. Aug. 18, 1789; d. Sept. 7, 1845.
779* JOHN,[8] b. Dec. 7, 1791; d. April 3, 1868.
780* RUTH,[8] b. Sept. 7, 1794; d. April 13, 1875.
781 JOSEPH,[8] b. March 5, 1797; d.   ; m.; one child, d. y.
782* ELIZABETH,[8] b. April 25, 1799; d.
783* FANNY,[8] b. June 21, 1801; d. Feb. 19, 1885.
784* AHIMAAZ,[8] b. April 1, 1804; d.
785* MARY,[8] b. Oct. 3, 1809.

Bazalael was a farmer, and lived in the town of Mansfield, Conn., and all of his children were born in that town. He died of dropsy, from which he suffered for more than two years. His widow survived him a few years.

Bazalael was a soldier in the Revolutionary war, entering the service when but sixteen years of age. Connecticut military records show that he joined Capt. James Dana's company, April 29, 1780. He was a devout Christian, kind and affectionate. He sent his children to church and to school faithfully, and they looked back to the recollections of their early life with pleasure. An incident occurred during the war of 1812 and 14, and related by Mrs. Mackenzie [who was Ruth Balch] to her daughter Helen Mar, is of interest in showing the energy and resources of the household. Bazalael's son John was suddenly summoned to the army, and had to go on the following day, but needed an extra coat of sheep's gray. A black and a white sheep were accordingly sheared, the wool mixed, carded, spun, woven into cloth, the cloth cut, made ready into a well-fitting coat, and warming John's back twenty-four hours after it had left the backs of the sheep. All these operations were performed in the family without outside aid.

Mrs. Mackenzie described her father to her daughter as a dark complexioned man, with dark hair and eyes. He was a man of mild disposition. It was his custom to tell his children, without scolding them, that they might go back to bed if they did not feel well after they had dressed and eaten breakfast!

379. Jonathan,[7] son of 182 Jonathan[6] and Abigail [Williams] Balch, was born at Boston, April 7, 1774, and died at that city in the summer of 1803. He married Miss Elizabeth Hastings, by whom he had two sons.

786 JONATHAN,[8] d. in infancy.
787 THOMAS HASTINGS,[8] d. in infancy.

Jonathan was a lumber merchant in Boston. He left land and a new dwelling house in Friend street, worth some six thousand dollars. His widow married William Dickenson, Aug. 14, 1808.

382. Samuel Williams,[7] son of 182 Jonathan[6] and Abigail [Williams] Balch, was born March 14, 1780, at Boston, Mass. The date of his death is not known. He was living in Dorchester, Oct. 13, 1813, as appears by Suffolk Deeds, Vol. 286, p. 193, but as he is not mentioned in his mother's will, dated Oct. 25, 1815, either by name or representative, it is reasonable to infer that he died between the above dates, and left no children.

384. David,[7] son of 182 Jonathan[6] and Abigail [Williams] Balch, was born at Boston, May 14, 1784. He was alive in 1818, and then junior member of the firm of Ridgway & Balch, of Philadelphia, Pa. This is all that is known regarding him.

385. Alexander,[7] son of 182 Jonathan[6] and Abigail [Williams] Balch, was born at Boston, March 9, 1786, and died July 5, 1812. He married, April 4, 1811, Ann, daughter of Col. Ebenezer and Mary [Glover] Clapp, of Dorchester. She was born December 8, 1792. They had one daughter.

788 ANN ALEXANDER,⁵ b. Feb. 4, 1813; m. Francis D. Kidder.

Alexander was a merchant, of the firm of Ridgway & Balch, of Philadelphia, Pa. His widow married John, son of Lewis Wheeler, of Boston.

389. Joshua,⁷ son of 186 Joshua⁶ and Rebecca [Hopkins] Balch, was born June 9, 1778, and died at Lyme, N. H., April 23, 1833. He was married June 15, 1800, to Miss Nancy P. Shaw, who was born December 17, 1780, and died January 24, 1850. Joshua was a farmer, and lived in the town of Lyme, N. H. They had eight children.

789* SAMUEL WEST,⁸ b. June 9, 1803; d. May 27, 1889.
790* JULIA,⁵ b. May 15, 1805; d. 1893.
791* DAN SHAW,⁸ b. March 16, 1807; d. Feb. 24, 1888.
792 FANNY,⁵ b. Feb. 28, 1809; d.; m. in October, 1833, to Francis A. Haynes.
793 ADNA,⁵ b. April 2, 1811; d. Oct. 16, 1816.
794 ASA,⁵ b. April 12, 1814; d. Nov. 6, 1820.
795* ADNA PERKINS,⁸ b. Nov. 30, 1817; d. May 28, 1889.
796* FRANCIS BROWN,⁵ b. Aug. 3, 1819; d. March 28, 1891.

390. Israel,⁷ son of 187 Israel⁶ and Hannah [Kimball] Balch, was born at Francestown, N. H., June 29, 1773, and died in the same town, May 3, 1847. He was married, in 1796, to Miss Elizabeth Epps, of Francestown. She died December 12, 1846, aged 74 years. Nine children was their issue, all born in Francestown.

797* MARY,⁸ b. Aug. 12, 1797; d. June 8, 1880.
798* SALLY,⁵ b. Jan. 29, 1799; d. Mar. 5, 1893.
799* MASON,⁸ b. Oct. 23, 1800; d. July 21, 1873.
800* BETSEY,⁵ b. Nov. 28, 1802; d. April 12, 1846.
801* NANCY,⁵ b. Sept. 26, 1804; d. Sept. 28, 1839.
802* HANNAH,⁵ b. May 18, 1807; d. Dec. 15, 1848.
803* SUSAN,⁵ b. Feb. 25, 1809; d. Oct. 22, 1854.
804* JOHN,⁸ b. May 19, 1812; d. Sept. 19, 1886.
805* ORRA A.,⁵ b. Dec. 20, 1813; d. March, 1878.

Israel⁷ was classed among the wealthy men of Francestown.

391. Hannah,⁷ daughter of 187 Israel⁶ and Hannah [Kimball] Balch, was born at Francestown, N. H., March 23, 1775. She married Bartholomew Pearson. They lived at Peterboro, N. H., and had seven children.

392. Sally,[7] daughter of 187 Israel[6] and Hannah [Kimball] Balch, was born at Francestown, N.H., October 13, 1778, and died at Swale, Steuben county, N. Y., April 1, 1856. She married Isaac Jones. They moved from Francestown to Stoddard, N. H., in the fall of 1828, and Mr. Jones died in the latter town. They had four children.

393. Polly,[7] daughter of 187 Israel[6] and Hannah [Kimball] Balch, was born at Francestown, November 4, 1780. She married Isaac Winchester, of Greenfield, N. H., August 1, 1799. They had ten children. For a time they lived at Hill, N. H., and then removed to Providence, R. I.

394. John,[7] son of 187 Israel[6] and Hannah [Kimball] Balch, was born at Francestown, N. H., October 1, 1782. When 20 years of age he went to Chester, Vt., at which place, on the 12th day of May, 1808, he married Miss Lydia, daughter of James and Lydia [Powers] Reed. John was a farmer, and lived and died in the town of Chester. Their eleven children were all born in Chester.

806* JOHN,[8] b. Dec. 28, 1803; d.
807* ACHSAH PHILENA,[8] b. Aug. 24, 1804; d.
808* CLARK,[8] b. May 29, 1807; d. May 24, 1882.
809* JOANNA,[8] b. June 1, 1809.
810* VARION,[8] b. 1811; d. July 1, 1864.
811* DANIEL,[8] b.   ; d.
812* MARANDA P.,[8] b. Oct. 3, 1824; d.
813 LYDIA,[8] b.   ; m. Rial Walters living at Rupert, Vt.
814 ADELINE,[8] b.   ; m. Edward Whiting, living at Whitehall, N. Y.
815 LOUISA,[8] b.   ; d.   ; m. Richard Stevens.
816 SARAH,[8] b.   ; d.   ; m. Thomas Murray, Whitehall, N. Y.

395. Joanna,[7] daughter of 187 Israel[6] and Mary [————] Balch, was born at Francestown, N.H., January 20, 1786. She married Daniel Symonds, they resided at Francestown, and had three children. A daughter was living at Lyndboro, N. H., in 1888.

396. Varion,[7] son of 187 Israel[6] and Mary [widow Fletcher] Balch, was born at Francestown, N. H., May 6, 1789, and died in the same town June 12, 1834. He married Mary,

daughter of William and Olive [Kindrick] Thompson. She
was born at Dalton, Mass., June 6, 1794, and was living in
January, 1886.   They had six children.

817   VARION,[8] b.   ; d. in infancy.
818* JOANNA,[8] b. Apr. 4, 1815; d. Apr. 26, 1892.
819* JAMES T.,[8] b. Apr. 18, 1817; d. Jan. 28, 1888.
820* PAMELA,[8] b. Dec. 21, 1821; d. Apr. 9, 1854.
821* OLIVE,[8] b. Apr. 5, 1825; d. June, 1865.
822* WILLIAM,[8] b. July 14, 1831.

Varion was a farmer and always lived in Francestown, and
died in the same house his father lived and died in at Balch
Hill.   It is reasonable to presume that he was named for his
great grandmother, Hannah Veren, although the family now
spell the name Varion.

397. Pamela,[7] daughter of 187 Israel[6] and Mary
[widow Fletcher] Balch, was born at Francestown, N. H.,
November 7, 1791 and died in the same town January 24, 1833.
She was married February 7, 1825 to Levi, son of Amos, and
Huldah [Kimball] Bachelder.   He was born at Francestown,
December 27, 1798 and died in that town June 24, 1875.
They had two sons both born in Francestown.

ELBRIDGE KIMBALL, b. May 13, 1826; m. Dec. 13, 1849, Miss Caroline Ann, daughter of Elisha Vose.   She was b. Oct. 11,
1828, at Francestown.   E. K. Bachelder is a mason [brick-
layer and plasterer] and lives at Francestown.   Their three
sons were b. in that town.   *Charles Levi*, b. June 24, 1851; m.
Chelsea, Mass., Nov. 28, 1873.   Miss Alice, daughter of
Moses, and Mary [Torrey] Sleeper of Quincy, Mass.
She d. at Nashua, N. H., Jan. 5, 1879.   One child, Ernest
Allen, b. Jan. 23, 1875; m. 2, at Minneapolis, Minn., Dec. 15,
1883, to Mrs. Etta Sperling, of Nashua, N. H.   They were
living in April, 1891, at West Medford, Mass.   *George
Arthur*, b. Feb. 14, 1860; m. Oct. 30, 1881, Miss Ada F.
Mills of Francestown, N. H.   One child, Nina May, b. June,
7, 1882.   They were living at West Medfeld, Mass., in Apr.
1891.   *John Henry*, b. Apr. 11, 1869; d. April 24, 1887.
GEORGE LEVI, b. Dec. 17, 1828; was living at Sunderland, Mass.
in April, 1891.

398. William,[7] son of 187 Israel[6] and Mary [widow
Fletcher] Balch, was born at Francestown, N. H., November
3, 1793, and died at Reading, Mass., January 19, 1877.   He

was married first, July 21, 1818, to Nabby, daughter of John Johnson. She was born at Francestown, February 18, 1797, and died July 16, 1836. They had two sons.

823   WILLIAM,[8] b. July 31, 1819; d. Nov. 5, 1829.
824* MARK,[8] b. Mch. 30, 1821; d. Dec. 16, 1878.

William was married second June 8, 1837, to Zebiah, daughter of Edward Johnson. She was born at Boston, Mass., January 24, 1807, and was living at Reading in 1889. No issue. William was buried at Francestown, N. H.

399. Ruth,[7] daughter of 187 Israel[6] and Mary [widow Fletcher] Balch, was born at Francestown, N. H., September 10, 1796. She married Isaac Jones, and they moved to Canistio, N. Y., where she died June 14, 1870.

402. Isaac,[7] son of 191 Isaac[6] and Olive [Grant] Balch, was born at Lyme, N. H., September 29, 1793, and died at North Thetford, Vt., December 27, 1873. He graduated from Dartmouth College in 1811. When a young man he settled at North Thetford, and there married Miss Sally Marshal by whom he had four children, all born at North Thetford.

825   SARAH E.,[8] b. Apr. 14, 1826; living at N. Thetford, Vt.
826* ALFRED,[8] b. Aug. 9, 1828; d. Nov. 26, 1869.
827* MARSHALL S.,[8] b. July 10, 1832; d. Mch. 18, 1874. unm.
828* CHARLES NEWTON,[8] b. Oct. 17, 1836.

404. Betsey,[7] daughter of 191 Isaac[6] and Elizabeth [Bell] Balch, was borne at Lyme, N. H., January 16, 1799, and died in the same town, March 24, 1873. She was married March 23, 1823, to John Flint. They resided at Lyme, and their four children were born in that town.

ELIZABETH BALCH, b. Oct. 5, 1824; m. a Mr. Stanley in 1867, and resides at Piermont, N. H. They have no children.
HANNAH SELINDA, b. Mar. 1, 1826; m. Nov. 8, 1859, Henry Newell, resides at Lyme. Two children, both b. at Lyme. *George Newell,* b. Oct. 13, 1860. *Mary E. Newell,* b. July 3, 1865.
DIANTHA, b. Mar. 4, 1827; unm. resides at Piermont, N. H.
LEVI SPAULDING, b. Mar. 8, 1829; d. in 1864; m. in Chicago in 1863, and died soon after. No issue.

406. Albert,[7] son of 191 Isaac[6] and Elizabeth [Bell] Balch, was born at Lyme, N. H., September 6, 1802. He married, Nov. 27, 1825, Miss Chloe, daughter of Lemuel and Mary Holt, they lived in Lyme, and all their children were born in that town. After the death of his wife Albert went to Wisconsin, and nothing more can be learned regarding him.

829 DOLLY ANN,[8] b. July 21, 1826; d. Oct. 11, 1849.
830 FREEMAN,[8] b. Aug. 27, 1828; m.; rem. West.
831 JOHN FRANCIS,[8] b. June 13, 1830.
832 HARVEY,[8] b. Aug. 21, 1833; d. Jan. 16, 1857.
833 ISAAC LEMUEL,[8] b. Dec. 30, 1835; m.
834 CHLOE HOLT,[8] b. Jan. 21, 1837; d. Dec. 21, 1858.
835 MARY ELIZABETH,[8] b. Apr. 24, 1839; unm. in 1864.
836 HARRIS ALLEN,[8] b. Apr. 24, 1842; d. Nov. 4, 1859.
837 ARTHUR NEWTON,[8] b. July 3, 1845.

407. Theodore,[7] son of 191 Isaac[6] and Elizabeth [Bell] Balch was born at Lyme, N. H., October 4, 1804, and died at Lyme, January 31, 1892. He was married March 22, 1831, to Miss Sally Lovejoy of Lyme. She died April 6, 1874. They had seven children.

838* THEODORE EDWIN,[8] b. Jan. 13, 1832; d. Jan. 12, 1896.
839* WILLIAM WORCESTER,[8] b. Apr. 27, 1834.
840* ISAAC FREEMAN,[8] b. Feb. 13, 1836.
841* JOHN CARROLL,[8] b. July 7, 1839; d. Aug. 27, 1889.
842* SARAH ELIZA,[8] b. June 18, 1841.
843* HANNAH SOPHRONIA,[8] b. June 25, 1843.
844* FRANK PIERCE,[8] b. Oct. 14, 1850.

408. John,[7] son of 191 Isaac[6] and Elizabeth [Bell] Balch, was born at Lyme, N. H., June 13, 1809, and died in 1846. He married Eunice P. [Sturtevant] Lyon, they resided at Cambridge, Mass., and had five children.

845* SARAH E.,[8] b. July 31, 1836.
846* ELLEN M.,[8] b. Aug. 7, 1838; d. Jan. 23, 1861.
847* LOUISE M.,[8] b. Dec. 24, 1840.
848* EUNICE P.,[8] b. Nov. 12, 1843.
849* JOHN H.,[8] b. July 16, 1847.

410. Lucinda,[7] daughter of 195 Israel[6] and Sarah [Arnold] Balch, was born at Mansfield, Ct., April 3, 1772, and died at Wellington, Ct. She married a Mr. Cushman, they lived in Mansfield, and had nine children. Among them were the following named.

ISRAEL CUSHMAN.
HARRY.
WILLIAM, d. at Belcher, Mass.
GEORGE, d. at New Britain, Ct.
ANGELINE, d. at Durham, Ct.

411. Arnold,[7] son of 195 Israel[6] and Sarah [Arnold] Balch, was born at Mansfield, Ct., February 8, 1775, and died at Rush, Susquehanna Co., Pa., October 10, 1848. He married Meribah, daughter of Ebenezer Leonard, of Burlington, Otsego Co., N. Y. She was born December 10, 1788, and died April 28, 1861, at Aldensville, Wayne Co., Penn. Arnold and Meribah had seven children.

850* ARCHIBALD,[8] b. Aug. 30, 1802; d. July 11, 1862.
851* ARNOLD,[8] b. Oct. 11, 1805; d. Feb. 25, 1881.
852* SALLY,[8] b. July 22, 1807; d. Jan. 21, 1841.
853* SUSAN,[8] b. Apr. 30, 1810; d. Nov. 8, 1885.
854* JANE,[8] b. July 7, 1814; d. 1889.
855* ABIGAIL,[8] b. Jan. 16, 1818; d. Nov. 6, 1888.
856* DIANA,[8] b. Dec. 16, 1822; d. June 4, 1892.

Soon after Arnold was married he moved to Montrose, Penn., and lived in a log house near where the court house now stands. Wild animals were in great abundance, and neighbors scarce. One night while Arnold and his wife were going home from a neighbor's, where they had been spending the evening, a panther took after them, jumping from one tree to another over their heads. They ran with all speed for life, and succeeded in reaching home in safety. The country being so wild and new, they returned to Otsego Co., N. Y., and there raised their family. All the children were born in Otsego County, N. Y., except Diana, who was born in Cortlandt Co., N. Y. About 1825 they returned to Penn. and settled at Rush, on the Wyalusing creek, where they continued to live until removed by death. By trade Arnold was a cabinet and wheel-head maker. [A wheelhead is a part of a large spinning wheel, which was used in making woolen yarn.]

412. Roger,[7] son of 195 Israel[6] and Sarah [Arnold] Balch, was born at Mansfield, Ct., May 17, 1779. His death

was caused by the kick of a horse. He died February 12,
1831, at Sherburn, and was buried in that town. When a
young man he went to Sherburn, Chenango Co., N. Y., and
continued to reside in that town. On the 2nd 'day of February, 1806, he married Miss Hannah, daughter of Stephen
Northrup. She was born at Salem, N. Y., June 16th, 1787,
and died at Lenox, N. Y., October 5, 1870. Roger and
Hannah had seven children, all born at Sherburne. Roger
was a farmer by occupation.

857* ORPHA B.,⁸ b. July 6, 1807; d. Sept. 6, 1891.
858* MARY P.,⁸ b. July 31, 1808; d. June 6, 1875.
859 RHODA,⁸ b. July 31, 1810; d. July 1, 1848.
860* MARILLA,⁸ b. Dec. 18, 1812; d. Dec. 24, 1895.
861 CHESTER A.,⁸ b. Nov. 29, 1816; d. Feb. 9, 1817.
862 LAVINIA,⁸ b. Feb. 23, 1818; m. Feb. 23, 1852, Enoch Northrup;
        d. s. p.
863* CYNTHIA L.,⁸ b. Oct. 6, 1821.

413. **Polly,**⁷ daughter of 195 Israel⁶ and Sarah [Arnold]
Balch, was born at Mansfield, Ct., April 10, 1785, and died
at New Lisbon, N. Y., January 11, 1844. She was buried at
Burlington, N. Y. About 1805 she was married to Russel
Babcock. He was born in Ct., June 27, 1786, and died at
New Lisbon Center, N. Y., January 8, 1861. Babcock was
a farmer. They resided at New Lisbon, and their ten
children were born in that town.

IRA BABCOCK, b. Nov. 2, 1806.
HARRIET, b. Feb. 21, 1809.
ASAHEL, b. May 17, 1812.
SALLY, b. May 10, 1814.
REBECCA, b. June 13, 1816.
CLARK P., b. Sept. 12, 1818.
CHESTER, b. Aug. 31, 1820.
MARSHALL, b. July 31, 1822.
PROSPER, b. Aug. 7, 1824.
SIDNEY, b. Nov. 5, 1826.

414. **Chester,**⁷ son of 195 Israel⁶ and Sarah [Arnold]
Balch, was born at Mansfield in 1788, and died at New
Haven, Ct., May 15, 1847, and buried in Grove St. Cemetery
in that city. He married Nancy, daughter of Stephen At-

water. She was born at Mt. Carmell, Ct., and died at New Haven, September 11, 1860. They had six children all born at New Haven.

864 SARAH,[8] d. y.
865 ANN,[8] d. y.
866 ELIZABETH,[8] d. y.
867 CHESTER,[8] d. of consumption in 1842, aged 19 years.
868 CHARLES,[8] drowned when a child.
869 NANCY E.,[8] b. in 1827, is now living unm. in New Haven, Ct.

Chester died of consumption. He was a hard working man, a kind and obliging neighbor. He owned his house in New Haven, and his daughter is now living in it.

415. Sylvester,[7] son of 195 Israel[6] and Sarah [Arnold] Balch, was born at Mansfield, Ct. He died in 1848. He married Miss Mary Albray. The Connecticut Records show that Sylvester enlisted as a private in Capt. Jabez Collins Company and served from August 18, 1814 to October 26, 1814. Sylvester and Mary had six children.

870 CATHERINE,[8].
871 MARY,[8].
872 IRA,[8] d. Dec. 4, 1881.
873 SYLVESTER,[8] d. 1873.
874 PETER,[8].
875 GEORGE,[8].

417. Henry Taylor,[7] son of 197 Henry[6] and Elizabeth [Kimball] Balch, was born at Mansfield, Ct., November 28, 1785, and died at Brockfield, La Salle Co., Ill., January 29, 1869. He was married to Catherine Thomas, September 11, 1808. She was born June 27, 1791, and died at Brockfield, Ills., September 22, 1869. About 1810 they removed from Mansfield to Richfield Springs, N. Y., and lived there for fifty years, and then they moved to Illinois. Their eldest son was born at Mansfield, Ct., the other eleven children were born at Richfield Springs, N. Y.

876* DAN C.,[8] b. July 14, 1809; d. Feb. 1, 1883.
877 HANNAH,[8] b. Mar. 8, 1811; d. June 9, 1856; m. Joseph Batchelder, Sept. 3, 1843.
878* HENRIETTA,[8] b. Apr. 1, 1818; d. Feb. 2, 1869.
879* CLARISSA,[8] b. Feb. 18, 1815.

880* JOSEPH CHAPMAN,⁸ b. Jan. 30, 1817; d. about 1891.
881   NANCY,⁸ b. Mar. 11, 1819; m. Amos Edmunds, Nov. 7, 1837.
882* MARIA,⁸ b. Feb. 7, 1821.
883* RHODA ANN,⁸ b. Sept. 26, 1823.
884* HENRY,⁸ b. Dec. 5, 1825.
885   WILLIAM,⁸ b. Jan. 13, 1828; d. Mar. 11, 1830.
886* MARTHA,⁸ b. Feb. 5, 1830.
887* SARAH A.,⁸ b. Oct. 4, 1832.

419. John,⁷ son of 197 Henry⁶ and Elizabeth [Kimball]
Balch, was born at Mansfield, Ct., May 10, 1790. He was
married March 15, 1811, to Mary, daughter of Nathan Wood
of Mansfield. They had two children both born at Mansfield.

888* JOHN AUSTIN,⁸ b. Jan. 24, 1812.
889* MARY ANN MARIA,⁸ b. Apr. 9, 1816.

In 1822 John removed from Mansfield to Marathon, Cortlandt Co., N. Y. He was a shoemaker by trade; in politics
he was a democrat. He never united with any church. His
wife was a Presbyterian.

421. Thomas,⁷ son of 197 Henry⁶ and Elizabeth [Kim-
ball] Balch, was born at Mansfield, Ct., November 6, 1794.
On the 19th of May, 1819, he married Eunice Hamilton of
Mansfield, by whom he had four children all born at Mansfield.

890* SOPHRONIA ANN,⁸ b. Jan. 25, 1820.
891   SAMUEL HENRY,⁸ b. June 20, 1823.
892* ROXANA MINERVA,⁸ b. Apr. 17, 1828.
894* MILO HAMILTON,⁸ b. June 17, 1835.

423. David Burnham,⁷ son of 211 David⁶ and Betty
[Burnham] Balch was born at Topsfield, Mass., June 29,
1784, and died in the same town, June 27, 1860. He married
Fanny, daughter of Abraham J., and Abigail [Burnham]
Channell, of Essex. She was born March 28, 1784, and died,
April 10, 1882.

895   HANNAH H.,⁸ b. July 8, 1810; m. Robert Channell.
896   ANSTISS PITMAN,⁸ b. Aug. 17, 1812; m. Moses Downes.
897   SARAH HODGE,⁸ b. Apr. 24, 1815; d. Mar. 26, 1886; m. Geo. C.
         Verney.
898   MARY ELIZABETH,⁸ b. Nov. 25, 1818; d. Oct. 26, 1884.
899* WILLIAM HENRY,⁸ b. Mar. 16, 1823; d. Aug. 30, 1855.

David Burnham, was a farmer, during the war of 1812-14,

he lived at Salem, Mass., and then at Durham, N. H., for several years, then returning to Topsfield he spent the remainder of his life there.

424. Israel,[7] son of 211 David[6] and his second wife Sarah [Peabody] Balch, was born at Topsfield, Mass., September 14, 1788, and died at Amesbury, Mass., July 7, 1858. He was married at Amesbury, in 1814, to Miss Nancy Goodwin, who was born October 12, 1793, and died at Amesbury in 1865. Four children were born to Israel and Nancy.

900* MARA,[8] b. July 20, 1816; unm.; d. Aug. 29, 1895.
901 ISRAEL,[8] b. July 20, 1817; d. May 20, 1821.
902* ISRAEL DANIEL PERKINS,[8] b. June 18, 1822,
903* DAVID LOWELL DEARBORN,[8] b. Oct. 13, 1828.

Doctor Israel Balch prepared himself for college, entering Dartmouth when eighteen years of age, and graduating at the end of a four years' course. He then went to Amesbury, Mass., and studied medicine three years in the office of Doctor French. He was gifted with a strong scientific mind. He took out several patents and made some very peculiar clocks. He wrote and delivered several lectures on scientific subjects. Many young men sought his office for instruction in medicine and surgery, navigation and higher mathematics. He was a strong advocate of temperance and a firm abolitionist.

He located first at Salisbury, Mass., and practiced there five years, then he removed to Amesbury where he spent the remainder of his life. He had the largest medical library in Amesbury or vicinity. He was a very successful practitioner of medicine and surgery.

He received no aid from his father to defray his educational expenses. He grandmother Peabody made him a present of $450, which was all the pecuniary aid he had that he did not earn himself.

425. Polly,[7] eldest daughter of 211 David[6] and Sarah [Peabody] Balch, was born at Topsfield, Mass., March 7, 1792, and died January 7, 1859. She was married April 2, 1808, to Henry Luscomb, who was born at Salem, Mass.,

April 13, 1785, and died December 11, 1861. He was a mariner, they lived at Topsfield, and Salem, Mass. They had ten children, the two eldest were born at Topsfield, the other eight at Salem.

THOMAS BALCH, b. Apr. 3, 1809; a shoemaker by trade.

ISRAEL, b. Apr. 8, 1811; a mariner.

HANNAH, b. Dec. 26, 1817.

MARY MUGFORD, b. Dec. 21, 1818; she married Samuel Richard Blisdale, a shoemaker. They had two children; *Mary Appleton*, b. Apr. 13, 1838; m. Horace Lane Hill, a cooper, [by whom she had three children: William Lane, b. Nov. 10, 1861; Mary Louisa, b. Apr. 6, 1865; Henry Frederick, b. Dec. 20, 1867]; *Eliza Thayer*, b. Nov. 14, 1840; m. Henry Frederick Danforth and had one child; Ella A., b. Jan. 8, 1860.

HENRY WILLIAM, b. Mar. 28, 1820.

AUGUSTUS FRANKLIN, b. 1825; a mariner.

CAROLINE, b. July 26, 1838.

SARAH ELLEN, b. Jan. 4, 1834.

GEORGE WARREN, b. Jan. 20, 1835. He was married Nov. 22, 1855, to Pamela Jones Wyman, b. May 3, 1839. They live at Webster, Me. Their children were b. at Salem Mass: *Henry*, b. Jan. 28, 1857; d. y. *Julia Frances*, b. July 17, 1859; m. Arthur Brookhouse; they live at Medford, and have one child, Albert Luscomb, b. Mar. 30, 1884. *Emma Louisa*, b. Aug. 3, 1862; d. y. *George Henry*, b. Jan. 14, 1867. *Mary Emma*, b. Nov. 11, 1869.

SARAH ELLEN, b. July 25, 1837; m. Herbert Ezekiel Larrabee. Two children: *Annie Maria*, b. Dec. 7, 1862; d. y. *Frederick Merrill*, b. Feb. 5, 1864.

428. Sally,[7] youngest daughter of 211 David[6] and Sarah [Peabody] Balch, was born at Topsfield, June 19, 1800.

She was married in 1822 to David Sanderson of Salem, Mass. They had one daughter, Lucy Ann, who married a Mr. Wright and lived at Topsfield.

All the knowledge we have in regard to these daughters is from their mother's will.

433. William,[7] son of 219 David[6] and Esther [Esty] Balch, was born at Topsfield, Mass. He married Mehitable Townsend, and first settled at Keene, N. H., where his eleven children were born. Afterwards he moved to Madison Co., N. Y., where he died. He was a member of the Baptist Church.

904 AARON,[8] b. May 10, 1792; d. June 10, 1792.
905 EPHRAIM,[8] b. Dec. 3, 1793; d. Sept. 9, 1799.
906* REBECCA,[8] b. Dec. 8, 1795; d. Sept. 27, 1873.
907 MEHITABLE,[8] b. Sept. 6, 1797; d. Sept., 1799.
908 MEHITABLE,[8] b. Jan. 16, 1800; d. Feb., 1881; m. Mr. Brown.
909 WILLIAM,[8] b. Jan. 11, 1803; d. July 21, 1828, at Keene, N. H.
910 EPHRAIM,[8] b. Feb. 2, 1805; d. May 2, 1889.
911 AARON,[8] b. Aug. 8, 1808; d. Aug. 27, 1886.
912 EMILY,[8] b. June 10, 1810; d. May 25, 1881; m. Thomas West.
913* CHARLES,[8] b. Feb. 22, 1814; d. July 6, 1882.
914* ARTEMIA,[8] b. Jan. 30, 1816; d.; m. Mr. Tarpy.

434. Lydia,[7] daughter of 219 David[6] and Esther [Esty] Balch, was born at Topsfield, Mass., in 1765, and died April 18, 1834. She was married to John, son of John and Hannah [Smith] Peabody, of Topsfield, May 6, 1781. Peabody was born in July, 1762, and died January 22, 1836. They had eight children.

ABIGAIL, b. in 1782; d. in 1857; m. Humphrey Wildes in 1804.
JOHN, b. Oct. 30, 1784; m. 1st, Lydia Symonds, Jan. 9, 1810; 2nd, Margaret Brown, of Hamilton. He had two sons by Margaret.
AARON B., b. Apr. 12, 1788; d. unm. in 1814.
HANNAH SMITH, b. Dec. 28, 1792; m. Sewell Lake, of Bucksport, Me., June 19, 1811.
DANIEL, } twins, b. Jan. 12, 1797 { d. unm. in 1833.
LYDIA, }   { m. Dec. 23, 1819, Francis Peabody, Amherst, N. H.
JOEL ROGERS, b. Nov. 29, 1800; d. July 24, 1861. He was a deacon of the church at Topsfield. Married 1st, Mary B. Safford, in May, 1827; married 2nd, Sarah Dole of Newbury, Mass., Dec. 6, 1841.
DAVID, b. Apr. 16, 1805, d. Oct. 17, 1839; m. Maria Bringham of Cambridgeport, Sept. 11, 1834. Was a minister at Lynn in 1832, and at Worcester in 1835; was Prof. of Rhetoric and Oratory at Dartmouth College in 1838.

435. David,[7] son of 219 David[6] and Esther [Esty] Balch, was born at Topsfield, Mass., September 1, 1771, and died in Keene, N. H., September 8, 1835. He was married November 2, 1799, to Abigail Wells, who was born January 12, 1773, and died at Keene, November 10, 1848. They resided in Keene and their seven children were born in that town.

915 ELIZA,[8] b. Nov. 13, 1800; d. Nov. 26, 1813.
916* LAURA ANN,[8] b. Nov. 11, 1802; d. Oct. 19, 1874.
917 HARRIET,[8] b. Sept. 16, 1805; d. Sept. 28, 1825.

918   CHARLOTTE,⁸ b. Aug. 31, 1807; d. Jan. 19, 1880.
919ᵉ   GEORGE A.,⁸ b. Oct. 13, 1809; d. Mar. 8, 1891.
920   NABBY ANN,⁸ b. Feb. 4, 1812; d. Feb. 8, 1818.
921   JAMES,⁸ b. Aug. 25, 1814; d. unm.

438. Mehitable,⁷ daughter of 220 John⁶ and Sarah [Baker] Balch, was born at Topsfield, June 26, 1772, and died September 16, 1864. She was married to Nathaniel Fisk, November 20, 1794. He was born December 2, 1764, and died November 13, 1849. Their issue was four children : Mehitable, b. Aug. 22, 1793; d. in 1796; Elsey, b. May 3, 1798; d.; Amos Fisk, b. May 26, 1801; d. Sept. 9, 1850; Rev. Jonas, b. Sept. 24, 1805; d.

440. John,⁷ son of 220 John⁶ and Sarah [Baker] Balch, was born at Topsfield, August 17, 1776, and died in the same town, October 24, 1837. In 1798 he married Mary, daughter of Andrew Elliot, of Middleton, Mass. They were published July 22, 1798. She was born in 1780, and died August 23, 1856, aged 76 years and seven months. They resided in Topsfield and had five children born to them in that town. This family were all physically large.

922   MARY,⁸ b. July 30, 1799; d. May 17, 1856; unm.
923   SARAH,⁸ bapt. Oct. 18, 1800; m. Mr. Cram.
924   ANDREW B.,⁸ b. Feb. 10, 1803; d. June 24, 1865; unm.
925ᵉ   JOHN CAPEN,⁸ b. 1805; d.
926ᵉ   NEHEMIAH,⁸ b. 1807; d. Jan. 2, 1884.

442. Hannah,⁷ daughter of 222 Robert⁶ and Sarah [Dodge] Balch, was born at Topsfield, Mass., August 18, 1770, and died at Johnson, Vt., March 20, 1867. She was married at New Boston, N. H., in 1791, to Thomas Baker, of Topsfield. They had seven children.

THOMAS, b.   ; d. Mar. 10, 1863; m. Mary C. Bingham, by whom he had eight children: *Henry L.*, b. June 29, 1837. *Thomas J.*, b. Aug. 3, 1839. *Frances K.*, b. Feb. 12, 1841. *Elias W.*, b. Dec. 9, 1843. *Sherman C.*, b. June 2, 1847. *Joseph*, b. June 11, 1850; d. in 1852. *Stillman J.*, b. June 18, 1853. *Mary C.*, b. May 14, 1858.
JOSEPH,¹ b. June 20, 1803; m. and had twelve children: *Joseph W.*, b. Mar. 13, 1831. *Hannah R.*, b. Aug. 28, 1832. *Thomas R.*, b. Sept. 11, 1833. *John S.*, b. May 19, 1835.

William H., b. Apr. 3, 1837. *Gardner M.*, b. Sept. 5, 1839.
Charity E. and *Chaney P.*, twins, b. May 9, 1841. *George W.*
b. Oct. 4, 1843. *Mary E.*, and *Moses F.*, twins, b. Aug. 11,
1845. *William W.*, b. Jan. 6, 1849.

Hannah [Balch] Baker, was left a widow at the age of
fifty. She moved to Johnson, Vt., in 1880 and united soon
after with the Congregational Church, of which she was an
esteemed member. She died in the family of her daughter,
Mrs. Moses Fullington, where she was cared for to the last
with exemplary tenderness. Eventful were the years through
which she passed, remembering distinctly when the first blow
for freedom was struck. She was thirteen years of age when
the sovereignty of our nation was conceded by the mother
country, eighteen when our present constitution went in
operation, forty-two when again arms were taken up against
England, ninety when our country was threatened with dis-
union, and still she lived on to see the most gigantic rebellion
put down that the world ever saw. All of these epochs in our
country's history were retained with unusual vividness in her
memory to the last. Her predominant traits of character
were industry, prudence, and piety, every one of which, even
industry she retained to the last.

443. Robert,[7] son of 222 Robert[6] and Sarah [Dodge]
Balch, was born at Topsfield, Mass., February 17, 1772, and
died at Jericho, Vt., March 4, 1842. He married Nabby
Cram, of Ware, N. H. She died at Jericho, April 17, 1842,
without issue. She was a cousin of John Cram, who married Robert's sister Sarah. In 1792, Robert, with his brother
Solomon, settled at Johnson, Vt. where they bought three
hundred acres of land near the center of the township.
There being a defect in the title they had to pay for their
land twice.

444. Solomon,[7] son of 222 Robert[6] and Sarah [Dodge]
Balch, was born at Topsfield, Mass., October 20, 1773, and
died at Johnson, Vt., October 22, 1854. He was married to
Ruth Knights, of Antrim, N. H., about 1801. She was born

July 22, 1777, and died Nov. 4, 1882. In 1792 Solomon left
the parental roof at New Boston, N. H., and settled at Johnson, Vt. upon a three hundred acre farm with his brother
Robert. There was born to Solomon and Ruth nine children.

927* PHEBE,⁵ b. Mar. 18, 1803 ; d. Mar. 7, 1841.
928* ROBERT,⁸ b. Aug. 2, 1804 ; d. Jan. 11, 1874.
929* RUTH,⁸ b. Sept. 7, 1806 ; d. Feb. 28, 1873.
930* SOLOMON,⁸ b. April 8, 1808 ; d. April 30, 1859.
931   SARAH,⁸ b. Feb. 26, 1810 ; d. April 10, 1845 ; m. Darius Clark, no
        issue.
932* ALLEN,⁸ b. Nov. 18, 1811 ; d. April 13, 1881.
933* FREDERICK P.,⁸ b. Oct. 26, 1813.
934* BETSEY,⁸ b. Dec. 10, 1815 ; d. Nov. 11, 1848.
935   FLORELLA,⁸ b. July 18, 1820 ; d. 1821.

Solomon was married a second time to the widow Philo-
mena [Marcy] Willey, of Jericho, Vt. He died March 31,
1849, aged 66 years, without issue.

Solomon cleared his share of the farm which he bought in
company with his brother Robert. He built a house and
barns, and a saw mill on a small stream that ran through his
farm. Upon this farm he spent the remainder of his life, respected by all who knew him. He was repeatedly elected as
selectman, and justice of the peace. He was a man of
strict integrity, and very exact in all his business dealings.
As showing the opinion his neighbors had of his honesty, the
following incident illustrates. An eccentric neighbor would
never measure anything unless he could get the "Squire's"
ten-foot pole, as no other was right.

Solomon was a portly gentleman, weighing 250 pounds,
erect, with a clear blue eye. When pleased, his eye had a
merry twinkle, but he could look as stern as the sternest.
He was very fond of company. The summer before he died
he made each of his grandsons a shot pouch of deer skin
with deer horn nozzles. In politics he was a whig.

446. Moses,⁷ son of 222 Robert⁶ and Sarah [Dodge]
Balch, was born at Topsfield, Mass., October 7, 1777, and
died at Johnson, Vt., May 7, 1813. He married first Nabby,
daughter of Nehemiah Dodge, of New Boston, N. H. In

1794 they moved to Johnson, Vt. Three children was the issue of this first marriage.

936 ELVIRA,[8] m. Mr. Tewksbury, of New Boston, N. H.
937 SARAH,[8] m. George Dunlap, of New Boston, N. H.
938 FRANKLIN,[8] d. y.

Moses married for his second wife Sally Willis of Wethersfield, Vt., who outlived him. Four sons was the issue of Moses and Sally.

939* JOHN,[8] b. Feb. 18, 1806.
940* SAMUEL,[8] b. June 23, 1808 ; d. Aug. 26, 1854.
941* MOSES,[8] b. Nov. 30, 1810 ; d. Mar. 17, 1891.
942* ABIJAH,[8] b. Mar. 16, 1813 ; d. Sept. 21, 1878.

447. John,[7] son of 222 Robert[6] and Sarah [Dodge] Balch, was born at Topsfield, Mass., June 25, 1779, and died at Jericho, Vt., June 20, 1822. He married Deborah Kenniston, of Weare, N. H. They lived at Jericho, Vt., and had eleven children. John was a farmer.

943 JOHN,[8] } twins, b. April 3, 1800 ; d. y.
944 DELIA,[8] }
945 ROBERT,[8] b. Feb. 2, 1802.
946* JOHN JEFFERSON,[8] b. June 27, 1804 ; d. Mar. 10, 1879.
947* ELIZA,[8] b. Mar. 3, 1806 ; d. Dec. 22, 1866.
948* ELIPHALET,[8] b. Dec. 29, 1807 ; d. May 28, 1873.
949* JULIA ANN,[8] b. Aug. 25, 1809; d. June 25, 1896.
950* HANNAH,[8] b. May 11, 1811.
951* WILLIAM PLUMBER,[8] b. March 13, 1813 ; d. Apl. 12, 1884.
952 ALLEN,[8] b. Mar. 27, 1815.
953* ROXANNA,[8] b. July 1, 1818; d. June 3, 1889.

449. Dilley,[7] daughter of 222 Robert[6] and Sarah [Dodge] Balch, was born at Topsfield, Mass., May 6, 1784, and died at Unity, N. H., October 19, 1864. She married Ezra, son of Capt. Ezekiel Cram, of Weare, N. H. He died October 28, 1856. They lived at Unity, N. H., and their five children were born in that town.

HIRAM and JAMES, d. y.
THOMAS JEFFERSON, b. in 1804 ; d. of apoplexy in a street car at Philadelphia, Pa., Dec. 20, 1883. Married Nov. 3, 1853, Mary, daughter of James Boggs, a merchant of Philadelphia. They had one child. *Ida Balch*, b. in 1858.

T. J. Cram graduated at West Point in 1826, commissioned to a second Lieutenantcy in the 4th U. S. Artillery in July, 1826. In

April, 1835, he was promoted to 1st Lieutenantcy. He resigned
his commission in Sept., 1836. Two years later in July, 1838, he
was appointed to a captaincy in the Topographical Engineers,
a rank which he retained for no less than twenty-five years. The
war of the Rebellion opened the path for advancement, and in
August, 1861, he at last obtained his long delayed majority. In
Sept., 1861, he was made a Lieut.-Colonel additional aid-de-camp.
In March, 1863, he was transferred to the engineers. He was
breveted Brigadier General of volunteers in March, 1865. In
November of the same year he was promoted to a colonelcy of
Engineers. In January, 1866, he was breveted Brigadier General, and Major General, in the regular army for faithful and
meritorious service during the war. He was retired from the
army in February, 1869, after an honorable career of forty-one
years in the military service of his country.

POLLY, b. in 1806 ; d. July 26, 1874 ; m. Harvey Bingham, of
Unity, N. H. They had two daughters, *Mary Matilda*, and
Helen Mar ; both married and were left young widows with
one son each.

ELIPHALET, b. in 1821 ; d. Aug. 12, 1868 ; m. Betsey Ann, daughter of Major Roys Jones, of Claremont, N.H. Eliphalet, with his
wife, settled at Racine, Wis. He was known in that state as
the Hon. E. Cram. They had three children, *Mary Elizabeth*,
Roys Jones, and *Arthur Balch*.

450. Betsey,[7] daughter of 222 Robert[6] and Sarah
[Dodge] Balch, was born at Topsfield, Mass., April 2, 1786,
and died at Washington, N. H., November 10, 1813. She
married in 1802, Samuel Philbrick Bailey, of Washington, N.
H. He was born February 27, 1780, and died in May, 1880,
having lived more than a century ; he descended from a long
lived and patriotic stock. His father, Jesse Bailey, was from
Haverhill, Mass., and was a soldier in the Revolution, and died
at Weare, N. H., aged near 84 years. His grandfather, Ebenezer Bailey, died at the age of 97 years.

451. Nancy,[7] daughter of 222 Robert[6] and Sarah
[Dodge] Balch, was born at Topsfield, Mass., June 10, 1789,
and died Jan. 30, 1850. She married Even Dow, of Weare,
N. H., and had two sons and one daughter. John, d. about
1865 ; Franklin, d. about 1870, and Lucretia.

452. Allen,[7] son of 222 Robert[6] and Sarah [Dodge]
Balch, was born at Topsfield, Mass., July 19, 1791, and died

ALLEN BALCH.

(452)

at Northfield, Vt., August 28, 1881. He married in 1812, Miss Hepzibah Dodge, of New Boston, N. H., who was born June 30, 1794, and died June 26, 1874. They had nine children.

954* WILLIAM D.,[8] b. Oct. 26, 1813; d. Oct. 12, 1862.
955* MARGARET D.,[8] b. May 13, 1815; d. Jan. 22, 1892.
956* SARAH L.,[8] b. May 16, 1818.
957* ELIZABETH C.,[8] b. Jan. 15, 1821.
958* JOHN A.,[8] b. June 23, 1823; d. July 28, 1891.
959* ALMA A.,[8] b. June 6, 1828.
960* EZRA D.,[8] b. May 6, 1830; d. Sept. 6, 1867.
961 ZILLAH K.,[8] b. March 5, 1832; d. unm. Dec. 30, 1862.
962* ANGIA H.,[8] b. Nov. 17, 1837; d. Jan. 31, 1880.

Allen Balch moved into the town of Northfield, Vt., in 1829. He always had the merited respect and confidence of his fellow citizens. His end was quite sudden, his daughter on returning from church one Sunday, found him lying upon the floor in an insensible condition, having had a stroke of paralysis. Allen and his wife belonged to the denomination of Freewill Baptists.

Allen Balch was a Democrat, but because Jackson vetoed the U. S. Bank act, he turned Whig, and continued as such the remainder of his life.

453. William,[7] son of 222 Robert[6] and Sarah [Dodge] Balch, was born at New Boston, N. H., July 20, 1793, and died at Madison, Lake Co., Ohio, August 27, 1885. He married Miss Mary Boyington, of Wethersfield, Vt., March 5, 1818. Mary was the daughter of John Boynton, and sister to Lucindia, the wife of 672 James Parker Balch.[8] She was born 30th of August, 1797, and died at Madison, Ohio, Jan. 2, 1851. They had six children all born at Madison, Ohio.

963* JOHN B.,[8] b. Jan. 21, 1819.
964 WILLIAM,[8] b. Sept. 11, 1821; d. July 11, 1834.
965* HIRAM A.,[8] b. Sept. 11, 1824.
966 OSCAR,[8] b. Oct. 30, 1834; d. Nov. 3, 1834.
967* MARY L.,[8] b. March 28, 1836.
968* GEORGE F.,[8] b. Aug. 20, 1843.

William married second Miss Mary Whitney, Feb. 5, 1853. No issue.

In 1818, he went to Ohio and located his future home, he then returned to Vermont, married his wife and returned to Madison, Ohio, where he spent the rest of his life, following the occupation of a farmer.

454. Rebecca,[7] daughter of 222 Robert[6] and Sarah [Dodge] Balch, was born at New Boston, N. H., December 19, 1796, and died September 22, 1876. She married Ezra Dodge of New Boston, January 5, 1815. He was born August 7, 1791, and died February 20, 1853. Rebecca was a member of the Presbyterian church. No issue.

455. Abigail,[7] daughter of 224 Cornelius[6] and Mehitable [Dwinell] Balch, was baptized at Topsfield, Mass., December 22, 1771. She was married first to Asa Bradstreet of Topsfield, November 30, 1790. He was born May 29, 1769. He died leaving Abigail a widow, and she married for her second husband, David Perkins. Whether she had children or not is not known.

457. Mehitable,[7] daughter of 224 Cornelius[6] and Mehitable [Dwinell] Balch, was born at Topsfield, Mass., in February, 1778, and died October 4, 1815. She married John Bradstreet, Jr., January 9, 1793. He was born December 9, 1771. Their issue was three children. Mehitable, b. Mar. 29, 1794; Cornelius, b. Oct. 30, 1796; Ruth, b. Feb. 16, 1799.

458. Perley,[7] son of 226 Roger[6] and Sarah [Perley] Balch, was born at Topsfield, Mass., August 5, 1783, and died in the same town, May 2, 1858. He was married November 11, 1808, to Sarah, daughter of Asa and Hannah [Johnson] Perkins. She was born May 3, 1789, and died March 23, 1865. They resided at Topsfield, and their six children were born there.

969* PERLEY,[8] b. Apr. 27, 1809; d. Feb. 9, 1881.
970 EUNICE,[8] b. Sept. 21, 1811; d. Dec. 31, 1878; m. Amos Perkins. No issue.
971* MEHITABLE,[8] b. May 16, 1814; d. 1891.
972* HUMPHREY,[8] b. May 18, 1818.
973ª JEREMIAH STONE,[8] b. May 17, 1823.
974* BENJAMIN JOHNSON,[8] b. Sept. 9, 1826.

464. Benjamin,[7] son of 282 Benjamin[6] and Susanna [Muliken] Balch, was born at East Bradford, Mass., July 21, 1798, and died at Haverhill, Mass., in 1842. He married Miss Marilda Goodale, and by her had eight children. They lived in Haverhill.

975[a] LEWIS,[8] b. Aug, 23, 1815; d. Apr. 21, 1891.
976[a] MARY ANN,[8] b. Apr. 23, 1818; d. July 27, 1834.
977   DANIEL,[8] Supposed to have been lost at sea.
978   ALBERT,[8] d.
979   SAPHRONIA,[8]
980   WARREN,[8]
981   CHARLES,[8]
982[a] SARAH GOODWIN,[8] b. May 19, 1836.
983   GEORGE W.,[8]
984   HARRIET,[8] d.
985   EUNICE LYDIA,[8] d.

466. Daniel,[7] son of 282 Benjamin[6] and Susanna [Muliken] Balch, was born at East Bradford, Mass., March 21, 1797, and died at Manchester, N. H., August 21, 1875. He was married October 15, 1822, to Miss Silence Clark Adams, of Medway, Mass. She was born at Holliston, Mass., July 1, 1801, and died at Manchester, N. H., March 2, 1872. They had seven children.

986   LOUISA SHATTUCK,[8] b. June 2, 1824, at Lowell; d. May 17, 1842.
987[a] ASAHEL ADAMS,[8] b. June 1, 1826, at Lowell; d. Jan. 16, 1869.
988[a] WALTER BYRON,[8] b. Aug. 9, 1828, at Lowell.
989   SARAH ADELINE,[8] b. Aug. 27, 1831, at Lowell; d. Dec. 14, 1848.
990   HANNAH MARIA,[8] b. Dec. 3, 1836; d. Feb. 3, 1837.
991   FRANCIS M,[8] b. June 16, 1840; d. Aug. 5, 1841.
992   EMILY CORNELIA,[8] b. Apr. 25, 1845; d. Feb. 13, 1846.

For a time they lived at Methuen, Mass., and then removed to Lowell. In 1844 he was elected a member of the state legislature and served one term. In 1847 they removed to Manchester, N. H. Daniel was a prominent member of the Masonic Fraternity.

467. William H.,[7] son of 282 Benjamin[6] and Susanna [Muliken] Balch, was born at East Bradford, Mass., October 21, 1798, and died in the same town February 14, 1835. He was married to Louisa, daughter of Meshack Shattuck. They resided at East Bradford, and had four children, all born in that town.

993° HENRY AUGUSTUS,[8] b. Sept. 3, 1824; d. Sept. 7, 1850.
994° REBECCA ANN,[8] b. May 8, 1828.
995 MARY HARRIS,[8] b. May 7, 1831; d. Sept. 14, 1838.
996 HELEN MARIA,[8] b. May 14, 1834; d. June 31, 1834.

Louisa, William H.'s widow, married for her second husband
Mr. Amos Parker.

468. Sophronia,[7] daughter of 232 Benjamin[6] and
Susanna [Muliken] Balch, was born at East Bradford, Mass.,
October 6, 1801, and died at Bradford, December 13, 1858.
She was married December 7, 1818 to John, son of David,
and Abigail Morse. He was born August 11, 1790, and died
June 30, 1879. They had five children born at Bradford.

> EMELINE ANN, b. Aug. 8, 1824, d. unm. April 21, 1884.
> CAROLINE E., b. June 20, 1826, d. Aug. 20, 1880; m. Samuel B.
> Perry, of Bradford, October 10, 1870. He d. Sept. 27, 1882,
> aged 49 years. No children.
> JOHN HOWARD, b.   ; d. Sept. 15, 1835.
> Two died young, unnamed.

470. Margaret,[7] daughter of 233 Wesley Perkins[6] and
Margaret [Lord] Balch, was born July 24, 1796, at Bradford,
Mass., and died January 4, 1872. She married Benjamin
Emerson, of Haverhill, Mass., April 27, 1815. He was born
at Boxford, Mass., Nov. 16, 1785, and died at Haverhill,
March 7, 1874. They had seven children all born at Haver-
hill.

> CHARLES, b. June 27, 1817; d. Aug. 6, 1890, m. Celinda George of
> Haverhill, who was born June 10, 1820; d. March 7, 1891.
> They had four children all born at Haverhill. *Charles W.,*
> b.   ; d. in infancy; *Charles,* b. July, 1845; d. Jan. 3, 1889;
> *George Leighton,* b. Nov. 5, 1849; m. Elizabeth Killam, Dec. 7,
> 1870. She was b. at Boxford, Aug. 26, 1848. They had three
> children born at Haverhill. William Wells, b. March 9, 1872;
> Cora Blanche, b. Nov. 22, 1874; George Edward, b. February
> 19, 1877.
> CAROLINE, b. Dec. 4, 1818; d. May 2, 1843.
> MARGARET ANN, b. Feb. 4, 1821; d. Jan. 24, 1843.
> GEORGE, b. Nov. 15, 1822; d. Nov. 16, 1822.
> JOHN BRADSTREET, b. Nov. 12, 1824; d. Aug. 25, 1825.
> JULIA MATILDA, b. March 25, 1829; d. Jan. 11, 1891.
> BENJAMIN LEVERATT, b. Aug. 16, 1834; m. Abbie Augusta
> McDuffee, July 20, 1861. She was born at Winthrop, Me.,

July 24, 1836. They had six children. *Edith*, b. at Cam‑
bridgeport, Nov. 23, 1862; died Nov. 23, 1862. *Carrie Augusta*,
twins, b. Cambridgeport, Nov. 23, 1862. *Lizzie Florence*, b.
Chelsea, Dec. 2, 1864. *Alice Marion*, b. Charlestown, April
23, 1867. *Frederick Benjamin*, b. Chelsea, May 4, 1871.
Rudolph Waldron, b. Chelsea, July 23, 1875.

471. Wesley,[7] son of 233 Wesley Perkins[6] and Marga‑
ret [Lord] Balch, was born at Haverhill, Mass., March 25,
1798, and died July 5, 1853. He was married January 29,
1822, to Ann Greenleaf, who died at Haverhill, September 19,
1865. They had three daughters all born at Haverhill.

997* Eliza Greenleaf,[8] b. May 16, 1825; d. Dec. 18, 1886.
998* Harriet Frances,[8] b. 1827; d. March 23, 1866.
999   Mary,[8] d. in infancy.

472. John,[7] son of 233 Wesley Perkins[6] and Margaret
[Lord] Balch, was born at Haverhill, January 7, 1800, and
died at Waldeboro, Me., May 28, 1868. He was married to
Sarah A. Samson, of Waldeboro, September 27, 1827. She
died May 21, 1866. They had two children, both born at
Waldeboro.

1000* Sarah Elizabeth,[8] b. Nov. 13, 1828.
1001   Charles Wesley[8], b. Nov. 13, 1834; d. March 19, 1861.

476. Sophia,[7] daughter of 233 Wesley Perkins[6] and
Margaret [Lord] Balch, was born at Haverhill, Mass., Sep‑
tember 5, 1807, and died at Thomaston, Me., March 22, 1855.
She married Dr. Moses R. Ludwig, of Thomaston, May 6,
1830, they were published March 20, 1829. Dr. Ludwig died
at Thomaston, September 7, 1870. They had 5 children, all
born at Thomaston.

Susan L., b. March 4, 1831; m. Rev. Oliver J. Fernald, Apr. 30,
1849. He was b. in Boston, Nov., 1822, and d. at T. May 7,
1861. They had five children, all born at Thomaston.
William Ludwig, b. Feb. 24, 1850; m. Ada F. Whitney of
Thomaston, Sept., 1873. *Minnie Hichborn*, b. Dec. 7, 1851.
Margaret Ludwig, b. Apr. 7, 1854. *Mary Frances*, b. Feb. 22,
1856. *Susan Ellen*, b. Nov. 5, 1858.
William A. T., b. Aug. 26, 1833; d. in infancy.
Mary Frances, b. June 16, 1835; m. Edward P. Merrill, of Cam‑
bridge, Mass. He was born at Otisfield, Me., Aug. 10, 1829.
They had four children, two eldest born at Thomaston, Me.,

the two youngest at Lynn, Mass. *Mary Sophia,* b. Feb. 2,
1857; d. Apr., 1884. *Helena Ludwig,* b. Apr. 24, 1858; d. June,
1867. *Oliver Fernald,* b. Jan. 5, 1863; d. June, 1868. *Edward
H.,* b. Nov. 1868; d. Nov., 1875.

MOSES MALONY, b. July 15, 1837; d. Dec. 6, 1858.
MARGARETTE C., b. Feb. 4, 1840; d. Aug. 22, 1846.

478. Susan Osborn,[7] daughter of 233 Wesley Perkins[6]
and Susan [Osborn] Balch, was born at Haverhill, Mass.,
June 11, 1811, and died in the same town, December 5, 1878.
She was married August 31, 1830, to John Davis of Haverhill. He was born at Bradford, May 14, 1805, and died at
Somerville, Mass., September 6, 1872. They had eleven children, all born at Haverhill.

    MARY BOARDMAN, b. Sept. 15, 1831; m. at Bradford, Mass., June
    4, 1867, to Jackson B. Swett, of Haverhill, whose first wife
    was 998 Harriet F., daughter of 471 Wesley Balch. He
    was born at Haverhill, Feb. 12, 1815, and d. at Haverhill, Oct.
    3, 1890. They had two children, both born at Haverhill.
    Mary Jackson, b. June 13, 1870. *Susan Ellen,* b. July 21,
    1873; d. Aug. 16, 1873.

    JOHN FRANCIS, b. Dec. 9, 1832; m. Nov. 30, 1858, Julia M. P.
    Brown, of Haverhill. She was b. at Bradford, Jan. 16, 1833.
    They had three sons, all born at Brooklyn, N. Y., where they
    reside. *Rev. Francis Howard,* b. Oct. 6, 1860; m. May 16, 1888,
    to Carrie A. Foote of Brooklyn. She was b. at Rush, N. Y.,
    March 2, 1861. They had one son: Francis Warren, b. Aug.
    9, 1889, at Franklin Falls, N. H. *John Herbert,* b. Oct. 9,
    1862; m. Katherine Kingsbury, of Bradford, Oct. 3, 1888.
    She was b. at Winooskie, Vt., July 11, 1863; d. Sept. 26, 1889.
    They had one son, born at Bradford. John Bradford, b.
    Sept. 26, 1889. *Robert Brown,* b. July 18, 1868.

    GUSTAVUS LUDWIG, b. Jan. 6, 1834; m. Adelaide A. Smith, of
    Haverhill, May 27, 1856. She was born at North Bridgewater,
    Mass., Aug. 28, 1833, d. at Haverhill, Nov. 22, 1884. They
    had one daughter born at Haverhill. *Annie Shumway,* b.
    April 27, 1866; d. Feb. 21, 1867.

    SUSAN ELLEN, b. Nov. 8, 1835; m. at Bradford, Mass., Nov. 24,
    1857, to William Warren Shumway, of Brooklyn, N.Y. He was
    b. at Medway, Mass., Sept. 26, 1830. They had seven children,
    the first born at Bradford, Mass., and the others at Brooklyn,
    N. Y.; *Warren Davis,* b. Oct. 17, 1858; *Susan Alice,* b. Dec. 18,
    1860; d. Oct. 21, 1873; *Frank Storrs,* b. March 12, 1862; *Annie
    Boardman,* b. Feb. 8, 1864, m. George H. Stevens, of Brooklyn,
    N. Y., Nov. 24, 1885. He was b. at Brooklyn, N. Y., Nov. 12,

1861; *Arthur Clifford,* b. Aug. 13, 1872; *William Warden,* b.
Nov. 10, 1876; *John Howard,* b. May 29, 1878; d. May 2, 1880.

CAROLINE MATILDA, b. June 12, 1837; d. Oct. 23, 1837.

HARRIETTE PARKER, b. Sept. 24, 1838; d. Aug. 21, 1839.

EDWARD ORESTES, b. Apr. 13, 1841; d. Sept. 4, 1842.

HARRIETTE ANNA, b. Apr. 15, 1842; m. Jan. 24, 1875, to John L.
Burst, of Fernandina, Fla. He was b. at Woodstock, Ills.,
March 25, 1849. They had four children; the first born at
Fernandina, Fla., and the others at Brooklyn, N. Y.; *Ellen
Maria,* b. Dec. 11, 1875, at Fernandina, Fla.; d. Aug. 20, 1888,
at Brooklyn, N. Y.; *Susan Grace,* b. Aug. 8, 1877, at Brook-
lyn, N. Y.; *John Gustavus,* b. March 23, 1880, at Brooklyn, N.
Y.; *William Corwin,* b. June 12, 1881, at Brooklyn, N. Y.

EMMA LOUISE, b. Sept. 7, 1845, m. in Bradford, Mass., June 22,
1869, to Charles H. Tufts, of Andover, Mass. He was born in
Boston. No issue.

HENRY LOWE, b. March 23, 1851, unm.

CARRIE LIZZIE BALCH, b. July 31, 1853; d. Feb. 26, 1857.

480. Wesley Perkins,[7] son of 236 John[6] and Phebe
[Harmon] Balch, was born at Beverly, Mass., September 2,
1794, and died at Medfield, Mass., September 23, 1856. He
married first Rebecca Battelle, of Dover, August 20, 1817.
She died January 8, 1820, leaving one son.

1002   ALBERT BATTELLE,[8] b. April 2, 1819. Is living at Arlington,
Mass., unm.

Wesley Perkins married second, Mary Baker of Dedham,
Mass., September 3d, 1821. She died in 1845, an issue of
three children.

1003*   WESLEY PERKINS,[8] b. June 20, 1822; d. Nov. 10, 1890.

1004*   MARY REBECCA H.,[8] b. Nov. 10, 1823.

1005   ELIZABETH C.,[8] b. Nov. 3, 1829; d. unm. in 1845.

Wesley Perkins married for his third wife a widow, Mrs.
Eliza A. Brackett, October 10, 1847, by whom he had two
children. She died at Lowell, Mass., August 29, 1892.

1006*   WILLIAM HENRY,[8] b. Apr. 3, 1849; unm. living in California.

1007*   ELIZABETH ARABELLA,[8] b. Sept. 23, 1851.

Wesley Perkins when a young man went to Medfield and
worked in a bakery. The firm for whom he worked failed.
and he commenced business for himself, which he carried on
successfully for many years. He was an enterprising, and
useful citizen, serving in several important town offices. He

was one of the principal supporters of the Baptist Church in
Medfield.

481. Phebe,[7] daughter of 236 John[6] and Phebe [Harmon]
Balch, was born at Beverly, Mass., April 18, 1797. She married Mr. Joseph Marshall, and lived at Medfield, Mass. She
had at least two children. Mary and Rebecca. Mary m.
Dr. Burpee, of Malden, now deceased.

483. John,[7] son of 236 John[6] and Phebe [Harmon] Balch,
was born at Beverly, Mass., May 1, 1801, and died in 1868, at
Boston, and was buried at Medfield. In 1827, he married
Miss Abigail Fairbanks, she was born at Medfield. For a
time they resided at Medfield, and then removed to Boston.
They had two children, both were born at Medfield.

1008* JOHN F.,[8] b. in 1829; d. Aug. 24, 1869.
1009   ELIZA E.,[8] b. in 1835; unm. is living at Boston.

484. Benjamin,[7] son of 236 John[6] and Phebe [Harmon]
Balch, was born January 11, 1804, at Quincy, Mass., and died
of pneumonia at Providence, R. I., April 28, 1888. His occupation was that of a baker. He was married four times : for
his first wife he married Chloe Smith, April 17, 1826. She
was born at Medfield, Mass., July 1, 1805, and died at Providence, R. I., May 12, 1837. She was the mother of four children.

1010* SARAH CLARK,[8] b. Sept. 5, 1827; d. May 20, 1853.
1011   CHOLE SMITH,[8] b. Sept. 20, 1829; d. Sept. 30, 1829.
1012   CLARISSA SMITH,[8] b. May 18, 1831; d. Nov. 30, 1834.
1013* CLARA ANNA,[8] b. Sept. 3, 1834.

Benjamin was married a second time November 28, 1837, to
Frances N., daughter of Matthew Robinson. She was born at
South Kingston, July 15, 1811, and died at Providence, June
16, 1845. She was the mother of three children, all born at
Providence, R. I.

1014   MARIA FRANCES,[8] b. Dec. 6, 1841; d. Jan. 3, 1842.
1015   AMELIA FRANCES,[8] b. Apr. 10, 1843; d. Sept. 18, 1845.
1016   MARY ROBINSON,[8] b. Mar. 6, 1845; d. Apr. 11, 1848.

Benjamin married for his third wife, Alice H., daughter of
Jeremiah N. Potter, the ceremony was performed January 20,

1846. Alice H. was born at South Kingston, R. I., and died at Providence, May 12, 1847. She had no children.

Benjamin was married a fourth time on the 31st of August, 1848, to Louise, daughter of Benjamin H. Fales. She was born at Wrentham, Mass., April 30, 1820, and was living at Providence at the time of Benjamin's death. Benjamin, and Louise had five children, all born at Providence.

1017   CHARLES WESLEY,⁸ b. Aug. 26, 1850; d. Aug. 12, 1851.
1018   WILLARD FALES,⁸ b. June 10, 1852; d. June 29, 1852.
1019* LOUISE MAYNARD,⁸ b. Sept. 27, 1856.
1020* FRANK BENJAMIN,⁸ b. Oct. 23, 1859.
1021   EDWARD ROBINSON,⁸ b. Sept. 27, 1863; d. Feb. 3, 1866.

485. Ebenezer Harmon,⁷ son of 286 John⁶ and Phebe [Harmon] Balch, was born at Quincy, Mass., January 28, 1806, and died at Boston, Mass., December 9, 1878, and was buried at Upton, Mass. He was married three times. He married first in 1829, Miss Betsey Childs. She was born at Mendon, Mass., in 1811, and died May 31, 1830. No issue. He was married second, November 23, 1830, to Sarah, daughter of Colonel Evro, and Judith [Chapin] Wood. She was born at Upton, Mass., March 19, 1809, and died at Glen Cove, N. Y., August 21, 1865, and was buried at Upton. To Eben. ezer H. and Sarah, were born four children.

1022* JANE REBECCA,⁸ b. Nov. 26, 1832, at Worcester, Mass.
1023* SARAH MARIA,⁸ b. Nov. 16, 1834, at Providence, R. I.
1024* ANNA BETSEY,⁸ b. Sept. 4, 1837; d. Feb. 13, 1890.
1025* FRANK WOOD,⁸ b. Sept. 1, 1841.

Ebenezer H. for his third wife married Fannie Maria Boyle. She was born at Cheltenham, Eng., November 29, 1822, and died in New York city without issue, June 5, 1875. Ebenezer H., lived in many places, among them were Mendon, Worcester and Boston, Mass., Philadelphia, Pa., and New York, N. Y. He was also engaged in divers kinds of business. At one time he owned the South Danvers iron foundery.

489. Thomas,⁷ son of 239 Rev. Benjamin⁶ and Joanna [O'Brien] Balch, was born at Scarboro, Me., October 2, 1765, and died at Waterloo, N. Y., January 16, 1840. He was married Nov. 10, 1798, to Elizabeth, daughter of John

Kingman, the ceremony being performed by his father at
Barington, N. H.   Elizabeth Kingman, was born August 16,
1774, and died at Bariugton, April 21, 1802.   They had three
children.

1026* JOANNA,⁸ b. May 5, 1794; d. Oct., 1863.
1027* BENJAMIN,⁸ b. May 2, 1796; d. Jan. 28, 1869.
1028* DOLLY,⁸ b. Sept. 10, 1799; d. July 28, 1870.

Thomas was married a second time, December 6, 1803, to
Judeth [Swain] Perhens, a widow with two sons. Perkins
and Goram. She was born August 10, 1773.   They had three
children.

1029   ELIZABETH,⁸ b. Feb. 4, 1805.
1030* LUCY C.,⁸ b. Dec. 22, 1807.
1031   LUCRETIA,⁸ b. Dec. 16, 1814; d. Feb. 4, 1833.

Thomas served during the Revolution, in the navy. He
was with his father in the Paul Jones Squadron. He served
also on the Privateer "Hannible," of which his uncle Jeremiah O'Brien was the commander. He was taken prisoner
and confined in the Jersey Prison Ship, at New York. He
was serving on board the "Alliance" when she was in the
terrific fight with a British Ship and British Brig, off Halifax,
and captured them both.   He also served on board the ship
Boston.

490. Benjamin,⁷ son of 239 Rev. Benjamin⁶ and Joanna
[O'Brien] Balch, was born at Dedham, Mass., January 5, 1768,
and was drowned at sea, April 10, 1809. He was with his
father and brother Thomas in the Navy, the two boys being
counted as one man on the pay rolls. His occupation was a
shipmaster ; he never married.

491. Mary,⁷ daughter of 239 Benjamin⁶ and Joanna
[O'Brien] Balch, was born at Mendon, N. H., June 11, 1770,
and died at Calias, Me., August 30, 1855. She was married to
Benjamin J. Garland, of Barington, N. H., the ceremony being
performed by her father, January 18, 1790. Garland was born
at Barrington, July 11, 1767, and died at Hamstead, N. H.,
November 18, 1835. Mary and Benjamin had eight children,
all born at Barrington, N. H.

DENNIS, b. May 27, 1791; d. 1879, at Calais, Me., Sept. 20, 1847.
BENJAMIN B., b. Feb. 6, 1793.
JOANNA, b. Sept. 23, 1796.
MARY, b. Sept. 9, 1799.
MARTHA, b. March 16, 1802; d. same month.
SUSAN, b. April 21, 1803; d. at Joliet, Ill., Sept. 26, 1838; m. a
    Mr. Wing.
JOHN JAY, b. July 21, 1806; d. at Joliet, Ill., Sept. 30, 1845.
EMILY, b. March 24, 1815; d. at Kent, Mich., March 23, 1842; m.
    a Mr. Harris.

492. John,[7] son of 239 Rev. Benjamin[6] and Joanna
[O'Brien] Balch, was born September 4, 1772, and died August 5, 1843, at Lubec, Me., having driven up from Trescott.
That day he had a paralytic stroke, and died almost immediately. His remains were taken back to Trescott for interment. On the 28th of December, 1802, he was married to
Miss Hannah Stone, and by her had fifteen children. The
ten eldest were born at Bangor, the other five at Trescott.
She died on the 30th of December, 1829, aged 46 years.

1032* JOHN,[8] b. Nov. 14, 1803, at Bangor; d. Jan. 29, 1861.
1033 JOANNA,[8] b. March 25, 1805, at Bangor; d. March 17, 1828; unm.
1034* HIRAM AUGUSTUS,[8] b. Sept. 14, 1806, at Bangor; d. Jan. 29,
      1872.
1035 ABIGAIL,[8] b. Nov. 15, 1807, at Bangor; d. Aug. 24, 1808.
1036* REBECCA,[8] b. Feb. 7, 1809, at Bangor; d. Feb. 20, 1864.
1037* LOUIS,[8] b. March 27, 1810, at Bangor; d. Dec. 23, 1837; unm.
1038* CHARLES,[8] b. Sept. 1, 1811, at Bangor; d.
1039* HANNAH,[8] b. Dec. 1, 1812, at Bangor; d. 1865.
1040 GEORGE WASHINGTON,[8] } twins, b. Mar. 18, 1815, d. July 19,1816.
1041 HORATIO GATES,[8]   }   d. Apr. 1, 1834.
      born at Bangor.
1042* HENRY,[8] b. July 15, 1819, at Bangor.
1043* GEORGE,[8] b. May 18, 1821, at Trescott; d. May 18, 1861.
1044 SARAH ANN,[8] b. Oct. 9, 1822, at Trescott; d. Dec. 22, 1843.
1045* LAFAYETTE,[8] b. Feb. 3, 1825, at Trescott; d. Nov. 25, 1862.
1046* ALBERT GALLATIN,[8] b. March 10, 1827, at Trescott; d. unm.,
      1860.

John[7] married for his second wife the widow Susan Minot,
July 25, 1832. They had no children. John Balch resided
at Bangor, Me., until about 1820, when he met with reverses
in business, which caused him to remove to Trescott, where

he continued to live. He was an educated and Christian gentleman. He was a justice of the peace, and performed the marriage ceremony for a great many in the vicinity of Trescott.

493. William,[7] son of 289 Rev. Benjamin[6] and Joanna [O'Brien] Balch, was born January 17, 1775, and died at Dedham, Mass., August 31, 1842. He was a classmate of Dr. Channing and Judge Story at Harvard. He was a chaplain in the U. S. navy, serving on the Congress* and Chesapeake. He preached at Salisbury, Mass., 1802–1816, and at Salem, N. H., 1819–1835. On the 31st day of October, 1805, he was married to Mary, daughter of Rev. Benjamin Wadsworth, D.D. and LL. D., and his wife Mary [Hobson] of Danvers, Mass. Mary [Wadsworth] Balch died of consumption, June 27, 1816, aged 41 years. Two children was the issue of this marriage.

1047* MARY WADSWORTH,[8] b. Aug. 10, 1806; d. April 11, 1881.
1048 ELIZABETH,[8] b. July 18, 1812; d. Dec. 28, 1834; m. Dr. Abraham Dearborn, of Methume, Jan. 18, 1834.

William married second, July 10, 1822, Miss Sarah, daughter of Isaac and Sarah C. Eaton, of Dedham. They had one son.

1049 BENJAMIN WADSWORTH,[8] b. Oct. 10, 1823; d. unm., at Chicago, Ill., Sept. 18, 1858.

494. George Washington,[7] son of 239 Rev. Benjamin[6] and Joanna [O'Brien] Balch, was born at Danvers, Mass., October 16, 1777, and died at Welden, N. C., June 21, 1826. He married Elizabeth Noble, of Portsmouth, N. H., and they moved to Weldon, N. C., where he engaged in mercantile business. In the war of 1812 he was sailing master on board a privateer, was captured, and imprisoned a year in Dartmoor.

All the children of George W. and Elizabeth died young, except one, who died at Boston, Mass.

1050. ELIZABETH,[8] b.   ; d. unm. 1839.

---

*Navy Dept. records.
Wm. Balch was appointed Chaplain to the " Congress," October 30, 1799, and discharged May 10, 1801.

495. **Horatio Gates,**[7] son of 289 Rev. Benjamin[6] and
Joanna [O'Brien] Balch, was born at Danvers, Mass., October 16, 1777, and was baptized with his twin brother, George
W., by the Rev. Mr. Holt, at Danvers, Oct. 26, 1777. He
died at Lubec, Me., in 1850. He studied medicine, and was
a physician of marked ability. The early part of his life was
spent in and near Bangor, where he married his first wife,
Miss Rhoda Dutton, a sister of Judge Dutton, a lawyer of
considerable note at Bangor. Horatio G. was quite prominent in politics, was a Democrat up to Van Buren's administration, when he became a Whig. He was a member of the
Legislature at Boston, before Maine was a separate state, and
also the first Representative from Washington county after
Maine became a state. In 1820 he was living at Lubec, Me.
In 1821 or 2 he moved to Machias, Me., and soon after received the office of high sheriff, which he held till 1830,
when he moved to Lubec again. That year he received the
appointment of inspector of customs at Lubec, under Jackson's administration, which office he held about nine years.
He was a member of the Congregational Church. He was
very benevolent, as many since his death have given testimony to his kindness and consideration of the poor. By his
first wife, Rhoda Dutton, he had eight children.

1051	HORATIO,[8] b.	; d., s. p., about 1845.
1052	GEORGE,[8] b.	; d., s. p., about 1845.
1053*	HARRIET,[8] b.	; d.
1054*	SOPHIA,[8] b.	; d.
1055	ELIZABETH,[8] b. in 1814; d., unm., in 1830.	
1056	JAMES,[8] b.	; drowned while skating at Machias.
1057*	EMILY,[8] b. Aug. 8, 1820; d. Dec. 13, 1892.	
1058	ANDREW,[8] b.	; drowned at sea.

Horatio G. married for his second wife Harriet Tanner Mc-
Lellan, of Portland, Me. To them were born three children.
Harriet T. died at Brooklyn, N. Y.

1059	EBENEZER MCINTOSH,[8] b.	; d. y.
1060*	JAMES RIPLY,[8] b. Nov. 22, 1831; d. April 18, 1895.	
1061*	HORATIO GATES,[8] b. June 15, 1840; d. March 7, 1894.	

496. **Joanna,**[7] daughter of 289 Rev. Benjamin[6] and Jo-

anna [O'Brien] Balch, was born July 3, 1780, and died in
1866. She was twice married. Her first husband was a Mr.
Stephens ; her second husband was Deacon Webster, of Salisbury, a relative of Daniel Webster. Joanna had one daughter, whether by her first or second husband is not known. Joanna inherited part of the manuscript sermons of her father
and grandfather.

497. Martha,[7] daughter of 239 Rev. Benjamin[6] and Joanna [O'Brien] Balch, was born Jan. 19, 1783, and died at
Methuen, Mass., in February, 1866. She was married on the
8th of June, 1806, to Richard Hackett, of Salisbury, Mass.
The marriage ceremony was performed by her father, the
Rev. Benjamin Balch. Hackett was born at Salisbury, and
died in that town, October, 21, 1814, at the age of thirty
years. He followed the occupation of his father, John
Hackett, who was a ship-builder, and built the U. S. ship Alliance. They had four children: James; Horatio Balch,
b. Dec. 27, 1808; d. Nov. 2, 1875; John, b. November,
1810 ; d. Aug. 16, 1815 ; Richard.

Martha married for her second husband Deacon Davidson.

498. Jeremiah O.,[7] son of 239 Rev. Benjamin[6] and
Joanna [O'Brien] Balch, was born at Barrington, N. H., July
31, 1785, and died at Chicago, Ill., November 4, 1875. His
remains were taken to Marshall, Mich., for interment. He
was married twice. His first wife was Sarah Penniman,
daughter of Jacob and Mary O'Brien Penniman, of Machias,
Me. They had four children.

1062* JACOB WILLIAM,[8] b. Nov. 19, 1817; d. Nov. 1, 1883.
1063* MARY CYNTHIA,[8] b. Oct. 12, 1820; d. 1874.
1065* HENRY CRAWFORD,[8] b. Dec. 18, 1824; d. July 30, 1861.
1066* FRANCIS STORMS,[8] b. Sept. 5, 1826; d. Aug., 1888.

Jeremiah O. married in the fall of 1827, for his second
wife, Elizabeth A. Haskell, daughter of Reuben S. Haskell.
She was born in 1806, and died at Marshall, Mich., in 1865.
To them were born five children.

1067 JEREMIAH O.,[8] b. Aug. 1, 1828; d. May 22, 1843.
1068 SARAH ELIZABETH,[8] b. July 16, 1830; d. Oct. 23, 1841.

1069* GEORGE WASHINGTON,[3] b. May 24, 1832.
1070* BENJAMIN,[3] b. Dec. 8, 1840; d. March 3, 1884.
1071* LAVINIA MELISSA,[3] b. June 25, 1843; d. July 12, 1887.

Jeremiah O. Balch moved to western New York about 1825. He first engaged in mercantile pursuits, but later, it being better suited to his education, he became an editor and publisher, as well as a practical printer. He published various newspapers in western New York, principally in Rochester. About 1835 he moved to Illinois, and later to Michigan, where his family followed in the spring of 1836. He was here considered one of the foremost and ablest editors of his day in Michigan. His work was chiefly done on the States-man and Telegraph, at Marshall, and the Whig, at Ann Arbor. In politics he was first an old-line Whig, and when the Republican party was formed joined its ranks and became a most staunch and energetic supporter of its principles. His was a trenchant pen, and a most scathing one when battling for his party. In the war of the rebellion he was universally for the Union, and notwithstanding his advanced years, did good service for the cause through the press. Nor was his hatred of disloyalty confined entirely to words, for when nearly or quite 80 years of age he raised his cane in the physical rebuke of disloyal utterances by a neighbor, with such effect as to break it, whereupon his loyal fellow-citizens and friends procured a very handsome new stick and present-ed it to him with much formality and words of high appro-bation. The last work on his paper was in denunciation of Andrew Johnson.

He was an accomplished Latin scholar and linguist, and was respected by the editorial fraternity and all as an upright and honorable citizen.

501. **Phineas Carleton,**[7] son of 250 Jonathan[6] and Abigail [Carleton] Balch, was born at Newburyport, Mass., June 20, 1797, and died at Rowley, Mass., January 24, 1880. He was a deacon in the church at Byfield, and was a christian gen-tleman of quiet virtues. He filled wisely and well many offices of trust in the town and church, and was highly

respected and beloved by all who knew him.   He married Jane
Kezer, daughter of Samuel and Olive [Kezer] Merrill of
Byfield.   She was born May 24, 1797.   They had but one child.

1072* REBECCA BAILEY,⁸ b. 1821.

502.   Leonard,⁷ son of 250 Jonathan⁶ and Abigail [Carle-
ton] Balch, was born at Newburyport, September 18, 1799,
and died at Groveland, Mass., August 9, 1871.   He was married first, July 8, 1823 to Mary A., daughter of Eben Hopkinson.   She died September 30, 1848, aged 45 years.   One
daughter was the issue of this marriage.

1073* ABIGAIL CARLETON,⁸ b. June 25, 1825.

For his second wife, Leonard married Hannah J. Parsons.
She was born in 1799, and died July 8, 1855, no issue.   On the
3rd of March, 1859, he took to himself a third wife, Reasanna
P., daughter of John and Nancy [Brown] Hooper, of Water-
borough, Me.   She was living at Groveland in 1886.

503.   William,⁷ son of 250 Jonathan⁶ and Abigail [Carle-
ton] Balch, was born at Newburyport, May 7, 1802, and died
October 25, 1841.   He was married May 3, 1825, to Abigail
B., daughter of Nathaniel Parker.   She was born at East Bradford, Mass., July 24, 1806, and died March 6, 1869, at North
Bridgewater, near Brockton, Mass.   After her husband's death
she resided at Groveland, but the last eight years of her life
she lived with her daughter, Clara M., in Richmond, and East
Machias, Me., and later at North Bridgewater.

William and Abigail had two children.

1074* MELVIN PARKER,⁸ b. Nov. 27, 1832, at E. Bradford.
1075* CLARA MARIA,⁸ b. Sept. 10, 1840; d. July 1, 1896.

505.   Thomas Hutchinson,⁷ son of 250 Jonathan⁶ and
Mehitable [Carleton] Balch, was born at East Bradford,
March 20, 1807.   On the 12th of November, 1838, he married
Sophia Buck, daughter of William and Abigail [Jaques]
Tenney of Groveland.   She was born May 7, 1811.   Thomas
H. and Sophia had seven children.

1076* WILLIAM,⁸ b. Oct. 9, 1840.
1077* HIRAM TENNEY,⁸ b. May 28, 1842.

THOMAS HUTCHINSON BALCH.

(505)

1078* CHARLES THOMAS,[3] b. Feb. 23, 1844; unm.
1079* ARTHUR CLIFFORD,[3] b. Oct. 22, 1846.
1080* EUSTIS,[3] b. Apr. 2, 1849.
1081 SOPHIA PRISCILLA,[3] b. Aug. 2, 1851; d. in June, 1855.
1082* GARDNER PICKARD,[3] b. July 7, 1856.

Thomas Hutchinson was a farmer, and superintendent of the burial ground at Groveland; also proprietor of " Balch Grove," a popular picnic ground on the Merrimac River. This grove gave the name to the town. It is a fine tract of pine-clad hills, and level ground, and can be reached by steamer on the river where there is a wharf for landing, or on the other side by a street railway, which connects Haverhill with Groveland about three miles distant. It was formerly known as " Uncle Billy's Grove." Thomas H. inherited this property from his uncle 249 William[6] whom he took care of in his old age. The old house in which the 58 Rev. William,[4] 127 Deacon William,[5] and his uncle 249 William,[6] had lived, he tore down and built a new one in which he resides at this time.

506. Jonathan,[7] son of 250 Jonathan[6] and Mehitable [Carleton] Balch, was born at East Bradford, October 5, 1808, and died November 15, 1892, at Groveland. He was married March 20, 1829, to Sally, daughter of Paul and Sally [Morse] Hopkinson, a cousin to his brother Leonard's wife. She was born September 24, 1810. They celebrated their golden wedding March 20, 1879, more than one hundred and fifty guests were present. Mr. Balch was great hearted, broad and liberal in his opinions. He stood against the slave power, when it cost reputation and caste to be an abolitionist. He was a great lover of music and was connected with a band of music in early life. As a neighbor and friend he was among the best, and as a husband and father he was not excelled by any in the community. He was thoroughly honest, upright and substantial.

Jonathan was a boot and shoemaker, and resided at Groveland. To him and his wife were born ten children.

1083* SARAH HUTCHINSON,[8] b. Sept. 21, 1829.
1084* HORACE MORSE,[8] b. Feb. 24, 1831; d. Sept. 14, 1892.

1085° ANN MARY,⁶ b. Nov. 17, 1832.
1086   GARDNER L.,⁶ b. Dec. 14, 1834; d. Jan. 12, 1835.
1087   GARDNER L., 2d,⁶ b. Feb. 9, 1836; d. Aug. 10, 1840.
1088° HARRIET LAPHAM,⁶ b. Aug. 28, 1838; d. Jan. 31, 1898.
1089   LEVERETT H.,⁶ b. May 18, 1841; d. June 4, 1844.
1090   LOUISA H.,⁶ b. June 9, 1843; d. Feb. 6, 1846.
1091   PRISCILLA K.,⁶ b. Aug. 14, 1845; d. Feb. 29, 1848.
1092° FRANK HENRY,⁶ b. July 18, 1851.

509.   Louisa,[7] daughter of 253 Benjamin[6] and Lois [Phippen] Balch, was born at Salem, Mass., July 12, 1802, and died June 1, 1887. She was married January 31, 1822, to Hon. George Savary, son of Maj. Thomas and Polly [Rollins] Savary, of Bradford, Mass. He was born January 30, 1793, and died March 28, 1854. He was State Senator from Essex. In 1848 he was candidate for Lieut. Governor.

Savary was a boot and shoe manufacturer, and trader at Groveland where he resided. Louisa was the mother of nine children, all born at Groveland.

> MARTHA WINGATE, b. May 10, 1823, m. Eldred, son of Dr. Benjamin Parker, in 1845; no children.
> GEORGE THOMAS, b. July 28, 1826, m. first, Margaret C., daughter of John Tappan; m. second, Jennie Goodale; children, *Annie Louise,* b. May 10, 1863, unm.; *George,* b. July 7, 1865. He is a minister in the Reform Episcopal church, at Newark, N. J.; m. Henrietta L. Johnson of Boston.
> FRANK, b. Sept. 5, 1829; m. June 14, 1861, to Esther A. Barnard of Worcester; children, *Caroline A.,* b. Jan. 24, 1864, an artist; *Martha P.,* b. Nov. 4, 1865.
> CLARA LOUISA, b. July 9, 1831; d. in infancy.
> MARY ROLLINS, b. Apr. 15, 1831; d. in infancy.
> WILLIAM HENRY, b. April 19, 1835. Graduated from Yale, 1857, is a Unitarian minister, and is pastor of the Dorchester St. Chapel, South Boston; m. a daughter of Rev. George W. Hosmer, D. D.; children, *Edward Hosmer,* a lawyer; *Sarah Kendall,* a teacher.
> LUCY ANN, b. in 1836; d. y.
> CLARA LOUISA, b. Dec. 24, 1837; unm.
> BENJAMIN BALCH, b. Apr. 17, 1840; m. Oct. 30, 1873 to Abby Dorr, of Medford; children, *Nellie Louise,* b. Dec. 27, 1890.

510.   Benjamin,[7] son of 253 Benjamin[6] and Lois[Phippen] Balch, was born at Salem, Jan. 25, 1804, and died in the same town where he always resided, November 5, 1863. On the

12th of February, 1829, he married Caroline L., daughter of
David and Mary [Pratt] Moore of Salem. She died June
13, 1880, in the 75th year of her age. Benjamin was a master mariner in the East India trade. Shortly after his marriage
he went as mate of the Glide to the Fiji Islands. The ship
was totally wrecked in a hurricane, and the crew, except a
few, killed. He was held by the natives, at that time utterly
barbarous, for over two years. They curiously tattooed his
hands, feet and portions of his body, and the colors held
bright to the day of his death. The story is told in a small
book entitled "The Wreck of the Glide." He was for some
voyages captain of the celebrated ship George, a clipper of
great local fame in the Calcutta trade. He was also wrecked
on the coast of Zululand, South Africa. Hot and unhealthy
climates broke down his constitution and he was an invalid
for several years. Benjamin and Caroline had three children.

1093 BENJAMIN FRANKLIN,⁸ b. April 18, 1833 ; d. Mar. 6, 1838.
1094* DAVID MOORE,⁸ b. Jan. 22, 1837.
1095* EDWARD FRANKLIN,⁸ b. Nov. 27, 1842 ; d. Aug. 29, 1892.

511. James,⁷ son of 253 Benjamin⁶ and Lois [Phippen]
Balch, was born at Salem, February 21, 1806, and died at
Half Day, Ill., in November, 1846, while on a visit to his
brother. He married Harriet Jane, daughter of Captain
William and Sarah Fowler [Herrick] Duncan, of Salem.
The ceremony was solemnized by Rev. Bishop Griswold,
June 27, 1833. She was born Sept. 21, 1807, and died Jan.
16, 1873. James was a watchmaker with his father in Sa-
lem. They had four children.

1096* WILLIAM DUNCAN,⁸ b. Sept. 28, 1834.
1097* CATHERINE D.,⁸ b. Sept. 22, 1836 ; d. February, 1892.
1098 ANNIE FOWLER,⁸ b. Sept. 28, 1839 ; d. unm. Mar. 14, 1887.
1099 JAMES,⁸ b. May 17, 1846 ; d. y. Oct. 17, 1847.

512. William,⁷ son of 253 Benjamin⁶ and Lois [Phip-
pen] Balch, was born at Salem, Mass., February 1, 1808, and
died in 1887. He was a clerk, and a farmer, and lived at Providence, Pawtucket, R. I., Chelsea, Mass., and Half Day, Ills.
He married twice, first in 1834 to Miss Marian Kittredge,

daughter of Dr. Benjamin Kittredge of Salem, by whom he
had seven children. She died May 27, 1849, aged 85, and
in the following year he married Miss Susan Thayer of Boston. There was no issue by his second marriage. Widow
living at Roxbury, Mass.

1100* WILLIAM FREDERICK,[8] b. July 16, 1836 ; d. Mar. 31, 1868.
1101* LUCY ANN,[8] b. Aug. 17, 1837 ; d. Oct. 21, 1881.
1102 BENJAMIN K.,[8] b. Nov. 5, 1840 ; drowned after 1865. d. s. p.
1103 EDWARD AUGUSTUS,[8] b. in Ills.; d. unm. in Cal.
1104* LOWELL THAYER,[8] b. Ills. May 21, 1848.
1105 LOUISA M.,[8] b.   ; d. y.

513. Moses Phippen,[7] son of 253 Benjamin[6] and Lois
[Phippen] Balch, was born at Salem, July 23, 1810. He
resided at many places in several states, and died March 13,
1888. On the 18th of August, 1839, he married Miss Adelia
M. Lauriet, of Chicago, daughter of the celebrated aeronaut.
She died April 19, 1887. Moses P. and Adelia had nine
children.

1106* GEORGE PHIPPEN,[8] b. June 18, 1840.
1107 ADEL MARIA,[8] b. June 18, 1842; unm.
1108* SARAH ELIZABETH,[8] b. Jan. 1, 1844.
1109 CLARA HUDSON,[8] b. Feb. 27, 1846 ; d. unm. Dec. 30, 1893.
1110 JAMES HENRY,[8] b. Oct. 4, 1849 ; unm.
1111 AUGUSTA L.,[8] b. Aug. 4, 1851 ; unm.
1112 LUCY ANN,[8] b. July 2, 1853; unm.
1113* LAURA OCTAVIA,[8] b. Jan. 18, 1858.
1114 LOUISA L.,[8] b. July 27, 1860.

514. Clarissa,[7] daughter of 253 Benjamin[6] and Lois
[Phippen] Balch, was born at Salem, June 22, 1812, and
died Feb. 28, 1842. She married in 1839 Charles Hodge, son
of John Rogers and 519 Hannah [Balch] Hudson. Charles
married for his second wife Mary Snowman, by whom he
had a son Charles; for his third wife he married Mary
Brooks. He is now living in New York City. Clarissa was
the mother of three children, Clara L., b.   ; d. William
Henry, b. in 1840 ; d. Annie, b. April 23, 1842 ; d.

518. Henry Freeborn,[7] son of 253 Benjamin[6] and
Lois [Phippen] Balch, was born at Salem, November 24,
1820. Was a mariner, sailed with his brother Benjamin.

Left the sea and lived for a time in Illinois. He went to California in 1852, and now lives at Knight's Ferry. He is the owner of a vineyard and fruit ranch, in Stainlaus Co., Knight's Ranch. He married Sarah, daughter of Elijah Fuller. No issue.

519. Hannah,[7] daughter of 257 Daniel[6] and Lucy [Hodge] Balch, was born at Newburyport, Oct. 14, 1784, and died at the same place March 20, 1828. She was married January 9, 1810, to John Rogers Hudson, son of Henry and Anna [Rogers] Hudson. He was born at Newburyport September 19, 1784, and died at Newburyport, April 15, 1831. Hannah and John R. had eight children. John Rogers, b. Nov. 15, 1810; d. 1888. Charles Hodge, b. Jan. 17, 1812; m. 514 Clarissa Balch. Lucy Ann, b. Oct. 5, 1813; is a Homœopathic physician. Fanny Elizabeth, b. Feb. 26, 1815; d. Feb. 7, 1816. Fanny Elizabeth, b. Feb. 3, 1817; d. Jan. 5, 1875; Mary Rogers, b. May 14, 1819. Henry James, b. June 29, 1821; graduated from Harvard, and afterwards from the Divinity School, and was a Unitarian clergyman; living at Plattsburg, N. Y. Sarah Hodge, b. Nov. 14, 1823; d. Oct. 29, 1856.

520. Elizabeth,[7] daughter of 257 Daniel[6] and Lucy [Hodge] Balch, was born at Newburyport, Mass., March 18, 1786, and died in that town, Oct. 17, 1873. She never married. She was remarkable for her great love of books, and desire for self improvement. She was given to works of charity, and fervently religious, a member and communicant of the Unitarian church.

521. Charles Hodge,[7] son of 257 Daniel[6] and Lucy [Hodge] Balch, was born at Newburyport, Mass., October 29, 1787, and died in the same town, November 18, 1852. He was for many years a selectman of Newburyport, and a representative in the state legislature. For two years he was state senator. In politics he was a Federalist. Although he received but a moderate schooling, he was a great reader, and was a self-made man. He was an attendant at the Unitarian church. He never married.

522. Daniel,[7] son of 257 Daniel[6] and Lucy [Hodge] Balch, was born at Newburyport, June 16, 1790, and died in the same town, November 17, 1858. He married Elizabeth, daughter of Ebenezer Gunnison. She was born at Dorchester, Mass., August 10, 1796, and died at Newburyport, November 16, 1863. For a time Daniel resided at Dorchester, and then at Newburyport. In politics he was a Federalist, and in church creed a staunch Unitarian. ˙When a young man, with a friend, he built an organ on which his brother William learned to play. Neither of the young men had ever learned the trade. Daniel and Elizabeth had four children, the eldest was born at Dorchester, the others at Newburyport.

1115* EBENEZER GUNNISON,[8] b. Sept. 18, 1819; d. Jan. 14, 1834.
1116* LUCY ELIZABETH,[8] b. Nov. 14, 1820; d. Apr. 16, 1867.
1117   CHARLES HODGE,[8] b. Nov. 5, 1822; d. unm. Aug. 7, 1845.
1118   SARAH HODGE,[8] b. Feb. 3, 1825; unm.

524. William,[7] son of 257 Daniel[6] and Lucy [Hodge] Balch, was born at Newburyport, Mass., July 20, 1795, and died in the same town, of pneumonia, January 26, 1886. On October 11, 1818, he married Hannah, daughter of Ebenezer Stone. She was born at Newburyport, December 14, 1796, and died in that town, March 8, 1864. William and Hannah had eleven children.

1119* WILLIAM CHARLES,[8] b. July 8, 1819; d. Feb. 12, 1895.
1120* SARAH STONE,[8] b. Feb. 5, 1821; d. Apr. 25, 1848.
1121* GEORGE EDWARD,[8] b. Aug. 7, 1822; d. Aug. 28, 1889.
1122* LEONADAS,[8] b. Aug. 7, 1824.
1123* LUCY HODGE,[8] b. Apr. 15, 1826.
1124   CHARLES CARROL,[8] b. Apr. 24, 1827; d. Sept. 1, 1827.
1125* ELIZABETH,[8] b. Sept. 6, 1828.
1126* MARY CAROLINE,[8] b. Oct. 18, 1829.
1127* HANNAH STONE,[8] b. Aug. 28, 1834.
1128* FANNY STONE,[8] b. Jan. 2, 1837.
1129* CHARLES CARROL,[8] b. May 9, 1841; d. unm. Aug. 27, 1863.

He was a man of strong sense and will, and one who had made his own fortune. During a long life he had commanded the universal respect, and he enjoyed the friendship, of a wide circle, and his advice in business matters was sought by many. While quite young he entered the store of Henry

WM. BALCH.

(524)

Frothingham, hardware dealer, as a clerk, and about 1822, he established himself in the same business, in Newburyport, and remained in trade for about fifteen years, and early in his career became interested in foreign freighting, which he carried on with the late Edmund Swett, and after retirement from the hardware business, he became part owner in a good many ships, trading to foreign ports. Mr. Balch also became interested in cotton manufacture, and was one of the first to introduce it in Newburyport. He had an interest in the Bartlett and Ocean Mills, and was for many years a director of the James, now the Victoria mill. He was also for a number of years a director of the Merchants Bank, a director of the Newburyport Mutual Fire Insurance Company, and Vice President of the Institute for Savings, which latter place he resigned about a year before his death, on account of age and increasing infirmities. He was a noted accountant and kept his own accounts by double entry. For more than half a century he was one of the active supporters of the First Religious Society, in Newburyport, filling many of its offices, and more than sixty years ago was organist of the church. Mr. Balch had a strong constitution, having never required the advice of a physician until he was taken with pneumonia a week before his death, though he had been gradually failing in strength for several years. He retained his faculties wonderfully until the last.

525. John Theodoric,[7] son of 257 Daniel[6] and Martha [Tarbox] Balch, was born at Newburyport, October 13, 1799, and was christened John Tarbox. He died February 24, 1847. He was considered quite a wit, and a star in society in his youth. He married Elizabeth Jones, daughter of George Thacher, of Biddeford, Me. Her father was a member of Congress from Massachusetts from April, 1789 to March, 1801, and at the time of his death was judge of the Supreme Judicial Court of Massachusetts. Mrs. Elizabeth Jones [Thacher] Balch was a very superior woman. They had five children.

1130* GEORGE THACHER,[8] b. Oct. 2, 1828, at Biddeford, Me.; d. April 15, 1894.

1131* THEODORIC AUGUSTUS,⁸ b. Jan. 16, 1832, at New York city.
1132* DANIEL WEBSTER,⁸ b. Nov. 14, 1834, at New York city.
1133* ELIZABETH THACHER,⁸ b. Dec. 27, 1837, at New York city.
1134* LAURA OTIS,⁸ b. Sept. 23, 1845, at Akron, Ohio.

532. Joseph,⁷ son of 261 John⁶ and Eunice [Bartlett] Balch, was born at East Bradford, December 5, 1785, and died at Boston, December 10, 1849. He was President of the Merchants Insurance Co., of Boston, from the time of its establishment to the day of his death, a period of over thirty years. No man in the city was more highly respected for the excellence of his private character, as well as for the promptness and fidelity with which he dispatched the business of his office. In the knowledge of the laws of Insurance, and their adaptation to business he had no superior. On the 13th of December, 1811, he married Caroline Ann Buckminster, daughter of Joseph Williams of Newburyport. She was born December 19, 1789, and died May 24, 1825. They had six children.

1135* CAROLINE WILLIAMS,⁸ b. Mar. 16, 1813.
1136 ANN BUCKMINSTER,⁸ b. Aug. 24, 1814; unm.
1137* SARAH BARTLETT,⁸ b. Nov. 24, 1817; d. Sept. 9, 1854.
1138* JOSEPH WILLIAMS,⁸ b. Aug. 3, 1819; d. Jan. 11, 1891.
1139 SUSAN WILLIAMS,⁹ b. June 28, 1821; unm.
1140 SOPHRONA,⁸ b. Mar. 20, 1823; d. unm. Feb. 16, 1883.

Joseph married for his second wife, Anne Lathrop, daughter of Dr. Nathan, and Sally Noyes of Newburyport, the ceremony was performed on the 22d of January, 1827. She was born December 21, 1801, and died at Cohasset, Mass., August 26, 1880. Joseph and Anne L. had five children.

1141 EUNICE ANN,⁸ b. Jan. 30, 1831; unm.
1142 MARY NOYES,⁸ b. Nov. 26, 1832; d. Apr., 1833.
1143 JOHN,⁸ b. Apr. 3, 1835; unm.
1144 FRANCIS,⁸ b. June 30, 1836; d. Sept. 11, 1836.
1145* FRANCIS VERGNIES,⁸ b. Feb. 3, 1839.

533. Eunice,⁷ daughter of 261 John⁶ and Eunice [Bartlett] Balch, was born at East Bradford, August 7, 1787. She married Enoch, son of Capt. Paul, and Mary [Jewett] Moody, of Byfield Parish, Mass. He was born July 21, 1772, and died in 1837. They resided at Hollowell, Me., and Newburyport, Mass. They had six children.

JOSEPH BALCH.
(1839).

ANN MEHITABLE, b. April 23, 1818, m. Isaac G. Braman, M. D., who married second 1135 Caroline Williams[6].

EUNICE BALCH, b. July 15, 1821; m. Joseph Williams, of Wilbraham, a school teacher.

SOPHRONIA LITTLE, b. April 20, 1824; m. Nathaniel Dole, her cousin, a broker, lived in New York city, Yonkers, N.Y., and Newburyport, Mass.

JOHN BALCH, b. Jan. 25, 1827; d. Sept. 12, 1837.

SARAH BALCH, b. Aug. 2, 1828; d. unm. Apr. 15, 1845.

JOHN HORACE, b. Mar. 7, 1831; d. Was in insurance business in New York city, and resided in Yonkers, where he died. He had two children. *Sophronia Moody*, b. 1853; *Caroline Moody*, b. 1856.

534. Hannah,[7] daughter of 261 John[6] and Eunice [Bartlett] Balch, was born at East Bradford, January 3, 1789. She married Ebenezer, son of Nathaniel, and Mary [Noyes] Dole, of Newburyport. Dole was a merchant at Hollowell, Me., and died there in 1847. Hannah was the mother of five children.

EBENEZER, b. in 1815; d. unm. June 7, 1846; graduated at Brunswick College, and Bangor Theological Seminary. He died at Hollowell.

HANNAH BALCH, b. May 19, 1817; died at Jamaica Plain, Mass., unm.

NATHANIEL, b. May 17, 1819, m. his cousin, Sophronia Little Moody. He was a stock broker in New York city, lived in Brooklyn, and Yonkers, N. Y., and Newburyport, Mass.

ANN BALCH, b. Apr. 16, 1822, m. Jules Stanis Lous De Lacroix, a planter, born at Rose Dale, La.

MARY BALCH, b. Oct. 16, 1824; unm.

535. Sarah,[7] daughter of 261 John[6] and Eunice [Bartlett] Balch, was born at East Bradford, December 21, 1790, and died at Georgetown, Mass., February 8, 1893. On March 22, 1837, she was married to Rev. Isaac Braman, of Georgetown, being his second wife. Rev. Dr. Braman was pastor of the South church for a period of sixty years, loved, honored and revered, and during this long pastorate he never received a salary exceeding $400 per annum. Dr. Braman died December 26, 1856, in his 89th year. Mrs. Braman visited Newburyport when in her 94th year. During the summer of her 98th year she attended church and visited among her neighbors. She retained her faculties remarkably and was a most

delightful and agreeable conversationalist and a very intelligent companion. Her memory was very accurate, and
she could readily locate all the different branches of her
family. She narrated with great vividness the scene of the
great fire in 1811, in Newburyport. She remembered "Lord"
Timothy Dexter, as he appeared on the streets with cocked
hat and cane, and wearing a blue cloak lined with a bright
red material ; of going to his funeral and seeing his dead
"lordship" in his coffin with his sword laid upon it, and many
other incidents in the life of this eccentric man. Mrs.
Braman held a reception upon her 102d birthday and over
one hundred persons paid her their compliments. She was
cheerful and in good health. About two weeks later when
walking across the room she fell, breaking her right arm near
the shoulder.   This accident upset her whole physical economy and she rapidly failed and died at the ripe old age of 102
years, 1 month and 18 days. She never had any children.
The funeral services were conducted by Rev. John Rounds
Smith, pastor of the Memorial Church, in which he was
assisted by several of her former pastors.

536. Sophronia,[7] daughter of 261 John[6] and Eunice
[Bartlett] Balch, was born at Newburyport, February 14,
1793, and died in that town, June 24, 1872. She was married
January 24, 1814, to Josiah, son of Josiah and Sarah [Tappan]
Little, of Newburyport. Little was born January 13, 1791,
graduated at Bowdoin in 1811, was an extensive land owner
and engaged in manufacturing, served two terms in the State
Senate of Massachusetts, was eminently a public spirited man,
and gave largely to benevolent objects. No issue.

538. Lydia Pillsbury,[7] daughter of 261 John[6] and
Eunice [Bartlett] Balch, was born at Newburyport, March 1,
1797, and died October 2, 1870. She was married April 15,
1822, to Jeremiah Pearson, son of Sewell, and Lydia [John-
son] Tappan. He was born July 6, 1795, and died April 7,
1869. He was President of the Marine Insurance Co., New
York city. They resided at Brooklyn, N. Y., and had seven
children.

MRS. SARAH (BALCH) BRAMAN.
(535)

JOHN SEWELL, b. June 28, 1823, marine ins. underwriter, m.
  Susan, daughter of Charles W. Storey, of Newburyport, June
  2, 1847. No issue.
SARAH ELIZABETH, twin to John S., m. Robert Dodge Merrill,
  United States Consul to Australia. No issue.
LYDIA BALCH, d. y.
LYDIA BALCH, b. Jan. 7, 1829, m. Reuben Langdon, of N.Y. city,
  had two children, both died young.
MARY NELSON, b. June 14, 1831, m. John Wheelwright. No
  issue.
JEREMIAH NELSON, b. in 1833, d. Sept. 5, 1884, m. Mary Pearson
  Spencer; three children. Was a commission merchant in N.
  Y. city, and held the important office of City Chamberlain.
FRANCES ROLLINS, b. Jan. 3, 1838, m. Stephen H. Tyng, Jr.; two
  children.

540. Mary,[7] daughter of 261 John[6] and Eunice [Bartlett]
Balch, was born at Newburyport, April 17, 1800. She was
married in April, 1831, to Hon. Jeremiah Nelson of Rowley,
Mass. He was born September 18, 1768, and died October 2,
1838. He graduated at Dartmouth College in 1790, and was a
merchant at Newburyport, and a member of Congress for many
years. They had four children. Mary Balch, b. May 29,
1832; Elizabeth Meyhill, b. Feb. 8, 1834 ; d. unm. June 14,
1851; Jeremiah, b. June 2, 1836 ; John, b. Jan. 6, 1839.

541. Lucy,[7] daughter of 261 John[6] and Eunice [Bartlett]
Balch, was born at Newburyport, October 11, 1801, and died
July 20, 1885. She was married twice, first October 11, 1821,
to Charles, son of Benjamin French, he was born March 4,1797,
and died April 4, 1825, leaving his widow with two children.

  BENJAMIN, b. Aug. 17, 1822; d. Aug. 12, 1847.
  CHARLES, b. Aug. 19, 1825; d. unm., Nov. 26, 1846.

For her second husband, Lucy married, September 28,
1835, Ebenezer, son of Dea. Benjamin, and Lydia [White]
Hale. He was born October 4, 1774, in Atkinson, N. H.,
and died February 19, 1848. They resided at Newburyport,
and had three children.

  LUCY BALCH, b. June 9, 1836, m. October 29, 1855, Benjamin,
  son of Benjamin, and Caroline [King] Hale. He was liberally educated, studied medicine and law, was a farmer at Newbury, Vt., and is now living at Newburyport, Mass. They

have had two children, *John White,* b. June 12, 1858. Graduated from the Chandler Scientific School, Dartmouth College in 1881, and is an inventor. He married Charlotte E. Mace, Nov. 10, 1892, and resides in Newburyport, Mass. *Mary Alice,* b. March 6, 1873; d. Aug. 8, 1873.

EBENEZER, b. Dec. 9, 1839; d. July 23, 1840.

EBENEZER THOMAS, b. May 9, 1842; d. Sept. 7, 1868.

542. John,[7] son of 261 John[6] and Eunice [Bartlett] Balch, was born at Newburyport, April 14, 1808, and was run over and killed at Topsfield, July 11, 1871, while feeding his horse. The horse took fright and ran, throwing him to the ground and the carriage wheel passed over his neck. For a time John was a dealer in leather, then he became agent and treasurer for the Bartlett steam mills, of Newburyport, also a director in the Ocean Bank, and president of the Mutual Insurance Company, of Newburyport. He was married first to Elizabeth, daughter of Sewall and Lydia [Johnson] Tappan. She was born August 5, 1804. By her he had four children.

1146   JULIA NORRIS,[8] b. Aug. 17, 1825; unm.
1147*   LUCY FRENCH,[8] b. Nov. 22, 1827; d. May 30, 1852.
1148   JOHN,[8] b. June 30, 1830; d. Oct. 15, 1835.
1149*   ELIZABETH TAPPAN,[8] b. Sept. 19, 1832.

John married again in 1834, Miss Laura Amelia Denny. She was born September 3, 1807, and died in July, 1886. By her he had five children.

1150*   ISAAC DENNY,[8] b. April 18, 1835; d. Feb. 16, 1889.
1151   LAURA A. D.,[8] b. Oct. 14, 1838; living at Newburyport, unm.
1152*   ALICE MARCH,[8] b. Sept. 16, 1840.
1153   JOHN SEWALL,[8] b. March 28, 1844; d. at Calcutta, Aug. 27, 1861.
1154*   MARY NELSON,[8] b. July 29, 1846.

543. Benjamin,[7] son of 261 John[6] and Eunice [Bartlett] Balch, was born at Newburyport, April 16, 1805, and died September 24, 1880. He was married in Boston, April 27, 1830, to Lydia Elizabeth Williams, who was born December 20, 1809. They lived in New York city, but the last few years of his life Benjamin passed in his native city. Benjamin and Lydia E. had four children.

JOHN BALCH.
(542)

WILLIAM SAVORY BALCH.
(546)

1155° MARIA WILLIAMS,[8] b. Jan. 28, 1831.
1156° FRANCES CAROLINE,[8] b. Feb. 28, 1833.
1157 CHARLES O.,[8] d. without issue.
1158 CHARLES TILTON,[8] d. without issue.

Benjamin was engaged in the insurance business. He was a remarkable man, far seeing and somewhat eccentric. His eccentricity rose to such a degree that his mind became somewhat unbalanced. He was considered one of the ablest statisticians in the country. Our present national banking law is nearly word for word as he designed it and advocated long before the civil war. He organized the first life insurance company in the country. The Pacific railroad schemes were originated by him before they were dreamed of by others. For more than fifty years he advocated the Darien ship-canal. A writer said of him : " He was called insane, but he knew more than any sane man he had ever met, particularly on the subject of banking and insurance."

546. William Savary,[7] son of 265 Samuel[6] and Betsey [Savary] Balch, was born at Portsmouth, N. H., December 15, 1799, and died at Groveland, January 22, 1871. He was married June 4, 1823, to Mary, daughter of Deacon Daniel and Sarah [Balch] Stickney, of East Bradford. She was his second cousin, and was born at East Bradford, June 22, 1800, and died at Groveland, February 2, 1874. Their eleven children were born at East Bradford, now Groveland, Mass., in the old William Savory house.

1159 AGNES E.,[8] b. Sept. 6, 1824; d. unm., Jan. 4, 1874. She lived with her father at Groveland, where she died.
1160° WILLIAM HEMAN,[8] b. Aug. 17, 1826; d. Sept. 19, 1886.
1161 SARAH S.,[8] b. July 7, 1828; d. Sept. 27, 1830.
1162 SAMUEL P.;[8] } twins, b. Oct. 3, 1830; d. y.
1163 DANIEL S.,[8] }
1164° DANIEL STICKNEY,[8] b. Dec. 11, 1831.
1165 GEORGE HENRY,[8] b. Feb. 16, 1833. Is a deaf mute, and lives on the old homestead in Groveland.
1166 SARAH HELEN,[8] b. July 20, 1835; unm., lives with George Henry.
1167° JOHN KIBBY PERRY,[8] b. Feb. 17, 1837.
1168 EDWARD PAYSON,[8] b. July 18, 1840; was a deaf mute, and was drowned in a tan vat in his father's yard.

1169   LOUIS,⁵ b. June 19, 1843; d. unm., Oct. 10, 1880; was a farmer,
        and lived upon the old homestead in Groveland.

William Savary resided at Groveland [East Bradford]
upon the estate of his maternal grandfather William Savory. He was a member of the State Legislature for several
terms, and filled many public offices of the town and parish.
His business was that of a tanner and dealer in boots and
shoes. He was generally called captain.

548. **Mary Elizabeth,**⁷ daughter of 265 Samuel⁶ and
Hannah [Widden] Balch, was born at Portsmouth, N. H.,
June 1, 1804, and died at Woburn, Mass., December 12, 1851.
She married first, June 27, 1822, Charles, son of Samuel and
Ann [Andrews] Wyman, of Woburn. Their six children
were all born at Woburn.

> CHARLES HENRY, b.   ; d. y.
> FRANCES, b. Feb. 19, 1825; m. Charles Thwing, a farmer at West
>   Boxford, Mass.
> MARY ELIZABETH, b. May 1, 1827; m. Sept. 8, 1853, Levi H. Rood
>   of La Salle county, Ill. He was born at Litchfield, Ct., Jan.
>   15, 1803, and died at La Salle, Ill., June 17, 1875.
> ANNA, b. June 15, 1829; m. Aug. 31, 1851, Claud B. King. He
>   was born May 25, 1825. They had ten children.
> CHARLES and CHARLES HENRY, twins, b.   ; d. y.

Mary Elizabeth⁷ married for her second husband, Moses
Morrill, of Woburn. He was born at Canaan, Vt., April 15,
1812, and died at Peabody, Mass., Jan. 8, 1857. By occupation he was a tanner and currier. The issue of this marriage
was three children.

> EDWIN, b. March 8, 1840; was killed at battle of Sabine Cross
>   Roads, La., April 8, 1864.
> JULIA, b. Feb. 20, 1842; m. Loren Augustus Perkins, of Prairie
>   du Sac, Wis., March 18, 1860. They have three children.
> MARTIE, b. July 3, 1850; is living with sister Julia in Wisconsin.

549. **Mehitable Melcher,**⁷ daughter of 265 Samuel⁶
and Hannah [Widden] Balch, was born at Portsmouth, N.
H., August 10, 1806, and died at the same town, August 20,
1873. She married about 1824, Samuel Cate, son of George
and Mary [Cate] Hodgdon. He was a farmer. They resided
at Portsmouth until after the birth of their three eldest chil-

dren, when they removed to Georgetown, Mass. where the other four were born. Then they returned to Portsmouth.

> GEORGE WILLIAM, b. in 1826; m. Ann Leach, of Kittery, Me. She d. at Groveland. They had ten children.
>
> NATHANIEL BALCH, b.   ; d. at Oak Alla, Ill., Dec. 14, 1857; m. Feb. 27, 1851, Lucindia Perley, daughter of Samuel and Letice [Sanborn] Verrill, of Minot, Me. She was born at Minot, Aug. 1, 1831. They resided at Oak Alla, Iroquois county, Ill., and had two children, *Nellie May*, b. Dec. 31, 1856; *Frank Edward*, b. May 1, 1858; d. June 28, 1866. Nathaniel's widow m. for her second husband 534 Samuel[7].
>
> ALFRED, b.   ; m. Emily Libby. They resided at Valley Springs, Dakota. Three children.
>
> HARRIET LAVINA, b.   ; d. in Canada; m. Charles Adams. Three children.
>
> SARAH, b. in 1838; d. at Portsmouth, June 14, 1860; m. first, John Neal, of Portsmouth; m. second, Charles Farrell, of Portsmouth. One child.
>
> HARLAN PAGE, b.   ; m. Miss Pickering, of Portsmouth. Two children.
>
> HENRY, b.   ; d. aged four years.

550. Nathaniel,[7] son of 265 Samuel[6] and Hannah [Widden] Balch, was born at Portsmouth, N. H., September 9, 1808, and died in that town, June 3, 1876. He was married April 8, 1835, to Elizabeth M., daughter of Mihil Tucker, of Portsmouth. She was born at Portsmouth, May 9, 1812. Their four children were all born at Portsmouth.

> 1170   WILLIAM WALLACE,[8] b. March 30, 1839; d. July 21, 1858, at sea, on a voyage from New Orleans to Liverpool, Eng.
>
> 1171* EDWARD H.,[8] b. Dec. 24, 1840.
>
> 1172   GEORGE T.,[8] b. Feb. 20, 1846; d. unm. March 1, 1869.
>
> 1173* MARTHA ELLEN,[8] b. March 30, 1851.

552. Eunice Jane,[7] daughter of 265 Samuel[6] and Abigail [Bartlett] Balch, was born at Portsmouth, N. H., August 23, 1822, and died at Cohasset, Mass., September 12, 1860. She married Squire L., son of Jonathan and Martha [Bartlett] Gove, of Deering, N. H. They had one son, George Gove, b. Aug. 19, 1857; d. Feb. 23, 1858.

554. Samuel,[7] son of 265 Samuel[6] and Abigail [Bartlett] Balch, was born at Portsmouth, N. H., September 28, 1825; died December 4, 1893, and was buried on the 7th, at

Groveland. He was a carpenter, and lived at Groveland,
Mass. Deacon Balch was one of the best of men, upright,
honorable, and sympathetic. He was quiet and unassuming,
but firm as a rock for the right. To him conviction was duty,
and he never faltered in doing what his hands found to do.
He was a member of the Congregational Church, and for
many years was one of its most respected deacons. He was
married first, October 13, 1855, to Miss Hannah Holton,
daughter of Thomas and Deborah [Perley] Savary, of East
Bradford. She was born March 26, 1825, and died at Groveland, November 24, 1860. No children.

Samuel married second, September 24, 1861, Lucindia Perley, widow of Nathaniel Balch Hodgdon, his nephew. No
children.

FIRST BRANCH.

Descendants of 5 Samuel.[1]

555. Joseph,[8] son of 277 Samuel[7] and Mercy [Atwood] Balch, was born in the town of Shoreham, Vt., and died at Frankfort, N. Y., about 1828. He married Miss Betsey Shrove by whom he had three sons, all of whom were born at Frankfort, N. Y.

1174[e] CHRISTOPHER S.,[9] b. Aug. 19, 1821; d. Oct. 22, 1861.
1175[e] JOHN HENRY,[9] b. Apr. 26, 1825; d. May 30, 1869.
1176[e] EBENEZER ATWOOD,[9] b. Mar. 26, 1827; d. Jan. 16, 1892.

556. John,[8] son of 277 Samuel[7] and Mercy [Atwood] Balch, was born at Athens, Vt., October 29, 1798, and died at Frankfort, N. Y., August 4, 1847. He was married January 1, 1825, to Margaret, daughter of Joseph and Catherine Hadcock. She was born at Deerfield, N. Y., December 15, 1806, and died at Utica, N. Y., May 18, 1887. John was a farmer and lived in the town of Frankfort. His nine children were born in that town.

1177   CALISTA A.,[9] b. Jan. 13, 1826; d. Oct. 17, 1882.
1178[e] JOSEPH,[9] b. Dec. 3, 1828.
1179[e] ANDREW J.,[9] b. Feb. 17, 1831; d. Dec. 30, 1889.
1180   WILLIAM W.,[9] b. July 21, 1833; d. May 24, 1887.
1181   AMELIA S.,[9] b. Nov. 18, 1835; d. Mar. 26, 1890.
1182[e] MARCUS D.,[9] b. Aug. 5, 1838.
1183   ESTHER MIRANDA,[9] b. Apr. 1, 1840; d. Feb. 1, 1859.
1184[e] ROSELLE,[9] b. Mar. 3, 1844.
1185   EUGENIE,[9] b. Feb. 13, 1847.

557. Delia,[8] daughter of 277 Samuel[7] and Mercy [Atwood] Balch, was born in 1800, and died at Utica, N. Y.

She married Joseph Tame and had three sons and four daughters.

558. Ebenezer,[8] son of 277 Samuel[7] and Mercy [Atwood] Balch was born about 1802 and died about 1868. He married, but had no children.

559. Adaline,[8] daughter of 277 Samuel[7] and Mercy [Atwood] Balch, was born April 15, 1804. She married a Mr. Houghton, and had sons and daughters, some of whom lived in Kenosha, Wis.

560. Olive,[8] daughter of 277 Samuel[7] and Mercy [Atwood] Balch, was born March 2, 1806, and died about 1876. She married Joseph Brown, her sister Abigail's widower. No issue.

561. Abigail,[8] daughter of 277 Samuel[7] and Mercy [Atwood] Balch, was born at Guilford, Vermont, January 4, 1791, and died January 8, 1853. She married, March 13, 1815, Joseph Brown, and had several children, one of whom, Mercy, married a Mr. Smith, and lived at Rodman, Jefferson Co., N. Y.

562. Mercy,[8] daughter of 277 Samuel[7] and Mercy [Atwood] Balch, was born March 2, 1812. She married twice but had no children. Her last husband was a Mr. Johnson. She was living in Somers, Wis., in 1891.

564. Charlotte,[8] daughter of 278 Josiah[7] and Sarah [Kimball] Balch, was born December 27, 1798. The date of her death is not known. She married James Greely. They lived at Lyndon, Vt., and had two children. James, m., lived at West Dedham, Mass., where he died leaving a widow and four children. Charlotte, m. George Bennett. They live at St. Johnsbury Center, Vt.

566. Sarah,[8] daughter of 278 Josiah[7] and Mercy [Sterns] Balch, was born March 11, 1808, and died November 23, 1884. She married Erastus Graves and lived at Lyndonville, Vt. Graves was born February 8, 1808, and died August 4, 1888. They had two daughters, both living unmarried at

Lyndonville, Vt. Susan M. Graves, b. Dec. 24, 1832 ; Rosaline Graves, b. Jan. 1, 1834.

567. Philander,[8] son of 278 Josiah[7] and Mercy [Sterns] Balch was born at St. Johnsbury, Vt., May 21, 1812, and died May 30, 1885. He was married September 24, 1838, to Jane A. Robinson, and had five children. They lived at Charlestown, Vt.

1186   Marium,[9] b.
1187   Martha,[9] b.
1188   Frederick,[9] b.
1189   Mercy,[9] b.   ; d.
1190* Emma M.,[9] b.

569. Leonard,[8] son of 278 Josiah[7] and Mercy [Sterns] Balch, was born December 8, 1816, and died at Baton Rouge, La. He enlisted in the 8th Vermont Infantry Volunteers, and died while in the service. He married Betsey, daughter of Samuel and Phebe Smith. She was born at Lyndon, Vt., December 22, 1816 ; and died May 8, 1898. To them were born four children at Lyndon, Vt.

1191   Charles N.,[9] b. Mar. 5, 1844; d. May 31, 1865.
1192   Adeline,[9] b. Nov. 24, 1847.
1193* Romanzo,[9] b. June 14, 1852.
1194   William,[9] b. Mar. 19, 1860; d. Mar. 9, 1872.

570. Mary Wilson,[8] daughter of 281 Nathaniel[7] and Sally [Bennett] Balch, was born at Athens, Vt., August 31, 1806, and died December 15, 1875. She was married to Jonathan Towne of Rockingham, Vt., February 25, 1835, the ceremony was performed by Chester W. Levings, a minister of the gospel.

571. Nathaniel Aldrich,[8] son of 281 Nathaniel[7] and Sally [Bennett] Balch, was born at Athens, Vt., January 22, 1808, and died at Kalamazoo, Feb. 1, 1894. Hon. Nathaniel A. Balch was endowed with a wonderful memory. When 17 he began life as a teacher. He graduated from Middlebury College with high honors in 1835. He was principal of Bennington Academy for two years, and during his spare time read law in the office of Gov. John S. Robinson. In 1837, he

moved to Kalamazoo, Mich., and became principal of the Huron
Institute, now known as the Baptist College. He was admitted
to the bar of the state of Michigan in 1840, and in 1842 was
elected prosecuting attorney for Kalamazoo Co., and the same
year was appointed by the circuit Judge to the same office
in Barry Co. He filled the office of president of the Kalamazoo Bar Association with credit and honor for more than
thirty years. He was licensed to practice before the Supreme
Court of the United States. In 1847 he was elected to the
State Senate for two years, where he exhibited great diligence
and caution. He was postmaster under Buchanan's administration for four years. He was engaged in over twenty murder trials some of which had national notoriety. Eminently
patriotic he has contributed to public and philanthropic enter-
prises liberally. He was a professed Christian in the Presbyterian church, a devout Bible student, an instructive Sabbath
School teacher, and an earnest friend of the temperance cause
and every other moral reform. He married first, Sarah M.,
daughter of Rev. Walter and Hannah [Mosher] Chapin. She
was born at Woodstock, Vt., May 14, 1817, and died at Kalamazoo, Mich., April 12, 1848. She was an accomplished lady
and a profound scholar. Nathaniel A. and Sarah M. had three
children all born at Kalamazoo.

1195* H. Anna,* b. July 12, 1840.
1196* Walter O.,* b. Apr. 9, 1843; d. Dec. 22, 1876.
1197 S. Eliza,* b. Oct. 12, 1845; d. Nov. 2, 1848.

In 1849, Nathaniel A. married his second wife, Miss Elizabeth E. daughter of Samuel and Eliza [Boyd] Dungan, of
Philadelphia, Pa. She was born at Philadelphia in 1825, and
died at Kalamazoo, January 8, 1880. She was a highly
accomplished lady, knew the French and Spanish languages,
was a remarkable conversationalist, a fine student of history, and possessed an extensive knowledge of great men,
both living and dead. They had two children.

1198 William Sidney,* b. Aug. 22, 1850; d. Oct. 15, 1850.
1199 Gertrude E.,* b. June 11, 1852; d. June 25, 1861.

The home of Nathaniel A. Balch was proverbial for the hospitality there extended. His mind was remarkably active nearly to the last.

572. Sarah Chamberlain,[8] daughter of 281 Nathaniel[7] and Sally [Bennett] Balch, was born at Athens, Vt., January 15, 1810, and died at the same town November 26,1841. She was married to the Rev. Hubbard Eastman, a Methodist minister, March 16, 1836. He was a son of John and Elizabeth Eastman, and was born at Grafton, Vt., January 22, 1809. They had but one child. Sarah L. Eastman, b. at Athens, April 9, 1838. She married first Edward, son of William and Hannah Gorton, May 28, 1862. He was born in the state of N. Y. Aug. 4, 1832, and died at Pepin, Wis., April 12, 1874. They had four children. Lottie E., b. July 20, 1866, at Kalamazoo, Mich.; Hugh H., b. May 14, 1870, at Pepin, Wis., d. Aug. 16, 1870 ; David E., b. June 10, 1871, at Pepin, Wis. ; Nellie A., b. May 25, 1874, at Pepin, Wis.

The widow Gorton married for her second husband, Oliver P. Carruth, January 31, 1880. He was born Sept. 8, 1828, at Lorraine, N. Y. No issue.

573. Drexa Webb,[8] daughter of 281 Nathaniel[7] and Sally [Bennett] Balch, was born at Athens, Vt., December 25, 1811, and died at St. Charles, Ills., June 18, 1887. She was buried in the North Cemetery at St. Charles. On April 18, 1837, she was married to Charles Haile, son of Amos and Nancy [Skinner] Haile. He was born at Acton, Vt., November 26, 1808. Haile was a farmer, and they lived at Brookline, Vt., until after the birth of their three eldest children, when they removed to St. Charles, Ills., where they had two more children. Charles Walter, b. May 13, 1838, d. Nov. 21, 1844 ; James Omar, b. Nov. 20,1839, d. March 26, 1863, at Vicksburg, Miss. A soldier in the Union army, and one of Gen. Steele's body guard. Nathaniel Amos, b. March 8, 1842. A member of the 27th Ills. Vols. served through the war, now living at Maple Park, Ills. Occupation a miller. Sarah D., b. June 19,1845, d. Oct. 9,1888, m. a Mr. Daly. Harriet L., b. Sept. 29, 1847, m. a Mr. Wright.

This family are Baptists, and Republicans in politics.

574. Samuel Raymond,[8] son of 281 Nathaniel[7] and Sally [Bennett] Balch, was born at Athens, Vt., March 22, 1814, and died at El Dorado, Kansas, Aug. 2, 1890. He was married May 12, 1858, at Kalamazoo, Mich., to Elizabeth Kendell, daughter of Albert and Betsey [Kendell] Woods· She was born at Windsor, Vt., April 6, 1826, and died at Kalamazoo, Nov. 29, 1866. Their seven children were all born at Kalamazoo.

1200* HERBERT MELVILLE,[9] b. July 13, 1854.
1201   SARAH ELVA,[9] b. Oct. 20, 1856; d. July 21, 1857.
1202* ELMER ADELBERT,[9] b. Sept. 25, 1857.
1203* LAURA ALICE,[9] b. Sept. 15, 1859.
1204   ALBERT SIDNEY,[9] b. Apr. 24, 1862.
1205* WILLIAM ARTHUR,[9] b. Aug. 28, 1864.
1206   URIEL KENDELL,[9] b. Oct. 17, 1866.

Samuel R. was a farmer and lived for many years at Kalamazoo, he then removed to El Dorado, Kansas. He was married a second time at Michowaka, Mich., to Mrs. Sarah B. Finley, no issue.

575. Lovina Cummins,[8] daughter of 281 Nathaniel[7] and Sally [Bennett] Balch, was born at Athens, Vt., December 30, 1815, and died September, 1895. She married Samuel C. Easau of Springfield, Mass., March 27, 1842. They had two daughters, Mary Lovina, b. Oct., 1844, d. at Kalamazoo, Mich., aged 17 years; and Alice. Soon after their marriage they moved to St. Charles, Ills., where their two daughters were born. They afterwards moved to Shermen, Texas.

576. Royal Tyler,[8] son of 281 Nathaniel[7] and Sally [Bennett] Balch, was born at Athens, Vt., December 17, 1817, and died at Oshtemo, Mich., September 12, 1884. On July 4, 1844, he was married to Miss Ruthana Grimes, daughter of Micah and Abigail [Woolly] Davis, at Athens, Vt., where she was born, October 26, 1826. She died at Oshtemo, Mich., September 28, 1889. They had seven children.

1207* JANE MARIA,[9] b. Sept. 18, 1845.
1208   RUTHANA AUGUSTA,[9] b. Sept. 12, 1847.

1209* SARAH LORINDA,[9] b. Nov. 29, 1849.
1210* ABBY ADELLA,[9] b. July 16, 1852.
1211* ROYAL CURTIS,[9] b. Apr. 26, 1856.
1212* EMMA MAY,[9] b. Aug. 21, 1858.
1213* ERNEST ALANSON,[9] b. June 23, 1867.

Royal Tyler was born upon the farm purchased by his grandfather. He possessed a mild disposition, but was firm in his convictions of right, and labored to improve the neighborhood in which he lived. He never used intoxicants or tobacco. He taught several terms of school successfully. In 1860 he joined the M. E. church at Oshtemo, continued a faithful member of the same until his death, and for many years he served as steward and trustee. He also was Sunday-school superintendent and class leader. As a neighbor he was loved and respected by all, as a husband loving and true, as a father he was kind and indulgent, no pains were spared nor labor unexpended if his family could be benefited thereby. He gave all his children the privilege of a liberal education, often saying, "An education is something that no one can take from you." He moved to Michigan in 1850, and purchased a farm near Kalamazoo, in which vicinity he lived until his death.

577. **Sybil Maynard**,[8] daughter of 281 Nathaniel[7] and Sally [Bennett] Balch, was born at Athens, Vt., November 22, 1819, died March 31, 1891, at St. Charles, Ill. She was married January 20, 1846, to Harlow, son of Gustavus A. and Pamela [McArthur] Hooker. He was born at St. Andrews, Prov. of Quebec, April 11, 1818. His mother, Pamela McArthur, was the daughter of Peter McArthur, a brother of Charles McArthur, father of Mrs. Mary Balch, wife of 309 Alvah Burchard Balch. Hooker follows the occupation of farming, and both he and his wife were members of the M. E. church. Their children were born in St. Charles. Adelbert Harlow, b. Oct. 4, 1847, d. Apr. 10, 1892. Adolphus Nathaniel, b. Feb. 22, 1849. Ceton Icilious, b. May 7, 1853. Emmarilla Augusta, b. Nov. 23, 1854. Lydia Annette, b. Aug. 21, 1857.

578. Amaziah Robinson,[8] son of 281 Nathaniel[7] and Sally [Bennett] Balch, was born at Athens, Vt., December 18, 1821, and died at Wayland, Mich., May 29, 1872. He was married first in 1846, to Abby, daughter of Micah and Abigail [Woolley] Davis, of Athens, Vt. She died June 7, 1851, leaving one son.

1214* DORR MICAH,[9] b. Jan. 11, 1848, at Athens, Vt.

In 1861 Amaziah married his second wife, Miss Mary Williams, formerly of Canada. The issue of this marriage was five children.

1215   EDGAR DOUGLASS,[9] b.   ; d. y.
1216   CORA BELLA,[9] b.
1217* NATHANIEL AMAZIAH,[9] b. Feb. 18, 1866.
1218   JAMES BIRD,[9] b.
1219* MARY ELIZABETH,[9] b. Jan. 9, 1872.

579. Arad Chickering,[8] son of 281 Nathaniel[7] and Sally [Bennett] Balch, was born at Athens, Vt., November 30, 1828. He was married April 20, 1853, to Elizabeth O., daughter of Daniel and Hannah [Pool] Emerson. She was born February 18, 1829, at Plainfield, N. H. To them have been born nine children.

1220* EMERSON B.,[9] b. Mar. 26, 1854.
1221* FRANK C.,[9] b. Oct. 4, 1855.
1222   SALLIE O.,[9] b. Oct. 12, 1857; d. Jan. 4, 1861.
1223   DANIEL W.,[9] b. Oct. 17, 1859; d. Jan. 3, 1861.
1224   LUCY J.,[9] b. July 18, 1861; d. Feb. 6, 1864.
1225   GRACE E.,[9] b. June 11, 1865; d. Dec. 3, 1871.
1226   GUY F.,[9] b. Oct. 31, 1866; d. Dec. 1, 1871.
1227* GLENN E.,[9] b. May 11, 1869.
1228* RALPH,[9] b. July 31, 1873.

Arad C. was postmaster at Dowagiac, Cass Co., Mich. for the two years of 1848-9, he has been Marshal, and for several years justice of the peace for Kalamazoo Co. He served in the Civil War as Captain of Co. "G" Thirteenth Regt. Mich. Vols. He was commissioned October 8, 1861, and resigned January 20, 1868. He was in command of his company at the battles of Shiloh, Stevenson, Perryville and Stone-River.

Arad C. is now engaged in farming, apiculture, and stock-raising at Kalamazoo.

580. Confucius Icilious,[8] son of 281 Nathaniel[7] and Sally [Bennett] Balch, was born at Athens, Vt., March 26, 1826. On April 10, 1852, he was married to Caroline A., daughter of Daniel and Emily [Loomis] Ryther.   She was born at Canton, N. Y., March 28, 1833. Their five eldest children were born at St. Charles, Ills., the two youngest at Kalamazoo.

1229   EMILY A.,[9] b. Mar. 1, 1855.
1230   SARAH A.,[9] b. Aug. 20, 1856; d. Nov. 21, 1859.
1231   CLARA O.,[9] b. Mar. 27, 1858.
1232   HERBERT B.,[9] b. Dec. 1, 1860.
1233   GEORGE R.,[9] b. June 20, 1862.
1234   LOUIS N.,[9] b. Apr. 28, 1865.
1235   CHARLES N.,[9] b. April 6, 1867; unm. a book-keeper at Chicago.

Confucius I. is a builder by trade, but is now engaged in farming and livery at Kalamazoo. He raises fine horses on his farm.

583. Coben,[8] son of 283 Coben[7] and Patty [Patch] Balch, was born at Guilford, Vt., May 2, 1807, and died at Grand Rapids, Mich., February 2, 1868. He was a farmer and lived at Irving, Mich.   In February, 1832, he married Amanda E., daughter of Jonathan and Polly Houghton. She was born November 1, 1811, and died November 8, 1863. They had eight children.

1236   COBEN,[9] b. Sept. 17, 1832; d. Sept. 19, 1832.
1237   MARTHA P.,[9] b. Feb. 10, 1834.
1238   MARY E.,[9] b. Nov. 7, 1837.
1239   SARAH A.,[9] b. Mar. 29, 1840; d. Sept. 30, 1869.
1240   HERMAN P.,[9] b. Nov. 3, 1842; d. y.
1241   WAITSTELLE B.,[9] b. Oct. 24, 1845; d. y.
1242   JOHN,[9] b. May 18, 1848; d. y.
1243   EUGENE H.,[9] b. March 8, 1850; d. Feb. 25, 1852.

Coben was an extensive dealer in cattle, and often went to Grand Rapids on business. On the first day of February, 1868, he stopped at a hotel in that town for dinner, it was not a house at which he had ever stopped before, the beef put upon the

table was exceedingly tough, and he remarked that it was some
of an old steer he used to have in his breaking team.   The
landlord hearing the remark was infuriated, and coming to
Coben's back attacked him, and before Coben could help himself had him upon the floor, and was jumping upon him.   The
man was taken off, and Coben was removed to another hotel.
Inflammation set in and on the following day he died.   The
landlord was tried and sentenced to prison for life.   Coben was
a strong man and well able to have protected himself had he
had a chance.

584.   Barnabas Dodge,[8] son of 283 Coben[7] and Patty
[Patch] Balch, was born at Athens, Vt., May 9, 1809, and died
November 30, 1872.   He was married first to Phebe Brown of
Barton, Vt., she died at Kalamazoo, Mich.   She was of Quaker
descent from Providence, R. I.   No issue.

He married a second time November 7, 1847, Miss Adeline
Ketchum.   She was born at Buffalo, N. Y., January 1, 1826.
They had three children, now living at Kalamazoo.

1244   PHEBE ELIZA,[9] b. Dec. 3, 1848.
1245* MARIA E.,[9] b. Feb. 1, 1851.
1246   HENRY DODGE,[9] b. Dec. 3, 1856.

588.   Sarah Marion,[8] daughter of 283 Coben[7] and Patty
[Patch] Balch, was born at Athens, Vt., March 26, 1817, and
died at Kalamazoo, July 8, 1891.   She married Henry Bishop
and had four children, three of them died in infancy.   Lucius
Bishop, b. April 2, 1848, m. and has two children, Charles
and Henry.

590.   Luther Chickering,[8] son of 283 Coben[7] and Patty
[Patch] Balch, was born at Athens, Vt., February 1, 1826,
and died May 7, 1888.   He was married to Sarah A. Pointer,
who was born September 12, 1828, and is now living at Kalamazoo.   The issue of this marriage was two children.

1247* FLORENCE GERTRUDE,[9] b. Nov. 28, 1851.
1248* CHARLES L.,[9] b. Jan. 14, 1855.

592.   Frederick,[8] only son of 285 Samuel[7] and Eunice
[Moses] Balch, was born at Salem, Mass., September 8,

1817, and died March 15, 1896. He had a beautiful home at West Somerville, and was a carpenter, doing business at Boston. He was a prohibitionist in politics, and an earnest Christian. In 1845, he was married to Hannah J., daughter of Cushman and Tabitha Perry, who was born at Charlestown, Mass., Nov. 8, 1817. They had five children born in Boston.

1249* JAMES F.,[9] b. Nov. 12, 1847; d. June 14, 1889.
1250* LYDIA A.,[9] b. Jan. 6, 1849.
1251* HANNAH M.,[9] b. Feb. 21, 1850; d. Feb. 22, 1891.
1252 JOSEPH,[9] b. June 20, 1852; d. Mar. 18, 1854.
1253 JOSEPH,[9] b. Aug. 24, 1859; unm.

593. Matilda,[8] daughter of 285 Samuel[7] and Eunice [Morse] Balch, was born at Salem, Mass., about 1820, and died at Boston, April 19, 1875. She was married April 30, 1840, to Joseph Lyon, of Hubbardston, Mass. He died in November, 1869. They had six children.

> CAROLINE M., b. Feb. 2, 1841, at Boston; m. Jan. 31, 1867, Albert Hall of Marshfield, Mass., a son of Luke and Elsie Hall. He was b. Dec. 31, 1839; issue one son, *Albert Percival*, b. at Chicago, Ills., Feb. 15, 1870.
>
> LUCY A., b. Nov. 6, 1843, at Boston; m. H. Floyd Faulkner, Nov. 27, 1867; he was born in Maine, and d. Sept. 25, 1875. They had four children, *William Floyd*, b. Nov. 10, 1868; *Eunice Florence*, b. Apr. 11, 1873; *Hollis Moore*, b. Sept. 10, 1874; d. Sept. 23, 1875; *Helena Kent*, b. Feb. 11, 1876; d. Aug. 20, 1876.
>
> JOSEPH, b. Feb. 17, 1845; m. Sept. 3, 1872, Miss Hattie S., dau. of Edward and Mary Parmenter, of Boston; she was b. Sept. 4, 1850; they had six children, *Joseph Willis*, b. Sept. 18, 1873; *Herbert Edward*, b. Nov. 17, 1875; *Fred Oscar Gray*, b. Mar. 20, 1878; *Hattie Alice*, b. Nov. 15, 1881; *Lester Packard*, b. Aug. 29, 1884; *Walter Mitchell*, b. Oct. 21, 1890.
>
> ASA, b. March 31, 1850; m. in Dec., 1880, to Alice Brown, who was b. in Maine, June 15, 1859; no issue.
>
> EUNICE MARIA, b. Feb. 9, 1853; m. Charles R., son of Jeremiah and Lucinda Robinson; he was born at Exeter, N. H., Oct. 21, 1844; they had two children, *Albert J.*, b. Nov. 1, 1876; d. Aug. 15, 1877; *Harold R.*, b. June 8, 1882, at Cambridge, Mass.
>
> FREDERICK BALCH, b. Apr. 12, 1861; d. unm. Mar. 4, 1887.

594. Almira,[8] eldest daughter of 286 Joseph[7] and Eliza [Legro] Balch, was born at Lancaster, N. H., December 19, 1811, and died at the same town, December 22, 1879. She was buried at Lancaster.

On January 1, 1840, she was married to James N., son of
Hezekiah and Abigail [Carr] Cloudman. He was born at
Rochester, N. H., December 10, 1811. They had four chil-
dren : Mary E. and Martha J., twins, b. Mar. 18, 1841 ;
Pircis A., b. Mar. 26, 1843 ; Joseph B., b. Nov. 30, 1845.

596. Amos,[8] son of 286 Joseph[7] and Eliza [Legro]
Balch, was born at Lancaster, N. H., November 1, 1815. He
always lived at Lancaster, and died there July 5, 1884. He
was married, November 30, 1841, to Esther A., daughter of
Luke and Sarah Woodward. She was born at Minot, Me.,
March 7, 1818, and died at Lancaster, January 2, 1880. Amos
was a farmer. Their four children were born at Lancaster.

1254* ADELINE R.,[9] b. Aug. 30, 1842.
1255* LUKE W.,[9] b. Dec. 23, 1846.
1256　HENRY H.,[9] b. Apr. 22, 1855; d. Feb. 11, 1857.
1257* EVA A.,[9] b. Jan. 3, 1858; d. Apr. 9, 1885.

597. Samuel B.,[8] son of 286 Joseph[7] and Eliza [Legro]
Balch, was born at Lancaster, N. H., July 11, 1817, and died
at Hollister, California, July 22, 1890. He was married
August 13, 1839, to Mary A. Holmes. She was born at
Jefferson, N. Y., January 20, 1814. She was a daughter of
Nathaniel and Mary Holmes. Their children were born at
Lancaster and Colebrook, New Hampshire.

1258* EMMELINE,[9] b. Oct. 22, 1841; m. M. C. Serles.
1259　EDGAR,[9] b. Nov. 3, 1845; d. Mar. 12, 1866; in the war three years.
1260　JANE,[9] b. June 15, 1847; m. Alfred Hurd.
1261* HARVEY,[9] b. Dec. 24, 1848.
1262* ADELAIDE,[9] b. Feb. 17, 1852; d. Oct. 21, 1894; m. F. E. Bilden.

600. Joseph H.,[8] son of 286 Joseph[7] and Eliza [Legro]
Balch, was born at Lancaster, N. H., March 7, 1822, and died
at New Iberia, Louisiana, December 2, 1869. He was married March 7, 1850, to U. S. Riles, a daughter of Joseph and
Celest [Dupny] Riles. She was born at Plaquemine, Louisiana, March 6, 1830, and died in the same town, December 12,
1861. They had six children, all born at Plaquemine.

1263* SARAH ADAMS,[9] b. Dec. 16, 1850.
1264　FRANK PIERCE,[9] b. July 3, 1852; d. Oct. 17, 1864.

1265* ELIZA C.,[9] b. Sept. 16, 1854.
1266* JOSEPH THOMAS,[9] b. June 7, 1856.
1267 LAURA C.,[9] b. Mar. 19, 1858; d. Apr. 8, 1860.
1268 M. HUBBARD,[9] b. Dec. 27, 1859; d. June 1, 1863.

On the 3rd day of July, 1862, Joseph H. married his second wife, the widow C. Olivia Marr, of Plaquemine, by her he had no issue. She was living at New Orleans, Louisiana, in 1888.

Joseph H. Balch studied law in the office of Gov. Williams at Lancaster, New Hampshire. About 1845 he went to Louisiana, and settled at Plaquemine. In 1864 he was a member of the State Legislature at New Orleans. In 1868 he removed to New Iberia, where he continued to reside till his death. Joseph H. Balch was one of the most prominent men in the community in which he lived, and was respected and beloved on account of his superior talents and amiable qualities. He died of pernicious malarial fever, leaving a widow and three children, upon whom the love and veneration of the community was most bountifully bestowed.

601. Frederick B.,[8] son of 286 Joseph[7] and Elizabeth [Legro] Balch, was born at Lancaster, N. H., February 16, 1825. On March 4, 1848, he married Thankful, daughter of John and Sarah Vincent, by whom he had one son, born at Manchester, at which place Frederick B. is now living.

1269 CHARLES,[9] b. Nov. 4, 1850; d. August 8, 1851.

603. Charles W.,[8] son of 286 Joseph[7] and Elizabeth [Legro] Balch, was born at Lancaster, N. H., February 6, 1829, and died December 9, 1888. He was a moulder. He married first Olive, daughter of Hiram and Belinda Higgins. She was born and died at West Boudoin, Me. They had two children, both born at West Boudoin, Me.

1270* EMMA E.,[9] b. July 13, 1855; d. June 2, 1880.
1271* CHARLES H.,[9] b. June 21, 1856; d. May 18, 1889.

Charles W. was married again, April 20, 1864, to Isabel M., daughter of William and Isabel M. [Morison] Gillfilan. She was born at Rygate, Vt., November 21, 1834; they have one daughter born at St. Johnsbury, Vt.

1272 DAISIE E.,[9] b. Sept. 23, 1868.

604. Eliza Ann,[8] daughter of 286 Joseph[7] and Elizabeth [Legro] Balch, was born at Lancaster, N. H., Feb. 24, 1832. She was married April 7, 1851, to James P., son of Stephen and Isabel [Perkins] Hayes of Guildhall, Vt. They live at Northumberland, N. H., and all their eight children were born at that town except Henry H., who was born at Lancaster. Charles T., b. June 13, 1852; William, b. July 11, 1853; Guy, b. Mar. 4, 1855; Henry H., b. Dec. 19, 1856; Nellie A., b. June 5, 1858, d. June 4, 1863; Isabel, b. Jan. 22, 1861; Frederick, b. Apl. 19, 1865; J. Melvin, b. April 9, 1868.

605. Elvira,[8] daughter of 292 Frederick B.[7] and Harriet [Benedict] Balch, was born at Alexander, N. Y., October 10, 1817. She was married Feb. 18, 1840, to William Hopkins, son of James and Sally Jones, who was born June 7, 1812, and died at Alexander, August 7, 1844. They had one child born at Alexander, Hopkins Earl, b. July 20, 1841, d. April 19, 1865.

Elvira married a second time, December 28, 1854, to Austin Richmond. They live at Alexander, N. Y., and have no children.

606. Emeline,[8] daughter of 292 Frederick B.[7] and Harriet [Benedict] Balch, was born at Alexander, N. Y., May 10, 1819. She was married August 14, 1845, to Frederick Leason, who was born at Batavia, N. Y., January 12, 1821, and died at Sheboygan Falls, Wis., October 19, 1864. They had four children. Frederick Grove, b. Aug. 11, 1848, m. Dec. 2, 1873 Mary Lois [Platt] Aiken, lives at Hingham, Wisconsin; Frank Eugene, b. April 7, 1850, unm., lives at Alvin, Texas; Park Benjamin, b. Mar. 2, 1852, unm., physician, lives in Chicago; Ida Emeroy, b. July 11, 1857, unm., lives at Sheboygan Falls.

608. Frederick A.,[8] son of 292 Frederick B.[7] and Harriet [Benedict] Balch, was born at Batavia, N. Y., August 21, 1824, and is living at Neillsville, Wisconsin. He was married August 9, 1852 to Henrietta, daughter of William

C. Caldwell. She was born at Greenville, N. Y., January
22, 1836, and died Nov. 11, 1895. They have five children.

1273   LEROY W.,[9] b. Mar. 22, 1854 ; d. Oct. 20, 1855.
1274* LOREN A.,[9] b. Nov. 4, 1856.
1275* RELLA W.,[9] b. Sept. 14, 1859.
1276   LILLIAN M.,[9] b. May 30, 1866; d. May 13, 1877.
1277* FREDERICK O.,[9] b. May 3, 1869.

612. Henry Brace,[8] son of 298 Jonathan[7] and Minerva
[Brace] Balch, was born at Harwinton, Ct., May 13, 1820.
He was run over and killed on the railroad at Cadillac, Mich.,
March 19, 1886. He was married twice, first to Lucy Aurora Brace, October 13, 1851. She was born in Canada, and
died at Meadville, Pa. They had one daughter born at Meadville.

1278* AURORA MARIA,[9] b. Oct. 19, 1852; d. Jan. 6, 1877.

Henry Brace married second, December 10, 1858, Julia
Elvira, daughter of Dr. S. S. Bates. She was born at Evens-
burg, Crawford Co., Pa., February 27, 1834, and died June 17,
1891, at Benzonia, Mich. Their three eldest were born at
Meadville, Pa., the youngest at Benzonia, Mich.

1279   CECIL HENRY,[9] b. Sept. 16, 1859; d. Sept. 5, 1860.
1280* HERBERT CORRIE,[9] b. Jan. 27, 1861.
1281* IDA MINERVA,[9] b. Mar. 26, 1863.
1282   RALPH WALKER,[9] b. Jan. 1, 1871; lives at Aneta, North Da-
       kota.

Henry Brace Balch for a time attended the Western Reserve College, at Hudson, Ohio, but did not graduate. After
leaving college, he travelled for the Bible Society in Virginia,
Illinois and Wisconsin. In 1849 he settled at Meadville
Pa., and opened a bookstore. In 1863 he removed to Titus-
ville, Pa., and travelled as agent for a Hartford publishing
house until 1869 when he removed to Benzonia, Mich. In
pushing his agency he was pleased to style himself "A Michigan Picket." Over this signature many readable articles
appeared in several of the Michigan newspapers in the
Grand Travers region, where his home was located. He was
outspoken in his hatred of tobacco, alcohol, and all kinds of
narcotics, and intoxicants. He and his wife were members

of the Congregational church. In politics he was a staunch Republican.

613. ´Jonathan Belden,[8] son of 298 Jonathan[7] and Minerva [Brace] Balch, was born at Harwinton, Ct., October 26, 1822, where he still lives, and his children were born. He is a carpenter, and is now in the carriage repairing and undertaking business. On January 1, 1844, he was married to Harriet N. Gibbs, of Montrose, Pa. She was born November 16, 1819, and died December 30, 1852, without issue.

Jonathan B. was married a second time January 24, 1855, to Charlotte Crosby, daughter of Isaac and Diana [Crosby] Warner, of Middleton, Ct. She was born September 2, 1828, and died April 15, 1895. Her sister Maria, married the Hon. Chauncey Shaffer, who was an eminent New York lawyer. Jonathan B. and Charlotte C. had four children.

   1283* CHARLES WARNER,[9] b. Mar. 30, 1856.
   1284* GEORGE HUMPHREY,[9] b. Aug. 28, 1858.
   1285* WALTER SHAFFER,[9] b. Sept. 29, 1860.
   1286* CARRIE MARIA,[9] b. Oct. 22, 1862.

614. James Shelton,[8] son of 298 Jonathan[7] and Minerva [Brace] Balch, was born at Harwinton, Conn., April 21, 1825, and is now living in the same town, and in the same house in which his mother and himself were born. He never married, is a farmer, was a member of the state Legislature in 1883.

620. Alida,[8] daughter of 301 Justin[7] and Maria [Veder] Balch. She married a Mr. Putnam, a druggist in New York city. They moved to Galveston, Texas, and had one child. All three died of yellow fever in Galveston.

621. Joseph,[8] son of 304 Gustavus[7] and Mary Ann [Van Sickles] Balch, was born at Johnstown, N. Y., May 18, 1844. He is a farmer at Mayfield, N. Y. He married Elbertine Wilkins, of Mayfield, N. Y. She was born at Kingsbury, May 25, 1844. No issue.

622. William Vistus,[8] son of 306 Vistus[7] and Margaret [Dockstader] Balch, was born December 17, 1849. He married Elizabeth Young, of Johnstown, and is a physician and

Albert V. Balch.

(623)

surgeon at East Galoway, New York. He graduated from the College of Physicians and Surgeons, New York City, in 1871. He married Elizabeth Young of Johnstown, N. Y. They have four children.

1287 WALTER ANDERSON,[9] b. Aug. 2, 1874.
1288 ETHEL M.,[9] b. Oct. 3, 1880.
1289 HAZEL Y.,[9] b. Dec. 6, 1884.
1290 MARJORIE K.,[9] b. May 11, 1890.

623. Albert Vestus,[8] son of 309 Alvah Burchard[7] and Mary [McArthur] Balch, was born at Plattsburgh, N. Y., July 21, 1828, and is now an insurance agent at Weyauwega, Wis.

He was married December 1, 1853, at Malone, N. Y., to Sarah T., youngest daughter of Rev. Dr. Ashabel and Fanny [Brush] Parmelee. The ceremony was performed by the bride's father. She was born at Malone, December 24, 1826, and died at Weyauwega, December 9, 1887. They had three daughters all born at Weyauwega.

1291* MARY JULIA,[9] b. Jan. 21, 1855.
1292* SARAH MARIA,[9] b. July 25, 1860.
1293* LAURA BERTHA,[9] b. Dec. 12, 1862.

Albert Vestus is a man of remarkable and sterling qualities. He received his education at the common district school, at select schools at Schuyler Falls and Keesville, N. Y., and finished at the Plattsburgh Academy at the age of sixteen. He was an apt scholar, possessing a retentive memory, and was quite an athlete. He could clear over 18 feet at a standing jump with dumbbells. On leaving school he entered on a mercantile career in New York city, but a serious illness led him to give it up. When twenty years of age he was employed as a teacher of convicts at Clinton state prison, after which he was appointed a keeper. In 1850 he located at Weyauwega, and was, in 1853, the first to make a purchase of land from the United States in the town, upon which he has lived continuously since that time. He there took a government contract of surveying, and through this work made himself thoroughly acquainted with the timber and mineral lands of Northern

Wisconsin, and became largely engaged as a land agent. He has been largely interested in the development of northern Wisconsin. He was postmaster from 1861 to 1867, was a member of the Legislature of Wisconsin in 1867, and has held some civil office almost continuously either in county or town since 1852. Early in life he united with the First Presbyterian church at Plattsburgh, N. Y., and was prominent in the organization of the Presbyterian church at Weyauwega, of which he has been an elder since 1857. He has represented the Winnebago County Presbytery three times in the General Assembly. He united with the Freemasons, and has taken the Royal Arch degrees. In politics he is a staunch Republican.

Albert V. was married again June 4, 1891, to Madeline, daughter of Maurice and Mary Ann [Dobler] Blind. She was born in Kiffis, Alsace Lorain, August 21, 1851. In the fall of 1875, she came to America. In 1881 she returned to Europe to perfect her German education at the University of Gottingen. Returning to America in two years, she entered the Millersburg Female College, at Millersburg, Kentucky, as a teacher of Modern Languages.

624. Clarissa,[8] daughter 309 Alvah Burchard[7] and Mary [McArthur] Balch, was born at Plattsburgh, N. Y., February 1, 1831, and died at Dayton, Wis., May 8, 1880. She was married to Lorin, son of Hiram Larkin, October 18, 1853. He was born at Beekmantown, N. Y., December 19, 1829. The ceremony was solemnized at her father's house in Plattsburgh. In the spring of 1854, they moved to Dayton, Wis., and Larkin followed the occupation of farming. He died suddenly of heart disease at Weyauwega, February 5, 1864. They were both members of the M. E. church. To them were born five children, all at Dayton. Alvah, b. Mar. 11, 1855; Hiram, b. Apr. 9, 1857, lives at Waukesha, Wis.; Mary L., b. Jan. 26, 1859, m. Aug. 19, 1885, to Robert McFetridge, and resides at Oshkosh, Wis.; Arthur, b. Apr. 27, 1861, lives at Surrounded Hill, Ark.; Albert, b. Apr. 9, 1863, lives at Waukesha, Wis.

GALUSHA B. BALCH, M. D.

Clarissa was married a second time, February 12, 1867, to Hiram Lynch, of Dayton. He was born in Penn., April 5, 1828, and by him she had four more children, all born at Dayton. Ernor, b. July 30, 1870, lives at Dayton, O.; Hattie, b. Oct. 30, 1872, killed by a falling tree in a wind storm Aug., 1888; Charles, b. Jan. 6, 1874, lives at Dayton, O.; Frederick, b. Feb. 19, 1876, lives in Milwaukee, Wis.

625. Galusha Burchard,[8] son of 309 Alvah Burchard[7] and Mary [McArthur] Balch, was born February 6, 1839, at Plattsburgh, N. Y., and now lives at Yonkers, N. Y. October 9, 1860, he was married to Harriet Cornelia, daughter of Truman Bishop and Mary Ann [Austin] Andrews, of Richmond, Mass., Rev. George F. Kettell, officiating. She was born at Addison, Stuben Co., N. Y., December 8, 1837. They had five children, the first born at Malone, the last at Yonkers and the others at Plattsburgh, N. Y.

1294• SAMUEL WEED,[9] b. Jan. 18, 1862.
1295 FREDERICK ANDREWS,[9] b. Dec. 14, 1868; d. Aug. 2, 1869.
1296• HARRIET ELIZABETH,[9] b. May 17, 1870.
1297 MARY LOUISE,[9] b. May 28, 1871; d. July 26, 1872.
1298• MARGARET ANDREWS,[9] b. June 1, 1875.

Galusha B. was born and reared upon the farm on which his grandfather located in 1800. He finished his schooling at the Plattsburgh Academy, and after teaching district schools for two seasons entered the Berkshire Medical College at Pittsfield, Massachusetts. Here he was under the tutilage of Dr. Harry Childs and his son, Dr. Timothy Childs. He then finished his medical education at the College of Physicians and Surgeons of the Medical Department of Columbia College at New York City, and graduated in 1860. After graduating he practiced first at Saranac, and then at North Lawrence, New York. At the outbreak of the Civil War he passed the examination of the board of examiners for medical staff appointments in New York regiments, and was commissioned assistant surgeon of the 98th New York Infantry, October 20, 1861. The regiment was at that time being recruited at Malone, N. Y.

In the spring of 1862 he went to the front with this regiment. It was assigned to the Army of the Potomac, and went to the Peninsula under General McClellan. Upon the taking of Yorktown he was detached from his regiment and assigned to duty in the general hospital there, and for a time was in charge of the steamer State of Maine, transporting sick to Baltimore. While thus engaged Dr. J. Simpson, the medical director at Baltimore, said in a letter to the Surgeon General that the condition in which the State of Maine arrived was highly creditable to Dr. Balch, that the sick were well cared for and that the sanitary condition of the vessel was in a much better state than that of the others that had lately arrived.

Contracting typho-malarial fever at Yorktown, he lay sick in hospital for about six weeks. Having returned to his regiment early in August before he had fully recovered, the condition of his health led him to resign on Sept. 20, 1862. Returning north he located, as soon as his health would permit, at Sheffield, Massachusetts, and practiced his profession till December, 1863, when, feeling restored to health, he accepted a commission as Assistant Surgeon of the Second Regiment of Veteran Cavalry, New York Volunteers. With this regiment he went to the Department of the Gulf in February, 1864, and was the only surgeon with the regiment during the Red River campaign of that year, and with it in the battles of Alexandria, Grand Ecore, Camptee, Pleasant Hill, Cane River and Yellow Bayou.

During the summer of 1864, and winter following, the regiment was stationed at Morganzia Bend on the Mississippi river, and was kept constantly scouting up and down both sides of the river between Baton Rouge and the mouth of the Red river, having frequent sanguinary skirmishes. The Doctor was almost always out with these scouting parties, and consequently was frequently exposed to the bullets of the enemy.

In March, 1865, the regiment was sent to Pensecola, Fla.,

and joined General Steel, who moved around into the rear of Mobile, Ala., to co-operate with General Canby in capturing that city. After the surrender of Fort Blakely the regiment moved out through the state of Alabama, and on April 11, fought the battle at Mt. Pleasant, one of the last of the war. After the surrender of all the opposing forces the regiment was sent to Talladega, Alabama, where it remained until it was mustered out on November 8, 1865.

In the spring of 1866 the Doctor located at Plattsburgh, N. Y., and purchased a drug store. This was destroyed by the great fire of Plattsburgh, in 1868. In 1872 he moved to Yonkers, N. Y., where he is now practicing his profession. In 1876 he was appointed Health Officer for the city and organized the Health Department and made it one of the best in the state at that time. This office he held two years.

In 1877 he was elected vice-president of the Westchester County Medical Society, and, in the year following, was chosen as its president and is still a member of that society. He was one of the organizers of the Yonkers Society for the Prevention of Cruelty to Children, and since its organization in 1881 has continued as its president at the unanimous desire of its directors. In 1867 he became a member of Clinton Lodge, 155, of F. and A. M., and has taken the Royal Arch and Council degrees. He served two years as thrice illustrious master of Nepperhan Council R. and S. M's, No. 70. During the year 1883 he was Commander of Kitching Post, No. 60, G. A. R., and was Commander of John C. Fremont Post, No. 590, for seven years. The Doctor and Mrs. Balch are members of the First Presbyterian Church. His first ballot was cast for Abraham Lincoln, in 1860, and he has voted the Republican ticket ever since. He was one of the organizers of the Yonkers Historical and Library Association and is its librarian. The work of compiling this Genealogy was taken up by him in 1874, and has occupied his spare moments for twelve years.

627. Betsey Selina,[8] daughter of 312 Horatio James[7]

and Sophronia [Allaird] Balch, was born in Canada East, November 21, 1830, and now resides at Olney, Illinois. She was married January 11, 1849, to Isaac, son of William Sutterfield, a farmer who was born at Highland Co., Ohio, January 1, 1826. They have had thirteen children, the eldest was born in Gibson Co., Ind., the others in Richland Co., Ill. Amanda Bristoe, b. Oct. 26, 1849; Lucinda Bell, b. Feb. 8, 1851; Sylvester, b. Sept. 16, 1852; Sophronia Walker, b. April 18, 1855; Mary Ann Kellogg, b. June 14, 1857; William A., b. Jan. 11, 1859, a school teacher; Margaret, b. Feb. 15, 1861, d. May 31, 1874; Isaac, b. Dec. 20, 1862, d. Feb. 7, 1863; Ephraim P., b. Jan. 7, 1864; Lizzie Stacey, b. Feb. 16, 1866; James M., b. April 27, 1868, d. June 4, 1874; Thomas, b. Oct. 17, 1870, d. Nov. 7, 1870; Theodore, b. Apr. 20, 1872, d. Aug. 22, 1873.

632. **Abigail Melissa,**[8] daughter of 312 Horatio James[7] and Sophronia [Allaird] Balch, was born in Knox Co., Ind., January 12, 1840. She was married January 11, 1860, to Isaac, son of James Garrett, of Gibson Co., Ind. He was born February 9, 1842. They reside at Wabash township, Gibson Co., Ind. P. O. address Owensville, Ind. Their eleven children were all born in Indianna. Aac, b. Nov. 18, 1860; d. Jan. 19, 1861. Alexander, b. Dec. 10, 1861; d. June 10, 1862. Elvira Christian, b. Mar. 20, 1863. Lemuel Ebenezer, b. Feb. 15, 1865; d. Dec. 20, 1867. Eveline, b. Jan. 20, 1867; d. June 15, 1868. Samantha Ellen, b. Sept. 17, 1868; d. Aug. 25, 1869. Elsie P., b. Sept. 18, 1871. Saphronia Catherine, b. Sept. 29, 1873; d. Oct. 23, 1877. William Henry, b. Sept. 22, 1877. Sarah Effa, b. Jan. 18, 1880; d. Sept. 12, 1880. Delia Florence, b. Oct. 4, 1881.

636. **Caroline E.**[8] daughter of 314 Chester[7] and Lucy [Smedley] Balch, was born November 12, 1822, at Plattsburgh, N. Y., and died in the same town June 8, 1842. She was married to John Banker, of Plattsburgh, November 12, 1841. No issue.

639. **Loesa M.**[8] daughter of 314 Chester[7] and Lucy

[Smedley] Balch, was born at Plattsburg, N. Y., August 18, 1829. She was married Feb. 22, 1855, to Calvin Deming, son of Nathan A. Vaughan, of Plattsburgh. He died at Amboy, Ills., March 26, 1886. C. D. Vaughan was a merchant at Amboy, Ills., where their six children were born. Lottie Louisa, b. Apr. 17, 1858, m. Dec. 25, 1878, to P. M. James, a lawyer, and resides at Amboy, Ills. Harriet Deming, b. Nov. 7, 1860. Frank Chester, b. Mar. 17, 1863 ; m. Feb. 25, 1891, Carrie J. Briggs. Fred Nathan, b. Feb. 1, 1865 ; m. Nov. 28, 1887, Elizabeth Jeannette Poland. Wallace Baker, b. Mar. 11, 1867 ; m. Jan. 18, 1893, Helen May Doty. Louie Smedley, b. Feb. 9, 1869.

642. **John Timothy,**[8] son of 314 Chester[7] and Lucy [Smedley] Balch, was born at Plattsburgh, N. Y., October 21, 1836. He is of a kind and gentle disposition, affectionate, jovial, and enjoys society. The strict puritanical ways of his father, and uncongenial feeling that existed between him and his stepmother, induced him to leave home in 1856. He went first to his sister's home at Amboy, Ills., and there he found employment with the Illinois Central R. R. Co. In the spring of 1858 he went South in the employ of the Mississippi Central R. R. and in 1860 was in the employ of the Mobile and Ohio R. R. He remained within the Confederate lines in the employ of this latter road until 1864, when he came through the lines at Vicksburg, Miss. Thence he went to St. Louis and was in the employ first of the Ohio and Mississippi, second as general baggage agent of the Wabash for seven years, and third at Union depot for six years. Since 1881 he has been assistant baggage agent at Union depot, Kansas City. He is a Democrat and a member of the Westminster Presbyterian Church at Kansas City. On June 20, 1872, he married Margaret J., daughter of Frank P. and Margaret Traynor. She was born at Davenport, Iowa, May 1st, 1854. They have one child.

1299 LOUISE MARY,[9] b. Jan. 3, 1874; a school teacher.

643. **Lucy Smedley,**[8] daughter of 314 Chester[7] and Lucy

[Smedley] Balch, was born Februrary 9, 1839, at Plattsburgh, N. Y., and died at Malone, N. Y., July 80, 1868. She was married to C. Halsey Vaughan, M.D., a brother of Charles Demming, her sister Loesa's husband. They moved to Illinois, but in 1861 returned east, and Dr. Vaughan entered the service as Assistant Surgeon of the 96th New York Volunteers, commissioned March 27, 1862, promoted to surgeon of the 48d New York Volunteers, May 18, 1864, and was mustered out on March 14, 1865. They had one son, Louis Hubbard, b. July 26, 1863; d. July 19, 1864.

645. Henry,[8] son of 317 Henry[7] and Fanny [Baker] Balch, was born at Plattsburgh, N. Y., about 1842. He has lived at Saranac and Plattsburgh, N. Y.

647. Manning B.,[8] son of 321 William Skinner[7] and Caroline M. [Martin] Balch, was born at Pownal, Vt., September 23, 1836. In 1859, he married Clementine, daughter of John H. and Eliza Wager, of Saratoga, N. Y., by whom he had one son who died in infancy. She died in August, 1860. He enlisted in the Union Army in 1861. In 1865 he became a lecturer for the Good Templars in Wisconsin, and afterwards in Massachusetts. In 1869 he entered the Methodist Episcopal ministry in the West Wisconsin conference, was presiding elder of the La Cross district in 1883, and of the Madison district in 1887.

On August 11, 1867, he married Hattie L., daughter of Hon. Dr. William and Mary [Beebe] Monroe, of Fayette, Wis. She was born July 31, 1846. They have had one son.

1300* WILLIAM MONROE,[9] b. Nov. 25, 1871.

648. Edward N.,[8] son of 321 William Skinner[7] and Caroline M. [Martin] Balch, was born at Williamstown, Mass., March 2, 1841. At the breaking out of the Civil War he was in Wisconsin, and enlisted in the twenty-second Wisconsin Volunteers. He died in the army hospital at Lexington, Ky., January 1, 1863, from exposure in the service. He never married.

649. Carrie V.,[8] daughter of 321 William Skinner[7] and

Vesta H. [Child] Balch, was born at Saratoga Springs, N. Y., June 24, 1860. She was married Nov. 17, 1880, to George D. son of Daniel and Fatima [Shedd] Harvey, of Auburndale, Mass., where they reside. He was born Dec. 20, 1840, and is a wholesale dry goods merchant at Boston, Mass. They have no children.

652. Jane Louisa,[8] daughter of 324 Henry[7] and Martha Ann [Fuller] Balch, was born at Sandisfield, Mass., September 18, 1838. She was married to Charles Stevens, son of Abner Stevens and Mary M. [Alford] Webster, January 1, 1865. He was born at Sandisfield, Mass., May 6, 1837, and died July 19, 1896. He owned extensive poultry yards at West Winsted, Conn.   They have two children both born in New York city. Celia Louise, b. Nov. 8, 1865, m. Oct. 7, 1891, Darwin S. Moore. Lillian Matilda, b. Oct. 31, 1867.

653. Cornelia Ann,[8] daughter 324 Henry[7] and Martha Ann [Fuller] Balch, was born at Sandisfield, Mass., November 19, 1845. She was married November 19, 1872, to William Edwin, son of Edwin Butler. He was born at Norfolk, Conn., November 16, 1849. He is a farmer and they live at Tolland, Mass., where their two children were born. Addie Cornelia, b. Nov. 19, 1878 ; Grace Eliza, b. July 24, 1885.

654. Edward Henry,[8] son of 324 Henry[7] and Martha Ann [Fuller] Balch, was born at Sandisfield, Mass., April 28, 1852. He was married May 20, 1870, to Emma E., daughter of Lewis G. Sage. She was born at Sandisfield, in October, 1853.   Edward H. is a farmer and resides at Southwick, Mass. They have one child, born at Sandisfield.

1301 WALLACE WILBUR,[9] b. Mar. 7, 1873.

655. Alonzo W.,[8] son of 326 Thomas[7] and Delia [Persons] Balch, was born at Hartford, Ct., September 16, 1837. He was married May 31, 1865, to Joanna B. Rohr, and lives in New York City. He is a wholesale dealer in teas and wines.

1302 DAVID CLARK,[9] b. April 27, 1866, at New York City.

656. Frederick A.,[8] son of 326 Thomas[7] and Delia [Persons] Balch, was born at Hartford, Ct., August 22, 1839.

He was a wood engraver, but lost his business owing to improved methods of illustration. Worry over this led to his untimely death on July 10, 1896. This was exactly seven years even to the hour and minute after the death of his son Claude. He was a man of scrupulous integrity, unselfish, and devoted to his family. On November 22, 1867, he married Celeste A. Brasier, daughter of Jean Claude Brasier De Latour, she was born at LaRoche [Haute-Saevoie], France, on January 10, 1842. She is a dressmaker in Brooklyn, New York. Two children have been born to them, both in Brooklyn, N. Y.

1303ᵃ ELEONORE MARIE AMELIE,⁹ b. Dec. 1, 1868.
1304 CLAUDE ALFRED,⁹ b. Oct. 11, 1873; d. July 10, 1889.

657. Margaret S.,⁸ daughter of 326 Thomas⁷ and Delia [Persons] Balch, was born at Hartford, Ct., October 12, 1842. She was married May 26, 1881, to Augustus F. Kummel. They reside at Hartford, Ct., and have no children.

658. Alfred P.,⁸ son of 326 Thomas⁷ and Delia [Persons] Balch, was born at Hartford, Ct., August 19, 1844. He was married October 31, 1879, to Grace L., daughter of J. C. Perkins, she was born at Calais, Me., June 12, 1851. They live at Winsted, Ct. and have two children, born at that place.

1305 ALICE MARGARET,⁹ b. Oct. 29, 1880.
1306 GRACE P.,⁹ b. Oct. 27, 1887.

659. Delia F.,⁸ daughter of 326, Thomas⁷ and Delia [Persons] Balch, was born at Hartford, Ct., October 7, 1848. She was married April 20, 1870, to Eugene H. Williams. He was born at Rockville, Ct., July 3, 1846, and is a wholesale dealer in confectionery at Hartford. He enlisted as a drummer boy in the fourteenth Connecticut Volunteers and served all through the Civil War. They have no children.

660. Ellen Elizabeth,⁸ daughter of 332, John Rogers⁷ and Elizabeth C. [Lawton] Balch, was born at Providence, R. I., on May 9, 1833. She married George O., son of

C. L. BALCH.

Nathaniel H. and Louisa Olmstead. He was born at Savannah, Georgia, December 30, 1830. They live at Providence, where Mr. Olmstead is engaged in mercantile pursuits. They have two children, born at Providence. Nathaniel B., b. Feb. 12, 1855; d. in Oct. 1857. Nellie L., b. Mar. 27, 1866.

661. Collins Lawton,[8] son of 332 John Rogers[7] and Elizabeth C. [Lawton] Balch, was born at Providence, R. I., July 6, 1834. He was married to Georgia Hardy of Brooklyn, N. Y., Oct. 11, 1859. They had two children.

1307 FRANK COLLINS,[9] died in infancy.
1308 GRACE COLLINS,[9] b. Nov. 13, 1865.

Collins Lawton is the last male descendant of 71 Timothy,[5] son of 22 Joseph[4] and Mary [Osgood] Balch, of Boston. He prepared for college at the Providence High School and entered Brown University in 1851. He pursued an English course, but left the University, in 1854, without graduating, to enter upon a business life in New York City, as a clerk in a dry goods commission house. After a few years he left to take charge of the business of a manufacturing jewelry firm. Next he went into the manufacturing and jobbing jewelry business on his own account, and subsequently became interested in the development of the then new material " celluloid " and is now one of the managers of the Celluloid Company. In 1864 he united with the First Presbyterian Church at Tremont, N. Y., then a suburb of New York city. In this church he has at different times filled the various offices trustee, deacon, and elder, and for fifteen years enjoyed the confidence of the church officers by being annually elected superintendent of the Sabbath School.

SECOND BRANCH.

Descendants of 6 Benjamin.[3]

663. Nathan,[8] son of 333 Hart[7] and Priscilla [Holt] Balch, was born August 29, 1773. He married and moved to Thompson, Ohio, with his family of 14 children, about 1828.

1309* JOEL,[9] b.   ; d.
1310   IRA,[9] was in Sou Prairie, Madison county, Wis., in 1856.
1311   CHARLES[9].
1312   WILLIAM[9].
1313   NATHANIEL[9].
1314   DANIEL[9].

664. Joel,[8] son of 333 Hart[7] and Priscilla [Holt] Balch, was born February 6, 1775, and died at Andover, October 27, 1845. He was married, July 4, 1796, to Betsey, daughter of William Stevens. She was born April 30, 1778, and died at Andover, Vt., December 31, 1810. They had six children, all born at Andover.

1315   PRISCILLA HOLT,[9] b. Nov. 6, 1797; d. June 4, 1813.
1316   BETSEY,[9] b. April 27, 1800; d. Nov. 10, 1871; m. Nathan Derby, in February, 1823.
1317* AARON LELAND,[9] b. June 17, 1802; d. Nov. 4, 1839.
1318* LOUISA MERREAM,[9] b. April 13, 1804.
1319* WILLIAM STEVENS,[9] b. April 13, 1806; d. Dec. 25, 1887.
1320   SUSAN,[9] b. Sept. 7, 1810; d. April 11, 1811.

Joel[8] was married a second time, February 6, 1812, to Abigail Joy Edwards. She was born at Johnson, R. I., March 9, 1786, and died at Andover, January 12, 1852. They had three children.

1321   SUSAN EDWARDS,[9] b. March 16, 1813; d. 1854.
1322   JOHN HART,[9] b. Sept. 25, 1816; d. July 12, 1841.
1323   MARIA,[9] b. June 23, 1820; d. April 4, 1848.

Joel Balch was a man of a strong and active mind, but had little opportunity for an education, having gone to Vermont among the first settlers there. His wife taught the first school in the town. He was not rich, but industrious and frugal, and lived comfortably, and enjoyed the respect and confidence of all who knew him. He never sought office, but was often called upon to serve as one of the selectmen, justice of the peace, representative to the Legislature, and in places of trust in the neighborhood and town. He was a great reader of the Bible, but could never agree with the close communion Calvinism of his day.

666. Deborah,[8] daughter of 333 Hart[7] and Dorcas [Somers] Balch, was born at Keene, N. H., November 13, 1780. She married Lemuel, son of Josiah and Hannah [Hobbs] Abbot, of Amherst, N. H. He was born May 13, 1764, and died January 19, 1841. They lived at Windham, Vt., and had seven children: Lemuel, b. April 3, 1799; Hart B., b. Dec. 29, 1800; Sally B., b. Nov. 17, 1802; Lucius, b. Feb. 3, 1804; Lucia, b. Aug. 5, 1807; Marcius, b. Dec. 1, 1809; Marcia, b. Nov. 26, 1811.

668. Asa,[8] son of 333 Hart[7] and Dorcas [Somers] Balch, was born May 12, 1786, and died at Andover, Vt., in 1872. He married Betsey Parker; both were quite old when married, and they had no issue.

669. Francis S.,[8] son of 333 Hart[7] and Dorcas [Somers] Balch, was born at Andover, Vt., September 2, 1788, and died at Shirley, Mass., August 25, 1857. On February 7, 1810, he married Sally, daughter of James Dickerson. She was born at Shirley, January 24, 1790, and died in that town, December 28, 1871, and was buried by her husband. Immediately after his marriage he went to live at Mitchelville (then a part of Shirley, now of Ayer), and engaged in flour-milling for Levi Dodge. He worked in the mill several years, then bought a farm near by. He was short of stature, of medium weight, and quick in his movements. He loved the country life, hunting and fishing. They had four children, all born in the town of Shirley.

1324* DORCAS,[9] b. Nov. 26, 1811; d. Oct. 23, 1886.
1325* FRANCIS,[9] b. March 10, 1814; d. Nov. 22, 1876.
1326* SARAH,[9] b. May 14, 1818.
1327* CHARLES C.,[9] b. Dec. 20, 1820; d. May 16, 1893.

670. Er,[8] son of 333 Hart[7] and Dorcas [Somers] Balch, was born at Andover, Vt., February 10, 1794, and died at

Leominster, Mass., January 5, 1854. He was married March 7, 1818, to Susan, daughter of John and Sarah [Richardson] Buss. She was born at Leominster, February 26, 1796, and died in that town, September 12, 1867. Er was a hotel keeper at Leominster for the last thirty years of his life. Both he and his wife were buried in that town, and their ten children were born there.

1328* SUSAN,[9] b. May 13, 1819; d. May 22, 1863.
1329* SARAH ANN,[9] b. May 20, 1821; d. Oct. 3, 1851.
1330* JOHN BUSS,[9] b. June 17, 1825; d. Oct. 27, 1851.
1331* DENEBIS,[9] b. June 6, 1829; d. Dec. 20, 1867.
1332* GEORGE LUCIUS,[9] b. April 8, 1831.
1333* FRANCIS ER,[9] b. Jan. 17, 1834.
1334* ADALINE ADAMS,[9] b. Nov. 26, 1837.
1335 HARRIET ELIZABETH,[9] b. Sept. 21, 1840; d. Aug. 9, 1860.

671. Sally,[8] daughter of 333 Hart[7] and Dorcas [Somers] Balch, was born October 7, 1795, and died at Charlestown, Mass., June 15, 1874. She married Obediah Parker, by whom she had several children, among them Jerome W. Parker, who lives at Charlestown, and is a butcher in Boston market.

672. James Parker,[8] son of 333 Hart[7] and Dorcas [Somers] Balch, was born at Andover, Vt., December 4, 1797, and died at Weathersfield, Vt., April 2, 1857. He was married to Lucinda, daughter of John Boynton, of Weathersfield. She was born at Weathersfield, July 28, 1795, and died at Newburyport, Mass., November 15, 1881. James P. was a farmer, and resided at Weathersfield, Vt., and their nine children were born in that town.

1336 HORACE LELAND,[9] b. Nov. 11, 1820; d. unm. in 1854.
1337* JOHN HIRAM,[9] b. Feb. 22, 1824.
1338* ELIZABETH MARY,[9] b. Jan. 18, 1827; d. July 16, 1894.
1339 JEANNETTE NANCY,[9] b. April 4, 1829; unm.
1340* JAMES NELSON,[9] b. May 26, 1832.
1341* GEORGE PARKER,[9] b. Jan. 18, 1834; d. Oct. 17, 1891.
1342* ISADORE LUCINDA,[9] b. Feb. 8, 1836; d. July 14, 1883.
1343* ELLEN JANE,[9] b. Aug. 20, 1838.
1344* CARRIE MARIA,[9] b. Dec. 7, 1841.

673. Jacob Abbot,[8] son of 333 Hart[7] and Dorcas [Somers] Balch, was born June 4, 1800, at Andover, Vt., and died at Newburyport, Mass., August 27, 1881. He was married at Chester, Vt., April 20, 1829, to Huldah J. Burton, daughter of Samuel Burton, one of the pioneers of Vermont. She was born at Andover, Vt., October 28, 1803, and died at Newburyport, Mass., August 28, 1893. Her mother was a cousin of Gen. Israel Putnam. At the time of Jacob Abbot's marriage, both he and Huldah were living at Andover, Vt., but the record of their marriage is at Chester, Vt. They had one daughter, born in Newburyport.

1345 HELEN B.,[9] b. Dec. 5, 1835; m. Moses H. Fowler, July 8, 1874.

674. Maria S.,[8] daughter of 334 Nathaniel[7] and Mary [Stillman] Balch, was born March 20, 1790. She married Dr. David Torry, and had two sons.

675. William,[8] son of 334 Nathaniel[7] and Mary [Stillman] Balch, was born March 11, 1792, and was lost at sea sometime after 1826, as he was in Boston in that year. He never married. William was, like many Balches, a sailor, and commanded several vessels in the merchant marine service.

676. Nathaniel,[8] son of 334 Nathaniel[7] and Mary [Stillman] Balch, was born at Boston, February 13, 1794. In 1826 he was a printer in Boston. In 1831 he was in Baltimore, Md., and probably died in that city a few years afterwards, unmarried.

677. Harriet,[8] daughter of 334 Nathaniel[7] and Mary [Stillman] Balch, was born at Boston, November 14, 1795. She married a Mr. Grafton.

678. Benjamin Stillman,[8] son of 334 Nathaniel[7] and Mary [Stillman] Balch, was born at Boston, July 9, 1797. Early in life he removed to Baltimore, Md. About 1857, he discovered a mode of rapidly cutting stencil plates by means of nitric acid, this proved valuable to him, but the fuming acid proved detrimental to his health, as he wrote in his last letter to his relatives in 1850.

679. Edward Lawrence,[8] son of 334 Nathaniel[7] and Susan [Young] Balch, was born at Boston, May 31, 1816, and was baptized at the " Old South Church" by Rev. Dr. Wisner. He died at Boston, November 21, 1869. On Sunday, Decem-1, 1844, he was married at Jamaica Plain, by the Rev. Dr. Gray, to Miss Martha Willis, third daughter of Bradford, and Rebecca [Atwood] Lincoln. She died at Boston, April 4, 1882, at the age of 71 years and eight days. They had two children, the first of whom was a daughter, b. Nov. 11, 1845, and died the next day.

    1346ᵃ WILLIAM LINCOLN,⁹ b. April 2, 1847.

Bradford Lincoln, the father of Mrs. Edward L. Balch, was descended—through Stephen Jr., David, Mathew, and Job, of Hingham, Mass., from Stephen Lincoln, who came from Windham, Eng., in 1638, and through his mother, Mercy Hersey, on her maternal side, from Gov. William Bradford, of the Plymouth Colony.

Edward Lawrence Balch when a very young man was employed for a short time in the office of the first city clerk of Boston,—which received its charter in 1822,—and was at an early age apprenticed to the printers trade, his employers being the Merriams at Brookfield, Mass. Returning to Boston, he made a specialty of music printing and for many years a large share of the music book and concert printing of the city issued from his office. For a time he had charge of the printing of "Dwight's Journal of Music." He was the first printer of the " Boston Musical Times " and of the " Congregational Quarterly " magazine. He was a patentee of a form of movable music type for school-chart printing. He was an officer of the Mendelssohn Choral Society, and an active member for years of the Handel and Hayden Society and the Massachusetts Charitable Mechanics Association.

    680. William Young,⁸ son of 334 Nathaniel⁷ and Susan [Young] Balch, was born at Boston, March 10, 1819, and died in that city December 17, 1872. He was a picture frame maker, and resided for several years at Hillsboro, Illinois. He was married October 24, 1844, by the Rev. James Angier, to Maria Swift, daughter of William, and Elizabeth Beal, of Milton, Mass. They had two daughters born at Milton.

DR. JOSEPH BALCH.
(1801)

1347   KATE,⁹ b. April 24, 1853.
1348ª ELLA M.,⁹ b. Sept. 29, 1857.

681. Joseph,⁸ son of 348 Joseph⁷ and Hannah [Pope] Balch, was born at Boston, Mass., July 16, 1796, and died at Providence, R. I., July 16, 1872. He settled in Providence at the age of 21 and was the head of the firm of J. Balch & Son, druggists. He was married at Providence, July, 1821, to Mary Ann, daughter of Eli and Hannah [Vaughn] Bailey. She was born June 25, 1800, and died January 9, 1879. They had nine children, all born at Providence.

1349ª JOSEPH POPE,⁹ b. Aug. 9, 1822; d. Dec. 2, 1872.
1350ª MARY ANN,⁹ b. Oct. 7, 1823; d. Aug. 31, 1889.
1351   JANE,⁹ b. Jan. 1825; d. 1826.
1352ª JANE ADAMS,⁹ b. Jan. 14, 1827; d. Jan. 4, 1893.
1353ª ELLEN HOWARD,⁹ b. Mar. 14, 1830; d. Oct. 6, 1865.
1354ª EDWARD AUGUSTUS,⁹ b. Apr. 2, 1832; d. Jan. 14, 1871.
1355ª ANNA,⁹ b. Mar. 12, 1835.
1356ª ABIGAIL POPE,⁹ b. Mar. 11, 1837; unm.
1357ª HANNAH RAYMER,⁹ b. Mar. 16, 1839; d. Dec. 18, 1891.

683. Abigail Bright,⁸ daughter of 343 Joseph⁷ and Hannah [Pope] Balch, was born at Boston, Mass., April 1, 1799. She was married October 13, 1824, to Stanton Bebee, of Little Compton, R. I.

THIRD BRANCH.

Descendants of 7 John.⁸

684. Hannah,⁸ daughter of 348 John⁷ and Lucy [Snow] Balch, was born at Keene, N. H., April 4, 1781, and died at Brattleboro, Vt., July 27, 1866. She was married to Abel Haynes, at Keene, N. H. in April, 1801. He was born March 3, 1780, and died September 29, 1822. He was a farmer at Landgrove, Vt., where they had always lived, and where their children were born.

CLARISSA, b. Mar. 7, 1802; d. at Westmoreland, N. H., Oct. 27, 1823.
LUCY ANN B., b. Oct. 23, 1806; d. at Landgrove, Vt., Oct. 12, 1833.
ABIGAIL S., b. Oct. 2, 1808; d. at Landgrove, Vt., Jan. 2, 1812.
JOHN ROBINSON, b. Sept. 22, 1811; d. at Landgrove, Vt., Oct. 7, 1879,
       was killed by a bull; m. Fannie Garfield, had one child,
       a daughter; he was a farmer.

ABIGAIL S., b. Oct. 6, 1814, lives at Putney, Vt.; m. Cincinnatus J.
    Taft, of Putney, Vt., a farmer, had one child, Ellen, d.
    y. Taft died in 1863.
MARIETTA P., b. Dec. 30, 1817; d. at Landgrove, Aug. 19, 1864; m.
    Almon Patterson, a miller, lived at Landgrove, had three
    sons and four daughters.
HENRY B., b. May 1, 1820; resides at Granville, Ills. has been mar-
    ried three times; has one son.

685.   Lucindia,[8] daughter of 348 John[7] and Lucy [Snow]
Balch, was born at Keene, N. H., March 23, 1783, and died at
Westmoreland, N. H., August 7, 1848.   She was married at
Keene, December 23, 1810 to Gaines Hall, who was born at
Raynham, Mass., June 12, 1780, and died at Westmoreland
November 30, 1871.   He was a farmer and for more than 50
years he was a deacon in the Christians Church.   They had
two sons and two daughters all born at Westmoreland.

ESTHER MASON, b. June 9, 1812; d. at Westmoreland, Sept. 6, 1889;
    m. at Westmoreland, Nov. 16, 1834, Mr. Prentis Daggett,
    who was born at Westmoreland, Aug. 25, 1807, and died
    in the same town, Oct. 29, 1881, occupation, farmer; poli-
    tics, Republican.
GAINS KIETH, b. Feb. 10, 1814; d. April 6, 1863; m. Nov. 1, 1837, to
    Mary Fuller, resides at Westmoreland.   He is a farmer,
    a member of the Christian Church, and a Republican.
    His wife Mary, died July 21, 1858, and he married 2nd,
    Cordelia Hubbard, Nov. 1858.   By his first wife he had
    seven children.
EMELINE, b. July 30, 1816; d. Sept. 26, 1816.
EMELINE, b. Feb. 2, 1818; d. Mar. 23, 1818.
LUCY SNOW, b. Feb. 18, 1820; d. Apr. 7, 1895; m. Feb. 28, 1844, Elisha
    Shelley, resided at Westmoreland, a farmer and a Repub-
    lican, he was born Aug. 27, 1822, no children.
SETH CHANDLER, b. Oct. 28, 1822; m. at Westmoreland, Oct. 23, 1847,
    Alfreda Pattan, they reside at Keene; have had five chil-
    dren; are members of the Christian Church; a farmer
    and a Republican.

686.   Nabby,[8] third daughter of 348 John[7] and Lucy
[Snow] Balch, was born at Westmoreland, N. H., March 28,
1785, and died in the same town August 17, 1830.   She was
married January 1, 1816, to Isaac Miller, who was born at
Westminster, Mass., July 12, 1789, and died at Worcester,
Mass., July 27, 1870.   He was a farmer at Westmoreland, N.

H. and Athol, Mass. They were Baptists and their children Universalists.

> MARY C., b. at Putney, Vt., Oct. 9, 1817; d. at Swansey, N. H., Nov. 15, 1845.
>
> JOHN BALCH, b. at Westmoreland, Jan. 28, 1819; d. at Brattleboro, Vt., Apr. 3, 1873; m. Apr. 25, 1842, Sabrina P. Stockwell, who was born at Brattleboro, Vt., Dec. 20, 1820. He was a tanner and currier. No issue.
>
> ABEL HAYNES, b. at Westmoreland, May 1, 1822; d. at Malone, N. Y., Aug. 30, 1877; m. Jan. 10, 1845, Martha Moody. He was a merchant.
>
> ISAAC JACKSON, b. at Westmoreland, May 1, 1825; d. at Brattleboro, Vt., Dec. 13, 1849; m. Celista C. Ward, who was born in 1827. They resided at Brattleboro, Vt. No issue.

687. Andrew,[8] eldest son of 348 John 7 and Lucy [Snow] Balch, was born at Keene, N. H., May 2, 1787, and died at Westmoreland, May 26, 1845, and was buried at Keene. On October 5, 1815, he was married at Westmoreland to Louisa, daughter of Noah and Olive [Staples] Fuller. She was born at Westmoreland, N. H., May 30, 1796, and died in the same town, November 26, 1870.

Andrew was a farmer and lived at Keene up to 1826, when he removed to Westmoreland. Their six eldest children were born at Keene, and the three youngest at Westmoreland. In politics Andrew was a Whig, and both he and his wife were members of the Baptist Church.

> 1358* LOUISA FULLER,[9] b. July 7, 1816.
> 1359* JAMES ANDREW,[9] b. Nov. 22, 1817; d. Oct. 11, 1876.
> 1360* LUCY SNOW,[9] b. Sept. 17, 1819.
> 1361 OLIVE AMELIA FULLER,[9] b. Aug. 11, 1821; d. July 23, 1822.
> 1362* PERLEY SNOW,[9] b. Sept. 15, 1823; d. Aug. 16, 1868.
> 1363 PHILINDA,[9] b. May 27, 1825; d. Sept. 3, 1826.
> 1364* BETSEY FULLER,[9] b. Aug. 21, 1827.
> 1365* MARY ELITIA,[9] b. June 2, 1831.
> 1366* JOHN EDWIN,[9] b. Apr. 27, 1833.

688. Ezra,[8] second son of 348 John[7] and Lucy [Snow] Balch, was born at Keene, N. H., in 1798, and died April 26, 1828, and was buried at Keene. He married in 1820, Dorcas Miller. She was born in 1799, and died March 28, 1877, and was buried at Keene. They were Baptists and had three children.

1367 SARAH ANN,[8] b. 1821; d. May 26, 1824.
1368* SARAH L.,[9] b. 1826; d. Feb. 26, 1860.
1369 EZRA W.,[9] b. 1829; d. in New Orleans, La., Jan. 5, 1858.

690. Timothy,[8] son of 349 Timothy[7] and Hannah [Damon] Balch, was born at Manchester, Vt., December 10, 1789, and died at Orwell, N. Y., August 10, 1843. About 1821 he married Hannah Randall. She was born in 1800, and died December 12, 1889. Timothy was a farmer and lived in the town of Orwell, N. Y. Their seven children were born in that town.

1370 JOHN,[9] b. Dec. 3, 1823; d. Sept. 19, 1842.
1371* EZRA W.,[9] b. Sept. 12, 1825; d. Sept. 18, 1862.
1372 HIRAM,[9] b. Jan. 8, 1828; went away and was never heard from.
1373* NANCY L.,[9] b. Dec. 26, 1832.
1374* LUCINDIA,[9] b. March 22, 1834.
1375 TIMOTHY,[9] b. Jan. 28, 1836.
1376 ANN,[9] b. March 20, 1842; m. first Thomas Thompson, second Horatio Tiffts.

691. John,[8] son of 349 Timothy[7] and Hannah [Damon] Balch, was born at Manchester, Vt., February 14, 1792, and died at Orwell, N. Y., March 10, 1882. He was married at Orwell, in 1821, to Eunice Stowell, of Orwell. They had ten children.

1377 LUCINDIA,[9] b. Dec. 6, 1823; d. Apr. 30, 1851.
1378 WALSTIN,[9] b. Jan. 2, 1826; d. Mch. 2, 1890.
1379 SUSANAH,[9] b. Nov., 1827; m. Nelson Rima, P. O. Demster, N. Y.
1380* WILLIAM,[9] b. Dec. 18, 1832.
1381* ORRIN H.[9] b. Mch. 31, 1835.
1382 HARRIET,[9] b. Mch. 18, 1838; m. a Mr. Wheeler, Horsehead, N.Y.
1383* IRA,[9] b. Feb. 22, 1840.
1384 LORETT,[9] b. 1842.
1385 ANN,[9] b. 1842.
1386* JOHN H.,[9] b. Jan. 24, 1849.

John Balch possessed a well-balanced organization and powers of endurance that well fitted him for the pioneer life in which he was brought up.

692. Susan,[8] daughter of 349 Timothy[7] and Hannah [Damon] Balch, was born at Manchester, Vt., August 22, 1794, and died June 2, 1880. She married Stephen Tift, March 1, 1818, and had four children:—Jarome, b. Sept. 13,

1819; d. Dec. 17, 1888; m. Lucinda Ritter, Dec. 19, 1858.
Amy M., b. Nov. 8, 1826; m. Henry K. Kain, Feb. 20, 1856.
Lafayette, b. June 19, 1829; m. Jane Ann Thomas, Feb. 5,
1851. Susannah, b. June 18, 1835; d. Aug. 18, 1865; m. E.
P. Potter, May 1, 1855.

693. Anna,[8] daughter of 349 Timothy[7] and Hannah
[Damon] Balch, was born at Manchester, Vt., August 27,
1798, and died at Orwell, September 21, 1840. She was
married at Orwell, April 16, 1817, to Edward, son of Allen
and Mary [Hall] Gilbert, of Orwell. He was born May 3,
1795, and died at Lorraine, N. Y., May 2, 1882. Mr. Gilbert
for his second wife married Polly, a younger sister of Ann.

Edward Gilbert and his wife Ann had nine children, all
born in the town of Orwell, N. Y. Hannah, b. March 7,
1819; Polly, b. June 26, 1821, m. first, March 19, 1843,
Samuel Hayt, m. second, May 10, 1846, a Mr. Spink; Nathaniel, b. July 8, 1823, d. May 1, 1893, m. Jan. 1, 1849,
Nancy Leech; Charlotte, b. Sept. 2, 1825, d. Jan. 28, 1847,
m. Mr. Luther James; Lucy, b. Aug. 19, 1827, d. Sept. 6,
1881, m. Oct. 20, 1851, Mr. Chancey James; John, b. Nov.
6, 1831, d. Jan. 27, 1853, at Orwell; Timothy, b. July 17,
1834, m. Sept. 20, 1857; Richard, b. July 17, 1840, d. Oct.
15, 1840.

694. Daniel,[8] son of 349 Timothy[7] and Hannah [Damon]
Balch, was born at Manchester, Vt., July 29, 1800, and died
May 25, 1874. He married Betsey West, who died September 1, 1787. They were members of the Methodist church,
and had five children.

1387   PHILO W.,[9] b. 1825; d. 1828.
1388   MARYETT,[9] b. 1826; d. 1828.
1389*   ABTIMICIA M.,[9] b. May 19, 1829.
1390   CALISTA,[9] b. Aug. 18, 1831; d. Dec. 21, 1893; m. Lewis Park-
       hurst, Dec. 30, 1857.
1391*   LUBANNAH,[9] b. June, 1833; d. Oct. 26, 1877.

695. Polly,[8] daughter of 349 Timothy[7] and Hannah
[Damon] Balch, was born at Manchester, Vt., October 31,
1803, and died at Orwell, September 18, 1893. She was mar-

ried, February 20, 1824, to Daniel, son of Dimmiet and Ruth [Goodenough] Damon. He was born at Manchester, Vt., Nov. 18, 1801. He was killed June 2, 1835; he was a constable, and went into the woods in the town of Boylston, N. Y., to serve some papers, and was there killed. He was a farmer, and resided in the town of Orwell; and their four children were born in that town.

> JOSEPH H., b. Nov. 24, 1825; d.   ; m. Aug. 31, 1862, Melissa Hedges.
> H. MARILLA, b. Sept. 12, 1828; d.   ; m. June 5, 1850, D. C. Bragdon.
> MARY M., b. April 4, 1832; d. March 5, 1893; m. Sept. 7, 1856, A. J. Potter.
> RUTH, b. May 17, 1835; m. Dec. 26, 1855, G. H. West.

Polly married second, March 19, 1843, Edward Gilbert, a widower of her sister Ann. They had one son, Herbert C., b. Oct. 12, 1844, at Orwell. He was a corporal in the 147th regiment, N. Y. vols., wounded at Gettysburg, came home on a furlough, went back, and was killed at Petersburg, Va., June 19, 1864.

698. Ebenezer,[8] son of 357 Cyrus[7] and Judith [Stone] Balch was born September 16, 1787, in the town of Westford, Vermont. He died in Alleghany Co., N. Y. aged 62 years. When he was four years of age, his father moved into the town of Enosburg, Vermont. About 1813 he married Lydia, daughter of Silas Shepard of Northern Vermont. She died in Meigs Co., Ohio, at the age of about 88 years. They were members of the M. E. church and lived in Alleghany Co., N. Y. Family tradition says that he was a volunteer in the battle of Plattsburgh. They had ten children.

1392* CYRUS DECATUR,[9] b. 1812; d. 1877.
1393 NELSON HORATIO,[9] b. 1815; left his home in Alleghany, N. Y., when 22 years of age and was never heard from afterwards.
1394* EBENEZER WASHINGTON,[9] b. 1819; d.
1395* CHRISTOPHER COLUMBUS,[9] b. 1821; d. 1848.
1396* JOHN QUINCY ADAMS,[9] b. April 6, 1825; d. Aug. 28, 1887.
1397 MARQUIS DE LAFAYETTE,[9] b.   ; d. at two years of age.
1398* ANDREW JACKSON,[9] b. Dec. 1, 1838; d. Nov. 3, 1894.
1399 SOPHRONA,[9] b.   ; d.   ; m. a Spaniard and went to Cuba.

1400 ACHSA,[9] b.   ; d.   ; m. a Spaniard and went to Cuba.
1401 MARIA,[9] b.   ; d. aged 17.
1402* BENJAMIN FRANKLIN,[9] b. 1842.

699. Mary,[8] daughter of 357 Cyrus[7] and Judith [Stone] Balch, was born August 20, 1791, and died March 25, 1862, at Elyria, Ohio, where she was buried. In 1850 she went to Ohio, where two of her brothers had made their homes. She lived a brave, trusting, unselfish, unwavering, noble, Christian life. Just one year before the day of her funeral she was stricken with typhoid fever from which she recovered but never rallied. She was married Dec. 31, 1810, to Seth, son of Timothy and Elizabeth Morgan. He was born at Westford, Vermont, October 15, 1791, where he died July 9, 1846. He constructed a log house on an uncleared farm in Westford, where their twelve children were born and named as follows : Orville, Timothy, Tyler, Seth, Elizabeth, Emily Caroline, Hampton, Harmon Cyrus, Elmina Smith, Allen Smith, Elizabeth Roenee, Cora Allen. They also adopted one child, Eliza Abigail. Five grew to maturity.

> EMILY CAROLINE, b. Aug. 25, 1818, d. at Elyria, Ohio, April 22, 1893; m. Jonas Cooke, April 25, 1838. Lived at Elyria, Ohio, San Diego, Cal. Six children, two surviving. *Herman C.* and *Janet M.* at San Diego.
>
> HARMON CYRUS, b. April 6, 1821.
>
> ELMINA SMITH, b. Nov. 19, 1823; d. Oct. 6, 1849.
>
> ELIZABETH ROENEE, b. Feb. 7, 1828; m. George W. Pettengill, Jan. 31, 1847. Live at Essex, Vermont. Nine children, four reaching maturity. *George H.* b. Dec. 1, 1847, d. Nov. 5, 1888; *Elmina M.*, b. Sept. 15, 1849, d. April 6, 1889; *Carrie H.* b. July 17, 1862; *Walter J.*, b. March 31, 1866.
>
> CLARA ALLEN, b. Sept. 5, 1830; m. Abel Cooley, Oct. 31, 1864, in Cleveland, Ohio. He died at their home in West Springfield, Massachusetts, Nov. 13, 1864. She lives at Westford, Vermont.

701. John,[8] son of 357 Cyrus[7] and Judith [Stone] Balch, was born January 29, 1794, and was drowned with nine others by the capsizing of a small boat in Lake Champlain, Aug. 21, 1834. He was buried at Addison, Vermont. He married about 1825, Miss Lucy Williams, a native of New Hampshire, and to them were born five children.

1403*   ELMINA M.,⁸ b. Feb. 6, 1826.
1404*   JOHN,⁸ b. Nov. 12, 1827.
1405*   EMELINE ROBINSON,⁸ b. May 4, 1830; d. Sept. 28, 1886.
1406*   MARTHA ELIZA,⁸ b. Sept. 15, 1832.
1407   ENOS CEYLON,⁸ b. Mar. 7, 1834, at Addison, Vt.; d. Sept., 1864,
        in the Union army at Fort Slocum, D. C., and was buried at
        Arlington. He was a member of Capt. Charles H. Long's
        Company, 1st N. H. Heavy Artillery.

702. Simeon,⁸ son of 357 Cyrus⁷ and Judith [Stone]
Balch, was born in 1796. He married second, about 1829, Miss
Sophronia, daughter of Capt. Coffin, of Nantucket, Mass.
They lived at Mt. Vernon, Fredericktown, Ohio, and later in
Missouri, where they both died.   They had five children.

1408   ALBERT GOODWIN,⁹ b. Aug. 22, 1830.
1409   GEORGIANNA,⁹ b. Oct. 9, 1836.
1410   EDWIN COFFIN,⁹ b. Nov. 12, 1838.
1411   MARY COFFIN,⁹ b. Dec. 14, 1840.
1412   WILLIAM COFFIN,⁹ b. Mar. 1, 1843; d. 1860.

Under date of Vergennes, Vermont, Dec. 12, 1891, Mr.
Geo. W. Grandey writes : " Simeon Balch, Enos B. Balch,
John Balch, and Elmina Balch, came from Enosburg, Franklin Co., Vt., nearly or quite 70 years ago.   Simeon was my
first School Master and taught in Panton many years.   Enos
worked on my father's farm in Panton and Addison and
boarded there.   Elmina boarded and lived in our family a
long time.   I attended the funeral of John Balch and the
others who were drowned in August, 1834, saw them all
taken from the Lake.   Simeon, after he left Panton, went
to Washington, Vt., and married.   My age 79.   Think I
must have been about 5 or 7 years old when Simeon, Enos,
and Elmina lived at our house."

703. Enos,⁸ son of 357 Cyrus⁷ and Judith [Stone] Balch,
was born in Enosburg, Vt., in 1796, '97,* and died at Cleve-

---

*Hemenway, Vermont, Historical Gazetter, Vol. II, page 133.
" As per record; ' June 4, 1798, Anna F. Farrar, daughter of Isaac B.
Farrar and Anna, his wife,' appears to be the first child born in town.
Although report has it, and it is believed, that Enos Balch was the first
child born in town, was named Enos in consideration of the fact, and
was cradled in a sap-trough. It is claimed that his father and mother

land, Ohio, in 1872. He married Emeline, daughter of Capt. Robinson, of Nantucket, Mass. They lived at Elyria, Ohio, and had no children, but adopted a girl, Amanda, who married N. D. White. She lived in Cleveland, and it was at her home that Enos died.

704. Cyrus,[8] son of 357 Cyrus[7] and Judith [Stone] Balch, was born at Enosburg, Vt., in April, 1799, and died at Rutland, Barry Co., Mich., August 7, 1878, and was buried in the same town. He was a farmer. For a time he lived in New York state where his two eldest children were born and died, then he moved to Carlisle, Ohio, where his six other children were born, finally he moved to Rutland, Barry Co., Mich. In August, 1830, he was married to Asenith, daughter of Moses and Sarah Robinson. She was born near Auburn, N. Y., August 4, 1808, and died at Rutland, Mich., September 27, 1882. He was a Republican, a soldier in the War of 1812, and a member of the M. E. church. Their children were eight in number.

1413 VIRGINIA,[9] b.   ; d.
1414 ELMINA,[9] b.   ; d.
1415 SARAH SOPHRONIA,[9] b. Dec. 1, 1836; d. Mar. 21, 1876.
1416* CYRUS MUNSON,[9] b. June 5, 1839.
1417* MARY ERMINA,[9] b. Sept. 10, 1842.
1418* CAROLINE ELIZABETH,[9] b. Jan. 15, 1845.
1419 EDWIN MOSES,[9] b. Feb. 6, 1848.
1420* JAMES WILLIAM,[9] b. Nov. 13, 1849.

705. Elmina,[8] daughter of 357 Cyrus[7] and Judith [Stone] Balch, was born at Enosburgh, Vt., in 1801, and died at Addison, Vt., September 4, 1838. She married Allen Smith. Of her children one is known named Cyrus, and one named Hiram.

706. Ely Stone,[8] son of 357 Cyrus[7] and Judith [Stone]

---

constituted the first family that wintered in town—the winter of 1796 and '97, on the Hoyt farm, so called, now owned by Bradley Bliss, situated on a swell of land in the west part of the town; then and now called Balch Hill. It is interesting to know that this first son of Enosburgh became a worthy minister of the Gospel, of the Methodist persuasion."

Balch, was born at Enosburg, Vt., February 18, 1808, and died at Conway, Mich., December 24, 1861, and was buried in the latter town. He was married first, October 80, 1827, to Philura, daughter of Moses, and Cynthia [Wilson] Southard. She was born in Vermont, December 8, 1808, and died at Pontiac, Mich., June 14, 1842. They had four children, the three first were born in Addison, Vt., the last at Summerfield, Mich.

1421° CYRUS HENRY,° b. Jan. 16, 1830; d. May 28, 1857.
1422° MARTHA HELEN,° b. Mar. 12, 1832.
1423   ALBERT ALLEN,° b. Oct. 2, 1833; d. Aug. 8, 1855.
1424° DELIA ANN ELMINA,° b. Sept. 14, 1836.

Ely Stone was married second, June 5, 1845, to Adeline Coffin. She was born at Nantucket, Mass., May 18, 1806, and died at Conway, Mich., August 18, 1858.   They had two children born at Conway.

1425   ADELINE COFFIN,° b. Apr. 27, 1846; d. Apr. 27, 1846.
1426° EMALINE,° b. July 31, 1847.

On October 14, 1859, Ely Stone Balch married Maria Wilcox. He was a farmer. About 1834, he moved with his family to Michigan in which state he continued to live, first at Pontiac, and finally in Conway.

709. Alden,[8] oldest son of 363 Abner[7] and Lydia P. [Alden] Balch, was born in 1798, and died in 1818.

711. Abner,[8] son of 363 Abner[7] and Lydia P. [Alden] Balch, was born January 1, 1804, and died November 18, 1888. He was a farmer also a carder, dyer and fuller, and was an exemplary man.   He married Lydia Woodbury, September 2, 1830.   They lived at St. Johnsbury, Bath, and Luninburg, Vt., and had seven children.

1427° ELIZA H.,° b. July 19, 1832; d. Dec. 8, 1868.
1428° ALMIRA,° b. July 2, 1834; d. Nov. 25, 1861.
1429° WILLIAM HENRY,° b. Jan. 11, 1837; d. Nov. 13, 1865.
1430   ALFRED,° b. June 11, 1839; killed at battle of Fair Oaks, June
          1, 1862, Fifth N. H. Volunteers.
1431° ELLEN J.,° b. Feb. 27, 1842.
1432   LEVI C.° b. 1841; d. Dec., 1850.
1433° BYRON BLISS,° b. Nov. 23, 1848.

712. Eliza,[8] daughter of 363 Abner[7] and Lydia P. [Alden] Balch, was born February 8, 1805, and died December 6, 1826. She married Aaron Hayes of Lebanon, N. H. They had one son born at Lebanon, Horace Alden, who was born July 26, 1826, and died October 3, 1895. He was married October 28, 1852, to Lucy Ann Fellows, who was born at Lyme, March 6, 1833. They had seven children, the first born at Windsor, Vermont, the second at St. Johnsbury and the others at Groveton, N. H. Charles Melroy, b. Oct. 28, 1853 ; Edith Balch, b. Sept. 15, 1857 ; Winifred Lucy, b. Apr. 1, 1861 ; John Alden, b. Nov. 6, 1864 ; Annie Grace, b. Dec. 28, 1867, d. June 29, 1868 ; William Henry, b. Apr. 4, 1871 ; Blanche Adelyn, b. Feb. 12, 1874.

713. Alfred,[8] son of 363 Abner[7] and Lydia P. [Alden] Balch, was born January 8, 1806, at St. Johnsbury, Vt. ; and died at Lebanon, N. H., April 11, 1892. He was a twin to Albert, who died the same year. He was married, September 3, 1848, to Elizabeth Fellows, daughter of Alvah and Elizabeth [Fellows] Cory, at Lebanon, N. H. She was born at Thetford, Vermont, June 19, 1826. They lived at Lebanon, N. H., until 1856, then in Illinois for two years, and afterward at Hanover, N. H. Mrs. Balch is now at Tiskilwa, Ill. The following are their children.

1434* ELLEN ALMIRA,[9] b. May 31, 1844.
1435* CHARLES PARKHURST,[9] b. Aug. 10, 1845.
1436* PLINNY EARL,[9] b. Jan. 25, 1847.
1437* FRANK MORTIMER,[9] b. June 10, 1849.
1438   NED EUGENE,[9] b. Feb. 25, 1851; unm; living in Chicago.
1439* ALICE MAUD,[9] b. Jan 21, 1853.
1440* ROSALIE,[9] b. Sept. 6, 1855.
1441* ALVAH ABNER,[9] b. Sept. 5, 1857.
1442   JESSIE,[9] b. May 1, 1859; d. unm. Jan., 1878.
1443   ALFRED ALDEN,[9] b. Oct. 4, 1865; unm.; living in Boston, Mass.
1444   CLARENCE HEPWORTH,[9] b. Jan. 5, 1868; unm.; living in Boston.

715. Lydia,[8] daughter of 363 Abner[7] and Lydia P. [Alden] Balch, was born in 1808 and died in 1829. She married her sister Eliza's widower, Aaron Hayes and had one child who died young.

716. Almira A.,[8] daughter of 363 Abner[7] and Lydia P. [Alden] Balch, was born August 5, 1811, and is living in Boston. She was married December 1, 1852, to Frank, son of David and Balinda [Hadlock] Rowell. He was born at Weare, N. H., February 1, 1832. They have no children. Mr. Rowell is a photographer.

717. Albert,[8] son of 363 Abner[7] and Lydia P. [Alden] Balch, was born in 1814, and was killed in a railroad accident, Feb., 1854. He was married to Lois Balcom, of Meriden, N. H. They lived at Lebanon, N. H., and St. Johnsbury, Vermont, and two children were born at each place.

1445 SUSAN,[9] b. ; d. y.
1446 CHARLES GLEASON,[9] b. ; was a soldier in the Union Army and was drowned at Hilton Head, N. C.
1447 JOSHUA,[9] b.
1448 ELIZABETH,[9] b.

719. Sarah Stanley,[8] eldest daughter of 367 Benjamin[7] and Sarah [Stanley] Balch, was born at St. Johnsbury, Vt., November 24, 1809 and lives at Sayre, Pa. She married Russell M. Badger, and by him had one son, Rollo M., b. Jan. 1, 1849; m. Mar. 19, 1879, Maria M. Hutchins.

721. Benjamin,[8] eldest son of 367 Benjamin[7] and Sarah [Stanley] Balch, was born at St. Johnsbury, Vt., June 13, 1812, and lived at Union, N. Y. He died July 15, 1894. About 1840, he married Lucy Cary, by whom he had six children. She was born August 22, 1818.

1449 JUDSON,[9] b. Sept. 6, 1842; d. in the army unm. in his 23d year.
1450 MARY,[9] b. Feb. 23, 1845; d. unm. in her 18th year.
1451* SARAH BELLA,[9] b. May 26, 1849.
1452 FRANK,[9]   }
1453 FREDERICK,[9]   } twins, b. July 28, 1852.
1454 NETTIE BEN,[9] b. June 18, 1858.

722. Matthew Stanley,[8] son of 367 Benjamin[7] and Sarah [Stanley] Balch, was born August 4, 1813, at St. Johnsbury, Vt., and died Oct. 20, 1844. About 1840 he was married to Maria Eldridge, by whom he had two children.

1455 CLARY,[9] b. June 27, 1841.
1456* ELNORA,[9] b. 1843; d.

725. James Britton,[8] son of 367 Benjamin[7] and Sarah
[Stanley] Balch, was born June 22, 1819, at St. Johnsbury,
Vt., and is now living at Nanticoke, N. Y.   He was married
at Union, N. Y., May 15, 1847, to Phoebe Eliza, daughter of
David and Esther (Hempstraugh) Decker.   She was born at
Campville, N. Y., June 18, 1818.   Their three eldest children
were born at Union, N. Y., and the youngest at Bingham-
ton.

1457   VIRGINIA,[9] b. May 1, 1848; unm.; lives at Union, N. Y.
1458* ESTHER ALICE,[9] b. Oct. 4, 1850.
1459* THUR,[9] b. Oct. 19, 1852.
1460* EMMA ANN STANLEY,[9] b. Mar. 25, 1856.

726. Lucy H.,[8] daughter of 367 Benjamin[7] and Sarah
[Stanley] Balch, was born Feb. 12, 1821.   She married
Thomas Twining, January 14, 1849, and to them was born
one son, Thomas Dick, b. Oct. 22, 1849.   He married in
1870, Dorinda M., daughter of James Cogswell, and to them
were born two children. Guy Elmer, b. Apr. 7, 1871 ; Merta,
b. Mar. 8, 1873.

727. Benjamin Franklin,[8] son of 367 Benjamin[7] and
Sarah [Stanley] Balch was born December 8, 1822.   He was
married August 4, 1851, to Miriam Clark, by whom he had
three children.   They live at Binghamton, N. Y.

1461   EMMET LEE,[9] b. May 10, 1854.
1462   EVERETT B.,[9] b. Dec. 19, 1860.
1463   ROSA L.,[9] b. Feb. 12, 1867.

728. Lydia M.,[8] daughter of 367 Benjamin[7] and Sarah
[Stanley] Balch, was born December 24, 1827, and was mar-
ried to Samuel Weed, March 4, 1856, and had three children.
Lilla B., b. Nov. 15, 1857 ; Samuel Everett, b. Aug. 14, 1859;
Nella M., b. Feb. 12, 1869.   She lives at Buffalo, N. Y.

729. Laura Olive,[8] daughter of 368 Sylvanus[7] and
Catherine [Wetherby] Balch, was born at Concord, Vermont,
June 24, 1820, and died at Littleton, New Hampshire, May
24, 1873.   She was married, in 1847, to Franklin, son of
Joseph Tilton, of Danville, Vermont.   He was a man of

prominence in Littleton, and a successful merchant. They had five children, all born in Littleton.

JOHN FRANKLIN, b.

WILLIAM HENRY, b. Jan. 23, 1852, a clothing merchant at San Francisco, Cal.

FREDERICK ALBERT, b.   ; d. May 30, 1898 at Spokane, Wash.; m. Hattie Grace Sample, of Littleton; children, *Luna Belle, Franklin Pearce, Isabel,* and *William Henry.*

MARY BALCH.

CARRIE, b.   ; m. Dr. M. F. Young, of Littleton, N. H. Two sons, *Riley Tilton* and *Willard F.*

730. John Wetherby,[8] son of 368 Sylvanus[7] and Catherine [Wetherby] Balch, was born at Concord, Vt., May 20, 1824. He was married July 23, 1849, to Miss Louisa C., daughter of Solomon and Sally Stevens of Barnet, Vt. She was born at Barnet, June 12, 1827, and died at Marshalltown, Iowa, February 11, 1887. They had two sons.

1464* ALBERT F.,[9] b. April 11, 1855.
1465* PHINEAS S.,[9] b. April 27, 1857.

John W. was a merchant and farmer at Littleton, N. H. for more than 20 years. In 1865, he removed to St. Johnsbury, Vt., and formed the company of "Ely, Balch & Co." manufacturers of hoes and forks. In 1887 he was living at St. Johnsbury, a dealer in furniture, under the firm name of "Hall & Balch."

731. Samuel Albert,[8] son of 368 Sylvanus[7] and Catherine (Wetherby) Balch, was born June 11, 1828, and died in San Francisco, California, May 14, 1895. He was married in New York city about 1862, to Agnes Lacy, a native of Ireland, and a Roman Catholic. She died Jan. 31, 1886, aged 52 years. They had two daughters, both born in New York.

1466* MARY E.,[9] b. June 22, 1863.
1467   ELIZA J.,[9] b. Aug. 23, 1867 ; d. Oct. 6, 1876.

Samuel Albert worked for many years for the Knickerbocker Ice Co., of New York, then he went to California and engaged in mining and farming. He then returned east and

engaged in the ice business again. About 1882 he returned
to the Pacific coast. He was of quiet, gentle disposition, but
extremely reticent, and never told his family who his relatives
were, or told his brother of his marriage. Because of his
prolonged absence from home, his daughter, Mrs. Smalley,
became anxious after his welfare, and in the spring of 1898
her husband looked in the New York directory, and finding
the son of the author of this Genealogy with a similar name,
called at his office and made known the facts concerning
his father-in-law's marriage. As Samuel Albert had not com-
municated with his brother in Vermont for some time, it
was not possible to obtain his address at the time. Early in
the next year, Samuel Albert suddenly appeared at his
daughter's home, was shown his genealogical record and admitted that it was correct. He remained for a few days and
then suddenly disappeared. Notice of his death was published in a San Francisco paper; it was cut out and sent to
the author of the Genealogy by a correspondent in Tacoma,
and through it Mrs. Smalley first learned of her father's death
just three months after it occurred.

732. Selinda,[8] daughter of 370 Adin[7] and Martha [Gee]
Balch, was born at Lunenburg, Vt., February 1, 1812. She
married, when quite young, a Mr. Carby, a farmer, and was
the mother of fourteen children, of whom none were twins.
They moved about considerably.

734. James,[8] son of 370 Adin[7] and Martha [Gee] Balch,
was born at Lunenburg, Vt., February 23, 1816, and died
February 27, 1894. He was a shoemaker. For many years
he played the bass viol in the Baptist Church choir at Lunenburg. He married Fannie Smith, who was born April 3,
1816, and died March 31, 1887. They had seven children,
all born in Lunenburg, Vermont.

1468[a] SYLVIA W.,[9] b. Sept. 29, 1839; d. Oct. 15, 1892.
1469[a] EMELINE M.,[9] b. Nov. 5, 1840; d. July 27, 1874.
1470[a] AUSTIN A.,[9] b. Jan. 8, 1842.

1471   WILLIAM J.,⁹ b. Oct. 18, 1843; d. July 8, 1868; m. Mary Hubbard.

1472   MATILDA C.,⁹ b. Aug. 17, 1845; m. June 3, 1874, Martin V. B. Vance.

1473* GARDNER H.,⁹ b. Dec. 7, 1848.

1474   LUCY E.,⁹ b. Aug. 8, 1852; m. John B. Blandin.

735. Edward Austin,⁸ son of 370 Adin⁷ and Martha [Gee] Balch, was born at Lunenburg, Vt., June 16, 1817, and died November 12, 1891, at Harmon, Illinois, where he was a farmer. He was a fine singer. He was married April 20, 1847, to Mary, daughter of William and Betsy [Davis] Ingerson. She was born at Jefferson, N. H., December 26, 1818. They had three children of whom one died young.

1475* LAURA L.,⁹ b. Feb. 15, 1848, at Lunenburg, Vt.

1476* GEORGE EDWARD,⁹ b. Oct. 25, 1853, at Jefferson, N. H.

736. William,⁸ son of 370 Adin⁷ and Martha [Gee] Balch, was born at Lunenburg, Vt., May 1, 1819, and died September 6, 1842. He married Lucy Ann Moss. A few minutes before his death he sang with great pathos the hymn "All is well."

737. Martha,⁸ daughter of 370 Adin⁷ and Martha [Gee] Balch, was born at Lunenburg, April 17, 1821. She married a well to do farmer, and lived on one farm all her life, and had five sons and three daughters. She was a most excellent woman and a fine singer.

738. Caroline Matilda,⁸ daughter of 370 Adin⁷ and Martha [Gee] Balch, was born at Lunenburg, Vt., April 21, 1824, and died at Pewamo, Mich., June 2, 1885. She was buried at Lebanon, Mich. She had a fine alto voice, trained for concert singing. On December 8, 1849, she was married to William Henry, son of George and Louisa [Hovey] Woodworth. He was born at Dorchester, N. H., on January 14, 1828. They had one son, Henry Dodge, b. March 10, 1851, at Salem Falls, N. H. He was married, Nov. 27, 1878, to Maggie H. Rose, daughter of Almon Rose and Caroline [Brown] Kraus. She was born at Lyons, Mich., March 5, 1856. Henry Dodge is a farmer at Pewamo, Mich. Their children are as follows: Bertha, b. Nov. 6, 1874; Vera, b. June 11, 1878; Bela, b. July 31, 1880; Vida, b. July 31, 1882; Thomas, b. March 4, 1887; Pliny Lawton, b. June 8, 1889; William Henry, b. Feb. 26, 1892; Caroline, b. April 28, 1893; Dorothy, b. April 13, 1895.

739. Rachel,[8] daughter of 370 Adin[7] and Martha [Gee] Balch, was born at Lunenburg, Vt., May 23, 1826, and lives at Pewamo, Michigan. She married, in 1857, George D. Pennington, who was born in England, and died at Pewamo, Mich., in April, 1867, from disease caused by service in the army. He was a cabinet maker at Pewamo.

Rachel married a second time, December 8, 1885, William H. Woodworth, whose first wife was her sister, Caroline M. His business is farming and lumbering. From 1873 to 1885 he was Judge of Probate for the county of Iona, Mich. Rachel was a fine singer. She has no children.

740. Elizabeth H.,[8] daughter of 370 Adin[7] and Martha [Gee] Balch, was born at Lunenburg, Vt., January 6, 1828, and died August 19, 1878. She married, first, Leonard Pierce, a well to do farmer. No issue. She married second a Mr. Neigh, by whom she had one child.

741. George Sherman,[8] son of 370 Adin[7] and Martha [Gee] Balch, was born at Lunenburg, September 16, 1833, and has always lived in that town, and is a manufacturer of sleighs, carriages and caskets. He was one of the Balch Concert Company. On April 6, 1853, he was married to M. Eliza, daughter of Rev. Jeremiah and Weltha [Wood] Glins, of Lunenburg. She was born in that town, February 8, 1835, and died there, July 28, 1887. Their five children were born in the same town.

1477* WILLIAM E.,[9] b. Feb. 3, 1854.
1478* GEORGE A.,[9] b. Sept. 27, 1855.
1479* HERBERT F.,[9] b. Sept. 28, 1857.
1480* KARL O.,[9] b. July 4, 1860.
1481 ANNIE W.,[9] b. Aug. 21, 1871.

742. Isaac A.,[8] son of 370 Adin[7] and Martha [Gee]

Balch, was born at Lunenburg, September 10, 1836. He was
married June 3, 1860, to Abbie J. Wallace, of Concord, Vt.
Shortly after his marriage he removed from Lunenburg to
Lyons, Michigan, where he was a successful teacher of music. He is the owner of a large farm, and has an apiary of
over 300 colonies of bees. He has no children.

743. **Louisa E.,**[8] youngest daughter of 370 Adin[7] and
Martha [Gee] Balch, was born at Lunenburg, Vt., March 16,
1838. She married, first, J. E., son of Rev. Jeremiah and
Weltha [Wood] Glins. He was born at Concord, N. H., in
1830, and was a teacher and composer of both instrumental
and vocal music. He volunteered and served in the civil
war as a band master. They had one son, Frank Gay, b.
April 22, 1869.

Louisa E. married second Peter J., son of Christien Speicher,
a farmer at Goble, Michigan. He was born April 8, 1835, at
Milford, Penn.; they have one son, Benjamin M., b. May 17,
1871.

Louisa E., at the age of ten years, traveled with her brother
Geo. S. and sisters Caroline and Rachel, giving concerts
through the Eastern States, under the name of the Balch
Family. Her first husband was one of the Concert Company.

For many years she has been a member and the leader of
the choir of the Baptist Church at Goble. Her two sons are
musical and are members of the band at Goble.

746. **Lura,**[8] daughter of 371 William[7] and Lucy [How-
land] Balch, was born at Lunenburg, Vt., September 1, 1822,
and died Oct. 17, 1893. She was married, December 14,
1844, to Caleb Johuson, a farmer, who was born at Lunenburg,
June 10, 1814; and died July 20, 1889. They always lived
at Lunenburg, and their children were all born in that town.

> WILLIAM, b. Oct. 31, 1845; m. Louisa Wheeler, Oct. 19, 1871. He
> is a farmer, and lives at Perris, Cal. They have three
> children: *Grace L.*, b. June 24, 1878; *Mabel B.*, b. Dec.
> 1, 1881; *Harry A.*, b. Aug. 18, 1885.
>
> WASHINGTON, b. May 19, 1848; m. Jenney Manley, Dec. 18, 1871.
> He resides at Grand Junction, Ia., and is an engineer.

They have four children: *Irving W.*, b. Aug. 8, 1876; *Ernest W.*, b. May 5, 1880; *Charlott G.*, b. Aug. 25, 1885; *Mildred P.*, b. Jan. 17, 1889.

JEROME, b. Nov. 21, 1849; d. Mar. 2, 1883; m. Lizzie L. Dodge, Nov. 21, 1877. He was a farmer; they had two children: *Vernon P.*, b. May 26, 1879; *Inez H.* b. Feb. 21, 1881.

LUCY M., b. June 21, 1854; m. Albert J. Morton, June 17, 1882. They have one daughter, *Laura B.*, b. Mch. 28, 1893.

ALONZO, b. Apr. 24, 1857.

BELINDA, b. Oct. 17, 1859; lives at South Lunenburg, Vt.

751. Electa,[8] daughter of 371 William[7] and Lucy [Howland] Balch. was born at Lunenburg, Vt., April 28, 1832, and died in the same town, March 13, 1888. She was married, September 14, 1854, to Timothy Powers, a farmer; he was born at Lunenburg, April 27, 1827. They always lived in Lunenburg, and their four children were born there.

JULIA A., b. Aug. 28, 1856; m. Jan. 27, 1880, Judson Olcot, a farmer. They live at Lunenburg, and have had three children: *Glen Edison*, b. Apr. 21, 1881; *Roy Berton*, b. Dec. 30, 1886; d. Sept. 4, 1888; *Nina Electa*, b. Oct. 7, 1889.

NELLIE A., b. Mar. 24, 1860; d. Feb. 12, 1890; m. Nelson D. Holmes, of Brockton, Mass., a carpenter.

EUGENE C., b. Apr. 30, 1864.

ERNEST W., b. Jan. 22, 1874.

753. George,[8] son of 372 James[7] and Nancy [Moore] Balch, was born at Lunenburg, Vt., August 5, 1821, and was killed by the cars at Davenport, Iowa, January 2, 1880, and was buried at Davenport. He was married at Concord, Vt., May 27, 1844, to Elizabeth H. Aldrich, who was born at Troy, Vt. They had two children.

1482° FRANK A.,[9] b. May 14, 1847.

1483 ELLEN,[9] b. Mar. 13, 1852; d. June 1, 1857.

After George's marriage they resided at Concord, Vt., for five years, then they removed to Milford, Mass., where they lived nine years, and then they removed to Davenport, Iowa, where his widow still resides.

754. Stephen Moore,[8] son of 372 James[7] and Nancy [Moore] Balch, was born at Concord, Vt., February 12, 1826. He was a commission merchant at San Francisco, California, where he died December 20, 1876; he was buried in the Masonic Cemetery of San Francisco. He was married in Boston, Mass., March 13, 1852, to Olive A. Kimball, of Kennebeck, Maine. She was born July, 1820. They had two children.

1484   ELLA A.,⁹ b. at San Francisco, July 13, 1858; d. Sept. 3, 1858.
1485⁰ ADDIE LOUISE,⁹ b. at Kennebeck, Me., Oct. 8, 1860.

755. **Susan,**⁸ daughter of 374 John⁷ and Lucy [Bowen] Balch, was born February 8, 1786. She married Alexander Harrison. They lived at Onondaga, N. Y., and their eight children were born in that town. Peggy Ann; Susan; Emerson; John; Sprague; Thomas; Alexander; Allet.

756. **Anna,**⁸ daughter of 374 John⁷ and Lucy [Bowen] Balch, was born October 4, 1787. She married Chauncey Brockett. They had four children; then they moved to Ohio, and nothing more is known of them; their children were Hosea, Nancy, Lucy Ann and Matilda.

758. **Lucy,**⁸ daughter of 374 John⁷ and Lucy [Bowen] Balch, was born November 20, 1791, and died at Norvell, Mich., October 10, 1861. She married William Marlatt, by whom she had four children, Maria, Lucy Ann, James and Seneca.

759. **John,**⁸ son of 374 John⁷ and Lucy [Bowen] Balch, was born December 20, 1793, and died at Norvell, Mich., October 10, 1868. He was married to Sybil, daughter of Lemuel Barrow. She was born in 1788, and died August 3, 1858. John resided at Marcellus, N. Y., and at Norvell, Mich. Their three children were born at Marcellus, N. Y.

1486⁰ ABIGAIL,⁹ b. Dec. 12, 1815; d. May 9, 1891.
1487⁰ JAMES,⁹ b. May 7, 1819; d. Feb. 14, 1892.
1488⁰ ADELPHIA,⁹ b. Dec. 12, 1821; d.

760. **Ira,**⁸ son of 374 John⁷ and Lucy [Bowen] Balch, was born May 20, 1796, and died at Sodus, N. Y., August 29, 1861. He was married about 1820 to Margaret, daughter of George Baker. She was born June 21, 1804, and died September 15, 1864. Ira was a farmer at Sodus, N. Y. Their

eight youngest children were born in that town, and the two eldest at Onondaga, N. Y.

　1489　Lita,[9] b. Sept. 18, 1822; d. unm., Oct. 30, 1838.
　1490*　Holland,[9] b. Jan. 31, 1825.
　1491*　Mary,[9] b. July 21, 1827; d. March 20, 1892.
　1492　Jane,[9] b. Nov. 9, 1829; lives at Mount Morris, Michigan.
　1493　Euphrasia,[9] b. July 21, 1832; d. July 12, 1860.
　1494*　Caroline,[9] b. May 28, 1835; d. Aug. 30, 1889.
　1495　Olive,[9] b. Feb. 11, 1838; d. Dec. 19, 1849.
　1496*　Orrin,[9] b. June 4, 1840.
　1497　John,[9] b. Jan. 15, 1843; lives at Mount Morris, Michigan.
　1498　Amanda,[9] b. Aug. 17, 1845; lives at Mount Morris; m. Granger.

762.　Calista,[8] daughter of 374 John[7] and Lucy [Bowen] Balch, was born August 12, 1801, and died at Onondaga, N. Y. She married Sylvester Harronn, by whom she had ten children, all born at Onondaga : Emma, Narcissa, Seth, Cornelia, Roxy, Albert, Alexander, Wesley, Fletcher, William.

763.　Celinda,[8] daughter of 374 John[7] and Lucy [Bowen] Balch, was born August 12, 1801, a twin to Calista. She married George Baker, and had six children ; Fanny, Laura, Byron, Elsie, Frank, Willard.

764.　David,[8] son of 374 John[7] and Lucy [Bowen] Balch, was born at Colerain, Massachusetts, July 2, 1804, and is living at Medina, New York. On February 20, 1831, he was married to Polly, daughter of Jude and Joyce [Baher] Comstock. She was born at Onondaga, N. Y., February 10, 1811, and died February 5, 1895. David is a farmer, and lived many years at Ridgeway, N. Y., where his six children were born.

　1499*　Jude Henry,[9] b. July 5, 1833.
　1500*　Lydia Almira,[9] b. Nov. 8, 1835.
　1501　Francis,[9] b. April 1, 1838; d. Aug. 21, 1838.
　1502*　William Jackson,[9] b. Feb. 18, 1843.
　1503*　Charles Irwin,[9] b. Feb. 10, 1849.
　1504*　Martha Ann,[9] b. Sept. 16, 1851.

765.　Stephen,[8] son of 375 William[7] and Elizabeth [Hall] Balch, was born at Mansfield, Ct., November 29, 1787, and died at Algonquin, Illinois, December 22, 1874, and was buried at Elgin, Illinois. Rev. William S. Balch officiated at

his funeral. He was a farmer, a Republican, and a member
of the Church of the Disciples. On December 25, 1809, he
married Polly, daughter of Zalmon Terrell. She was born
February 7, 1790, and died at Elgin, February 10, 1872.
They had twelve children, all born in the state of New York.

1505* HORACE,[9] b. Jan. 2, 1811.
1506* JASPER,[9] b. Sept. 11, 1812; d. Jan. 19, 1891.
1507* DIANTHA,[9] b. Sept. 16, 1814; d. Dec. 9, 1848.
1508 PHOEBE,[9] b. June 15, 1817; d. unm. March 26, 1836.
1509* PHILANDER,[9] b. Feb. 18, 1819.
1510* LAURA,[9] b. July 10, 1821; d. July 2, 1891.
1511* ALBERT,[9] b. March 30, 1823.
1512* MATILDA,[9] b. Sept. 17, 1825.
1513* LUCINDA,[9] b. Nov. 30, 1827.
1514 NELSON,[9] b. Oct. 20, 1829; d. unm. Jan. 2, 1853.
1515* HARRIET,[9] b. Feb. 4, 1832.
1516* MELINDA,[9] b. Nov. 2, 1835; d.

769. Phebe,[8] daughter of 375 William[7] and Elizabeth
[Hall] Balch, was born at Onondaga, N. Y., June 26, 1796,
and died at Marcellus, N. Y., in 1875. She was married October 26, 1810, to Seneca Hunt, of Onondaga. He was the
son of Seneca Hunt, and was born June 19, 1766, and died
at Onondaga, March 31, 1847. He was a carpenter, and they
resided at Onondaga and Marcellus, N. Y. They had ten
children : Stephen, b. Aug. 10, 1812 ; Jehial, Sarah Ann,
Jasper, Senaca, Betsey Ann, Adeline, William, Henry, Cor-
ridon.

774. Marvin,[8] son of 876 Israel[7] and Sarah [——]
Balch, was born at Mansfield, Ct., March 1, 1793. Whether
he married or not has not been ascertained. The Connecticut Records show that Marvin enlisted from Groton in Amos
Chaffe's company, serving from Aug. 23 to Oct. 26, 1814.

778. Ann,[8] daughter of 377 Bezaleel[7] and Ruth [Davis]
Balch, was born at Mansfield, Ct., August 18, 1789, and died
at South Coventry, Ct., September 7, 1845. She was married
to Samuel, son of Jerome Topliff, of Coventry, October 28,
1819. He was born at South Coventry, October 8, 1789, and
died in the same town August 29, 1850, and both he and his

wife were buried in that town.   He was a farmer.   They had seven children all born at Coventry.

SAMUEL D., b. July 13, 1820.

AARON P., b. May 20, 1822; d. May 28, 1833.

DAVID B., b. Oct. 31, 1823; d. June 12, 1831.

JOHN S., b. July 9, 1824; m. Zerviah F. Standish, June 2, 1851, who was born Mar. 17, 1825. She was a sister to Lucius Green Standish, who married Mary, the youngest daughter of Bezaleel Balch.   John S. and Zerviah F. had two children. *Miles Standish*, b. March 23, 1852; m. Mary Kenyon, and resides at Andover, Ct. *Fanny S.*, b. Oct. 17, 1853; d. Dec. 23, 1863.

ANDREW J., b. Mar. 23, 1828; m. first, Mary Bascom, had one child *Mary*, b. in 1861.

RHODA ANN, b. Oct. 13, 1830; d. June 15, 1847.

DAVID W., b. June 29, 1833.

779.   John,[8] son of 377 Bezaleel[7] and Ruth [Davis] Balch, was born at Mansfield, Ct., December 7, 1791, and died at Momence, Ill., April 3, 1868.   He was married April 10, 1816, to Almira Stowell, who was born at Mansfield, Ct., June 21, 1793, and died at Momence, May 17, 1886.   He was a stonemason, and resided most of his life in Cortland Co., N. Y. He enlisted in a Connecticut regiment in 1814, but the war closed before the regiment was sent into the field.

1517• FIDELIA ANN,[9] b. June 9, 1825.

1518   HORACE ORLANDO,[9] b. Mar. 31, 1827; lived at Wichita, K.

1519• EMMA MELVINA,[9] b. Oct. 11, 1831.

1520• MARY JANE,[9] b. April 9, 1833.

1521• JOHN RANSOM,[9] b. Jan. 18, 1835.

1522   BETSEY ROXANA,[9] b. July 30, 1841.

780.   Ruth,[8] daughter of 377 Bezaleel[7] and Ruth [Davis] Balch, was born at Mansfield, Ct., September 7, 1794, and died at Blauvelt, New York, April 18, 1875.   She was buried in New York Bay Cemetery at Jersey City, N. J.   She was married October 23, 1822, to Philip Mackenzie, a ship carpenter. He was born at Ross Shire, Scotland, June 24, 1788, and died in New York city, October 30, 1842.   They had five children, the three eldest were born at Springfield, Mass., the other two at New York city.

PHILIP WALLACE, b. Jan. 27, 1824; d. May 24, 1891.   He was an inventor and manufacturer.

HELEN MAR, b. Sept. 23, 1825; resides at Pearl River, New York, is a teacher and writer. She is a member of the Episcopal Church, and an active member of the Woman's Christian Temperance Union.

WALTER SCOTT, b. Aug. 18, 1828; d. spring of 1871, was a jeweler. He removed to California in 1852, and died there.

ANDREW, b. Oct. 10, 1831. He has been a machinist, but is now at Pearl River. He enlisted as a private in the 170th New York Infantry Volunteers and served from Sept. 6, 1862, to the close of the war, was wounded near Petersburg, Va., June 16, 1864.

MARY FANNY, b. Sept. 12, 1834. Is a teacher, and has been engaged in schools in New York city and vicinity. She is a member of the Episcopal church, and interested in the temperance cause.

This family are Republicans. Mrs. Mackenzie was a Congregationalist. Before her marriage she was a school teacher, and through her life she took a deep interest in education and missionary work.

782. **Elizabeth,**[8] daughter of 877 Bezaleel[7] and Ruth [Davis] Balch, was born at Mansfield, Ct., April 25, 1799, and died January 3, 1877, at Colchester, Ct. She married James Ashton, of Ashton, England, and had three children.

OLIVER CROMWELL, b. July 28, 1832 ; m. first, Oct. 22, 1860, Eunice S. Marsh, of Colchester, Ct.; m. second, June 24, 1896, Mrs. Ouiss J. Gilman.

ELIZABETH, b. May 2, 1835; m. Dec. 18, 1865, John H. Talcott; lives at Silver Creek, N. Y.

JAMES T., b. Aug. 1, 1836; m. Sept. 19, 1865, Mary Lou Stevens, of Bryan, Ohio, where they reside; children, *Clara E.*, *James T.*, *Fred W.*, *Walter S.*, *Emma Lou.*

783. **Fanny,**[8] daughter of 877 Bezaleel[7] and Ruth [Davis] Balch, was born at Mansfield, Connecticut, June 21, 1801, and died at Tolland, Connecticut, February 1, 1885. She was a woman of great courage and endurance. She was married to Jabez, son of David and Mercy (Clark) West, of Lebanon, Connecticut. He was born in that town February 22, 1799, and died at Tolland, August 11, 1869. He was a blacksmith and farmer. Their nine children were all born at Colchester, Ct.

MARY E., b. Feb. 19, 1825; m. Feb. 19, 1845, Albert W. Lamb.
He left for California in 1850, and was never heard from.
She was at Hartford, Ct.; two sons, *Frank A.* and *Adelbert W.*

FANNY H., b. April 3, 1827; m. Apr. 3, 1844; William O. Thompson. He died Oct. 12, 1860. She lives at Waterbury, Ct.;
two daughters, *Mary F.* and *Julia H.*

AURELIA M., b. Nov. 28, 1828; d. Dec. 17, 1882; m. Charles H.
Stebbins; one son, *Charles F.*

SUSAN M., b. Apr. 29, 1831; d. Apr. 8, 1892; m. Sept. 19, 1852,
Thomas Burt, at Tolland, Ct. He d. Apr. 8, 1881; children,
George W. and *Susan M.* live at Holyoke, Mass.

CAROLINE N., b. Feb. 23, 1833; m. May, 1853, James W. Burton.
He d. Jan., 1882; three children, *William J.*, *Carrie E.*, and
Lillian F.

JABEZ C., b. Jan. 6, 1835; d. Apr. 11, 1865.

ORREN C., b. Jan. 18, 1837; m. Amanda Waller; one daughter,
Fanny; m. second, Elizabeth M. Fuller; one daughter, *Grace
Balch.*

JULIUS C., b. Jan. 14, 1839; m. Martha J. Charter; children, *Julius
S., Nettie R., Walter P., Howard, Evelyne H., Byron E.*

WILLIAM W., b. Oct. 28, 1841; d. Apr. 29, 1844.

784. Ahimaaz,[8] son of 377 Bezaleel[7] and Ruth [Davis]
Balch was born at Mansfield, Ct., April 1, 1808, and is not
now living. He married Sarah Way, of Colchester, Ct., and
had one son by her.

1523* JOHN,[9] b.

Ahimaaz married second, Eliza, daughter of Nehemiah
Lee, of Colchester, Ct., and by her he had two more children.

1524* BETSEY MORGAN,[9] b.
1525* FRANCES ANN,[9] b.

785. Mary,[8] daughter of 377 Bezaleel[7] and Ruth [Davis]
Balch, was born at Mansfield, Ct., Oct. 3, 1809. She is living
at Springville, N. Y. On September 7, 1834, she was married
to Lucius Green Standish, who was born Sept. 7, 1812, and
died May 3, 1882. He was a blacksmith. Their three children were born at Colchester, Connecticut.

MARY PAMELA, b. Mar. 20, 1840; m. Henry Miller, of Colchester, and they now reside in that town.

JULIA FRANCES, b. Nov. 27, 1843; m. Henry Ware, June 20, 1878.
They reside at Springville, N. Y. Ware is road master on
the Rochester and Pittsburg R. R.; one son, *Lloyd*, b. June
29, 1879.

GEORGE GEER, b. Apr. 6, 1846; m. Nov. 22, 1883, Evalyn M.
Webb, of Willimantic, Ct. She died June 28, 1886. One son,
Henry Webb, b. Sept. 24, 1884, George G. is head of the firm
of Standish & Thompson, boot and shoe dealers at Danbury,
Ct. He m. second, Oct. 12, 1891, Harriet, daughter of Dr.
George and Anna Miner. She was b. New York City, June
9, 1864. Three sons: *Myles*, b. Aug. 18, 1892; *Livingston Miner*,
b. Mar. 29, 1894; *George Winthrop*, b. Jan. 17, 1896.

787a. Thomas Sumter,[8] son of 382* Samuel Williams[7]
and Maria Randolph [Holmes] Balch, was born February 29,
1812, at Rio Janeiro, Brazil, and died unmarried in 1884 in
Texas.

787b. Maria Glorianna,[8] daughter of 382* Samuel
Williams[7] and Maria Randolph [Holmes] Balch was born
May 20, 1814, at Rio Janeiro and lives at New Brighton,
Staten Island.

787c. Emilia Abigail,[8] daughter of 382* Samuel
Williams[7] and Maria Randolph [Holmes] Balch, was born
July 1, 1816, at Roxbury, Massachusetts. She lived at New
York City from 1823 to 1886, and now lives at New Brighton,
Staten Island.

787d. Natilie Catharine,[8] daughter of 382* Samuel
Williams[7] and Maria Randolph [Holmes] Balch, was born in
1817 at Good Luck, New Jersey, and is living at Matteawan,
New York. She was married in 1845 to William C. Free-
man, a lawyer in New York City. Their children are as
follows: William Randolph, born Nov. 20, 1847, and died in
Texas, 1892; Josephine Augusta, born April 20, 1851, m.
John Wesley Chandler, a flour merchant in Chicago; Catha-
rine Maria, born November, 1859, m. Aaron Tice and lives at
Matteawan, New York.

787e. Louisa Anna Davidson,[8] daughter of 382*
Samuel Williams[7] and Maria Randolph [Holmes] Balch was
born December, 1819, at New Orleans, where she died unmarried, Nov. 20, 1885.

---

*See Addenda for additional records of 382 Samuel Williams Balch.

788. Ann Alexander,[8] daughter of 385 Alexander[7] and Ann [Clapp] Balch, was born February 4, 1818, and died in Boston, May 12, 1885. She was married February 28, 1834, to Francis Dana Kidder, a merchant of Boston. They had one child, Frances Ann, born in Boston, June 14, 1835. She was married December 8, 1870, to Zabdiel Boylston Adams, M. D., son of Zabdiel Boylston Adams, M. D., and Sarah May [Holland] Adams, of Boston. He settled in Framingham in 1867, and they have two children, Frances Boylston, b. 1872; Zabdiel Boylston, b. 1875.

789. Samuel West,[8] son of 389 Joshua[7] and Nanny P. [Shaw] Balch, was born at Lyme, N. H., June 9, 1803, and died May 27, 1889. He married December 23, 1835, Joanna E., daughter of Adna and Frances [Campbell] Perkins. She was born May 31, 1812, and died June 27, 1875. They had twelve children born at Lyme, New Hampshire.

1526* ANNAH MARIA,[9]
1527* LUCRETIA SOPHIA,[9] } twins, b. July 5, 1837.
1528* FRANCES CAMPBELL,[9] b. Oct. 2, 1839.
1529 SARAH PERKINS,[9] b. Apr. 24, 1842; lives at Lyme, N. H.
1530 WEST SHAW,[9] b. July 9, 1843; d. Nov. 14, 1844.
1531 WEST SHAW,[9] b. May 16, 1845; d. May 18, 1848.
1532* CHARLES CARROL,[9] b. Aug. 23, 1847.
1533* WEST SHAW,[9] b. May 16, 1849.
1534 JOHN BUNYAN,[9] b. Mar. 17, 1850; d. Feb. 12, 1853.
1535 HARRIET BEECHER,[9] b. Jan. 3, 1853; d. June 13, 1859.
1536 ELLEN RUGGLES,[9] b. Dec. 1, 1854; d. May 30, 1859.
1537 ELIZABETH PRITCHARD,[9] b. Dec. 12, 1856; d. Dec. 20, 1860.

790. Julia,[8] daughter of 389 Joshua[7] and Nanny P. [Shaw] Balch, was born at Lyme, N. H., May 15, 1805, and died in 1898. She was married February 8, 1829, to Jonathan Kittredge. He was born July 17, 1793, graduated at Dartmouth in 1813, read law in New York city, and settled at Canaan, N. H., and represented the town for several years in the state legislature. He was appointed Chief Justice of the Court of Common Pleas, and removed to Concord, N. H., where he continued to reside until his death, which occurred April 8, 1864. He was distinguished as a pioneer in the temperance movement. A lecture by him was the first delivered and published in the state, January 8, 1827. They had nine children: Edgar Perry, b. Apr. 6, 1830; d. Mar. 5, 1832. Julia Apphia, b. Oct. 18, 1831; d. Feb. 13, 1861, m. James Monroe Fallansbee, Jan. 2, 1854. Alfred Hamilton, b. July 31, 1833; m. Susan Frances Keefer, Jan. 11, 1865. Edward Cornelius Delevan, b. Dec. 29, 1834; d. Jan. 20, 1879; m. Rosaline Holmes, May 9, 1871. Augustus Greeley, b. Sept. 30, 1836; d. Jan. 23, 1868. Ellen Maria, b. Dec. 7, 1838; d. Aug. 11, 1839. Jonathan Perry, b. Dec. 18, 1840; resides at Concord, N. H. Henry and Fannie.

791. Dan Shaw,[8] son of 389 Joshua[7] and Nanny P. [Shaw] Balch, was born at Lyme, N. H., March 16, 1807, and died at Minneapolis, Minn., February 24, 1888. He was married November 2, 1834, to Dorothy Marston, daughter of Richard and Lettace Whittier. She was born at Grafton, N. H., March 8, 1816, and died at Minneapolis, Minn., July 21, 1886. They lived at Canaan, N. H., Bradford, Vt., Boscawen, Concord and Fisherville, N. H. In May, 1855, they moved to Minneapolis, Minnesota. They had eleven children.

1538* FOSTER LAMSON,[9] b. Sept. 19, 1835, at Canaan, N. H.
1539   ADELINE PRICHARD,[9] b. Jan. 18, 1837.
1540* HENRY FRANCIS,[9] b. Nov. 17, 1838.
1541* MARTHA JANE,[9] b. Nov. 8, 1842.
1542* DAN WHITTIER,[9] b. Sept. 28, 1844.
1543* FRED KITTREDGE,[9] b. Mar. 2, 1847.
1544* CHARLES JOSEPH,[9] b. Dec. 8, 1848.
1545* GEORGE SHAW,[9] b. Apr. 8, 1851.
1546* WILLIAM CLARK,[9] b. Sept. 18, 1853.
1547* KATE GAGE,[9] b. Nov. 9, 1857.
1548* EVA DOROTHY,[9] b. June 8, 1860.

795. Adna Perkins,[8] son of 389 Joshua[7] and Nanny P. [Shaw] Balch, was born at Lyme, N. H., November 30, 1817, and died at Hanover, N. H., May 28, 1889. He married first December 23, 1841, Julia A. Drake, by whom he had three children.

1549 HELEN A.,[9] b. May 8, 1843; d. at Hanover, N. H., Nov. 18, 1868.
1550 FRANK K.,[9] b. Feb. 23, 1845; died at Panama, United States of
         Columbia, April 13, 1883.
1551 EDWARD P.,[9] b. Feb. 1, 1850; d. at Shakopee, Minn., in 1876.

Julia A. Drake died. Abner P. married, October 17, 1855, Susan Brewster Bibby, of Paterson, N. J. She died at Hanover, N. H., March 3, 1889, aged 55 years. They had seven children, three dying unnamed.

1552 WILLIAM VAN BEAVERHENDT,[9] b. Oct. 5, 1857; d. Dec. 1, 1858.
1553* JULIA GOUVERNEUR,[9] b. Nov. 9, 1861.
1554 EMILY MONTAGUE,[9] b. Nov. 18, 1867; d. Dec. 10, 1868.
1555 HENRY KEMBLE,[9] b. Mar. 7, 1874.

796. Francis Brown,[8] son of 389 Joshua[7] and Nanny P. [Shaw] Balch, was born at Lyme, New Hampshire, August 3, 1819, and died at Winchester, New Hampshire, March 28, 1891, and was buried in the same town. He was a currier. He was married December 16, 1849, to Louisa, daughter of Omri and Hannah Dyke. She was born at Lyme. They had seven children, one unnamed, all born at Lyme, except the youngest, who was born at Haverhill, N. H.

1556 NELSON KENT,[9] b. Feb. 11, 1851; d. Aug. 27, 1863.
1557* ADELIA ANN,[9] b. Jan. 11, 1853.
1558 JULIA KITTRIDGE,[9] b. Nov. 1, 1855; d. Aug. 25, 1863.
1559* ALICE LOUISA,[9] b. Dec. 18, 1857; d. Aug. 26, 1887.
1560 FRANCIS BROWN,[9] b. July 6, 1860.
1561* HERBERT NEWTON,[9] b. July 11, 1868.

797. Mary,[8] daughter of 390 Israel[7] and Elizabeth [Epps] Balch, was born at Francestown, N. H., August 12, 1797, and died at Troy, N. H., June 8, 1880. She was married December 30, 1821 to William Taylor, of Greenfield, N. H. He died Nov. 6, 1876, and both he and his wife were buried at Francestown, in which town he was a farmer and always lived. They had five children, twin sons died in infancy.

MARY ELIZABETH, b. July 9, 1824, was married at Francestown, Sept. 30, 1847 to Milton C. Dickey. He died July 15, 1879. After their children were born they moved to Missouri. Mrs. Dickey and her children live at Cadet, Missouri. *Charles W.*, b. Jan. 22, 1849; unm. *Mary Francella*, b. June 15, 1850; m. at Madrid, Mo., Sept. 12, 1878, to Alonzo L. Secoy, by whom she has two children, Charles M. and Cora L. *Frederick T.*, b. Apr. 1, 1858; was married at Madrid, Mo., Mar. 19, 1874 to Christine A. Secoy. Their children were Wilfred T., Maud E., Ida Mabel. *Walter E.*, b. Sept. 29, 1863. *Mabel J.*, b. Sept. 17, 1865.

NANCY ANN, b. May 17, 1825; married Nov. 10, 1847, Calvin C.
Lord, of Ossipee, N. H. They lived in Francestown, where
they both died and were buried. Their children, *George Calvin,* b. Nov. 30, 1848; m. Oct. 15, 1879, Addie Brown. *Ida F.*
b. Dec. 11, 1851; m. Sept. 28, 1875, Edward B. Richardson.

SARAH FRANCES, b. Oct. 23, 1829; was married Sept. 2, 1850, to
Charles Whitney. They have three children all living at
Troy, N. H. *Ella F.,* b. Sept. 26, 1854; married George F.
Kimball, Aug. 21, 1877. He died April 26, 1881. They had
two children, Edward W., b. July 11, 1878. Mary F., b.
July 28, 1879; d. Aug. 19, 1880. *Cora M.,* b. May 29, 1858,
married Melvin T. Stone, M. D., Jan. 26, 1882; three children,
Mary F. Stone, b. Apr. 29, 1886; d. April 15, 1891; Mildred T.,
b. Mar. 17, 1889; Dorothy C., b. Apr. 25, 1896. *Charles W.,*
b. Mar. 14, 1861; married Lizzie L. Hayward, Nov. 26, 1884;
one child, Doris B., b. Sept. 20, 1888.

798. Sally,[8] daughter of 390 Israel[7] and Elizabeth [Epps]
Balch was born at Francestown, N. H., January 29, 1799, and
died March 5, 1892. She was married in January, 1856, to
William Holt, of Greenfield, N. H., in which town they lived.
Mr. Holt died in June, 1873. Mrs. Holt at the age of 87
was able to sew and care for her home. She had no children.

799. Mason,[8] son of 390 Israel[7] and Elizabeth [Epps]
Balch, was born at Francestown, N. H., October 23, 1800,
and died in the same town July 21, 1873. He married first
Sabina Holmes, Apr. 17, 1826, who died September 24, 1831,
aged 24 years, leaving two children.

'1562* MASON HOLMES,[9] b. Nov. 22, 1829.
'1563* MARY ANN,[9] b. Mar. 14, 1827; d. Sept. 30, 1858.

Mason was married a second time at Francestown, Oct. 7,
1886 to Hannah, daughter of Joshua and Hannah [Ingalls]
Holt, of Greenfield. She was born May 3, 1796. They had
one son, born in Greenfield.

'1564* CHARLES EDWARD,[9] b. Mar. 17, 1843; d. Oct. 18, 1884.

Mason Balch was a farmer and lived at Francestown. He
married a third time Mrs. Elizabeth (Gould) Styles, of Greenfield, who is living at Milford, N. H. No issue.

800. Betsey,[8] daughter of 390 Israel[7] and Elizabeth
[Epps] Balch, was born at Francestown, New Hampshire,

November 28, 1802, and died April 12, 1846, at Francestown. She was married Apr. 5, 1824 to Nahum Farnum, of Frances-. town, and had three children.

> SARAH JANE, b.   ; she married Dr. Hardy Atwood, June, 1845. He died in Virginia during the war. They lived at Manchester, N. H. and had two children, *Jennie* and *Walter* who lived at Manchester.
>
> MARIA, b. Aug., 1828; d. Aug., 1847.
>
> ISRAEL B., b. July 17, 1832; m. Apr. 27, 1858; lives at Derry Depot, N. H.

801. Nancy,[8] daughter of 390 Israel[7] and Elizabeth [Epps] Balch, was born at Francestown, September 26, 1804, and died September 28, 1839. She was married in 1827 to William Hopkins, of Francestown. He died April 2, 1859. They resided at Francestown, and had two children.

> ORRA ANN, b. Aug. 23, 1835; married Nov. 27, 1877, Ambrose Gould, of Greenfield, N. H. He died July 15, 1883, and his widow is now living at Greenfield.
>
> WILLIAM CLEAVES, b. Aug. 16, 1837; married at Manchester, Oct. 16, 1859, Lucetta Wood of Topsham, Vt. They have four children. *Arthur William*, b. Aug. 29, 1867. *Guy Anson*, b. Nov. 19, 1872. *Ray Cleaves*, b. May 19, 1875. *Orra Lucetta*, b. Jan. 1, 1882. William Cleaves Hopkins has lived at Manchester and Portsmouth, and in 1886 was living at Nashua, N. H. He served three years with a N. H. battery in the Army of the Potomac.

802. Hannah,[8] daughter of 390 Israel[7] and Elizabeth [Epps] Balch, was born at Francestown, N. H., May 18, 1807, and died Dec. 15, 1848. She married Ebenezer Boyd, of Francestown, who died in 1839. They lived in Francestown, and their three children were born there. Page I. was living at Dover, Kansas, in 1886. George F., was living in Oregon, in 1886. Charles Henry, b. Nov. 4, 1836, died Jan. 5, 1868, at Manchester, N. H. On Nov. 26, 1863, he married Lizzie Cregin, of Francestown. He was a Congregational minister of exceptional earnestness and talent.

803. Susan,[8] daughter of 390 Israel[7] and Elizabeth [Epps] Balch, was born at Francestown, N. H., February 25, 1809, and died Oct. 22, 1854. She married Horace Hopkins,

of Francestown, in Sept., 1830, where their three children
were born.

> SARAH FRANCES L. married Daniel Patch, who lives at New-
> port, N. H. They had one son *William*, who is married and
> lives at Manchester, N. H.
> DEAN N. married Nellie Gilman, lives at Francestown, N.
> H. One daughter, *Mary*, lives with her parents.
> HARVEY, M. D. Married Mattie A. ———— Has two children,
> lives at Manchester, N. H.

804. John,[8] son of 390 Israel[7] and Elizabeth [Epps]
Balch, was born at Francestown, N. H., May 19, 1812, and
died Sept. 19, 1886. He was a farmer at Francestown, N. H.
He was married April 26, 1836, to Roxie Dutton, daughter of
Ruben Dutton. She was born at Lyndborough, N. H., April
11, 1818, and died at Francestown, October 5, 1865. They
had seven children, the eldest was born at Lyndborough, the
other six at Francestown.

1565* ISRAEL D.,[9] b. Mar. 4, 1839.
1566 ELIZABETH E.,[9] b. Apr. 11, 1841; d. July 26, 1860.
1567* ORRIN J. L.,[9] b. May 19, 1843; d. Jan. 14, 1895.
1568 ALFONSO L.,[9] b. Aug. 25, 1845, d. Feb. 24, 1861.
1569 HARLON P.,[9] b. Mar. 15, 1848; d. Sept. 19, 1871.
1570 JOSEPHINE H.,[9] b. Mar. 25, 1851; d. Feb. 5, 1861.
1571 EUGENE,[9] b. Aug. 6, 1854; d. Mar. 10, 1861.

805. Orra A.,[8] daughter of 390 Israel[7] and Elizabeth
[Epps] Balch, was born at Francestown, N. H., December 20,
1813, and died in March, 1878. She married Deacon Merrill
C. Dodge, of Francestown, in May, 1844. He died in March,
1884. They resided at Greenville, N. H., and both died and
were buried in that town. They had one child which died in
infancy.

806. John,[8] son of 394 John[7] and Lydia [Read] Balch,
was born at Chester, Vt., December 28, 1808, and died January 8, 1873. He was married to Julia Ann Pond. She was
born at Wrentham, Massachusetts, May 22, 1808, and died
July 11, 1896, at Hartland, Vermont. They lived at Hartland, and afterwards at Granville, N. Y. Their children were
as follows:

1572* HARVEY JOHN,[9] b. July 22, 1829.
1573* ELIZABETH M.,[9] b. December 14, 1830.
1574* LOWELL LEVI,[9] b. Jan. 22, 1832.
1575 WILLIAM MASON,[9] b. Oct. 11, 1834; d. Oct. 22, 1848.
1576 DANIEL EVERETT,[9] b. Sept. 30, 1836; d. Aug. 30, 1888.
1577 CHARLES E.,[9] b. Aug. 12, 1840; d. Sept. 12, 1842.
1578* AMANDA C.,[9] b. Aug. 15, 1844; d. May 14, 1871.
1579* MARY ANN,[9] b. May 7, 1848.

807. Achsah Philena,[8] daughter of 394 John[7] and
Lydia [Read] Balch, was born at Chester, Vermont, August
24, 1805, and died Jan. 1, 1894. She married Hiram, son of
Adolphus Whitney, of Westminster, Vermont. He was born
at Sherburne, Vermont, May 28, 1810, and died November 21,
1889. They had eight children, the first unnamed.

HULDAH D., b. Feb. 16, 1833; d. Nov. 22, 1833.
HULDAH ANN, b. Feb. 9, 1835; d. 1881; m. her cousin, 1574 Lowell Levi Balch,[9] which see.
HIRAM H., b. May 23, 1836; d. Oct. 10, 1844.
SARAH JOSEPHINE, b. Feb. 23, 1838; d. Oct. 3, 1844.
SANFORD M., b. Dec. 10, 1840; m. Addie M. Marcy, July 7, 1869; two children, *Fred S.* and *Mary A.*; lives at Taftsville, Vt.
JOHN B., b. July 8, 1844; m. Jan 1, 1864, his cousin 1578 Amanda Balch,[9] which see.
HIRAM, b. Dec. 21, 1846; d. Feb. 18, 1849.

808. Clark,[8] son of 394 John[7] and Lydia [Read] Balch,
was born at Chester, Vt., May 29, 1807, and died in the same
town, May 24, 1882. On February 25, 1829, he married Miss
Sabrina Pamela Shelden, of Chester, Vermont. She was
born February 24, 1813.

Clark was a farmer and lived at Chester, Vt., and his 16
children were born in that town.

1580 ISRAEL,[9] b. Dec. 28, 1829; d. y.
1581 PAMELA C.,[9] b. June 4, 1832; d. Sept. 23, 1893; m. Herman Merrill
1582 SARAH,[9] b. Oct. 20, 1833.
1583 ORRA ANN,[9] b. Dec. 30, 1835.
1584 PHEBE,[9] b. May 24, 1837; d. aged 17 years.
1585 SUSAN A.,[9] b. Feb. 20, 1838; d. Sept. 5, 1891; m. Nutting Parker.
1586 HIRAM W.,[9] b. Mar. 26, 1840.
1587 JOHN C.,[9] b. Nov. 4, 1841; lives Bellows Falls, Vt.
1588 ELIZABETH E.,[9] b. Sept. 10, 1843; d. y.
1589 HENRY,[9] b. Nov. 6, 1844; d. aged five years.
1590 JULIA J.,[9] b. Aug. 3, 1848; d. June 17, 1882.

1591 EMMA J.,⁹ b. Jan. 29, 1851; d. Oct., 1892; m. Woodworth.
1592 JAMES S.,⁹ b. Mar. 28, 1853.
1593 DANIEL,⁹ b. Feb. 23, 1855; d. Apr. 21, 1855.
1594 FILENA,⁹ ⎫
1595 FILENDA,⁹ ⎬ twins, b. May 8, 1859.

809. Joanna,⁸ daughter of 394 John⁷ and Lydia [Read] Balch, was born at Chester, Vt., February 15, 1809, and is living at Manchester, N. H. She married first Silas, son of Josiah and Ann [Harding] Lamb, who was born at Pomfret, Vt., April 16, 1808, and died at Stockbridge, Vt., October 14, 1837. They had one son, who was born at Pomfret, Vt. Alfred S., b. Dec. 14, 1835. He is living at Manchester, N. H.

Joanna married for her second husband, Derstin Kendall, who was born at Cavendish, Vt., October 6, 1806, and died at Manchester, N. H., June 8, 1890. They had one daughter born at Sheffield, Vt.; Clara E., b. May 22, 1851.

810. Varion,⁸ son of 394 John⁷ and Lydia [Read] Balch, was born at Chester, Vt., about 1811, and died in the same town July 1, 1864. He married and has one daughter living.

1596 SUSAN,⁹ married a Mr. Glynn, and lives at North Springfield, Vt.

811. Daniel,⁸ son of 394 John⁷ and Lydia [Read] Balch, was born at Chester, Vt. The dates of his birth and death are not known. He married, lived at North Granville, N. Y., and had children.

1597 WALTER,⁹

812. Maranda P.,⁸ daughter of 394 John⁷ and Lydia [Read] Balch was born at Chester, Vt., October 3, 1824, and died August 19, 1892. She married Laban B., son of Jonathan Bradley. He was born at Sheffield, Vt., December 21, 1827, and died November 22, 1894. They had two children born at Sheffield.

JOSEPHINE, S., b. Aug. 26, 1851; m. Azro J. Gray, Aug. 26, 1872; lives at Sheffield, Vt.

MARY A., b. Mar. 14, 1858; d. July 10, 1884; m. Geo. B. Newell, May 20, 1879.

814. Adeline,⁸ daughter of 394 John⁷ and Lydia [Read] Balch, married Edward Whitney, whose brother married her sister 807 Achsah Philena Balch. They had four children, Frederick ; George Henry ; Marion ; Louisa.

818. Joanna,[8] daughter of 396 Varion[7] and Mary [Thompson] Balch, was born at Francestown, N. H., April 4, 1815, and died April 26, 1892. She was married, November 17, 1835, to John K. Cristy. They lived at New Boston, N. H., where their nine children were born.

> JAMES C., b. Oct. 31, 1836; d. Jan. 25, 1837.
>
> JOHN R., b. Jan. 8, 1838; d. Dec. 22, 1838.
>
> REBECCA C., b. 1840; d. 1842.
>
> MARY ELIZABETH, b. July 1, 1842; d. June 7, 1871; m. Solomon Dodge, Aug. 9, 1862; had five children: *Effie E.*, b. May 31, 1863, m. George W. Carr; *Carrie M.*, b. April 12, 1866, m. Chas. M Gaffield; *Nellie R.*, b. Oct. 19, 1867, m. Frank E. Rowe; *Millie Belle*, b. Oct. 16, 1869, d. y.; *Mary E.*, b. May 30, 1871, d. y.
>
> PAMELA, b. Sept. 24, 1845; d. May 17, 1874; m. James B. Whipple, August, 1866; no issue.
>
> CYNTHIA A., b. Aug. 4, 1848; d. unm. July 3, 1871.
>
> REBECCA C., b. Feb. 16, 1850; d. Jan. 2, 1873; m. Chas. W. Dodge, Sept. 17, 1870; no issue.
>
> MARTHA J., b. April 24, 1853; d. July 5, 1888; m. George Stearns, no children.
>
> VARION B., b. Nov. 24, 1856; d. June, 1857.

819. James T.,[8] son of 396 Varion[7] and Mary [Thompson] Balch, was born at Francestown, N. H., April 18, 1817, and died at Antrim, N. H., January 28, 1888. He held several positions of trust. He married Lois, daughter of Josiah and Polly [White] Robbins, of Antrim. She was born March 8, 1817. They had four sons, born in Antrim.

1598* CHARLES F.,[9] b. Nov. 29, 1844.

1599 GEORGE W.,[9] b. July 31, 1848; was drowned May 8, 1852.

1600* WILLIAM A.,[9] b. Nov. 4, 1856.

1601* JOHN A.,[9] b. Feb. 28, 1860.

820. Pamela,[8] daughter of 396 Varion[7] and Mary [Thompson] Balch, was born at Francestown, N. H., December 21, 1821, and died April 9, 1854, at Lyndeborough. She married Franklin Senter. They lived at Lyndeborough, N. H., and had four children. Mary Ann, b. Feb. 27, 1847, d. Feb. 18, 1882; Juliette, b. Oct. 16, 1848; William Franklin, b. Jan. 31, 1851; George Riley, b. Dec. 25, 1852.

821. Oliva,[8] daughter of 396 Varion[7] and Mary

[Thompson] Balch, was born at Francestown, N. H., April 5, 1825, and died June, 1865. She married William Cristy. They lived at New Boston, N. H., and had two children, one of whom was James William.

822. William,[8] son of 396 Varion[7] and Mary [Thompson] Balch, was born at Francestown, N. H., July 14, 1831, and is a foreman at Nashua, New Hampshire. He was married first at Harvard, November 3, 1852, to Hannah Crosby Worster, who was born at Harvard, Massachusetts, August 28, 1836, and died at Nashua, N. H., July 28, 1854. They had one daughter, born at Harvard, Massachusetts.

1602   HANNAH PAMELA,[9] b. March 4, 1854: d. Oct. 7, 1889.

William was married second at Caro, Mich., September 26, 1870, to Sarah Ann, daughter of William and Sarah Hoyt. She was born at Craftsbury, Vt., November 3, 1845, and died at Nashua, N. H., November 23, 1880. They have one son.

1603* WILLIAM HOYT,[9] b. April 3, 1874.

824. Mark,[8] son of 398 William[7] and Nabby [Johnson] Balch, was born at Francestown, March 30, 1821, and died December 16, 1878, and was buried at Francestown. On the 2d of May, 1850, he married Laurilla H. Farnum, of Francestown. She is not living.

826. Alfred,[8] son of 402 Isaac[7] and Sally [Marshall] Balch, was born at Lyme, N. H., August 9, 1828, and died at Marble Hill, Mo., November 26, 1869. He married and had four children.

1604   CHRISTIANA,[9] b. 1860.
1605   SARAH,[9] b. 1863.
1606   ANNIE,[9] b. 1867.
1607   ISAAC NEWTON,[9] b. 1868.

When fifteen years of age Alfred went to Cambridge, Mass., to live with his uncle, 408 John Balch. Upon his uncle's death he assisted in settling up the affairs. Then he went into the express business, and next became connected with the Penny Post in Boston. He moved west in the spring of 1858, and went to farming. All through the civil war he served in the Union army.

827. **Marshall S.,**[8] son of 402 Isaac[7] and Sally [Marshall] Balch, was born at Lyme, N. H., July 10, 1832, and died at Boston, Mass., March 13, 1874, and was buried at North Thetford, Vt. For 22 years he was with the Boston Penny Post. He never married.

828. **Charles Newton,**[8] son of 402 Isaac[7] and Sally [Marshall] Balch, was born at Lyme, N. H., October 17, 1836. He is a farmer, and lives at North Thetford, Vt. He married Julia A. Mayo, of Lyme, N. H. She was born July 31, 1847, and died February 29, 1896. They had two daughters, both born at North Thetford.

1608 ANNIE B.,[9] b. June 24, 1874.
1609 JULIA MAY,[9] b. July 13, 1884; d. March 2, 1896.

838. **Theodore Edwin,**[8] son of 407 Theodore[7] and Sally [Lovejoy] Balch, was born at Lyme, N. H., January 13, 1832, and died at Wakefield, January 12, 1896. He was married September 3, 1856, to Ellen R., daughter of John and Rebecca [Coffin] Sanborn. Their three eldest children were born at Hopkinton, New Hampshire, and their youngest child at Wakefield, Massachusetts.

1610 ELLEN,[9] b. July 18, 1857; d. same day.
1611 EDWIN RANDOLPH,[9] b. Oct. 23, 1858; d. April 27, 1863.
1612 MARY ELLEN,[9] b. Oct. 26, 1864; m. June 4, 1896, H. G. Gowing.
1613 ANNIE GERTRUDE,[9] b. Sept. 8, 1872.

Theodore Edwin Balch was elected chancellor of the Central University of Iowa, and removed from Wakefield, Massachusetts, to Pella, Iowa, to fill that position. He was elected treasurer of Roger Williams University, at Nashville, Tennessee, and removed from Pella to Nashville, to accept the office. He returned to Wakefield in 1887, and from then until his death was general agent of the Watchman. He was financial agent of Colby Academy in N. H., selectman, overseer of poor, member of school board, trustee of Public Library and trustee of Savings Bank.

839. **William Worcester,**[8] son of 407 Theodore[7] and Sally [Lovejoy] Balch, was born at Lyme, N. H., April 27,

1884. He was married June 9, 1858, to Wealthy A. Flint. They live at Lyme Centre where he is a farmer. They have adopted three children who have taken the name of Balch.

1614   ROSA M., b. July 9, 1856.
1615   GEORGE B., b. March 23, 1858; d. June 12, 1896; m. no children.
1616   HATTIE J., b. Aug. 14, 1866.

840. Isaac Freeman,[8] son of 407 Theodore[7] and Sally [Lovejoy] Balch, was born at Lyme, N. H., February 13, 1836. He was married September 3, 1867, to Sarah Sanborn. They had two children, both born at Lyme.

1617   ELLA MARIA,[9] b. Mar. 9, 1869.
1618   THEODORE EDWIN,[9] b. Sept. 13, 1870.

Isaac Freeman is a farmer at Webster, N. H. In 1861 he enlisted in the First New Hampshire Battery, and was honorably discharged in January, 1863, on surgeons' certificate of disability, caused by disease contracted in the service.

841. John Carroll,[8] son of 407 Theodore[7] and Sally [Lovejoy] Balch, was born at Lyme, N. H., July 7, 1839, and died at Lyme, N. H., August 27, 1889. He was married first, in May, 1864, to Sarah H. Baker, she died March 17, 1883, without issue. He was married second, February 10, 1885, to Josie A. Lane, by whom he has one daughter, born at Manchester.

1619   MAY LENA,[9] b. Dec. 1, 1885.

John C. Balch resided at Manchester, N. H., occupation, a time keeper. In August, 1862, he enlisted in the Tenth N. H. Volunteers and was honorably discharged therefrom March 19, 1863, on Surgeon's certificate of disability, caused by a fall on a transport going from Aquai Creek, to Newport News, Va.

842. Sarah Eliza,[8] daughter of 407 Theodore[7] and Sally [Lovejoy] Balch, was born at Lyme, N. H., June 18, 1841. She was married September 9, 1868, to Joseph N. Flint. They have one child, born in Lyme, Cara Hope, b. March 6, 1875.

843. Hannah Sophronia,[8] daughter of 407 Theodore[7] and Sally [Lovejoy] Balch, was born at Lyme, N. H., June 25, 1843. She was married March, 17, 1861, to Moses A. Flint.

They moved from Manchester, N. H., to Deep River, Iowa. In 1885 they moved to the state of Washington, and are now living there at Rankin. They had six children, the eldest was born at Manchester, the others at Deep River. Edwin Atwood, b. Dec. 3, 1862. Theodore Balch, b. Nov. 28, 1865. Sarah Elizabeth, b. Apr. 27, 1868 ; m. Nov. 19, 1885, to David Scovel. Levi Carroll, b. Dec. 28, 1871 ; d. Mar. 5, 1876. Moses Delos, b. Sept. 30, 1873. Emma Frances, b. Apr. 27, 1877.

844. Frank Pierce,[8] son of 407 Theodore and Sally [Lovejoy] Balch, was born at Vershire, Vermont, October 14, 1850. He was married March 6, 1880, to Hannah Lytle. He is a farmer at Methuen, Massachusetts, and has two children.

1620 Bernice Lillian,[9] b. Jan. 12, 1882.
1621 Frankie.

845. Sarah E.,[8] daughter of 408 John and Eunice P. [Lyon] Balch, was born at Cambridge, Mass., July 31, 1836. She was married May 20, 1854, to Milton, son of Daniel and Sally Branch. They reside at Waterville, Me., and have six children. Walter N. b. Dec. 20, 1856 ; m. Aug. 9, 1885, Hattie Thornton. Edward R., b. June 28, 1860 ; m. Jan. 20, 1884, Gertrude Rideout. Leonard, b. Nov. 25, 1862 ; d. unm. Mar. 8, 1882. John B. b. Aug. 8, 1864. Frank M. b. Jan. 9, 1870. Ethel M. b. Dec. 21, 1879.

846. Ellen M.,[8] daughter of 408 John[7] and Eunice P. [Lyon] Balch was born at Cambridge, Mass., August 7, 1838, and died at Waterville, Maine, January 23, 1861, the fifth anniversary of her marriage. She was married January 23, 1856, to Asa R. son of John and Mary [Cree] Clifford. He was born April 12, 1820. They had three children, born at Waterville, Maine.

Fidelia A., b. Dec. 17, 1857; m. Nov. 27, 1878, Frank B. Teague, of Skenhegen, Me., where they live and have two children. *Henry F.*, b. June 25, 1880; *Nellie M.*, b. May 30, 1882.
Cora E., b. Feb. 11, 1859; m. Oct. 12, 1878, Frank W. Davis; they reside at Waterville, Me., and have three children. *Stella*

M., b. Dec. 18, 1879; *Harrison M.*, b. Aug. 28, 1888; *Ellen M.*, b. Mar. 10, 1890.

ELLEN M., b. Jan. 18, 1861; m. Nov. 4, 1879, to Frank E. Sturtevant; they live at Waterville, Me., and have the following children: *Bertie E.*, b. Jan. 8, 1881; *Leslie H.*, b. Dec. 27, 1885; *Della*, b. Aug. 18, 1889.

847. Louisa M.,[8] daughter of 408 John[7] and Eunice P. [Lyon] Balch, was born at Cambridge, Mass., Dec. 24, 1840. She was married November 28, 1866, to Asa R. Clifford, whose first wife was her sister Ellen M.   They reside at Waterville, Me., and have five children.   Eunice B., b. Mar. 8, 1869; m. Oct. 10, 1891, Olie Willey.   Edith S., b. Apr. 16, 1871; m. May 5, 1890, Fred B. Grimes.   John C., b. Nov. 11, 1872; m. Dec. 7, 1895, Mary D. Trafton.   Jennie M., b. Aug. 6, 1877. Theodore A., b. May 26, 1880.

848. Eunice P.,[8] daughter of 408 John[7] and Eunice P. [Lyon] Balch, was born at Cambridge, Mass., November 12, 1843, and died December 17, 1891.   She was married October 4, 1865, to William E. Shedd.   They resided at West Somerville, Mass., and had two children.   Horace S., b. Aug. 4, 1866, d. Nov. 11, 1886 ; Annie L., b. July 29, 1871 ; m. June 8, 1892, Augustus O. Clark.

849. John H.,[8] son of 408 John[7] and Eunice P. [Lyon] Balch was born at Cambridge, Mass., July 16, 1847, and is a merchant at Cambridge, Mass.   He was married June 28, 1886, to Minerva A. Booth and has three children.

1622 GRETCHEN,[9] b. June 4, 1888.
1623 JOHN,[9] b. Nov. 16, 1889.
1624 CLARKSON,[9] b. March 29, 1892.

850. Archibald,[8] son of 411 Arnold[7] and Meribah [Leonard] Balch, was born in Otsego Co., New York, August 30, 1802; and died at Westfield, Pennsylvania, July 11, 1862. He was a house-carpenter and farmer.   He owned at one time a chair factory and afterwards a saw and shingle mill.   He was married to Mary Sweet.   She was born July 30, 1802, and died at Westfield, December 11, 1854.   They had three children.

1625* HENRY R.,[9] b. Dec. 23, 1826.
1626* ALPHONZO BURDETT,[9] b. Apr. 13, 1832.
1627* HELEN ADALAID,[9] b. Mar. 7, 1839.

851. Arnold,[8] son of 411 Arnold[7] and Meribah [Leonard] Balch, was born at Cooperstown, New York, October 11, 1805, and died at North Jackson, Pennsylvania, February 25, 1881. He was married June 15, 1826, to Sarah, daughter of Justice Leonard. She was born at Stevenstown, New York, February 15, 1801, and died at Jackson, Pa. August 27, 1831. Arnold was an ordained minister of the Baptist denomination. He was also a farmer, and lived at Jackson, Pa.   Their three children were born in that town.

1628   CHESTER,[9] b. Mar. 24, 1827; d. Apr. 3, 1827.
1629   CATHERINE,[9] b. Mar. 4, 1829; d. Oct. 27, 1830.
1630* MILTON,[9] b. Jan. 2, 1831.

852. Sally,[8] daughter of 411 Arnold[7] and Meribah [Leonard] Balch, was born at Cooperstown, N. Y., July 22, 1807, and died January 21, 1841, at Rush, Pennsylvania, where she was buried. She was married September 21, 1826, to Henry Joslin, son of Asa, and Elizabeth Kinne. He was born at Otsego Co., N. Y., July 21, 1803, and died at Stevensville, Pa., May 30, 1875, and was buried at Wyalusing, Pennsylvania. He was first a shoemaker, and afterwards a farmer. They had six children.

MERIBAH ELIZABETH, b. June 8, 1827, at Hartwick, N. Y.; m. first, Jan. 10, 1847, Henry L. Fessenden, at Wyalusing, Pa. He was born in 1822, and d. Oct. 21, 1868. They were both members of the Baptist church. Meribah E. m. second, Oct. 21, 1872, B. A. Pettes, who was born in 1820, and d. in 1887, Meribah had six children by her first husband, none by her second. *Sally Esther*, b. at Montrose, Pa., Oct. 28, 1847; d. May 26, 1874, m. F. B. Ryder in 1865. *Hosea*, b. at Montrose, Pa., Aug. 17, 1849, m. Stella Jones, Jan. 7, 1880; *Martha Meribah*, b. at Wyalusing, Pa., June 8, 1851; d. Nov. 9, 1870. *Theodore Augustus*, b. at Terrytown, Pa., May 14, 1853, m. Dec. 25, 1873, to Hattie Wells; d. Mar. 1890; *James Edward*, b. at Terrytown, Pa., Jan. 15, 1856, m. Anna Stevens, Jan. 1, 1877; *Charles Ellery*, b. Mar. 28, 1858; d. August 31, 1861.

MINERVA, b. at Harwick, N. Y., Oct. 13, 1829; d. Aug 7, 1830, at Harwick.

FRANKLIN EVERET, b. at Harwick, Oct. 13, 1831; d. at Morris
Farm, Va., Oct. 13, 1863; m. Mar. 16, 1851, to Elizabeth Place,
by whom he had four children. *Gilbert*, b. at Terrytown, Pa.,
Feb. 22, 1852; m. Catherine Capwell, July 5, 1875. *Josephine*,
b. at Terrytown, Pa., Apr. 22, 1855; m. Elwood Capwell, Mar.
11, 1878. *Jacob*, b. at Frenchtown, Pa., June 25, 1857; m.
Catherine Proof, Apr. 22, 1882. *Byron*, b. in Ohio, Sept. 14,
1859; m. Sept. 22, 1883. Laura Place.

Franklin E. with two half brothers enlisted in 1862, into Co.
"A" 141, Pa. Vols. and was shot through the body and killed
on his thirty-second birthday. He was Orderly Sergeant of
his company, and was about to be promoted to a lieutenant.
He was a brave soldier, loved and respected by both officers
and men.

LUCINDA, b. at Hartwick, Oct. 11, 1833; m. first, Valentine Brown,
Jan. 9, 1856. He died Feb. 9, 1879. Brown was a Methodist,
Lucinda a Baptist. They had two children, both b. in Illi-
nois. *Jane*, b. Mar. 25, 1857; m. at Montrose, Pa., in 1881, to
Frank Campbell. *Henry*, b. Mar. 15, 1860; m. Oct. 1, 1880, to
Ette Gannon. Lucinda m. second, in 1893, T. E. Philips a
Baptist minister.

ORVIL W., b. at Rush, Pa. Mar. 25, 1836; m. Apr. 15, 1862, to
Catherine Richards, their four children were born at Terrytown, Pa. where they live with their parents on their
farm. Parents and children are members of the Baptist
church. *Helen*, b. Jan. 19, 1864; m. Nov. 23, 1887, Derr Bow-
men; *John*, b. Nov. 5, 1865; m. Mar. 23, 1893, Margaret Can-
non; *Mary*, b. Oct. 6, 1867; *Burroughs*, b. Nov. 30, 1870.

HELEN, b. May 31, 1838, d. Oct. 9, 1863; m. George Brown, in 1885,
had three children. *Ida Eudora, Samuel* and *John*.

853. Susan,[8] daughter of 411 Arnold[7] and Meribah
[Leonard] Balch, was born at Burlington, New York, April
30, 1810, and died at Seward, Nebraska. November 8, 1885.
She was married April 8, 1826, at Truxton, New York, to
Ebenezer M. Ellsworth. They resided at Burlington and
Cooperstown, New York, at Rush, and Auburn, Pa., at sev-
eral places in Iowa, and last at Seward, Nebraska. They had
nine children.

GEORGE A., b. at Burlington, Feb. 13, 1828; d. at Prescott. Ara.,
July 3, 1882; m. Mar. 15, 1853, Margaret Hulick, at Ainsworth,
Iowa. Three children, *Charlotte P.*, m. Geo. Brobaker, Los
Angeles; *Maryettee*, m. Charles Glover, Oskaloosa, Ia.; *James*,
d. 1884.

CHANDLEE W., b. at Cooperstown, July 15, 1831; m. Sept. 16,
1852, to Helen E. Maxson, of Fredonia, Iowa. A farmer at
San Diego, Cal. They have nine children. *Oliver James*, b.
Feb. 26, 1856, m. Laura Mullhorn; *George L.*, b. Feb. 17, 1858,
m. Ida Finney; *Clara A.*, b. Jan. 15, 1860, m. T. B. Thompson; *Emma*, b. Sept. 25, 1862, m. L. C. Chusemann; *Elmer O.*,
b. Feb. 1, 1866, m. Emma Christmas; *Laura A.*, b. July 17,
1870, m. W. R. Guy; *Molley H.*, b. Nov. 3, 1873, m. A. F.
Crowell.

SUSAN D., b. at Rush, Pa., Jan. 30, 1833; m. Mar. 8, 1851, to John
Hood, of Washington Co., Ia. They had ten children. *Annie
M.*, b. June 18, 1855; *Susan D.*, b. Dec. 9, 1860, m. J. J.
Emmerson, Feb. 2, 1881; *Wilfred B.*, b. April 17, 1862; *Frank
W.*, b. July 11, 1865, d. Mar. 8, 1874; *Emma J.*, b. Feb. 22,
1867; *Nancy D.*, b. Mar. 7, 1870, m. Oct. 1, 1885, to S. A. Don-
alson; *Martha M.*, b. May 7, 1873.

NANCY P., b. at Auburn, Pa., Apr. 11, 1837; now lives at San
Diego, California; m. Feb. 11, 1861 to Charles C. Jobes. He
was proprietor of the Seward Broom Factory, at Seward,
Nebraska, and their four children were born in that town.
Joseph Weeks, b. Feb. 27, 1865; *Frank Henry*, b. July 9, 1867;
Susan Emeline, b. Aug. 21, 1869.

OLIVE P., b. Feb. 14, 1840, at Auburn; d. Sept. 14, 1854, at Fredonia.

FRANCIS M., b. Mar. 3, 1844, at Rush; m. Feb. 22, 1871, to Emma
Smith, at Seward. Francis M. is a lawyer at Colfax, Wash.

ELIZABETH E., b. Feb. 6, 1847; d. Apr. 14, 1876, at Mt. Pleasant, Ia.

CHARLES A., b. Mar. 10, 1850; d. Mar. 14, 1877, at Jessup, Ga.;
m. Jan. 1873, to Ivy Newell.

MERIBAH D. J., b. Sept. 2, 1853; in Louesa Co., Ia.; m. Dec. 1,
1874 to John A. Stephens, of Union Co., Iowa.

854. Jane,[8] daughter of 411 Arnold[7] and Meribah [Leon-
ard] Balch, was born at Truxton, New York, July 7, 1814,
and died November 29, 1889. She was married at Sherburn,
N. Y., March 7, 1832, to William P. Tefft. He was born in
Vermont, January 16, 1779, and was a farmer at Port Alle-
ghany, Pa., when he died June 8, 1862. He was a son of
Oliver and Deborah Tefft. They had seven children. Mary
Jane, b. April 19, 1833, m. 1855, B. F. Jackson; Julia, b.
May 15, 1836, d. Dec. 21, 1892, m. Geo. Salisbury; William,
b. 1839, d. 1841; Arnold, b. Mar. 15, 1841, d. Nov. 20, 1856;
Diana, b. 1844, m. 1863, N. R. Page; Victoria, b. 1847, m.
Edgar Burr; Fitz James, b. May 11, 1850, m. Susie Burr.

855. Abigail,[8] daughter of 411 Arnold[7] and Meribah [Leonard] Balch, was born at Burlington, N. Y., January 16, 1818, and died November 6, 1888. She was married March 1, 1840, to David Bonnel, at Rush, Pa. They had two children born at Rush. Sally C., b. Mar. 14, 1841; Abel R., b. Aug. 22, 1844, d. Jan. 24, 1866.

Mr. Bonnel died at Rush, and Abigail married for her second husband Thomas C. Hoover. He was born July 27, 1828, and died September 13, 1879. To them were born four children. Arnold G., b. Dec. 26, 1852, d. Sept. 28, 1881; Archibald, b. Dec. 28, 1855; Frank, b. May 19, 1858; Meribah S., b. Mar. 19, 1861, d. Mar. 13, 1866.

856. Diana,[8] daughter of 411 Arnold[7] and Meribah [Leonard] Balch, was born in Cortlandt Co., N. Y., December 16, 1822, and died June 4, 1892. She was married first to William D. Dennison, March 8, 1846. Dennison was born April 18, 1821, and died at Gainsville, Florida, October 13, 1859. He was the son of Dr. Mason Dennison, of Montrose, Pa. They had one son, Mason W., b. Apr. 20, 1847, at Montrose, Pa., who is a civil engineer.

Diana married for her second husband Levi Marsh, June 15, 1869, and lived at Maple Works, Wisconsin. He died in 1893.

857. Orpha B.,[8] daughter of 412 Roger[7] and Hannah [Northrup] Balch, was born at Sherburne, N. Y., July 6, 1807, and died September 6, 1891, at Fulton, N. Y. She was married, May 6, 1828, to Albert P. King, of Sullivan, N. Y. They had seven children, the youngest died young. Amos N., b. Mar. 27, 1829; Alfred J., b. Dec. 2, 1831, d. Jan. 26, 1832; Celestia E., b. Jan. 12, 1834, m. D. M. Cox, Granby, N. Y.; Ann Maria, b. May 16, 1836, d. Feb. 9, 1870, m. John A. Cox, Hannibal, N. Y.; Jennie H., b. Apr. 14, 1845, m. Amasa B. Keeney, lives at North Hannibal, N. Y.; Albert J., b. Dec. 5, 1847.

858. Mary P.,[8] daughter of 412 Roger[7] and Hannah [Northrup] Balch, was born at Sherburne, N.Y., July 31, 1808,

and died June 6, 1875. She was married, October 11, 1829,
to Charles, son of Stephen and Joanna Mills Benedict. He was
born at Sherburn, New York, May 6, 1808; Benedict's 2d wife.
No issue. The Benedict Genealogy gives her name Cornelia.

860. **Marilla**,[8] daughter of 412 Roger[7] and Hannah
[Northrup] Balch, was born at Sherburne, N. Y., December
18, 1812, and died December 24, 1895, at Whitelaw, N. Y.
She was married, March 27, 1834, to Seymour H. Barnes, of
Lenox, N. Y.; they had six children. Catherine M., b. Dec.
31, 1835, lives at Canastota, N. Y.; Albert S., b. Sept. 1, 1837,
m. Carrie C. Ward in Sept., 1865; Emma C., b. Feb. 8, 1839,
m. B. F. Harpham, Feb. 28, 1861; Chester E., b. July 3, 1842,
d. Mar. 2, 1860; Mary L., b. Feb. 14, 1846, d. Dec. 19, 1877;
Fannie A., b. Mar. 16, 1860, m. June 1, 1887, Rev. Lansing
Van Auken, of Troy, N. Y.

863. **Cynthia L.**,[8] daughter of 412 Roger[7] and Hannah
[Northrup] Balch, was born at Sherburne, N. Y., October 6,
1821. She was married January 5, 1853 to Zerah R. Niles,
of Cooperstown, N. Y. They live at Oneida, N. Y. They
have four children. Arthur S., b. March 17, 1855; Ebbert R.,
b. March 6, 1858; Irving Balch, b. July 6, 1860; Minnie E.,
b. Oct. 31, 1864.

876. **Dan C.**,[8] son of 417 Henry Taylor[7] and Catherine
[Thomas] Balch, was born at Mansfield, Ct. July 14, 1809,
and died at Euclid, N. Y., February 1, 1883. He was a farmer, and a member of the M. E. Church. On April 11,
1831, he was married to Matilda Gammet, by whom he had
three daughters.

1631* PAMELA,[9] b. Jan. 18, 1842; d. Dec. 19, 1872.
1632 RHODA ANN,[9] b.   ; m. Eckert, lives Euclid, N. Y.
1633 EDSON,[9] b.   ; d. y.

878. **Henrietta**,[8] daughter of 417 Henry Taylor[7] and
Catherine [Thomas] Balch, was born at New Haven, April
1, 1813, and died at Richfield, Otsego Co., N. Y., February
2, 1869.   She was married first to Andrew Chrisman, July
27, 1835, and second to Henry Oxner, who died at Richfield,
April 14, 1868.

879. Clarissa,[8] daughter of 417 Henry Taylor[7] and
Catherine [Thomas] Balch, was born at Richfield Spa, N.
Y., February 18, 1815. She was married Jan. 22, 1837, to
Leroy Robinson, and was living at Newell, Iowa.

880. Joseph Chapman,[8] son of 417 Henry Taylor[7] and
Catherine [Thomas] Balch, was born at Richfield, N. Y., January 30, 1817, and died about 1891. He was a mason, and
lived last at Sand Bank, N. Y. He was married February 7,
1844, to Sarah J. daughter of William Rose. She was born at
Fly Creek, N. Y., Oct. 13, 1824, and died at Albion, N. Y., April
25, 1868. They had six children, the five eldest were born at
Richfield, the youngest at Albion, N. Y.

1634 ESTELLA,[9] b. Nov. 6, 1844.
1635 DELAS,[9] b. May 21, 1846.
1636 JOHN,[9] b. June 17, 1850; d. Mar. 11, 1863.
1637 EMELY,[9] b. Aug. 19, 1853.
1638 ALBERT,[9] b. Aug. 28, 1856; d. Feb. 17, 1857.
1639 DARWELL,[9] b. Sept. 4, 1862.

Joseph C. was married second September 18, 1864, to Mary
J., daughter of Terance Sheridan. She was born in Ireland,
September 17, 1829. By this marriage Joseph C. had four
children, all born at Albion, N. Y.

1640 ELIZA A.,[9] b. Aug. 14, 1865.
1641 CHARLES,[9] b. Jan. 20, 1867.
1642 JAMES,[9] b. July 3, 1868.
1643 MARY,[9] b. Dec. 11, 1871.

882. Maria,[8] daughter of 417 Henry Taylor[7] and Catherine [Thomas] Balch, was born at Richfield, N. Y., February
7, 1821. She was married October 24, 1844, to George
Washington Rose of Otsego, N. Y. He was born April 10, 1821,
and died in March, 1894. He was a farmer. Their residences
have been Richfield, N. Y., Brockfield, Ill. and Marseilles,
Ill. They had six children, the three eldest were born at
Richfield, the others at Brockfield, Ill. William. H.,
Catherine V., George Washington, Albert, Emma, Truman.

883. Rhoda Ann,[8] daughter of 417 Henry Taylor[7] and
Catherine [Thomas] Balch, was born at Richfield, N. Y.,

September 26, 1823. She was married Dec. 12, 1857, to
Thomas, son of William Holt. He was born in New York
March 24, 1826. He is a farmer, and is living with his wife
at Seneca, Ill. They had five children. The eldest was born
at Richfield, N. Y., the other four at Brockfield, Ill.   Martha
A., b. Nov. 5, 1852, m. March 10, 1879, Nathaniel Baker;
John A., b. Nov. 10, 1856, d. Dec. 15, 1856; Sarah A., b.
March 18, 1858, d. Feb. 17, 1862; Nellie F., b. Feb. 20,
1860, d. Aug. 21, 1860; Aveline R., b. Jan. 7, 1863, m. Dec.
29, 1880, Frank L. Covell.

884. Henry,[8] son of 417 Henry Taylor[7] and Catherine
[Thomas] Balch was born at Richfield, N. Y., December 5,
1825, and is living at Schuyler Lake, N. Y. He married first
Emma Delong by whom he had one daughter who is now
married.

1644 EMMA,[9] b.   ; m.

Henry married second, Lovanda Sitts, by whom he has
one daughter.

1645 MAY,[9] b.   ; m. William Fay.

886. Martha,[8] daughter of 417 Henry Taylor[7] and Catherine [Thomas] Balch, was born at Richfield, N. Y. February
5, 1830; she married, first, John Shaul, June 3, 1855. She was
living at Forest City, Iowa, in 1887. Shaul was a farmer; they
moved to Iowa about 1862; they have six children; the three
eldest were born at Brockfield, Ill., the other three in Iowa.
Monroe, b. Feb. 25, 1857, d. Sept. 14, 1865; Julia, b. Dec. 2,
1859; Cornelus, b. May 5, 1860; Edward, b. March 13, 1863;
William, b. Aug. 29, 1864; Dora, b. Jan. 5, 1866. Shaul
died, and Martha married John Reynolds, who died without
issue.

887. Sarah A.,[8] daughter of 417 Henry Taylor[7] and
Catherine [Thomas] Balch, was born at Richfield, N. Y.,
October 4, 1832. She was married September 23, 1849, to
Alexander Shaul. He is a farmer, and they are living at
Armstrong, Iowa. They have two children. Charles C.,
b. July 9, 1850; Henry Alexander, b. Feb. 1, 1854.

888. John Austin,[8] son of 419 John[7] and Mary [Wood] Balch, was born at Mansfield, Conn., January 24, 1812, and was a farmer at Killawog, N. Y. in March, 1886. He is a Democrat and Spiritualist. In 1839 he was married to Minerva Lynde, who died in 1886. They had two children.

1646 IRA,[9] b. 1840; unm., a farmer.
1647 PAMELA,[9] b. 1843; d. 1848.

889. Mary Ann Maria,[8] daughter of 419 John[7] and Mary [Wood] Balch, was born at Mansfield, Ct., April 9, 1816; she married Harmon Mackey by whom she had two children. Marvin Mackey married Miranda Jennings; Lucy Mackey married William Wheaton, one child Florence Wheaton. This family are all Methodists.

890. Sophronia Ann,[8] daughter of 421 Thomas[7] and Eunice [Hamilton] Balch, was born at Mansfield, Ct. January 25, 1820. She married a Mr. Lawrence Wood and resided at East Winsor, Ct.

892. Roxana Minerva,[8] daughter of 421 Thomas[7] and Eunice [Hamilton] Balch, was born at Mansfield, Ct., April 17, 1828. She married first Rufus Fielden Conant, son of Edmund, and grandson of Sylvester and a lineal descendant from Roger. He was born May 27, 1827, at Mansfield, Ct., where he always lived. He died in 1865. They had two children. Isadorus, b. March 12, 1849. Mary Ann Jeannette, b. August 17, 1850.

Roxanna M. married for her second husband a Mr. Merrick. They lived at Atwoodville, Conn.

894. Milo Hamilton,[8] son of 421 Thomas[7] and Eunice [Hamilton] Balch, was born at Mansfield, Conn., June 17, 1835, and was living at Mansfield, Ct., in 1886.

899. William Henry,[8] son of 423 David B.[7] and Fanny [Channell] Balch, was born at Topsfield, Mass., March 16, 1823, and died in the same town, August 30, 1855. He married Hannah Lowell, who was born in 1816. They had one son.

1648 DAVID HENRY,[9] died at Amesbury, Mass., the last male descendant of David Burnham.

900. Mara,[8] daughter of 424 Dr. Israel[7] and Nancy [Goodwin] Balch, was born at Salisbury, Mass., July 20, 1816, and died at Amesbury, Mass., August 29, 1895. She was a lady of excellent mind and memory. She rendered great assistance to this Genealogy in giving the biography of her father and the records of his family. She never married.

902. Israel Daniel Perkins,[8] son of 424 Dr. Israel[7] and Nancy [Goodwin] Balch, was born at Amesbury, Mass., June 18, 1822. In 1850 he married Margaret Cherry, who was born in 1822 at North Balmore, Ireland. She died in 1867. They had four children.

1649   ANNA FRANCES,[9] b. Oct. 23, 1854; d. 1856.
1650   NELLIE AUGUSTA,[9] b. Nov. 21, 1856; d. Nov. 21, 1856.
1651*   IDA FRANCES,[9] b. Dec. 3, 1857.
1652   ARTHUR ISRAEL,[9] b. Dec. 3, 1859.

Israel D. P. was married a second time in 1868 to Margaret Kenedy. She was born at North Andover, Mass., December 20, 1833. They had two children.

1653   HERMON FREDERICK,[9] b. June 12, 1869; d. July 18, 1881.
1654   NELLIE JOSEPHINE,[9] b. May 6, 1871.

903. David Lowell Dearborn,[8] son of 424 Dr. Israel[7] and Nancy [Goodwin] Balch, was born at Amesbury, Mass., October 18, 1828. On January 10, 1854 he was married to Miss Judith Ann Boardman, who was born at Newburyport, Mass., in 1832. No issue.

906. Rebecca,[8] daughter of 433 William[7] and Mehitable [Townsend] Balch, was born December 3, 1795, and died September 27, 1873. She married a Mr. Farnham in N. H. He was a ship blacksmith. They moved to Bangor, Me., where he had a large shop.

913. Charles,[8] son of 433 William[7] and Mehitable [Townsend] Balch, was born February 22, 1814, and died July 6, 1882, at Ogden, Iowa. He was a farmer and Baptist. He was married in 1835 to Harriet, daughter of Nathan Hines of Schoharie, N. Y. She was born March 18, 1805, and died March 28, 1882, at Oran, N. Y. They had four children.

1655* WILLIAM HENRY,⁹ b. Nov. 7, 1836.
1656* ELIZA JANE,⁹ b. Sept. 2, 1838; d. May 9, 1885.
1657* CHARLES D.,⁹ b. Aug. 18, 1840.
1658* HARRIET CORNELIA,⁹ b. Feb. 8, 1844.
1659* MARIA,⁹ b. May 26, 1846.

916. Laura Ann,⁸ daughter of 435 David⁷ and Abigail
[Wells] Balch, was born at Keene, N. H., November 11,
1802, and died at Winchendon, Mass., Oct. 19, 1874. She
was buried at Keene, N. H. She married Daniel Jackson,
and had seven children. They lived at Winchendon, Mass.
David W., b. Oct. 27, 1829 ; Harriet A., b. Sept. 16, 1831, d.
Jan. 5, 1882 ; James W., b. Sept. 22, 1834 ; Charles A., b.
Nov. 24, 1837, d. Nov. 29, 1842 ; Eliza N., b. Oct. 12, 1839, d.
May 7, 1842 ; Sarah C., b. Sept. 16, 1841 ; George A., b. Feb.
5, 1844.

919. George A.,⁸ son of 435 David⁷ and Abigail [Wells]
Balch, was born in Keene, N. H., October 13, 1809, and died
in Worcester, Mass., March 8, 1891, and was buried at Keene.
He was a mechanic, and was engaged in railroading for the
Cheshire R. R. He was a strong Republican. On November
13, 1831, he was married to Jemima Clark, who was born in
Chesterfield, N. H., July 25, 1805, and died in Keene, Sep-
tember 2, 1850. They had three children, all born in
Keene.

1660 GEORGE W.,⁹ b. Dec. 23, 1832; d. Apr. 18, 1848.
1661* MARTHA A.,⁹ b. Aug. 19, 1834; d. Mar. 5, 1883.
1662* MARY A.,⁹ b. July 11, 1837.

George A. married second, September 1, 1851, Maria Sanderson, who was born in Springfield, Vt., July 9, 1815, and
died in Keene, May 14, 1888. They had two children, both
born in Keene.

1663* EMMA M.,⁹ b. Sept. 5, 1852.
1664* CHARLES A.,⁹ b. Nov. 23, 1854.

925. John Capen,⁸ son of 440 John⁷ and Mary [Elliot]
Balch, was born at Topsfield, Mass., in 1805, and died at
Lynn, Mass. He was a man of great piety. He was married
twice. The name of his second wife was Mary Ann Collin-

son. A diary by Mary Endicott of Danvers, notes the date of death and age of a Rebecca Balch, who was probably his daughter. The diary says that she was the only child of a widowed mother.

1665 REBECCA P.,[9] b. 1837; d. Mar. 20, 1864.

926. Nehemiah,[8] son of 440 John[7] and Mary [Elliot] Balch, was born at Topsfield, Mass., in 1807, and died in that town January 2, 1884. He was married April 23, 1829, to Mary Ann Lovett. She was born June 22, 1806, at Newbury-port. They had three children, all born at Topsfield.

1666* NEHEMIAH CHARLES,[9] b. Feb. 6, 1834.
1667 EDWIN WALLACE,[9] b. Aug. 27, 1837; d. Mch. 8, 1838.
1668* GEORGE EDWIN,[9] b. Jan. 23, 1839; d. June 11, 1874.

Nehemiah Balch was a man of sterling integrity, kind and sympathetic. Nearly forty years of his life was spent in the employ of C. Herrick & Co., where as overseer, and at one time as director, he gained the confidence of all with whom he came in contact.

He served the town in many places of trust. In 1861, '62, he was treasurer, and had much to do with the recruiting for the war. In 1850 he represented the town in the legislature and took a lively interest in the contest for the senate, between Sumner and Winthrop. He was a member of the Congregational church for fifty-three years. Mrs. Balch was a woman of great persistency and remarkably well read, especially of religious and theological works.

927. Phebe,[8] daughter of 444 Solomon[7] and Ruth [Knights] Balch, was born at Johnson, Vt., March 18, 1808, and died March 7, 1841, in the same town where she had always lived. She married Charles H. Clark, a farmer, and had five children. Augusta M., b. Aug. 20, 1829 ; Amelia A., b. Sept. 3, 1831 ; Solomon, b. July 15, 1833, d. 1836 ; Byanoe, b. Nov. 16, 1835 ; Charles, b. Feb. 22, 1838.

928. Robert,[8] son of 444 Solomon[7] and Ruth [Knights] Balch, was born at Johnson, Vt., August 2, 1804, and died in the same town January 11, 1874. He was married April 22,

1828, to Lydia, daughter of Seth Pike. She was born at Brookfield, Vt., October 2, 1805. Robert was a farmer, and lived at Johnson, Vt., where his eight children were born.

1669* RUTH CLEMENTINE,⁹ b. Jan. 17, 1830.
1670 CAROLINE MARY,⁹ b. Apr. 7, 1832; d. Aug. 10, 1841.
1671 VERNON WATERMAN,⁹ b. July 16, 1834; d. Feb. 18, 1842.
1672* LOUISA PIKE,⁹ b. Nov. 1, 1836; d. Aug. 6, 1862.
1673 SOLOMON,⁹ b. Apr. 9, 1840; d. Oct. 5, 1852.
1674* CAROLINE MARTHA,⁹ b. Aug. 28, 1843.
1675* JULIA ETTA,⁹ b. Mar. 5, 1846.
1676 ROBERT,⁹ b. May 16, 1849; d. Aug. 24, 1869.

929. Ruth,⁸ daughter of 444 Solomon⁷ and Ruth [Knights] Balch, was born at Johnson, Vt., September 7, 1806, and died in the same town February 28, 1873. She married John A. Clark, who was born August 31, 1804, and died May 9, 1874. They had six children, all born at Johnson, Vt.

FREDERICK, b. Oct. 17, 1835.
JANE, b. Apr. 22, 1838; m. first Lucius S. Rand, Oct. 28, 1863. Rand was born Mar. 4, 1835, and died Mar. 31, 1877; they had two children. John C., b. June 9, 1865; and an unnamed son, d. y. Jane [Clark] Rand m. second Samuel H. Smith, Nov. 6, 1882. Smith was born Jan. 11, 1834.
SOLOMON B., b. Dec. 25, 1839; d. Jan. 11, 1872.
JENNETT, b. Mar. 28, 1842; m. Lewis D. Smith, Jan. 1, 1861.
JOHN A., b. Jan. 17, 1847; d. Apr. 10, 1847.
RUTH A., b. May 8, 1848; d. Sept. 8, 1852.

930. Solomon,⁸ son of 444 Solomon⁷ and Ruth [Knights] Balch, was born at Johnson, Vt., April 8, 1808, and died at Waterville, Vt., April 30, 1859, and was buried at Johnson. He was married first in March, 1832, to Hannah Clark. She was born at Johnson, Vt., and died at Waterville, in August, 1841. They had two children.

1677* RUTH K.,⁹ b. Apr. 11, 1833.
1678* ENOS,⁹ b. Dec. 16, 1835.

In December, 1842, Solomon married his second wife, Maria A. Hurlburt, of Waterville. They had three children.

1679* MARY,⁹ b. in 1844; d. in Kansas.
1680* MARTHA,⁹ b. in 1846; d. at Waterville.
1681* FIDELIA,⁹ b. in 1848.

932. Allen,[8] son of 444 Solomon[7] and Ruth [Knights] Balch, was born at Johnson, Vt., November 13, 1811, and died in the same town, April 13, 1881. He was married July 23, 1842, to Jane, daughter of Joseph Andrews, of Johnson. Their five children were all born in Johnson, Vt.

   1682* ALMA H.,[9] b. Nov. 6, 1843; d. Mar. 1889.
   1683* EDWIN K.,[9] b. Oct. 12, 1846; d. Dec. 19, 1895.
   1684 ALLEN,[9] b. Mar. 12, 1849; d. May 9, 1849.
   1685 WARREN,[9] b. Apr. 28, 1852; d. July 2, 1856.
   1686* ADDIE,[9] b. Dec. 25, 1857; d. Sept. 7, 1885.

Allen was ambitious to leave home when he was of age, but one trip as a yankee pedler satisfied him. He bought the old farm on which he was raised, and built a new house near the old one in which he lived the remainder of his life. He was a quiet, hard working man, fond of fun in a quiet way, a Republican, an earnest Christian, a member of the Baptist church, a good neighbor, a kind father, and respected by all who knew him.

933. Frederick P.,[8] son of 444 Soloman[7] and Ruth [Knights] Balch, was born at Johnson, Vt., October 26, 1813, and is a farmer at Masena, New York. He married February 12, 1847, Elvira Clark, of Johnson. She died February 18, 1898. They had one son.

   1687* FRED,[9] b. October 21, 1848.

934. Betsey,[8] daughter of 444 Solomon[7] and Ruth [Knights] Balch, was born at Johnson, Vt., December, 10, 1815, and died November 11, 1848. She was married in December, 1841, to John T. Fullington, of Cambridge, Vermont. They had one son, George H., who is a merchant at Idana, Kansas.

939. John,[8] son of 446 Moses[7] and Sally [Willis] Balch, was born at Johnson, Vt., February 18, 1806. He was married December 2, 1831, to Lydia A. Andrews. She was born at Johnson, February 28, 1811, and died at Newport, Vt., October 19, 1866. John was a farmer and carpenter, and was living at Newport, Vt., in 1887. They had eight children, all born at Johnson.

1688 SARAH, J.,[9] b. Sept. 11, 1832.
1689 OTIS P.,[9] b. Feb. 28, 1835.
1690 JOHN,[9] b. July 23, 1837; d. Mar. 28, 1861.
1691 JOSEPH A.,[9] b. Oct. 11, 1839.
1692 SEREA A:,[9] b. Aug. 15, 1841; d. Aug. 20, 1841.
1693 CHAT M.,[9] b. July 14, 1842; d. Nov. 20, 1862.
1694 MARY J.,[9] b. May 14, 1844.
1695 SAMUEL A.,[9] b. Apr. 22, 1847.

John was married again September 15, 1867, to Sarah G. Hazelton. No issue.

940. Samuel,[8] son of 446 Moses[7] and Sally [Willis] Balch, was born at Johnson, Vt., June 23, 1808, and died at Manchester, N. H., August 26, 1854. He was married April 2, 1835, to Nancy Maria Bartlett. She was born at Unity, N. H., March 23, 1818, and died at Manchester, April 12, 1884. They had three children.

1696* SUSAN ELIZABETH,[9] b. Dec. 27, 1835.
1697* GEORGE GRANVILLE,[9] b. Aug. 17, 1837; d. Dec. 20, 1865.
1698 SARAH MARIA HERBERT,[9] b. Jan. 7, 1840; d. unm. Apr. 14, 1856.

Samuel was a farmer, and lived at Manchester, N. H. His widow Nancy, married Charles C. Huntoon. No issue.

941. Moses,[8] son of 446 Moses[7] and Sally [Willis] Balch, was born at Johnson, Vt., November 30, 1810, and died Mar. 17, 1891. He was married August 14, 1831, to Mary Ann, daughter of Moses Burnham, of Chester, Vt. She was born at Chester, Vt., December 23, 1813. They have had eight children, all born at Johnson, except their youngest son, Samuel H., who was born at Goffstown, N. H.

1699 MARTHA M.,[9] b. Sept. 18, 1832; d. unm., at New Boston, N. H. June 23, 1851.
1700* PROLINA L.,[9] b. Dec. 24, 1834; d. June 18, 1878.
1701* ELIZABETH A.,[9] b. Feb. 22, 1837.
1702* WAYLAND F.,[9] b. May 28, 1839.
1703* SARAH A.,[9] b. Oct. 31, 1841.
1704* ELLEN ASINITH,[9] b. Feb. 14, 1844.
1705* CHARLES S.,[9] b. Feb. 5, 1848.
1706* SAMUEL H.,[9] b. Oct. 1, 1854.

942. Abijah,[8] son of 446 Moses[7] and Sally [Willis] Balch, was born at Johnson, Vt., Mar. 16, 1813, and died in

the same town in which he was born and always lived, Sept.
21, 1878. He was buried in North Hyde Park, Vt. Abijah
was a farmer. On February 10, 1838, he was married to
Eliza Nites. She was born at Enosburg, Vt., July 23, 1815.
Their four children were born at Johnson, Vt.

    1707   HIAL B.[9] b. April 1, 1889 ; d. June 8, 1839.
    1708* WILLARD M.,[9] b. Apr. 17, 1840 ; d. Dec. 17, 1881.
    1709   FREDERICK V.,[9] b. Mar. 16, 1842 ; d. Feb. 2, 1852.
    1710* ALMON,[9] b. Nov. 20, 1847.

  946. John Jefferson,[8] son of 447 John[7] and Deborah
[Kenniston] Balch, was born at Jericho, Vt., June 27, 1804,
and died March 10, 1879, at Kennebunkport, Me., where he
had gone because of his eldest son's illness. He was a farmer.
He was married in November, 1827, to Abigail G. Mudgett.
She died at Lyndeborough, New Hampshire, March 16, 1879,
within twelve days of the death of her husband and their
eldest son. All three died of pneumonia. They lived at
Lyndeboro and were much esteemed for their uniform kindness and generosity. Prior to 1862 they lived at New Boston, New Hampshire.

    1711* JOHN W.,[9] b. September 10, 1828 ; d. Mar. 4, 1879.
    1712* MOSES M.,[9] b. Sept. 11, 1831.
    1713* MARY EMILY,[9] b. July 17, 1840.

  947. Eliza,[8] daughter of 447 John[7] and Deborah [Ken-
niston] Balch, was born at New Boston, N. H., March 8,
1806, and died at LeClaire, Iowa, December 22, 1866. She
was married May 25, 1823, to Ezekiel, son of Philip and
Hannah [Hackett] Peaslee, who was born at Lewiston, Me.,
October 5, 1802, and died at LeClaire, Ia., July 14, 1880. They
lived at Middletown, Mass., until 1887, when they removed
to LeClaire. They had six children, the five eldest were born
at Middletown, Mass., the youngest at LeClaire. John B.,
b. Sept. 10, 1824, m. Nov. 1, 1855, Isabelle Barr; Phillip O.,
b. May 28, 1828, d. unm. 1850; Hannah M., b. Jan. 27, 1830,
d. Mar. 22, 1851, m. Nov. 7, 1847, Silas Lancaster; Julia A.
Peaslee, b. Mar. 3, 1838, m. Aug. 14, 1853, David T. Stonebraker, lives at Melvern, Kansas; George P., b. May 3, 1886,

d. April 1, 1867, m. July 5, 1863, Melissa Lewis; Orrin H.,
b. Jan. 23, 1848, m. Jan. 24, 1868, Anna E. Stonebraker, live
at LeClaire, Iowa.

948. Eliphalet,[8] fourth son of 447 John[7] and Deborah
[Kenniston] Balch, was born at New Boston, New Hampshire, December 29, 1807, and died May 28, 1873, at Jericho,
Vt., where he was a farmer. He was married Nov. 9, 1831,
to Lucretia Maria, daughter of Pittman Barker. She was
born in Tinmouth, Vt., June 17, 1812, and died at Jericho,
Vt., March 29, 1890.

    1714   HENRY JOHN,[9] b. Nov. 24. 1832; d. Feb. 12, 1853.
    1715* HELEN ABIGAIL,[9] b. Sept. 5, 1834; d. Aug. 16, 1881.
    1716   GEORGE HIRAM,[9] b. Oct. 27, 1836; d. Feb. 9, 1853.
    1717* BARKER SAWYER,[9] b. July 28, 1838.
    1718   OLIVE SAWYER,[9] b. April 2, 1840; d. Feb. 6, 1853.
    1719   NOAH WOODMAN,[9] b. Jan. 28, 1842; d. Feb. 16, 1853.
    1720   ANN ELIZA,[9] b. Nov. 29, 1844; d. Feb. 16, 1853.
    1721* FAYETTE,[9] b. August 23, 1848; d. Sept. 30, 1886.
    1722* EFFIE JANE,[9] b. Sept. 16, 1850.

The entire family with the exception of the father were
sick with scarlet fever, and five died in ten days.

949. Julia Ann,[8] daughter of 447 John[7] and Deborah
[Kenniston] Balch, was born at New Boston, N. H., August
25, 1809, and died June 25, 1896. She lived at Hookset,
N. H. She married January 24, 1835, Ayers, son of Ayers
and Sarah Worth. He was a farmer, and was born August
10, 1808, at Center Harbor, N. H., and died Nov. 21, 1875,
at Moultonboro, where they lived. They had two children.
Julia Maria, b. Dec. 14, 1836, d. December 25, 1836, m. Aug.
6, 1854, Elisha Slager; William Balch, b. May 26, 1844, d.
May 3, 1863, in the army.

950. Hannah,[8] daughter of 447 John[7] and Deborah
[Kenniston] Balch, was born at New Boston, N. H., May 11,
1811, and is living at Waltham, Mass. She was married in
1836 to George Washington Haseltine, who was born February 18, 1812, and died August 27, 1864. They had ten children. George Hector, b. June 29, 1837, d. July 25, 1889;

Wright Augustus, b. Dec. 2, 1888, d. July 21, 1847 ; William Harrison, b. Nov. 30, 1840, d. Feb. 22, 1881 ; Charles Sewell, b. June 5, 1842, d. June 29, 1885 ; John R., b. Feb. 2, 1844, d. May 10, 1896 ; Hannah, b. Sept. 7, 1845 ; Edwin, b. Nov. 20, 1847, d. Feb. 28, 1885 ; Augustus, b. Oct. 17, 1849 ; Helen, b. August 10, 1851, d. Sept. 27, 1855 ; Emma, b. Aug. 19, 1855, d. Sept. 30, 1855.

951. William Plummer,[8] son of 447 John[7] and Deborah [Kenniston] Balch, was born at New Boston, N. H., March 13, 1818, and died at South Weare, N. H., April 12, 1884, and was buried in the Hillside cemetery at South Weare. He was a farmer, in politics a democrat. He was married February 15, 1846 to Sarah C. daughter of Samuel and Delila [Welch] Gove. She was born at South Weare, February 15, 1821. The family are Universalists. They always lived at South Weare, where their four children were born.

    1723* HENRY H.,[9] b. Jan. 16, 1847.
    1724* DELILA GOVE,[9] b. Sept. 16, 1848.
    1725* ALMENA M.,[9] b. Mar. 11, 1850.
    1726* EMMA D.,[9] b. July 18, 1855.

953. Roxanna,[8] youngest daughter of 447 John and Deborah [Kenniston] Balch, was born at New Boston, N. H., July 1, 1818, and died at Goffstown, June 3, 1889. She was married at Stoddard, N. H., April 14, 1872, to Samuel Nichols, who was born at Stoddard, March 11, 1831, and is a dry goods peddler, living at Hopkinton, New Hampshire. They had no children.

954. William D.,[8] son of 452 Allen[7] and Hepzibah [Dodge] Balch, was born at New Boston, N. H., October 26, 1818, and died at New Orleans, La., October 12, 1862. He enlisted in 1861, in Co. K, seventh regiment, Vermont Volunteers.

955. Margaret D.,[8] daughter of 452 Allen[7] and Hepzibah [Dodge] Balch, was born at Unity, N.H., May 13, 1815, and died at Antrim, N. H., January 22, 1892. She married James C. Brackett. He was born June 27, 1815, and died Septem-

ber 21, 1889, and was buried with Masonic rites at Antrim
where they lived, and were members of the Methodist church.

CLARENCE A., b. Mar. 2, 1840; m. Laura Oliver, of Walpole,
    Mass., lives at Chelsea, Mass., a physician.
CHARLES P., b. June 9, 1842; lives at Antrim, a merchant.
ESTELA O., b. Jan. 28, 1851; m. Fred L. Nay, a photographer and
    engraver, they live at Antrim.

956. Sarah L.,[8] daughter of 452 Allen[7] and Hepzibah
[Dodge] Balch, was born at New Boston, N. H., May 16,
1818, and lives at Jackson, Michigan. She was married
August 19, 1838, to Samuel O. Knapp, who died suddenly
January 6, 1883. He was born in 1816, at Royalton, Vt.
He was superintendent of a woolen manufactory connected
with the Michigan State Prison. Afterward he made valuable investments in Lake Superior mining property. He was
a prominent member of the Methodist Church. He was a public spirited, high minded, and generous citizen, courteous
and genial. They had no children.

957. Elizabeth O.,[8] daughter of 452 Allen[7] and Hepzibah [Dodge] Balch, was born at Unity, N. H., Jan. 15, 1821.
She was married November 19, 1843, to Charles S. Philips.
He is a miller at Watertown, New York. They are members
of the Methodist church, and have one son, George Henry,
b. April 2, 1854, who is with his father in the milling business.

958. John A.,[8] son of 452 Allen[7] and Hepzibah [Dodge]
Balch, was born at Unity, N. H., June 23, 1823, and died at
Iola, Wisconsin, July 28, 1891. He was married first, in
1852, to Caroline Stevenson, of Keeseville, New York. She
was born in 1837, and died September 26, 1878. They had
six children.

1727* JENNIE LAURA,[9] b. March 25, 1853,
1728* CLARA LOUISA,[8] b. Jan. 20, 1855.
1729* ELIZABETH D.,[9] b. Nov. 27, 1856.
1730* MARY KATE,[9] b. July 20, 1858.
1731* CHARLES P.,[9] b. April 21, 1860.
1732 JOHN A.,[9] b. Feb. 3, 1864; d. July 6. 1876.

In 1882 John married his second wife, a Miss Pope, of

Shawano, Wis. She was born at Wurtemburg, Germany,
April 10, 1842. As a boy John A. was full of mischief and
fun. When 20 years of age he bought his time from his
father for forty dollars, and in the early spring of 1844 left
home for Keeseville, New York, to learn flour milling. From
Burlington, Vermont, he walked twelve miles across Lake
Champlain, on the ice, which was deemed unsafe for teams.
He remained at the mill until 1849, and then, on December
18, took passage, with three others, on the brig "Orbit,"
from New York, around the Horn, to San Francisco. The
journey took four months and twenty days, and cost two
hundred dollars. John worked a short time in the gold
mines at Weaver Creek, was taken sick, spent all his money,
and then went to Oregon, landing at the site of the present
city of Portland. Here he soon found employment as a carpenter, first at five, and then at eight dollars a day, with
tools and board. After a time he returned to the California
mines, and was doing very well, when news of his mother's
illness led him to sell out and return home by way of the
isthmus. Soon after his return he married and took charge
of the flour mill at Peru, New York. In 1858 he took charge
of the mill at Ausable Forks, New York, and two or three
years later he moved to Iola, Wisconsin. He was a Democrat, and a hard working, honest, temperate man.

959. Alma A.,[8] daughter of 452 Allen[7] and Hepzibah
[Dodge] Balch, was born at Unity, N. H., June 6, 1828.
She never married. Her father gave her the old homestead
and personal property at Northfield, where she now lives.
She is a lady of ability and kindly disposition, and has rendered much assistance in collecting material for this Genealogy.

960. Ezra D.,[8] son of 452 Allen[7] and Hepzibah [Dodge]
Balch, was born at Charlestown, N. H., May 6, 1830, and
died at Iola, Wisconsin, Sept. 6, 1867. He was married January 1, 1850, to Martha E. Nye, of Northfield, Vermont, and
removed to Iola in 1855. He was a farmer, a member of the

Methodist church, superintendent of the Sabbath school, and class leader. He also held various town offices. His six children were born at Iola, except the two eldest, who were born at Northfield.

1733　ARABELLA S.,[9] b. Sept. 26, 1850; d. Sept. 13, 1862.
1734*　OSSIAN E. D.,[9] b. July 21, 1853.
1735*　ALLEN E.,[9] b. Oct. 7, 1855.
1736*　ETTA ALMA,[9] b. Feb. 10, 1858.
1737*　ORRELIA E.,[9] b. Mar. 3, 1861.
1738*　MATTIE E.,[9] b. May 19, 1867.

962. Angia H.,[8] daughter of 452 Allen[7] and Hepzibah [Dodge] Balch, was born at Northfield, Vt., November 17, 1837, and died at Montpelier, Vt., January 31, 1880. She was married to George Wheeler, April 2, 1860, at Montpelier; they resided in that town and kept the Union Hotel.

963. John B.,[8] son of 458 William[7] and Mary [Boynton] Balch, was born at Madison, Ohio, January 21, 1819. He was married January 29, 1838 to Mary Ann Stoddard, who was born at Madison, Ohio, in 1818, and died at Fon du Lac, Wisconsin, December 14, 1851. They had seven children, five eldest were born at Madison, the two youngest at Fon du Lac.

1739*　JOHN ALLEN,[9] b. Jan. 26, 1839.
1740*　WILLIAM HENRY,[9] b. Apr. 10, 1840; d. Jan. 14, 1868.
1741　OSCAR FITSLAND,[9] b. 1842; d. y.
1742*　ANN ELIZA,[9] b. Apr. 8, 1844.
1743*　OSCAR NELSON,[9] b. May 16, 1846; d. 1873.
1744　JASPER HIRAM,[9] b. Jan. 10, 1848; d. y.
1745*　JULIA ANN,[9] b. Dec. 4, 1851.

John B. married second, January 28, 1852, Ellen O., daughter of Levi Stevens. She was born at Russell, N. Y., May 20, 1834. He was divorced from her in 1875. They had eight children.

1746　HARRISON F.,[9] b. Nov. 28, 1852; d. 1862.
1747*　LAURA ELLEN,[9] b. Aug. 29, 1854.
1748*　FRANCES AMELIA,[9] b. Mar. 28, 1856.
1749　JOHN BYRON,[9] b. June 20, 1857; d. July 22, 1859.
1750*　FRED WILLARD,[9] b. June 15, 1860.
1751　FITCH B.,[9] b. Oct. 1861; d. 1862.

1752* NINA JESSIE,⁹ b. Oct. 25, 1863.
1753* HATTIE,⁹ b. Nov. 18, 1869.

After his first marriage, John B. engaged in farming at Madison, Ohio, for about ten years, when he lost everything by fire but $35 which was in his pocket. He then moved to Fon du Lac, Wis., and with his strong mental and physical energy, he was soon engaged in farming and land speculating. In 1862, he turned to well sinking for salt and oil, in Michigan, Pennsylvania and Kansas. In 1871, he engaged in the successful cultivation of cranberries at Bennington, Wisconsin. In 1877, he married his third wife, Margaret D. Nute, who had no children.

965. Hiram Allen,⁸ son of 453 William⁷ and Mary [Boynton] Balch, was born at Madison, Ohio, September 11, 1824. He was married first, June 4, 1850, to Martha A., daughter of Judge Daniel and Polly [Ross] Curtis of Joliet, Illinois, formerly of Pennsylvania. A daughter was born to them but both mother and child died October 16, 1854. Hiram A. married again August 15, 1866, to Emilia Houghton, daughter of Jasper and Melvina [Conroy] Curtis, of St. Albans, Vt. She was born in that town January 10, 1839. They had two children.

1754 MELVINA CURTIS,⁹ b. July 3, 1867; d. July 17, 1867.
1755* WILLIAM ALLEN,⁹ b. Aug. 27, 1869.

Hiram was educated at Madison Academy and Kirtland Institute, and in 1844 at the latter had charge of the classes in chemistry and penmanship. In 1846 took up daguerreotyping and went South. In 1849, he settled in Joliet, Illinois. His photographs won premiums wherever exhibited. He traveled through Kentucky and Tennessee from 1859 until the breaking out of the war, and then came to Cairo, Illinois. Soon after the capture of Memphis, he opened a gallery there and remained until 1869. In 1869 he bought one thousand acres of land in Arkansas, and tried farming for three years, but his crops were destroyed by drought and cattle. He then engaged again in photography at Hot Springs, Arkansas, and was burned out in the great fire of 1879. In 1880, he received an appointment in the Census Bureau at Washington, D. C., and since 1882 has been a clerk in the Pension Bureau. He is a Republican, an Episcopalian and is a member of the Masonic fraternity and Odd Fellows.

967. Mary L.,[8] daughter of 453 William[7] and Mary [Boynton] Balch, was born at Madison, Ohio, March 28, 1836. She was married July 27, 1854, to William Y. Duke, who was born at Manchester, England, August 24, 1832, and died at Onarga, Illinois, November 28, 1877. He was the son of William and Ann Duke. They had eight children.

> WILLIAM F., b. at Madison, Ohio, Apr. 15, 1855; graduated at the Commercial College at Grand Prarie, Seminary, Onarga, Illinois. He is a partner of the firm Duke Brothers, stockmen and fruit growers, at Hotchkiss, Colorado. He married October 10, 1894, Bertha Merrifield; they had one child *Wanda E.*, b. Aug. 22, 1895.
>
> GEORGE H., b. at Loda, Ills., March 13, 1857; is a member of the firm Duke Brothers. He graduated at the Commercial College, Onarga, Illinois. He married, July 12, 1885, Gertrude M. Miller; children *Helen M.*, b. July 6, 1886; *George W.*, b. Nov. 1, 1888; *Homer A.*, b. July 12, 1892.
>
> ADA MARY, b. at Ash Grove, Ills., Sept. 13, 1859; d. Aug. 1, 1877.
>
> NETTIE E., b. at Ash Grove, Ills., Jan. 25, 1862; married Dec. 25, 1881, Horace F. Dent, a traveling merchant; children, *Edna*, b. Chicago, Dec. 8, 1881; *Vivian*, b. Florida, Sept. 16, 1883; *Ada*, b. Kansas City, Mo., July 18, 1887; *Orville*, b. Kansas City, Dec. 20, 1889.
>
> EDWARD M., b. at Ash Grove, Ills., Oct. 12, 1866; is a member of the firm of Duke Brothers. He married, Nov. 17, 1891, Maud E. Doughty; children, *Horace E.*, b. Sept. 15, 1892; *Bruce E.*, b. Aug. 6, 1894.
>
> CHARLES A., b. at Onarga, Ills., Dec. 26, 1868; d. Jan. 12, 1870.
>
> CLARA E. b. at Onarga, Ills., Oct. 19, 1870; m. Jan. 15, 1893, Fred W. Simonds, wholesale book business; child *Elinor*, b. Chicago, Dec. 25, 1893.
>
> JESSIE E., b. at Onarga, Ills., June 11, 1877; is a teacher in the High School, at Onarga, Illinois.

When the civil war broke out, William Y. Duke enlisted in the 76th Illinois Infantry Volunteers, with which regiment he served nearly three years as first Sergeant of his company.   He was wounded in the Mobile campaign, in the spring of 1865, from which wound he never recovered, and finally died from its effects.   Mr. Duke was a carriage maker by trade.

968.   George F.,[8] son of 453 William[7] and Mary [Boynton] Balch, was born August 20, 1843, at Madison, Ohio, where he is a farmer.   He was married October 5, 1865, to Emma, daughter of Edwin Warner.   She was born at Madison, Ohio.   They have one son, born at Madison.

1756 WILLIAM,[9] b. Mar. 18, 1873.

969.   Perley,[8] son of 458 Perley[7] and Sarah [Perkins] Balch, was born at Topsfield, Mass., April 27, 1809, and died at Lowell, February 9, 1881.   He was a teacher at Lowell. He married Susan H. Glazier, by whom he had one child.

1757 MARY ABBY,[9] b. March 10, 1844, at Lynn, Mass.; a teacher at Lowell.

971.   Mehitable,[8] daughter of 458 Perley[7] and Sarah [Perkins] Balch, was born at Topsfield, May 16, 1814, and died July 24, 1891.   She married William G. Lake, November 25, 1834.   Their four children were born at Topsfield, Massachusetts.   Marietta B., b. Dec. 13, 1835; d. Nov. 15, 1845; Susan J., b. June 24, 1838; Perley B., b. March 9, 1843; William G., b. Feb. 27, 1851.

972.   Humphrey,[8] son of 458 Perley[7] and Sarah [Perkins] Balch, was born at Topsfield, May 18, 1818, and is living at Topsfield.   On April 10, 1842, he was married to Hannah P., daughter of Peter and Mehitable Bradstreet. She was born March 5, 1823, and died June 19, 1891.   She was a descendant of Governor Bradstreet, and was born on the historical Governor Bradstreet farm in Topsfield, which came down to her in regular descent.   She was highly accomplished, of lovely character, and possessed of much of the spirit of Ann [Dudley] Bradstreet, the first American poet.   Humphrey and Hannah had four children.

1758 HUMPHREY PORTER,[9] b. May 28, 1844; d. May 23, 1847.
1759* EDWARD PERLEY,[9] b. Jan. 13, 1850.

1760* GILBERT BROWNELL,[9] b. Feb. 9, 1856.
1761* ANNA BRADSTREET,[9] b. Feb. 18, 1860.

973.　Jeremiah,[8] son of 458 Perley[7] and Sarah [Perkins] Balch, was born at Topsfield, May 17, 1823, and is living at Salem, Mass.　He and his children are excellent musicians. He was married, Oct. 24, 1849, to Mary Shepherd, of Salem. They have had six children.

1762　HARRIET W.,[9] b. June 3, 1850; d. July 5, 1853.
1763* MARY AUGUSTA,[9] b. June 16, 1853; d. March 31, 1888.
1764　JEREMIAH PERKINS,[9] b. April 12, 1855; d. May 24, 1856.
1765　CLARENCE LINWOOD,[9] b. May 21, 1857; d. unm. Sept. 1, 1882.
1766　JEREMIAH SHEPHERD,[9] b. Nov. 6, 1859.
1767　EDWARD FOREST,[9] b. April 7, 1862.

974.　Benjamin Johnson,[8] son of 458 Perley[7] and Sarah [Perkins] Balch, was born at Topsfield, September 9, 1826, and is living in Topsfield, upon the farm owned by his great grandfather, 115 John[5] Balch.　On May 2, 1858, he married Eliza, daughter of Oliver Killam, of Boxford.　She died January 22, 1868, leaving one child.

1768* FLORENCE ELIZA,[9] b. Sept. 3, 1859.

Benjamin J. married second, September 26, 1871, Caroline P., daughter of Jewett and Mary [Perkins] Pingree, a bright and intelligent lady.

1769　FRANKLIN,[9] b. Jan. 15, 1876; student Boston University Law School.

FOURTH BRANCH.

Descendants of 9 Freeborn.[8]

975.　Lewis,[8] son of 464 Benjamin[7] and Marilda [Goodale] Balch, was born at Haverhill, Mass., August 23, 1815, and died at West Troy, N. Y., April 21, 1891, and was buried at Balston, N. Y.　He was married, December 22, 1844, to Sarah, daughter of Henry and Isabel Tucker.　She was born at Greenwich, N. Y., May 5, 1824.　Lewis and his wife were members of the Episcopal church.　They had eight children.

1770 CHARLES H.,[9] b. Dec. 18, 1846; d. unm.
1771 SARAH M.,[9] b. Jan. 27, 1848.
1772 CORA R.,[9] b. Aug. 30, 1850; d. unm.
1773* MARY E.,[9] b. July 5, 1853.
1774* BENJAMIN H.,[9] b. Dec. 22, 1855.
1775 ALBERT W.,[9] b. Jan. 13, 1860; d. unm.
1776 LEWIS F.,[9] b. Apr. 15, 1862; d. unm.
1777 GEORGE W. L.,[9] b. Sept. 5, 1868.

976. Mary Ann,[8] daughter of 464 Benjamin[7] and Ma-
rilda [Goodale] Balch, was born April 23, 1818, and died at
Milford, N. H., July 27, 1884.   She married Harvey Sweet.
He died at Milford, April 3, 1858.   They had one daughter.
Mary Esther, b. at Milford, June 13, 1855 ; m. Albert H.
Morton, May 1, 1877.   They had two children[4]: Ethel, b. Dec.
4, 1878, d. Jan. 1, 1879 ; Earle, b. June 6, 1881.

982. Sarah Goodwin,[8] daughter of 464 Benjamin[7] and
Marilda [Goodale] Balch, was born at Methuen, Mass., May
19, 1836.   She was married, May 17, 1854, to John Murry
Sunt, who was born at Saco, Me., May 7, 1833.   He is a shoe-
maker and farmer, and they live at South Berwick, Maien.
They had two children.

> SARAH MARILDA, b. May 18, 1855, at Haverhill, Mass., d. Sept.
> 12, 1885, at South Berwick; m. Herbert W. Butler, a sales-
> man, April 30, 1874.   Butler was born at Malden.   Four
> children: *Herbert L.*, b. at Haverhill, Oct. 4, 1875.   *Grace
> H.*, b. at South Berwick, Jan. 3, 1877; d. June 7, 1877.   *Effy
> May*, b. at South Berwick, June 20, 1879.   *Leroy Sheldon*, b.
> at Portsmouth, N. H., Mch. 7, 1881.
>
> SUSAN ELLEN, b. Jan. 2, 1863, at Haverhill; d. Nov. 8, 1869, at
> Haverhill.

987. Asahel Adams,[8] son of 466 Daniel[7] and Silence C ·
[Adams] Balch, was born at Lowell, Mass., June 1, 1826, and
died at Manchester, N. H., January 16, 1869.   He was State
Representative from Manchester from 1865 to 1869, and was
a prominent Mason.   He was married, February 4, 1854, to
Izetta Theresa Thompson, of Manchester.   She was born at
Fryeburg, Me., July 7, 1835, and died at Lowell, Mass.,
August 26, 1889.   They had four children, all born at Man-
chester.

1778 FRANK BUSH,[9] b. Aug. 16, 1855; d. Dec. 8, 1883, at Pomona, Fla.
1779 LOUISA SHATTUCK,[9] b. July 12, 1860. Living at Lowell, Mass.
1780 EDWARD EVERETT,[9] b. Jan. 17, 1865; unm.
1781 ASAHEL ADAMS,[9] b. Aug. 14, 1869; unm.

988. Walter Byron,[8] son of 466 Daniel[7] and Silence C.
[Adams] Balch, was born at Lowell, Mass., August 9, 1828·
He was married November 10, 1859, to Miss Augusta Evelyn Demeritt, of Durham, N. H. They have had three children, the eldest was born at Durham, the other two at Manchester.

1782 WALTER ADAMS,[9] b. Jan. 31, 1861; d. Mch. 5, 1880, at Man-
         chester.
1783* FANNIE AUGUSTA,[9] b. May 19, 1867.
1784   ALICE EVELYN,[9] b. May 14, 1876.

993. Henry Augustus,[8] son of 467 William H.[7] and
Louisa [Shattuck] Balch, was born at East Bradford, Mass.,
September 3, 1825, and died September 7, 1850. He married
Lauretta C. Whitcomb, of Fairlee, Vt., in 1848. They had
one child.

1785* LOUISA SHATTUCK,[9] b. in 1849.

994. Rebecca Ann,[8] daughter of 467 William H.[7] and
Louisa [Shattuck] Balch, was born at East Bradford, May 7,
1828. She married Abel, son of John Stickney, of Groveland,
March 13, 1856. They had three children, all born at Groveland. John Henry, b. Feb. 22, 1859; Frank Wallace, b. June
5, 1864; Louisa Shattuck, b. Mar. 14, 1868, d. Sept. 13, 1868.

997. Eliza Greenleaf,[8] daughter of 471 Wesley[7] and
Ann [Greenleaf] Balch, was born at Haverhill, Mass., May
16, 1825, and died December 18, 1886. She was married first,
at Thomaston, Me., to Parker McCobb, of Waldoboro, Me.
He died at St. Augustine, Fla. She married for her second
husband, John A. Low, of Concord, N. H. He died in December, 1865. She had no children.

998. Harriet Frances,[8] daughter of 471 Wesley[7] and
Ann [Greenleaf] Balch, was born at Haverhill, Mass., in
1827, and died in the same town, March 23, 1866. She married Hon. Jackson B. Swett, State Senator from Haverhill,

May 2, 1854.   He was born at Haverhill, February 12, 1815, and died in the same town October 8, 1890.   She was Swett's second wife ; his third was her cousin Mary Boardman Davis, daughter of 478 Susan Osborn Balch.   They had four children, all born at Haverhill.   Wesley Balch, b. Sept. 20,1855, d. Apr. 11, 1858 ; Harry and Willie, twins, b. Jan. 3, 1858, d. Jan. 4, 1858 ; Alice Balch, b. June 27, 1860, d. Aug. 8, 1860.

1000.   **Sarah Elizabeth.**[8] daughter of 472 John[7] and Sarah Ann [Samson] Balch, was born at Thomaston, Maine, November 13, 1828.   She was married, June 6, 1848, to Thomas Genthner.   He died at Waldoboro, Maine, March 2, 1872.   They had three children :

> EDWARD KAVANAGH, b. Mar. 26, 1849; m. Anna M. M'Carrison, of Portland, Me., June 3, 1890.   She died at Portland in March, 1891.   Edward K. Genthner is a physician at Portland.
> DELIA JARVIS, b. March 29, 1851; m. at Waldoboro, Jan. 12,1891, Herbert A. Hastings, of Westboro, Mass.   They live at Somerville, Mass., and have one child: *Gladys Balch*, b. Jan. 19, 1893, at Waldoboro.
> ELIZABETH FARLEY, b. Oct. 4, 1864.

1003.   **Wesley Perkins,**[8] son of 480 Wesley Perkins, and Mary [Baker] Balch, was born at Medfield, June 20, 1822, and died November 10, 1890.   He married Almira Patterson Smith, in June, 1848.   She was born May 11, 1826, and is living in Boston.   They had one child.

1786   MARY ELIZABETH,[9] b. March 4, 1849; d. April 22,1852.

In 1860 he was a leading merchant in Boston, doing business in grain and flour.   Few men in this country have been more successful in trading and breeding famous horses.   The stallion Fearnaught and the mare Purity he sold for $25,000 each.

1004.   **Mary Rebecca H.,**[8] daughter of 480 Wesley Perkins[7] and Mary [Baker] Balch, was born at Medfield, November 10, 1823, and lives at Brookline, Massachusetts.   She married George William Pettes, a journalist and author, at Roxbury, Mass., December 8, 1846.   He died at Brookline, March 18, 1892.   They had six children :   Elizabeth Law-

rence, b. July 25, 1848, m. Henry Hall Tuttle, June 8, 1879,
he died July 19, 1888; George Wesley, b. May 5, 1850,
unm.; James Lawrence, b. Sept. 9, 1851, unm.; Ada Percy,
b. Oct. 9, 1856, unm.; Helen Huntington, b. Oct. 19, 1858, d.
Aug. 21, 1859; Helen Frances, b. Dec. 18, 1860; unm.

1006. **William Henry,**[8] son of 480 Wesley Perkins[7]
and his third wife, Eliza A. [Brackett] Balch, was born at
Medfield, April 3, 1849, is not married; is living at Santa
Barbara, California; a merchant and ship owner.

1007. **Elizabeth Arabella,**[8] daughter of 480 Wesley
Perkins[7] and his third wife, Eliza A. [Brackett] Balch, was.
born at Medfield, Sept. 23, 1851. She is not married, and
lives in Boston, Massachusetts.

1008. **John F.,**[8] son of 483 John[7] and Abigail [Fair-
banks] Balch, was born at Medfield, in 1829, and died in New
York city, August 24, 1869. He was married July 23, 1860,
to Elvira J., daughter of Walter James. She was born at
Boston, November 1, 1834, and died at New York city, January 6, 1894, and was buried at Medfield, Mass. They had
four children, the first born in Boston, the others in New
York city.

1787   EVA JAMES,[9] b. Dec. 24, 1863.
1788   IDA RICHARDSON,[9] b. Sept. 9, 1865; d. July 21, 1866.
1789   ELIZABETH RICHARDSON,[9] b. April 2, 1867; d. July 25, 1867.
1790   JOHN WALTER,[9] b. April 27, 1869; d. Oct. 11, 1869.

1010. **Sarah Clark,**[8] daughter of 484 Benjamin[7] and
Chloe [Smith] Balch, was born at Mendon, Mass., September
5, 1827, and died in Dayton, Ohio, May 20, 1858, and was
buried at Dayton. She was married January 12, 1845, to
Asahel P. Clark, who was born at Medfield, Mass., and died
in Providence, R. I., February, 1875. They had two children: Amelia J., b. February, 1846; Anna Louisa, b. November, 1852, d. January, 1855.

1013. **Clara Anna,**[8] daughter of 484 Benjamin[7] and
Chloe [Smith] Balch, was born in Providence, R. I., September 3, 1834, and is living in Chicago, Illinois. She was mar-

ried December 21, 1858, to Sylvanus Holbrook Southwick, son of Jonathan F. Southwick. He was born at Uxbridge, Mass., Jan. 15, 1835. They have no children.

1019. Louise Maynard,[8] daughter of 484 Benjamin[7] and his fourth wife, Louise [Fales] Balch, was born in Providence, R. I., September 27, 1856. She is a teacher, unmarried, and lives at Pasadena, California, with her mother and brother.

1020. Frank Benjamin,[8] son of 484 Benjamin[7] and his fourth wife, Louise [Fales] Balch, was born at Providence, R. I., October 23, 1859, and is a salesman of saddlery hardware. In 1895 he moved from Providence to Los Angeles, California. He is not married, and lives at Pasadena.

1022. Jane Rebecca,[8] daughter of 485 Ebenezer H.[7] and Sarah [Wood] Balch, was born November 26, 1832, at Worcester, Massachusetts, and lives at Boston. She was married April 15, 1851, to Eben Sears, who was born in Boston, July 15, 1829. They live in that city, and have four children.

> EBEN WARDEN, b. Aug. 1, 1854, at Watertown; m. Caroline Roos, July 23, 1879, b. Boston, Dec. 7, 1857. Children: *Eben Warden*, b. Boston, May 18, 1880; *Richard Willard*, b. Dorchester, Oct. 11, 1881; *Nathaniel Philip*, b. Winthrop, Mass., Oct. 29, 1883; *Florence Hazel*, b. Malden, Mass., Nov. 16, 1886; *Winthrop Montgomery*, b. Winthrop, Sept. 7, 1893.
>
> FLORENCE, b. Dec. 20, 1856, at Watertown, Mass.; m. Henry Tolman, Jr., of Boston, December 6, 1877. Children: *Henry*, b. Boston, Oct. 15, 1879; *Richard Sears*, b. Newton, Sept. 30, 1881.
>
> MARY CREASE, b. Aug. 18, 1859, at Watertown, Mass.; unm.; is an artist; and was commissioner to the Columbian Exposition from Massachusetts.
>
> EMMA ELIZABETH, b. Jan. 12, 1861, at Watertown, Mass.; unmarried.

1023. Sarah Maria,[8] daughter of 485 Ebenezer H.[7] and Sarah [Wood] Balch, was born November 16, 1834, at Providence, R. I. She was married November 8, 1855, to Charles A. Ramsdell, who was born January 10, 1836, at Milford, New Hampshire, and has a clothing store at Winchester, Massachusetts. They have two children, both born in Boston.

IDA M., b. Aug. 30, 1856; m. first, Feb. 18, 1884, to William
Thomson, of Winchester, Mass. He died March 3, 1891,
leaving no children. She married second, October 23, 1895,
Jean Louis Victor Gustave Bélichon, of Paris, France. They
are artists, living in Paris.

CLIFFORD, b. Aug. 17, 1863; m. first, Aug. 9, 1884, Mary S. Ir-
win. She died at Dorchester, Mass., Sept. 12, 1888, leaving
no children; m. second, at Roxbury, Mass., March 9, 1892,
Carrie E. Felch. Children: *Laurice C.*, b. at Forest Hill,
Mass., Oct. 21, 1894; d. Nov. 16, 1894; *William Eben*, b. at
Providence, R. I., May 4, 1895.

1024. Anna Betsey,[8] daughter of 485 Ebenezer H.[7] and
Sarah [Wood] Balch, was born September 4, 1837, at Providence, R. I., and died at Chicago, Illinois, February 13, 1890,
and was buried at Rose Hill. She was married in October,
1877, to Leonard St. John, M.D., of St. Catherines, Ont.,
Canada. They lived in Chicago, and had no children.

1025. Frank Wood,[8] son of 485 Ebenezer H.[7] and Sarah
[Wood] Balch, was born September 1, 1841, at Providence,
R. I., and lives at Chicago, Illinois. He was educated at
Williston Seminary, East Hampton, Massachusetts. On
September 12, 1862, he was mustered as a private in Com-
pany F. 44th Massachusetts Volunteer Militia, a nine-months'
regiment, and saw service principally in North Carolina. He
was honorably discharged June 18, 1862, and engaged in the
coal trade, which business he still continues. He was married
April 19, 1876, to Lucy Cudworth, daughter of James M. and
Lucy [Cudworth] Ellis, of Syracuse, and granddaughter of
General John Ellis. They have had three children.

1791 LOUI,[9] b. Sept. 1877, d. y.
1792 ISABELLA ELLIS,[9] b. March 18, 1880, at Chicago.
1793 ELLIS ST. JOHN,[9] b. Apr. 17, 1883, d. July 11, 1883.

1026. Joanna,[8] daughter of 489 Thomas[7] and Elizabeth
[Kingman] Balch, was born May 5, 1794, and died October,
1863. She married November 13, 1820, John B. Elliott, who
was born June 21, 1789. They had eight children. John O.,
b. Jan. 13, 1822, d. March 19, 1822; Ezekiel B., b. July 16,
1823, d. 1888; Thomas B., b. July 24, 1824, d. 1881; Sarah

FRANK W. BALCH.

(1025)

E., b. Nov. 23, 1827 ; Emily Joanna, b. Oct. 14, 1829 ;
Martha Joanna, b. May 17,1831, d. ; Lucretia Ann, b. ; Jacob
Henry, b.

1027. **Benjamin,**[8] son of 489 Thomas[7] and Elizabeth
[Kingman] Balch, was born at Barrington, N. H., May 2,
1796, and died at Syracuse, N. Y., January 28, 1869. He
was married April 24, 1819, to Ann Van Benthuysen, of
Troy, N. Y. She was born October 9, 1795. They lived in
Syracuse, N. Y., and had six children.

1794   SARAH ELIZABETH,[9] b. Apr. 13, 1820; unm.; d. April 4, 1895.
1795   THOMAS,[9] b. May 22, 1822; d. y.
1796*   JOANNA,[9] b. May 22, 1823; d. Jan. 14, 1877.
1797*   GEORGE H.,[9] b. July 1, 1825; unm. d. May 15, 1892.
1798*   BENJAMIN JAMES,[9] b. Aug. 27, 1828; d. Oct. 7, 1887.
1799*   JOHN W.,[9] b. Aug. 10, 1837.

Benjamin,[8] was a skilful joiner and pattern maker. This
family were dark complexioned, tall, and finely developed.

1028. **Dolly,**[8] daughter of 489 Thomas[7] and Elizabeth
[Kingman] Balch, was born at Barington, N. H., September
10, 1799, and died July 28, 1870. She was married March
25, 1829, to Jeremiah Caverno, of Stafford. He was born
March 17, 1797 and died November 14, 1872.

1030. **Lucy O.,**[8] daughter of 489 Thomas[7] and Judith
[Perhens] Balch, was born December 22, 1807. She was
married April 19, 1827, to Charles C. Elliott, who was born
November 4, 1805. They had one son, Ezekiel O., b. June
1, 1831.

1032. **John,**[8] son of 492 John[7] and Hannah [Stone]
Balch, was born at Bangor, Me., November 14,1803, and died
suddenly of heart disease at Roxbury, Mass., January 29,
1861. He married March 19, 1833, Mary E. Chaloner.
They had eleven children.

1800*   JOHN WILLIAM,[9] b. Feb. 1, 1834.
1801*   LOUIS C.,[9] b. Oct. 13, 1835; d. unm. Jan. 6, 1854.
1802*   MARY LOUISE,[9] b. Apr. 11, 1837; unm.
1803*   HANNAH ELIZABETH,[9] b. Apr. 13, 1839; d. Mar. 5, 1865.
1804*   ANNA MARIA,[9] b. Aug. 12,1841; unm.
1805*   HENRY CLAY,[9] b. Dec. 7, 1843; unm.
1806*   AMORY OTIS,[9] b. Jan. 7, 1846; d. unm. Sept. 21, 1866.

1807   HENRIETTA RING,[9] b. Dec. 13, 1847.
1808*   ALICE HALL,[9] b. Oct. 15, 1849.
1809*   GEORGE HALEY,[9] b. Oct. 6, 1851.
1810   ZOE TRACY,[9] b. July 15, 1853; unm.

Capt. John Balch spent the active years of his life at Trescott, Me., where he was largely engaged in ship-building, and advanced that branch of industry to a state of great prosperity in that part of the country.   He represented his fellow townsmen repeatedly in the legislature and other public offices.   He was an active friend of the temperance cause, and other objects of social progress and enterprise.

Several years before his death, he removed from Maine to Roxbury, Mass, and was engaged in commerce with England, Australia, and the Pacific coast.   Severe reverses in business marked his last years, but they were borne with singular fortitude, and served only to bring out other and brighter sides of his character which had less opportunity to display themselves during his days of prosperity.

1034. **Hiram Augustus,**[8] son of 492 John[7] and Hannah [Stone] Balch, was born at Bangor, Maine, September 14, 1806, and died January 29, 1872, at Lubec, where he was buried. When a young man he went to Trescott, Maine, where he built and owned several sawmills, engaged in ship building, and owned several vessels. In 1846 he removed his business to Lubec, and soon after was elected to the state legislature. He lived upon his father's old homestead at Trescott, and in the latter years of his life also owned a summer residence at Calais, Me. He was married December 30, 1835, to Martha, daughter of Capt. John and Mary [Schofield] Maryman. She was born at Brunswick, Maine, in 1807, and died at Lubec, October 17, 1870. They had five children, born at Trescott.

1811*   HIRAM AUGUSTUS,[9] b. Sept. 13, 1837; d. Jan. 22, 1894.
1812*   HANNAH STONE,[9] b, Oct. 24, 1839; d. March 17, 1886.
1813*   HARRIET M.,[9] b. Nov. 4, 1842.
1814   MARY SUSAN,[9] b. April 4, 1845; d. Jan. 7, 1873.
1815   ALBERT BENJAMIN,[9] b. Oct. 11, 1848; unm.; a school teacher, lives at Pee Ell, Washington.

1036. Rebecca,[8] daughter of 492 John[7] and Hannah [Stone] Balch, was born at Bangor, Me., February 7, 1809, and died February 20, 1864. She married John Monroe. He died December 12, 1884, and was a grandson of Capt. Varden, of the British navy. They lived six years at St. George, New Brunswick, where their three eldest children were born. Then they moved to St. Johns, where their two youngest children were born.

> SARAH MARIA, b. Aug. 17, 1834; m. George T. Smith, of the Provincial Militia of New Brunswick, and lives at Tacoma, Wash. They moved west in 1869, and are members of the Congregational Church. Their children are as follows: *Lafayette Balch*, a grocer at Tacoma, m. Nov. 17, 1882, Phebe Adell Woodruff; *Eva Gertrude*, a teacher at Tacoma; *Lillian Rebecca*; *George William*, a grocer at Tacoma; *Izola Balch*.
>
> HANNAH, b. Nov. 13, 1835; lives at Ludington, Mich.; m. Edwin Wheaton, who died March 31, 1869, at St. Johns, N. B. They have two sons: *Frederick Albert*, b. December, 1862; hotel clerk at Cheboygan, Mich.; *John Balch*, b. November, 1863; lives in Chicago.
>
> GEORGE ALPHONSE, b. 1838; d. 1839.
>
> JOHN HARRISON, b. 1842; d. 1843.
>
> JOHN ALBERT, b. June 24, 1847; d. June 10, 1895; m. Kate Monroe, who lives at Houghton, Mich. They had one daughter, *Eva J.*, b. Sept. 17, 1870, m. June 27, 1895, Frank Kopp, of Houghton.

After the death of her mother, Rebecca assumed the management of the household. She was noted for her amiability and deeds of charity, and was a devout Christian, and a member of the Wesleyan Methodist Church.

1037. Louis,[8] son of 492 John[7] and Hannah [Stone] Balch, was born at Bangor, Me., March 27, 1810. He was a sea captain, and owned the vessel which he commanded. In a gale on December 23, 1837, when on a voyage from New York to Charleston, he was knocked overboard and drowned.

1038. Charles,[8] son of 492 John[7] and Hannah [Stone] Balch, was born at Bangor, September 1, 1811. He owned and commanded a sailing vessel. His home was at Trescott. He was married, but died January 29, 1890, without issue, at Trescott, Maine.

1039. **Hannah,**[8] daughter of 492 John[7] and Hannah [Stone] Balch, was born at Bangor, Maine, December 13, 1818, and died at Chippewa Falls, Wisconsin, July 19, 1865. She was a woman of pure Christian spirit, manifest in all her life. On June 8, 1834, she married George Gillmor, of St. George, N. B. He was largely engaged in the lumber trade. He left St. George in 1857, and moved with his family to Chippewa Falls, where he died, June 7, 1861. They were members of the Baptist church, and had twelve children: Horatio Gonzala, b. April 30, 1835, d. Dec. 27, 1867; Rosalba Elisabeth, b. Sept. 25, 1836, d. Jan. 29, 1838; George Alonzo, b. Oct. 24, 1837, lives at Chippewa Falls, Wisconsin; John Balch, b. Jan. 2, 1839, d. Dec. 10, 1875; Rosalba Ellen, b. April 4, 1840, d. Sept. 15, 1842; Rosina Grace, b. March 28, 1843, lives at St. George, New Brunswick; Sarah Balch, b. Sept. 13, 1844, d. Jan. 15, 1864; Daniel Webster, b. May 28, 1845, is a minister at Creston, Iowa; Anna Sophia, b. April 11, 1847, d. Aug. 29, 1871; Zachary Taylor, b. Oct. 15, 1848, d. Oct. 10, 1868; Joseph Judson, b. April 13, 1852, d. April 28, 1852; Hannah Rebecca, b. April 18, 1856, lives at Chippewa Falls.

1042. **Henry,**[8] son of 492 John[7] and Hannah [Stone] Balch, was born at Bangor, Me., July 15, 1819, and is a mining engineer in San Francisco, California. He never married. For seven years he was superintendent of the Comstock gold mines.

1043. **George,**[8] son of 492 John[7] and Hannah [Stone] Balch, was born at Trescott, Me., May 18, 1821, and died at Placer county, Cala., May 18, 1861. He went to California in 1850, with his brothers, around the Horn, and in a few years amassed a fortune in mining. In 1855 he came east to visit his relatives. On his return to California he met a lady on the steamer, whom he afterwards married. Three years after his marriage he died, leaving all his property to his widow and baby girl, then eight months old. His widow married a Mr. Sullivan. She is insane.

1816 NELLIE,[9] b. about 1858; d. in 1876.

1045. Lafayette,[8] son of 492 John[7] and Hannah [Stone] Balch, was born at Trescott, Me., February 8, 1825, and died at San Francisco, Cal., November 25, 1862.   He owned a line of packets that ran between San Francisco, Oregon and Puget Sound.   He was a sea captain, and commanded the ship Sacramento, in which he and his brothers sailed around the Horn in 1850.   He was a member of the first Territorial Legislature of Washington.

1046. Albert Gallatin,[8] son of 492 John[7] and Hannah [Stone] Balch, was born at Trescott, Me., March 10, 1827, and died unmarried about 1860.   He went to California, and engaged in mercantile pursuits in a town near San Francisco.

1047. Mary Wadsworth,[8] daughter of 493 Rev. William[7] and Mary [Wadsworth] Balch, was born at Salisbury, Mass., August 10, 1806, and died at Newton, Mass., April 11, 1881.   She married Horatio Balch Hackett, D. D., LL.D , September 22, 1834.   He was the second son of Richard and 497 Martha [Balch] Hackett and was born in Salisbury, Mass., December 27, 1808, and died in Rochester, New York, November 2, 1875.   They had four children, born at Newton Centre.

> HORATIO BALCH, b. July 5, 1841; m. Dec. 23, 1874, Sarah Maria Field.   They live at Newton and have had four children. *William Field,* b. Oct. 13, 1876· *Howard,* b. Apr. 11, 1879; *Bertha,* b. July 7, 1883; *Sarah Balch,* b. Apr. 23, 1887.
> MARY WADSWORTH. b. Sept. 12, 1843, unm., lives at Newton.
> WILLIAM RICHARD, b. Mar. 27, 1846; d. Sept. 19, 1849.
> BENJAMIN WADSWORTH, b. Jan. 5, 1849; m. Nov. 13, 1878, Alice Harriet Abbott, two children. *Bessie Wadsworth,* b. at Newton, Aug. 24, 1879, d. May 13, 1891; *Leon,* b. at Cambridge, Mass., Oct. 20, 1882.

Dr. Hackett graduated at Amherst College in 1830, and studied theology at Andover.   Afterwards he studied the German language at Halle and Leipsic, and the Greek language at Athens.   He taught for a year at Mt. Hope College, Baltimore, and while there changed his views on baptism. He was ordained a Baptist clergyman. He was professor of ancient languages in Brown University from 1835 to 1839, when he became professor of New Testament Exegesis in Newton Theological Institution. In 1868 he resigned his professorship at Newton and became editor of the American Edition of Smith's Bible Dictionary. In 1870 he accepted the professorship of New Testament Exegesis at Rochester Theological Seminary, and retained it until his death. Among his numerous published works are " A Commentary on the Original Text of the Acts of the Apostles," " Illustrations of Scripture," and " Christian Memorials of the War." A volume entitled "Memorials of Horatio Balch Hackett," was published under the auspices of the Rochester Theological Seminary.

1053. Harriet,[8] daughter of 495 Dr. Horatio Gates[7] and Rhoda [Dutton] Balch. She married Uriah, son of Capt. Coolidge, commander in the revenue service. They had three children, all now dead. Julia Dutton, Edith and Frank.

1054. Sophia,[8] daughter of 494 Dr. Horatio Gates[7] and Rhoda [Dutton] Balch, She married Lowell Chase. They had one child, Elizabeth.

1057. Emily,[8] daughter of 495 Dr. Horatio Gates[7] and Rhoda [Dutton] Balch, was born at Lubec, Maine, August 8, 1820, and died at Weaverville, Cal., Dec. 13, 1892. She was married in June, 1844, to J. J., son of Capt. John Ames. He was born in 1820, and died at San Diego, Cal., in 1861. They had two children, both born at Calais, Maine: George G., b. April 2, 1845, d. April 2, 1847, at Calais, Me.; Helen P., b. Sept. 3, 1847, d. unm. May 29, 1865, at Peabody, Mass.

1060. James Ripley,[8] son of 495 Dr. Horatio Gates[7] and Harriet Turner [McLellan] Balch, was born November 22, 1831, at Lubec, Me. He was a merchant, and resided at Weaverville, Cal., where he died, April 18, 1895. He was married October 8, 1867, to Margaret, daughter of John Robb.

She was born at Lewis, N. Y., February 12, 1848. They have had seven children, all born at Weaverville, California.

1817   JAMES HORATIO,[9] b. July 30, 1868; d. March 11, 1869.
1818*   EMILY AMES,[9] b. May 19, 1870.
1819   ALICE,[9] b. Jan. 5, 1872; d. Jan. 19, 1872.
1820   HENRY RIPLEY,[9] b. April 12, 1873.
1821   EDWARD,[9] b. April 24, 1878; d. Feb. 5, 1885.
1822   HELEN PATIA,[9] }
1823   HORATIO[9],   } twins, b. Oct. 13, 1881. { d. Feb. 10, 1887.

1061. Horatio Gates,[8] son of 495 Dr. Horatio Gates[7] and Harriet Turner [McLellan] Balch, was born at Lubec, Me., June 15, 1840, and died at Weaverville, Cal., March 7, 1894. He was a seaman, and did not marry.

1062. Jacob William,[8] son of 498 Jeremiah O.[7] and Sarah [Penniman] Balch, was born November 19, 1817, at Lubec, Me., and died at New Westminster, British Columbia, November 1, 1888. He was married in 1844 to Sarah A., daughter of True and Lydia Bradbury, of Lubec. She was born at Lubec, July 12, 1823, and died at Boston, Wash., July 10, 1892. About 1865 his family removed from Machias, Maine, to Washington Territory, where he had made a home, and was engaged in the lumber trade. They had nine children. All were born at Machias, except the youngest, who was born at Port Gamble, Wash.

1824*   FRANK TRUE,[9] b. March 24, 1845.
1825   SARAH P.,[9] b. Dec. 28, 1847; m. McQuillen; lives at Seattle, Wash.
1826   HENRY C.,[9] b. Feb. 6, 1850; d. Feb. 19, 1850.
1827   LIZZIE M.,[9] b. Feb. 25, 1851; d. June 13, 1856.
1828   AUGUSTUS LEROY,[9] b. March 6, 1853; d. Oct. 19, 1878.
1829   LAURA P.,[9] b. Feb. 8, 1856; m. Hall; lives at Port Townsend, Wash.
1830   KATE M.,[9] b. May 6, 1860; m. White; lives at Suez, Wash.
1831*   MINNIE B.,[9] b. Sept. 20, 1862.
1832   TERESIA T.,[9] b. Feb. 17, 1869; d. May 17, 1891.

1063. Mary Cynthia,[8] daughter of 498 Jeremiah O.[7] and Sarah [Penniman] Balch, was born October 12, 1820, and died November 18, 1873. She was married at Machias,

Maine, December 31, 1837, to Robert Dutch Foster. He died August 29, 1866. They lived and died at St. Louis, Missouri, and had eight children: Helen Maria, Helen Jane, Charles Henry, Mary Elizabeth, Sarah Frances, Eugene and Ella, twins; Ignatus Sargent. Of these two grew up.

> HELEN JANE: b. Feb. 3, 1840; m. April 2, 1863, Charles LaSalle Gilpin. Three children: *Adele Locke*, b. March 20, 1864; m. Spencer Ervin, of Philadelphia; *Robert Porter*, b. Feb. 26, 1868, d. May 25, 1878; *Charles Edward*, b. Nov. 15, 1872.
>
> CHARLES HENRY, b. Dec. 15, 1841; d. Dec. 6, 1895; m., 1865, Charlotte Remer, at Kosciusko, Miss. Children: *Charles Henry, Robert Balch*, live at New Orleans, La.

1065. Henry Crawford,[8] son of 498 Jeremiah O.[7] and Sarah [Penniman] Balch, was born at East Machias, Me., December 18, 1824, and died at Williamsburg, N. Y., July 30, 1861, and was buried at Kingston, N. Y. He was a dry goods merchant, first at Montgomery, Ala., and afterwards at New York city. He was married to Catherine A., daughter of Robert W. Newton, of Hope, New Jersey, where she was born November 22, 1825. She lives at Sioux City, Iowa. They had four children.

1833   HENRY NEWTON,[9] b. Oct. 7, 1850; d. May 27, 1853. :
1834*   IDA MAY,[9] b. June 29, 1853.
1835*   CHARLES TAYLOR,[9] b. Oct. 22, 1856.
1836*   EDWARD CRAWFORD,[9] b. July 17, 1858.

1066. Francis Storms,[8] son of 498 Jeremiah O.[7] and Sarah [Penniman] Balch, was born September 5, 1826. He died, unmarried, August, 1888, in New York city. He was one of the early residents of Washington Territory. He returned east, and was appointed an acting assistant paymaster in the U. S. navy, March 29, 1865; served on the Curlew, Mississippi squadron, and afterwards on the "Woxsaw." Discharged October 17, 1866.

1069. George Washington,[8] son of 498 Jeremiah O.[7] and Elizabeth A. [Haskell] Balch, was born in Vienna (now Phelps), N. Y., May 24, 1832. He was married at Detroit,

Mich., June 8, 1858, to Mary E. Cranage, by whom he has had six children, the third born at Mt. Clemens, and the others at Detroit, Michigan.

1837   GEORGE C.,⁹ b. Oct. 27, 1859.
1838*   THOMAS B.,⁹ b. Oct. 22, 1861.
1839*   MARY E.,⁹ b. Sept. 25, 1863.
1840   HOWARD,⁹ b. Aug. 7, 1867; d. Feb. 18, 1869, at Detroit.
1841   KATE D.,⁹ b. Dec. 23, 1869.
1842   FREDERICK A.,⁹ b. July 3, 1874.

George W. Balch was trained early to business pursuits, first in Michigan, and next at Chattanooga, Tenn., where, at the age of 17, he engaged in the dry goods business. About 1851 he became also connected with the telegraph, which was then first introduced in that region. Knowledge of this business he had previously acquired at the North. He was the first, and for a time the only practical telegrapher in East Tennessee. In 1852 he returned North, and regularly entered the telegraph service, first at Detroit, Michigan, then at Chicago, and returning again to Detroit, in 1853-4, he there became superintendent of the Western Union Telegraph Company. In 1865 he was appointed assistant general superintendent of that company, with headquarters at Rochester, N. Y. In 1866 he removed to New York city, as assistant to I. H. Wade, president Western Union Telegraph Company. In 1867-8 he returned to Detroit and engaged in commercial business. In 1871 he was elected president of the common council, and for a time was acting mayor. Subsequently he served three years as president of the Board of Education of that city. He was president of the American District Telegraph Company and of the Telephone and Telegraph Construction Company, and also of the Michigan Bell Telephone Company and of the Michigan Telegraph Company, and also president of the Detroit Electrical Works. Later he entered on railroad construction, and became vice-president of the Detroit, Butler & St. Louis Railroad Company (an adjunct of the Wabash R. R. Co.) For 25 years he was engaged in the grain business at Detroit, and for the past twenty years, in connection therewith, conducted the grain business in New York city, retaining residence, however, continuously in Detroit, Mich. As chairman of the New York Produce Exchange Canal Committee, he promoted the improvement of the New York state canals, under whose efforts the present $9,000,000 improvement of the state canals was mainly brought about.

1070. **Benjamin,**[8] son of 498 Jeremiah O.[7] and Elizabeth A. [Haskell] Balch, was born at Leroy, N. Y., December 8, 1840, and died March 3, 1884, at Burlington, Vt. He was twice married, first to a Miss Fish, second to Miss Jane E. Wilkins, and had no children.

1071. **Lavinia Melissa,**[8] daughter of 498 Jeremiah O.[7] and Elizabeth A. [Haskell] Balch, was born June 24, 1843, at Marshall, Mich., and died at Bellevue, Mich., July 12, 1887. She was married December 6, 1865, to Abram G., son of Edward Butler, of Marshall, Mich. He was born in that city, August 15, 1841. They had eight children, one born at Marshall, Michigan, two at Detroit, three at Chicago, Illinois, and two at Bellevue, Michigan. Grace Dency, b. Nov. 11, 1866 ; Maynard Balch, b. Sept. 28, 1868 ; Josephine, b. Nov. 11, 1870 ; Florence, b. Feb. 26, 1877 ; Samuel Abram, b. Jan. 15, 1880 ; Abram G., b. Aug. 19, 1881 ; Ada Havel, b. March 10, 1885 ; Lavinia M., b. March 4, 1887.

1072. **Rebecca Bailey,**[8] daughter of 501 Phineas Carleton[7] and Jane Kezer [Merrill] Balch, was born July 21, 1821, and died June 16, 1887, the result of a fall from a hammock. She married Joshua N. Foss, in 1856. He was a farmer and fire insurance agent at Rowley, Massachusetts. He died January 11, 1894. They had no children.

1073. **Abigail Carleton,**[8] daughter of 502 Leonard[7] and Mary A. [Hopkinson] Balch, was born at East Bradford, Massachusetts, June 25, 1823. She was married to Ebenezer

Carleton, who was born October 20, 1820. They had four children:

ALVIN BYRON, b. May 9, 1842; m. July 25, Kate Fitzsimmons.

PHINEHAS BALCH, b. July 2, 1846; m. Dec. 28, 1871, Julia E. Fenton. Three children: *George Henry*, b. Oct. 8, 1872; *Mabel Louise*, b. Oct. 8, 1874; *Daniel Barton*, b. May 16, 1880.

HARRIOT LAPHAM, b. Dec. 21, 1854; m. July 4, 1872, Newton Tilton. Two children: *Leonard Alvin*, b. June 30, 1873; *Mary Elizabeth*, b. Aug. 30, 1877.

MARY ANN, b. ; d. y.

1074. Melvin Parker,[8] son of 503 William[7] and Abigail B. [Parker] Balch, was born at East Bradford [Groveland], November 27, 1832. He was married at Lynn, April 12, 1863, to Ada R. Huntley, of Lynn. He became intemperate and violent, and in 1873 his wife obtained a divorce. He then disappeared, and it is not known what became of him. They had two children, both of whom are living with their mother.

1843 AMY G.,[9] b. at Kasson, Minn., Nov. 22, 1865.

1844 ETHEL M.,[9] b. at Lynn, Mass., March 29, 1869.

1075. Clara Maria,[8] daughter of 503 William[7] and Abigail B. [Parker] Balch, was born at East Bradford [Groveland], September 10, 1840, and died July 1, 1896. She was married February 20, 1859, to Alfred, son of Thomas Laws, who was born in Washington, N. H., June 26, 1831. He graduated at Dartmouth, for a time was a school teacher, and is now in the insurance business at Brockton, Mass. Their children were as follows: Amma, b. Nov. 2, 1861, d. Aug. 14, 1866; Walter, b. June 14, 1864, d. Aug. 14, 1866; Frank A., b. May 28, 1867, at North Bridgewater, Massachusetts; Mary L., b. July 28, 1869, d. Sept. 24, 1869.

1076. William,[8] son of 505 Thomas Hutchinson[7] and Sophia B. [Tenney] Balch, was born at East Bradford [Groveland], October 9, 1840. He was married July 8, 1866, to Martha S., daughter of Charles and Rebecca C. [Palmer] Harriman. They reside in Brockton, Mass., and have no children.

1077. Hiram Tenney,[8] son of 505 Thomas Hutchinson[7] and Sophia B. [Tenney] Balch, was born at East Bradford [Groveland], May 28, 1842. He was married February 23, 1864, to Mary Sophia, daughter of Daniel and Ascenath [Parker] Morse, of Bradford, Mass. She was born at Bradford, January 25, 1842. They live at Newburyport, and their four children were born at. Groveland.

1845   HERMAN MORSE,[9] b. June 5, 1865; d. Sept. 6, 1866.
1846   JOHN PEMBERTON,[9] b. July 13, 1867; unm.
1847ª WILLIAM,[9] b. Aug. 18, 1869.
1848   LEONARD PARKER,[9] b. Dec. 29, 1871; unm.

Hiram T. enlisted in company B, 48th Regiment, Massachusetts Volunteers, August 18, 1862. This was a nine months' regiment. It was sent to the Department of the Gulf, and served its full time in Louisiana. He was honorably discharged September 3, 1863. He re-enlisted August 23, 1864, in company M, 4th Massachusetts Heavy Artillery, and was honorably discharged July 17, 1865. He is an engineer.

1078. Charles Thomas,[8] son of 505 Thomas Hutchinson[7] and Sophia B. [Tenney] Balch, was born at East Bradford [Groveland], February 23, 1844. He was with the firm of Pemberton & Balch, at Newburyport. The firm was dissolved after the burning of the shop, in 1888. He has held many town offices, and was a member of the Massachusetts Legislature from Groveland in 1895.

1079. Arthur Clifford,[8] son of 505 Thomas Hutchinson[7] and Sophia B. [Tenney] Balch, was born at East Bradford [Groveland], October 22, 1846. He was married to Mary Darling, widow of Leonard Darling, and daughter of Elbridge and Lucy [Runnells] Smith, of Haverhill. They live at Groveland, and have one child.

1849   CLIFFORD TENNEY,[9] b. Oct. 16, 1884.

1080. Eustis,[8] son of 505 Thomas Hutchinson[7] and Sophia B. [Tenney] Balch, was born at East Bradford

[Groveland], Mass., April 2, 1849. He is a carpenter and builder, and lives at Oakland, California. He was married June 2, 1886, to Georgianna M., daughter of John McDougald and Matilda [Irving] Post. She was born at Sutter's Creek, December 26, 1859. Their children were born at Oakland, California.

 1850 SOPHIA MATILDA,[9] b. Dec. 28, 1888.
 1851 HENRIETTA,[9] b. June 17, 1890.
 1852 THOMAS EUSTIS,[9] b. May 16, 1893.

 1082. Gardner Pickard,[8] son of 505 Thomas Hutchinson[7] and Sophia B. [Tenney] Balch, was born at Groveland, Massachusetts, July 7, 1856. He was married August 28, 1886, to Sophia George, daughter of Moses and Eliza A. [Estabrook] Williams. She was born January 28, 1868, at West Newbury, Mass. They have one child.

 1853 MALCOLM WILLIAMS,[9] b. Sept. 2, 1894.

Gardner Pickard graduated from Dartmouth College in 1881, was first sub-master of the High and Putnam School, at Newburyport, and is now principal of schools in Swampscott, Mass., and master of the Phillips High School.

 1083. Sarah Hutchinson,[8] daughter of 506 Jonathan[7] and Sally [Hopkinson] Balch, was born September 21, 1829. She was married Oct. 25, 1849, to Charles Putnam, son of Thomas and Deborah Savary. He was born May 20, 1828, and died Nov. 11, 1893. She resides at Groveland, and has three children : William P., b. April 10, 1852, m. Aug. 8, 1879, Alice M. Richardson ; Elizabeth M., b. May 27, 1859, d. April 8, 1863; Annie W., b. July 25, 1866.

 1084. Horace Morse,[8] son of 506 Jonathan[7] and Sally [Hopkinson] Balch, was born February 24, 1831, and died Sept. 14, 1892, in California. He married first Sarah L. G. Ayers, in 1854. She was the widow of Joseph U. York. They had no children. He married second Louise Pettigrew, by whom he had one son. They lived in San Francisco.

 1854 ALVIN H.,[9] b. May, 1873; d. Aug., 1893.

1085. Ann Mary,[8] daughter of 506 Jonathan[7] and Sally [Hopkinson] Balch, was born November 17, 1832. She was married February 23, 1854, to Luther K., son of Joseph Kimball and Lucy [Jameson] Pemberton. He was born August 10, 1830, and was a member of the firm of Pemberton & Balch, until the shop was burnt in 1888. He is a contractor for children's shoes, and lives in Groveland.

1088. Harriet Lapham,[8] daughter of 506 Jonathan[7] and Sally [Hopkinson] Balch, was born at Groveland, August 28, 1838, and died Jan. 31, 1893, in Wisconsin. She was married, in 1854, to George W., son of James A. and Grace M. [Walker] Banks, of Yorkshire, Eng. He died in March, 1895. They lived at Monroe, Wisconsin. Harold, b. April 13, 1856 ; Fred A., b. April 17, 1858 ; Philip, d. y.; George, b. July 1, 1866 ; Harriet M., b. Sept. 17, 1875 ; Ralph, b. Dec. 20, 1877, d. y.

1092. Frank Henry,[8] son of 506 Jonathan[7] and Sally [Hopkinson] Balch, was born July 18, 1851, and lives in Groveland, Mass. He was married September 26, 1872, to Marcy, daughter of Charles and Charlotte [Brock] Ruddock, of West Newbury, Mass. They have no children.

1094. David Moore,[8] son of 510 Benjamin[7] and Caroline L. [Moore] Balch, was born at Salem, Mass., January 22, 1837, and is a chemist at Coronado, Cal. He was married December 26, 1876, to Emma A., only daughter of Joseph Swasey. She was born June 16, 1851. Their children are:

1855 CAROLINE MOORE,[9] b. Oct. 24, 1877.
1856 ALICE GIFFORD,[9] b. Dec. 26, 1878; d. next day.
1857 MARY ELIZABETH,[9] b. May 28, 1881.
1858 EMMA LOUESE,[9] b. Jan. 2, 1883, at Lugonia, Cal.

David M. graduated from Harvard College in 1854. To him is due the credit of much of the work in collecting the matter for this Genealogy. His searches among the official records of Massachusetts has been extensive, and his care to have his work correct is characteristic of his Balch heredity.

An article by him, of great historical value, entitled "The Old Planters," was published in the "Salem Gazette," May 10, 1878, and in the Balch Leaflets. He resided in Salem until about 1880, when he went to California to cultivate oranges. For a time he lived at Lugonia, and since 1888 he has been at Coronado Beach.

1095. **Edward Franklin,**[8] son of 510 Benjamin[7] and Caroline L. [Moore] Balch, was born at Salem, November 27, 1842, and died Aug. 29, 1892. He was married June 5, 1873, to Elizabeth S., daughter of Thomas and Mary [Dustin] Perkins. They had three children, all born at Salem.

1859 EDITH PERKINS,[9] b. Aug. 26, 1874.
1860 ELIZABETH,[9] b. Nov. 11, 1876.
1861 FRANK,[9] b. Oct. 31, 1880.

Edward Franklin received his education at the private schools of Salem, Mass. He first tried a business career, but not being suited, entered the machine shop of the Naumkeag Cotton Mills, at Salem, remained for five years, and rose to the position of superintendent. Next he resigned to accept the agency of the Dwight Mills at Chicopee. He remained there two years, when the agency of the Naumkeag Mills became vacant, and he was called to the position, which he filled up to the time of his death.

1096. **William Duncan,**[8] son of 511 James[7] and Harriet Jane [Duncan] Balch, was born at Salem, Sept. 28, 1834. He lives at Malden, Massachusetts, and is a jeweler at Boston. He served in the 50th Massachusetts Volunteers during the civil war, in Gen. Auger's division, 19th Army Corps, Department of the Gulf. He was married August 2, 1871, to Caroline Elizabeth, daughter of Col. David and Caroline P. Stanwood, of Brunswick, Maine, where she was born, November 18, 1832. They have no children.

1097. **Catherine Duncan,**[8] daughter of 511 James[7] and Harriet Jane [Duncan] Balch, was born at Salem, Mass., September 22, 1836, and died at Brooklyn, N. Y., in February, 1892. She was married June 1, 1857, to James D. Nairne, of Scotland. He studied dentistry, but did not practice, and was a lace importer and dealer in New York city. They lived in Brooklyn, and all their children were born there. Katherine D., b. April 14, 1858, d. at Edinburg, June 4, 1860; James D., b. Aug. 22, 1860; Elizabeth D., b. July 15, 1862; Lillian, b. July 25, 1864; Harriet D., b. Sept. 25, 1867; William H., b. Jan. 25, 1871; Frank B., b. Aug. 2, 1873.

1100. William Frederick,[8] son of 512 William[7] and Marian [Kittridge] Balch, was born July 16, 1836, and died March 31, 1868. He lived at Salem and Pawtucket, Mass., Half Day, Ill., and New York city. He was married February 11, 1857, to Martha C. Darg, who was born in Louisiana. She died about 1885, in Texas, leaving one daughter.

1862 AMY C.,[9] b. 1859; m. Canning; no children.

William F. was the author of a paper on the "Balch Genealogy," in the New England Genealogical and Historical Register, for July, 1855. He was a physician, and practiced in New York city.

1101. Lucy Ann,[8] daughter of 512 William[7] and Marian [Kittridge] Balch, was born August 17, 1837, and died October 21, 1881. She married, April 17, 1862, Capt. George R. Durand, of the United States navy. They had three children, born at Pawtucket, Rhode Island: Susan Marian, b. Jan. 29, 1868; Lucy Balch, b. Sept. 30, 1865; William Balch, b. Feb. 26, 1871. They live in Buffalo, N. Y.

1102. Benjamin K.,[8] son of 512 William[7] and Marian [Kittridge] Balch, was born November 5, 1840, and was drowned at Pawtucket, Rhode Island, in August, 1870. He was married October 8, 1864, to Elizabeth Robinson, and left no children.

1104. Lowell Thayer,[8] son of 512 William[7] and Marian [Kittridge] Balch, was born at Half Day, Illinois, May 21,

1848, and lives at Pawtucket, Rhode Island. He was married June 14, 1868, to Martha Travis, daughter of George and Laureney [Marchant] Thompson, at Pawtucket. Her father was born in Lancashire, England, and her mother in Massachusetts. She was born in Pawtucket, June 14, 1852, and died in the same town, December 18, 1874. They had three children, born at Pawtucket.

1863* WILLIAM,[9] b. Feb. 16, 1869.
1864* EDWARD KITTRIDGE,[9] b. May 5, 1871.
1865* MARTHA THOMPSON,[9] b. Dec. 11, 1874.

1106. **George Phippen,**[8] son of 513 Moses Phippen[7] and Adelia M. [Lauriat] Balch, was born at Barre, Mass., June 18, 1840. He is a watchmaker, and resided at DeKalb, Illinois. He is now at Lynn, Mass. He was married Dec. 25, 1870, to Isadore Cornish.

1866 DANIEL LAURIAT,[9] b. Oct. 9, 1876.
1867 AUSTIN CORNISH,[9] b. June 12, 1878.

1108. **Sarah Elizabeth,**[8] daughter of 513 Moses Phippen[7] and Adelia M. [Lauriat] Balch, was born at Lynn, Mass., January 1, 1844. She was married November 17, 1869, to Frederick L. Fiske, of Charlestown. They live at Everett, Mass., and have two children. William Lincoln, b. July 29, 1873, m. Clara Deihl, Sept. 9, 1894; George Frederick, b. Sept. 18, 1877.

1113. **Laura Octavia,**[8] daughter of 513 Moses Phippen[7] and Adelia M. [Lauriat] Balch, was born January 18, 1858. She was married August 5, 1877, to Robert R. Jones. They live in Boston, Mass. They have one child, Clara Rosanna, b. May 26, 1878.

1115. **Ebenezer Gunnison,**[8] son of 522 Daniel[7] and Elizabeth [Gunnison] Balch, was born at Dorchester, N. H., September 18, 1819, and died at Newburyport, January 14, 1884. He went on several whaling voyages when a young man, after which he entered a hardware store, where he remained up to a few years before his death. He was a deacon

in the Unitarian church, a Republican, and much respected
in the community in which he lived. In 1851 he married
Eliza Hall, and had five children.

1868   DANIEL,[9] b.   ; d. y.
1869*   DANIEL,[9] b. 1853.
1870*   LUCY ANN,[9] b. April 6, 1857; d. March 29, 1888.
1871*   GEORGE H.,[9] b. 1861; d. Feb. 15, 1895.
1872   CHARLES HODGE,[9] b. 1862; d. unm. March 24, 1883.

1116. Lucy Elizabeth,[8] daughter of 522 Daniel[7] and
Elizabeth [Gunnison] Balch, was born at Newburyport, No-
vember 14, 1820, and died April 16, 1867. She was married
June 25, 1844, to David Merritt, of Salem, and had one child,
Elizabeth Balch, b. March 29, 1851.

1119. William Charles,[8] son of 524 William[7] and Hannah [Stone] Balch, was born at Newburyport, July 8, 1819,
and died February 12, 1895, at Dorchester, Massachusetts.
He graduated at Phillips Academy, Exeter, after which he
was in a hardware store in Boston. Then he was agent of a
steam cotton mill in Newburyport for many years. He was
an alderman and school committeeman in that city. In politics he was a Democrat. He married Elizabeth Ann Hamilton, of Portland, Me., November 12, 1846. She was born
November 16, 1825, and died September 17, 1894. They had
eight children.

1873*   WILLIAM,[9] b. March 20, 1848.
1874*   GERTRUDE ARLINE,[9] b. Oct. 24, 1849.
1875*   WALTER HAMILTON,[9] b. Aug. 28, 1851.
1876*   ARTHUR STONE,[9] }
1877   ERNEST HODGE,[9] } twins, b. Oct. 13, 1853, { d. April 22, 1854.
1878*   EDITH ASHTON,[9] b. Jan. 12, 1856.
1879*   GERALD SPOFFORD,[9] b. Feb. 16, 1859; d. July 22, 1896.
1880   HORACE PEARSON,[9] b. Feb. 13, 1861; d. Jan. 12, 1863.

1120. Sarah Stone,[8] daughter of 524 William[7] and Hannah [Stone] Balch, was born at Newburyport, February 5,
1821, and died April 25, 1848. She was devoted to works of
charity, possessed a superior mind, was an expressive singer,
had a charming manner, and such beauty, both of person and

character, that even after fifty years she still seems a vivid inspiring reality to all who knew her. She was married September 25, 1844, to Frederick Beck, of Boston, who was born May 9, 1818. They had two children.

> FREDERICK ALLEYNE, b. Oct. 17, 1845; m. Nov. 3, 1866, Sarah E. Piper, of Newburyport. They live at Portland, Oregon, and have five children and three grandchildren.
>
> ALICE FOSTER, b. Jan. 8, 1847; m. June 1, 1877, Charles W. Lovett, of Boston. He died Feb., 1890. She lives in Marshfield.

1121. **George Edward,**[8] son of 524 William[7] and Hannah [Stone] Balch, was born at Newburyport, August 7, 1822, and died in the same town, August 23, 1889. He graduated at Exeter Academy. At the age of 22 years he was given the command of the bark Oberlin, and five years later commanded the full-rigged ship, "The Columbus," from Boston to Akyab. While bound from Akyab for Flushing the upper cabin was broken down by a tremendous sea during the night, which took him with it, head first, through the lee bulwarks to his waist, when the boards sprung back and held him half in and half out of the ship. While in this position one knee was severely injured by a loose spar, and he was insensible when rescued. While expecting every minute that they might founder, they sighted a Dutch vessel in distress, with missionaries on board. Captain Balch had his men carry him on deck to see the situation and give orders. Volunteers went to the relief of the vessel. The Dutch sailors were drunk when rescued, and at their urging some of their chests were taken off, but instead of clothing, they contained whiskey. Unknown to the officers, this was given freely to the men, and all hands refused to man the pumps. Captain Balch, though suffering excruciating pain, with pistol in hand, quelled the mutiny. For this act of humanity and heroism he was given a gold medal by the South Holland Institute. The cyclone lasted three days. Seventeen days later they made the Isle of France. A physician there proposed to amputate his leg, but Captain Balch would not consent,

and it was saved. On his homeward voyage, in April, 1851,
in the storm that carried away the Minot Ledge lighthouse,
the ship was wrecked, and they were left upon the back of
Cape Cod for forty-eight hours, when they were taken off
naked and barely alive. He had a third narrow escape.
When four days out from Boston, his ship, the "Howadji,"
was struck by lightning, and he and his crew were rescued by
another ship just before theirs went down.

Captain Balch was married October 21, 1852, to Elizabeth
Johnson, daughter of Peter LeBreton, of Newburyport. She
was born April 17, 1826. They have four children.

1881* Le Breton,[9] b. April 10, 1855.
1882* Sarah Beck,[9] b. July 29, 1857.
1883* Lewis,[9] b. Feb. 25, 1861.
1884 Georgianna Elizabeth,[9] b. Jan. 17, 1865.

1122. Leonidas,[8] son of 524 William[7] and Hannah
[Stone] Balch, was born at Newburyport, August 7, 1824.
He is not married, was a clerk, and lives at Newburyport.

1123. Lucy Hodge,[8] daughter of 524 William[7] and
Hannah [Stone] Balch, was born at Newburyport, April 15,
1826. She is not married, lives at Newburyport, and has
been of much assistance in gathering material for this Genealogy.

1125. Elizabeth,[8] daughter of 524 William[7] and Hannah
[Stone] Balch, was born at Newburyport, September 6, 1828.
She was married October 22, 1863, to Eliphalet Griffin. They
live at Newburyport, and have two children : Hannah Balch,
b. Aug. 26, 1864 ; Life, b. June 17, 1867, he married, May
23, 1895, Mary Elizabeth Davis.

1126. Mary Caroline,[8] daughter of 524 William[7] and
Hannah [Stone] Balch, was born at Newburyport, October
18, 1829, where she now lives. She married Charles P. Morrison, April 23, 1864. He enlisted as a private in company
A, Eighth Regiment, Massachusetts Volunteers, and served
with that regiment for four months at Washington and Bal-

timore. He was next commissioned second lieutenant in
company A, 48th Massachusetts Volunteers, and served with
Gen. Banks in the Department of the Gulf, participated in
the battle of Plain's Store, and was one of the few volunteers in the sortie of the Forlorn Hope during the siege of
Port Hudson. He made music a profession, at Newburyport,
Mass., till 1867; then at Worcester, Mass., until 1879, when
he became professor of music at Washington University, St.
Louis, Mo. He is the author of "Morrison's Collection of
Church Music," "In Memoriam," and other pieces. They
have had no children.

1127. **Hannah Stone,**[8] daughter of 524 William[7] and
Hannah [Stone] Balch, was born at Newburyport, August
28, 1834, and lives at Brookline, Massachusetts. She was
married May 17, 1855, to George Richard Coffin. He was
born at Castine, Maine, February 12, 1832, and died August
20, 1894, at Brookline, Massachusetts. They had eight children: George, b. March 6, 1856, at Jamaica Plain; Frederick Seymour, b. May 19, 1860, at Newburyport; Winthrop,
b. June 8, 1863, at Boston; Gertrude Richards, b. March 4,
1866, d. June 26, 1868; Anna Balch, b. June 8, 1867, at
Roxbury, m. May 10, 1893, Edward Everett Elms, two children; Laura Stone, b. July 15, 1869, at Roxbury; Henry
Richards, b. June 21, 1871, at Roxbury; William Balch, b.
Dec. 30, 1877, at Auburndale, Massachusetts.

1128. **Fanny Stone,**[8] daughter of 524 William[7] and
Hannah [Stone] Balch, was born at Newburyport, 'January
2, 1837. For several years she has been president of the day
nursery for the children of the poor, in St. Louis, Missouri.
She was married Sept. 30, 1863, to Calvin Milton Woodward,
who was a captain in the 48th Regiment, Massachusetts Volunteers, during the civil war. In 1865 he was appointed
professor of mathematics and applied mechanics in Washington University, St. Louis, Mo. He held the office of dean of
the Polytechnic School for twenty-five years. He is the

author of a work on the " Theory and Construction of the
St. Louis Bridge." They have had nine children: Alice
Balch, b. July 25, 1864, d. May 19, 1865 ; Clara Lincoln, b.
July 20, 1865; Bertha, b. Aug. 29, 1867, d. Dec. 21, 1870;
Fanny Louise, b. Dec. 9, 1869; Hilda, b. Aug. 21, 1871 ;
Margaret, b. Feb. 7, 1874; Alexander, b. Sept. 5, 1876, d.
July 1, 1877; Calvin Balch, b. Oct. 27, 1878, d. Jan. 19,
1888 ; Henry Bridge, b. Sept. 3, 1880, d. Feb. 25, 1883.

1129. **Charles Carrol,**[8] son of 524 William[7] and Hannah
[Stone] Balch, was born at Newburyport, May 9, 1841. He
graduated at Harvard in 1862, and decided to study medicine.
He was drowned, August 27, 1863, while bathing at Salisbury
Beach.

1130. **George Thacher,**[8] son of 525 John Theodoric[7] and
Elizabeth Jones [Thacher] Balch, was born at Biddeford,
Me., October 2, 1828, and died very suddenly in New York
city, April 15, 1894, and was buried at Troy, N. Y. He was
married, November 8, 1859, to Harriet Delafield, daughter of
Hon. John P. Cushman, a judge of the New York Supreme
Court, living at Troy. She lives at Saratoga. They have
had no children.

Colonel George T. Balch graduated from West Point Military Academy in 1852, and soon after was commissioned a
lieutenant of artillery. In April, 1861, he was ordered to
Fort Pickens, Florida, with the artillery under the command
of Colonel Harvey Brown. The war department soon
recognized his remarkable organizing and executive abilities,
and called him to the Ordnance Bureau at Washington,
where he remained until the close of the war. The com-
pleteness of his organization in the ordnance department
enabled all the accounts to be closed and the force of clerks
reduced to the few needed in times of peace, almost as soon
as the troops were mustered out. Having been promoted
through the various grades to that of lieutenant colonel during the war, he resigned at its termination, and formed the

COL. GEORGE THACHER BALCH.
(1130)

Remington Plow Company. Not meeting with success in this undertaking, he soon terminated his connection with it, and passed into the service of the receiver of the Erie Railway Company, to straighten out its affairs. While in this position he thoroughly inventoried the property of the company, and in this work discovered to them real estate titles amounting to over one million dollars that had been overlooked and forgotten. At the direction of Mayor Hewitt, of New York city, in 1886, he made a careful study and investigation of the health department and of the street paving contracts of the city, and in this capacity made a scathing report on the repaving of Fifth Avenue and many other frauds perpetrated on the city by contractors. From his investigation of the health department he was led to the study of the foreign-born residents of New York city. His remarkable ability for thorough and accurate work came to the attention of the Board of Education of New York, and led to his appointment as actuary of that board. His original and thorough methods in these various capacities have been embodied in various books and reports from his pen. " A General Classification of Railway Rights, Realities and Personalities," J. J. Little & Co., printers, New York, 1878, concisely sums up his methods of taking the inventory of the Erie Railway Company's property. " The Sewage Question in Saratoga " appears in a report from the Board of Sewer Commissioners to the Board of Trustees of that village in 1885. " Teaching Patriotism in Our Public Schools," The D. Van Nostrand Co., publishers, brings timely before the American public the importance and the methods of inculcating loyalty to the country and its flag.

1131. Theodoric Augustus,[8] son of 525 John Theodoric[7] and Elizabeth Jones [Thacher] Balch, was born in New York city, January 16, 1832, and is a farmer, and resides at Akron, Ohio. He was married October 8, 1868, to Ann E., daughter of Justin Gale, late of Akron, O., but originally from Wells

River, Vt. She was born September 28, 1831. They have no children.

1132. Daniel Webster,[8] son of 525 John Theodoric[7] and Elizabeth Jones [Thacher] Balch, was born in New York city, November 14, 1834, and lives in San Francisco, California. He was married April 25, 1868, to Nellie Dingle Holmes. She was a daughter of John Dingle, and took the name of Holmes upon her mother's second marriage. She was born in Syracuse, N. Y., June 18, 1844. They have five children, three born in Virginia City, Nevada, and two born in San Francisco, California.

1885	GEORGE THACHER,[9] b. Feb. 27, 1869.
1886	DANIEL HERBERT,[9] b. Sept. 5, 1870; d. Oct. 11, 1896.
1887	MAUD,[9] b. June 15, 1873.
1888	JOHN ADRIAN,[9] b. Aug. 6, 1876.
1889	DANIEL FRASER,[9] b. Jan. 19, 1882.

Daniel Webster left his home in Akron, Ohio, at the age of thirteen, shipped as a sailor from Newburyport, Mass., and made several voyages. In 1850 he went to California, and has since resided in that state and Nevada. By profession he is an assayer, but has been interested in railways and mining. In 1886 he was president of the Nevada and Oregon R. R. and secretary of the California Rock Drill Co. He is the inventor of an improved method of working ores by the cyanide process.

1133. Elizabeth Thacher,[8] daughter of 525 John Theodoric[7] and Elizabeth Jones [Thacher] Balch, was born in New York city, December 27, 1837. She was married March 18, 1863, to Gilbert Saltonstall, son of James Sumner and Frances [Saltonstall] Carpenter. He was born at Medina, Ohio, April 17, 1836. He is an officer in the U. S. army, with rank of major. They have had the following children: George Balch and James Thacher, twins, b. Jan. 18, 1866, at Akron, Ohio, both d. y. ; Laura Balch, b. March 29, 1868, at Chattanooga, Tenn.; Dudley Saltonstall, b. Feb. 26, 1870, at

Nashville, Tenn.; Edward Laramie, b. Jan. 14, 1873, at Fort Laramie, Wyoming Ter.; Elizabeth Frances, b. June 22, 1878, at Fort Hartsuff, Neb.; Anna Thacher, b. Jan. 25, 1882, d. Aug. 27, 1883.

1134. **Laura Otis**,[8] daughter of 525 John Theodoric[7] and Elizabeth Jones [Thacher] Balch, was born at Akron, O., September 23, 1845. She is not married, and is living in Youngstown, O.

1135. **Caroline Williams**,[8] daughter of 532 Joseph[7] and Caroline A. B. [Williams] Balch, born at Boston, Mass., March 16, 1813. She was married Nov. 3, 1840, to Dr. Isaac Gordon Braman, whose first wife was Ann Mehitable Moody, daughter of 533 Eunice[7]. They lived at Georgetown, Mass., until about 1848, when they moved to Brighton, now a part of Boston, where he practiced for about thirty-three years. During the greater part of this time he was in charge of the medical department of the arsenal at Watertown, Mass., as acting assistant surgeon, United States army. He was also coroner and justice of the peace. They had two children.

> CHANDLER BALCH, b. August 19, 1841, at Georgetown; d. Aug. 15, 1868. He was acting assistant surgeon United States army, and while stationed at Baton Rouge, Louisiana, was killed by a brother officer. He was married Aug. 13, 1867, at Terra Haute, Indiana, to Cecilia O. Gage.
>
> JOSEPH BALCH, b. Feb. 15, 1845, at Brighton (now in Boston), Massachusetts. He is practicing law with his wife in New York city. They are commissioners for all the states and many foreign countries, and are also passport and consular agents and customs notaries. Mr. Braman enlisted at Boston, Dec. 7, 1861, in Capt. James M. Magee's cavalry company, the "Mounted Rifle Rangers," known as Butler's Body Guard, at first attached to the 30th Regiment, Massachusetts Volunteers. Being disabled, he was discharged at New Orleans, Louisiana, June 21, 1862. He re-enlisted at Boston, May 16, 1864, in the 12th Unattached Company, Massachusetts Volunteers, and served at Provincetown, Mass. On July 21, 1864, he was commissioned captain of company D, 47th Regiment, Massachusetts Volunteers, and was discharged August 4, 1864. He is a Master Mason, Odd Fellow,

and a member of Lafayette Post, Grand Army of the Republic. On Sept. 10, 1867, he was married at Brighton, to Ella Frances, daughter of Abram W. and Sophronia Swift [Ellis] Collins. They have had five children, the four eldest born at Brighton, Mass., and the youngest at Los Angeles, California. *Joseph Milton*, b. July 13, 1869, d. Nov. 14, 1869; *Susan Caroline*, b. Oct. 6, 1870; *Joseph Chandler*, b. Aug. 5, 1872; *Herbert*, b. Nov. 15, 1875; *Ella Angela*, b. April 5, 1874.

1137. Sarah Bartlett,[8] daughter of 532 Joseph[7] and Caroline A. B. [Williams] Balch, was born at Boston, Mass., November 26, 1817, and died at Jamaica Plain, September 9, 1854. She was married June 6, 1838, to Stephen Minot, son of Capt. William Gordon and Hannah [Minot] Weld, of Boston. He was born at Boston, September 29, 1806, and graduated from Harvard College in 1826. His sterling worth, elastic spirits, and strong social sympathies made him the most popular member of his class. In 1858 he was chosen by the legislature one of the overseers of Harvard College. To Stephen M. Gordon and Sarah B. Weld were born seven children, two of whom died in infancy : Hannah Minot, b. July 18, 1839; Stephen Minot, b. Jan. 4, 1842 ; m. Eloise Rodman ; Alice Buckminster, b. Feb. 28, 1844 ; Caroline Balch, b. Jan. 15, 1846, m. S. S. Gray ; Edith, b. Aug. 4, 1848.

1138. Joseph Williams,[8] son of 532 Joseph[7] and Caroline A. B. [Williams] Balch, was born in Boston, August 8, 1819, and died at Jamaica Plain, Massachusetts, January 11, 1891. He married, first, June 8, 1846, Maria, daughter of George Hallet, of Boston. She was born in that city, March 15, 1820, and died at Gloucester, Mass., August 16, 1857, leaving four children.

1890[e] GEORGE HALLET,[9] b. May 27, 1847; d. unm., Feb. 25, 1894.
1891 AGNES GORDON,[9] b. Feb. 12, 1849.
1892[e] HENRY GORDON,[9] b. Sept. 15, 1853.
1893 CHARLES BUCKMINSTER,[9] b. June 18, 1856; d. Dec. 28, 1881, in Orange, Cal.

Joseph W. was married, second, September 27, 1859, to

JOSEPH WILLIAMS BALCH.
(1129)

Agnes Love, daughter of Franklin and Agnes Love [Brad-lee] Greene, of Boston. She was born in Boston, July 23, 1832, and died September 6, 1893. They had four children :

1894* JOSEPH,[9] b. Feb. 3, 1861.
1895* FRANKLIN GREENE,[9] b. April 26, 1864.
1896* JOHN,[9] b. May 4, 1865.
1897 EMILY GREENE,[9] b. Aug. 17, 1869.

He was tall and well proportioned, a man of sterling integrity, and excellent business ability. In 1838 he entered the Boylston Fire and Marine Insurance Company as its secretary. In 1853 he became its president, and held the position until it was ruined by the great Boston fire of Saturday, November 9, 1872. The next Monday a new company, now known as the Boylston Insurance Company, was formed, and he was chosen its president, and retained the office to the time of his death. He was also president of the Boston and Providence Railroad, and of the Boston Fire Underwriters' Union, vice-president of the Provident Institution for Savings, and a trustee of the Roxbury Latin School. He was a trustee of Forest Hill cemetery corporation for twenty-one years, and was its president from 1876 to 1889.

No man ever bequeathed to the community the recollection of more kindly traits of character, a warmer and more sympathetic nature, or was more conscientious in adherence to the right, than Joseph Balch. He was a loyal friend, a kind and thoughtful neighbor, a public-spirited citizen, and a large-hearted Christian gentleman.

1145. Francis Vergnies,[8] son of 532 Joseph[7] and Anne Lathrop [Noyes] Balch, was born in Boston, February 3, 1839. He took the degree of A. B., in 1859, at Harvard College, and in 1860 graduated from Harvard Law School, and was admitted to the bar. He first became a partner with Francis Winthrop Palfrey, and came into professional relations with George S. Hillard. In 1862 he joined the Twentieth Massachusetts Infantry Volunteers, of which his partner, Mr. Palfrey, was lieutenant colonel, but fell out after a few months, on account of sickness, without having been in any engagement. After a prolonged convalescence, he re joined, in the practice of his profession, Col. Palfrey, who had been wounded and discharged. In 1868 he married his cousin, Ellen Maria, daughter of Francis V. and Elizabeth [Porter] Noyes, and great granddaughter of William Bartlett, of Newburyport, a successful merchant. She was born July 11, 1837. They had eight children.

1898   CATHERINE,[9] b. June 14, 1864; d. April 24, 1865.
1899   ANNE LATHROP,[9] b. July 29, 1865.
1900* EMILY GREENE,[9] b. Jan. 8. 1867.
1901* ELIZABETH,[9] b. Aug. 29, 1868.
1902   ELLEN,[9] b. Jan. 10, 1872; d. Dec. 7, 1874.
1903* FRANCIS NOYES,[9] b. Nov. 23, 1873.
1904   ALICE,[9] b. July 12, 1876.
1905   MARION CASARES,[9] b. Feb. 25, 1879.

In 1864 Francis V. became the clerk of the Senate Committee on Foreign Relations, and also for two years was private secretary of Senator Sumner. Later he was made general executor and one of the literary executors by Mr. Sumner. In 1867 he was admitted to the law office of William Minot, where he remained for several years, and attained a position of high standing. He is now the senior partner in the law firm of Balch & Rackemann, his specialty being conveyancing and trust law.

1147. Lucy French,[8] daughter of 542 John[7] and Elizabeth [Tappan] Balch, was born at Newburyport, Mass., November 22, 1827, and died at Baltimore, Maryland, May 30, 1852. She was married May 31, 1848, to John L., son of Hon. John Merrill, of Newburyport, Mass. He was born January 24, 1824. They had two daughters, born at Baltimore, Md.

CATHERINE ELIZABETH, b. May 27, 1849. She married Stuart Lindsley, of Orange, N. J., and had five children: *George Leonard*, b. May 30, 1882, at East Orange, N. J.; *Lucy Merrill*, b. Dec. 12, 1884, at Carson City, Colo.; *Alice*, b. Sept. 1,

Isaac Denny Balch.
(1150)

1888, at Orange, N. J.; *Horace Nelson*, b. April 12, 1889, at Orange; *Girard*, b. May 3, 1891, at Orange.

LUCY L., b. Jan. 27, 1852; d. July 12, 1852.

1149. **Elizabeth Tappan**,[8] daughter of 542 John[7] and Elizabeth [Tappan] Balch, was born at Newburyport, Mass., September 19, 1832. She was married September 26, 1860, to John L. Merrill, whose first wife was her sister, Lucy French. They live at East Orange, New Jersey, and have had six children.

> ALICE BALCH, b. March 16, 1862, at West Orange, N. J. She was married Oct. 10, 1884, to Henry F. Camblos, M. D., of Philadelphia, Penn. They have three children.
>
> GEORGE DENNY, b. Jan. 1, 1864, at West Orange, N. J. Married, April 26, 1888, to Miss Elizabeth A. Haines, of Brooklyn, N. Y. Lives at East Orange.
>
> JOHN LENORD, b. Sept. 17, 1866, at Orange.
>
> JOSEPH MOULTON, b. Feb. 3, 1870, at East Orange.
>
> JULIA BALCH,   } twins, b. May 17, 1873; { d. Aug. 5, 1874.
> ELIZABETH TAPPAN, }

1150. **Isaac Denny**,[8] son of 542 John[7] and Laura Amelia [Denny] Balch, was born at Newburyport, April 18, 1835, and died unmarried, February 16, 1889, at East Orange, New Jersey. In 1856 he graduated at Bowdoin College, studied law, and practiced at Cincinnati until the breaking out of the civil war, when he volunteered in a three months' regiment at Washington. Afterwards he practiced law in New York city. About 1869 he was appointed chief clerk of the law department in one of the divisions of the New York Custom House. Ten years later, under General Merritt, he was appointed a deputy collector in the rotunda, and also special deputy collector, with power to represent the head of the custom house when absent. In this position he introduced many reforms in the methods of transacting the business. In 1882 he resigned, and devoted himself thereafter mainly to stock brokerage business. He was a man of decided ability and of unwavering integrity. He was buried at Newburyport.

1152. **Alice March**,[8] daughter of 542 John[7] and Laura

Amelia [Denny] Balch, was born at Newburyport, September 16, 1840. She was married November 2, 1864, to Abiel Abbot, a commission merchant in New York city. They live at East Orange, New Jersey, and have had eight children: Laura Kendrick, b. Oct. 12, 1865; Alice Balch, b. Feb. 11, 1867; Mary Wade, b. Dec. 29, 1869, d. Jan. 10, 1870; Arthur Denny, b. Dec. 21, 1870, d. Aug. 6, 1871; Fanny Holmes, b. June 17, 1872; Alfred Ernest, b. Jan. 12, 1875; Julia Wade, b. March 18, 1877; Helen Denny, b. July 11, 1880.

1154. **Mary Nelson**,[8] daughter of 542 John[7] and Laura Amelia [Denny] Balch, was born at Newburyport, Mass., July 29, 1846, where she now lives. She was married October 19, 1869, to George Whitfield Blood, of Charlestown, Mass. He died November 12, 1876. They had three children : John Balch, b. July 21, 1870, at Newburyport; Grosvenor Tarbell, b. Aug. 22, 1872 ; George Whitfield, b. March 26, 1877.

1155. **Maria Williams**,[8] daughter of 543 Benjamin[7] and Lydia Elizabeth [Williams] Balch, was born at Newburyport, Mass., January 28, 1831. She married Elias Nason, of Hollowell, Me. He was a flour merchant at Fall River, Mass. They had three children ; two d. y.

1156. **Frances Caroline**,[8] daughter of 543 Benjamin[7] and Lydia Elizabeth [Williams] Balch, was born at Newburyport, Mass., February 28, 1833, and died at St. Louis, Mo. She married George Perrin, and had four children : George, b. 1853 ; Charles O., d. y. ; Charles T., d. y. ; Anna Tilletson.

1160. **William Heman**,[8] son of 546 Capt. William Savary[7] and Mary [Stickney] Balch, was born at East Bradford, [Groveland] Mass., August 17, 1826, and died at Malden, Mass., September 19, 1889. He succeeded his father in the manufacture of boots and shoes for the western trade, and carried on a wholesale business in Boston. He married first,

DANIEL STICKNEY BALCH.
(1164)

June 17, 1852, Susan, daughter of Capt. Benjamin and Anna [Lapham] Parker. She was born in East Bradford, April 7, 1829, and died in Malden, July 19, 1874. Their four children were born in Groveland.

1906 MARY A.,[9] b. Nov. 29, 1855; d. May 28, 1856.
1907 ANNIE P.,[9] b. Feb. 7, 1860.
1908 WILLIAM,[9] b. Dec. 31, 1863; d. Aug. 17, 1864.
1909 BENJAMIN K.,[9]
1910 FREDERICK,[9] twins, b. Oct. 12, 1866; prop's Malden Express.

William H. married second, November 25, 1881, Sophia, daughter of Aaron and Susanna [Burbank] Atwood, of Groveland.

1164. Daniel Stickney,[8] son of 546 Capt. William Savary[7] and Mary [Stickney] Balch, was born at East Bradford [Groveland], December 11, 1831. He moved to Lyons, Iowa, and with his brother, John Kirby Perry, established a large boot and shoe wholesale trade. He is the American Express agent at Lyons, and is secretary of Pioneer Camp, No. 1, Modern Woodmen of America. He was married August 20, 1861, to Mary Jane, daughter of Moses and Abigail B. [Ladd] George, of East Haverhill, Mass., where she was born, January 1, 1834. The family are members of the Congregational church, where he is a deacon. Their three children were born in Lyons.

1911* LOUISA ANNIE,[9] b. April 7, 1864.
1912* CLIFTON FLETCHER,[9] b. March 4, 1867.
1913 JENNIE FULLINGTON,[9] b. Aug. 26, 1870.

1167. John Kirby Perry,[8] son of 546 Capt. William Savary[7] and Mary [Stickney] Balch, was born at East Bradford [Groveland], Mass., February 17, 1837. He moved to Lyons, Iowa, in 1858, and carried on a wholesale boot and shoe business for twenty-five years. In 1877 he took the first telephone to Iowa, and built the first telephone exchange in the West. Many parts of this he invented. He has held the offices of president and general manager of the Northwestern Bell Telephone Co., president of Lyons Pressed and

Paving Brick Co., director and superintendent Lyons Water Works Co., and treasurer and superintendent Lyons & Fulton Bridge Co. He is a member of the Sons of the American Revolution. He was married August 10, 1870, to Sarah Amelia, daughter of Orville and Sarah Hayes [Cone] Barbour, of Harwinton, Ct., where she was born, May 12, 1846. She died in New Britton, December 18, 1884, and was buried at Harwinton. They had one child, born at Lyons, Iowa.

1914 MARY ELIZABETH,[9] b. May 16, 1872.

John Kirby Perry Balch married second, January 15, 1891, Frances Ellen Crosby, of Malden, Massachusetts. She was born at Cambridge, May 11, 1853. They had one child.

1915 MARY EAMS,[9] b. Dec. 9, 1891; d. same day.

1171. **Edward H.,**[8] son of 550 Nathaniel[7] and Elizabeth, M. [Tucker] Balch, was born at Portsmouth, December 24, 1840, and lived at Exeter, New Hampshire. He was married in 1864, to Julia H. Philbrick, of Rye, N. H. She died at Portsmouth, November 23, 1884. They had one child, born at Rye.

1916 ELIZA GRACE,[9] b. July 4, 1865; d. Nov., 1887; m. John Jenner.

Edward H. was married second, April, 1889, to Olive Willey, of Concord, N. H. She died in October, 1891.

1173. **Martha Ellen,**[8] daughter of 550 Nathaniel[7] and Elizabeth M. [Tucker] Balch, was born at Portsmouth, N. H., March 30, 1851. She was married September 24, 1877, to Charles E., son of Charles F. Trefether, of Rye, N. H., where he is a carpenter and farmer. They have had ten children: Susie Ellen, b. July 1, 1878, d. Jan. 6, 1880; Austen Wallace, b. Sept. 5, 1880; George Chester, b. Feb. 15, 1882; Arthur Elwyn, b. April 24, 1883; Elmer Balch, b. July 10, 1885; Willie Marshall, b. Dec. 24, 1887; Julia Alice, b. Feb. 5, 1888; Raymond Hall, b. Aug. 10, 1889; Maria Elizabeth, b. April 19, 1891; Ruth Mabel, b. May 5, 1893.

JOHN KIRBY PERRY BALCH.

(1167)

NINTH GENERATION.

FIRST BRANCH.

Descendants of 5 Samuel.[3]

Descendants of 21 Samuel.[4]

1174. Christopher S.,[9] son of 555 Joseph[8] and Betsey [Shrove] Balch, was born at Frankfort, N. Y., Aug. 19, 1821, and died October 22, 1861, at North Easton, N. Y. He was a farmer, and lived in the town of Easton, N. Y. He married Susan M. Robinson, of Easton, N. Y., on Jan. 12, 1848. She was born October 5, 1823, and died Feb. 12, 1878.

  1917 WILLIAM H.,[10] b. June 29, 1854; d. Jan. 3, 1870.

  1918* EDWIN,[10] b. Aug. 21, 1859.

1175. John Henry,[9] son of 555 Joseph[8] and Betsey [Shrove] Balch, was born at Frankfort, N. Y., April 26, 1825, and died at Cambridge, N. Y., May 30, 1869. He was married December 15, 1847, to Abby Ilzaide, daughter of John and Amelia Lee. She was born at Cambridge, March 22, 1820, and died in the same town, October 8, 1881. They had two children, both born on the home farm in Cambridge.

  1919* AMELIA E.,[10] b. Feb. 18, 1849; d. Jan. 18, 1886.

  1920* FANNIE M.,[10] b. May 16, 1853.

1176. Ebenezer Atwood,[9] son of 555 Joseph[8] and Betsey [Shrove] Balch, was born at Frankfort, N. Y., March 26, 1827. He resided at Greenwich, N. Y., where he died, January 16, 1892, and was buried at Schaghticooke, N. Y. On February 20, 1856, he was married to Hannah, daughter of Robert and Abbie Hoag, who was born at Pittstown, N. Y., July 3, 1833. They had three children.

1921*   ALLAN C.,[10] b. March 13, 1864.
1922   ELIZABETH A.,[10] b. March 10, 1871.
1923   HOWARD J.,[10] b. March 10, 1873.

Ebenezer A. first farmed with his brother Christopher, then engaged in the sale of jewelry and maps, was next a station agent at Valley Falls, and afterwards engaged in real estate transactions. At Cambridge he had a grocery store, and lastly a shirt factory.

1178.   Joseph,[9] son of 556 John and Margaret [Hadcock] Balch, was born at Frankfort, N. Y., December 3, 1828, and was married July 4, 1850, to Margaret Morehouse, who was born July 23, 1880. Their children were as follows :

1924*   ROZENA,[10] b. March 31, 1851; d. April 16, 1884.
1925*   JOHN A.,[10] b. Dec. 16, 1853.
1926*   MERRETT A.,[10] b. June 28, 1857.
1927*   ADAH E.,[10] b. April 25, 1859.
1928*   WILLETT F.,[10] b. March 14, 1863.
1929   G. FRANK,[10] b. July 14, 1868.
1930   WARREN D.,[10] b. Jan. 31, 1871.
1931*   F. CORA,[10] b. Aug. 29, 1873.
1932   GERTRUDE M.,[10] b. Jan. 16, 1877.

1179.   Andrew J.,[9] son of 556 John and Margaret [Hadcock] Balch, was born at Frankfort, N. Y., February 17, 1831, and died at Marcy, N. Y., December 30, 1889, and was buried at Frankfort. He was a carriage maker at Utica, N. Y., and was married December 19, 1854, to Caroline, daughter of Michael and Hannah Reymore. She was born at Constantia, N. Y., December 9, 1834. They had seven children, the first three born at Frankfort, N. Y., the next two at Mansfield, and the last two at Albert Lea, Minnesota.

1933   CARRIE E.,[10] b. Aug. 16, 1856; d. June 3, 1861.
1934*   CHARLES HERBERT,[10] b. July 22, 1858.
1935*   FREDERICK W.,[10] b. Jan. 23, 1861.
1936*   WILLIAM DELL,[10] b. Dec. 23, 1866.
1937*   GEORGE A.,[10] b. June 5, 1869.
1938   CORA BELLE,[10] b. Sept. 22, 1871; d. Nov. 11, 1873.
1939   MYRTLE BELLE,[10] b. Feb. 12, 1875.

1182.   Marcus D.,[9] son of 556 John[8] and Margaret [Hadcock] Balch, was born at Frankfort, N. Y., August 5, 1838. He has been engaged in farming, but is now a builder at Utica, N. Y. He was married January 21, 1869, to Miss Adeline M., daughter of James S. and Lucy Harvey. She was born at Frankfort, N. Y., January 24, 1846. They have four children, all born at Utica, N. Y.

1940 EVA M.,[10] b. April 6, 1870.
1941* BURTON M.,[10] b. Jan. 15, 1874; lives in Brooklyn.
1942 FLORENCE L.,[10] b. Dec. 16, 1878.
1943 BESSIE M.,[10] b. Nov. 12, 1882.

1184. Roselle,[9] son of 556 John[8] and Margaret [Hadcock] Balch, was born at Frankfort, N. Y., March 3, 1844, and is in the real estate business in Utica, N. Y. He was married, in 1868, to Ida, daughter of Charles Hubbell, of Frankfort. They have three children.

1945 ORVILLE,[10] b. 1869; m. Ella Dell.
1946 REBA,[10] b. June, 1881.
1947 MAY,[10] b. 1885.

1190. Emma M.,[9] daughter of 567 Philander[8] and Jane A. [Robinson] Balch. She married H. R. Bailey, and they lived at East Charleston, Vt.

1193. Romanzo,[9] son of 569 Leonard[8] and Betsey [Smith] Balch, was born at Lyndon, Vt., June 14, 1852, and is a machinist at St. Johnsbury, Vt. He married first, August 15, 1872, Abbie, daughter of Jeremiah Leighton. She was born at Danville, Vt., and died at St. Johnsbury, Vt., July 26, 1886. They had two children, born at St. Johnsbury.

1948 HARRY EDWIN,[10] b. May 8, 1873.
1949 LEONARD GEORGE,[10] b. June 6, 1876.

Romanzo was married second, September 10, 1887, to Mrs. Luella Stanton, a daughter of Benson and Mary Etta Aldrich. She was born at Topsham, Vt., August 24, 1854. They have two children, both born at St. Johnsbury.

1950 BENSON ALDRICH,[10] b. July 9, 1888.
1951 LYLE W.,[10] b. Aug. 14, 1890.

1195. H. Anna,[9] daughter of 571 Nathaniel Aldrich[8] and

Sarah M. [Chapin] Balch, was born at Kalamazoo, Mich.,
July 12, 1840. She was married October 25, 1864, to John,
son of Paulus and Gooltze den Bleyker. He was born September 5, 1839, at Isle Texel, Holland, Europe. They are
living at Kalamazoo, and their nine children were all born in
that city. Paul, b. Sept. 14, 1865 ; Sara, b. April 28, 1867 ;
Gertrude, b. Jan. 12, 1869; Johnnie, b. Jan. 12, 1871, d.
July 22, 1873 ; Harry, b. Aug. 2, 1873 ; Walter, b. Oct. 30,
1876 ; Mattie, b. April 27, 1879, d. July 4, 1887 ; Anna, b.
Nov. 29, 1881 ; and a twin to Anna, who died young.

1196. Walter O.,[9] son of 571 Nathaniel Aldrich[8] and
Sarah M. [Chapin] Balch, was born at Kalamazoo, Mich.,
April 9, 1843, and died at Kalamazoo, December 22, 1876. He
was married September 29, 1868, to Helen M., daughter of
Rev. S. W. Burton, of Wattsburg, Pa. No issue. He was
a graduate from the law department of the University of
Michigan, was admitted to the bar in 1866, and associated
himself with the firm of Balch, Smiley & Balch. He was
forcible in argument, an able and ready writer, and a regular
correspondent of several newspapers and magazines. His
health was always delicate. He remained in the firm for
nearly eight years, but owing to delicate health, was unable
to practice for the last three or four. For a time he was as-
sociate editor of the Austin (Tex.) News. In 1876 he returned to Kalamazoo, and died after a long and painful illness. His noble Christian qualities of mind and heart en-
deared him to all who knew him.

1200. Herbert Melville,[9] son of 574 Samuel Raymond[8]
and Elizabeth Kendell [Woods] Balch, was born at Kalamazoo, Mich, July 13, 1854, and is a farmer at El Dorado, Kansas. He was married December 2, 1877, to Mrs. Elita Prin-
dle. They have one child.

1952 RAYMOND,[10] b. Sept. 6, 1878.

1202. Elmer Adelbert,[9] son of 574 Samuel Raymond[8]
and Elizabeth Kendell [Woods] Balch, was born at Kalama--

zoo, Mich., Sept. 25, 1857, and was married October 28, 1877, to Josephine Chapman. They reside at Kalamazoo, and have six children.

    1953 GEORGE ADELBERT,[10] b. July 12, 1879.
    1954 CLARENCE EUGENE,[10] b. May 9, 1880.
    1955 WALTER A.,[10] b. Nov. 22, 1881.
    1956 HOMER,[10] b. July 8, 1883.
    1957 JESSIE,[10] b. Feb. 2, 1889.
    1958 JAMES,[10] b. Oct. 7, 1893.

1203. Laura Alice,[9] daughter of 574 Samuel Raymond[8] and Elizabeth Kendell [Woods] Balch, was born at Kalamazoo, Mich., September 15, 1859. She was married at Somerville, Mass., March 17, 1885, to Charles Haynes, son of Charles Davis and Hannah Louise [Haynes] Chapman. He was born at Oldtown, Maine, August 26, 1858, is a farmer, and they live at Goodale's Corner, Maine.

1205. William Arthur,[9] son of 574 Samuel Raymond[8] and Elizabeth Kendell [Woods] Balch, was born at Kalamazoo, Michigan, August 28, 1864, and was married November 26, 1891, to Dora Pines.

1207. Jane Maria,[9] daughter of 576 Royal Tyler[8] and Ruthana Grimes [Davis] Balch, was born at Athens, Vt., September 18, 1845, and lives at Helena, Montana. She graduated from Kalamazoo High School in 1868, and was a successful teacher. She was married May 4, 1870, to Albert Sergeant, son of Clark and Catherine [Sergeant] Kellogg, who was born at Oshtemo, Mich., November 80, 1842. They are Presbyterians, and have had five children, three born at Oshtemo, Michigan, and two at Boulder, Montana. Julia Clark, b. April 5, 1871, m. Nov. 12, 1894, Wm. Fergus, of Whitehall, Montana; Ruth Elsie, b. Jan. 31, 1875. Frederick William, b. Jan. 13, 1877, d. June 22, 1880; Sarah Augusta, b. March 5, 1886; Ernest Wickes, b. April 19, 1889, d. Sept. 19, 1889.

1209. Sarah Lorinda,[9] daughter of 576 Royal Tyler[8] and Ruthana Grimes [Davis] Balch, was born at Athens,

Vt., November 29, 1849. She graduated at the Kalamazoo
High School in 1868, and is now a teacher. She is a member
of the Methodist Episcopal Church.

' 1210. **Abby Adella,**[9] daughter of 576 Royal Tyler[8] and
Ruthana Grimes [Davis] Balch, was born at Kalamazoo,
Mich., July 16, 1852. She was married February 12, 1879,
to Frank Cherevoyx, son of George Washington and Ruth
Rosett Hall. He was born August 15, 1851. They are mem-
bers of the Methodist Episcopal church. Their children are
Walter Albert, b. Nov. 4, 1879, at Kalamazoo, Mich.; Royal
Tyler, b. Jan. 7, 1881, at Oshtemo, Mich.; Jennie Rosetta, b.
Feb. 19, 1885, at Portage, Mich.; Frank Nathan, b. Aug. 10,
1891, at Kalamazoo.

1211. **Royal Curtis,**[9] son of 576 Royal Tyler[8] and Ruthana Grimes [Davis] Balch, was born at Oshtemo, Mich
igan, April 26, 1856, where he is a farmer. He was married October 6, 1880, to Alice Nellie, daughter of William
C. and Mary Ann [Kempsey] Wild. She was born at Oshtemo, October 6, 1856. The family are Methodists, and their
children were born at Oshtemo.

1959   CLARENCE LEIGH,[10] b. Oct. 28, 1882.
1960   JOHN VINCENT,[10] b. Aug. 28, 1884.
1961   ELWYN CURTIS,[10] b. Aug. 5, 1886.
1962   RUTH A.,[10] b. Sept. 11, 1891.
1963   VERA,[10] b. May 20, 1893.
1964   ROYAL T.,[10] b. Jan. 3, 1895.

1212. **Emma May,**[9] daughter of 576 Royal Tyler[8] and
Ruthana Grimes [Davis] Balch, was born at Oshtemo, Mich.,
August 21, 1858. She was married October 6, 1880, to Seth
Edson, son of William and Maria [Smith] Combs. He was
born at Brandon, Oakland county, Mich., November 23, 1856,
and is a music dealer at South Haven, Mich. Their children
are: Earl Edson, b. March 7, 1882; Emma Leoti, b. Dec. 9,
1889.

1213. **Ernest Alanson,**[9] son of 576 Royal Tyler[8] and
Ruthana Grimes [Davis] Balch, was born at Oshtemo, Mich.,

June 23, 1867, and lives in Chicago, Illinois. He graduated
from Kalamazoo college in 1888, and in 1889 took the degree
of M. A. at the University of Michigan. He was married
April 2, 1890, to Bertha Low, daughter of Osmond Monroe
and Harriet E. [Kennicott] Stevens. She was born October
29, 1867.

1965 KENDELL MONROE,[10] b. April 13, 1892; d. Aug. 30, 1892.
1966 HELEN HARRIET,[10] b. Dec. 20, 1893.

1214. Dorr Micah,[9] son of 578 Amaziah Robinson[8] and
Abby [Davis] Balch, was born at Athens, Vermont, January
11, 1848. He was married in 1886, to Phœbe D., daughter of
Samuel S. and Lucretia [Bangs] Loomis. She was born at
Milton, Canada East, Nov. 30, 1847. They now live at New
Richmond, Wisconsin, and have three children, born at Min-
neapolis, Minnesota.

1967 SIDNEY ALANSON,[10] b. Oct. 27, 1887.
1968 RAYMOND EDISON,[10] b. May 6, 1889.
1969 GRACE ADELLA,[10] b. Oct. 2, 1890.

1217. Nathaniel Amaziah,[9] son of 578 Amaziah Robinson[8] and Mary [Williams] Balch, was born at Wayland,
Michigan, February 18, 1866. He was married in December,
1886, to Ella Curtis. She was born May 1, 1867, at Pine
Grove, and died Feb. 1, 1893, at Plainwell, Michigan, where
Nathaniel A. is now in business as a merchant. Their children are :

1970 HOYD,[10] b. Aug. 20, 1887.
1971 JAMES B.,[10] b. Jan. 21, 1893.

Nathaniel A. married second, Bridget Storms, daughter of
J. M. and Bessie Storms. She was born March 10, 1873. By
her he has no children.

1219. Mary Elizabeth,[8] daughter of 578 Amaziah Robinson and Mary [Williams] Balch, was born at Wayland,
Michigan, January 9, 1872. She was married December 10,
1891, to John S., son of Sherman G. and Sarah T. Forbes.
He was born Nov. 28, 1865, at Belleville, Alabama. They

have one child, born at Plainwell, Michigan : Sherman
Balch, b. Nov. 9, 1894.

1220. **Emerson B.,**[9] son of 579 Arad Chickering[8] and
Elizabeth O. [Emerson] Balch, was born at Kalamazoo, Michigan, March 26, 1854, and is engaged in farming and lumbering at Marble, Michigan. He was married April 22, 1885, to
Carrie, daughter of John W. and L. M. Austin. She was
born at Gouverneur, N. Y., Oct. 17, 1859. They have two
children born at Allegan, and one at Marble.

1972 GUY,[10] b. Sept. 26, 1886.
1973 RAY,[10] b. April 14, 1890; d. Aug. 26, 1890.
1974 ROY,[10] b. March 27, 1893.

1221. **Frank O.,**[9] son of 579 Arad Chickering[8] and Elizabeth O. [Emerson] Balch, was born at Kalamazoo, Mich.,
October 4, 1855, and is a civil engineer at Hastings, Michigan. He was married December 5, 1887, to Ida L., daughter
of James N. and Susan H. Stearns, who was born at Medina,
New York, September 20, 1861. They have one child, born
at Hastings, Mich.

1975 JOSEPHINE LOUISA,[10] b. Dec. 27, 1888.

1227. **Glen E.,**[9] son of 579 Arad Chickering[8] and Elizabeth O. [Emerson] Balch, was born at Kalamazoo, May 11,
1869, and is a civil engineer in the government lake survey.
He is unmarried.

1228. **Ralph,**[9] son of 579 Arad Chickering[8] and Elizabeth O. [Emerson] Balch, was born at Kalamazoo, July 31,
1873, and is a medical student at the Michigan University.

1229. **Emily A.,**[9] daughter of 580 Confucius Icilious[8]
and Caroline A. [Ryther] Balch, was born at St. Charles, Illinois, March 1, 1855, is unmarried, was the principal of the
Lovell street school in Kalamazoo, Mich., and is now teaching
at Aurora, Illinois.

1231. **Clara O.,**[9] daughter of 580 Confucius Icilious[8]
and Caroline A. [Ryther] Balch, was born at St. Charles,
Ill., March 27, 1858. She was married November 25, 1890,

to Charles A., son of Blamford and Sarah [Potter] Pierce,
and resides at Elgin, Illinois. They have two children:
Louise Winefred, b. April 12, 1892 ; Marion Alice, b. March
31, 1896.

1232. Herbert B.,[9] son of 580 Confucius Icilious[8] and
Caroline A. [Ryther] Balch, was born at St. Charles, Illinois,
December 1, 1860, and lives in Chicago, Illinois. He was
married July 6, 1882 to Nettie Grace Ridge, who was born
June 5, 1862, at Dayton, Ohio.

1976 EMMA E.,[10] b. Oct. 7, 1883; d. Jan. 20, 1890.
1977 MABEL GRACE,[10] b. Dec. 15, 1889.

1233. George R.,[9] son of 580 Confucius Icilious[8] and
Caroline A. [Ryther] Balch, was born at St. Charles, Illinois,
June 20, 1862, and is the purchasing agent of the Cincinnati,
Hamilton and Dayton R. R. Co., at Cincinnati, Ohio. He
was married October 22, 1890, to Edith, daughter of W. D.
and Helen Woodford, who was born August 19, 1867, at Kalamazoo, Michigan.

1234. Louis N.,[9] son of 580 Confucius Icilious[8] and
Caroline A. [Ryther] Balch, was born at St. Charles, Ill.,
April 28, 1865. He married Nellie Mullin, October 14, 1894,
in Chicago, Ill. He is a bookkeeper.

1978 LOUIS RAYMOND,[10] b. Sept. 11, 1895.

1237. Martha P.,[9] daughter of 583 Coben[8] and Amanda
E. [Houghton] Balch, was born at Lyndon, Vermont, February 10, 1834, and was married October 26, 1856, to John
J., son of Isaac and Hannah Henderschott. They have lived
at Irving, Mich., on the same farm, since they were married.
Their children are as follows: Lizzie Amanda, b. March 3,
1859, graduate homœopathic department, University of Michigan, class of 1888, and is practicing at Irving, Mich.; Mary
Gertrude, b. June 4, 1861, d. Dec. 12, 1863 ; Florence Edith,
b. March 4, 1865, graduate pharmacy department, University
of Michigan, class of 1887, m. Dec. 19, 1889, Frederick J.
Henning, of Detroit; Nellie Blanche, b. June 14, 1867 ;

Grace Leone, b. Dec. 2, 1870 ; Ella Pearl, b. Feb. 5, 1874, graduate Michigan State Normal School, class of 1895, teacher at Jackson, Mich.

1238. Mary E.,[9] daughter of 583 Coben[8] and Amanda E. [Houghton] Balch, was born November 7, 1837, and lives at Middleville, Michigan. She married John Campbell, December 25, 1861. He is a merchant and farmer. Their children are : Coben, b. Oct. 8, 1862, d. 1873 ; Amanda, b. April 27, 1865; Sarah Elizabeth, b. May 7, 1867, d. March 26, 1869 ; Edna, b. March 10, 1877. Amanda married Archie Orr, Sept. 24, 1885, and lives at Peoria, N. Y.

1239. Sarah A.,[9] daughter of 583 Coben[8] and Amanda E. [Houghton] Balch, was born March 29, 1840, and died September 30, 1869. She married January 8, 1860, George W. Slade, and had one daughter : Lulu Bishop Slade, b. November 5, 1863. She married, Dec. 2, 1885, Frank A. Stead, of Waterloo, Iowa. They live at Hopkinton, Iowa, and have four children.

1245. Maria E.,[9] daughter of 584 Barnabas Dodge[8] and Adeline [Ketchum] Balch, was born February 1, 1851. She married Lucien Everett, son of Dr. R. A. and Abbie H. E. Axtell, March 16, 1875. Edith, b. March 6, 1876 ; Bessie, b. June 18, 1878; May, b. Jan. 2, 1881, d. Feb. 10, 1891 ; Louise, b. Nov. 27, 1883 ; Henry Sylvester, b. Jan. 15, 1887 ; Everett Balch, b. Aug. 17, 1889.

1247. Florence Gertrude,[9] daughter of 590 Luther Chickering[8] and Sarah A. [Pointer] Balch, was born at Kalamazoo, Mich., November 28, 1851. She married A. J. Mills, who was born January 9, 1851. He is a lawyer, and has been judge of the circuit court in Kalamazoo county. They have two daughters, both born at Kalamazoo : Florence Gertrude, b. July 14, 1875 ; Mabel Clara, b. Aug. 21, 1877.

1248. Charles L.,[9] son of 590 Luther Chickering[8] and Sarah A. [Pointer] Balch, was born at Kalamazoo, Mich.,

January 14, 1855. He married Mary, daughter of William and Fannie McLain. She was born April 25, 1853. They live in Lawton, Mich., and have two children.

    1979 BERTHA,[10] b. Feb. 8, 1878.
    1980 BARNEY,[10] b. Jan. 12, 1881.

    1249. James F.,[9] son of 592 Frederick[8] and Hannah J. [Perry] Balch, was born at Boston, Mass., November 12, 1847, and died June 14, 1889. He married Angeline Maria Kauldack, of Boston, in the fall of 1872. She died at Worcester, Mass., in the fall of 1887. No issue.

    1250. Lydia A.,[9] daughter of 592 Frederick[8] and Hannah J. [Perry] Balch, was born at Boston, Mass., January 6, 1849. She was married October 1, 1868, to Henry Edwin, son of William and Mary Jane Warner, of Clarmont, N. H. He died at Tewksbury, Mass., April 18, 1881. Lydia A. is living at West Somerville, Mass. They had no children.

    1251. Hannah M.,[9] daughter of 592 Frederick[8] and Hannah J. [Perry] Balch, was born at Boston, Mass., February 21, 1850, and died February 22, 1891. She was married Dec. 25, 1873, to Isaac S. Foster, of Brewster, Mass. They had two children, born in Boston: Albert W., b. Oct. 20, 1874; Frederick Balch, b. July 7, 1876.

    1254. Adeline R.,[9] eldest daughter of 596 Amos[8] and Esther A. [Woodward] Balch, was born at Lancaster, N. H., Aug. 30, 1842, where she now lives. She was married June 13, 1860, to Charles H. Stebbins. They lived at Elkhart, Indiana, in 1886 and 1887 ; Wichita, Kansas, to 1889 ; Denver, Colorado, to 1893 ; Kirksville to 1895, and in 1896 are at their birthplace. They have had three children: Etta E., b. Jan. 22, 1862, d. Aug. 11, 1862; Bert L., b. July 10, 1868; Fred D., b. March 22, 1875. Bert L. married September 18, 1888, Eva B. Rydman. They live at Elkhart, Ind.

    1255. Luke W.,[9] eldest son of 596 Amos[8] and Esther A. [Woodward] Balch, was born at Lancaster, N. H., December 23, 1846, and lives at Sloan, Missouri. He was married first, June 10, 1871, to Clara B. Rundlett. She died November 25, 1873. He was married second, October 26, 1881, to Clara J. Davis, of New York city, a granddaughter of Acey Kinne, reviser of Blackstone.

1257. **Eva A.,**[9] youngest daughter of 596 Amos[8] and Esther A. [Woodward] Balch, was born at Lancaster, N. H., January 3, 1858, and died April 9, 1885. She was married September 26, 1880, to James Alden Stebbins, a brother of her sister Adeline's husband. They had one daughter, Lila E., b. May 17, 1881.

1258. **Emeline,**[9] daughter of 597 Samuel B.[8] and Mary A. [Holmes] Balch, was born at Lancaster, New Hampshire, October 22, 1841, and is living at Hollister, California. She was married March 3, 1857, to Milan C., son of Milan and Candice [Putnam] Serles, of New York. He was born June 9, 1835. They have had five children, three dying young. Martha L., b. Dec. 16, 1859; James E., b. Feb. 24, 1867.

1261. **Harvey,**[9] son of 597 Samuel B.[8] and Mary A. [Holmes] Balch, was born at Colebrook, N. H., December 24, 1848, and is living at Sloan, Missouri. He was married March 21, 1875, to Amanda Lanel. Their children are as follows:

1981 HARVEY,[10] b. Jan. 13, 1876.
1982 FRED,[10] b. Sept. 30, 1878.
1983 ALMA,[10] b. Sept. 14, 1880.
1984 BERTHA,[10] b. Oct. 13, 1882.
1985 ESMA,[10] b. Jan. 2, 1884; d. May 6, 1885.
1986 MABEL,[10] b. Jan. 25, 1886.
1987 LEE,[10] b. Jan. 9, 1888.
1988 EARL,[10] b. March 23, 1890.
1989 LUKE,[10] b. March 15, 1895.

1262. **Mary Adelaide,**[9] daughter of 597 Samuel B.[8] and Mary A. [Holmes] Balch, was born at Lancaster, New Hampshire, February 17, 1852, and died at San Diego, California, October 21, 1894. She was married August 13, 1873, to Frank E., son of William O. and Nancy J. [Whipple]

Belden. They had five children: James Edgar, b. June 1, 1874; Marvin Deloss, b. May 21, 1875; George W., b. May 31, 1876, d. y.; Sylvia Ellinor, b. Aug. 5, 1877; Julius T., b. Oct. 11, 1887, d. y.

1263. **Sarah Adams,**[9] eldest daughter of 600 Joseph H.[8] and U. S. [Riles] Balch, was born at Plaquemine, La., December 16, 1850. She was married February 23, 1870, to L. O. Hacker, a lawyer at New Iberia, La. He graduated in letters at the College of the Immaculate Conception, at New Iberia, La. They are Roman Catholics, and six children were born in New Iberia: Sarah Emily, b. Dec. 12, 1870; Lewis Wellington, b. Feb. 1, 1872; Mary Meade, b. April 19, 1874; John Hubbard, b. Aug. 19, 1877; Mary Edna, b. July 19, 1879; L. O. Hacker, Jr., b. July 29, 1883.

1265. **Elisa O.,**[9] daughter of 600 Joseph H.[8] and U. S. [Riles] Balch, was born at Plaquemine, La., September 16, 1854. She was married Oct. 24, 1876, to A. J. Mignes, a pilot on the Mississippi river, and lives at New Iberia. They are Roman Catholics, and have two children, both born at New Iberia: Kate, b. Aug. 29, 1877; L. Wellington, b. Dec. 3, 1879.

1266. **Joseph Thomas,**[9] son of 600 Joseph H.[8] and U. S. [Riles] Balch, was born at Plaquemine, La., June 7, 1856. He was married October 18, 1876, to Adorestine Bourk, of New Iberia, La. He is a printer and a Roman Catholic. Their three children were born in New Iberia, La., where they now reside.

1990 ADVEY,[10] b.
1991 HUBBARD,[10] b.
1992 AGNES,[10] b.

1270. **Emma E.,**[9] eldest daughter of 603 Charles W.[8] and Olive [Higgins] Balch, was born at West Boudoin, Maine, July 18, 1855, and died June 2, 1880. She was married October 14, 1874, to Henry Paine Bonney, of Hooksett, N. H. They had one child, Nona, b. April 11, 1875.

1271. Charles H.,[9] only son of 603 Charles W.[8] and
Olive [Higgins] Balch, was born at West Boudoin, Maine,
June 21, 1856, and died May 18, 1889. He was married first,
March 12, 1884, to Jeannette, daughter of Hosea Gray. They
had one son.

1993 HOSEA,[10] b, April, 1886; d. March, 1894.

Charles H. married second, May 26, 1887, Mrs. Jennie E.
(Ames) Goodwin, of Lancaster, N. H. They had two children.

1994 NORA MAY,[10] b. Feb. 8, 1888.
1995 CHARLES ASA,[10] b. April 8, 1889.

1274. Loren A.,[9] son of 608 Frederick A.[8] and Henrietta [Caldwell] Balch, was born at Trenton, Wisconsin, November 4, 1856, is a stenographer and salesman at Neillsville,
Wisconsin, and is manager of the Neillsville Novelty M'f'g
Co. He was married March 7, 1881, to Mary Austin, at Racine, Wisconsin, and divorced in February, 1889. He married second, Rose Isabella, daughter of Thomas Robinson,
on May 15, 1895, at Neillsville. He has had no children.

1275. Rella W.,[9] son of 608 Frederick A.[8] and Henrietta
[Caldwell] Balch, was born at Sheboygan Falls, Wisconsin,
September 14, 1859. He is head of the firm of Balch &
Tragsdorf, shippers of produce, at Neillsville, Wisconsin. He
was married November 22, 1881, to Nettie B., daughter of
Charles C. Whipple. She was born at Lima, Wis., April 16,
1860. They have two sons, born at Neillsville.

1996 LELAND R.,[10] b. March 10, 1883.
1997 HAROLD C.,[10] b. Aug. 27, 1890.

1277. Frederick O.,[9] son of 608 Frederick A.[8] and
Henrietta [Caldwell] Balch, was born at Hingham, Wisconsin,
May 3, 1869, and is a travelling salesman living at Neillsville,
Wisconsin. He was married July 27, 1892, to Grace Louise,
daughter of James and Ruane (Allison) Flynn. She was
born August 9, 1870, at Madison, Wisconsin.

1998 FAVILLE CLEON,[10] b. June 1, 1895.

Descendants of 22 Joseph.[4]

1278. Aurora Maria,[9] daughter of 612 Henry Brace[8] and Lucy Aurora [Brace] Balch, was born in Meadville, Pa., October 19, 1852, and died at Benzonia, Mich., January 6, 1877. She was married November 12, 1875, to George Buck, who was born June 16, 1851, at Wheatland, Hillsdale county, Mich. They had no children.

1280. Herbert Corrie,[9] son of 612 Henry Brace[8] and Julia Elvira [Bates] Balch, was born in Meadville, Pa., January 27, 1861. He was a sash and blind maker at Travers City, Michigan, until 1890, when he removed to Benzoa, Michigan, and has taken charge of a planing mill for the Case Brothers Lumber Company. He is a Republican. He was married June 30, 1885, to Clara Jane Chandler, who was born in Chicago, October 2, 1865. They are members of the Methodist church, and had one child.

1999 HINE EDWARD,[10] b. Sept. 5, 1895; d. Sept. 22, 1895.

1281. Ida Minerva,[9] daughter of 612 Henry Brace[8] and Julia Elvira [Bates] Balch, was born in Meadville, Pa., March 26, 1863. She is a professional nurse in Chicago, where she was married, November 28, 1895, to Dr. Benjamin L. Babcock, who was born March 12, 1862, at Huron, Michigan.

1283. Charles Warner,[9] son of 613 Jonathan Belden[8] and Charlotte Crosby [Warner] Balch, was born at Harwinton, Ct., March 30, 1856, and is a stenographer, living in New York city. He was married December 22, 1885, to Isabel Brevoort, daughter of Richard and Jane [Ker] Wickstead, of New York city. She was born Sept. 5, 1859. They have two children.

2000 HOWARD KELLOGG,[10] b. Nov. 21, 1886.
2001 CLARENCE WICKSTEAD,[10] b. Nov. 9, 1890.

1284. George Humphrey,[9] son of 613 Jonathan Belden[8] and Charlotte Crosby [Warner] Balch, was born at Harwinton, Ct., August 28, 1858, and lives at Morris, Conn.

He is an engraver. He was married to Nettie, daughter of
Joseph and Althea [Foster] Cook, of Harwinton. Their
children are as follows:

2002 CHARLOTTE EMMA,[10] b. Nov. 7, 1877.
2003 ARTHUR HUMPHREY,[10] b. April 6, 1879.
2004 MABEL ALTHEA,[10] b. June 16, 1880.
2005 FRANKLIN HENRY,[10] b. Jan. 18, 1887.
2006 KATIE LAURA,[10] b. Nov. 10, 1888.
2007 CHARLES EDGAR,[10] b. March 31, 1892.
2008 GEORGE JONATHAN,[10] b. Feb. 13, 1894.

1285. Walter Shaffer,[9] son of 613 Jonathan Belden[8]
and Charlotte Crosby [Warner] Balch, was born at Harwinton, Connecticut, September 29, 1860, where he is in the
mercantile business. He was married July 2, 1887, to Ellen
J., daughter of Horace W. and Sarah A. Fisher, of Stratford,
Conn.

2009 MABEL WOOD,[10] } twins, b. Feb. 28, 1888.
2010 MAUD THOMAS,[10] }
2011 WALTER FISHER,[10] b. July 22, 1889.

1286. Carrie Maria,[9] daughter of 613 Jonathan Belden[8]
and Charlotte Crosby [Warner] Balch, was born at Harwinton, Ct., October 22, 1862. She was married January 26,
1888, to Dennis G., son of Edward E. and R. L. Baker. He
has a market and grocery store at Harwinton, Conn. They
have one child, Addie Louise, b. March 18, 1889.

1291. Mary Julia,[9] daughter of 628 Albert Vestus[8] and
Sarah T. [Parmelee] Balch, was born at Weyauwega, Wisconsin, January 21, 1855. She was married September 29,
1877, to Frank W., son of Reuben B. and Ruth Ann [Ring]
Houghton. The ceremony was performed by the Rev. Dr.
Steele, at the residence of her father in Weyauwega.
Mr. Houghton was born at Rochester, N. Y., Dec. 21,
1849. He is a lawyer, in the successful practice of his
profession at Oshkosh, Wisconsin, where they reside.
They had five children, the two oldest born at Wausau, and the others at Oshkosh, Wisconsin. Laura Madge,
b. Oct. 6, 1878; Mary Ruth, b. Nov. 13, 1879; Albert Balch,

b. Aug. 27, 1882; Frank Wilbur, b. July 30, 1884; Harry Abner, b. Dec. 16, 1886.

1292. Sarah Maria,[9] daughter of 623 Albert Vestus[8] and Sarah T. [Parmelee] Balch, was born at Weyauwega, Wisconsin, July 25, 1860. She was married at the residence of her father in Weyauwega, April 20, 1891, to Dr. Charles D., son of Charles M. and Janet Fenelon, who was born in Weyauwega, May 17, 1863. Dr. Fenelon graduated in 1885 from the Wisconsin State University, was principal of the High School in Weyauwega for three years, then attended the Rush Medical College at Chicago, and graduated in 1891. He is practising at Phillips, Wisconsin. They have one daughter, Eunice, b. Dec. 24, 1894.

1293. Laura Bertha,[9] youngest daughter of 623 Albert Vestus[8] and Sarah T. [Parmelee] Balch, was born at Weyauwega, Wisconsin, December 12, 1862. She was married at the residence of her father, in Weyauwega, September 15, 1886, to Rev. Thomas E., son of Rev. Edward and Millia [Webb] Barr, of Frankfort, Ind. The groom's father performed the ceremony. Rev. Mr. Barr was born April 21, 1860. He and Laura Bertha were classmates, and graduated together, in 1885, from Lake Forest University, with the first and second honors of the class, the former being valedictorian and the latter salutatorian. Mr. Barr then attended Princeton (N. J.) Theological Seminary. In the summer of 1886 he was settled over the Presbyterian church at Snow Shoe, Pennsylvania. In June, 1887, he was settled as pastor of the Presbyterian church in Beloit, Wisconsin; in 1890 at Racine, Wisconsin; in 1892 at the First Presbyterian church, Kalamazoo, Michigan, and after one year of service became pastor of the First Congregational church in the same city. Their children are as follows: Edward Balch, b. June 16, 1887; Sarah Katharine, b. April 7, 1889; Millia Jennie, b. Sept. 4, 1891; Henrietta Rood, b. Sept. 15, 1893.

1294. Samuel W.,[9] son of 625 Galusha Burchard[8] and

Harriet C. [Andrews] Balch, was born at Malone, New York, January 18, 1862, and lives at Yonkers, New York. In 1883 he took the degree of engineer of mines, at the School of Mines, Columbia College, and has since been engaged in mechanical engineering and patent soliciting, with an office in New York city. He has contributed scientific articles to various periodicals, and has assisted in the editing of this Genealogy.

1296. **Harriet Elizabeth,**[9] daughter of 625 Galusha Burchard[8] and Harriet C. [Andrews] Balch, was born at Plattsburg, N. Y., May 17, 1870. In 1892 she took the degree of bachelor of science at Wellesley College, and is now a student in the senior class at the Women's Medical College, New York city.

1298. **Margaret Andrews,**[9] daughter of 625 Galusha Burchard[8] and Harriet C. [Andrews] Balch, was born at Yonkers, N. Y., June 1, 1875. She is now a student at Wellesley College, where she is making a specialty of literature and history.

1300. **William Monroe,**[9] son of 647 Manning B.[8] and Hattie L. [Monroe] Balch, was born at Monroe, Wisconsin, Nov. 25, 1871. He graduated from the University of Wisconsin in 1891, and received the degree of master of letters from the institution in 1896. He studied law the year following graduation, but entered the ministry in 1892. He is now a member of the West Wisconsin Conference of the Methodist Episcopal Church, and pastor at River Falls, Wisconsin. He has also served one year as state secretary of the Epworth League. He was married June 27, 1893, to Beulah G. Richards, of Mineral Point, Wisconsin. They have one daughter.

2012 MARY MONROE,[10] b. May 9, 1894.

1303. **Eleonore Marie Amelie,**[9] daughter of 656 Frederick A.[8] and Celeste A. Brasier [De LaTour] Balch, was born December 1, 1868. She was married June 27, 1894, to

Samuel W. Balch.
(1294)

Georges Paul Alba de Cazeneune. He was born in Faulsuse France, May 11, 1870, and is an actor. They have one child, Paul Auguste, b. Jan. 11, 1896.

SECOND BRANCH.

Descendants of 6 Benjamin.[2]

Descendants of 31 Joseph.[4]

1309. Joel,[9] son of 668 Nathan Balch, was born in Rutland county, Vermont, and was living at Fon du Lac, Wisconsin, in 1856. He married Louisa Manley. Their children were :

    2013 GEORGE.[10]
    2014* WILLIAM L.,[10] b. Dec. 22, 1833.
    2015 SPENCER.[10]
    2016 LOUISA.[10]
    2017 SYLVIA.[10]
    2018 MARTIN.[10]

1317. Aaron Leland,[9] son of 664 Joel[8] and Betsey [Stevens] Balch, was born at Andover, Vt., June 17, 1802, and died at Swanzey, Mass., November 4, 1839. He was married in New York city, December 25, 1826, to Eliza, daughter of Richard Vaughan. She was born at Bristol, England, in 1798, and died at Baltimore, Md., in 1871. They had four children.

    2019 WILLIAM S.,[10] b   ; d. y.
    2020 WILLIAM S.,[10] b.   ; d. y.
    2021 LELAND JOEL,[10] b. 1832; d. Nov., 1875.
    2022* WILLIAM EUGENE,[10] b. 1839, in Swanzey, Mass.

Aaron Leland Balch was a Universalist clergyman. He was brought up under the strictest kind of Calvanistic Baptist doctrine, and his means of education and improvement in early life were much restricted. He graduated in 1836 from the Norwich (Vt.) University, at the age of 21, and went to live in New York city. He commenced his ministerial labors at Woburn, Mass., and next removed to Newport, N. H., where he resided until June, 1839, when he settled with the societies in Fall River and Swanzey.

1318. Louisa Marium,[9] daughter of 664 Joel[8] and
Betsey [Stevens] Balch, was born at Andover, Vt., April 13,
1804 and died February 5, 1892. She was married March 8,
1827, to John L. Clay, of Galesburg, Ill. He was born October 3, 1802, and died October 29, 1877. Their children were
as follows:—Alonzo C., b. Feb. 18, 1828, lives at Galesburg,
Ill.; William L., b. Aug. 31, 1831, lives at Woodhull, Ill.;
Eliza A., b. March 31, 1833; d. Jan. 29, 1835; Warren W.
W., b. June 12, 1835, d. Jan. 7, 1861; Hiland H., b. Jan. 3,
1838; lives at Galesburg, Ill.

1319. William Stevens,[9] son of 664 Joel[8] and Betsey
[Stevens] Balch, was born at Andover, Vt., April 13, 1806,
and died at Elgin, Ill., December 25, 1887. He was married
August 6, 1829, to Adeline Gale, daughter of John Capron,
of Winchester, N. H. She was born May 19, 1809, and died
in New York city, May 24, 1854, and was buried in Greenwood cemetery. They had eight children.

2023* ADA LOUISA,[10] b. Sept. 25 1830.
2024* EMMA ELIZABETH,[10] b. March 23, 1832.
2025* WILLIAM DELOS,[10] b. June 2, 1834.
2026* ESTELLE MARIA,[10] b. June 23, 1836.
2027* CHARLES LELAND,[10] b. March 25, 1840; d. Aug. 20, 1872.
2028* MARY ELENA,[10] b. Oct. 9, 1842; d. June 18, 1876.
2029* EDWARD ERNEST,[10] b. Aug. 13, 1844.
2030* JOHN JOEL,[10] b. May 16, 1852.

Rev. William S. married, July 28, 1856, for his second
wife, Mrs. Mary Ann Waterhouse, daughter of John Dalley.
She was born in New York city, December 25, 1832. They
had three children.

2031* MINNA SEAMAN,[10] b. July 12, 1858.
2032 CLARENCE ELLSWORTH,[10] b. March 24, 1860; d. Dec. 24, 1864.
2033* GEORGE WARREN,[10] b. Nov. 12, 1861.

Rev. William Stevens Balch received fellowship as a minister of the General Convention at Saratoga, N. Y., in September, 1827, and ordination in Claremont, N. H., in June,
1828. Up to 1831 he preached in the various towns of
Windham county, Vermont, and then, after spending a year

REV. WM. STEVENS BALCH.
(1819)

at Watertown, he removed to Claremont, N. H., and supplied there, and in Hartland and Springfield, Vt., and Newport, N. H., until a new church in Claremont was finished. Here he was very actively employed in all kinds of missionary work. In March, 1836, he was settled over the society in Providence, R. I., which was divided between restorationism and ultra Universalism. In two years the large church was crowded, and a second society was formed in the city. Having become interested in what was known as the "Dorr" movement, and freely expressing his wish to have a "Republican form of government," by a constitution, and seeing a political storm brewing, he accepted the call from New York, and settled there in November, 1842.

After seventeen years' hard work in preaching, lecturing, and writing on religious and moral reform topics, he went to Ludlow, Vt., and supplied in various places. At Galesburg, Ill., he preached five years, and removed to Hinsdale in 1870. In 1871 he went to Elgin, Ill. In 1877 he started for California, but stopped for three years as a supply at Dubuque, Iowa.

When in Providence, R. I., Mr. Balch gave a course of lectures on "Language," which were published in 1838. He also wrote a "Grammar of English Language," explained according to the principles of truth and common sense, which passed through four editions. In 1849 his volume, "Ireland as I Saw It," was issued, and in 1881, "A Peculiar People," the first edition of which sold in eight weeks. He was the author of a "Sunday School Manual," published in 1887.

His business capacity was evinced in his raising funds for the theological school at Canton, N. Y., taking charge of the location, plan, and rearing of the building, and selection of the principal. He afterwards completed the raising of a large fund for the institution. He devoted much time to the business of making the Christian Ambassador of New York a denominational paper, and placing it on a sound financial basis. His work in these particulars was well and faithfully done.

His character is summed up as follows by Dr. J. G. Adams, in "Fifty Notable Years": "Mr. Balch was always a ready and popular speaker. Although in favor of fraternal organization for the good of the cause, yet his ideas in reference to creed and to centralized authority were not accordant with those of many other of his brethren, who hold in high estimation the work he had done in the spirit and truth of the gospel.

"His eminent services to the church and cause of righteousness entitle him to be ranked as one of the foremost preachers of his generation. His active and able participation in the temperance cause, and all other moral questions brought before the American people, clearly rank him as one of our most worthy and respected citizens. His pronounced convictions and firmness in maintaining them, with his bold and fearless hatred and denunciation of evil, are characteristic of the family.

"Dr. Balch had a commanding presence, a powerful physique, a strong and active mind, a lofty ideal, and a tender heart. He maintained a pure heart and a spotless life. He sympathized with all ranks and conditions of men, and no one stood more clearly, consciously and heartily than he on that plane of intellectual hospitality which is as wide as the race. He was an ardent and practical lover of all that was good and noble in man, and an ardent and practical hater of all selfishness, meanness, greed, hypocrisy and pretence. His influence for good was great and wide."

1324. Dorcas,[9] daughter of 669 Francis S.[8] and Sally [Dickerson] Balch, was born at Shirley, Mass., November 26, 1811, and died at North Leominster, October 23, 1886. She was married April 14, 1833, to George Rice, who was born at Boylston, Mass., August 10, 1811. They lived at Northboro and Leominster, and had one child, born at the former place: Sarah L., b. Aug. 17, 1836.

1325. Francis,[9] son of 669 Francis S.[8] and Sally [Dickerson] Balch, was born on his father's farm at Shirley, Mass., March 10, 1814, and died at North Leominster, November 22, 1876.   He was married April 9, 1836, to Eliza, a daughter of John Butler.   She was born in Leominster, Mass., August 6, 1812, and died in the same town, May 13, 1879.   They had three children.

2034* OSCAR ABBOTT,[10] b. Jan. 25, 1837.
2035* ELLEN M.,[10] b. July 8, 1844.
2036 REVILLA M.,[10] b. Jan. 10, 1846.

Francis engaged first in cotton and then in paper manufacture.   This he followed by other pursuits, such as farming, wood cutting, butcher business, milk business, and trading in real estate.   He was a man full of business, and of sterling integrity, always ready to assist his friends and neighbors. His wife was famous for her cooking and her pies.

1326. Sarah,[9] daughter of 669 Francis S.[8] and Sally [Dickerson] Balch, was born at Shirley, Mass., May 14, 1818. She was married December 1, 1841, to Oliver F. Lawrence, of Harvard, Mass.   They lived at Shirley, and have had six children, two born in Fitchburg, Mass., four in Shirley : George F., b. Nov. 1, 1843 ; Enoch H., b. April 24, 1845, d. y. ; Sarah E., b. Feb. 2, 1848, d. y. ; Edward A., b. Oct. 21, 1851 ; Herbert E., b. July 21, 1854 ; Austin E., b. Feb. 22, 1856.

1327. Charles C.,[9] son of 669 Francis S.[8] and Sally [Dickerson] Balch, was born on the farm at Shirley, December 20, 1820, and died May 16, 1893.   He was a carpenter. On his monument are graven words that fittingly describe him, " Faithful and true."   He was married, May 9, 1847, to Lucena Olive, daughter of Abel and Nicena [Ballou] Bliss.   She was born in Royalston, Mass., July 3, 1825.   The family have been influential members of the Baptist church. They have had but one child, who was born in Royalston.

2037 EMMA LUCENA,[10] b. Oct. 12, 1850; married, Dec. 18, 1886, Waldo F. Cummings.

1328. **Susan,**[9] daughter of 670 Er[8] and Susan [Buss]
Balch, was born in Leominster, Mass., May 13, 1819, and died
in the same town, May 22, 1863. She was married August
7, 1839, to her brother-in-law, Joel Crosby, son of Henry and
Frances [Crosby] Allen, who was born September 2, 1817.
He was a merchant, and held various town offices. Their
four children were born in Leominster.

> FANNY CROSBY, b. July 14, 1843; unm.; lives in Leominster.
> HANNAH BLANCHARD, b. July 9, 1846; m. Oct. 23, 1873, Eugene
> A. Bennet; he d. March 5, 1877.
> ALICE GERTRUDE, b. Dec. 6, 1849; m. June 10, 1868, Frank L.
> Croker, of Leominster; he d. July 31, 1873; one son, *Allen
> Crosby*, b. Nov. 17, 1870; m.·second, Nov. 20, 1883, Joel G.
> Taylor, of Leominster.
> JENNIE CATHERINE, b. Dec. 10, 1852; m. Dec. 27, 1876, Charles
> S. Perry, of Leominster; have one child, *Edith Martha*, b.
> June 9, 1878.

1329. **Sarah Ann,**[9] daughter of 670 Er[8] and Susan
[Buss] Balch, was born in Leominster, Mass., May 20, 1821,
and died October 3, 1851. She was married in September,
1841, to George William, son of William and Mary [Hills]
Wilder, of Leominster. He was born July 8, 1816, and died
March 19, 1889. They lived in Worcester, Mass., where their
two children were born.

> GEORGE EDWARD, b. Feb., 1843; d. May 4, 1844.
> ANNETTE ELIZABETH, b. Feb. 26, 1845; m. in Leominster, Jan.
> 8, 1867, to George W., son of George W. and Maria (Worces-
> ter) Chute, of Leominster. He was b. at Canton, Mass.,
> April 14, 1841. They have two children: *Ethel Sarah*, b.
> Jan. 2, 1873; *Josephine Wilder*, b. March 2, 1875.

1330. **John Buss,**[9] son of 670 Er[8] and Susan [Buss]
Balch, was born in Leominster, Mass., June 17, 1825, and
died in Boston, Mass., October 27, 1851. He was married
August 20, 1850, to his sister-in-law, Susan Thurston, daugh-
ter of Henry and Frances [Crosby] Allen. She was born
October 2, 1824. They had one child.

2038 ELIZABETH FRANCES,[10] b. March 22, 1852.

1331. **Deneris,**[9] daughter of 670 Er[8] and Susan [Buss]

Balch, was born at Leominster, Mass., June 6, 1829, and died December 20, 1867. She was married February 7, 1850, to George W. Pierce, M. D. He was born October 15, 1819, and died May 1, 1886. They had seven children.

> SARAH EVE, b. Feb. 24, 1852; m. Sept. 17, 1873, Edwin C. Farwell, who was b. Aug. 2, 1851. They have three children: *Harold Crosby*, b. Feb. 1, 1877, d. Dec. 22, 1877; *Minnie Gregory*, b. Sept. 21, 1878; *Chester Warren*, b. Nov. 3, 1880.
>
> MARY AGNES, b. April 2, 1854; d. Nov. 27, 1864.
>
> HELEN BELL, b. Dec. 21, 1855.
>
> GEORGE BALCH, b. Dec. 26, 1860; m. June 11, 1888, Addie Lincoln Shattuck. They have two children: *Marion*, b. Dec. 11, 1893; *Mildred Lincoln*, b. Sept. 6, 1895.
>
> HENRY WILLIAM, b. June 7, 1863; d. Aug. 6, 1864.
>
> SUSIE, b. May 27, 1864; d. July 22, 1864.
>
> HATTIE ELIZABETH, b. Oct. 9, 1865; m. Aug. 7, 1889, George H. Woodbury, dentist, who was born Mar. 17, 1864. They have three children: *Vernon Pierce*, b. Feb. 22, 1893; *Helen*, b. June 5, 1894; *Paul Henry*, b. Dec. 14, 1895.

1332. George Lucius,[9] son of 670 Er[8] and Susan [Buss] Balch, was born at Leominster, Mass., April 8, 1831, and lives at Cambridge, Mass. He was married November 4, 1863, to Lucia, daughter of Addison and Fanny [Wright] Dunham, of Westminster, Vt. She was born January 16, 1841. They had three children.

2039* JOHN ER,[10] b. Nov. 6, 1864.

2040 FANNY EMILY,[10] b. June 7, 1868; unm.; lives at Cambridge.

2041* HELEN FRANCES,[10] b. July 3, 1871.

1333. Francis Er,[9] son of 670 Er[8] and Susan [Buss] Balch, was born at Leominster, Mass., January 17, 1834, and is a hotel proprietor at Paris, Tennessee. He was married November 27, 1855, to Mary Ellen, daughter of Lysander and Emily [Brown] Conant, who was born at Louisville, Kentucky, March 5, 1833. To them have been born five children.

2042* FREDERIC HORACE,[10] b. Sept. 20, 1856.

2043* ADDIE AUGUSTA,[10] b. May 9, 1858.

2044 RUTH FRANCES,[10] b. Sept. 9, 1866; d. Dec. 29, 1869.

2045 WILLIAM FRANK,[10] b. April 2, 1870.

2046 MARION FRANKLIN,[10] b. Sept. 18, 1871.

In 1887 Francis E. kept the Hotel Pemberton, at Hull, Massachusetts. For seven years he was steward at Memorial Hall, Harvard College.

1334. **Adaline Adams**,[9] daughter of 670 Er[8] and Susan [Buss] Balch, was born at Leominster, Mass., November 26, 1837, where she now lives. She was married December 29, 1863, to Charles, son of Seth and Anna Tisdale. He was born September 10, 1833, and died in April, 1875. They had four children : Louis Francis, b. May 18, 1864, d. Feb. 23, 1884; Walter Seth, b. Aug. 9, 1865; Susie Balch, b. May 30, 1867, d. Dec. 18, 1884; Charles Er, b. Sept. 25, 1875.

1337. **John Hiram**,[9] son of 672 James Parker[8] and Lucinda [Boynton] Balch, was born in Weathersfield, Vt., February 22, 1824, and died January 7, 1897. He was a merchant at Newburyport, Mass., and was married June 22, 1854, to Lydia J. S., daughter of Jonathan Coffin. She was born at Fultonborough, N. H., March 7, 1833. They have had three children.

2047[e] HORACE LELAND,[10] b. Jan. 9, 1856.
2048[e] NETTIE COFFIN,[10] b. June 16, 1859.
2049[e] JOHN HIRAM,[10] b. Feb. 4, 1866.

1338. **Elizabeth Mary**,[9] daughter of 672 James Parker[8] and Lucinda [Boynton] Balch, was born January 18, 1827, and died July 16, 1894, at Newburyport. She was married November 9, 1847, to Pliny Gay. They lived at Colorado Springs, Colo., for a few years, and then returned to Newburyport, Mass. Mr. Gay died at Newburyport, August 4, 1892. They had one child, Fred H., born in 1849, who is living, unm., at Colorado Springs.

1340. **James Nelson**,[9] son of 672 James Parker[8] and Lucinda [Boynton] Balch, was born at Weathersfield, Vt., May 26, 1832, and is the head of the firm Balch, Price & Co., importers, manufacturers, and dealers in straw goods, furs, hats and millinery goods, at Brooklyn, N. Y. On September 20, 1858, he was married to Sarah, daughter of Edward S.

Wm. L. Balch

and Sarah F. Leslie, of Newburyport, Mass. They have no children.

1341. George Parker,[9] son of 672 James Parker[8] and Lucinda [Boynton] Balch, was born at Weathersfield, Vermont, January 18, 1834, and died at Newburyport, Mass., October 17, 1891. He was a dealer in coal and wood. He was married September 1, 1869, to Mary Elizabeth, daughter of Charles A. and Frances Stevens. She was born at Castine, Maine, October 16, 1843. They had two children.

2050   MABEL FRANCES,[10] b. June 18, 1875.
2051   CARRIE BOYNTON,[10] b. Aug. 18, 1877.

1342. Isadore Lucinda,[9] daughter of 672 James Parker[8] and Lucinda [Boynton] Balch, was born at Weathersfield, Vt., February 8, 1836, and died at Newburyport, Mass., July 14, 1883. She was married at Weathersfield, Dec. 16, 1856, to Warren Currier, and had three sons: Warren Thomas, b. Nov. 29, 1857, m. Feb. 5, 1885, to Effie Carolena Hodge; Frank Balch, b. Dec. 4, 1863, m. Nov. 4, 1889, Annie Knowlton Tuck; William Swasey, b. April 25, 1868.

1343. Ellen Jane,[9] daughter of 672 James Parker[8] and Lucinda [Boynton] Balch, was born at Weathersfield, Vt., August 20, 1837. She was married January 24, 1865, to Orlando Alford, of Brookline, Mass. They had two children: Martha, b. Feb. 3, 1867; Edward Balch, b. Sept. 13, 1871.

1344. Carrie Maria,[9] daughter of 672 James Parker[8] and Lucinda [Boynton] Balch, was born at Weathersfield, Vt., December 7, 1841. She was married November 23, 1868, to John Gardner Little, a farmer at Turkey Hill, Newburyport. They have no children.

1346. William Lincoln,[9] son of 679 Edward Lawrence[8] and Martha Willis [Lincoln] Balch, was born April 2, 1847, at Roxbury, Massachusetts, where he now lives. On the maternal side he is descended from Gov. Bradford, of the Plymouth colony. Learning all the details of the printer's

art from his father, he has always been connected with newspapers and literature, and has had experience in almost every
department of newspaper work, besides contributing to peri-
odical fiction. He prepared the chapters in this volume on
the origin of the name, the coat of arms, and the early English home of the family. He was night editor of the old
Boston Daily News, and is now engaged in similar work on
the Boston Herald, and is a member of the Boston Press
Club. On April 17, 1893, he was married to Nora E., daughter
of James and Eliza Ann [Colburn] Emerson, of Glover, Vt.

1348. Ela M.,[9] daughter of 680 William Young[8] and
Maria Swift [Beal] Balch, was born September 29, 1857, at
Milton, and lives at East Milton, Massachusetts. She was
married in Boston, January 17, 1883, to Joseph Albert, son
of John A. and Mahala L. Simpson, of East Milton. Their
children are George Albert, b. Feb. 29, 1884, and William
Beal, b. Aug. 8, 1887.

1349. Joseph Pope,[9] son of 681 Joseph[8] and Mary Ann
[Bailey] Balch, was born at Providence, R. I., August 9,
1822, and died in the same city, December 2, 1872. He was
married at Providence on July 14, 1853, to Laura Tiffany,
daughter of John A. Field, of that city. They had three
children.

2052   MARY HOWARD,[10] b. Jan. 22, 1855; unm.
2053   LAURA FIELD,[10] b. Feb. 11, 1857; d. Oct. 13, 1859.
2054* JOSEPH,[10] b. July 16, 1860.

Joseph Pope Balch, although prepared for college, evinced
such a desire for mercantile life, that, at the age of 14 years,
he entered his father's drug store as clerk, and eventually
became a partner. In 1841 he joined the Providence Marine
Corps of Artillery, and the exciting season of the following
year intensified his military ardor. In 1857 he was commissioned brigade major and inspector of the Second Brigade of
Rhode Island. He was appointed one of the majors of the
First Regiment in 1861, and accompanied its second detach-

ment to Washington, where he was untiring in his efforts toward improving its discipline and equipment. On the appointment of Col. Burnside to the command of a brigade, Major Balch succeeded to the command of the regiment, and in the battle of Bull Run was distinguished for his coolness, steadiness and courage. This gained for him from the President the brevet of Lieutenant-Colonel, Colonel, and Brigadier General of volunteers in the army of the United States. After the disbandment of the First Regiment, in August, 1861, he continued to render valuable services to the state and country in enlisting and organizing regiments and batteries for the war. On May 26, 1863, General Balch was commissioned brigadier-general of the Second Brigade of Rhode Island militia. In October of that year the brigade, consisting of over three thousand men, was reviewed by Governor James Y. Smith, and conceded to have furnished the finest military display ever witnessed in the state. He was social in his habits, devoted in his attachments, and generous in his hospitality. He was a member of the Rhode Island Society for the Encouragement of Domestic Industry, and was also a member of the Providence Franklin Society.

Death came to him suddenly. While home from his store for dinner, he was taken with an internal hemorrhage, from which he died in a few hours.

1350. **Mary Ann,**[9] daughter of 681 Joseph[8] and Mary Ann [Bailey] Balch, was born at Providence, R. I., October 7, 1823, and died August 31, 1889. She was a remarkable woman, both socially and publicly. She represented Rhode Island, in 1876, at the Centennial in Philadelphia, and founded the Rhode Island Institute for the Deaf. She was married December 16, 1845, to Henry Lippitt. He was born October 9, 1818, and died Jan. 5, 1891. He was Governor of Rhode Island in 1875-6. They had eleven children.

CHARLES WARREN, b. Oct. 8, 1846; Governor of Rhode Island, 1895-6; m. Margaret Bahara Farnum, Feb. 23, 1886; she was born June 29. 1860. Six children: *Charles Warren*, b. May 29, 1887, d. Dec. 27, 1893; *Alexander Farnum*, b. Feb. 28, 1890, d. Jan. 1, 1894; *Jeanie Barhara*, b. Jan. 5, 1892, d. Dec. 26, 1893; *Charles Warren*, b. May 15, 1894; *Alexander Farnum*, b. March 11, 1896.

HENRY MERRIMAN, b. Sept. 17, 1848; d. March 10, 1856.

JOSEPH BALCH, b. July 9, 1850; d. Nov. 18, 1851.

JEANIE, b. Jan. 6, 1852, m. April 18, 1893, William B. Weeden, widower of 1357 Hannah Raymond⁹. They live at Providence and Matunuck, Rhode Island.

GEORGE ERNEST, b. April 1, 1853; d. March 24, 1856.

FREDERICK. b. Feb. 1, 1855; d. April 1, 1856.

HENRY FREDERICK, b. Oct. 12, ¦1856; m. Dec. 15, 1881, Marie Louise, daughter of Tully D. and Louisa Holmes Bowen, She was born Dec. 19, 1859. Children: *Mary Louise*, b. March 8, 1883; *Henry*, b. July 13, 1886; *Frances*, b. Feb. 10. 1891: *Robert*, b. Feb. 19, 1893, d. Aug. 5, 1895.

MARY BALCH, b. July 14, 1858; m. Jan. 17, 1892, Charles John, son of Charles and Sarah [Bishop] Steedman, of South Carolina, admiral United States navy.

ROBERT LINCOLN, b. March 22, 1860; m. Nov. 17, 1883, Mabelle C. Brayton. They had one child: *Mabelle Clifton*, b. Dec. 1, 1884.

ABBY FRANCES, b. Oct. 31, 1861; m. Jan. 25, 1893, Duncan, son of Archibald and Mary Jane [Grahame] Hunter, of Scotland. He was born July 3, 1863. Children: *Mary Lippitt*, b. Dec. 11, 1893; *Francis Grahame*, b. May 19, 1895.

ALFRED, b. Feb. 6, 1863; d. y.

1352. Jane Adams,⁹ daughter of 681 Joseph⁸ and Mary Ann [Bailey] Balch, was born at Providence, R. I., January 14, 1827, and died in Providence, R. I., January 4, 1893. She was married June 5, 1849, to Albert S. Gallup. They resided in New York city, and had three children : Albert, b. June 9, 1853, d. Dec. 24, 1892 ; Howard, b. Sept. 14, 1854, living in London ; Jeanie, b. Nov. 14, 1864, m. Rev. Henry Mottet, D. D., New York.

1353. Ellen Howard,⁹ daughter of 681 Joseph⁸ and Mary Ann [Bailey] Balch, was born at Providence, R. I., March 14, 1830, and died October 6, 1865. She was married May 19, 1856, to Rev. Jared M. Heard. He was born March 16, 1832, and died in March, 1862. They had two children :

Jeanie, b. April, 1858, d. 1860 ; Mabel Balch, b. May 8, 1861, d. Jan. 8, 1879.

1354. Edward Augustus,[9] son of 681 Joseph[8] and Mary Ann [Bailey] Balch, was born in Providence, R. I., April 2, 1832, and died Jan. 14, 1871, in that city. He was a member of the firm of J. Balch & Son, druggists. He married, May 13, 1853, Anna L., daughter of Capt. William and Harriet Comstock. She was born April 20, 1836. They resided in Providence, R. I., and their three children were born in that city.

2055   HARRIET COMSTOCK,[10] b. March 9, 1857; unm.
2056°   ANNA AUGUSTA,[10] b. Oct. 29, 1858.
2057   MARY SPRAGUE,[10] b. Aug. 3, 1865; unm.

1355. Anna,[9] daughter of 681 Joseph[8] and Mary Ann [Bailey] Balch, was born March 12, 1835, at Providence, Rhode Island, where she now lives. She was married June 5, 1856, to James Robinson, who was born May 19, 1831, and died Aug. 16, 1875. They resided in New Bedford, Mass. They had two children : Caroline, b. Sept. 7, 1860 ; William Atmore, b. July 25, 1865.

1356. Abigail Pope,[9] daughter of 681 Joseph[8] and Mary Ann [Bailey] Balch, was born in Providence, R. I., March 11, 1837. She remained at home, and took care of her invalid mother and her orphan niece, Mabel Heard.

1357. Hannah Raymer,[9] daughter of 681 Joseph[8] and Mary Ann [Bailey] Balch, was born March 16, 1839, at Providence, Rhode Island, and died December 18, 1891. She was married December 5, 1867, to William B. Weeden, who was born September 1, 1834. He is a woolen manufacturer, and author of " Economic and Social History of New England." They had seven children :   John Edward and William Wager, twins, b. Feb. 5, 1869; Eliza Barnes, b. Aug. 1, 1870, m. March 1, 1892, Samuel Slater Durfee, have one child, Dorothy, b. Aug. 9, 1895 ; Raymer Balch, b. Nov. 5, 1877 ; James Vaughn, b. June 5, 1879 ; Mary Bailey, b. June 14, 1880 ; Ellen Howard, b. Dec. 8, 1882.

Mr. Weeden married second, Jeannie, daughter of Henry and 1850 Mary Ann[9] [Balch] Lippitt. She is a trustee of the institution founded by her mother.

THIRD BRANCH.

Descendants of 7 John.[3]
Descendants of 39 John.[4]

1358. Louisa Fuller,[9] daughter of 687 Andrew[8] and Louisa [Fuller] Balch, was born at Keene, N. H., July 7, 1816, and lives at Westmoreland, N. H., where she was married, September 28, 1838, to Warren Shelley, son of Barney and Lydia Shelley. He was born October 29, 1809, and died September 24, 1893, at Westmoreland, where he was a farmer. In politics he was a Republican. They are Baptists. They had no children.

1359. James Andrew,[9] son of 687 Andrew[8] and Louisa [Fuller] Balch, was born at Keene, N. H., November 22, 1817, and died at Arlington, Mass., October 11, 1876. He was married at Keene, N. H., in April, 1844, to Philena C. Robinson. They had two children, both born at South Acton, Mass.

.2059* ANDREW CARPENTER,[10] b. June 22, 1847; d. July 19, 1894.
  2060 MARIA PHILENA,[10] b. Oct., 1849; d. March, 1873, at Chelsea.

James Andrew was a carpenter. In 1846 he moved to South Acton, Mass., and in 1867 he went to live at Chelsea, Mass., where he resided until his death, which was sudden. For 23 years he was a deacon in the Baptist church at Acton. He was a Republican, and was universally esteemed as a conscientious and consistent Christian.

1360. Lucy Snow,[9] daughter of 687 Andrew[8] and Louisa [Fuller] Balch, was born at Keene, New Hampshire, September 17, 1819, and lives at Wilson [Witoka P. O.], Minnesota. She was married at Westmoreland, New Hampshire, November 29, 1842, to her second cousin, Francis, son of Martin

and Lucindia [Gilbert] Snow. He was born at Westmoreland, April 5, 1820, and died at Saxton River, June 13, 1898,
where they moved in 1881.

1362. **Perley Snow,**[9] son of 687 Andrew[8] and Louisa
[Fuller] Balch, was born at Keene, N. H., September 15,
1823, and was killed by falling from a load of hay, August
16, 1868. He was a Democrat, and a soldier in the civil
war. He was married at Keene, April 12, 1848, to Mary E.,
daughter of Levi and Sophronia Pond, who was born at
Keene, December 28, 1827. They had seven children, the
last of whom died young, all born at Keene, N. H.

    2061 LUCIUS EDWIN,[10] b. Aug. 30, 1849; d. Feb. 11, 1850.
    2062 MARY ELIZABETH,[10] b. Feb. 8, 1852; d. Dec. 6, 1853.
    2063* ELLA SOPHRONIA,[10] b. July 18, 1854.
    2064 ELIZABETH ANNA,[10] b. Feb. 26, 1857; d. unm. Sept. 3, 1880.
    2065 MARY ELLEN,[10] b. July 27, 1861; d. Aug. 13, 1861.
    2066 JULIA ELLEN,[10] b. May 19, 1866; d. Oct. 31, 1866.

1364. **Betsey Fuller,**[9] daughter of 687 Andrew[8] and
Louisa [Fuller] Balch, was born at Westmoreland, N. H.,
August 21, 1827, and lives at Keene, N. H. She was married at Westmoreland, April 1, 1847, to Joseph, son of Barney and Clarinda [Wilbur] Shelley, of Westmoreland. He
was born at Westmoreland, August 20, 1824, and died September 1, 1886. He was postmaster of Westmoreland for 15
years previous to his death. He was a Republican, and a
Seventh-Day Adventist. They had four children.

        WARREN WINFIELD, b. Nov. 22, 1849; m. Millie Streeter, of
          Westmoreland; has one daughter, *Ethel Shelley*, b. Dec.,
          1875.
        LOUISA JOSEPHINE, b. Feb. 27, 1848; m. Warren Wilbur, of
          Westmoreland, where they live, and have had four daughters
          and two sons.
        MARY EMELINE, b. Nov. 13, 1851; m. John D. Brown, of Chicago,
          Ill., in which city they live. They have one daughter,
          Florence.
        ALICE LUCILLA, b. Sept. 12, 1857; m. William Bretton, of Keene,
          N. H.; live in that city; no children.

1365. **Mary Elitia,**[9] daughter of 687 Andrew[8] and Louisa [Fuller] Balch, was born at Westmoreland, N. H., June 2, 1831. She was married at Westmoreland, January 22, 1857, to Charles Jefts, of Chester, Vt. They live at Owatonna, Minn. He is a merchant and a Democrat. They are Baptists, and have no children.

1366. John Edwin,[9] son of 687 Andrew[8] and Louisa [Fuller] Balch, was born at Westmoreland, N. H., April 27, 1833, and lives at Wilson [Witoka P. O.], Minnesota. He is a Republican, and a member of the Congregational church. He was married at Warren, Minn., September 5, 1859, to Lydia Martha, daughter of Levi and Martha [James] Reynolds. She was born in Ohio, November 25, 1841, and died at Ellington, Minn., February 9, 1869. They had four children.

2067* FRANCIS EDWIN,[10] b. Aug. 28, 1860.
2068* MARTHA LOUISA,[10] b. Dec. 7, 1862; d. Dec. 30, 1891.
2069   MARY IDA,[10] b. Oct. 22, 1865; d. Jan. 3, 1884.
2070* LEVI ANDREW,[10] b. Jan. 12, 1869.

John E. Balch was married a second time, July 15, 1869, to Margaret, daughter of John and ―― [Barbary] Wagner, who was born at Buffalo, New York, March 11, 1854. They had five children, all born at Wilson, Minn.

2071   LUCY JANE,[10] b. March 17, 1874.
2072   JOHN ADAMS,[10] b. April 23, 1876; d. Sept. 1, 1877.
2073   LYDIA ALICE,[10] b. July 24, 1879.
2074   JOHN EDWARD,[10] b. July 26, 1881.
2075   MARY ELIZA,[10] b. March 1, 1887.

1368. Sarah L.,[9] daughter of 688 Ezra[8] and Dorcas [Miller] Balch, was born at Keene, N. H., in 1826, and died in the same place, February 26, 1860. She married Clark Farrar.

1371. Ezra W.,[9] son of 690 Timothy[8] and Hannah [Randall] Balch, was born at Orwell, N. Y., September 12, 1825, and died September 18, 1862. He enlisted in company G, Twenty-fourth New York Infantry Volunteers. At the second battle of Bull Run, August 31, 1862, he was shot

through the left leg, above the knee, taken prisoner, and for
six days received little care. He was then taken to the Clifton Hospital at Washington, where his leg was amputated.
The stump became gangrenous, and ten days later secondary
hemorrhage took place, and he bled to death. He never married.

1373. **Nancy L.**,[9] daughter of 690 Timothy[8] and Hannah [Randall] Balch, was born at Orwell, N. Y., December
26, 1832. She was married December 13, 1849, to Wilbur,
son of William and Mary Blount. He was born August 10,
1819, at Barre, N. Y., and is a farmer at Ricard, N. Y. They
have five children : Nettie H., b. Dec. 13, 1850 ; Mary A.,
b. Oct. 1, 1852 ; Lewis P., b. Nov. 12, 1854 ; Herbert W.,
b. April 26, 1859 ; Cora B., b. Sept. 9, 1869.

1374. **Lucindia**,[9] daughter of 690 Timothy[8] and Hannah
[Randall] Balch, was born at Orwell, New York, March 22,
1834. She was twice married, first to Mr. B. Wells, and
second, on Dec. 8, 1890, to John, son of George H. and Polly
Chago. He was born June 23, 1841, at Sandy Creek, N. Y.,
where they live.

1380. **William**,[9] son of 691 John[8] and Eunice [Stowell]
Balch, was born at Orwell, New York, December 18, 1832,
and is a farmer at Mannsville, N. Y. He was married December 17, 1854, to Sarah M., daughter of Hiram and Polly
[Hill] Wheeler. She was born at Ellisburg, New York, February 2, 1835. Their four children were born at Ellisburg.

2076[a] ELLA,[10] b. Dec., 1858.
2077[a] IRA F.,[10] b. Jan. 2, 1862.
2078[a] MELVIN W.,[10] b. Jan. 9, 1865.
2079[a] DORA G.,[10] b. Dec. 30, 1871.

1381. **Orrin H.**,[9] son of 691 John[8] and Eunice [Stowell]
Balch, was born at Orwell, N. Y., March 31, 1835. He was
married September 4, 1856, to Catherine E., daughter of
Amos G. and Phebe [Steanburgh] Currey. She was born at
Oswego, October 22, 1834, and died at Mannsville, N. Y.,

October 14, 1876. They had five children ; the three eldest were born at Oswego, the two youngest at Orwell.

2080* CARRIE E.,[10] b. July 28, 1857.
2081* FREDERICK O.,[10] b. Oct. 28, 1861.
2082* HORACE E.,[10] b. July 7, 1865.
2083* IDA E.,[10] b. Nov. 2, 1867.
2084 ROSA MAY,[10] b. Sept. 10, 1871.

Orrin H. Balch married second, Clara C. [Vernam] Brown, a widow. They have one daughter, born at Mannsville.

2085 SADIE E.,[10] b. April 3, 1884.

Orrin H. served during the civil war in the 147th regiment, New York Infantry Volunteers. He is a member of Calvin Burch Post, No. 345, at Ellisburg, New York. He is a carriage ironer and general blacksmith.

1383. Ira,[9] son of 691 John[8] and Eunice [Stowell] Balch, was born at Orwell, N. Y., February 22, 1840. He was married March 18, 1860, to Mary E., daughter of Hiram and Polly [Hill] Wheeler. She was born December 30, 1839, at Mannsville, N. Y., where they now live, and he is a milk dealer. They have two children.

2086 ETTA L.,[10] b. Sept. 6, 1862, at Oswego, N. Y.
2087 HERBERT W.,[10] b. Oct. 15, 1870, at Ellisburg, N. Y.

1386. John H.,[9] son of 691 John[8] and Eunice [Stowell] Balch, was born January 24, 1849, at Orwell, New York, where he has a farm. He was married twice, first, August 28, 1868, to Mary E., daughter of Charles and Eliza Cutler, of Oak Grove, Wisconsin. She died at Orwell, November 3, 1878. They had three children, born at Orwell.

2088 CHARLES E.,[10] b. July 4, 1869.
2089 GEORGE W.,[10] b. May 26, 1871.
2090 ARTHUR A.,[10] b. Nov. 3, 1873.

John H. was married second, July 4, 1879, to Sarah E., daughter of Morgan and Frances [Hines] Greenfield. They have had three children, all born at Orwell.

2091 ROYCE H.,[10] b. June 4, 1880.
2092 JOHN H.,[10] b. Feb. 2, 1887.
2093 ORLO M.,[10] b. May 25, 1892.

1389. Artimicia M.,[9] daughter of 694 Daniel[8] and Betsey [West] Balch, was born May 19, 1829. She married Oct. 19, 1852, Nelson, son of John and Polly Carswell. He was born at Orwell, New York, where he was a farmer. March 30, 1868, he enlisted in a New York regiment, went to the front, and died in the service. After his death his widow went with her family to live in a part of the house with her sister Lurannah, who married Jonas Carswell, a brother to Nelson. The four children of Artimicia M. and Nelson Carswell were all born at Orwell : Bertha Teressa, b. March 5, 1854, d. April 9, 1874; Paris DeWitt, b. March 5, 1857, d. March 27, 1858 ; Paris DeWitt, b. May 16, 1859, d. -June 24, 1859 ; Nelson Leroy, b. Nov. 16, 1861, d. Jan. 17, 1878.

1391. Lurannah,[9] daughter of 694 Daniel[8] and Betsey [West] Balch, was born in June, 1833, and died of consumption, October 26, 1877. She was married December 30, 1857, to Jonas Carswell. He served in the Union army during the civil war. He died January 28, 1878.

1392. Cyrus Decatur,[9] son of 698 Ebenezer[8] and Lydia [Shepard] Balch, was born in 1812, in northern Vermont, and died in Meigs county, Ohio, in 1877. In 1832 he married Margaret Wakely, who was born in 1817, and died in 1862. They had six children, two born in Warren county, Pa., and four in Athens county, Ohio.

2094* SAMUEL,[10] b. June 26, 1833.
2095 EBENEZER,[10] b. 1835; d. 1837.
2096 MARY JANE,[10] b. 1840; lives at Hollister, Ohio.
2097 SOPHRONA,[10] b. 1843; lives Chicago Junction, Ohio.
2098* CYRUS,[10] b. July 5, 1850; d. Aug. 1, 1881.
2099 MARIA,[10] b. 1854; lives Bear Lake, Michigan.

Cyrus Decatur[9] married second, Winifred Logan, in 1863. By her he had five children.

2100 GEORGE,[10] b. 1864; d. 1869.
2101 LAURA,[10] b. 1866; d. 1869.
2102 HOWARD C.,[10] b. Aug., 1872; lives Meigs county, Ohio.
2103 EMMETT,[11] b. 1875; adopted to Wesley Benson.
2104 HATTIE,[11] b. 1876; d. 1877.

Cyrus Decatur was a farmer. Soon after his marriage he moved from Alleghany county, N. Y., to Warren county, Pa., where their two eldest children were born. Then they moved to Athens county, Ohio, and later to Meigs county, in the same state.

1394. **Ebenezer Washington,**[9] son of 698 Ebenezer[8] and Lydia [Shepard] Balch, was born about 1819, and was killed by being knocked from a car into a coal shaft. He married Catherine Smith, in Athens county, Ohio. They had two children.

2105 EBENEZER,[10] b.
2106 LYDIA,[10] b.

1395. **Christopher Columbus,**[9] son of 698 Ebenezer[8] and Lydia [Shepard] Balch, was born about 1821, and died in 1848. He was married to Charlotte Pierce in 1845. She was born in England, and died at Knight's Creek, Alleghany county, N. Y., in February, 1873. Soon after his marriage he enlisted in the army and went to Mexico. He served through nearly the whole of the Mexican war, when he died. They had one son.

2107* GEORGE W.,[10] b. Dec. 20, 1846.

1396. **John Quincy Adams,**[9] son of 698 Ebenezer[8] and Lydia [Shepard] Balch, was born in New York state, April 6, 1825, and died at St. Louis, Mo., August 28, 1887. He was married in 1849, in Athens county, Ohio, to Sarah, daughter of John Burton. Burton was a soldier in the war of 1812. They had eight children.

2108 ALICE,[10] b.
2109 HARRIET ANN,[10] b.
2110 ELI,[10] b.   ; d. y.
2111 QUINCY ADAMS,[10] b.   ; lives in St. Louis.
2112 EBENEZER,[10] b.   ; lives in St. Louis.
2113* GEORGE H.,[10] b. 1859; lives in St. Louis.
2114 KATIE GENEVA,[10] b.
2115 IDA BELL,[10] b.

John Q. A. Balch served through the Mexican war; was in

the battles of Palo Alto, Monterey, Chepultepec, Contreras, and at the capture of the City of Mexico. He was a farmer, and a member of the Baptist church.

1398. Andrew Jackson,[9] son of 698 Ebenezer[8] and Lydia [Shepard] Balch, was born in Alleghany county, N. Y., December 1, 1838, and died at Galena, Kansas, November 3, 1894. He married Elizabeth Watts, in Athens county, Ohio, August 6, 1859. She was born in Athens county, Ohio, June 4, 1842. She was the daughter of Richard and Cassie Watts. Andrew J. enlisted in company I, 92d Ohio Volunteers, and was with that regiment in many battles. He was a boot and shoe maker. Their children were:

2116* CASSANDRA,[10] b. June 21, 1860.
2117* RICHARD JOHNSON,[10] b. Nov. 6, 1863.
2118 CORA,[10] b. Feb. 2, 1868.
2119* NELLIE,[10] b. Dec. 5, 1871; m.
2120* LUCY,[10] b. Dec. 17, 1873; m.
2121 HELEN,[10] b. Jan. 27, 1875.
2122 WILLIAM A.,[10] b. Oct. 27, 1876; lives at Galena, Kansas.
2123 ELIZABETH,[10] b. Nov. 23, 1878.

1402. Benjamin Franklin,[9] son of 698 Ebenezer[8] and Lydia [Shepard] Balch, was born in Wayne county, N. Y., in 1842. He was married to Miss Rebecca Walker, in Meigs county, Ohio. She died December 19, 1884. They had four children.

2124 ANDREW J.,[10] b.
2125 BENJAMIN F.,[10] b.
2126 MARY M.,[10] b.
2127* QUENNIE V.,[10] b. 1871.

On the third of April, 1861, Benjamin Franklin Balch enlisted in company A, 17th Ohio Infantry, a three months' regiment. They were in the first battle of Bull Run, under Gen. Hunter, above the bridge. He was captured, paroled, went home to Ohio, was exchanged July 29, re-enlisted into company O, 18th Ohio, on the 7th of the following month, for three years. At the battle of Stone River, Tenn., he was badly wounded, and left on the field for dead, and put in

Pine Forest prison for eight and a half months, was then taken to Mobile, and from thence to Andersonville, where he remained nearly nine months. He kept the record of dates by cutting notches on a stick. Finally he escaped at night through a tunnel, and after great hardships, reached Gen. Sherman's lines, 15 miles south of Dalton, barefooted, bareheaded, and scarcely a garment left on his emaciated body, which was reduced from 175 to 115 pounds weight. After 15 days' rest, he went to Washington, was interviewed by President Lincoln, and given some money by him with which to go home to Ohio. In Key's "Andersonville Prison" he is spoken of as the man who acted as prosecutor at the trial of the New York toughs, which resulted in the hanging of several of them for murder. Soon after his return home from Washington he re-enlisted into company I, 92d Ohio Volunteers. At the battle of Columbia, S. C., he was permanently disabled by a wound in his left hand.

1403. **Elmina M.,**[9] daughter of 701 John[8] and Lucy [Williams] Balch, was born at Burlington, Vt., February 6, 1826, and lives at Morrisonville, N. Y. She was married November 25, 1845, to Edger, son of Shadrach and Susan Place. He was born at Shelburn, Vt., December 2, 1825, and is a blacksmith. They had four children.

> MARY ELIZA, b. Nov. 25, 1846, at Burlington, Vt.; d. Dec. 25, 1890; m. Wm. V. Greeley. Children: *Clara Elmina, Edward Peck.*
>
> EDWARD EUGENE, b. June 9, 1848, at Addison, Vt.; m. Ida A. Loyd. Two daughters: *Jessie May, Alice Elmina.*
>
> GEORGE SHADRACH, b. Feb. 6, 1850, at Vergennes, Vt.; m. first, Julia Ladue; second, Lilia J. Blanchard. Daughter, *Ruth Galusha.*
>
> FRANK CEYLON, b. May 6, 1857, at Morrisonville, N. Y.; m. Maggie S. Chalmers; no children.

1404. **John,**[9] son of 701 John[8] and Lucy [Williams] Balch, was born at Burlington, Vt., November 12, 1827, and is an ordained minister in the Iowa Wesleyan Methodist Conference. He married, May 5, 1845, Eunice, daughter of

Henry and Sally Baldwin, who was born at Crown Point, N.
Y., March 10, 1830. They have had seven children.

2128* MARY ELIZA,[10] b. May 28, 1849.
2129 WILLIAM WARNER,[10] b. Nov. 16, 1853; d. July 16, 1856.
2130* MELISSA MARIA,[10] b. Sept. 15, 1856.
2131* WILLIAM WARNER,[10] b. June 10, 1859.
2132* BENJAMIN ILIFF.[10] b. April 18, 1861.
2133* LUCY ELMINA,[10] b. Aug. 16, 1863.
2134* MIRIAM ELIZABETH,[10] b. Sept. 10, 1870.

1405. **Emeline Robinson,**[9] daughter of 701 John[8] and
Lucy [Williams] Balch, was born at Westford, Vt., May 4,
1830, and died September 28, 1886. She was married first to
Ruben Heath, by whom she had one son, George E., who
lives at Gardner, Mass.

Emeline R. was divorced from Heath, and married Lincoln
Whitcomb, by whom she had one son, William L., who lives
in Boston.

1406. **Martha Eliza,**[9] daughter of 701 John[8] and Lucy
[Williams] Balch, was born at Addison, Vt., September 15,
1832, and lives at Jay, N. Y. On January 1, 1855, she married Arthur, son of Jesse and Laura Benedict. He was born
October 7, 1832. Their children are ; Mary Jane, b. May
5, 1856 ; Laura Adelaide, b. Dec. 19, 1859 ; Walter Wesley,
b. Dec. 11, 1864 ; Richard Arthur, b. Sept. 15, 1869.

1416. **Cyrus Munson,**[9] son of 704 Cyrus[8] and Asenith
[Robinson] Balch, was born at Carlisle, Ohio, June 5, 1839.
He is an engineer at South Haven, Mich. He served in the
army during the civil war. He was married July 18, 1864,
to Mercy M., daughter of Peter and Mandana Frear. She
was born at Collamer, Ohio. They had five children, one
born at Grafton, Ohio, one born at Hastings, Michigan, and
the others at South Haven.

2135 MARY E.,[10] b. June 15, 1865; d. Jan. 18, 1872.
2136 AGNES F.,[10] b. July 27, 1868.
2137 KITTIE MINNIE,[10] b. Dec. 9, 1870.
2138 CARRIE ALICE,[10] b. Dec. 29, 1876.
2139 CHARLES ALBERT,[10] b. Jan. 18, 1882; d. Feb. 5, 1882.

1417. Mary Ermina,[9] daughter of 704 Cyrus[8] and Asenith [Robinson] Balch, was born at Carlisle, Ohio, September 10, 1842. She was married March 10, 1866, to William, son of Joel Taylor. He died at Parma, Mich., April 29, 1866. No children.

1418. Caroline Elizabeth,[9] daughter of 704 Cyrus[8] and Asenith [Robinson] Balch, was born at Carlisle, Ohio, January 15, 1845. She was married January 27, 1869, to Frank, son of James and Mary Campbell. He was born at Princeton, Canada, May 30, 1846, and is a farmer at Winsor, N. D. They have had three children, all born at Rutland, Mich. Bert, b. Oct. 10, 1868 ; Ella, b. Nov. 30, 1870, d. Oct. 10, 1880 ; Ray, b. Sept. 10, 1882.

1420. James William,[9] son of 704 Cyrus[8] and Asenith [Robinson] Balch, was born at Carlisle, Ohio, November 13, 1849. He is a stock ranchman, and lives at Jamestown, N. D. He was married March 18, 1868, to Henrietta Amelia, daughter of Timothy M. and Sarah [Palmer] Bush. She was born at Fitchville, Ohio, February 22, 1850. They have had four children, all born at Hastings, Mich.

2140 GEORGE B.,[10] b. Dec. 22, 1868.
2141 FRANK,[10] b. Nov. 13, 1870.
2142 IDA,[10] b. March 16, 1873.
2143 EDITH,[10] b. March 29, 1880.

1421. Cyrus Henry,[9] son of 706 Ely Stone[8] and Philura [Southard] Balch, was born at Addison, Vt., January 16, 1830, and died at Saginaw, Mich., May 23, 1857. He was married August 13, 1854, to Harriet M., daughter of Jerrious and Irene [Ashman] Bissett, who was born at Milford, Mich., June 2, 1840. They lived at Saginaw, Mich., where he was engaged in the sawmills, and was killed while attending a lathe saw, by a piece of lumber crushing his skull. He was a fine looking man, and much liked by all who knew him. They had one child.

2144 ELENOR MALICA,[10] b. Feb. 27, 1857; unm.

1422 **Martha Helen**,[9] daughter of 706 Ely Stone[8] and Philura [Southard] Balch, was born at Addison, Vt., March 12, 1832. She was married June 25, 1859, to Amos Fowler, son of James and Abigail [Fowler] Barnard. He was born at Cohocton, N. Y., July 2, 1820. He is a farmer; lived at Handy, Michigan, where their children were born: Albert Dwight, b. Nov. 7, 1860; Captola Verginia, b. Feb. 2, 1863, d. Jan. 17, 1865; Fred Johnson, b. May 23, 1865; Sir Willard, b. Aug. 16, 1866; Helen Gladstone, b. Nov. 20, 1867; Charles Henry, b. July 7, 1875.

1424. **Delia Ann Elmina**,[9] daughter of 706 Eli Stone[8] and Philura [Southard] Balch, was born at Summerfield, Mich., September 14, 1836. She was married December 7, 1856, to Charles Bulsby, son of Platt and Elenor [Ricar] Johnson. He was born June 3, 1835, at Pontiac, Michigan, where he is a farmer, and their five children were born. Albert Henry, b. Oct. 26, 1857; Frederic and Eli, twins, b. Dec. 27, 1861, d. y.; Alonzo J., b. April 16, 1865; Arthur Finsted, b. Oct. 12, 1874.

1426. **Emaline**,[9] daughter of 706 Eli Stone and Adeline [Coffin] Balch, was born at Conway, Mich., July 31, 1847. She married, June 18, 1878, Horatio M., son of Jerrious and Irene [Ashman] Bissett. He was born at Milford, Oakland county, Mich., April 6, 1843, and is a sailor. They have six children; the eldest was born at Pontiac, the others at Au Gres, Michigan: Helen Mabel Irene, b. Aug. 22, 1879; Edith Blanche, b. June 21, 1881; Grace Coffin, b. April 27, 1883; Grover C. Balch, b. June 16, 1885; Charles Gardner, b. June 26, 1887; Maud Charlien, b. Aug. 6, 1889.

1427. **Eliza H.**,[9] daughter of 711 Abner[8] and Lydia [Woodbury] Balch, was born at Concord, Vermont, July 19, 1832, and died at Littleton, New Hampshire, December 8, 1868. She was married June 19, 1853, to Harvey P., son of Samuel and Fanny P. Ross. He was born at Bath, New Hampshire, January 18, 1831, and is an express messenger and farmer. They lived at Bath, and had three children, two born at Bath and one at Littleton. Samuel, b. June 1, 1855 ; Mary Ellen, b. July 24, 1858 ; Ellwood Jackman, b. Sept. 28, 1863.

1428. Almira,[9] daughter of 711 Abner[8] and Lydia [Woodbury] Balch, was born at Concord, Vermont, July 2, 1834, and died at Bath, New Hampshire, November 25, 1861. She was married November 7, 1859, to Sumner W., son of Jonathan and Lucretia Lewis. He was born at Concord, April 6, 1829, and died at West Concord, November 30, 1885. He was a machinist, and they lived at West Concord, where their only son was born, Frank Balch, b. Aug. 30, 1861. He is a druggist at Whitefield, N. H. He was married Sept. 27, 1888, to Lizzie E., daughter of Clarence H. and Lucy O. [Burroughs] Dudley. She was born at Concord, April 30, 1866. They had no children.

Sumner W. Lewis served through the civil war in the Eighth Vermont Infantry, and rose from the ranks to a lieutenancy. He married second, August 8, 1872, Sabrina, daughter of Asa and Mary [Powers] Smith, who was born at Lunenburg, June 4, 1847, and died at West Concord, April 18, 1885. They had one son, Fred A., b. July 26, 1876.

1429. William Henry,[9] son of 711 Abner[8] and Lydia [Woodbury] Balch, was born January 11, 1837, and died at Bath, N. H., November 13, 1865. He was a mechanic, and lived at Bath. He married in 1860, Caroline Ann Buswell, of Lebanon, N. H. She died Sept. 18, 1882. They had two children.

2145   Joseph,[10] b.   ; d. y.
2146* Alfred C.,[10] b. Nov. 28, 1862.

1431. Ellen J.,[9] daughter of 711 Abner[8] and Lydia [Woodbury] Balch, was born February 27, 1842. She was married November 29, 1871, to Andrew C. Rollins, a railroad conductor. He was the son of John D. and Sarah H. Rollins, and was born July 9, 1843. They have one child, born at White River Junction, Vt., George R., b. Feb. 22, 1873.

1433. Byron Bliss,[9] son of 711 Abner[8] and Lydia [Woodbury] Balch, was born at Bath, N. H., November 23, 1848. He has a drug store at Chicopee, Mass. He was married November 25, 1875, to Edna M., daughter of Warren and Mary G. Simonds. She was born at Templeton, Mass., October 3, 1856. They have two children, both born at Springfield, Mass.

2147 MAUDE LYDIA,[10] b. Oct. 20, 1876.
2148 GEORGE WARREN,[10] b. Oct. 5, 1882.

1434. Ellen Almira,[9] daughter of 713 Alfred[8] and Elizabeth [Cory] Balch, was born at Lebanon, N. H., May 31, 1844. She married June 22, 1872, Theodore Francis, son of Edwin S. and Clara [Reed] Hovey. They live in Boston, Mass., and have two children : Clara May, b. Sept. 10, 1875 ; Alfred Balch, b. Dec. 6, 1876.

1435. Charles Parkhurst,[9] son of 713 Alfred[8] and Elizabeth [Cory] Balch, was born at Lebanon, N. H., August 10, 1845, and is superintendent of an elevator at Johnsonville, Tennessee. He married Mollie A. Estes, who died Nov. 25, 1890. They had four children.

2149 JESSIE M.,[10] b. June 9, 1881; d. Aug. 29, 1881.
2150 LUCIEN,[10] b. Mar. 17, 1883.
2151 ALICE MAUD,[10] b. Jan. 27, 1887.
2152 CHARLES PARKHURST,[10] b. Oct. 17, 1890 ; d. Nov. 4, 1890.

1436. Pliny Earl,[9] son of 713 Alfred[8] and Elizabeth [Cory] Balch, was born at Lebanon, N. H., January 25, 1847. He was married June 27, 1874, to Annie E., daughter of Harbard and Phoebe [Garrison] Fansler. She was born April 20, 1851, at Belleville, Ind. They live at Plainfield, Ind., where he is a carriage painter. They have four children.

2153* CORA MABEL,[10] b. Sept. 1, 1875.
2154 ALFRED CLARENCE,[10] b. June 6, 1878.
2155 HARBARD FANSLER,[10] b. April 28, 1880.
2156 GRAYDON A.,[10] b. July 27, 1891.

1437. Frank Mortimer,[9] son of 713 Alfred[8] and Eliza-

beth [Cory] Balch, was born at Lebanon, N. H., June 10,
1849. He married Mrs. Stella Walker Emerson, daughter of
Thomas and Maria [Gould] Walker. They live at Wakefield, Massachusetts, and have no children.

1439. **Alice Maud,**[9] daughter of 713 Alfred[8] and Elizabeth [Cory] Balch, was born at Lebanon, N. H., January 21,
1853. She was married September 4, 1879, to Algernon M.,
son of Calvin and Jane [Greeley] Stevens. He was born
June 27, 1846, at Tiskilwa, Ill. He is a stockman, and they
live at Janesville, Minn., and have two children: Calvin
Balch, b. July 6, 1886, d. Oct. 6, 1886; Rosalie Cora, b. Jan.
9, 1889, at Tiskilwa, Ill.

1440. **Rosalie,**[9] daughter of 713 Alfred[8] and Elizabeth
[Cory] Balch, was born at Lebanon, N. H., September 6,
1855. She was married September 6, 1876, to Charles M.,
son of Bradford Newcomb and Lydia [Alden] Stevens. He
was born February 6, 1848, at Tiskilwa, Ill. They live at
Tiskilwa, and have had four children, born in that town:
Alfred Newcomb, b. Jan. 13, 1879, d. July 4, 1880; Arline
Alice, b. May 10, 1880; John Alden, b. Oct. 26, 1882, d.
Dec. 15, 1884; Charles Harold, b. Jan. 29, 1884, d. Aug. 22,
1889.

1441. **Alvah Abner,**[9] son of 713 Alfred[8] and Elizabeth
[Cory] Balch, was born September 5, 1857, and lives at Columbus, Ohio. He was married October 27, 1887, to Jennie,
daughter of John G. and Elizabeth [Weaver] Bassey, who
was born March 8, 1865, at Jasper, Ohio.

1451. **Sarah Belle,**[9] daughter of 721 Benjamin[8] and
Lucy [Cary] Balch, was born May 26, 1849. She was mar-
ried December 10, 1873, to William G. Smith. Daughter,
Gale Balch, b. Oct. 4, 1874.

1452. **Frank,**[9] son of 721 Benjamin[8] and Lucy [Cary]
Balch, was born July 28, 1852, and lives at Union, N. Y. He
was married December 22, 1878, to Jenny Williams. They
have had three children.

2157 BULA,[10] b   ; d. in infancy.
2158 LAURA,[10] b. July 1, 1877.
2159 IRENE,[10] b. Jan. 12, 1886.

1456. Elnora,[9] daughter of 722 Matthew Stanley[8] and Maria [Eldridge] Balch, was born in 1848, in St. Johnsbury, Vt., and is not living. She married James Layton, by whom she had four children. Only one, a daughter, survived her.

1458. Esther Alice,[9] daughter of 725 James Britton[8] and Phoebe Eliza [Decker] Balch, was born at Union, N. Y., October 4, 1850. She was married at Owego, N. Y., September 20, 1876, to Edgar Zabriskie, who is an adjuster and public accountant. He was born in New York city, April 1, 1840. They reside at Omaha, Neb., and have had three children, the youngest of whom is living. Albert C., born Feb. 12, 1878, d. June 18, 1878 ; Helen B., b. May 4, 1882, d. May 7, 1882 ; Edgar Britton, b. Jan. 28, 1888.

1459. Thur,[9] son of 725 James Britton[8] and Phoebe Eliza [Decker] Balch, was born at Union, N. Y., October 19, 1852. He was married October 80, 1890, to Anna, daughter of Adolph and Bertha [Lohman] Nissen. He is now in business in Chicago, and is a member of the Board of Trade. They have one child.

2160 RUTH,[10] b. Oct. 31, 1891.

1460. Emma Ann Stanley,[9] daughter of 725 James Britton[8] and Phoebe Eliza [Decker] Balch, was born at Binghamton, N. Y., March 25, 1856, and is living in Chicago. She was married Dec. 13, 1879, to Henry Lane Carpenter, who was born Aug. 15, 1856, at Lone Rock, Wisconsin, and died Dec. 8, 1883, at Papillion, Nebraska. They had two children, one of whom died young. The other, Mildred Henry, b. Dec. 28, 1883, is living at Union, N. Y.

1464. Albert F.,[9] son of 730 John Wetherby[8] and Louisa C. [Stevens] Balch, was born at Littleton, N. H., April 11, 1855. He graduated at Cornell University in 1877 ; then he entered the employ of the Fairbanks, of St. Johnsbury,

Vt., as cashier. After remaining in the service of this firm a few years, he moved to Marshalltown, Iowa, and went into the Marshalltown State Bank. He was married January 20, 1888, to Nettie McVey, of Burlington, Iowa.

2161 LOUISA RUTH,[10] b. Nov. 20, 1888.

1465. Phineas S.,[9] son of 730 John Wetherby[8] and Louisa C. [Stevens] Balch, was born at Littleton, N. H., April 27, 1857. He was a clerk in the First National Bank of St. Johnsbury, Vt., for a few years, and then moved to Marshalltown, Iowa. He was married September 20, 1883, to Nellie Willigrod, of Marshalltown, Iowa.

2162 CATHERINE LOUISA,[10] b. Sept. 10, 1885.
2163 JOHN W.,[10] b. July 15, 1887.

1466. Mary E.,[9] daughter of 731 Samuel Albert[8] and Agnes [Lacy] Balch, was born in New York city, June 22, 1863. She was married January 18, 1882, to George H. Smalley. He is a member of the New York fire department, and lives at No. 5 Watts street, New York. They had one child, Frank, born January 5, 1883, died July 26, 1883.

1468. Sylvia W.,[9] daughter of 734 James[8] and Fanny [Smith] Balch, was born Sept. 29, 1839, at Lunenburg, Vermont, and died October 15, 1892. She was married January 1, 1863, to Luie B. Hartshorn, who lives at St. Johnsbury, Vermont. Their children are: Kate, b. Nov. 6, 1863, m. M. L. Miner; James E., b. Aug. 26, 1865; Fanny Fern, b. March 3, 1868, m. Gilbert E. Woods.

1469. Emeline M.,[9] daughter of 734 James[8] and Fanny [Smith] Balch, was born November 5, 1840, at Lunenburg, Vermont, and died July 28, 1874. She was married August 3, 1871, to John B. Blandin. They had one son, Lyman. After her death he married her sister 1474 Lucy E.

1470. Austin A.,[9] son of 734 James[8] and Fanny [Smith] Balch, was born at Lunenburg, Vermont, January 8, 1842, and is a merchant at Penacook, New Hampshire. He was married December 14, 1865, to Mary E., daughter of Jonathan and Hannah Whipple. She was born at Northumberland, N. H., May 24, 1865. They have two children.

2164ª HATTIE MAE,[10] b. Nov. 11, 1866.
2165ª JAMES WHIPPLE,[10] b. Dec. 28, 1870, at Lancaster, N. H.

1473. Gardner H.,[9] son of 784 James[8] and Fanny [Smith] Balch, was born December 7, 1848, at Lunenburg, Vermont, where he now lives. He married, September 1, 1870, Augusta M. Hartshorn. She was born February 10, 1854. They have had six children, all born in Lunenburg, the last of whom died young.

2166 LORENZO H.,[10] b. Sept. 27, 1873.
2167 MYRA A.,[10] b. Feb. 10, 1876.
2168 EUGENE G.,[10] b. Oct. 27, 1878.
2169 CHARLES H.,[10] b. Aug. 25, 1884.
2170 ERNESTENE,[10] b. March 1, 1888.

1475. Laura L.,[9] daughter of 785 Edward A.[8] and Mary [Ingerson] Balch, was born at Lunenburg, Vt., February 15, 1848. She was married May 12, 1878, to Mahlon M., son of William W. and Michael [Holcomb] Young. He was born at Stephentown, N. Y., December 31, 1836. They live at Dixon, Illinois, and have three children: Edward Clare, b. April 2, 1879 ; Homer Lyle, b. July 30, 1881 ; Enla, b. March 30, 1883.

1476. George Edward,[9] son of 785 Edward A.[8] and Mary [Ingerson] Balch, was born at Jefferson, N. H., October 25, 1853, and is a farmer at Water Valley, Mississippi. He was married February 17, 1878, to Caroline M., daughter of John and Caroline [Bell] Law. She was born October 29, 1852, at Scarboro, Ontario, Canada. They have two children, born at Harmon, Illinois.

2171 BERTRAM CLINT,[10] b. Jan. 15, 1880.
2172 ALICE VERE,[10] b. July 6, 1881.

1477. William E.,[9] son of 741 George Sherman[8] and Eliza M. [Glins] Balch, was born at Lunenburg, Vt., February 8, 1854. He holds the position of state taxidermist. He has rendered much assistance in obtaining records of the descendants of 179 Lieut. Benjamin. He was married September 27, 1876, to Ella, daughter of Jourden and Lois A. [Powers] Marr. She was born at Lewiston, Maine, January 27, 1857. They have two children.

2173 FLORENCE M.,[10] b. Sept. 14, 1877.
2174 WALTER H.,[10] b. Feb. 14, 1888.

1478. George A.,[9] son of 741 George Sherman[8] and Eliza M. [Glins] Balch, was born at Lunenburg, Vt., September 27, 1855, and is a casket manufacturer at Lunenburg. He was married June 28, 1882, to Harriet B., daughter of Joseph H. and Harriet [Miles] Benton. She was born at Bradford, Vt., February 3, 1858.

1479. Herbert F.,[9] son of 741 George Sherman[8] and Eliza M. [Glins] Balch, was born at Lunenburg, Vt., September 28, 1857, and is a clerk in the employ of the Boston & Maine road, residing at Lyndonville, Vermont. He was married October 5, 1879, to Susan E., daughter of Arthur H. and Louisa W. [Phelps] Dean. She was born at Lunenburg, Vt., December 29, 1857. They have one child, born at Lyndonville, Vt.

2175 GRACE D.,[10] b. Aug. 18, 1886.

1480. Karl O.,[9] son of 741 George Sherman[8] and Eliza M. [Glins] Balch, was born at Lunenburg, Vt., July 4, 1860. He was married February 24, 1887, to Mabel Thomas, daughter of C. W. and S. [Bell] Thomas, of Lunenburg. She was born at Lunenburg, December 4, 1866. They reside at Lunenburg. He is a wholesale dry goods agent.

1482. Frank A.,[9] son of 753 George[8] and Elizabeth H. [Aldrich] Balch, was born at Concord, Vt., May 14, 1847. He was married December 30, 1868, to Mary Emma Smith. She was born in Philadelphia, Pa., July 24, 1849. Their home is in Davenport, Iowa, and they have five children.

2176* JAMES E.,[10] b. Jan. 27, 1870.
2177 GRACE ALDRICH,[10] b. Aug. 28, 1871.
2178* EDWIN FRAZER,[10] b. July 29, 1873.

2179 GEORGE HENRY,[10] b. Sept. 25, 1874.
2180 FRANK A.,[10] b. Sept. 2, 1876.

About 1885 Frank A. went to Omaha, Nebraska, and engaged in hotel keeping for six years. During the World's Columbian Fair he was the manager of the Revere House, in Chicago.

1485. Addie Louise,[9] daughter of 754 Stephen Moore[8] and Olive A. [Kimball] Balch, was born at Kennebec, Maine, October 8, 1860. She was married at San Francisco, California, September 15, 1884, to Arthur F., son of James and Frances R. Thane. He is a commission merchant in San Francisco, where they are living. They have two children : Arthur C., b. May 18, 1886; Alma, b. Dec. 11, 1887.

Descendants of 40 Israel.[4]

1486. Abigail,[9] daughter of 759 John[8] and Sybil [Barrow] Balch, was born at Marcellus, N. Y., December 12, 1815, and died at Marietta, N. Y., May 9, 1891. She married Samuel D. Hall, who was born at Onondaga, N. Y., December 8, 1812, and died February 16, 1894. They lived at Marietta, N. Y., and had one son, Charles J., b. Oct. 3, 1850. He married Eliza Champlain, Jan. 6, 1875, and has one son, Frederick D., b. March 25, 1876.

1487. James,[9] son of 759 John[8] and Sybil [Barrow] Balch, was born at Marcellus, N. Y., May 7, 1819, and died February 14, 1892, and was buried in Amber Cemetery, Orisco, N. Y. He was a farmer, a republican and a Universalist. He was married July 28, 1845, to Laura, daughter of Jonah and Susan Henderson. They had two children.

2181 JAY,[10] b. Nov. 30, 1858; d. Jan. 27, 1861.
2182ᵉ DELLA E.,[10] b. Apr. 24, 1865.

1488. Adelphia,[9] daughter of 759 John[8] and Sybil [Barrow] Balch, was born at Marcellus, N. Y., December 12, 1821. She died at Norvel, Mich. She married Edward Fay, a farmer. They had two sons. George H. is dead. He was a lawyer at Jackson, Mich. Charles is a doctor, graduated at the Ann Arbor Medical College.

1490. Holland,[9] son of 760 Ira[8] and Margaret [Baker] Balch, was born at Onondaga, N. Y., January 31, 1825. He is a carpenter at Sodus, N. Y. He was married November 22, 1848, to Jane E., daughter of John and Helen Lund. She was born in Yorkshire, England, January 15, 1831. They have had five children.

2183 HELEN L.,[10] b. Jan. 12, 1852, at Sodus, N. Y.
2184* CHARLES M.,[10] b. Sept. 2, 1855, at Sodus, N. Y.
2185 JULIA A.,[10] b. Nov. 5, 1857, d. Dec. 10, 1862.
2186 HARRIET M.,[10] b. Oct. 20, 1860, at Genessee, N. Y.
2187 JENNIE E.,[10] b. Sept. 22, 1867, at Sodus, N. Y.

1491. Mary,[9] daughter of 760 Ira[8] and Margaret [Baker] Balch, was born at Onondaga, N. Y., July 21, 1827, and died at Sodus, New York, March 20, 1892. She was married February 20, 1851, to Robert, son of William Lund. He was born May 2, 1811, in Yorkshire, Eng., and died March 6, 1872, at Sodus. They had four children, all born at Sodus. Martha Augusta, b. Nov. 12, 1855; James Helson, b. Aug. 29, 1862; George Elmer, b. Feb. 20, 1865, d. Feb. 1, 1877; Edward Orrin, b. July 23, 1868.

1494. Caroline,[9] daughter of 760 Ira[8] and Margaret [Baker] Balch, was born at Sodus, N. Y., May 28, 1835, and died at Sodus, New York, August 30, 1889. She was married September 12, 1859 to Walter, son of Ephrim Tetor. He was born at Sodus, October 4, 1837. They resided at Sodus where their four children were born. Mary Ella, b. April 8, 1861; George Elmer, b. Feb. 24, 1863; Rose Adella, b. Aug. 31, 1868; Emily Eliza, b. Dec. 29, 1871.

1496. Orrin,[9] son of 760 Ira[8] and Margaret [Baker] Balch, was born at Sodus, N. Y., June 4, 1840. He was married December 29, 1863, to Hannah Adelade, daughter of Elisha Burdick. She was born March 2, 1845, in Delaware Co., N. Y. Orrin is a farmer, at Poplar Grove, Illinois, where their five children were born.

2188 THOMAS JOHN,[10] b. July 10, 1865; d. Oct. 15, 1875.
2189 WILLIAM HENRY,[10] b. Sept. 4, 1868.

2190 CAROLINE AMANDA, [10] b. Aug. 14, 1871.
2191 MARY LOUISA,[10] b. Nov. 5, 1874, d. Mar. 17, 1877.
2192 PHEBE JANE,[10] b. Apr. 12, 1878.

Orrin and his wife separated November 17, 1880, the children going with their mother, and they reside at Ogden, Illinois, and he was married again December 2, 1885, to Hannah Ester McCann. She was born in Pennsylvania, in 1866 and died at Poplar Grove, December 14, 1895.

2193 LILLIAN ELSY,[10] b. Jan. 31, 1892.

1499. Jude Henry,[9] son of 764 David[8] and Polly [Comstock] Balch, was born at Ridgeway, N. Y., July 5, 1833, and resides at Janesville, Wisconsin. He graduated from the Buffalo, N. Y., Commercial College ; was three years a student at Wilson Collegiate Institute, N. Y.; one year as teacher at Oxford Institute, Michigan ; served three terms as clerk of the lower house, and one term as clerk of the Senate of Wisconsin ; two terms as deputy register of deeds, Rock County, Wisconsin ; two years as justice of the peace and four years as city assessor. Since 1886 he has been bookkeeper in the Rock County National Bank. He was married March 20, 1858, at Oakland, Mich., to Olivia L. Newman. They have three children.

2194 FRANK ERVYN,[10] b. Jan. 12, 1859, d. Apr. 17, 1861.
2195[c] FRED JAY,[10] b. July 17, 1862.
2196[c] CARLYN JUDE,[10] b. July 19, 1865.

1500. Lydia Almira,[9] daughter of 764 David[8] and Polly [Comstock] Balch, was born at Ridgeway, N. Y., November 8, 1835. She was married December 31, 1863, to Truman A. Bacon, of Ridgeway, they reside at Medina, N. Y., and have two children. Louis Allen, b. Feb. 14, 1865, m. Dec. 10, 1893, Anna House ; Nellie Diantha b. Sept. 28, 1869.

1502. William Jackson,[9] son of 764 David[8] and Polly [Comstock] Balch, was born at Ridgeway, N. Y., February 18, 1848, and lives on the old homestead at Medina, N. Y. He was married at Medina, February 18, 1869, to Edna M., daughter of John and Huldah [Bullard] Leighton. She was born March 29, 1845, and died February 16, 1875. They had two children.

2197 AILEEN EDNA,[10] b. Sept. 19, 1870, d. Apr. 30, 1879.
2198 BARRY LEIGHTON,[10] b. May 1, 1874.

William J. was married second at Ridgeway, N. Y., January 29, 1880, to Eva F., daughter of James and Jane [Powell] Hesse. She was born December 28, 1857. They have one child.

2199 VERA EVELYN,[10] b. July 18, 1882.

1503. Charles Irwin,[9] son of 764 David[8] and Polly [Comstock] Balch, was born at Ridgeway, N. Y., February 10, 1849. He was married at Ridgeway, N. Y., February 27, 1884, to Jennie L. Hesse, who was born at Medina, N. Y.

2200 EDMUND IRWIN,[10] b. Aug. 5, 1886.
2201 MABLE JENNIE,[10] b. Dec. 6, 1887.
2202 OLGA HESSE,[10] b. Apr. 30, 1890.
2203 PERCIA EVELYN,[10] b. July 31, 1891.

1504. Martha Ann,[9] daughter of 764 David[8] and Polly [Comstock] Balch, was born at Ridgeway, N. Y., September 16, 1851. She was married at Ridgeway, October 17, 1883, to Jay E. Allis. They live at Medina, N. Y., and have one child. Raymond Erwin, b. Aug. 19, 1889.

1505. Horace,[9] son of 765 Stephen[8] and Polly [Terrell] Balch, was born at Covington, New York, January 2, 1811, and lives at Oleander, California. He was married February 6, 1832, to Mary Manning, who was born in New York state, January 4, 1811, and died in Kansas, January 19, 1881. They had six children.

2204 GEORGE,[10] b. Sept. 6, 1833; lives at Lone Star, Cal.; six children, three living.
2205* LUCINDA,[10] b. Nov. 12, 1835; d. Oct. 18, 1864.
2206* EMILY,[10] b. April 12, 1841.
2207* MATILDA,[10] b. July 27, 1845; d. Mar. 24, 1868.
2208 MARY ANNIE,[10] b. April 7, 1848; m. 2213 Homer P. Balch.
2209 LUCY JANE,[10] b. Oct. 8, 1850; d. Nov. 2, 1863.

Horace married second, Mrs. Sarah Penfield, August 6, 1882. She died July 6, 1884.

1506. Jasper,[9] son of 765 Stephen[8] and Polly [Terrell] Balch, was born at Covington, Onondaga County, N. Y., September 11, 1812 and died January 19, 1891, at Welda, Kansas. He was married September 3, 1832, to Betsey, daughter of Josiah Manning, of Leroy, N. Y. She was born at Leroy, February 19, 1816. They had four children, all born in Genessee County, New York.

2210* MARGARET A.,[10] b. Sept. 27, 1833; d. Apr. 27, 1881.
2211* AMELIA M.,[10] b. July 11, 1835; d. May 18, 1876.
2212   MERCY O.,[10] b. Apr. 27, 1838; d. Oct. 25, 1865; m. Elijah Justice.
2213* HOMER P.,[10] b. Feb. 6, 1840; d. Dec. 19, 1883.

1507. Diantha,[9] daughter of 765 Stephen[8] and Polly [Terrell] Balch, was born at Covington, N. Y., September 16, 1814, and died December 9, 1848. She was married to Marquis Langtoss. No issue.

1509. Philander,[9] son of 765 Stephen[8] and Polly [Terrell] Balch, was born at Covington, N. Y., February 18, 1819, and is living at Elgin, Illinois. He was married November 10, 1842 to Eleanor H. Driscoll, by whom he had eight children, all the living ones being married.

2214   EDWIN E.,[10] b. Sept. 16, 1843; lives at Elgin, Ill.
2215   ALBERT,[10] b. July 2, 1845; d. May 2, 1853.
2216   WILLIAM C.,[10] b. Dec. 28, 1846; d. Dec. 14, 1882.
2217   HENRY,[10] b. Jan. 21, 1849; lives at Henrietta, Mich.
2218   JAMES O.,[10] b. Nov. 12, 1850; lives at Mills City, Oregon.
2219   CHARLES C.,[10] b. Aug. 21, 1852; lives at Charlotte, Mich.
2220   ELLEO,[10] b. Jan. 2, 1854; d. Oct. 4, 1866.
2221   ADELE,[10] b. Mar. 2, 1857; d. Aug. 12, 1863.

Eleanor H. died October 2, 1866, and Philander married second November 27, 1867, Addie N., daughter of John Curtis, of Dalton, Mass., by whom he had two daughters, both born at Church Hill, Mississippi.

2222   ADELE,[10] b. Nov. 7, 1868; m. Eams, Elgin, Ill.
2223   CLARA L.,[10] b. Nov. 14, 1874; m. Cole, Pecos Valley, N. M.

1510. Laura,[9] daughter of 765 Stephen[8] and Polly [Terrell] Balch, was born at Covington, N. Y., July 10, 1821, and

died July 2, 1891. She was married April 7, 1844, to Enoch
M. Winslow, M. D. He graduated from Ann Arbor, Mich.,
and is living at Parma, Mich. They have one son, Frank, b.
in 1857.

1511. Albert,[9] son of 765 Stephen[8] and Polly [Terrell]
Balch, was born at Covington, N. Y., March 30, 1823, and is
a farmer at Oleander, California. When sixteen years of age
he became a member of the Church of the Disciples. About
1856 he united with the Adventists for whom he has
preached. Before the war he was an Abolitionist, after the
war a Greenbacker. He was married first, June 1, 1854, to
Emeline, daughter of Nelson Baker. She was born in March,
1830, and died at Minneapolis, Minnesota, Dec. 1, 1867.
They had three children, all born at Naperville, Illinois.

2224ᵃ LEWIS NELSON[10], b. Mar. 9, 1855.
2225   CARRIE ARLOTTIE[10], b. Jan. 21, 1859; d. May 23, 1861.
2226   ELLIOTT THOMPSON[10], b. Sept. 24, 1860; lives at Leavenworth,
       Wash.

Albert married for his second wife, Almira Dart, a sister
of Jabez who married 2211 Amelia M.[10] She was born at
Bedford, Canada, April 19, 1842. They have five children.
The four eldest were born at Elmdale, Kan., the youngest at
Colfax, Colorado.

2227ᵃ CARRIE MAY[10], b. Feb. 15, 1871,
2228   ALBERT EUGINE,[10] b. June 1, 1873.
2229   MARY LILLIAN,[10] b. Nov. 29, 1877; d. June 17, 1882.
2230   LAURA EMILY,[10] b. June 20, 1880.
2231   GRACE EDITH,[10] b. July 6, 1884.

1512. Matilda,[9] daughter of 765 Stephen[8] and Polly
[Terrell] Balch, was born at Covington, N. Y., September
17, 1825. She was married December 10, 1845, to David S.
Babbitt. They live at Elgin, Illinois, and have three
daughters.

LULU M., b. Nov. 7, 1846, at Elgin, Ill.; d. unm. March 6, 1892.
ADDIE, b. Sept. 16, 1848, at Naperville, Ill.; m. Sept. 20, 1867, to
    W. H. Chapman. They reside at Elgin, Ill., and have three
    children, *Frank W.* b. June 14, 1869; m. Linda Morris; *Ella
    L.* b. Jan. 29, 1871; m. W. H. Morgan; *Genevieve L.* b. Mar.
    17, 1878.

JENNIE, b. July 4, 1857 at Naperville, Ill.; m. May 20, 1885, Oliver
N. Owens, at Elgin, Illinois. He is a merchant, and they reside at McHenry, Illinois. One daughter, *Ethel May*, b. Apr.
15, 1886.

1513. Lucinda,[9] daughter of 765 Stephen[7] and Polly
[Terrell] Balch, was born at Darien, N. Y., November 30,
1827. She was married Dec. 10, 1845 to Solomon Malton
Babbitt who was born at Austinburg, Ohio, August 27, 1823.
He is a banker. They reside at Oakland, Cal., and have had
five children. Mary F. b. Nov. 22, 1846, at Naperville, Ill.;
m. Feb. 14, 1878, to Zachery T. Gilpin, one son; Emma
Grace, b. Nov. 6, 1849, d. April 19, 1864; Ella Florence, b.
Dec. 4, 1855, d. April 8, 1870; Harriet Adele, b. Aug. 10,
1868, at Algonquin, Ill., m. Mar. 19, 1890, Edwin W. Owen;
Walter L. b. Sept. 22, 1871, d. Aug. 4, 1872.

1515. Harriet,[9] daughter of 765 Stephen[8] and Polly
[Terrell] Balch, was born in New York State, February 4,
1832. She was married to DeWitt Clinton Fox. He is an
engineer and they reside at Dayton, Nevada, and have had
two children. Alice, b. July 10, 1854, d. Aug. 21, 1858;
Charles, b. Apr. 27, 1857.

1516. Melinda,[9] daughter of 765 Stephen[8] and Polly
[Terrell] Balch, was born in New York State, November 2,
1835. She was married December 24, 1862, to Willet, son
of Robert Phillips. He was born June 11, 1834, at Nesham-
ing Falls, Penn., and is a farmer. They live at Algonquin,
Illinois, and have had four children, all born at Algonquin.
Nettie, b. Dec. 14, 1863; Alice Ray, b. Aug. 18, 1867, d.
Aug. 29, 1867; Frederick, b. May 14, 1869; Cora Maudline,
b. Nov. 26, 1870; d. Apr. 20, 1872.

1517. Fidelia Ann,[9] daughter of 779 John[8] and Almira
[Stowell] Balch, was born at Virgil, N. Y., June 9, 1825,
She married Daniel, son of Ezra and —— [Hotchkiss]
Maltby. He served during the last nine months of the civil
war in a New York regiment. In 1865, they removed to

Hagerty, Wisconsin, where Mr. Maltby died and his widow was living in 1887. They had three children all born in the state of New York. Hester Ann, b. Nov. 27, 1858; John Ezra, b. Dec. 30, 1859; Mary D., b. Feb. 7, 1864.

1519. Emma Melvina,[9] daughter of 779 John[8] and Almira [Stowell] Balch, was born at Cortland, N. Y., October 11, 1831, and lives in Wichita, Kansas. She was married March 4, 1853, to Edwin Adams, by whom she had three children; all were born at McLean, N. Y.

> RANDOLPH, b. Nov. 28, 1853.
> MATIE D., b. May 9, 1856, m. F. T. Tombs, lives East London, Ontario.
> HATTIE D., b. Jan. 25, 1860; m. F. Tenney, lives at Cortland, N. Y.

Mr. Adams died, and Emma M. married second, Urban S., son of Placid and Clotine Gabrielle [Tousigan] Beaudet, who was born near Quebec, October 11, 1838. They had three children all born at Auburn, N. Y.

> W. IRVING, b. Nov. 9, 1870.
> CLARA M., b. May 8, 1872.
> HORACE FREDERIC, b. Oct. 13, 1873.

1520. Mary Jane,[9] daughter of 779 John[8] and Almira [Stowell] Balch, was born at Summer Hill, N. Y., April 9, 1833. She was married May 6, 1855, to William D., son of Samuel and Lucy [Comstock] Lane, who was born at Trumensburg, N. Y., April 23, 1834. He enlisted in Co. E, Eighth Minnesota Infantry Volunteers, and served in the Indian War until 1864, when he was mustered out. He then moved to Momence, Illinois, and engaged first in the drug trade, and then in the grocery business. He was postmaster at Momence, from 1870 to 1884 and is now a dealer in general merchandise. They are Methodists and have four children.

> EMMA ESTELLA, b. May 23, 1856, at Momence, Ills. She married May 10, 1881, Herbert E. Conant, of New Haven, Vt. He is a carpenter at Momence, and they have one child *Flora*, b. in 1882.

CORA ETHLEEN, b. May 8, 1860, at Minneapolis, Minn., m. March
    2, 1882, to Frederick Brandt, of Chicago.   They reside at
    Momence, and have two daughters, *Irene* and *Viola.*
FRANK EUGENE, b. March 14, 1862, at Minneapolis, Minn., is a
    dealer in general merchandise at Momence; unm.
GRACE ELENOR, b. Oct. 17, 1876, at Momence.

1521. John Ransom,[9] son' of 779 John[8] and Almira
[Stowell] Balch, was born at Cortland, N. Y., January 18,
1835.   He married Margaret, daughter of Amos and Rebecca
Snyder.   She was born at Dryden, N. Y., April 23, 1830
They have had seven children.   The five eldest were born at
Cortland, N. Y., the other two at Stockbridge, Wisconsin.

2232 ELSA R.[10] b. Oct. 28, 1858; d. December 31, 1861.
2233 ALIDA E.,[10] b. Dec. 1, 1859; d. Jan. 13, 1861.
2234 ALBERT E.,[10] b. Nov. 2, 1861; d. Feb. 22, 1862.
2235* FREDERICK R.,[10] b. Mar. 16, 1863.
2236* LEWELLIE L.,[10] b. April 21, 1866.
2237 LENA L.,[10] b. July 30, 1867; d. October 12, 1885.
2238 EDITH M.,[10] b. July 12, 1872.

1523. John,[9] son of 784 Ahimaaz[8] and Sarah [Way]
Balch, was born at Colchester, Conn., and married Lucy,
daughter of Gardner Wickwire of that place where their
children were born.

2239 IDA,[10] b.   ; m. Wm. Wagner, of Colchester.
2240 ETTA,[10] b.   ; m. Frank Brown, of Colchester.
2241 ABBIE,[10] b.

1524. Betsey Morgan,[9] daughter of 784 Ahimaaz[8] and
Eliza [Lee] Balch, was born at Colchester, Connecticut, and
was married March 9, 1863, at Norwich, Ct., to George Marcus, son of Jabez and Eunice Bailey Rockwell, who was born
March 23, 1840.

1525. Frances Ann,[9] daughter of 784 Ahimaaz[8] and
Eliza [Lee] Balch, was born at Colchester, Ct.   She married
Charles King and had two children.   Minnie and Winnie.

1526. Annah Maria,[9] daughter of 789 Samuel West[8]
and Joanna E. [Perkins] Balch, was born at Lyme, N. H.,
July 5, 1837.   She was married October 24, 1865 to Simeon

Hunt. They lived at East Providence, R. I., and have three children. William West, b. April 22, 1868; Fred Balch, b. Jan. 8, 1872, d. Aug. 10, 1882; John Archie, b. Nov. 3, 1878. William W. is married and has one child.

1527. Lucretia Sophia,[9] daughter of 789 Samuel West[8] and Joanna E. [Perkins] Balch, is a twin to Annah Maria, and was married May 2, 1865, to Joseph P. Marsh. They live at Farmington, Minnesota, and have two children, Lucy Ellen, b. Feb. 14, 1868; Charles Balch, b. Oct. 7, 1870. Lucy E. married Mr. Seely and has two children.

1528. Frances Campbell,[9] daughter of 789 Samuel West[8] and Joanna E. [Perkins] Balch, was born at Lyme, N. H., October 2, 1839. She was married December 30, 1873, to James H. Holmes. They live at Lyme, N. H., and have had two children. Charles Balch, b. August, 1874, d. July, 1875; Harry Balch, b. Sept. 11, 1875.

1532. Charles Carroll,[9] son of 789 Samuel West[8] and Joanna E. [Perkins] Balch, was born at Lyme, N. H., August 23, 1847. He was married June 18, 1876, to Abbie M., daughter of Oliver and Abbie Maria Chaffee. They live at East Providence Centre, R. I., and have one child.

2242   GRACE ABBY,[10] b. Mar. 28, 1877.

1533. West Shaw,[9] son of 789 Samuel West[8] and Joanna E. [Perkins] Balch, was born at Lyme, N. H., May 16, 1849, and is a farmer at Lyme, New Hampshire. He was married first April 2, 1872, to Mary E. daughter of Sidney S. and Louisa Grant. She died October 10, 1885. Their children were as follows.

2243   FREDERICK WEST,[10] b. Aug. 10, 1874, d. July 10, 1875.
2244   FRANK FOSTER,[10] b. Oct. 24, 1876. Lives at Lyme, N. H.
2245   ANNA LOUISA,[10] b. July 31, 1880, d. April 3, 1898.

West Shaw was married second, June 2, 1888, to Julia F., daughter of Alfred W. and Edna E. Pusher. They have one child.

2246   RALPH WEST,[10] b. Mar. 15, 1894.

1538. Foster Lamson,[9] son of 791 Dan Shaw[8] and Dorothy Marston [Whittier] Balch, was born at Canaan, N. H., September 19, 1835, and is the head of the firm of Balch & Wetherbee, grading contractors, Minneapolis, Minnesota. He was married January 14, 1863, to Nancy McArthur, daughter of John Morris. She was born at Chillicothe, Ohio, October 4, 1829, and died at Minneapolis, Minn., April 26, 1886. They had five children. The four eldest were born at Shakopee, Minn., the youngest at Minneapolis.

2247* ROBERT MORRIS,[10] b. April 7, 1864.
2248* FRANK SHAW,[10] } twins, b. Nov. 16, 1865. } d. Oct. 15, 1866.
2249 EMMA ROGERS,[10]
2250* GERTRUDE,[10] b. March 24, 1869.
2251 HELEN,[10] b. March 11, 1875.

Foster L. was married second, January 28, 1889, to Helen Maria Lord. She was the widow of John Newton, and daughter of Samuel and Philura Parker Lord. She was born at Putney, Vt., January 7, 1838.

1540. Henry Francis,[9] son of 791 Dan Shaw[8] and Dorothy Marston [Whittier] Balch, was born at Bradford, Vt., November 17, 1838, and is a railroad contractor, living at Minneapolis, Minnesota. He was married June 18, 1862, to Evalyn, daughter of James Kendrick. She was born at Claremont, N. H., September 20, 1838. To them have been born three children, all at Minneapolis.

2252* ALICE KENDRICK,[10] b. March 3, 1864.
2253* MARY EVALYN,[10] b. June 25, 1866.
2254 AGNES LOUISE,[10] b. Feb. 24, 1871.

1541. Martha Jane,[9] daughter of 791 Dan Shaw[8] and Dorothy Marston [Whittier] Balch, was born at Boscawen, N. H., November 8, 1842. She was married October 4, 1866, to Henry L., son of Joseph Moses. He was born at Wellington, Maine, July 23, 1835, and is a farmer at Pasadena, California. Their two children were born at Empire, Minnesota. Addie Helen, b. June 4, 1867 ; Eva Maud, b. June 8, 1874.

1542. Dan Whittier,[9] son of 791 Dan Shaw[8] and Doro-

thy Marston [Whittier] Balch, was born at Concord, N. H.,
September 28, 1844. He was married June 6, 1871, to Maria
L., daughter of Ireneus Perkins. She was born at Lyme, N.
H., July 31, 1849. He is a farmer at Lakeville, Minnesota,
where their children were born.

    2255 LOUIS PERKINS,[10] b. April 20, 1872; d. July 19, 1873.
    2256 FRED KITTREDGE,[10] b. May 28, 1874.
    2257 ELLA WINIFRED,[10] b. June 12, 1877.
    2258 HERBERT WYLAND,[10] b. July 3, 1879.
    2259 EDNA IRENE,[10] b. June 25, 1882.

    1543. Fred Kittredge,[9] son of 791 Dan Shaw[8] and
Dorothy Marston [Whittier] Balch, was born at Boscawen,
N. H., March 2, 1847. He was married November 2, 1880,
to Etta M., daughter of Samuel A. Perkins. She was born
at Buckland, Massachusetts, August 18, 1862. He is a railroad and dock contractor at Lakeville, Minnesota, where
their children were born.

    2260 EDNA L.,[10] b. Dec. 24, 1883.
    2261 DELIA MARIA,[10] b. Oct. 6, 1889; d. Jan. 28, 1891.
    2262 EARL HENRY,[10] b. Nov. 28, 1893.

    1544. Charles Joseph,[9] son of 791 Dan Shaw[8] and
Dorothy Marston [Whittier] Balch, was born at Fisherville,
N. H., December 8, 1848, and is an engineer and electrician,
living at Owatonna, Minnesota. He was married February
5, 1890, to Nellie A., daughter of George Thomas and Nancy
Cordelia Welch. She was born at Burlington, Iowa, October
15, 1869.

    1545. George Shaw,[9] son of 791 Dan Shaw[8] and Doro-
thy Marston [Whittier] Balch, was born at Fisherville, N.
H., April 8, 1851. He was married March 30, 1881, to Mary
F., daughter of Ebenezer Parker. She was born at Grafton,
N. H., October 16, 1857. He is a farmer at Empire, Minn.

    2263 GEORGE EBEN,[10] b. Jan. 8, 1888.

    1546. William Clark,[9] son of 791 Dan Shaw[8] and Dor-
othy Marston [Whittier] Balch, was born at Fisherville, N.
H., September 18, 1853, and lives at Oakland, California. He

was married November 2, 1879, to Annie S., daughter of Allison Houck. She was born at Lakeville, Minn., May 6, 1859. Their eldest child was born at Preston Lake, Wisconsin, the youngest at Oakland, and the others at Minneapolis.

2264 CLIFFORD ALLISON,[10] b. June 27, 1880.
2265 CHARLOTTE,[10] b. June 19, 1882; d. y.
2266 EDWIN,[10] b. July 7, 1887; d. y.
2267 CHOATE NEWTON,[10] b. June 13, 1889.
2268 ROBERT ELMER,[10] b. June 3, 1894.

1547. Kate Gage,[9] daughter of 791 Dan Shaw[8] and Dorothy Marston [Whittier] Balch, was born at St. Anthony, Minn., November 9, 1857. She was married November 27, 1878, to Albert, son of Alexander Record. He was born at Columbus, Indiana, November 22, 1849, and is a carpenter at Oakland, California. They have five children: Henry Albert, b. Jan. 27, 1880; Winnifred Dorothy, b. April 19, 1882; Leon Willis, b. April 4, 1884.

1548. Eva Dorothy,[9] daughter of 791 Dan Shaw[8] and Dorothy Marston [Whittier] Balch, was born at Empire, Minnesota, June 8, 1860. She was married December 19, 1889, to Eugene, son of Elijah and Esther [Geiger] Griswold. He was born at Quincy, Illinois, July 14, 1848, and is a chemical manufacturer at San Francisco, California. Their children are as follows: Geneva Esther, b. April 6, 1891; Edwin, b. Nov. 17, 1892.

1553. Julia Gouverneur,[9] daughter of 795 Adna Perkins[8] and Susan Brewster [Bibby] Balch, was born at Hanover, N. H., November 9, 1861. She was married September 1, 1889, to Dr. Norman St. George, who graduated at Dartmouth in 1888. They first settled at Fall River, but in 1892 they removed to Boston.

1557. Adelia Ann,[9] daughter of 796 Francis Brown[8] and Louisa [Dyke] Balch, was born at Lyme, N. H., January 11, 1853. She was married November 28, 1872, to Henry Colby, son of Luther P. and Martha [Howe] Tenney. He was born November 25, 1851, and is a carpenter at Winchester, N. H. They have four children, two born at Newport, and two at Winchester, New Hampshire. Charles Adna, b. July 16, 1876; Guy West, b. July 29, 1879; Frank Balch, b. Jan. 30, 1882; Ralph Linwood, b. Aug. 8, 1885.

1559. **Alice Louisa,**[9] daughter of 796 Francis Brown[8] and Louisa [Dyke] Balch, was born at Lyme, N. H., December 18, 1857, and died at Winchester, N. H., August 26, 1887. She was married June 19, 1880, to Charles Edward, son of Frank and Maria [Ripley] Hildreth. He was born at Winchester, N. H., October 8, 1855. They lived at Winchester, and had one child: Linwood B., b. July 30, 1881; d. Aug. 2, 1882.

1561. **Herbert Newton,**[9] son of 796 Francis Brown[8] and Louisa [Dyke] Balch, was born at Haverhill, N. H., July 11, 1868, and is a carpenter at Winchester, New Hampshire. He was married December 21, 1891, to Emma Elizabeth, daughter of George A. and Emma [Whitney] Stone. She was born at Gardner, Mass., June 21, 1874.

1562. **Mason Holmes,**[9] son of 799 Mason[8] and Sabina [Holmes] Balch, was born in Francestown, N. H., Nov. 22, 1829. He married Maria Nay, of Peterboro, N. H. They had one child, who died in infancy.

1563. **Mary Ann,**[9] daughter of 799 Mason[8] and Sabina [Holmes] Balch, was born in Francestown, N. H., March 14, 1827, and died Sept. 30, 1858. In June, 1855, she was married to Deacon Levi Bradford, of Francestown. He died Nov. 19, 1884. They lived, died, and were buried in Francestown. They had one daughter: Ella, b. April 17, 1856, who lives in Francestown.

1564. **Charles Edward,**[9] son of 799 Mason[8] and Hannah [Holt] Balch, was born in Greenfield, N. H., March 17, 1843, and died at Manchester, N. H., Oct. 18, 1884. He was married July 30, 1867, to Emeline R., daughter of Rev. Nahum Brooks, who was born in Laconia, N. H., September 2, 1842. They had no children.

Col. Charles Edward Balch was noted for his strict integrity, persistent devotion to business, and cordiality of nature. He was cashier of the Manchester National Bank from its organization, in 1865, until January, 1884, when he became one of the directors. For 21 years he was a trustee of the Manchester Savings Bank, and in July of 1883 was appointed its treasurer. He received his military title by serving two years on the staff of Gov. Head. He was a member of the Franklin Street Society, and contributed liberally to its advancement.

1565. Israel D.,[9] son of 804 John[8] and Roxie [Dutton] Balch, was born in Francestown, March 4, 1839. He was married to Addie H. Hardy, May 12, 1861. She was a daughter of Herman Hardy, of Francestown, and was born in Francestown, June 8, 1838, and died in Boston, Mass., October 15, 1884. They had three children.

  2269 LIZZIE A.,[10] b. Mason Village, Jan. 26, 1863; d. Oct. 12, 1865.
  2270 LILLIAN A.,[10] b. E. Cambridge, Mass., June 27, 1872.
  2271 PERCY I.,[10] b. E. Cambridge, Mass., Jan. 16, 1876.

Israel D. married second, Aug. 15, 1894, Sadie G., daughter of John W. and Ruth [Gage] Burnham, of Bennington, N. H. They live at Ludlow, Vermont, where he is proprietor of the Goddard House.

1567. Orrin J. L.,[9] son of 804 John[8] and Roxie [Dutton] Balch, was born in Francestown, N. H., May 19, 1843, and died January 14, 1895. He was married May 19, 1864, to Josie S., daughter of George and Mary [Persons] Nay, of Peterboro, N. H. She was born in Peterboro, September 2, 1842. She now lives at Amoskeag, near Manchester, N. H., and has had eight children.

  2272* ETTA L.,[10] b. June 5, 1865.
  2273 EUGENE,[10] b. June 6, 1867; d. Oct. 6, 1867.
  2274* PERLEY O.,[10] b. May 8, 1868.
  2275 LEROY O.,[10] b. July 29, 1873.

2276   FREDERICK H.,[10] b. May 29, 1877.
2277   ETHEL R.,[10]
2278   EDITH M.,[10] } twins, b. Aug. 29, 1878; } d. Oct. 29, 1878.
2279   HARRY H.,[10] b. Oct. 17, 1884; d. July 29, 1889.

1572. Harvey John,[9] son of 806 John[8] and Julia Ann [Pond] Balch, was born in Windsor county, Vermont, July 22, 1829, and lives at Elbow, New York. He has had seven children, five born at Granville, and one at Chestertown, N. Y.

2280*   JOHN HARVEY,[10] b. Jan. 5, 1850.
2281   LOWELL JOSIAH,[10] b. Feb. 7, 1852; lives at Loch Muller, N. Y.
2282   ELIZA ANN,[10] b. April 2, 1854; m. Maxam; lives at Mukwon-
       ago, Wis.
2283   CHARLES ANDREW,[10] b. May 29, 1856; lives at Elbow, N. Y.
2284   MASON W.,[10] b. Nov. 3, 1858; lives at Elbow, N. Y.
2285   ELLA ALMIRA,[10] b. April 23, 1860.
2286   MARY,[10] b.

1573. Elizabeth M.,[9] daughter of 806 John[8] and Julia Ann [Pond] Balch, was born December 14, 1830, and lives at Rutland, Vermont. She was married November 13, 1849, to Marzuis Campbell, and has three children: Edgar L., b. Nov. 24, 1859; Henry C., b. March 9, 1865; Margett C., b. 1866.

1574. Lowell Levi,[9] son of 806 John[8] and Julia Ann [Pond] Balch, was born January 22, 1832, and lives at Tafts-ville, Vermont. On June 13, 1852, he married his cousin, Huldah Ann, daughter of Hiram and 807 Achsah Philena [Balch] Whitney. They had eight children, born in Hart-land, Vermont. The sixth died young.

2287*   CLARA ADELIA,[10] b. March 12, 1855.
2288*   ELIZABETH CAMPBELL,[10] b. July 21, 1858.
2289*   SARAH ANNA,[10] b. Dec. 11, 1860.
2290*   IDORA PHILENA,[10] b. March 27, 1863.
2291*   ELLEN GERTRUDE,[10] b. Feb. 1, 1865.
2292*   HARVEY HIRAM,[10] b. May 9, 1868.
2293   ELERIE AUSTIN,[10] b. Sept. 26, 1876.

Lowell Levi married second, May 30, 1886, Mrs. Lucina [Hadley] Hatch.

1578. Amanda Cordilia,[9] daughter of 806 John[8] and Julia Ann [Pond] Balch, was born Aug. 15, 1844, at Granville, New York, and died May 14, 1871, at Rutland, Vermont. She was married at North Granville, New York, Jan. 1, 1864, to her cousin, John B., son of Hiram and 807 Achsah Philena [Balch] Whitney. They had four children. Mary E., born July 1, 1867, d. Feb. 18, 1868 ; Elbert E., b. Sept. 9, 1869 ; John Henry and James Hiram, twins, b. May 14, 1871, d. y.

John B. enlisted August 19, 1862, with his brother, Sanford M., in company B, Twelfth Vermont Regiment, Volunteer Infantry, and were both discharged July 14, 1863.

John B. was married again at Port Henry, New York, January 6, 1873, to Martha A. Taggart. She was born April 4, 1851, at Stockholm, Vermont. They live at San Francisco, California, where John B. is president and general manager of the United States Standard Weight and Measure Association, and have one child, Frank Lowell, born March 4, 1877.

1579. Mary Ann,[9] daughter of 806 John[8] and Julia Ann [Pond] Balch, was born May 7, 1848, and was married first, June 13, 1866, to Henry S., son of John S. Willard. They have the following children :

> JOHN S., b. Aug. 13, 1867.
>
> NELLIE C., b. March 29, 1870; m. Henry H. Haley, June 4, 1887; one son, *Walter H.*, b. Sept. 9, 1888; m. second, Edward S. Hale, Oct. 24, 1892; two sons, *Warren E.*, b. May 13, 1893; *Harold W.*, b. Nov. 17, 1894.
>
> MABEL M., b. April 7, 1872; m. Fred O'Neal, Oct. 23, 1892; one daughter, *Mary A.*, b. June 29, 1896.
>
> ELMER ELLSWORTH, b. Nov. 19, 1874; m. Rose L. Harlow, Feb. 16, 1895; one son, *Earle E.*, b. Dec. 23, 1895.

Mary Ann married second, June 21, 1884, Samuel W. Davis. They live at Hartland, Vermont.

1598. Charles F.,[9] son of 819 James T.[8] and Lois [Robbins] Balch, was born in Antrim, N. H., November 29, 1844. He was married November 17, 1870, to Ellen O. Fleming, who was born at Bennington, N. H., April 10, 1851. They reside at Bennington, N. H., and have two children.

2294 CHARLOTTE E.,[10] b. Oct. 7, 1871, at Antrim.
2295 JAMES HARVEY,[10] b. Oct. 23, 1876, at Bennington.

1600. William A.,[9] son of 819 James T.[8] and Lois [Robbins] Balch, was born in Antrim, N. H., November 4, 1856. He lives at Antrim, and is a dealer in coal, ice and lumber. He was married July 16, 1879, to Marietta J., daughter of William and Charlotte Smith. She was born November 30, 1860. They have one son.

2296 HARRY E.,[10] b. Nov. 30, 1880.

1601. John A.,[9] son of 819 James T.[8] and Lois [Robbins] Balch, was born in Antrim, N. H., February 28, 1860. He is a merchant, and since 1893 has been town clerk at Antrim. He married Lena L., daughter of Milton and Hattie [Elliot] Tenney. She was born at Somerville, Mass., March 16, 1865. They have three children, born in Antrim.

2297 IVON A.,[10] b. Jan. 12, 1884.
2298 INA L.,[10] b. May 28, 1885.
2299 ALFRED T.,[10] b. April 4, 1888.

1603. William Hoyt,[9] son of 822 William[8] and Sarah Ann [Hoyt] Balch, was born April 3, 1874, at Nashua, New Hampshire, and is a civil engineer in the senior class at Dartmouth College.

1625. Henry R.,[9] son of 850 Archibald[8] and Mary [Sweet] Balch, was born at Richfield, N. Y., December 28, 1826. He married Delia Bellows, who was born December 7, 1830. They live at Knoxville, Pennsylvania, and have three children.

2300* FREDERICK VOLNEY,[10] b. Sept. 2, 1850; lives at Galeton, Penn.
2301 RAY S.,[10] b. Aug. 26, 1859; on way to Alaska when last heard from.
2302 NEVADA,[10] b. April 10, 1872; lives at Hornellsville, N. Y.

1626. Alphonso Burdette,[9] son of 850 Archibald[8] and Mary [Sweet] Balch, was born in Otsego county, N. Y., April 13, 1832, and is a farmer at Knoxville, Pennsylvania. He was married October 15, 1855, to Rhoda M., daughter of Abram and Nabbie [Burlingame] Smith. She was born at

Smithville, R. I., May 11, 1833. Their four children were born at Deerfield,⁅Pennsylvania.

2303ᵉ CASSIUS VERNON,¹⁰ b. March 6, 1857.
2304ᵉ HERBERT A.,¹⁰ b. Feb. 1, 1860.
2305 OSCAR BURDETT,¹⁰ b. May 6, 1869; lives at Oak Park, Ill.
2306 FOSTER H.,¹⁰ b. July 22, 1875.

1627. Helen Adalaid,⁹ daughter of 850 Archibald⁸ and Mary [Sweet] Balch, was born March 7, 1839, at Knoxville, Pennsylvania. She was married at Leominster, Wisconsin, September 13, 1860, to Oscar Selleck, of Janesville, Wisconsin, where they now live and their two children were born : Mary Adela, b. Jan. 24, 1863 ; William Hatch, b. Oct. 22, 1873.

1630. Milton,⁹ son of 851 Arnold⁸ and Sarah [Leonard] Balch, was born at North Jackson, Penn., January 2, 1831. He was a merchant at North Jackson until 1891, after which he took a farm in the western part of the town. For nineteen years he was town treasurer. He was married February 22, 1852, to Ammoratta C., daughter of Luther H. Cawles. She was born at Warren, Pennsylvania, October 3, 1833. They have two daughters, born at New Milford.

2307 SARAH MAY,¹⁰ b. May 25, 1856; unm.
2308ᵉ EMMA M.,¹⁰ b. Sept. 26, 1858.

1631. Pamela,⁹ daughter of 876 Dan C.⁸ and Matilda [Grant] Balch, was born January 18, 1842, and died December 19, 1872. She married Van Rensselaer Phillips, and they lived at Ashtebula, Ohio.

Descendants of 47 David.⁴

1651. Ida Frances,⁹ daughter of 902 Israel Daniel Perkins⁹ and Margaret [Cherry] Balch, was born December 8, 1857, at Amesbury, Mass. She was married in 1883 to Edgar Augustus Davis. They had one daughter, Mary Nelson, b. in 1884.

1655. William Henry,⁹ son of 918 Charles⁹ and Harriet [Hines] Balch, was born at Nelson, N. Y., November 7, 1836, and is engaged in farming and apiculture at Oran, New York. He was married July 3, 1868, to Elizabeth Polly, daughter of Arvin Albro, of Cuyler, N. Y., where she was born, August 16, 1848. They have had four children, all born at Cazenovia, N. Y.

2313* CHARLES ARVIN,[10] b. June 17, 1869.
2314 LILLIE MARIA,[10] b. Nov. 6, 1870; d. Nov. 24, 1873.
2315 CLARA LOUISA,[10] b. Dec. 19, 1877.
2316 ERNEST HENRY,[10] b. July 12, 1882.

1656. **Eliza Jane,**[9] daughter of 913 Charles[8] and Harriet [Hines] Balch, was born at Nelson, New York, September 2, 1838, and died May 9, 1885. She was married November 5, 1864, to John F., son of John H. Loope, of Solon, New York. He was born at Solon, August 28, 1843, and is living at Cortland, New York. They have had six children. The eldest was born at Solon; the other five were born at Ogden, Iowa, where she died. Florence J., b. March 26, 1868, m. J. W. Harris; George W., b. June 9, 1870, d. March 11, 1894; Lola W., b. June 20, 1872; John, b. Feb. 25, 1876, d. in infancy; John, b. Jan. 27, 1878, d. in infancy; Charles W., b. Nov. 25, 1881.

1657. **Charles D.,**[9] son of 913 Charles[8] and Harriet [Hines] Balch, was born at Nelson, N. Y., August 18, 1840, and was married June 20, 1866, to Sylvia A., daughter of William Blivin, of Edgerton, Wisconsin, where she was born, June 4, 1845. They have had five children, all born at Milton, Wisconsin.

2317 CORA M.,[10] b. Oct. 8, 1867.
2318 WILLIAM A. B.,[10] b. March 3, 1870.
2319 LOUA B.,[10] b. April 25, 1873.
2320 HOMER F.,[10] b. March 3, 1875.
2321 ERVINE C.,[10] b. Aug. 19, 1881; d. Aug. 19, 1884.

Charles D. Balch is a farmer at Milton Junction, Wisconsin. During the civil war he served in company F, sixteenth Wisconsin Volunteers, and was with Gen. Sherman in his march to the sea. He has been justice of the peace in Milton, and is a member of the S. D. B. church, at Rock River, Wisconsin.

1658. Harriet Cornelia,[9] daughter of 913 Charles[8] and Harriet [Hines] Balch, was born at De Ruyter, N. Y., February 8, 1844, and was married February 2, 1862, to William, son of Alexander Doran. He was born at Truxton, N. Y., May 30, 1834, and is a farmer at Milton, Wisconsin. They have had four children: Frank L., b. at Taylor, N. Y., Jan. 20, 1863; Nellie E., b. at Pompey, N. Y., Aug. 28, 1864; Jennie J., b. at Manlius, N. Y., Feb. 28, 1867; George B., b. at Milton, Wis., Dec. 7, 1872.

1659. Maria,[9] daughter of 913 Charles[8] and Harriet [Hines] Balch, was born May 26, 1846. She was married first, April 21, 1877, to James R., son of Alexander Wade, of Schuyler, N. Y. He was born May 13, 1825, and died October 21, 1877. At the age of 24 he became principal of schools at Buffalo, and held the position for ten years. He was a lawyer at Boone, Iowa.

Maria [Balch] Wade married second, May 21, 1880, Herman D., son of James W. Hall, of Alegon county, Michigan, where he was born, June 13, 1854. They have had three children, born at Beaver, Iowa: Ivie, b. Aug. 16, 1881; Bessie, b. July 11, 1883; James W., b. Aug. 19, 1884, d. March 21, 1885.

1661. Martha A.,[9] daughter of 919 George A.[8] and Jamima [Clark] Balch, was born at Keene, N. H., August 19, 1834, and died at Brattleboro, Vt., March 5, 1883, and was buried in the same town. She was married May 6, 1857, to George M., son of Mason Fay, who was born at Walpole, N. H., October 30, 1832. They had three children, all born at Walpole: Mary L., b. Jan. 9, 1859; Addie M., b. Sept. 5, 1860; Emma J., b. Sept. 15, 1864.

1662. Mary A.,[9] daughter of 919 George A.[8] and Jamima [Clark] Balch, was born at Keene, N. H., July 11, 1837.

She was married May 2, 1861, to Frederick A., son of Phineas and Fanny Chapin. He was born at Charleston, N. H., April 9, 1831. They lived at Oakdale, Mass., and had no children.

1663. **Emma M.**,[9] daughter of 919 George A.[8] and his second wife Maria [Sanderson] Balch, was born at Keene, N. H., September 5, 1852, and was married August 9, 1876, to George C., son of Andrew and Jane Wilson. He was born at Ovid, N. Y., August 18, 1849. They live at Worcester, Mass., and have one child, Herbert C., b. May 17, 1878, at Worcester.

1664. **Charles A.**,[9] son of 919 George A.[8] and Maria [Sanderson] Balch, was born at Keene, N. H., November 23, 1854, where he is a sash and blind manufacturer. He was married August 31, 1880, to Sarah Kenna.

1666. **Nehemiah Charles**,[9] son of 926 Nehemiah[8] and Mary Ann [Lovett] Balch, was born at Topsfield, Mass., February 6, 1834. He was married Jan. 5, 1859, to Martha Abby, daughter of Isaiah and Elizabeth P. Rogers. She was born at Ipswich, Mass., September 27, 1836. They have four children, all born at Ipswich, Mass.

2322 LENETTE P.,[10] b. Feb. 4, 1863.
2323 GRACE W.,[10] b. Sept. 14, 1866.
2324 BERTRAM C.,[10] b. Feb. 2, 1871.
2325 ELLIOTT R.,[10] b. Aug. 22, 1872.

Nehemiah Charles is a spring maker and also a musician, living at Lowell, Mass., and since 1883 has been with the Lamson Store Service Company. Previous to 1883 he was first engaged in the dry goods business. His health failing, he became a reporter, then a book dealer.

1668. **George Edwin**,[9] son of 926 Nehemiah[8] and Mary Ann [Lovett] Balch, was born at Topsfield, Mass., January 23, 1839, and died at Boston, June 11, 1874. He was acting hospital steward with a Massachusetts regiment during the war. He married Annie H. Morse, by whom he had three children, born in Boston.

2326 GEORGE E.,[10] b. March 18, 1867.
2327 ALICE,[10] b. in 1870; d. Feb. 6, 1874.
2328 RALPH A.,[10] b. Dec. 30, 1871; living at Boston, Mass.

1669. Ruth Clementine,[9] daughter of 928 Robert[8] and Lydia [Pike] Balch, was born at Johnson, Vt., January 17, 1830, and was married March 28, 1854, to William H. Porter, M. D., a son of Vine Porter, He was born at Morristown, Vt., May 10, 1830, and is a practicing physician at Surry, N. H., where their four children were born : Myron H., b. Jan. 3, 1855 ; Charles H., b. Jan. 29, 1858, d. Jan. 29, 1861 ; Ellen H., b. Dec. 26, 1861 ; Kate H., b. Jan. 26, 1865.

1672. Louisa Pike,[9] daughter of 928 Robert[8] and Lydia [Pike] Balch, was born at Johnson, Vt., November 1, 1836, and died at Cambridge, Vt., August 6, 1862. She was married May 15, 1859, to Daniel, son of John and Lavinia Prince, who was born at Johnson, Vt., May 23, 1830. He served during the civil war in the Eighth Vermont Volunteers, company E. He is a farmer, and lives at Cambridge, Vt. They have had two children : Minnie, b. May 5, 1860, at Johnson, Vt., d. Aug. 2, 1867; Stella L., b. Feb. 9, 1862, at Cambridge, Vt., m. Feb. 28, 1882, Fred Putnam.

1674. Caroline Martha,[9] daughter of 928 Robert[8] and Lydia [Pike] Balch, was born at Johnson, Vt., August 28, 1843. She was married November 14, 1865, to Levi B. Adams, who was born at Eden, Vt., March 19, 1838, and died at Morristown, Vt., July 30, 1877. He was a son of James and Lucy [Ritterbush] Adams. He served three years during the civil war in company D, First Vermont Artillery. They had five children, all born at Johnson, except the youngest, who was born at Morristown, Vt. : James H., b. May 7, 1866, d. June 8, 1866 ; Persis B., b. May 15, 1867, m. Nov. 24, 1885, to James M. Tinker, of Morristown; Guy C., b. Jan. 22, 1869; Azariah M., b. Dec. 30, 1873 ; Lucy J., b. Aug. 5, 1877, d. Jan. 30, 1878.

1675. Julia Etta,[9] daughter of 928 Robert[8] and Lydia

[Pike] Balch, was born at Johnson, Vt., March 5, 1846, and was married January 15, 1884, to Herbert W., son of Clark B. and her cousin, Ruth K. [Balch] Page. He was born at Waterville, Vt., September 14, 1858, is a farmer, and lives at Johnson, Vt. They have an adopted son, Lynn R., b. Feb. 20, 1875, and one daughter, Cynthia J., b. July 20, 1885.

1677. **Ruth K.,**[9] daughter of 930 Solomon[8] and Hannah [Clark] Balch, was born at Waterville, Vt., April 11, 1833. She married Clark B. Page, by whom she had two children: Cynthia, m. Harry Grand, and had two sons and three daughters; Herbert W., b. Sept. 14, 1858, m. his mother's cousin. 1675 Julia Etta Balch.

1678. **Enos,**[9] son of 930 Solomon[8] and Hannah [Clark] Balch, was born at Waterville, Vt., December 16, 1835, where he now lives. He married Hannah Lowater. Their children are as follows:

2329 HASKELL,[10] b. 1858.
2330 HEZMON,[10] b. 1860; d. y.
2331* FLORA,[10] b. 1862.
2332 PERSA,[10] b. 1866; d. y.
2333 ELMER,[10] b. 1868.
2334 ABBY,[10] b. 1869; d. y.
2335 ALICE,[10] b. 1872.
2336 ADELL,[10] b. 1874.
2337 HARRIET,[10] b. 1877.

1679. **Mary,**[9] daughter of 930 Solomon[8] and Maria A. [Hurlburt] Balch, was born in 1844, and died in Kansas. She married Milton Gilman Kenson. They had one son, William Gilman.

1680. **Martha,**[9] daughter of 930 Solomon[8] and Maria A. [Hurlburt] Balch, was born in 1846, and died at Waterville, Vermont. She married Charles Bixby, and they had two children: Mira, Renor.

1681. **Fidelia,**[9] youngest daughter of 930 Solomon[8] and Maria A. [Hurlburt] Balch, was born in 1848, and married David Prince Johnson. They had seven children: Myron, Clare, Charles, Martha, d. y.; Mary, John, Hannah.

1682. Alma H.,[9] daughter of 932 Allen[8] and Jane [Andrews] Balch, was born at Johnson, Vt., November 8, 1843, and died in March, 1889. She was married October 4, 1866, to Herbert C., son of Hiram A. Larkin. He was born at St. Armand, P. Q., October 4, 1841, and is a farmer. In 1882 they moved from Vermont to Mechanicsburg, Ohio, where they live. Their four children were born at Johnson : Allen A., b. July 25, 1867 ; Jennie V., b. Nov. 7, 1869 ; Bertie, b. Feb. 24, 1871 ; Mary, b. Jan. 23, 1874.

1683. Edwin K.,[9] son of 932 Allen[8] and Jane [Andrews] Balch, was born at Johnson, Vt., October 12, 1846, where he died, December 19, 1895, as the result of an accident seventeen months previous. He was a carpenter, and from 1881 to 1889 lived in Mechanicsburg, Ohio. He was married December 25, 1871, to Abbie J., daughter of Hiram A. Larkin. She was born May 4, 1845, at St. Armand, P. Q. Their two children were born at Johnson.

2338 INA M.,[10] b. Oct. 1, 1872.
2339 WARREN S.,[10] b. Feb. 24, 1874.

1686. Addie,[9] daughter of 932 Allen[8] and Jane [Andrews] Balch, was born at Johnson, Vt., December 25, 1857, and died in the same town, September 7, 1885. She was married February 14, 1884, to George Hall, of Connecticut. They had one daughter, born at Johnson, Jan. 1, 1885.

1687. Fred,[9] son of 933 Frederick P.[8] and Elvira [Clark] Balch, was born at Massena, N. Y., October 21, 1848. He was married November 8, 1869, to Ettie, daughter of James Murray. She was born September 80, 1848. Their four children were born at Massena, N. Y.

2340° FRED J.,[10] b. April 15, 1870.
2341° FRANK W.,[10] b. Aug. 1, 1873.
2342 ELVIRA,[10] b. April 3, 1876.
2343 JESSIE,[10] b. Aug. 25, 1881.

Fred is a steam fitter and machinist. He lives at Massena Springs, New York.

1696. Susan Elizabeth,[9] eldest daughter of 940 Samuel[8] and Nancy Maria [Bartlett] Balch, was born at Dalton, New Hampshire, December 27, 1835. She was married April 9, 1857, to Rufus Howard Pike, who was born at Londonderry, N. H., and died January 8, 1895. His widow lives at Manchester, N. H., where their two children were born. Sarah Helen, b. Aug. 21, 1859, d. y.; Florence Maria, b. Oct. 15, 1861, m. June 2, 1891, Willis Byron Kendall.

1697. George Granville,[9] son of 940 Samuel[8] and Nancy Maria [Bartlett] Balch, was born at Unity, N. H., August 17, 1837, and died at Port Royal, S. C., December 20, 1865, and was buried at Manchester, N. H. He was a mechanic. He married Harriet Whittier, who lives at Lynn, Mass. They had three children, all of whom died young.

2344 LIZZIE.[10]
2345 SAMUEL.[10]
2346 HARRIET.[10]

1700. Prolina L.,[9] daughter of 941 Moses[8] and Mary Ann [Burnham] Balch, was born at Johnson, Vt., December 24, 1834, and died at Epsom, N. H., June 18, 1878, and was buried at Goffstown, N. H. She was married July 8, 1856, to William L. Otis, of New Boston. They had four children : Frederic C., b. April 26, 1857, m. Dec. 7, 1880, to Minnie Johnson, lives at East Boston, Mass.; Grace M., b. Dec. 13, 1866, d. January 20, 1889; m. Feb. 14, 1886, to Frederick Waldo, of New Boston, N. H., Roscoe E., b. Feb. 21, 1870, living at East Boston, Mass.; Sarah B., b. May 24, 1876, d. at Epson, Feb. 25, 1877.

1701. Elizabeth A.,[9] daughter of 941 Moses[8] and Mary Ann [Burnham] Balch, was born at Johnson, Vt., February 22, 1837, and was married March 23, 1858, to Ira Christie, of New Boston, N. H., where they reside, and have four children : Martha and Mary, twins, living at Manchester, N. H.; Herbert, b. 1861, m. Avila Pinkney ; Blanche, m. Harry Morgan.

1702. Wayland F.,[9] son of 941 Moses[8] and Mary Ann
[Burnham] Balch, was born at Johnson, Vt., May 28, 1839,
and was married July 24, 1865, to Sarah F. Richardson, of
Westford, Mass., where they live, and have three children.

2347ª LENA E.,[10] b. 1866.
2348 AGNES D.,[10] b. 1870.
2349 MARY G.,[10] b. 1875.

1703. Sarah A.,[9] daughter of 941 Moses[8] and Mary Ann
[Burnham] Balch, was born at Johnson, Vt., October 31,
1841. She was married July 4, 1860, to Kirk C. Bartlett, of
Manchester, N. H. They reside in Manchester, and have
one daughter, Florence G., b. May 16, 1863, m. Nov. 10,
1887, Dr. Fred F. Fisher.

1704. Ellen Asinith,[9] daughter of 941 Moses[8] and Mary
Ann [Burnham] Balch, was born at Johnson, Vt., February
14, 1844, and was married June 11, 1767, to Royal H. Robie,
of Goffstown, N. H. They reside at Palatka, Fla., and have
one daughter, born at Creston, Iowa : Edna Lavina, b. Oct·
7, 1873, who was married at Palatka, Aug. 11, 1896, to Harry
E· Stewart.

1705. Charles S.,[9] son of 941 Moses[8] and Mary Ann
[Burnham] Balch, was born at Johnson, Vt., February 5,
1848, and was married at Dumberton, N. H., November 10,
1883, to Mary A. Moses. They reside at Goffstown, N. H.,
and have one daughter.

2350 FLORENCE J.,[10] b. Jan. 26, 1885.

1706. Samuel H.,[9] son of 941 Moses[8] and Mary Ann
[Burnham] Balch, was born at Goffstown, N. H., October 1,
1854, and was married April 26, 1881, to Ella L. Mudgett, of
Ware, N. H. They reside at Westford, Mass.

2351 GEORGE M., b. Oct. 26, 1888.

1708. Willard M.,[9] son of 942 Abijah[8] and Eliza [Nites]
Balch, was born at Johnson, Vt., April 17, 1840, where he
was a farmer, and died December 17, 1881. He was married
June 30, 1860, to Ann E., daughter of Peter and Olive

[Graves] Masure, who was born at Cambridge, Vt., December 6, 1842. Their three children were born in Johnson.

2352 EVA ELIZA,[10] b. Feb. 1, 1862; d. May 15, 1862.
2353 FREDERICK,[10] b. Aug. 13, 1864.
2354 HATTIE E.,[10] b. Sept. 9, 1866.

1710. **Almon,**[9] son of 942 Abijah[8] and Eliza [Nites] Balch, was born at Johnson, Vt., November 20, 1847, where he is engaged in farming. He enlisted in February, 1865, in the Eighth Vermont Infantry, but saw no field service. He was married November 9, 1869, to Mary E., daughter of Daniel and Elizabeth [Robinson] Hughes, who was born March 31, 1847, in Ohio. They have had four children. The three eldest were born at Sagone, Illinois, the youngest at Monticello, Illinois.

2355 EMMA ESTELLA,[10] b. Sept. 6, 1870.
2356 EDNA MAY,[10] b. April 5, 1872; d. Dec. 5, 1880.
2357 WILLIAM,[10] b. Nov. 21, 1873.
2358 CHARLES VERNON,[10] b. Oct. 16, 1875.

1711. **John W.,**[9] son of 946 John Jefferson[8] and Abigail G. [Mudgett] Balch, was born at New Boston, N. H., Sept. 10, 1828, and died at Kennebunkport, Maine, March 4, 1879. He was a ship carpenter, and also engaged in farming and in coast surveying. On January 25, 1852, he married Sarah E. Wormwood, who was born February 24, 1835, at Kennebunkport, Maine, where she now lives and her children were born.

2359* DANIEL ELLRIDGE,[10] b. April 22, 1853.
2360 GEORGE WILLIS,[10] b. Dec. 8, 1855.
2361 CHARLES FREDERICK,[10] b. Dec. 19, 1858.
2362 IDA ELIZABETH,[10] b. June 7, 1862; d. Nov. 1, 1865.
2363* LILL DORA,[10] b. Sept. 27, 1867.
2364 HENRY ROBIE,[10] b. June 27, 1869.
2365 FLORENCE,[10] b. May 31, 1873; d. Jan. 5, 1874.

1712. **Moses M.,**[9] son of 946 John Jefferson[8] and Abigail G. [Mudgett] Balch, was born at Sunapee, N. H., September 11, 1831, and is a lumber dealer at New Ipswich, N. H. In his business he lost his right hand. He was married November 20, 1856, to Harriet E. Stiles, of Wilton, N. H.

They have four children, the first born at Weare, and the others at Temple, N. H.

2366 ANNA J.,[10] b. Nov. 11, 1858.
2367* ELLER M.,[10] b. July 3, 1862.
2368* ABBY L.,[10] b. Feb. 1, 1870.
2369* ALBRO L.,[10] b. Jan. 8, 1878.

1713. Mary Emily,[9] daughter of 946 John Jefferson[8] and Abigail G. [Mudgett] Balch, was born at New Boston, N. H., July 17, 1840, and was married Oct. 16, 1864, to David G. Dickey, of Deering, N. H. He is a farmer. During the civil war he served in the Second New Hampshire regiment, and as a result of this service his health was seriously injured, having been in thirteen actual engagements and suffered many hardships. They reside at Lyndeboro, N. H., and have had one son, Neil J., b. Dec. 14, 1871 ; d. Feb. 18, 1883.

1715. Helen Abigail,[9] daughter of 948 Eliphalet[8] and Lucretia M. [Barker] Balch, was born at Fairhaven, Vt., September 5, 1834, and died in Johnson, Vt., August 16, 1881. She was married November 9, 1859, to Julious, son of Julious Bliss. He was born at Jericho, Vt., April 15, 1833, is a farmer, and lives in Morrisville, Vermont. They had four children. All were born in Jericho.

> ANNA ELIZA, b. July 23, 1860; m. George Charles Cooke, at Morristown, Vt., Aug. 19, 1891. One child, *Lena May*, b. Aug. 8, 1894.
> ELMER, b. Dec. 1, 1861; m. Elsie Estella Gould, at Stowe, Vt., Nov. 1, 1893.
> IDA FLORA, b. Jan. 7, 1864; m. John E. Woodworth, at Morristown, Vt., Jan. 22, 1891. One child, *John Sedgwick*, b. April 17, 1892; d. Sept. 13, 1893.
> JESSIE LUCRETIA, b. July 2, 1866; m. William W. Fairbanks, at Stowe, Vt., Nov. 1, 1893.

1717. Barker Sawyer,[9] son of 948 Eliphalet[8] and Lucretia M. [Barker] Balch, was born at Jericho, Vt., July 28, 1838, and was married March 18, 1868, to Anna Jane, daughter of Uzziel Whitcomb. She was born November 21, 1848. They live in Richmond, Vt., where he is engaged in farming, and their three children were born.

2370e FRANK ARTHUR,[10] b. April 25, 1870.
2371 CHARLES SUMNER,[10] b. June 1, 1873; d. July 9, 1883.
2372 JENNIE MABEL,[10] b. April 17, 1885.

1721. **Fayette,**[9] son of 948 Eliphalet[8] and Lucretia M. [Barker] Balch, was born at Jericho, Vt., August 23, 1848, and died in the same town, September 30, 1886, where he was a farmer. He was married March 18, 1874, to Mary Janette, daughter of Manasseh Osgood. She was born at Westford, Vt., August 6, 1844.

1722. **Effie Jane,**[9] daughter of 948 Eliphalet[8] and Lucretia M. [Barker] Balch, was born at Jericho, Vt., September 16, 1850. She was married April 20, 1875, to Dennis Eugene, son of Orlin Rood. He was born at Jericho, February 17, 1848, is a harness maker at Jericho, where their three children were born : Maude Alice, b. June 3, 1876 ; Madge Lucretia, b. Jan. 2, 1879; Helen Myra, b. June 21, 1880.

1723. **Henry H.,**[9] son of 951 William Plummer[8] and Sarah C. [Gove] Balch, was born at South Weare, N. H., January 16, 1847, is a farmer, and resides at South Weare, N. H. He is a Democrat, a Universalist, and a member of Mount William Lodge, I. O. O. F. He was married February 2, 1868, to Maria R., daughter of William and Mary P. Emery. She was born at North Weare, July 26, 1845. They have two children, both born at South Weare.

2373 EVA L.,[10] b. March 3, 1873.
2374 MYRTIE M.,[10] b. Jan. 2, 1875.

1724. **Delila Gove,**[9] daughter of 951 William Plummer[8] and Sarah C. [Gove] Balch, was born at South Weare, N. H., September 16, 1848. She was married December 30, 1870, to Edwin J., son of William and Eliza Tenney. He is a Republican. They are Universalists, and have one child, born at North Weare, where they live : Fred P., b. December 8, 1871.

1725. **Almena M.,**[9] daughter of 951 William Plummer[8]

and Sarah C. [Gove] Balch, was born at South Weare, N. H., March 11, 1850. She was married in August, 1881, to David N. Butterfield. They reside at North Lyndeboro, New Hampshire, post-office New Boston, and are Universalists. They have three children, all born at New Boston: Addie J., b. Jan. 25, 1882, d. Dec. 24, 1891; Mary Ella, b. Dec. 17, 1884; Florence E., b. Dec. 27, 1886; George N., b. March 29, 1888.

1726. **Emma D.**,[9] daughter of 951 William Plummer[8] and Sarah C. [Gove] Balch, was born at South Weare, N. H., July 18, 1855. She was married December 24, 1876, to George F., son of Raymond and Roxanna Hadley. He is a Democrat. They are Universalists, and live at Weare Centre, where their only child was born: Emma B., b. June 26, 1881.

1727. **Jennie Laura**,[9] daughter of 958 John A.[8] and Caroline [Stevenson] Balch, was born at Keeseville, N. Y., March 25, 1853. She was married June 3, 1869, to John W. Bishop, a lawyer, who is now a partner in the Underwood Veneer Company, at Wausau, Wisconsin. They have adopted two children: Chester E., b. March 18, 1882; Rena May, b. Oct. 16, 1888.

1728. **Clara Louisa**,[9] daughter of 958 John A.[8] and Caroline [Stevenson] Balch, was born at Peru, New York, January 20, 1855. She was married May 12, 1871, to Edson J. Goodrick, who is a lawyer. He was born June 21, 1878. They live at Oshkosh, Wisconsin, and have had three children: Raleigh Allen, b. Nov. 18, 1872, d. Aug. 8, 1896; Arthur Balch, b. Sept. 3, 1874; Edson J., b. June 21, 1878, d. May, 1895.

1729. **Elizabeth D.**,[9] daughter of 958 John A.[8] and Caroline [Stevenson] Balch, was born at Peru, N. Y., November 27, 1856, and lives at Dufur, Oregon. She was married December 29, 1872, to Alpha K. Dufur, at Oshkosh,

Wis. He owned a valuable flour mill at Dufur, and died
February 19, 1896. They had three children: Edna C., b·
Dec. 29, 1873, d. Nov. 12, 1882; Merritt Howe, b. March 16,
1875, d. Dec. 3, 1882; Daisy E., b. Jan. 23, 1880.

1730. Mary Kate,[9] daughter of 958 John A.[8] and Caro-
line [Stevenson] Balch, was born at Ausable Forks, N. Y.,
July 20, 1858. She was married August 2, 1886, to George
Milton Rock, an engineer. He was born September 17, 1856.
They live at Altoona, Wisconsin, and have four children:
John Allan, b. April 29, 1887; George Milton, b. Jan. 27,
1889; Hazel, b. Aug. 3, 1881; Frank Abner, b. Sept. 9,
1892.

1731. Charles P.,[9] son of 958 John A.[8] and Caroline
[Stevenson] Balch, was born at Iola, Wis., April 21, 1860,
and is a druggist at Dufur, Ore. He was married at Dufur,
June 28, 1891, to Mrs. Lois, daughter of Andrew J. Dufur,
Jr. Andrew J. was a cousin of Alpha K. Dufur, who mar-
ried 1729 Elizabeth D. Balch.

1734. Ossian E. D.,[9] son of 960 Ezra D.[8] and Martha
E. [Nye] Balch, was born at Northfield, Vt., July 21, 1853.
He was a farmer at Northfield, Vermont, and married, May 3,
1880, Sarah Green, of Amherst, Nova Scotia. They have
two children, one born at Amherst, N. S., the other at Barre,
Vermont.

  2375 LESTER W.,[10] b. July 1, 1881.
  2376 CARRIE M.,[10] b. Aug. 6, 1882.

1735. Allen E.,[9] son of 960 Ezra D.[8] and Martha E. [Nye]
Balch, was born at Northfield, Vt., October 7, 1855, and is a
stone cutter at Barre, Vermont. He married Etta Corliss, of
Ellenburg, N. Y., and they are members of the M. E. Church.
They have three children.

  2377 ORSON ALLEN,[10] b. Dec. 7, 1879.
  2378 ARABELLA ETTA,[10] b. Nov. 22, 1881.
  2379 LENA ETHEL,[10] b. Dec. 31, 1883.

1736. Etta Alma,[9] daughter of 960 Ezra D.[8] and Martha E. [Nye] Balch, was born at Iola, Wis., February 10, 1858. She married Ransom B. Vaughn, a blacksmith. They live at Barre, Vt., are members of the Methodist church, and have one child, Clarence, b. March 30, 1882.

1737. Orrelia E.,[9] daughter of 960 Ezra D.[8] and Martha E. [Nye] Balch, was born at Iola, Wis., March 3, 1861. She married Walter Kimball, of Worcester, Mass. He is a farmer, and they live at Coldbrook, Massachusetts. They had one child, Allen W., b. Feb. 23, 1885.

1738. Mattie E.,[9] daughter of 960 Ezra D.[8] and Martha E. [Nye] Balch, was born at Iola, Wis., May 19, 1867. She married Vernon E. Lindsey, a stone cutter at Barre, Vermont. They are members of the Methodist church, and have one child, a son, b. Jan. 3, 1886.

1739. John Allen,[9] son of 963 John B.[8] and Mary Ann [Stoddard] Balch, was born at Madison, Ohio, February 2, 1839. He was married August 13, 1862, to Mary E., daughter of Isaac and Charlotte Van Duzar. They have had three children.

   2380 LOTTIE ANN,[10] b. Nov. 25, 1863, at Saginaw, Mich.; d. Oct. 2, 1871, at Tipton, Ind.
   2381 HENRY ALLEN,[10] b. March 18, 1870, at Clifton, Ill.
   2382 GEORGE PERCY,[10] b. July 18, 1873, at West Unity, Ohio.

John Allen is a man of liberal views. He enlisted August 12, 1862, in the 72d Illinois Regiment, and served three years as a non-commissioned officer. He was with his regiment in all its campaigns and battles, except for three months while a prisoner of war at Cahaba, Alabama. He is a railroad contractor at Frankfort, Indiana, and his wife is the state organizer of the Women's Christian Temperance Union.

1740. William Henry,[9] son of 963 John B.[8] and Mary Ann [Stoddard] Balch, was born at Madison, Ohio, April 10, 1840, and died of small-pox in the army hospital at La Grange, Tennessee, Jan. 14, 1863. He was well formed and graceful. He enlisted at the same time with his brother, John

A., and went to the front. Between them there was an unusual fraternal love.

1742. **Ann Eliza,**[9] daughter of 963 John B.[8] and **Mary** Ann [Stoddard] Balch, was born at Madison, Ohio, April 8, 1844. After her mother's death she lived at Berlin, Wisconsin, and taught school. She was married at Eureka, Wisconsin, February 18, 1864, to William H., son of Israel and Elizabeth [Getman] Williams. He was born in Herkimer County, N. Y., February 17, 1836. He served for three years in the Third Wisconsin Battery and was the only man who was not out of the command for a single day. He had a farm at Aurora, Wisconsin, until 1884, when they removed to Raymond, South Dakota, for a time. They now live at Meadow Valley, Wisconsin. They have had seven children, the six eldest born at Aurora, the youngest at Winnebago, Wisconsin: Melvin Henry, b. May 19, 1866, m. Delvina Bertrand; Grace Julia, b. Sept. 5, 1867, m. Samuel Stewart; Gertrude Eliza, b. Dec. 16, 1869, m. Charles Hazelton; Roger, b. April 14, 1872, d. July 23, 1873; Ralph Ovette, b. July 24, 1874; Henry Oscar, b. Aug. 13, 1881; William, b. May 30, 1884, d. June 3, 1884.

1743. **Oscar Nelson,**[9] son of 963 John B.[8] and Mary Ann [Stoddard] Balch, was born at Madison, Ohio, May 16, 1846, and died, unmarried, at Aurora, Wisconsin, in 1873. He was in business with his brother, John Allen.

1745. **Julia Ann,**[9] daughter of 963 John B.[8] and Mary Ann [Stoddard] Balch, was born at Fon du Lac, Wisconsin, December 4, 1851, ten days before her mother's death. She commenced teaching at the age of eighteen and taught several terms at Necedah, Wisconsin. She was married in 1874 at Aurora, Wisconsin, to E. O., son of Nehemiah D. and Lucy [Brook] Rundell. He was born at Russell, N. Y., July 10, 1846. He is a farmer and cranberry grower at Aurora, where their two children were born: Nina L., b. July 16, 1875; Hayes A., b. Nov. 21, 1876.

1747. Laura Ellen,[9] daughter of 963 John B.[8] and Ellen O. [Stevens] Balch, was born at Fon du Lac, Wisconsin, August 29, 1854. She was married at Necedah, Wisconsin, in 1873, to Edwin, son of Edwin C. and Emily Bullis. He was born at Poton Creek, Dane County, Wisconsin, January 15, 1849. They lived at Scranton, Wisconsin, for five years, at La Crosse for two years, in Dakota for two years, at De Kalb, Illinois, and at Chicago, where they now live. Mr. Bullis has been in railroad employ, except during his residence at Dakota, where he owned a farm. They have two children ; John C., b. Feb. 24, 1874, at Scranton, Wisconsin; Bessie L., b. June 9, 1880, at La Crosse.

1748. Frances Amelia,[9] daughter of 963 John B.[8] and Ellen O. [Stevens] Balch, was born at Aurora, Wisconsin, March 28, 1856. She was married in 1874 at Balch's Ranch, Wisconsin, to George, son of John Hockenhull, who was born at Oak Creek, Wisconsin, November 6, 1851, and is a merchant at Alton, Kansas. They have one child, Olive, b. July 15, 1876, at Berlin, Wisconsin.

1750. Fred Willard,[9] son of 963 John B.[8] and Ellen O. [Stevens] Balch, was born at Aurora, Wisconsin, June 15, 1860, and is engaged in cranberry culture at Daly, Wisconsin. He was married in 1885 to Rilda, daughter of John Darling. She was born at Crystal Lake, Wisconsin, June 25, 1861. They reside at Balch's Ranch, Wisconsin, and have three children :

2383 GLADYS MYRTLE,[10] b. Jan. 14, 1886.
2384 GARNET BLANCHE,[10] b. July 18, 1891.
2385 JOHN WILLARD,[10] b. Apr. 16, 1896.

1752. Nina Jessie,[9] daughter of 963 John B.[8] and Ellen O. [Stevens] Balch, was born at Saginaw, Michigan, October 25, 1863, and is a successful real estate and merchandise broker at Minneapolis, Minnesota. She is the only woman thus occupied in the city and is also an acceptable writer of stories for magazines. On May 27, 1896, she was married to Winter Davis, son of General Levi A. Nutting, of Faribault, Minnesota.

1753. **Hattie,**[9] daughter of 963 John B.[8] and Ellen O. [Stevens] Balch, was born at Aurora, Wisconsin, November 18, 1869. She was educated at Fon du Lac, Wisconsin, and was married November 27, 1888, to Joseph A. Gosselin of Minneapolis, Minnesota, where they live and their three children were born: Hazel L., b. March 12, 1890; Guy Balch, b. March 31, 1891; Jessie O., b. Aug. 17, 1893.

1755. **William Allen,**[9] son of 965 Hiram Allen[8] and Emily H. [Curtis] Balch, was born in Chicago, Illinois, August 27, 1869, and was married on June 11, 1895 to Clara Comstock, daughter of Dudley W. and Martha Parham Farlin of Washington, D. C. He was educated in the public and private schools of Washington, later taking up the study of architecture, which is now his profession. He went to Chicago in 1892 and was employed in the construction department of the World's Fair until April, 1894, when he entered the office of D. H. Burnham & Co., architects, with whom he has remained.

1759. **Edward Perley,**[9] son of 972 Humphrey[8] and Hannah P. [Bradstreet] Balch, was born at Topsfield, Mass., January 13, 1850, and is a publisher living at West Newbury, Mass. He married Miss Mary H. Orne.

1760. **Gilbert Brownell,**[9] son of 972 Humphrey[8] and Hannah P. [Bradstreet] Balch, was born at Topsfield, Mass., February 9, 1856. He married Miss Mary E. Perkins. No issue. He graduated from Dartmouth College in 1877. He is in business with his brother, Edward P., and resides in Boston.

1761. **Anna Bradstreet,**[9] daughter of 972 Humphrey[8] and Hannah P. [Bradstreet] Balch, was born at Topsfield, Mass., February 18, 1860. She married Frederick Jordon.

1763. **Mary Augusta,**[9] daughter of 973 Jeremiah
Stone[8] and Mary [Shepherd] Balch, was born at Salem,
Mass., June 16, 1853, and died March 31, 1888. She mar-
ried Thurton Perkins and had two children : Sallie M., b.
June 19, 1876, and Mollie W., b. July 15, 1880.

1768. **Florence Eliza,**[9] daughter of 974 Benjamin
Johnson[8] and Eliza [Killam] Balch, was born at Topsfield,
Mass., September 3, 1859. She taught music for three years
at the Weslean Female Seminary at Oxford, Ohio, and is
now a teacher of vocal music at Mt. Holyoke Seminary.

FOURTH BRANCH.

Descendants of 9 Freeborn.[3]

Descendants of 51 Freeborn.[4]

1773. **Mary E.,**[9] daughter of 975 Lewis[8] and Sarah
[Tucker] Balch, was born at West Troy, N. Y., July 5, 1853.
She was married April 15, 1873, to Edwin Plantz, who was
born at Gloversville, N. Y., June 15, 1847. They live at
Saratoga Springs, and have had eight children : Lillian,
b. March 14, 1874; Lewis Henry, b. Jan. 14, 1876, d. May,
1881 ; George, b. Sept. 24, 1878 ; Harry, b. Sept. 11, 1880, d.
February, 1882 ; Henry, b. Aug. 11, 1882; Viola, b. June
11, 1884 ; Edward, b. June 14, 1886 ; William J., b. March
31, 1888.

1774. **Benjamin H.,**[9] son of 975 Lewis[8] and Sarah
[Tucker] Balch, was born at Greenwich, N. Y., December
22, 1855, and was married May 8, 1877, to Lavira, daughter
of George and Eunice [Merrill] Luffman. She was born at
Balston Spa, October 14, 1853. They live at Balston, N. Y.,
and have had four children, born in that town.

2386 EDWIN H.,[10] b. Dec. 23, 1879.
2387 BENJAMIN H.,[10] b. April 15, 1881; d. June 27, 1882.
2388 SARAH E.,[10] b. April 2, 1884.
2389 HOWARD E.,[10] b. Sept. 11, 1887.

1783. **Fannie Augusta,**[9] daughter of 988 Walter Byron[8] and Augusta Evelyn [Demeritt] Balch, was born at

Manchester, New Hampshire, May 19, 1867, and was married in 1893 to Morris Lamprey, of Manchester.

1785. **Louisa Shattuck,**[9] daughter of 993 Henry Augustus[8] and Lauretta C. [Whitcomb] Balch, was born in 1849. She married Oscar J. Gilbert, of Lowell, Mass., and had a number of children.

Descendants of 52 Benjamin.[4]

1796. **Joanna,**[9] daughter of 1027 Benjamin[8] and Ann [Van Benthusen] Balch, was born May 22, 1823, and died January 14, 1877. She was married June 18, 1850, to Wayland C. Parker, and had no children.

1797. **George H.,**[9] son of 1027 Benjamin[8] and Ann [Van Benthusen] Balch, was born July 1, 1825, and died May 15, 1892. He was not married, a baker, and lived at Syracuse, New York.

1798. **Benjamin James,**[9] son of 1027 Benjamin[8] and Ann [Van Benthusen] Balch, was born August 27, 1828, and died October 7, 1887. He was an iron moulder at Syracuse, New York, where he was born and died. He was married December 29, 1863, to Lizzie Gray, who was born at Knox, N. Y. They had one child.

2390 CORA ELLA,[10] b. Jan. 30, 1865.

1799. **John W.,**[9] son of 1027 Benjamin[8] and Ann [Van Benthusen] Balch, was born August 10, 1837, at Manlius, N. Y., and is a brass molder at Syracuse, N. Y. He was married June 1, 1860, to Addie A., daughter of Robert P. and Mary A. Aylsworth, of Syracuse, N. Y., who was born July 16, 1843, and died March 16, 1870. They had two children.

2391* IDA ANN,[10] b. March 18, 1861.
2392* ESTHER JOANNA,[10] b. June 4, 1862.

John W. married second, September 26, 1872, Harriet A. Aylsworth, a sister of his first wife, and they had two children.

2393 FRANK JEROME,[10] b. Nov. 21, 1873.
2394 FLORENCE MAY,[10] b. May 17, 1878.

1800. John William,[9] son of 1032 John[8] and Mary E. [Chaloner] Balch, was born at Trescott, Me., February 1, 1834. He was married November 27, 1862, to Mary E., daughter of Ellery Turner. She was born at North Cutler, Me., June 20, 1840, and died at sea near Rio de Janeiro, July 6, 1889. They had no children.

John W. served in the U. S. navy during the civil war. He entered the service as acting master, September 4, 1861, and was ordered to the " Florida." He was detached November 13, 1862, and ordered to command the " Houquah." On June 19, 1865, he was granted leave of absence, and was discharged October 20, 1865. During his service he was promoted to acting volunteer lieutenant, was captured, and held a prisoner of war in Salisbury, N. C., and in Libby, at Richmond, Va. Was lieutenant commanding the " Houquah," in the North Atlantic Squadron, January 15, 1865, and participated in the capture of Fort Fisher. He is a master mariner in the merchant service, and since 1870 has been most of the time upon the Pacific coast, making his home in San Francisco. He is master of the ship John A. Briggs.

1801. Louis O.,[9] son of 1032 John[8] and Mary E. [Chaloner] Balch, was born at Trescott, Me., October 13, 1835. He never married. He was his father's chief clerk, cashier and bookkeeper. He made a trip to France, arriving home Sunday, December 23, 1855, sick with what proved to be small-pox, of which he died January 8, 1856. He was of a noble, gentle and kind nature.

1802. Mary Louise,[9] daughter of 1032 John[8] and Mary E. [Chaloner] Balch, was born April 11, 1837, and lives at Brookline, Massachusetts. She is a woman of rare business capacity, and owns the " Louisburg," the principal summer hotel at Bar Harbor, Maine.

1803. Hannah Elizabeth,[9] daughter of 1032 John[8] and Mary E. [Chaloner] Balch, was born at Trescott, Maine,

April 18, 1839, and died at Detour, Michigan, March 5, 1865.
She was married November 2, 1858, to Rev. Samuel Brooks,
who is a professor in the theological college at Kalamazoo,
Michigan. His brother was the president of that institution
for thirty years. Rev. Samuel Brooks was a missionary at
Sault de Ste Maria at the time of the death of his wife. They
had two children: Helen, b. Sept. 10, 1859, and Elizabeth
Maria, b. Feb. 27, 1865, d. Nov. 28, 1869. Helen was born
at Beverly Farms, Mass., and married, Oct. 24, 1888, Henry
S. Mahon, a lawyer. They live at Duluth, Minnesota, and
have had three children: Winifred Balch. b. March 16,
1890; George Brooks, b. Sept. 10, 1891, d. y.; Helen, b.
Oct. 28, 1892.

1804. **Anna Maria,**[9] daughter of 1032 John[8] and Mary
E. [Chaloner] Balch, was born at Trescott, Me., August 12,
1841, lives at Brookline, Massachusetts, and is a teacher.

1805. **Henry Clay,**[9] son of 1032 John[8] and Mary E.
[Chaloner] Balch, was born at Trescott, Maine, December 7,
1843, and is living in New Orleans. He served for three
years in the Union army, and fought among others in the
battles of Bull Run, Williamsburg and Centreville.

1806. **Amory Otis,**[9] son of 1032 John[8] and Mary E.
[Chaloner] Balch, was born at Trescott, Maine, January 7,
1846, and died unmarried, September 21, 1866. He was a
lieutenant in the 86th United States Colored Infantry, and
fought, among others, in the battles of Fredericksburg, An-
tietam, and Blue Mountain.

1808. **Alice Hall,**[9] daughter of 1032 John[8] and Mary
E. [Chaloner] Balch, was born at Trescott, Maine, October
15, 1849. She married, October 15, 1879, William F. Root.
They live at Buffalo, N. Y. They had three children: Harold, b. July, 1884, d. y.; Florence Madeline, b. July 22,
1885, d. Jan. 21, 1890; Ernest N., b. Nov. 22, 1891, d. May
24, 1893.

1809. George Haley,[9] son of 1032 John[8] and Mary E. [Chaloner] Balch, was born at Moose River, Me., October 6, 1851, and is living at South Boston, Mass.   He is a printer in Boston, and was married, January 12, 1877, to Manetta Maria, daughter of Thomas Barnard Green.   She was born at South Boston, August 12, 1856.   They have four children, born at South Boston.

2395   GEORGE LOUIE,[10] b. March 18, 1878.
2396   ELIZABETH,[10] b. Oct. 26, 1880; d. Dec. 5, 1880.
2397   MARY ELIZABETH,[10] b. Jan. 6, 1882.
2398   NETTIE LOUISA,[10] b. May 31, 1887.

1811. Hiram Augustus,[9] son of 1034 Hiram Augustus[8] and Martha [Maryman] Balch, was born at Trescott, Me., September 18, 1837, and died January 22, 1894.   He was married March 25, 1866, to Catherine, daughter of Stephen D. and Winifred B. Ruddell.   She was born at Lancaster, Missouri, March 25, 1847.   About 1858 he emigrated from Maine to the Pacific coast.   For ten years he lived at Olympia, and for fifteen at Oakville, Wash.   While crossing the Chehalis river, from Oakville to his ranch, in a canoe, it was upset, and in attempting to save his child, George, they were both drowned.   His wife and other children, who were in the boat at the time, were rescued.   He was an industrious and successful farmer.   There were seventeen children, three of whom died unnamed.

2399*   WINIFRED HANNAH,[10] b. Feb. 2, 1867.
2400*   MARTHA,[10] b. Oct. 7, 1868.
2401   CALLIE ANN,[10] b. Aug. 24, 1870.
2402   BENJAMIN ALBERT,[10] b. April 9, 1872.
2403   STEPHEN DALY,[10] b. March 18, 1875.
2404   HENRY,[10] } twins, b. June 4, 1877.
2405   HARRIET,[10] }
2406   KATIE,[10] b. Sept. 12, 1879.
2407   HIRAM AUGUSTUS,[10] b. May 5, 1882.
2408   JOHN,[10] b. March 15, 1884.
2409   TRESCOTT,[10] b. March 19, 1886.
2410   CHARLES,[10] b. July 30, 1888.
2411   GEORGE,[10] b. June 22, 1890; drowned Jan. 22, 1894.
2412   WILLIAM LAFAYETTE,[10] b. Sept. 18, 1893.

1812. **Hannah Stone,**[9] daughter of 1034 Hiram Augustus[8] and Martha [Maryman] Balch, was born at Trescott, Maine, October 24, 1839, and died at Lubec, Maine, March 17, 1886. She was married at Lubec, February 15, 1866, to Abner MacFadden, a sea captain. He was born in 1835, and died June 1, 1892. They had three children, born at Trescott: Martha Balch, b. Nov. 24, 1867; Lewis Balch, b. Sept. 22, 1869; Mary Harriet, b. Sept. 12, 1871.

1813. **Harriet M.,**[9] daughter of 1034 Hiram Augustus[8] and Martha [Maryman] Balch, was born at Trescott, Maine, November 4, 1842, and lives at Cape Elizabeth, Maine. She was married December 6, 1879, to Albert W. Fickett. They have no children.

1818. **Emily Ames,**[9] daughter of 1060 James Ripley[8] and Margaret [Robb] Balch, was born May 19, 1870, at Weaverville, Cal. She was married June 19, 1889, to Dr. W. H. LaBaree, a dentist at Weaverville. They have one child, a daughter, Margaret Balch, b. Dec. 19, 1895.

1824. **Frank True,**[9] son of 1062 Jacob William[8] and Sarah Ann [Bradbury] Balch, was born at Machias, Me., March 24, 1845, and is a merchant at Boston, Wash., and a member of the State Legislature in 1897. He was married January 15, 1887, to Sarah Esther, daughter of Alanson B. and Matilda Smith. She was born February 19, 1851, at Ulster, Penn. They have four children. The two eldest were born at Quillenute, and the two youngest at Boston, Wash.

2413 AUGUSTUS WILLIAM,[10] b. Nov. 4, 1887.
2414 TRUE BRADBURY,[10] b. April 30, 1889.
2415 HENRY WIRE,[10] b. March 25, 1891; d. Sept. 30, 1891.
2416 PENN NEY,[10] b. Aug. 30, 1892.

1831. **Minnie B.,**[9] daughter of 1062 Jacob William[8] and Sarah Ann [Bradbury] Balch, was born at Machias, Maine, September 20, 1862. She was married December 18, 1884, to James Edwin McLean, son of Charles Ryne and Susan

Carlile [Carter] Higgins. He was born November 10, 1854, at Wentworth, Nova Scotia. They live at Tyee, Washington, where their children were born: Susie Edith, b. June 29, 1885; Frank Truman, b. Jan. 14, 1887; George Carlile, b. March 4, 1888; Agnes Louisa, b. July 28, 1889; Ethel, b. Dec. 20, 1890; William Buth, b. April 2, 1892; Berttie, b. Aug. 13, 1893.

1834. **Ida May,**[9] daughter of 1065 Henry Crawford[8] and Catherine A. [Newton] Balch, was born at Kingston, N. Y., June 29, 1853. She was married October 30, 1884, to Rev. Harvey Hostetler, a Presbyterian minister. They live at Sioux City, Iowa.

1835. **Charles Taylor,**[9] son of 1065 Henry Crawford[8] and Catherine A. [Newton] Balch, was born at Brooklyn, N. Y., October 22, 1856, and is a manufacturer of cloaks and suits in New York city. He was married to Annie, daughter of M. J. Calverley, of Brooklyn, N. Y., April 18, 1882. She was born at Brooklyn, July 2, 1859. They have had four children, the first and third born at Brooklyn, New York, and the second and fourth at East Orange, New Jersey.

2417   ANNA LAURETTA,[10] b. Feb. 13, 1883; d. Dec. 1, 1894.
2418   CHARLES H.,[10] b. April 2, 1885.
2419   WALTER NEWTON,[10] b. Dec. 16, 1886.
2420   KITTY IRINE,[10] b. Oct. 27, 1888.

1836. **Edward Crawford,**[9] son of 1065 Henry Crawford[8] and Catherine A. [Newton] Balch, was born at Brooklyn, N. Y., July 17, 1858. He is a manufacturer of cloaks and suits in New York city, and lives at Maplewood, New Jersey. He was married March 20, 1879, to Kittie L., daughter of John A. McKinney. She was born in New York city, February 27, 1861. They have four children, three born in New York city, and one at Maplewood, New Jersey.

2421   EDWARD CRAWFORD,[10] b. Dec. 27, 1879.
2422   IDA MAY,[10] b. Feb. 28, 1882.
2423   HENRY NEWTON,[10] b. June 13, 1884.
2424   EVERETT PURDY,[10] b. Jan. 22, 1893.

1838. Thomas B.,[9] son of 1069 George Washington[8] and Mary E. [Cranage] Balch, was born at Detroit, Mich., October 22, 1861. He is unmarried, and until 1895 was associated in business with his father, with office in the Produce Exchange, New York city.

1839. Mary E.,[9] daughter of 1069 George Washington[8] and Mary E. [Cranage] Balch, was born at Mt. Clemens, Mich., September 25, 1865. She was married to F. T. Ranney. They have no children.

Descendants of 58 William.[4]

1847. William,[9] son of 1077 Hiram Tenney[8] and Mary Sophia [Morse] Balch, was born at Groveland, August 18, 1869. He was married January 15, 1891, to Nellie, daughter of Benjamin Stevens.

2425 MARGUERITE STEVENS,[10] b. Aug. 26, 1892.
2426 RAYMOND TENNEY,[10] b. Dec. 8, 1894.

1863. William,[9] son of 1104 Lowell Thayer[8] and Martha T. [Thompson] Balch, was born at Pawtucket, R. I., February 16, 1869, and is on the Boston police force. He was married November 30, 1892, to Nora Fickett, of Millbridge, Maine.

1864. Edward Kittridge,[9] son of 1104 Lowell Thayer[8] and Martha T. [Thompson] Balch, was born at Pawtucket, R. I., May 5, 1871, and is with Fleischman & Co., compressed yeast, Boston, Mass. He was married July 25, 1894, to Esther L. Brown.

1865. Martha Thompson,[9] daughter of 1104 Lowell Thayer[8] and Martha T. [Thompson] Balch, was born at Pawtucket, R. I., December 11, 1874. She married Thomas C. Stewart, of New York city. They live in Brooklyn, N. Y., and have two children: William Lowell, b. Oct. 24, 1892, and Grace Evlyn, b. Sept. 15, 1895.

1869. Daniel,[9] son of 1115 Ebenezer Gunnison[8] and Eliza [Hall] Balch, was born at Newburyport, Mass., in

1853. He was married August 25, 1874, to Isabella Hall Burnham. They live at Newburyport, and have one son.

2427 EBEN GEORGE,[10] b. Oct. 12, 1875.

1870. Lucy Ann,[9] daughter of 1115 Ebenezer Gunnison[8] and Eliza [Hall] Balch, was born at Newburyport, Mass., April 6, 1857, and died in the same town, March 29, 1888. She was married June 16, 1884, to William Clark Morse.

1871. George H.,[9] son of 1115 Ebenezer Gunnison[8] and Eliza [Hall] Balch, was born at Newburyport, Mass., in 1861, and died February 15, 1895. He was married October 14, 1882, to Annie Eliza Davidson. Their children are:

2428 CHARLES HALL,[10] b. Mch. 22, 1884.
2429 ANNIE REBECCA,[10] b. Oct. 2, 1886.
2430 MARION ELIZA,[10] b. Sept. 27, 1888.
2431 LILLIAN PEARLE,[10] b. Jan. 17, 1890.
2432 GEORGE EBEN,[10] b. Mch. 16, 1893.

1873. William[9] son of 1119 William Charles[8] and Elizabeth Ann [Hamilton] Balch, was born at Newburyport, Mass., March 20, 1848, and lives at Dorchester, Massachusetts. He is not married. He graduated at the Brown High School, at Newburyport, in 1864, and was the valedictorian of his class. He was in cotton, metal and insurance business until 1885, and since then has been with the firm of Howe, Balch & Co., Boston and Calcutta.

1874. Gertrude Arline,[9] daughter of 1119 William Charles[8] and Elizabeth Ann [Hamilton] Balch, was born at Newburyport, Mass., October 24, 1849. She was married in Boston, Oct. 24, 1877, to William Henry Brewster, of Boston. He is president of the New England Burglary Insurance Company, which he organized. They live in Boston, and have no children.

1875. Walter Hamilton,[9] son of 1119 William Charles[8] and Elizabeth Ann [Hamilton] Balch, was born at Newburyport, Mass., August 28, 1851. He was in the lumber business for over twenty years, and since 1894 has been in the life insurance business in Boston. He was married October 3, 1874, to Sarah H. Cate, of Gardner, Maine. They have one child.

2433 GERTRUDE,[10] b. Dec. 13, 1886.

1876. Arthur Stone,[9] son of 1119 William Charles[8] and Elizabeth Ann [Hamilton] Balch, was born at Newburyport, Mass., October 18, 1853. He is a member of the firm of Howe, Balch & Co., dyestuffs and importers, Boston and Calcutta. He was married March 17, 1880, to Ella, daughter of Moses H. and Ellen M. [Low] Shaw, and widow of Frank W. Friend, of Gloucester, Mass. They have one child, and one adopted.

2434 ELLEN FRIEND,[10] b. July 29, 1877, of Frank W. and Ella (Shaw) Friend.
2435 EDITH,[10] b. Jan. 9, 1881.

1878. Edith Ashton,[9] daughter of 1119 William Charles[8] and Elizabeth Ann [Hamilton] Balch, was born at Newburyport, Mass., January 12, 1856. She graduated at the High and Pitman schools of Newburyport. She was married October 17, 1877, to Moses Foster Sweetser. He is an author of artists' biographies, a series of American guide books, King's Handbooks, and other works. They have had two children: Harold, b. June 17, 1880, d. June 6, 1894; Arthur, b. July 16, 1888.

1879. Gerald Spofford,[9] son of 1119 William Charles[8] and Elizabeth Ann [Hamilton] Balch, was born at Newburyport, Mass., February 16, 1859, and died July 22, 1896. He was note teller in the Maverick National Bank of Boston, and was married February 16, 1891, to Lydia Estelle, daughter of George W. and Caroline M. [Stanyan] Towle, of Walpole, Massachusetts. They had two children.

2436 ELEANOR,[10] b. Dec. 27, 1891; d. Dec. 2, 1892.
2437 ELIZABETH,[10] b. Dec. 26, 1894; d. Mar. 8, 1895.

1881. LeBreton,[9] son of 1121 George Edward[8] and Eliz-

GEORGE HALLET BALCH.
(1880)

: was the fourth generation in lineal descent of insurance underwriters. For portraits of
ancestors see pages 170, 174, 414.

abeth Johnson [LeBreton] Balch, was born at Newburyport,
Mass., April 10, 1855, and is in the wholesale beef business
at Ogden, Utah. He was married October 15, 1895, to Mary
Maude, daughter of Samuel Franklin and Alice Louise Harris. She was born February 28, 1875. They have one son.

2438 GEORGE EDWARD,[10] b. Aug. 22, 1896.

1882. **Sarah Beck,**[9] daughter of 1121 George Edward[8]
and Elizabeth Johnson [LeBreton] Balch, was born at Newburyport, July 29, 1857, where she now lives. She is not
married, and is an artist and engraver on silver.

1883. **Lewis,**[9] son of 1121 George Edward[8] and Elizabeth Johnson [LeBreton] Balch, was born at Newburyport,
Mass., February 25, 1861. He built a factory for manufacturing patent leather at Amesbury, Massachusetts, and is
now a dealer in wool in Boston. He was married May 20,
1890, to Margaret Currier, daughter of Henry M. and Sarah
[Currier] Cross. They live in Newburyport, and have one
child.

2439 ELLEN LEWIS,[10] b. Aug. 11, 1898.

1890. **George Hallet,**[9] son of 1138 Joseph Williams[8]
and Maria [Hallet] Balch, was born at Boston, May 27, 1847,
where he died, unmarried, February 25, 1894. He was with
the Boylston Insurance Company, succeeded his father as its
president, and held the office at the time of his death. He
was a man of the strictest integrity and highest business
principles, and a true friend.

1892. **Henry Gordon,**[9] son of 1138 Joseph Williams[8]
and Maria [Hallet] Balch, was born at Dedham, Mass., September 15, 1858. He is president of the First National Bank
at Laramie, Wyoming. He was married January 15, 1889,
to Harriet Crandell, daughter of Levi and Anne [Charles-
worth] Crow. She was born at Troy, N. Y., July 9, 1861.
They have two children, born at Bozeman, Montana.

2440 GORDON HENRY,[10]
2441 MARJORY HALLET,[10] } twins, b. Oct. 10, 1890.

1894. **Joseph,**[9] son of 1138 Joseph Williams[8] and Agnes
L. [Greene] Balch, was born February 3, 1861, at Jamaica
Plain, which is his residence. He is in the wool business in
Boston, and is prominent in outdoor sports at Dedham.

1895. **Franklin Greene,**[9] son of 1138 Joseph Williams[8]
and Agnes L. [Greene] Balch, was born at West Roxbury,
Mass., April 26, 1864. He is a surgeon to out-patients at
Carney Hospital and at the Massachusetts General Hospital,
Boston, Mass. He took the degree A. B. at Harvard Uni-
versity in 1888, and in 1892 the degrees of M. D. and A. M.
He was married at Jamaica Plain, Boston, November 6, 1894,
to Lucy Rockwell, daughter of Charles Pickering and Cor-
nelia [Rockwell] Bowditch. She was born at Geneseo, N.
Y., August 24, 1868. Her mother was the daughter of Judge
Rockwell, of Pittsfield, Mass.

2442 FRANKLIN GREENE,[10] } twins, b. May 8, 1896.
2443 CHARLES BOWDITCH,[10] }

1896. **John,**[9] son of 1138 Joseph Williams[8] and Agnes
L. [Greene] Balch, was born at Jamaica Plain, Mass., May 4,
1865, and is an electrical engineer. He was married at Dubuque, Iowa, February 16, 1897, to Katharine Kellogg, daughter of George Lansing and Margaret Kellogg [Rockwell]
Torbert. She was born August 2, 1872, at Utica, N. Y.
They live at Jamaica Plain, Mass.

1900. **Emily Greene,**[9] daughter of 1145 Francis Vergnies[8] and Ellen Maria [Noyes] Balch, was born January 8,
1867, at Jamaica Plain, Massachusetts. She took the degree
of A. B. from Bryn Mawr in 1889, and won the European
fellowship prize. She has since been a student along economic and social lines at Boston, Paris, and the University of
Berlin. In 1896 she became assistant in economics at Wellesley College.

1901. **Elizabeth,**[9] daughter of 1145 Francis Vergnies[8]
and Ellen Maria [Noyes] Balch, was born August 29, 1868,
at Jamaica Plain, Massachusetts. She took special courses

at Radcliffe College, being especially interested in history.
She has since taught successfully at Louisville, Kentucky.

1903. Francis Noyes[9] son of 1145 Francis Vergnies[8]
and Ellen Maria [Noyes] Balch, was born November 23, 1873,
at Jamaica Plain, Massachusetts. He graduated in 1896 from
Harvard University, with honorable mention in natural history, and is taking a post graduate course in zoology and
cognate branches.

1911. Louisa Annie,[9] daughter of 1164 Daniel Stickney[8]
and Mary Jane [George] Balch, was born at Lyons, Iowa,
April 7, 1864, and is a teacher there in the public schools.
She is not married.

1912. Clifton Fletcher,[9] son of 1164 Daniel Stickney[8]
and Mary Jane [George] Balch, was born at Lyons, Iowa,
March 4, 1867, and lives at Winona, Minnesota, where he is
a storekeeper for the Chicago and Northwestern Railroad.
He was married at Clinton, Iowa, October 19, 1891, to Ida
B. A., daughter of Chauncey R. and Hattie A. Dickinson.
She was born at Clinton, Iowa, March 29, 1871. They have
one daughter, born at Winona.

2444 GLADYS IRENE,[10] b. Aug. 15, 1892.

1914. Mary Elizabeth,[9] daughter of 1167 John Kirby
Perry[8] and Sarah Amelia [Barbour] Balch, was born at Lyons,
Iowa, May 16, 1872. She graduated in 1894, with the degree
of Bachelor of Laws, from Smith College, Northampton,
Massachusetts, and in 1896 from the Connecticut State Nor-
mal School, New Britain, Connecticut.

TENTH GENERATION.

FIRST BRANCH.

Descendants of 5 Samuel.[3]
Descendants of 21 Samuel.[4]

1918. Edwin,[10] son of 1174 Christopher S.[9] and Susan M. [Robinson] Balch, was born at Easton, N. Y., August 21, 1859, and is a member of the firm of Mealey & Balch, at Greenwich, N. Y. He married, November 25, 1885, Nellie M. Stephenson, of Cambridge, N. Y. She died Feb. 3, 1891, aged 29 years. They had one child.

2445 LILLIE S.,[11] b. June 8, 1886.

Edwin married second, January 11, 1893, Anna M. Ensign, of Easton, N. Y. They have one child.

2446 ENSIGN C.,[11] b. March 6, 1894.

1919. Amelia E.,[10] daughter of 1175 John Henry[9] and Abby Ilzaide [Lee] Balch, was born at Cambridge, N. Y., February 18, 1849, and died at Mayville, N. Y., January 18, 1886, and was buried at Cambridge. She was married November 24, 1877, to Charles A., son of Waterman and Harriet Thayer Tinkeom. He was born at Mayville, N. Y., May 1, 1845. They had one daughter, Florence J., b. June 9, 1880.

1920. Fannie M.,[10] daughter of 1175 John Henry[9] and Abby Ilzaide [Lee] Balch, was born at Cambridge, May 16, 1853. She was married March 18, 1873, to Moses A., son of John and Eliza Hill, who was born at Shushan, N.Y., August 14, 1848, and is a farmer. They live at Coila, N. Y., and have eleven children, born in the town of Cambridge: John

Henry, b. Feb. 4, 1874; Ann Eliza, b. Aug. 15, 1875, d. Jan. 23, 1894; Charlie E., b. Jan. 2, 1877; Abbie Ilzaide, b. Aug. 28, 1878; Gertrude L., b. April 6, 1880; Mary E., b. Nov. 8, 1881; George A., b. June 26, 1884; Minnie W., b. March 26, 1886; Edith S., b. Sept. 14, 1888; Fred J., b. Sept. 22, 1891; Marguerite, b. June 2, 1894.

1921. Allan C.,[10] son of 1176 Ebenezer Atwood[9] and Hannah [Hoag] Balch, was born March 13, 1864. He graduated from Cornell in 1891, and was one of the leading men in his class. He was married April 30, 1891, to Janet, daughter of David and Maria Christina Soledad Jacks, of Monterey, California. He is an electrician at Los Angeles, California.

1924. Rozena,[10] daughter of 1178 Joseph[9] and Margaret [Morehouse] Balch, was born March 31, 1851, and died April 16, 1884. She was married February 23, 1870, to John Tubbs. They had three children, two d. y.   Mr. Tubbs is dead also. Eugenie, b. 1892.

1925. John A.,[10] son of 1178 Joseph[9] and Margaret [Morehouse] Balch, was born December 16, 1853. He was married January 27, 1871, to Sarah Mulholland. They have had seven children.

1926. Merrett A.,[10] son of 1178 Joseph[9] and Margaret [Morehouse] Balch, was born June 28, 1857. He was married January 7, 1877, to Amanda Auchard. They have no children.

1927. Adah E.,[10] daughter of 1178 Joseph[9] and Margaret [Morehouse] Balch, was born April 25, 1859. She was married April 1, 1883, to Samuel Bonar. They have three children.

1928. Willett F.,[10] son of 1178 Joseph[9] and Margaret [Morehouse] Balch, was born March 14, 1868. He was married April 9, 1882, to Emma M. Owens. They have four children.

1931. F. Cora,[10] daughter of 1178 Joseph[9] and Margaret [Morehouse] Balch, was born August 29, 1873. She was married December 22, 1891, to Albert Brown.

1934. Charles H.,[10] son of 1179 Andrew J.[9] and Caroline [Reymore] Balch, was born at Frankfort, New York, July 22, 1858, and owns a foundry at Anamoosa, Iowa. He was married February 6, 1884, to Lillie Chisman, of Anamoosa. They have three children.

2447 MYRTLE,[11] b. 1884.
2448 GRACE,[11] b. 1886.
2449 HARRY,[11] b. 1890.

1935. Frederick W.,[10] son of 1179 Andrew J.[9] and Caroline [Reymore] Balch, was born at Frankfort, N. Y., January 23, 1861, and is a stencil cutter and rubber stamp maker at Utica, N. Y. On June 27, 1888, he was married to Carrie, daughter of Walter and Laura Edgerton. She was born at Bridgeport, N. Y., August 6, 1861. They have one child, born at Utica, N. Y.

2450 FLOYD,[11] b. March 22, 1889.

1936. William Dell,[10] son of 1179 Andrew J.[9] and Caroline [Reymore] Balch, was born at Mansfield, Minnesota, December 23, 1866, and is senior member of the firm of Balch Brothers, lithograph printers and rubber stamp manufacturers at Utica, New York. On November 6, 1895, he was married to Nellie Stone, of Utica.

1937. George A.,[10] son of 1179 Andrew J.[9] and Caroline [Reymore] Balch, was born at Mansfield, Minnesota, June 5, 1869, and is junior member of the firm of Balch Brothers, at Utica, New York. He was married September 21, 1892, to Ella M. Robards, of Utica. They have one child.

2451 MARGUERITE,[11] b. Dec. 21, 1893.

1941. Burton M.,[10] son of 1182 Marcus D.[9] and Adeline M. [Harvey] Balch, was born at Utica, New York, January 15, 1874. He took the degree of A. B. at Hamilton College, in 1895, and is professor of mathematics at the Boys' High School, in Brooklyn, New York.

SECOND BRANCH.

Descendants of 6 Benjamin.[3]
Descendants of 31 Joseph.[4]

2014. William L.,[10] son of 1309 Joel[9] and Louisa [Manley] Balch, was born at Leroy, Ohio, December 2,2 1833, and is living at Fremont, Indiana. Before the war he was a carpenter. He was married December 22, 1864, to Susan E., daughter of William and Lucy Davis. She was born at Canton, Ohio, March 31, 1843. Their children are as follows :

2452 OLIVE E.,[11] b. Sept. 12, 1865.
2453 MERIL A.,[11] b. July 30, 1867.
2454* EDWIN WILLIAM,[11] b. Sept. 23, 1869.
2455 ERNEST J.,[11] b. Sept. 30, 1868.

2022. William Eugene,[10] son of 1317 Aaron Leland[9] and Eliza A. [Vaughan] Balch, was born in 1839, at Swanzey, Massachusetts, and is manager for R. Wallace & Sons' Mfg. Co., silversmiths, Fifth avenue, New York city.

2023. Ada Louisa,[10] daughter of 1819 William Stevens[9] and Adeline Gale [Capron] Balch, was born at Newton, Mass., September 25, 1830, and was married first to Leonard Wheeler, of New York, April 16, 1851. He was born at Brattleboro, Vt., June 6, 1830, and died in the same town, December 23, 1853. They had no children. She was married second, December 25, 1857, to Sidney A. Miller, of Brattleboro, Vt., who was born July 26, 1826. They are living at Omaha, Neb., and have had three children. Estelle Louisa, b. Feb. 4, 1861, d. Aug. 9, 1861; Elena Capron, b. Nov. 14, 1863, d. March 27, 1864; Henry Capron, b. Jan. 25, 1865.

2024. Emma Elizabeth,[10] daughter of 1819 William Stevens[9] and Adeline Gale [Capron] Balch, was born at Newton, Mass., March 28, 1832. She was married at New York city, June 25, 1857, to Lynes S. Dickinson. They reside at Elgin, Ill., and have two children. Augustus J., b. July 4, 1863; Emma Balch, b. March 20, 1868.

2025. William Delos,[10] son of 1819 William Stevens[9] and Adeline Gale [Capron] Balch, was born at Claremont, N. H., June 2, 1834, and is vice-president of the National Bank at Charles City, Iowa. He was married first to Ellen M., daughter of H. B. Melville, of New York city. She was born in that city, August 16, 1838, and died at Ludlow, Vt., September 26, 1864. They had four children, the first born at New Brunswick, N. J., the others in New York city.

2456   NELLIE M.,[11] b. Oct. 25, 1858; d. Dec. 28, 1864, at Ludlow, Vt.
2457   CHARLES DELOS,[11] b. Feb. 12, 1860; d. Dec. 4, 1864, at Ludlow, Vt.
2458* ESTELLE LOUISE,[11] b. Oct. 9, 1861.
2459   WILLIAM HARVEY,[11] b. June 19, 1863; d. Sept. 11, 1863.

William Delos was married second at Charles City, Iowa, Feb. 11, 1868, to Maria, daughter of Dr. William M. Palmer, of Charles City. She was born at Palmyra, Maine, March 7, 1835. They have had four children, all born at Charles City.

2460   PALMER,[11] b. Jan. 10, 1869; d. Sept. 8, 1870.
2461* MARGARET,[11] b. May 5, 1872.
2462   GALE,[11] b. Nov. 9, 1873; d. Sept. 19, 1874.
2463   STEVENS DELOS,[11] b. Feb. 2, 1877.

2026. Estelle Maria,[10] daughter of 1819 William Stevens[9] and Adeline Gale [Capron] Balch, was born at Providence, R. I., June 28, 1836, and lives in New York city. She was married in New York, December 25, 1857, to William B., son of Josiah W. and Laura [Britton] Fairfield, of Hudson, N. Y. He was born August 24, 1835, and died October 11, 1879. He was a judge in the Iowa courts. They had three children, born at Charles City. Ada Laura, b. Dec. 11, 1858 ; Margaret Ashleigh, b. March 26, 1866, d. Aug. 15, 1866 ; Mildred Britton, a twin to Margaret.

2027. Charles Leland,[10] son of 1819 William Stevens[9] and Adeline Gale [Capron] Balch, was born at Providence, R. I., March 25, 1840, and died in New York city, August 20, 1872, and was buried at Greenwood. He was a teacher of elocution. He was married at Galesburg, Ill., April 28, 1868, to Mattie Jones. They had one child.

2464   MILDRED,[11] b.   ; m. Genie Wallace, Chicago, Ill.

2029. Edward Ernest,[10] son of 1319 William Stevens[9] and Adeline Gale [Capron] Balch, was born in New York city, August 13, 1844, and is assistant cashier of the Omaha National Bank. He was married at Omaha, Neb., October 12, 1868, to Elizabeth, daughter of Dugald and Harriet Stewart. She was born April 5, 1853. They have had three children.

2465   CHARLES STEWART,[11] b. Feb. 23, 1870; d. Sept. 16, 1870.
2466* ERNA CAPRON,[11] b. June 11, 1871.
2467* THEDE ADELINE CAPRON,[11] b. Jan. 21, 1873.

2030. John Joel,[10] son of 1319 William Stevens[9] and Adeline Gale [Capron] Balch, was born at New York, May 16, 1852, and lives at Mont Clare, Ill. He was married at Rockford, Illinois, April 6, 1880, to Eva, daughter of Robert S. and Mariette [Fay] West. They have had three children.

2468   CLARENCE ARTHUR,[11] b. Mar. 31, 1881; d. Aug. 18, 1881.
2469   ALICE MAY,[11] b. Mar. 12, 1885, at Papillion, Neb.
2470   WILLIAM STEVENS,[11] b. Feb. 18, 1892, at Mont Clare, Ill.

2031. Winna Seaman,[10] daughter of 1319 William Stevens[9] and Mary Ann [Dalley] Balch, was born at Ludlow, Vt., July 12, 1858, and lives at Elgin, Illinois. She was married at Dubuque, Iowa, May 21, 1879, to Joseph Newman. They have four children: Balch W., b. April 6, 1880; Mary Emma, b. April 28, 1882; Winna Louise, b. May 17, 1885; Margaret, b. Oct. 6, 1889.

2033. George Warren,[10] son of 1319 William Stevens[9] and Mary Ann [Dalley] Balch, was born at Ludlow, Vermont, November 12, 1861, and was married at Englewood, Illinois, November 12, 1885, to Eva L. Ranstead.

2034. Oscar Abbott,[10] son of 1325 Francis[9] and Eliza [Butler] Balch, was born at Leominster, Mass., January 25, 1837, and is proprietor of the grist mill at North Leominster. He was married October 30, 1861, to Julia Ann, daughter of Nathaniel Norris. She was born at New Hampden, N. H., June 29, 1836, and died at Ayer, Mass., July 29, 1881. They had five children, one born at Mason, N. H., two at Groton Junction, and two at Ayer, Massachusetts.

2471° FRANCIS ABBOTT,[11] b. Oct. 9, 1865.
2472° MARION ALICE,[11] b. Nov. 20, 1867.
2473° GEORGE WALTER,[11] b. Aug. 21, 1870.
2474 MARY ADDIE,[11] b. June 9, 1875.
2475 HELEN REVELLA,[11] b. May 3, 1878.

2035. Ellen M.,[10] daughter of 1325 Francis[9] and Eliza [Butler] Balch, was born at Shirley, Mass., July 8, 1844. She was married September 1, 1870, to George S. Pierce, of Leominster, Mass. He was born September 15, 1840. They live at Leominster, and have no children.

2039. John Er,[10] son of 1332 George Lucius[9] and Lucia [Dunham] Balch, was born at Brattleboro, Vt., November 6, 1864. He is a cutter, and lives at Cambridge, Mass.

2041. Helen Frances,[10] daughter of 1332 George Lucius[9] and Lucia [Dunham] Balch, was born at Boston, Mass., July 3, 1871. She was married December 29, 1891, to Henry Clinton, son of James and Mary E. [Tufts] Durgin, of Arlington, Mass. They have one son, born at Waltham, Mass., James Clinton, b. April 7, 1893.

2042. Frederic Horace,[10] son of 1333 Francis Er[9] and Mary Ellen [Conant] Balch, was born at Leominster, Mass., September 20, 1856. He was married December 31, 1890, to Cynthia Freeman, daughter of Thomas and Lydia Miles, of Middlefield, Nova Scotia. They have had two children, born at Jamaica Plain, Massachusetts.

2476 FRANK WILFRED,[11] b. Jan. 9, 1892; d. Aug. 14, 1894.
2477 WILFRED VEYSEY,[11] b. June 30, 1896.

2043. Addie Augusta,[10] daughter of 1333 Francis Er[9] and Mary Ellen [Conant] Balch, was born in Lawrence, Iowa, May 9, 1858, and lives at Watertown, Massachusetts. She was married January 8, 1886, to Edwin Curtis, son of Joseph Curtis and Maria Nancy [Gregg] Richardson. They have one son, Carl Balch, b. Aug. 1, 1887.

2047. Horace Leland,[10] son of 1337 John Hiram[9] and Lydia J. S. [Coffin] Balch, was born at Newburyport, Mass., January 9, 1856, and resides in Brooklyn, N. Y. Since 1879 he has been a wholesale shoe dealer in New York city. He was married October 16, 1884, to Kate B., daughter of Mortimer C. and Amelia [Bell] Ogden. She was born in Brooklyn, N. Y., April 1, 1859. They have two children, both born in Brooklyn.

2478 GLADYS B.,[11] b. April 24, 1886.
2479 MORTINA L.,[11] b. Sept. 20, 1889.

2048. Nettie Coffin,[10] daughter of 1337 John Hiram[9] and Lydia J. S. [Coffin] Balch, was born at Newburyport, Mass., June 16, 1859. She was married June 19, 1895, to Dr. John Kelso, son of Joseph Harradon and Mary A. [Kelso] Warren. They live at Worcester, Massachusetts.

2049. John Hiram,[10] son of 1337 John Hiram[9] and Lydia J. S. [Coffin] Balch, was born at Newburyport, February 4, 1866, and is a coal dealer at Newburyport, Mass. He was married October 10, 1889, to Blanche, daughter of Julius and Mary A. [Knapp] LeLeurch. She was born February 11, 1866. They have one child.

2480 LELAND,[11] b. July 31, 1890.

2054. Joseph,[10] son of 1849 Joseph Pope[9] and Laura Tiffany [Field] Balch, was born at Providence, R. I., July 16, 1860, and is a clerk in the Providence Institute for Savings. He was married in Providence, R. I., October 28, 1885, to Nellie Wheaton, daughter of A. Crawford and Lucretia C. [Whipple] Greene. Their son is the sixth of the same name in the direct line of descent.

2481 JOSEPH,[11] b. Nov. 13, 1890.

2056. Anna Augusta,[10] daughter of 1354 Edward Augustus[9] and Anna L. [Comstock] Balch, was born in Providence, R. I., October 29, 1858. She was married May 6, 1886, to Charles Value, son of Joshua Bicknell and Louise [Value] Chapin. He was born January 17, 1856, and in 1892 was superintendent of health and city register of Providence, R. I. They have one child, Howard Miller, b. May 11, 1887, at Providence.

THIRD BRANCH.

Descendants of 7 John.[3]

Descendants of 39 John.[4]

2059. Andrew Carpenter,[10] son of 1359 James Andrew[9] and Philena C. [Robinson] Balch, was born June 22, 1847, at West Acton, and died July 19, 1894, at Chelsea, Massachusetts. He was a house painter, and was married January 4, 1871, to Emma Louise, daughter of William and Priscilla Warren. She was born January 17, 1850, at Chelsea, where she lives. They had three children, born in Boston.

2482 EDITH MARIA,[11] b. Nov. 10, 1873.
2483 WARREN ANDREW,[11] b. March 11, 1878.
2484 ERVILLE GUY,[11] b. April 27, 1884.

2063. Ella Sophronia,[10] daughter of 1362 Perley Snow[9] and Mary E. [Pond] Balch, was born at Keene, N. H., July 18, 1854. She was married at Keene, March 27, 1873, to Edwin H. Stone. They live at Keene, and have one child George, b. July, 1877.

2067. Francis Edwin,[10] son of 1366 John Edwin[9] and Lydia Martha [Reynolds] Balch, was born at Warren, Minn., August 28, 1860, and is a farmer at Wilson, Minnesota. He was married in July, 1888, to Olive, daughter of Elbragre and Emily [Dutcher] Perry. They have three children.

2485 CECIL FRANCIS,[11] b. June 1, 1884.
2486 IDA MAY,[11] b. Nov. 11, 1887.
2487 JOHN E.,[11] b. Nov., 1891.

2068. Martha Louisa,[10] daughter of 1366 John Edwin[9] and Lydia Martha [Reynolds] Balch, was born at Warren, Minn., December 7, 1862, and died December 30, 1891. She was married in November, 1882, to Frank Hutton. They resided first in Dakota, and afterwards at Spokane, Wash., and had one child, Ida Martha, b. Sept., 1888.

2070. Levi Andrew,[10] son of 1866 John Edwin[9] and Lydia Martha [Reynolds] Balch, was born at Ellington, Minn., January 12, 1869. He was married at Winona, Minn., September 20, 1890, to Pearl, daughter of William and Emily [Nichols] Spencer.

> 2488 LYDIA EMILY,[11] b. June 20, 1891.
> 2489 LAURA,[11] b. April, 1892.
> 2490 GENEVA,[11] b. Mar. 12, 1895.

2076. Ella,[10] daughter of 1380 William[9] and Sarah M. [Wheeler] Balch, was born at Ellisburg, N. Y., in December, 1858, and was married July 24, 1879, to Fred G., son of Luther Fish. He was born at Ellisburg, N. Y., in April, 1855. They live at New Castle, Indiana. Their only child was born at Ellisburg: Anna Bell, b. March 10, 1880.

2077. Ira F.,[10] son of 1380 William[9] and Sarah M. [Wheeler] Balch, was born at Ellisburg, N. Y., January 2, 1862, and is a farmer at Mannsville, N. Y. He was married September 30, 1885, to Amelia, daughter of Daniel and Caroline [Sily] Casler. She was born at Boylston, N. Y., April 28, 1867. They have three children, all born at Ellisburg.

> 2491 VERA E.,[11] b. Dec. 8, 1886.
> 2492 VERNESS S.,[11] b. Feb. 9, 1888.
> 2493 VALNEY W.,[11] b. Dec. 24, 1889.

2078. Melvin W.,[10] son of 1380 William[9] and Sarah M. [Wheeler] Balch, was born at Ellisburg, N. Y., January 9, 1865, and is a farmer at Mannsville, N. Y. He was married September 26, 1888, to Nellie S. daughter of Francis and Melissa [Clark] Torrey, who was born January 26, 1870.

> 2494 RONALD W.,[11] b. Jan. 17, 1890; d. May 22, 1890.

2079. Dora G.,[10] daughter of 1380 William[9] and Sarah M. [Wheeler] Balch, was born at Ellisburg, N. Y., December 30, 1871. She was married May 14, 1890, to Charles A. Snyder. He was born at Boylston, N. Y., in June, 1865.

2080. Carrie E.,[10] daughter of 1381 Orrin H.[9] and Catharine E. [Currey] Balch, was born at Oswego, N. Y., July 28, 1857. She was married June 24, 1877, to Theodore M. Rounds, of Mannsville, where they live and have two children: Edith A., b. Feb. 24, 1879; Lafayette M., b. May 27, 1882.

2081. Frederick O.,[10] son of 1381 Orrin H.[9] and Catharine E. [Currey] Balch, was born at Oswego, N. Y., October 28, 1861. He was married June 21, 1888, to Susannah E. Wilson. She was born August 26, 1864. They live at Mannsville, N. Y., and have two children.

2495 Frederic A.,[11] b. Nov. 1, 1888, at Oswego, N. Y.
2496 Catherine J.,[11] b. March 29, 1891, at Mannsville, N. Y.

2082. Horace E.,[10] son of 1381 Orrin H.[9] and Catharine E. [Currey] Balch, was born at Oswego, N. Y., July 7, 1865. He was married April 27, 1887, to Minna Armstrong. They have one child.

2497 Ralph E.,[11] b. Jan. 1, 1891.

2083. Ida E.,[10] daughter of 1381 Orrin H.[9] and Catharine E. [Currey] Balch, was born at Orwell, N. Y., November 2, 1867. She was married May 7, 1890, to George Carpenter.

2094. Samuel,[10] son of 1392 Cyrus Decatur[9] and Margaret [Wakely] Balch, was born in Warren county, Pa., June 26, 1838, and is a farmer at Evans, West Virginia. He was married June 18, 1869, to Martha H., daughter of Timothy B. and Sina Vining, who was born in Meigs county, Ohio, June 3, 1843. They have six children, all born in Meigs county, Ohio.

2498* William W.,[11] b. March 2, 1870.
2499   Quincy Adams,[11] b. July 14, 1872.
2500   Delbert C.,[11] b. Jan. 17, 1874.
2501   Cora B.,[11] b. Sept. 27, 1876.
2502   Dock Vining,[11] b. Feb. 7, 1880.
2503   Corna Nell,[11] b. Aug. 2, 1883.

Samuel[10] enlisted in June, 1862, in the Second Regiment

of Ohio Heavy Artillery, and served as sergeant of company
" K," until the close of the war. For more than two years
he was ranking sergeant of the regiment. He was offered a
commission, but declined the promotion.

2098. Cyrus[10] son of 1892 Cyrus Decatur[9] and Margaret
[Wakely] Balch, was born in Athens county, Ohio, July 5,
1850, and was drowned at Nelsonville, Ohio, August 1, 1881,
where he was a miner. He was married March 10, 1870, to
California Almira, daughter of Timothy B. and Sina Vining.
She was born April 7, 1852, in Meigs county, Ohio. They
had four children, born in Meigs county, O.

2504 CYRUS EDGAR,[11] b. Jan. 18, 1870.
2505 WALLACE DEVALSON,[11] b. June 29, 1872; engaged in railroading.
2506 LELAND LESLIE,[11] b. July 6, 1875.
2507 ERNEST EUGENE,[11] b. May 29, 1881.

2107. George W.,[10] son of 1395 Christopher Columbus[9]
and Charlotte [Pierce] Balch, was born at Granger, N. Y.,
December 20, 1846. He was married at Knight's Creek, N.
Y., July 25, 1865, to Thresa Kent, who was born in Tioga
county, N. Y., October 11, 1845. They have no children. He
enlisted November 14, 1861, as a private in company I, 76th
N. Y., and was in the Army of the Potomac. After the battle of Williamsburg, Va., he was sent to Mount Pleasant
Hospital at Washington, from which he was discharged from
the service in June, 1862, for general disability. He is a
farmer at Harrisville, Michigan, and is an agent for agricultural machinery.

2113. George H.,[10] son of 1396 John Quincy Adams[9]
and Sarah [Burton] Balch, was born in Kansas in 1859, and
is a landscape gardener in St. Louis, Mo. He was married
March 22, 1881, to Maggie Elizabeth, daughter of Henry
Sumering. She was born at Buffalo, N. Y., in 1857. They
have had nine children.

2508 IDA MAY,[11] b. 1882.
2509 JULIA,[11] b. 1883.
2510 KATIE,[11] b. May 2, 1884; d. July 29, 1884.

2511　Sarah,[11] b. 1886.
2512　Maggie,[11] b. Dec. 11, 1887; d. Oct. 21, 1888.
2513　George B.,[11] b. 1888.
2514　Robert,[11] b. 1890.
2515　Gertrude,[11] b. Sept., 1891.
2516　Albert H.,[11] b. May 6, 1893.

2116. **Cassandra,**[10] daughter of 1898 Andrew Jackson[9] and Elizabeth [Watts] Balch, was born June 21, 1860, and married February 4, 1884, Joel A. Edmonds. They live at Bethpage, Missouri.

2117. **Richard Johnson,**[10] son of 1898 Andrew Jackson[9] and Elizabeth [Watts] Balch, was born November 6, 1863, at Shade, Ohio. He lived for a time at Seneca, Missouri, and served in the State Assembly and Senate, and was a member of the Supreme Judicial Convention held at St. Louis in 1892. He now lives at Galena, Kansas. He was married February 6, 1892, to Ida M., daughter of Robert A., and Eliza E. Mayfield. She was born at Erie, Missouri, September 18, 1872. They have one child, born at Erie, Missouri.

2517　Ray Vest,[11] b. Jan. 5, 1892.

2119. **Nellie,**[10] daughter of 1898 Andrew Jackson[9] and Elizabeth [Watts] Balch, was born in Nelsonville, Ohio, December 5, 1871, and lives at Galena, Kansas. She was married December 17, 1888, to Penrose Eyster.

2120. **Lucy,**[10] daughter of 1898 Andrew Jackson[9] and Elizabeth [Watts] Balch, was born at Charlestown, W. Va., December 17, 1873, and lives at Galena, Kansas. She was married October 4, 1891, to George B. Lamb. He died January 25, 1895. Their children are one girl and one boy: Fay, b. July 10, 1892; Loyd, b. Jan. 5, 1894.

2123. **Lillian Judith,**[10] daughter of 1898 Andrew Jackson[9] and Elizabeth [Watts] Balch, was born November 23, 1878, and is a teacher, with her sister Cora, in the public schools at Galena, Kansas. She was named Elizabeth Judith, but has preferred the name Lillian.

2127. **Queenie V.,**[10] daughter of 1402 Benjamin F.[9] and Rebecca [Walker] Balch, was born in 1871. She married James T. Watkins, a plumber and gas fitter at Sedalia, Missouri. They have two children.

2128. **Mary Eliza,**[10] daughter of 1404 John[9] and Eunice [Baldwin] Balch, was born at Vergennes, Vermont, May 28, 1849. She was married November 25, 1895, to Adoniram Judson, oldest son of Elisha Hogle and Abbie [Huff] Gleason, of Genesee county, New York. He was born April 28, 1854, at Newark, Illinois, and is engaged in the harness business at Holstein, Iowa.

2130. **Melissa Maria,**[10] daughter of 1404 John[9] and Eunice [Baldwin] Balch, was born at Eldorado, Iowa, September 15, 1856. She was married September 15, 1874, to Arthur Corner, son of John and Sarah [Daniels] Calvert. He was born in Morgan county, Ohio, April 9, 1848, and is a farmer at Galva, Iowa. They have had six children : Burtis Earl, b. July 9, 1875, at College Springs, Iowa, d. Oct. 12, 1875 ; Evert Leroy, b. March 24, 1877, at Elgin, Iowa ; Walter Alfred, b. Sept. 18, 1879, at Elgin, Iowa ; Edna Maud, b. Feb. 6, 1883, at Lake View, Iowa ; Eunice Edith, b. Aug. 9, 1885, at Odebolt, Iowa ; Josephine, b. May 22, 1894, at Galva, Iowa.

2131. **William Warner,**[10] son of 1404 John[9] and Eunice [Baldwin] Balch, was born at Beaver, Minn., June 10, 1859, and is a carpenter, living at Gary, South Dakota. He was married February 20, 1884, to Almina, daughter of John and Almira Shannon. She was born July 13, 1861, in Floyd county, Iowa. They have two children.

2518 Oscar Earl,[11] b. May 4, 1885, at Charles City, Iowa.
2519 Eunice Bernetta,[11] b. July 21, 1896, at Gary, South Dakota.

2132. **Benjamin Iliff,**[10] son of 1404 John[9] and Eunice [Baldwin] Balch, was born at Beaver, Minn, April 18, 1861, and is a farmer at Early, Iowa. He was married September 13, 1884, to Hessa Rosetta, daughter of Cornelius C. and

Sophia McGilvra. She was born in 1867. They have had four children.

2520 ENOS CEYLON,[11] b. July 29, 1885.
2521 CLAUD LYLE,[11] b. Nov. 29, 1886; d. May 23, 1890.
2522 MABEL ELSIE,[11] b. March 2, 1891.
2523 BENJAMIN CYRUS,[11] b. Sept. 2, 1895.

2133. Lucy Elmina,[10] daughter of 1404 John[9] and Eunice [Baldwin] Balch, was born at Beaver, Minn., August 16, 1863, and was married February 22, 1883, to Bascum Somers, son of Sampson and Fanny Haworth. He was born May 27, 1862, in Dark county, Ohio, and is a carpenter and builder at Galva, Iowa. They have seven children: Clarence Elbert, b. Jan. 21, 1884; John Arthur, b. May 14, 1885; Pearl Edith, b. Oct. 10, 1887; Nathaniel, b. May 30, 1889; Hazel Dell, b. Aug. 25, 1890; Floyd Balch, b. Jan. 9, 1893; Dalton Cyrus, b. May 7, 1895.

2134. Miriam Elizabeth,[10] daughter of 1404 John[9] and Eunice [Baldwin] Balch, was born at Elgin, Iowa, September 10, 1870. She was married October 1, 1890, to Andrew T., son of Cyrus M. and Marietta [Rollins] Glass. He was born September 30, 1862, at River Falls, Wis., and is a buttermaker at Monticello, Iowa. They have one child: Ernest Rollins, b. July 14, 1891, at Monticello, Iowa.

2146. Alfred C.,[10] son of 1429 William Henry[9] and Caroline Ann [Buswell] Balch, was born at Bath, N. H., Nov. 28, 1862. He is purchasing agent for Rand, McNally & Co., printers and publishers, Chicago, Ill. He was married first, October 18, 1887, to Fannie, daughter of John and Ellen Fenton. She was born at Zanesville, Ohio, Nov. 18, 1868, and died at Chicago, Ill., May 9, 1892, leaving no children.

Alfred C. married again October 10, 1893, at Milwaukee, Wis., Sophie, daughter of Moses and Bertha [Blatskovitch] Bloomfield. She was born in Vienna, Austria, February 28, 1875. They have one child.

2524 WALTER BUSWELL,[11] b. Oct. 1, 1895.

2153. Cora Mabel,[10] daughter of 1436 Pliny Earl[9] and Annie E. [Fansler] Balch, was born at Greencastle, Indiana, Sept. 1, 1875. She was married September 1, 1895, to Benjamin Corey Vestal, who was born December 29, 1869, and is a farmer.

2164. Hattie Mae,[10] daughter of 1470 Austin A.[9] and Mary E. [Whipple] Balch, was born at Northumberland, N. H., May 11, 1866. She was married September 1, 1892, to Doctor Edwin L. Harris, of Clinton, Mass. Hattie Mae has inherited the fine musical taste that made her great aunts so famous. She has a fine, well cultivated soprano voice.

2165. James Whipple,[10] son of 1470 Austin A.[9] and Mary E. [Whipple] Balch, was born at Lancaster, N. H., December 28, 1870. He is a member of the firm of Gordon & Balch, contractors for painting and dealers in painters' supplies, at Berlin, N. H. His specialty is fine lettering and fresco painting.

2176. James E.,[10] son of 1482 Frank A.[9] and Mary Emma [Smith] Balch, was born at Davenport, Iowa, January 27, 1870. He was manager of the Colonnade Hotel in New York city until 1895, and is now proprietor of the Puritan Laundry.

2178. Edwin F.[10] son of 1482 Frank A.[9] and Mary Emma [Smith] Balch, was born at Davenport, Iowa, July 29, 1873, where he now lives at the old home.

Descendants of 40 Israel[4].

2182. Della E.,[10] daughter of 1487 James[9] and Laura [Henderson] Balch, was born at Marcellus, N. Y., April 24, 1865. She was married December 30, 1886, to Peter, son of Dennis and Anna Fitz Patrick. He was born September 8, 1861, and is a merchant at Marietta, N. Y., where they live. Their children are: Mamie Edna, b. Nov. 19, 1887, at Otisco, N. Y.; Howard J., b. Aug. 2, 1889.

2184. Charles M.,[10] son of 1490 Holland[9] and Jane E.

[Lund] Balch, was born at Sodus, N. Y., September 2, 1855, and was married, first, January 1, 1878, to Martha J., daughter of David Harner. She was born at Sodus, August 17, 1857, and died in the same town, August 26, 1879. They had one child, born one week before its mother's death.

2525 ADA M.,[11] b. Aug. 18, 1879.

Charles M. married second, March 12, 1890, Eva Augusta, daughter of Charles Hewson. She was born March 22, 1861. They have two children.

2526 IOLA BELL,[11] b. Sept. 15, 1892.
2527 RAYMOND CHARLES,[11] b. May 5, 1896.

2195. Fred Jay,[10] son of 1499 Jude Henry[9] and Olive L. [Newman] Balch, was born July 17, 1862. He is in the employ of the Oregon Railway and Navigation Company, at Portland, Oregon. He is not married.

2196. Carlyn Jude,[10] son of 1499 Jude Henry[9] and Olive L. [Newman] Balch, was born July 19, 1865, at Milton, Wisconsin. He was married December 5, 1887, to Grace Darling, daughter of C. T. and Hannah M. Woolsey. She was born at Albia, Iowa, December 12, 1868. They reside at Pocatello, Idaho. He is chief clerk in the superintendent's office, Union Pacific Railway. They have no children.

2205. Lucinda,[10] daughter of 1505 Horace[9] and Mary [Manning] Balch, was born November 12, 1835, and died October 18, 1864. She married a Mr. Murphy. Her children are: Mary, Annie, Emma, and Lizzie.

2206. Emily,[10] daughter of 1505 Horace[9] and Mary [Manning] Balch, was born April 12, 1841. She married George Collett. They live at Garnett, Kansas. Their children are Charley, Alice, Walter, and Willis.

2207. Matilda,[10] daughter of 1505 Horace[9] and Mary [Manning] Balch, was born July 27, 1845, and died March 24, 1868. She married Charles Britton. They have one child, Minnie.

2210. Margaret A.,[10] daughter of 1506 Jasper[9] and

Betsey [Manning] Balch, was born in Genesee county, N. Y.,
September 27, 1833, and died in Anderson county, Kansas,
April 27, 1881. She was married February 25, 1858, to Del-
ivan Perry. He was born November 8, 1825, and died in
Chase county, Kansas, November 6, 1875. They had six
children, three born at Warrenville, Illinois, and three in
Chase county, Kansas.

> ANNA A., b. Feb. 12, 1859; m. WilliamVineyard; lives Marion, K.
> HOMER D., b. Oct. 7, 1860; d. Jan. 3, 1866.
> CHARLOTTE B., b. Nov. 6, 1862; m. April 10, 1881, Alvah R.
> Ivans; d. Dec. 28, 1890.
> FRANK T., b. Aug. 11, 1867; m. Myrtle Dye; lives Oleander, Cal.
> ELLA O., b. Sept. 2, 1870; m. Marion Calder; lives Oleander, Cal.
> FREDERICK N., b. Feb. 4, 1872; lives Marion, K.

2211. Amelia M.,[10] daughter of 1506 Jasper[9] and Betsey
[Manning] Balch, was born in Genesee county, N. Y., July
11, 1835, and died in Chase county, Kansas, May 18, 1876.
She was married June 20, 1858, to Jabez Dart, a brother of
Almira, second wife of 1511 Albert.   He died August 28,
1871, in Chase county, Kansas, aged 36.   They had four
children : William J., b. Feb. 21, 1859, m. Alice Hayes,
lives Farmington, Or. ; Albert M., b. April 19, 1865, m. his
cousin, 2227 Carrie May Balch[10]; Momer M., b. Nov. 16,
1867, m. Alice Calder, lives Hanford, Cal. ; Mary Alice, b.
Dec. 21, 1870, m. Robert White, lives Easton, Cal.

2213. Homer P.,[10] son of 1506 Jasper[9] and Betsey
[Manning] Balch, was born in Genesee county, N. Y., February 6, 1840, and died at Moline, Ka., Dec. 19, 1883.   He
was married Sept. 3, 1865, to his cousin, Mary Annie[10],
daughter of 1505 Horace[9] and Mary [Manning] Balch, of
Welda, Ka.   They had one child, born in Chase county, Ka.

> **2528** IDA EMMA,[11] b. Oct. 6, 1868; lives at Garnett, K.

Homer P. Balch was a soldier in the Union army during
the civil war, serving in a regiment of Kansas volunteers.
He was mustered out in July, 1865, and his early death was
the result of exposures while in the army.   His wife lives at
Oleander, Cal.

2224. Lewis Nelson,[10] son of 1511 Albert[9] and Emeline [Baker] Balch, was born at Naperville, Ill., March 9, 1855, and is a farmer at Waitsburg, Washington. He was married, first, September 14, 1876, to Beatrice Guidotti, who was born in England, April 14, 1857, and died Aug. 10, 1886. They have five children.

2529 DEMONT VINCENT,[11] b. Oct. 20, 1877; d. Dec. 9, 1883.
2530 MADOLENA E.,[11] b. Dec. 6, 1878.
2531 EMILY BLANCHE,[11] b. Feb. 7, 1881.
2532 ROBERT I.,[11] b. March 27, 1883.
2533 ALBERT E.,[11] b. Oct. 1, 1885.

Lewis Nelson married, second, Dec. 2, 1889, to Eunice Johnson. She was born at Jackson, Ohio, September 21, 1854. They have four children.

2534 ARTHUR ROSCOE,[11] b. Feb. 2, 1891.
2535 BEATRICE ARVENA,[11] b, July 14, 1892.
2536 LEWIS JOHNSON,[11] b. June 17, 1894.
2537 MARJORIE H.,[11] b. Nov. 8, 1895.

2227. Carrie May,[10] daughter of 1511 Albert[9] and Almira [Dart] Balch, was born at Elmdale, Kansas, February 15, 1871. She was married August 22, 1890, to her cousin, Albert N., son of Jabez and 2211 Amelia M. [Balch] Dart. They live at Hanford, California, and have one child, Gertrude May, b. Aug. 11, 1891.

2235. Frederick R.,[10] son of 1521 John Ransom[9] and Margaret [Snyder] Balch, was born at Cortland, N. Y., March 16, 1863; is living at Antigo, Wis.

2236. Llewellyn L.,[10] daughter of 1521 John Ransom[9] and Margaret [Snyder] Balch, was born at Cortland, N. Y., April 21, 1866. She was married at Antigo, Wis., September 5, 1885, to Eugene Tuttle.

2247. Robert Morris,[10] son of 1588 Foster Lamson[9] and Nancy McArthur [Morris] Balch, was born at Shakopee, Minn., April 4, 1864. He is a hardware salesman at Minneapolis, Minnesota. He was married June 30, 1891, to Winnifred, daughter of Orton Skinner and Catherine [Leonard]

Clark. She was born at Buffalo, N. Y., September 27, 1870. They have one child.

2538 MYRON CLARK,[11] b. Jan. 1, 1894.

2248. Frank Shaw.[10] son of 1538 Foster Lamson[9] and Nancy McArthur [Morris] Balch, was born at Shakopee, Minn., November 16, 1865. He is a bookkeeper for the gaslight company at Minneapolis. He was married July 23, 1891, to Margaret Darling, daughter of John Hogen and Margaret [Reynolds] Mendenhall.

2250. Gertrude,[10] daughter of 1538 Foster Lamson[9] and Nancy McArthur [Morris] Balch, was born at Shakopee, Minn., March 24, 1868. She was married November 25, 1891, to Nahum Malcomb, son of Nahum Mitchell and Sarah Agnes Tribou. He was born March 7, 1861, at Mystic, Conn., and is credit man for Longley, Low & Alexander, at Chicago.

2252. Alice Kendrick,[10] daughter of 1540 Henry Francis[9] and Evalyn [Kendrick] Balch, was born at Minneapolis, Minn., March 3, 1854. She was married September 28, 1887, to Joseph Gault, son of James and Mary Hamilton. He was born at Hanover, Ohio, October 30, 1857. He is an agent for the Red Line at Minneapolis. They have four children : Ruth Evalyn, b. July 18, 1888 ; Margaret, b. Sept. 28, 1890 ; Joseph Gault and John Balch, twins, b. Aug. 28, 1894.

2253. Mary Evalyn,[10] daughter of 1540 Henry Francis[9] and Evalyn [Kendrick] Balch, was born at Minneapolis, Minn., June 25, 1866. She was married December 15, 1886, to Llewellyn, son of William and Nancy Groff. He was born at La Crescent, Minnesota, December 10, 1861. They live at Minneapolis, and have two children : Henry Balch, b. Sept. 22, 1888 ; Richard Llewellyn, b. May 21, 1890.

2272. Etta L.,[10] daughter of 1567 Orrin J. L.[9] and Josie S. [Nay] Balch was born at Mason Village, N. H., June 5,

1865. She was married Jan. 30, 1888, to Howard D. Halstead. Since 1890 she has parted from her husband and has lived with her mother. They have five children: Orrin H., b. Dec. 13, 1884 ; Perley O., b. Oct. 25, 1885, d. Oct. 19, 1886 ; Roy E., b. Dec. 23, 1886 ; George S., b. June, 1887, d. y.; Florence L., b. Nov. 3, 1889, d. Aug. 5, 1890.

2274. Perley O.,[10] son of 1567 Orrin J. L.[9] and Josie S. [Nay] Balch was born at Manchester, N. H., May 8, 1868. He was married June 6, 1889, to Sadie M. Daniels, of Wilton, N. H. They lived at Amoskeag, New Hampshire, and have three children :

2539 ALFRED S.,[11] b. Oct. 1, 1890.
2540 MARION L.[11] b. June 1, 1893; d. July 23, 1894.
2541 CLARENCE M.,[11] b. Dec. 4, 1895.

2280. John Harvey,[10] son of 1572 Harvey John[9] Balch, was born January 5, 1850, at Whitehall, New York, and lives at Chestertown, New York. He was married June 8, 1873, to Annie E., daughter of Courtney and Mary Ann [Prescott] Seage. They have had five children, born at Chestertown, N. Y.

2542 ELLEN ELMIRA,[11] b. July 22, 1874.
2543 MARY ANN,[11] b. Dec. 28, 1877.
2544 JENNIE DELL,[11] b. Sept. 15, 1883; d. July 8, 1889.
2545 SUSIE WHIPPLE,[11] b. Nov. 4, 1886.
2546 ELIZABETH ANN,[11] b. Dec. 28, 1895.

2287. Clara Adelia,[10] daughter of 1574 Lowell Levi[9] and Huldah Ann [Whitney] Balch, was born at Hartland, Vermont, March 12, 1855. She was married April 8, 1875, to Nahum C. Solger. He is a carpenter for the C. B. & Q. Railroad, at Aurora, Illinois, where they moved in 1883. They have had six children, one born at Hartford, Vermont, one born at Hartland, Vermont, and the others at Aurora, Illinois; Lizzie A., b. June 10, 1876 ; Nora C., b. Feb. 25, 1878 ; Ellen E., July 13, 1885 ; Leonard Roy, b. Aug. 6, 1887 ; Marguerite H., b. Sept. 28, 1891 ; Mildred G., b. Oct. 31, 1894, d. Nov. 29, 1894.

2288. Elizabeth Campbell,[10] daughter of 1574 Lowell Levi[9] and Huldah Ann [Whitney] Balch, was born at Hartland, Vermont, July 21, 1858.   She was married April 18, 1891, to John Long, who is a shoemaker at White River Junction, Vermont.   They have no children.

2289. Sarah Anna,[10] daughter of 1574 Lowell Levi[9] and Huldah Ann [Whitney] Balch, was born December 11, 1860, at Hartland, Vermont.   She removed to Aurora, Illinois in 1882.   On August 23, 1886, she was married to Leslie L. Dickey, of Hartford, Vermont.   They have two children born at Aurora, Illinois.   Leslie L., b. July 26, 1887 ; Lillian H. b. Dec. 14, 1891.

2290. Idora Philena,[10] daughter of 1574 Lowell Levi[9] and Huldah Ann [Whitney] Balch, was born March 27, 1863, at Hartland, Vermont.   She married Charles E. Small, of the same town, September 5, 1887.   They have lived at Windsor, Vermont, since 1890, and have two children.   Gertie E. b. Feb. 5, 1890, at Hartland; Hilda A., b. May 8, 1893, at Windsor.

2291. Ellen Gertrude,[10] daughter of 1574 Lowell Levi[9] and Huldah Ann [Whitney] Balch, was born February 1, 1865.   She was married July 3, 1886, to Lucius J. Whitney. He was born August 18, 1865, and died May 8, 1889.   They had one son, Allen Deane, b. Hartland, January 7, 1888.   On June 21, 1892, Ellen Gertrude married second Charles E. Cowdrey of Windsor, Vermont, where they now live.

2292. Harvey Hiram,[10] son of 1574 Lowell Levi[9] and Huldah Ann [Whitney] Balch, was born May 9, 1868, at Hartland, Vermont, and was married June 14, 1893, to Angie, daughter of Frank Parker.   They live at Hartland, Vermont, and have one child.

2547 FLORENCE.[11]

2300. Frederick Volney,[10] son of 1625 Henry R.[9] and Delia [Bellows] Balch, was born at Port Alleghany, Pennsylvania, September 2, 1850, and lives at Galeton, Pennsylvania. He is a locomotive engineer. He was married October 24, 1874, to Mary L., daughter of Archibald D. Knox, of Knoxville, Pennsylvania. They have one daughter, born at Janesville, Wisconsin.

2548 NEENAH,[11] b. Apr. 16, 1877.

2303. Cassius Vernon,[10] son of 1626 Alfonso Burdett[9] and Rhoda M. [Smith] Balch, was born at Deerfield, Pa., March 6, 1857, and lives at Sabinsville, Pennsylvania. He was married May 24, 1885, to Nellie Houland, who was born at Pomfret, Connecticut, November 8, 1858. They have three children.

2549 JESSIE,[11] b. June 8, 1886.
2550 EDNA,[11] b. Feb. 23, 1888.
2551 DIGHT VERNON,[11] b. Dec. 11, 1892.

2304. Herbert A.,[10] son of 1626 Alfonso Burdett[9] and Rhoda M. [Smith] Balch, was born at Deerfield, Pennsylvania, February 1, 1860. He was married in October, 1880, to Harriet A. Burlingame, who was born at Deerfield in April, 1863. They live at Middlebury, Penn., and have two children.

2552 LUTHER W.,[11] b. Nov. 2, 1881.
2553 HENRY H.,[11] b Nov. 20, 1883.

2308. Emma M.,[10] daughter of 1630 Milton[9] and Ammoratte C. [Cowles] Balch, was born at New Milford, Pa., September 26, 1858. She was married September 24, 1875, to Charles, son of George LaGier. He was born September 5, 1851, and is a farmer at Lestershire, New York. They have had five children, all born at North Jackson: Frank, b. Aug. 3, 1877; Cora May, b. May 24, 1879; Verna Ettie, b. June 18, 1881; Fred Thurman, b. July 22, 1883; Aida Bell, b. Nov. 9, 1885, d. May 18, 1886; Arthur Milton, b. June 27, 1887.

Descendants of 47 David.[4]

2313. Charles Arvin,[10] son of 1655 William Henry[9]

and Elizabeth Polly [Alger] Balch, was born at Cazenovia, N. Y., June 17, 1869. He graduated at the Cazenovia Seminary, Cazenovia, N. Y., in 1891. He then attended Rev. A. B. Simpson's Missionary Training School in New York city, and in September, 1895, joined the Susquehanna Conference of the Free Methodist Church. He has preached in Elmira and Auburn, New York, and studied in Auburn Theological Seminary. He was married July 11, 1891, at Cork County of Herkimer, N. Y. They have one son, born at Auburn, New York.

2554 BENJAMIN TITUS ROBERTS, b. Jan. 7, 1895.

2326. George E.,[10] son of 1961 George Edward and Annie H. [Morse] Balch, was born at Boston, Mass., March 18, 1867, and is secretary of the Eclipse Hay Press Co., at Kansas City, Missouri. He was married November 11, 1895, to Ola L., daughter of F. D. and L. Atkins.

2331. Flora,[10] daughter of 1675 Enos[9] and Hannah [Showater] Balch, was born at Hyde Park, Vt., in 1862, and married Frank Laraway. They have had three children, two sons and one daughter.

2340. Fred J.,[10] son of 1687 Fred[9] and Ettie [Murray] Balch, was born at Massena, N. Y., April 15, 1870, and is a telegraph operator and cashier at Rouse's Point, New York, in the freight office of the Vermont Central Railroad. He married, January 8, 1896, Grace Laura, daughter of Julius and Adelia Wilson, of Rouse's Point.

2341. Frank W.,[10] son of 1687 Fred[9] and Ettie [Murray] Balch, was born at Massena, New York, August 1, 1868, where he is a farmer on his grandfather's place. He was married February 12, 1896, to Annie, daughter of John W. and Mary Ann Bero. She was born at Hogansburg, New York, in 1874.

2347. Lena E.,[10] daughter of 1702 Wayland F.[9] and Sarah F. [Richardson] Balch, was born in 1866, and was married in 1887 to Edwin B. Currier. They have two children : Edna F., b. 1888 ; Mary G., b. 1889.

2359. Daniel Ellridge,[10] son of 1711 John W.[9] and Sarah E. [Wormwood] Balch, was born at Kennebunkport, Me., April 22, 1858. He is a farmer, and a member of the Congregationalist Church. He was married February 13, 1884, to Mary J., daughter of Leonard Miller, of Kennebunkport, where she was born May 31, 1862. They reside and their children were born at Kennebunkport.

2555 JOHN NEIL,[11] b. Nov. 1, 1884.
2556 SUSAN MAY,[11] b. April 15, 1886.

2363. Lill Dora,[10] daughter of 1711 John W.[9] and Sarah E. [Wormwood] Balch, was born at Kennebunkport, Me., September 27, 1867. She married, October 7, 1884, George Cluff, of Kennebunkport, where they live and have four children : Bertha Bell, b. May 22, 1885 ; Grace May, b. Aug. 21, 1886 ; Rowena Billings, b. Sept. 21, 1890 ; Sarah Emily, b. May 29, 1893.

2367. Eller M.,[10] daughter of 1712 Moses M.[9] and Harriet E. [Stiles] Balch, was born at Temple, N. H., July 3, 1862, and was married January 24, 1883, to Albert F. Walker, of New Ipswich, N. H. They have two children : Robert B., b. June 19, 1886 ; Lena F., b. Dec. 27, 1887.

2368. Abby L.,[10] daughter of 1712 Moses M.[9] and Harriet E. [Stiles] Balch, was born in Temple, N. H., February 1, 1870, and was married April 26, 1892, to Wilbur L. Phelps, of New Ipswich, N. H.

2370. Frank Arthur,[10] son of 1717 Barker Sawyer[9] and Ann Jane [Whitcomb] Balch, was born in Richmond, Vermont, April 25, 1870. He graduated from Dartmouth College in 1894, and is a professor at Norwich University, Northfield, Vermont.

FOURTH BRANCH.
Descendants of 9 Freeborn.[3]
Descendants of 52 Benjamin.[4]

2391. Ida Ann,[10] daughter of 1799 John W.[9] and

Addie A. [Aylsworth] Balch was born March 18, 1861, at Syracuse, New York, and was married May 27, 1884, to Edward T., son of Richard Austin and Rachel A. Yoe. He was born April 14, 1857, at Peoria, Illinois, and is a letter carrier at Syracuse, New York, where their children were born. Harry Austin, b. Jan. 20, 1886; Bessie May, b. March 14, 1888; John William, b. March 20, 1890.

2239. Esther Joanna,[10] daughter of 1799 John W.[9] and Addie A. [Aylsworth] Balch, was born June 4, 1862, at Syracuse, New York, and was married May 4, 1886, to James, son of James and Barbara Eggenberger, who was born August 11, 1854, in Switzerland, and is principal of schools at Dolgerville, New York. They had one child, born in Syracuse. James Balch, b. March 31, 1889, d. Jan. 22, 1891.

2399. Winifred Hannah,[10] daughter of 1811 Hiram Augustus[9] and Catherine [Ruddell] Balch, was born February 2, 1867, at Olympia, Washington, and was married September 27, 1885, to George E., son of Luther and Rachel Lawrence, who was born at Calais, Maine, and is a carpenter and builder. They have had two children; Edith, b. May 22, 1887; Leo, b. Aug. 22, 1889.

2400. Martha,[10] daughter of 1811 Hiram Augustus[9] and Catherine [Ruddell] Balch, was born October 7, 1868, at Olympia, Washington, and was married to William Elsworth, son of William and Elizabeth Menish. He was born May 27, 1862, at Paterson, New Jersey, and is a stationary engineer at Houquin, Washington, where their children were born. Anna May, b. June 26, 1889, d. Nov. 7, 1892; William H., b. March 15, 1891, d. Nov. 26, 1892, Glen E., b. Sept. 21, 1893.

ELEVENTH GENERATION.

SECOND BRANCH.

Descendants of 6 Benjamin.[3]
Descendants of 81 Joseph.[4]

2454. Edwin William,[11] son of 2014 William L.[10] and Susan E. [Davis] Balch, was born September 23, 1869, and is a proprietor of the Plymouth Mail, at Plymouth, Michigan.

2458. Estella Louise,[11] daughter of 2025 William Deloss[10] and Ellen M. [Melville] Balch, was born October 9, 1861, in New York City, and was married June 17, 1885, to William Samuel Harwood. They live at Chicago, Illinois.

2461. Margaret,[11] daughter of 2025 William Deloss[10] and Maria [Palmer] Balch, was born May 5, 1872, at Charles City, Iowa, and was married September 5, 1894, to James A. Case, a banker at Charles City.

2466. Erna Capron,[11] daughter of 2029 Edward Ernest[10] and Elizabeth [Stewart] Balch, was born June 11, 1871, at Omaha, Nebraska, and was married October 3, 1894, to Isaac Albemarle Coles.

2467. Thede Adeline Capron,[11] daughter of 2029 Edward Ernest[10] and Elizabeth [Stewart] Balch, was born at Omaha, Nebraska, January 21, 1873, and was married October 23, 1894, to Abraham Lincoln Reed. They have one child, Elizabeth Balch, born July 24, 1895.

2471. Francis Abbott,[11] son of 2034 Oscar Abbott[10] and Julia Ann [Norris] Balch, was born October 9, 1865, at Mason, New Hampshire, and is a teacher at Hoboken, New Jer-

(442)

sey. He was married June 24, 1891, to Bertha A., daughter of Franklin and Almeda [Dight] Lawton of Shirley, Mass. She was born August 11, 1867, and died December 1, 1892. They had no children.

2472. **Marion Alice,**[11] daughter of 2034 Oscar Abbott[10] and Julia Ann [Norris] Balch, was born November 20, 1867, at Groton Junction, Mass., and is living at Ashland, Mass. She married William Dadman, of Sudbury, Mass., and they have three children. Herbert, Bessie and Frank.

2473. **George Walter,**[11] son of 2034 Oscar Abbott[10] and Julia Ann [Norris] Balch, was born August 21, 1870, at Groton Junction, Mass., and was married in March, 1895, to Estella I. Cox.

THIRD BRANCH.

Descendants of 7 John.[8]
Descendants of 39 John.[4]

2498. **William W.,**[11] son of 2094 Samuel[10] and Martha H. [Vining] Balch, was born March 2, 1870, in Meigs county, Ohio, and is a farmer at Evans, West Virginia. He was married December 26, 1890, to Lillie, daughter of Preston and Clara Barnet. They have one child, born at Rock Castle, West Virginia.

2557   MATTIE,[12] b. Nov. 8, 1891.

MARY ELIZABETH BALCH, B. L.
(1914.)

.URA BERTHA [BALCH] BARR, B. A. HARRIET ELIZABETH BALCH, B. S., M. D.
(1893.) (1896.)

OUR COLLEGE GIRLS.

PREFACE TO MARYLAND FAMILY.

Two families bearing the Balch name appear about the middle of the eighteenth century in Maryland. Their descendants are now settled chiefly in the southern states, southern Indiana and Illinois, Missouri and Kansas. Persistent efforts to trace their ancestry has yielded but little trustworthy information, but in the absence of other British records, it is to be presumed that they came from the family in Somersetshire, England.

A few land records have been found in Maryland. The earliest is in the land office at Annapolis, in which the name is spelled with a "t," and is as follows:

"I, John Baltch, do assign over unto John Lloyd all my right, title and interest of one Right due unto me for my Transportation in this Province, as witness my hand this 30th day of December, 1663.

The mark of X JOHN BALTCH."

Witness,

DAN'L JENIFER.

From time of the very first settlements, in 1634, land was to be obtained in the first instance only as a premium to encourage settlement. A single man was given 100 acres, which was subject to a nominal yearly rental. This land he could transfer for a consideration, as the above entry shows.

In 1683 the Proprietory proclaimed new "Conditions of Plantation," as the term ran, by which any one could obtain warrants for any quantity of land, not already disposed of, by the payment of a small amount of purchase money, and afterwards of a trifling annual "quit rent." This system continued until after the Revolution.

The next entry containing the name Balch, which has

(446)

been found in the Maryland records, was made seventy-five years after John Baltch disposed of his right. It shows that there was a grant for a tract of land called "Balch's Abode," amounting to 86 acres, and lying in Baltimore county, on the north side of Deer creek. It was surveyed for John Balch, October 1, 1738, and patented to him December 14, 1739.

In the same locality the conveyance of a tract of land called "Bond's Hope" to James Balch, by Jacob Giles and Isaac Webster, on November 2, 1743, is shown by the records in the clerk's office of the Superior Court of Baltimore.

Four eminent Presbyterian clergymen of the Scotch-Irish type are first found on the north side of Deer creek, in what is now Hartford county, then Baltimore county, Maryland. One of these was Rev. Dr. Hezekiah Balch, of Greenville College, Tennessee. The three others, Rev. Hezekiah James, Rev. Dr. Stephen Bloomer, and Rev. James Balch, were brothers, and had three other brothers, Amos, William Goodwin and John, who followed agricultural pursuits. They were born in the order named, between 1741 and 1760, and the six brothers were sons of James Balch.

While three grandchildren of James Balch were living, three apparently inconsistent traditions were reduced to writing.

One of these traditions is from Rev. Thomas Bloomer, son of Rev. Stephen Bloomer Balch. It is that his great-grand-father, the father of James, was named John. He wrote a poem on the stamp act, was married in Wales, probably to a Bloomer, and came to Maryland about 1720 or 1725, and settled on Deer creek, but removed to Mecklenburg in 1769. With him was a brother, probably named Hezekiah, who was the father of Rev. Dr. Hezekiah Balch.

The second tradition is from Mrs. Albina Bloomer Mann, daughter of Rev. James Balch. It is that her paternal ancestor, of the fifth or sixth generation back, was kidnapped with other boys and girls on the coast of Wales, to be brought to America and sold to planters for a sufficient length of time to pay their ocean passage. He fell in love with a fair captive named Ann Bloomer, and in due time they were married. After taking them, the captain of the vessel became suspicious of detection, and set them ashore on the coast of Scotland, where they remained for several years, were married, and then emigrated to America. Dr. Calvin W. Balch has also given this tradition, except as to the marriage, and says that it was James, the father of Rev. James Balch, who was taken to Scotland, and there apprenticed to a shoemaker. While playing on the beach the steward of a vessel stopping for water offered him passage to Georgetown, which he gladly accepted.

The third tradition is from Zeno Campbell, who married Ann Kincade, daughter of William Goodwin Balch. It is that the first Balch was Hezekiah, of Cecil county, Maryland. He was stolen away from his people when quite a child, it is thought from Wales. He married a woman named Bloomer, and they had three sons and a daughter—James, John, Thomas, and Rachel. James married Ann Goodwin, and they, with their family, came to Mecklenburg county, North Carolina.

In the absence of facts, speculation on the relative credibility of these traditions is of little use. The story of the kidnapping is described by Dr. Calvin W. with minuteness of detail and assurance as to its accuracy, but it is not held by the descendants of either Rev. Stephen Bloomer or John, but those of the latter have such a story concerning an ancestor in a female line.

The characteristics of the family, observable in both the earlier and the later generations, are a general adherence to the Presbyterian denomination, high morality, decision of character, general intelligence and unflinching courage, coupled with keen penetration and self-confidence amounting sometimes almost to intolerance. Ever true to the land they live in, each earnestly battled in the civil strife for the side his state espoused.

In what follows the male descendants of James Balch, of Rev. Dr. Hezekiah Balch, and of William Balch, who is said to have been a brother of Hezekiah, will be quite fully traced. There are also several families in North and South Carolina who are probably related, but they have given no information.

JAMES BALCH.

FIRST GENERATION.

1. **James Balch,**[1] concerning whose parents no records have been found, is said by tradition to have been the son of John and Ann [Bloomer] Balch. On November 2, 1743, he purchased a place known as "Bond's Hope," on the north side of Deer creek, in Baltimore county, now Hartford county, Maryland. He married Ann Goodwin, probably a year or so after this purchase. They removed to Mecklenburg county, North Carolina, probably in 1769. Their children were as follows:

   2* ELIZABETH,[2] b. ; d.
   3* HEZEKIAH JAMES,[2] b. 1745; d. 1776.
   4* STEPHEN BLOOMER,[2] b. April 5, 1747; d. Sept. 22, 1833.
   5* JAMES,[2] b. Dec. 25, 1750; d. Jan. 12, 1821.
   6* MARGARET ANN,[2] b. 1752; d. 1848.
   7* AMOS,[2] b. ; d. after 1834.
   8* RHODA,[2] b. ; d.
   9* RACHEL,[2] b. ; d.
  10* WILLIAM GOODWIN,[2] b. ; d. Oct. 14, 1822.
  11* JOHN,[2] b. Nov. 1760; d. May 27, 1849.
  12* JANE,[2] b. ; d.

SECOND GENERATION.
Descendants of James Balch.

2. **Elizabeth,**[2] daughter of 1 James[1] and Ann [Goodwin] Balch, was born on the North side of Deer creek in Maryland, and was married to James Ashmore and had seven children: William, James, Samuel, Amos, Hannah, Margaret, and Rhoda.

3. **Hezekiah James,**[2] eldest son of 1 James[1] and Ann [Goodwin] Balch, was born about 1745, and died early in life unmarried in the spring of 1776. In 1766, he graduated

(450)

from Princeton College, and was licensed by the Donegal, Pennsylvania, Presbytery. In 1768 it was ordered that he supply four sabbaths north of the Kittatinning hills for which the Synod was to allow him four pounds. In 1770 he was ordained by the Donegal Presbytery, and in the same year the Presbytery of Orange was formed in North Carolina, and he together with Rev. Dr. Hezekiah Balch, whose relationship has not been proven, and several others, were erected into it by the Synod. He was for about seven years a pastor of the united congregations of Poplar Tent and Rocky River, in Mecklenburg county. His name does not appear on the church records after 1774, when he was reported absent from the Synod of Philadelphia.

In the convention at Charlotte of May 19 and 20, 1775, which declared independence of the British Crown, he was a prominent actor, and was one of the committee who prepared the Mecklenburg Declaration of Independence. To his eloquence on that occasion, is attributed its unanimous adoption on May 20, 1775. At a railroad meeting, in 1847, at Poplar Tent church, funds were raised for a suitable monument to his memory. There was present, Abijah Alexander, then ninety years of age, who had been present at the funeral, and was able to point out the precise place of burial in the graveyard of the church.

4. **Stephen Bloomer,**[2] son of 1 James[1] and Ann [Goodwin] Balch, was born April 5, 1747, and died September 22, 1833, at Georgetown, District of Columbia. He was married July 10, 1781, to Elizabeth, daughter of Col. George Beall who received from Queen Anne a grant of land which included nearly the whole of Georgetown. She died June 27, 1827. They had eleven children.

13* HARRIET,[8] b. 1786; d. 1841.
14* ALFRED,[8] b.   ; d. 1836.
15* LEWIS PENN WITHERSPOON,[8] b. Dec. 31, 1787; d. Aug. 29, 1866.
16 JANE,[8] b.   ; d. y.
17* GEORGE NINAN BEALL,[8] b.   ; d. 1831.

18 HEZEKIAH JAMES,² b. ; d. unm. 1827.
19° THOMAS BLOOMER,² b. July 28, 1798; d. 1878.
20° ANNA ELEANORA,² b. ; d.
21° ELIZABETH MARIA,² b. ; d.
22° JANE WHANN,² b. 1805; d.

Rev. Stephen Bloomer Balch, S. T. D., graduated from
Princeton College in 1774, and took charge of a classical
academy at Lower Marlborough, Maryland, over which he
presided until 1801. He was appointed Captain of his pupils
who were old enough to be enrolled in the state militia, and
was in actual service for two years. In 1780 he commenced
his ministerial work in Georgetown, and organized and presided over the Bridge street Presbyterian church to the day
of his death. On November 5, 1828, he married Mrs. Elizabeth King who lived only eighteen days after their marriage.
His third wife was Mrs. Jane Parrott whom he married
November 9, 1830. In a letter to his brother James, dated
Georgetown, January, 14, 1805, he describes his family as
follows: "My own family is large. We have had ten children: two of them are dead: eight survive. My two eldest
sons are now at Princeton College. Alfred the eldest will
graduate next Fall. Lewis Penn Witherspoon the Fall after
next. They both promise well so far. Two others of my
sons George Ninan Beall Balch & Hezekiah James Balch
are both in stores in this town & draw wages for their services. My youngest son Thomas Bloomer Balch is at the
Latin school in town. My eldest daughter Harriet is in her
20th year & is a fine blooming girl and might be well
married if she choose but she appears to be averse from matri-
mony as yet. We have other two daughters Anna Eleanora
& Elizabeth Maria both young, but they are promising. If
things are to turn out well we are to expect another son or
daughter before long."

5. James,² son of 1 James¹ and Ann [Goodwin] Balch,
was born on the north side of Deer Creek, in Maryland, December 25, 1750, and died January 12, 1821, at White's

Prairie, Sullivan county, Indiana. In 1772 he married Susanna Lavinia Garrison, who was born February 13, 1758, and died in 1834, and was buried in Pleasant Prairie cemetery, Coles county, Illinois. They had ten children.

23* Amos Prido,* b. 1775; d. Aug. 27, 1846.
24* Ann Wilks,* b. Feb. 17, 1776; d. Feb. 12, 1882.
25 Martha,* b.   ; d.   ; m. John McMillan, Russelville, Kentucky.
26* Mary,* b.   ; d.
27* Elizabeth Roe,* b. Jan. 16, 1788; d. May 22, 1863.
28* Ethelinda,* b.   ; d.
29* Albina Bloomer,* b. Nov. 25, 1797; d. Nov. 17, 1882.
30* Calvin,* b.   ; d.
31* John Luther,* b. Dec. 27, 1800; d. Oct. 3, 1870.
32* Jonathan Edwards,* b. 1808; d.

Rev. James Balch was nearly six feet in height, well proportioned, and of erect presence. He was a man of clear perceptions, of strong convictions, always active, courteous and kind, and did much to allay prejudice and inspire hope in the dark days of the Revolution. He earnestly labored for the education of all classes, as the hope of the country under a free government. But sparceness of population, scarcity of money, and the Revolutionary struggle and Indian raids rendered the introduction of any general educational system next to impossible. Families gathered into communities and hamlets for mutual protection, and their farms radiated around these centres, often at a distance of several miles. Guns were carried into the fields when men went to plow or harvest the grain. Only a small portion of these early pioneers could either read or write, and some of them cherished such an obstinate prejudice against educated people that it was difficult to maintain schools of the most primary character.

In the fall of 1786 he was called by the congregation at Sinking Springs through the Presbytery of Abingdon, at an annual salary of seventy pounds Virginia money. In May, 1787, his name first appears on the rolls of the Synod as licensed by the Presbytery of Abingdon, Maryland. At this same meeting of the Synod, Abingdon was charged with irregularity in licensing him, as he was said to be under suspension by the Presbytery of Orange, but the Synod decided that he was a proper candidate for the Presbytery of Abingdon, since he had been restored to church membership by the Presbytery of Hanover. The cause of the suspension does not appear on the record of the Synod. He commenced his labors at Sinking Spring in 1786, was over that church nine years, and was dismissed in 1795. Next he moved to Poplar Creek, near the line of Anderson and Roan counties, Tennessee, and here organized the Poplar Creek church. In the summer of 1798 he was on his way to Russelville, Kentucky, and in 1799 was supplying the churches of Mount Tabor and Concord, Kentucky. A peculiar nervous epidemic prevailed through the region, and during church services strong men became so overcome with a sense of sin that they fell prostrate, as if slain in battle, and women would jerk their heads with such force that their hair would crack like a whip. Many ministers regarded this as a special work of the Holy Spirit, and taught that if it were resisted the spirit would not always strive, but take everlasting flight. Rev. Mr. Balch opposed these views, and proved his position when preaching in a church noted for these outbursts by successfully commanding their omission. In 1816 he moved from Russelville, Kentucky, to the home of his son-in-law, on Turman's Creek, in Sullivan county, Indiana. He began his work here at once by preaching in private houses, in barns and groves, and soon a hewed log meeting house, known as Hopewell Presbyterian Church, was erected, the first in the county, if not in the state. By its door he was buried. Nearly sixty years after his remains were removed to the Presbyterian cemetery, north of Graysville, and there stands a modest marble monument erected by his descendants.

6. **Margaret Ann,**[2] daughter of 1 James[1] and Ann [Goodwin] Balch, was born in 1752 on the north side of

Deer creek, in Maryland, and died in the spring of 1848. She married Alexander Kelso, a wheelwright. He was in the Revolution. After leaving North Carolina they moved to Knoxville, Tennessee. His conscience led him to give his slaves their freedom, and to move away from slavery, about 1820, into Indiana. Alexander and Margaret Ann Kelso both lived to be nearly a hundred years old, and had six children—Charles, Dorcas, Nelvey, Mary, Ann Goodwin, and James Balch. All were Presbyterians and strong abolitionists. Charles and James Balch Kelso were farmers, and the latter was a soldier in the war of 1812, and was at the battle of Cowpens. H. A. Kelso, M. D., of Paxton, Illinois, is a grandson, and Margaret Ann [Kelso] Dryden, of Neoga, Illinois, a granddaughter.

7. **Amos,**[2] son of 1 James[1] and Ann [Goodwin] Balch, was born on the north side of Deer Creek, in Maryland, and went with his father's family first to North Carolina, then to East Tennessee, and finally to Kentucky. He died after 1834 in Bedford county, Tennessee. He married Ann, daughter of Samuel Patton, who was born about December 1, 1760, and died April 5, 1824. They had seven children.

33 ANN,[3] b. Nov. 22, 1785; d.
34 BARBARA,[3] b. Feb. 6, 1788; d. ; m. Joseph Alexander.
35* RHODA,[3] b. Oct. 28, 1790; d. 1859.
36 PEGGY,[3] b. Mar. 20, 1793; d.
37* JOHN BLOOMER,[3] b. July 19, 1795; d. April 24, 1864.
38* ALFRED MOORE,[3] b. Jan. 23, 1798; d. Dec. 2, 1856.
39* SAMUEL PATTON,[3] b. Sept. 7, 1800; d. 1877.
40* JAMES CALVIN,[3] b. April 19, 1803; d. April, 1857.

Amos was a Presbyterian. He served nine months in the Revolutionary war, and in 1812 applied for a pension. In a letter dated March 9, 1834, he wrote the following to his son, Alfred Moore: "I truly rejoice that you live in a state where the curse of slavery dare not show its head, and where republican principles prevail. With regard to myself, I still teach school not far from Lexington (Tenn.). I still board

at Mr. Wadley's. I enjoy tolerable health for a person of my
age. I expect to continue my school till the middle of August next."

8. **Rhoda,**[2] daughter of 1 James[1] and Ann [Goodwin]
Balch, was born on the north side of Deer Creek, in Maryland. She did not marry, and was a strong-minded, self-
poised woman, strong in the old-fashioned Presbyterian faith,
and considered one of the cleverest women in Tennessee.

9. **Rachel,**[2] daughter of 1 James[1] and Ann [Goodwin]
Balch, was born on the north side of Deer Creek, in Mary-
land. She married John Houston, and lived on Pistol creek,
Blount county, Tennessee.

10. **William Goodwin,**[2] son of 1 James[1] and Ann
[Goodwin] Balch, was born on the north side of Deer Creek,
in Maryland, and died October 14, 1822, at the home of his
nephew, 17 George N. B. Balch, near Moulton, Alabama.
While but a child, his father moved to Mecklenburg county,
North Carolina. He was a farmer, and removed with his
family to Shelbyville, Tennessee, and finally to Alabama. He
married Elizabeth, daughter of John and Martha Rodgers, in
North Carolina. She died in August, 1837. They had five
children.

41* HEZEKIAH JAMES,[3] b. March 21, 1780; d. Sept. 4, 1836.
42 MARTHA RODGERS,[3] b. 1783; d. Sept. 3, 1823; m. 17 George N. B.
       Balch.
43* THERON EUSEBIUS,[3] b. Dec. 12, 1787; d. Nov. 1, 1838.
44 PHILONIDES,[3] b.   ; d.
45* ANN KINCADE,[3] b. Jan. 8, 1794; d. Feb. 9, 1875.

11. **John,**[2] son of 1 James[1] and Ann [Goodwin] Balch,
was born about November, 1760, and died May 27, 1849,
near Dandridge, Tennessee, where he was buried. He married Barbara, an older sister of Ann Patton, who married 7
Amos Balch. They had six children.

46 ANN,[3] b. Jan. 5, 1789; d.
47* RACHEL PATTON,[3] b. Jan. 12, 1791; d. July 19, 1877.
48 BETSY,[3] b. Sept. 28, 1793; d.

49   CATHERINE,[3] b. Feb. 5, 1796; d.
50* JAMES PATTON,[3] b. July 25, 1796; d. June 29, 1879.
51   BARBARA THOMPSON,[3] b. Sept. 27, 1809; d.

For a short time John was in the Revolution, being but a lad, and was at Sumpter's defeat in South Carolina when the men were compelled to flee in wild confusion, without putting on their shoes.   He was also in a battle in which about 800 Whigs gained a victory over 1000 Tories, but lost five of their captains.   He was an uncompromising Whig, and voted for Harrison and for Clay.   In Hopewell Church, at Dandridge, he was an elder under Rev. Robert Henderson, son-in-law of Rev. Dr. Hezekiah Balch.   Because of his hasty temper, however, he resigned from the eldership.   He was an old bluestocking Presbyterian, but was led into Hopkinsianism, with which his pastors were in strong sympathy.

12. Jane,[2] daughter of 1 James[1] and Ann [Goodwin] Balch, is said by tradition to have married a Mr. Rankin, and that many ministers upon the Assembly roll are her descendants.

THIRD GENERATION.
Descendants of James Balch.

13. Harriet,[3] daughter of 4 Rev. Stephen Bloomer[2] and Elizabeth [Beall] Balch, was born at Georgetown, D. C., in 1786, and died in 1841.   In 1809 she married first James Reid Wilson, of the United States navy, and in 1826 she became the second wife of General Alexander Macomb, who was Commander-in-Chief of the United States army, and fought in the battle of Plattsburg, in 1814.   She possessed a stately and commanding appearance and great decision of character.

14. Alfred,[3] son of 4 Rev. Stephen Bloomer[2] and Elizabeth [Beall] Balch, was born at Georgetown, D. C., and died in 1836.   He graduated at Princeton College in the fall of 1805, and became a law partner of James K. Polk.   He was ap-

pointed by President Polk a judge of the United States District Court in Florida. He also lived at Nashville, Tennessee, and was a judge in that city. He possessed considerable property, which passed to his nephews, 65 Robert M.[4] and 66 Charles C.[4] He first married Miss Lewis, and afterwards Miss Newman, and they had one son.

   52 ALFRED,[4] b. ; d. 1853.

   15. Lewis Penn Witherspoon,[3] son of 4 Rev. Stephen Bloomer[2] and Elizabeth [Beall] Balch, was born December 31, 1787, and died August 29, 1868. He married Elizabeth Emeline Weaver and they lived at Leesburg, Virginia, and had twelve children of whom six grew up.

   53* LEWIS PENN WITHERSPOON,[4] b. Feb. 1, 1814; d. June 4, 1875.
   54   CATHERINE,[4] b. ; d. ; m. Rev. Freeman Clarkson.
   55* VIRGINIA,[4] b. March 18, 1818.
   56* THOMAS,[4] b. July 23, 1821; d. March 29, 1877.
   57* ALEXANDRINE MACOMB,[4] b. 1828.
   58* STEPHEN FITZHUGH,[4] b. March 14, 1830; d. May 20, 1893.

   Judge Lewis P. W. graduated from Princeton College in 1806, studied law with Roger Brooke Taney, afterwards Chief Justice of the United States Supreme Court, and was a judge in the highest state court in West Virginia. He became a strong Abolitionist, and impoverished himself by liberating his slaves and sending them to Liberia. On one occasion during the civil war, when there was fighting near his house and bullets were flying thick, although quite aged, he came out and cheered the Union forces. In the Historical Magazine for September, 1868, he gives his experience as a private soldier in 1814, at Baltimore in a regiment of Loudon, Virginia militia.

   17. George Ninan Beall,[3] son of 4 Stephen Bloomer[2] and Elizabeth [Beall] Balch, was born at Georgetown, D. C., and died in 1831 ; was a farmer near Moulton, Alabama, near Charlestown, Virginia. He married his cousin 42 Martha Rodgers Balch, and they had four children.

   59   ELIZABETH BEALL RODGERS,[4] b. 1813; d. Aug. 27, 1823.
   60   WILLIAM GOODWIN,[4] b. 1817; d. Sept. 10, 1823.

61 ALFRED,[4] b. 1819; d. Aug. 2, 1828.
62* GEORGE BEALL,[4] b. Jan. 3, 1821.
George N. B. married second, Anna Beall.

19. **Thomas Bloomer,**[3] son of 4 Stephen Bloomer[2] and Elizabeth [Beall] Balch, was born at Georgetown, D. C. in July 28, 1793 and died in 1878.   He married in 1820, Susan, daughter of Charles Carter, and a cousin of General Robert E. Lee. She was born December 25, 1801, in Virginia, and died in 1878.   They had nine children.

68* ANN CARTER,[4] b. 1821; d.
64* ELIZABETH,[4] b. ; d.
65* ROBERT M.,[4] b. May 7, 1826; d. 1871.
66* CHARLES CARTER,[4] b. 1828.
67 CHALMERS,[4] b. ; d.
68 BLOOMER,[4] b. ; d.
69* MARY L.,[4] b.
70* JULIA R.,[4] b.
71 WILLIAM,[4] b. ; a lawyer, Washington, D. C.

Rev. Dr. Thomas B. Balch graduated from Princeton College in 1813, and also received the degree of S. T. D. He was quiet and popular, and was characterized by Daniel Webster as the most learned man he ever knew.   Dr. Balch was a Presbyterian clergyman for over thirty years.   For ten years he lived at Snow Hill, Maryland, and had charge of three churches, one of them being the Rehobah, the first Presbyterian church planted in America by the pioneer Makennie. Mrs. Balch died quite suddenly after a life of usefulness and devotion.

20. **Anna Eleanora,**[3] daughter of 4 Stephen Bloomer[2] and Elizabeth [Beall] Balch, was born at Georgetown, D. C. She married Captain James C. Wilson, and lived in Washington for forty years.

21. **Elizabeth Maria,**[3] daughter of 4 Stephen Bloomer[2] and Elizabeth [Beall] Balch, was born at Georgetown, D. C. She married Rev. Septimis Tustin, a Presbyterian minister who was chaplain of the United States Senate for many years.

22. **Jane Whann,**[3] daughter of 4 Stephen Bloomer[2]

and Elizabeth [Beall] Balch, was born at Georgetown, D. C. She married Rev. William Williamson, a fine classical scholar. They lived in Washington, D. C.

23. **Amos Prido,**[3] eldest son of 5 Rev. James[2] and Susanna L. [Garrison] Balch, was born in North Carolina in 1775, and died August 27, 1846, at Greenville, Illinois. He first married Martha Leach who was born in Tennessee, and died about 1825. They had eight children.

72* SELINA M.,[4] b. Oct. 10, 1803; d. Sept. 14, 1878.
73* STEPHEN WITHERSPOON,[4] b. Dec. 27, 1806; d. Sept. 19, 1866.
74* ARMSTEAD BLUFORD,[4] b. Jan. 21, 1809; d. March 8, 1837.
75* CALVIN WHITFIELD,[4] b. April 25, 1811; d. March 17, 1894.
76   LAVINIA,[4] b.
77   EMELINE HARRISON,[4] b. Nov. 27, 1813; d. 1822.
78* JONATHAN JAMES PRESTON,[4] b. Jan. 27, 1816.
79* MARTHA ELVIRA,[4] b. Sept. 30, 1821; d. April 11, 1896.

In April, 1826, Amos Prido married second, Mary Sawyer, who was born in Logan county, Kentucky. They had nine children.

80* MONROE YOUNG,[4] b. May 7, 1827; d. March 11, 1863.
81* SYLVESTER NEWTON,[4] b. Aug. 23, 1829; d. Jan. 1, 1873.
82* JANE ELIZA,[4] b. May 22, 1831.
83   JOHN SHEALS,[4] b. April 9, 1833; d. unm. Jan. 30, 1853.
84* FELIX MARION,[4] b. Jan. 1, 1835; d. November 28, 1876.
85* MARIA THERESA,[4] b. July 22, 1838; d. April 5, 1867.
86* RACHEL VASHTI,[4] b. Aug. 3, 1840.
87* CAROLINE MELISSA, b. April 5, 1842.
88* CHARLOTTE MALETHA,[4] b. July 4, 1844.

Amos Prido with his brother-in-law William White went from Russelville, Kentucky, to Busiro Prairie, Knox county, Indiana, where they arrived August 1, 1815.   The location proving unhealthy, he and several other families, after a search, moved north in the fall to Turman's settlement. Ten or twelve years later he moved to Illinois, and lived first at Shelbyville, and finally at Greenville. He was a farmer and was an elder in the Presbyterian Church.

24. **Ann Wilks,**[3] daughter of 5 Rev. James[2] and Susanna L. [Garrison] Balch, was born at Greenville, Tennes-

see, February 17, 1776, and died in Fountain county, Indiana, February 12, 1832.   In the spring of 1796 she married William, son of William and Mary White, who was born March 27, 1776, in Washington county, Virginia, and died March 21, 1878, in Fountain county, Indiana.   They lived for a time in Greene county, Tennessee, and then bought land in Roan and Anderson counties, and by accident their house was built on the county line.   William White was the captain of a militia company for several years. During the war of 1812, his company was kept busy with the Indians who had been supplied with arms by the British. His company under Gen. Jackson was in the engagement of January 22, 1814, on the Tallapoosa river at the mouth of Emuckfaw creek, and also in the celebrated fight at Horse-Shoe Bend on the Tallapoosa on March 27, 1814.   In 1815 Capt. White led his brother-in-law Amos Prido Balch and other emigrants to Busero Prairie, Knox county, Indiana. While living in Tennessee they cultivated flax, which they spun, made into cloth, and into the tent in which they lived for a time at Busero Prairie.   In the fall, they moved north to Turman's settlement and Capt. White built a cabin three miles south of the present village of Fairbanks.   He owned 1,500 acres of land on Helts Prairie in Vermilion county, and a large tract of river-bottom land now known as White's Prairie.   They had eight children born in Roan county, Tennessee, except the youngest, who was born in Sullivan county, Indiana.   William Bloomer, b. Nov. 1, 1797, d. Jan. 10, 1847, m. Elizabeth I. White; Sarah Lavinia, b. Nov. 1, 1801, d. March 28, 1875, m. Thomas Turman; James Anderson, b. Oct. 4, 1805, d. 1890, m. Martha R. Elder; Serena Delia, b. July 13, 1809, m. Joseph Coats, lives Vreedenburg, Ind.; Selina Huntington, b. Aug. 4, 1812, d. Dec. 19, 1832; Adaline Harrison, b. 1813, d., m. Joseph Steely; Albert Franklin, b. June 21, 1821.

Albert Franklin White, LL. D., graduated from Wabash

College in 1843, and from Lane Theological Seminary in 1846. He was married June 24, 1846, to Caroline LaMonte, who was born at Middleburg, Scoharie county, New York, Oct. 14, 1821. They lived in Attica, Indiana, until the fall of 1852, when they went to California. There he had charge successively of the Presbyterian churches in Redwood City, Oakland, Carson City, San Leandro, and Los Angeles. He was superintendent of public instruction for two years in Nevada, was chaplain in the legislature for two sessions, and for more than four years was state mineralogist. He is the author of Reports on the Mineralogy of Nevada, and a Genealogy of James Balch and his descendants from which extracts have been made for this Genealogy.

26. **Mary**[8] daughter of 5 Rev. James[2] and Susanna L. [Garrison] Balch, was born in east Tennessee, and died in Boone county, Missouri. She married first, Thomas Henderson, and they had four children: James Balch, Michael Davis, Thomas Calvin, who died in the Confederate army; Serena Jane.

Mary married second Samuel Mitchell, who died in Boone county. They had five children: Matilda, b. 1818; Samuel Young, who died during the civil war; Ethelinda Albina, and Francina Jane, both of whom died in early life; Hezekiah Bloomer, b. 1830.

27. **Elizabeth Roe,**[8] daughter of 5 Rev. James[2] and Susanna L. [Garrison] Balch, was born January 16, 1788, in east Tennessee, and died May 22, 1863, in Parke county, Indiana. She was married in 1809 to Henry Rose Anderson, who was born April 21, 1788, and died in Parke county, Indiana, January 1, 1847. They lived in Logan county, Kentucky, until 1816, when they moved to Indiana, and in 1819 settled in Parke county. They had eight children: James Calvin, b. Jan. 29, 1810, d. March 31, 1858; Margaret Ethelinda, d. y.; Henry Harrison, b. Nov. 28, 1813, d. June 25, 1888; Granville Washington, b. Oct. 17, 1816, d. May 21, 1863; William

White, b. Oct. 2, 1818, d. Jan. 10, 1856 ; Angeline S. b. 1821, d. y.; John Moreland, b. Feb. 25, 1824, d. in Kansas ; Eliza A. b. Sept. 29, 1827. Henry H. married Dec. 27, 1816, Melinde Allen, lived at Rockville, Indiana, and left many descendants.

28. **Ethelinda**,[3] daughter of 5 Rev. James[2] and Susanna L. [Garrison] Balch, was born in East Tennessee, and died at Princeville, Randolph county, Illinois. She married Steele Rankin, and they had seven children : David Steele, Mary, Amos, John, Hamilton, Marthe, Theopolis.

29. **Albina Bloomer**,[3] daughter of 5 Rev. James[2] and Susanna L. [Garrison] Balch, was born in East Tennessee, November 25, 1797, and died near Kaskaskia, Illinois, November 17, 1882. She was married July 4, 1815, at Russelville. Kentucky, to John, son of Robert M. and Mary [Huston] Mann, who was born February 1, 1796, near Abbeyville, South Carolina, and died upon his farm near Kaskaskia, March 7, 1881. They lived a happy married life of sixty-six years, and had eleven children.

> SUSANNA LAVINA, b. 1816; d. y.
>
> WILLIAM YOUNG, b. 1818; d. y.
>
> WILLIAM HOUSTON, b. Jan. 21, 1820; m. Jan. 3, 1843, Martha Pettit, lived at Kaskaskia until 1884, now lives at Salina, Kansas. Children: *Mary Ellory*, b. May 6, 1847; m. John W. Burke. *Emma Jane*, b. Aug. 13, 1853; m. George C. Griswold. *Lavina Louis*, b. May 8, 1855. *Laura Elma*, b. Jan. 12, 1864; d. July 18, 1874.
>
> JOHN PRESTON, b. Feb. 6, 1822; served three years with the Fifth Illinois Cavalry, and is a lawyer at Rockwood, Illinois; m. Nancy Clendenin. Children: *Emily*, m. J. Hollowman; *Nancy*; *Alice*, m. R. Bilderback. *Samuel*; *Sadie*.
>
> ROBERT CLINTON, b. Feb. 18, 1824: d. Oct. 2, 1863, volunteered in the 22d Illinois Infantry, and was wounded at the battle of Chickamauga, was a blacksmith at Chester and Preston, Illinois; m. Ellen Pollock, Children: *Conway*, d. in the army; *Elwood Wallace*, editor Decatur, Illinois, m. Jennie Culbertson. *Joseph*, m. Mary Shultz.
>
> JAMES LUTHER, b. Feb. 3, 1826; was a captain in the 80th Illinois Infantry, but was soon discharged for disability. He is in the grain trade at Cutler, Illinois; m. first, Rachel A. Crawford;

one son, *Albert C.* a physician; m. second, Sallie Baldridge. Children: *James L.*, *William*, *Eva*, *Clinton*, *Charles.*

JONATHAN BALCH, b. Jan. 5, 1828; served three years in the 80th Illinois Infantry; is a farmer in Randolph county, Illinois; m. Harriet Webb. Children: *John Owen*, m. Laura Griswold. *Edward Webb*, m. Emma Marshall. *Hattie*, m. Edward Griswold.

ALBINA LOUISA, b. Aug. 24, 1830; d. Dec. 21, 1858; m. Henry Bilderback; one son, *Charles*, m., killed by a horse.

CALVIN ANDERSON, b. July 4, 1833; was a Lieutenant in the Fifth Illinois Cavalry, and was captured while on the way to destroy a railroad in Mississippi, was confined at Libby Prison, at Charlestown, and in North Carolina, in all thirteen months, when he escaped; is a physician at Gardin Plain, Kansas; m. Emily C. Young. Children: *Walter Huston*, *Emily Albina*, *Cornelius Hanford*, *Angeline.*

ALFRED MATTHEWS, b. Aug. 17, 1837; is a Presbyterian minister at Osawatomie, Kansas; m. Sallie Hood. Children: *Alfred Horace*, a dentist. *Homer Burns*, a journalist in Kansas City. *Sarah Belle*, *Cora Huston.*

MARY JANE, b. Oct. 4, 1841; m. Alfred W. Wright, a Presbyterian minister, now superintendent of missions in Minnesota. Children: *Albina May*, *Hattie*, *Charles*, *Clinton*, *Esther.*

During the war with Great Britain John Mann volunteered in the Fourteenth Regiment of Kentucky militia, and was in the battle of New Orleans, on January 8, 1815. In 1816 he moved into Indiana, and after living three years in Sullivan county, secured a farm near the present site of Rockville, where their first winter was spent in a comfortable shelter of split rails and bed quilts, on the edge of a dense forest. Deer and wild turkey were abundant. That was the happiest winter of their lives. By spring a set of house logs were hewn a few acres were ready for the plow, and a little later they were happy in the possession of a home of their own. The children were taught the Shorter Catechism, and hymns from Watts and McClellan's selections were sung to the accompaniment of the spinning wheel. In 1827 they moved to Kaskaskia, where he was an active elder in the church for over 45 years. He was a blacksmith, but also carried on a farm. His first vote was for Jackson, then he was a Whig and lastly a Republican.

30. **Calvin,**[3] son of 5 Rev. James[2] and Susanna L. [Garrison] Balch, was born in Tennessee, and went with his parents to Russelville, Kentucky, and also to Sullivan county, Indiana, in 1817. His first wife was Mary Peoples, of Bussero Prarie, Indiana. She lived but a short time, and he married Patsy McClure, of Vincennes. He died a few years after his second marriage.

31. **John Luther,**[3] son of 5 Rev. James[2] and Susanna L. [Garrison] Balch, was born at Russelville, Kentucky, December 27, 1800, and died upon his farm at Lerna, Illinois, October 8, 1870. He was married November 10, 1829, to Melinda Newton, daughter of John and Margaret [Lester] White, who was born in Roan county, Tennessee, May 4, 1808, and died at Lerna, Illinois, January 10, 1865. They had eight children.

89* ALFRED BOLIVAR,[4] b. Sept. 8, 1830.
90* ALBINA,[4] b. Sept. 7, 1832.
91* ALEXANDER HOUSTON,[4] b. April 18, 1834; d. June 1, 1868.
92 MARY MELINDA,[4] b. Jan. 9, 1836; d. unm. Aug. 2, 1894.
93 JAMES,[4] b. Dec. 12, 1837; d. Feb. 25, 1859.
94* WILLIAM,[4] b. Jan. 23, 1840.
95 MARTHA,[4] b. May 11, 1842.
96 ANGELINE ELIZABETH,[4] b. Sept. 1, 1844; d. Dec. 31, 1896.

John Luther moved in 1831, with his wife and child and a colony of Presbyterians, to Pleasant Grove township, Coles county, Illinois, which was then sparsely settled, and located on a farm of 200 acres. St. Louis was their nearest market for farm produce, and it had to be hauled 150 miles with horses or oxen over rough roads. The nearest store was ten miles away. In his house raising he was assisted by Thomas Lincoln, the father of Abraham Lincoln. The house covering and floors were of split lumber, and the work was done with imperfect farm tools, no luxuries, and scant necessities. He taught the first school in the township, and assisted in organizing the first Sunday school. For it he purchased a library, which he brought 75 miles on horseback. Out of this school grew the Pleasant Prairie Presbyterian Church.

His health failing, he sold his live stock, rented his farm, and spent three years in Randolph county, Illinois, and there wrote articles for the local papers on the political issues. He was a Whig, and afterwards a Republican. He and his wife were Presbyterians, and she was a good illustration of Solomon's description of a virtuous woman.

32. Jonathan Edwards,[3] son of 5 Rev. James[2] and Susanna L. [Garrison] Balch, was born at Russelville, Kentucky, in 1803, and died in Shawnee county, Kansas, February 20, 1860. About 1823 he married Elizabeth, daughter of John and Margaret [Lester] White, who was born in Roan county, Tennessee, and died in 1880. They had nine children.

97* ALBINA JANE,[4] b. 1824.
98* JAMES A.,[4] b. 1826.
99   VIOLINDA,[4] b. 1826; d. 1863; m. H. M. Robinson.
100* ELIZABETH,[4] b. 1830.
101* EVALINE,[4] b. 1832.
102* SUSANNAH LAVINA,[4] b. 1834.
103* MARY,[4] b. 1836; d. 1876.
104* JOHN MITCHELL,[4] b. 1838.
105* SARAH CAROLINE,[4] b. 1840.

35. Rhoda,[3] daughter of 7 Amos[2] and Ann [Patton] Balch, was born October 28, 1790, in Tennessee, and died in 1859. She married James Patton, and their children were as follows: James, d. 1840; George, d. 1851; Benjamin F., b. 1828, d. 1861; Eliza, b. 1836, d. about 1880.

37. John Bloomer,[3] son of 7 Amos[2] and Ann [Patton] Balch, was born July 19, 1795, and died April 24, 1863, near Sardis, Mississippi. He was a farmer in Tennessee until 1840, when he moved to Panola county, Mississippi. He was an old line Whig, and greatly regretted the secession of Mississippi. In January, 1817, he married Sarah Cook, who was born in 1801, and died in 1852, in Panola county. They had ten children.

106   EMILY,[4] b. Nov. 28, 1818; d. unm. 1864.
107* RUFUS COLWELL,[4] b. Jan. 20, 1819.

108   MARY ANN,[4] b. 1821; d. 1870; m. A. Baker.
109* AMANDA,[4] b. 1822; d. Nov., 1886.
110* MINOS NEWTON,[4] b. Nov. 11, 1823; d. June 7, 1885.
111* JOHN C.,[4] b. April 18, 1826; d. Jan. 15, 1883.
112* LYDIA,[4] b. April 14, 1827.
113   JANE,[4] b. 1829.
114* ELIZA TENNESSEE,[4] b. Jan. 15, 1880.
115   HELEN,[4] b. 1832.

38. Alfred Moore,[3] son of 7 Amos[2] and Ann [Patton] Balch, was born in Logan county, Kentucky, January 23, 1798, and died in Coles county, Illinois, December 2, 1856. He was a farmer in Bedford county, Tennessee, until 1830, when he moved with his family to Illinois, and settled near the present site of Lerna.   On July 1, 1819, he married Elizabeth Gammill, and they had eight children.

116* ANN JANE,[4] b. June 22, 1820; d. March, 1860.
117   NANCY CAROLINE,[4] b.   ; d. aged 30 years.
118   WILLIAM,[4] b.   ; d. y.
119   RHODA E.,[4] b.   ; d. aged 18 years.
120* GEORGE BELL,[4] b. Nov. 1, 1828; d. Sept. 4, 1886.
121* JAMES ALEXANDER,[4] b. Oct. 20, 1832; d. Jan. 4, 1869.
122   SAMUEL,[4] b.   ; d. aged 6 years.
123   JOHN,[4] b.   ; d. aged 20 years.

39. Samuel Patton,[3] son of 7 Amos[2] and Ann [Patton] Balch, was born September 7, 1800, and died in 1877, in Tippah county, Mississippi. He married Hannah Yates, and they had three children.

124   THOMAS W.,[4] b.
125   RHODA,[4] b.
126   MATILDA,[4] b.   ; m. Philip Carlton, no children.

40. James Calvin,[3] son of 7 Amos[2] and Ann [Patton] Balch, was born in Logan county, Kentucky, April 19, 1803. and died at Sparta, Tennessee, in April, 1857. He was a machinist at Murfreesborough, Tennessee, and was married December 30, 1828, to Eliza Jane, daughter of David Hazlett, who was born in Rutherford county, Tennessee, in November, 1808, and died in Carroll county, August 18, 1840, Their children were as follows:

127   MARGARET A. L.,[4] b. Dec. 10, 1829; d. Sept. 1884; m. Woodsen T. Harrison.

128*   DAVID LAWSON,⁴ b. Dec. 7, 1831.
129   SARAH J. B.,⁴ b. May 11, 1834; d. Dec. 1872; m. Milton L. Bentley.
130   SAFFRONIA,⁴ b. April 19, 1837.

James C. married second, August 26, 1844, Anna Elizabeth Cosby, who was born in Giles county, Tennessee, and died in December, 1855. They had six children.

131   GRACIE PORTER,⁴ b. June 1, 1845.
132*   HENRY TAYLOR,⁴ b. Nov. 7, 1846.
133   CHARLES LOUIS,⁴ b. Feb. 10, 1849.
134   DEMIELL NEWMAN,⁴ b. Jan. 5, 1851.
135   MARY ELIZA,⁴ b. Dec. 27, 1852; d. Feb. 7, 1855.
136   ELIZABETH WARREN,⁴ b. Nov. 17, 1855; d.

41. Hezekiah James,³ son of 10 William Goodwin² and Elizabeth [Rodgers] Balch, was born March 21, 1780, in North Carolina, and died September 4, 1836, in Coles county, Illinois. He was a Presbyterian, a farmer, and a school teacher. On October 30, 1799, he married Mary, daughter of David and Mary McCord, in Madison county, Kentucky. She was born March 14, 1778. They lived in Logan county, Kentucky, until 1808, then in Giles county, Tennessee, and after 1830 in Illinois. Their children were as follows :

137   ELTHANA ALLISON,⁴ b. July 23, 1800; d. 1880; m. Gersham Bills.
138*   LEVICA,⁴ b. Jan. 14, 1807; d. 1879.
139*   WALLACE WATTS,⁴ b. April 25, 1809; d. June 3, 1886.
140   ELIZA MARIA,⁴ b. Jan. 13, 1813; d. Dec. 13, 1829 in Lawrence
          Co., Ala.
141*   HEZEKIAH JAMES EMMET,⁴ b. Sept. 5, 1819; d. April 14, 1885.

43. Theron Eusebius,³ son of 10 William Goodwin² and Elizabeth [Rodgers] Balch, was born December 22, 1787, and died November 1, 1838, in Pleasant Grove township, Coles county, Illinois. He was in the war of 1812, and taught school and farmed. On May 28, 1811, he married Alpha, daughter of John and Ann Boyd, who was born in 1793, and died in Dane county, Wisconsin, in August, 1881. She possessed a fine intellect, and was a woman of untiring industry. A slave woman whom she inherited remained with them, although offered her liberty. They moved into Coles county in 1832, were Presbyterians, and had twelve children.

142* JULIA MARIA,⁴ b. Feb. 27, 1812; d. March 31, 1894.
143* WILLIAM BOYD,⁴ b. Sept. 1, 1813, d. March 20, 1884.
144* JOHN MOOREHEAD,⁴ b. Feb. 3, 1816; d. Feb. 15, 1868.
145* EMILY CLARISSA,⁴ b. May 31, 1818.
146* MARTHA JANE KINCADE,⁴ b. Aug. 7, 1822; d. June 1881.
147   ALMA CAROLINE,⁴ b. Nov. 17, 1826; d. July 31, 1884.
148   ELIZABETH ANN,⁴ b. July 29, 1830; d. March 21, 1841.
149   THERON EUSEBIUS,⁴ b. Jan. 12, 1824; d. Aug. 29, 1835.
150* CORNELIA TUSTON, b. Dec. 24, 1829; d.
151* GEORGE BELL,⁴ b. March 4, 1832.
152   ALPHA CAROLINE,⁴ b. Feb. 7, 1835; m. Charles Skinner, Long
      Prairie, Minn.
153   THERON HEZEKIAH EUSEBIUS,⁴ b. Oct. 7, 1838.

45. Ann Kincade,³ daughter of 10 William Goodwin³
and Elizabeth [Rodgers] Balch, was born January 8, 1794,
in Madison county, Kentucky, and died February 9, 1875, at
Neoga, Illinois. She was married about 1811 to Zeno Campbell of Mecklenburg county, North Carolina, whose mother,
Martha, was a sister of his wife's mother. He was born
December 30, 1787, and died May 25, 1867. In 1880 they
moved to Campbell, Illinois. They had eight children : Martha Rodgers, b. Aug. 12, 1813, d. Jan. 12, 1892, m. Nathan
Gould ; Elizabeth Amanda, b. Nov. 28, 1815, d. Feb. 7, 1887,
m. 144 John M. Balch ; Andrew Ames, b. Aug. 10, 1821, d.
March 26, 1840 ; Alpha C., b. Dec. 18, 1822, d. June 16,
1877, m. W. N. Morrison ; Harriet Ann, b. April 5, 1827, d.
Jan. 12, 1892, m. Austin Rice , William Tell, b. Dec. 20,
1829, d. y.; Darthula O., b. Sept. 13, 1832, d. Jan., 1895, m.
Frank Campbell ; Emma, b. Sept. 14, 1834, d. April 22, 1895,
m. Joseph Gould.

47. Rachel Patton,³ daughter of 11 John³ and Barbara
[Patton] Balch, was born January 12, 1791, and died July
19, 1877. In 1808 she married William Mathes, son of
George and grandson of Alexander Matthews, as the name
was formerly spelled, of Virginia. He was born in Jonesborough, Tennessee, was a farmer, an elder in the Presbyterian church at Dandridge, a magistrate, and held the office of
county trustee. They had eight children.

GEORGE A., b.   ; March 30, 1846, in Rogersville, Tenn.; was a
    Presbyterian clergyman.
JOHN PINKNEY, b. Oct. 28, 1812; d. Feb. 15, 1870; a physician.
WILLIAM ALFRED, b. Sept. 28, 1814; a minister in the Cumberland
    Presbytery living at Mount Horeb, Tenn.; m. Margaret Maria,
    daughter of Edward and Elizabeth [Hood] Hart. They had
    eight children. *James Harvey*, Captain in Confederate army,
    editor at Memphis, Tenn.; m. Mildred Spotswood [Dan-
    dridge] Cash. Children: Mildred Overton, Lee Dandridge,
    Benjamin, James Harvey, Talbot Spotswood. *Edward Hart*,
    a lawyer at Ozark, Ark. *John Theron*, San Antonio, Tex.
    Cordelia J., m. Shelley Hewen, Little Rock, Ark. *Dr. George
    Anderson*, d. July 31, 1881, in Confederate army, an editor at
    Brownsville, Tenn. *Rachel Emma*, d. 1896; m. James S. Bar-
    ton, a lawyer at McMinnville, Tenn. *Nathaniel Beecher*, a
    Presbyterian clergyman at West End, Atlanta, Ga.; m. Cora
    Clarke.
SERENA ANN, b. Aug. 3, 1819; d. July 22, 1884; m. Samuel Biddle.
    No children.
THERON, b. July 15, 1828; d. unm. Aug. 2, 1850.
MILTON HOUSTON, b. Dec. 8, 1825; d. unm. May 25, 1845.
LUTHER McEWEN, b. May 5, 1829; d. unm. June 30, 1844.
ALEXANDER WASHINGTON, b. Sept. 19, 1833; d. unm.

50. James Patton,[3] son of 11 John[3] and Barbara [Pat-
ton] Balch, was born July 25, 1798, and died June 29, 1879.
He was a man of untiring energy and decision of character.
He married Polly Russell, August 22, 1820, who died Nov.
21, 1879. They had no children.

FOURTH GENERATION.
Descendants of James Balch.

53. Lewis Penn Witherspoon,[4] son of 15 Judge Lewis
Penn Witherspoon[3] and Elizabeth [Weaver] Balch, was born
February 1, 1814, at Leesburg, Virginia, and died June 4,
1875, at Detroit, Michigan, and was buried at Holderness,
New Hampshire. He married first, Anna, daughter of Judge
William and Augusta Jay, and a sister of John Jay. They
had four children, born in New York city.

154   AUGUSTA J.,[5] b. Dec. 26, 1839; d. 1888; m. G. A. Peabody, Salem,
    Mass.

155* ELIZABETH,[5] b. April 20, 1845; d. May 25, 1890.
156 ANNA,[5] b. ; d. y.
157* LEWIS,[5] b. July 7, 1847.

Rev. Dr. Lewis P. W. married second, April 25, 1850, Emily, daughter of Timothy and Catherine [Holme] Wiggin, of Hopkinton, N. H. She was born in London, Eng., Oct. 15, 1826, and died at Washington, D. C., April 2, 1891.

158* ALFRED HOLME,[5] b. Feb. 28, 1851.
159* WILLIAM RALSTON,[5] b. Dec. 9, 1852.
160 CATHERINE HOLME,[5] b. Oct. 20, 1854; unm.
161* HENRY HERBERT,[5] b. May 7, 1856.
162 EMILY,[5] b. April 8, 1858; d. April 25, 1890.
163* ERNEST BERKELEY,[5] b. Jan. 15, 1860.
164* ADELINE,[5] b. Aug. 9, 1861.
165* ELLEN MARY,[5] b. Feb. 25, 1864.
166 EDITH CAZENOVE,[5] b. May 29, 1866.
167* STEPHEN ELLIOTT,[5] b. March 5, 1869.

Rev. Dr. Lewis P. W. attended three years at West Point Military Academy, and one year at Princeton College, where he graduated in 1834. He next entered the General Theological Seminary in New York, was ordained deacon, and was in charge of St. Andrew's church, Philadelphia, for ten months. While still deacon he was called to St. Bartholomew's church, New York, where he remained from 1837 to 1850, and cleared the church of debt. He was then obliged to leave New York for his health, and for five years he was rector of the parishes of Chester and West Chester, Pennsylvania. For five years he was rector of Christ church, Baltimore, Maryland, and during the winter of 1858 and 1859 was in charge of Christ church, Savannah, Georgia. From 1859 to 1866 he was rector of Emanuel church, Newport, Rhode Island, and was for six months at Bristol, Rhode Island. He was secretary of the House of Bishops from 1858 to 1866. From 1866 to 1871 he was canon of the Cathedral of Montreal, Canada, chaplain to the Metropolitan, and secretary of the Montreal Diocesan Synod. Over the Church of the Ascension, Baltimore, Maryland, he was rector from 1871 to 1878. Next in Huron, Canada, he was archdeacon of Kent, canon of the Cathedral, chaplain to the Bishop, president of the Hellmuth Boys' College, and vice-president of the Girls' College until November, 1874, when he became rector of Grace church, Detroit, Michigan, where he remained to the time of his death, six months afterwards.

Dr. Balch was a man of most charming manners. As a preacher he was at once impressive and powerful, and at times eloquent. His sermon at Newport on the death of Lincoln produced an effect on those who heard it which is still remembered. He had an extraordinary power of raising money for churches in debt. He secured the discharge of the indebtedness of eleven churches during the forty years of his ministry.

55. Virginia,[4] daughter of 15 Judge Lewis P. W.[3] and Elizabeth [Weaver] Balch, was born March 18, 1818, and lives at Washington, D. C. She was married to Dr. Charles H. Stephen, and they lived first at Baltimore, Maryland, and afterwards at Leetown, West Virginia, where he died. They had one daughter, Elizabeth Juliana, who married Dr. James R. Rogers, and they had two children : Charles Stephen, b. Aug. 1, 1870, lives in New York city ; Kathrine Elizabeth, b. Aug. 14, 1872, lives in Washington.

56. Thomas,[4] son of 15 Judge Lewis P. W.[3] and Elizabeth [Weaver] Balch, was born July 23, 1821, and died in Philadelphia, March 29, 1877. In 1852 he married Emily, daughter of Joseph Swift, of Philadelphia. They had four children.

168 EDWIN SWIFT,[5] b. ; a lawyer in Philadelphia.
169 ELISE WILLING,[5] b.
170 JOSEPH SWIFT,[5] b.
171 THOMAS WILLING,[5] b.; a lawyer in Philadelphia.

Thomas Balch studied at Columbia College, read law, and was admitted to the Philadelphia bar in 1850. Here he served in the city councils and presided over important committtees. For the Historical Society of Pennsylvania he ed-

REV. LEWIS P. W. BALCH.

ited the Shippen Papers, which related to the provincial history of the state. He also edited the Maryland Papers and
others for the Seventy-Six Society. Between 1859 and 1878
he travelled extensively in Europe, with headquarters in
Paris, and wrote in French a history of the part taken by
France in the establishment of American independence.
Among his other essays was one on Calvinism and American
Independence, and his last paper was before the Social Science Association on Free Coinage and Self-Adjusting Ratio,
in which he advocated the restoration of the bi-metallic
standard.

57. **Alexandrine Macomb,**[4] daughter of 15 Judge
Lewis P. W.[3] and Elizabeth [Weaver] Balch, was born in
1828, at Leetown, West Virginia, and lives at Baltimore, Md.
She was married in 1847 to Rev. George D. Cummins, D. D.
who became the leader in the reform movement of the broad
church school, which ended in the establishment of the Reformed Episcopal Church in America, of which he was the
first bishop. He was a rector at Norfolk and Richmond,
Virginia, Washington and Chicago. He died June 26, 1876.
Mrs. Cummins is a woman of strong character and great personal beauty, whose influence had much to do with the ulti-
mate determination of the reform movement. They had three
children: Elizabeth, d. Jan. 1890, m. Dr. Thomas C. Peebles;
George L. C., m. Sallie Branon ; Ella, m. Alfred E. Hatch.

58. **Stephen Fitzhugh,**[4] son of 15 Judge Lewis P. W.[3]
and Elizabeth [Weaver] Balch, was born March 14, 1830, at
Frederick, Maryland, and died May 20, 1893, at Philadelphia,
Pennsylvania. He graduated from Gettysburg, West Point,
and the Medical University of Maryland. For twelve years
he practiced in Iowa. Then he became first assistant surgeon
with the 19th Iowa Infantry, but broke down after three
months' service, and was afterwards stricken with paralysis.
He was married May 15, 1857, to Matilda Aletha, daughter
of Capt. Hezekiah Boteler. She was born July 24, 1848, at
Pleasant Valley, Maryland. The family were Presbyterians,

and they had thirteen children, the sixth born at Leetown, West Virginia, and the others at Adel, Iowa.

172   ALETHA ELIZABETH,[5] b. April 13, 1858; d. Dec. 9, 1858.
173   FLORA WILLIS,[5] b. May 15, 1859.
174   STEPHEN MACOMB,[5] b. Sept. 3, 1861; d. Oct. 5, 1863.
175   ROSALIE,[5] b. Oct. 3, 1863; d. May 21, 1880.
176   CATHARINE VIRGINIA,[5] b. Jan. 27, 1865; m. Rev. John Camp-
          bell.
177   EMILY ALEXANDRINE,[5] b. Sept. 19, 1866; m. Geo. W. Oram;
          lives in Philadelphia.
178*   WILLIAM L. H.,[5] b. Feb. 3, 1868.
179   ALEXANDER,[5] b. Oct. 4, 1869; d. Oct. 9, 1869.
180   BOTELER,[5] b. Jan. 1, 1871; d. May 19, 1888.
181   BESSIE,[5] b. Aug. 19, 1872; m. Dr. U. Grant Bickell.
182   MARGARET MAY,[5] b. March 7, 1875; m. Mr. Morton.
183*   LEWIS ROYAL,[5] b. Aug. 21, 1877.
184   BIRDIE,[5] b. Jan. 8, 1879.

62. **George Beall,**[4] son of 17 George Ninan Beall[3] and Martha Rodgers [Balch] Balch, was born January 3, 1821, at Shelbyville, Tennessee, and lives at Baltimore, Maryland. He was married first, December 26, 1844, to Julia Grace, daughter of Charles and Cassandra Vinsen. She was born February 22, 1825, at Washington, D. C. Their children were as follows:

185   GEORGE VINSEN,[5] b. Nov. 11, 1845; m., one child.
186   STEPHEN BLOOMER,[5] b. March 7, 1848.
187   JULIA GRACE,[5] b. Aug. 18, 1850.
188   MARGARET CASSANDRA,[5] b. Jan. 26, 1857.
189   HARRIET ANN,[5] b. May 29, 1859.

Admiral George B. was married second at New Castle, Delaware, on Sept. 12, 1865, to Mary Ellen, daughter of Hon. James and Hannah W. Booth. Her father was chief justice of Delaware, and she was born June 28, 1835, at New Castle. Their children were as follows:

190   ALFRED,[5] b. April 9, 1868.
191   ANNA BOOTH,[5] b. June 3, 1870; m. Rev. George W. Lay, Con-
          cord, N. H.
192   FRANCIS DUPONT,[5] b. Feb. 15, 1872.
193   AMY ROGERS,[5] b. Nov. 12, 1874.

Admiral George B. entered the United States Navy, December 30, 1837, as a midshipman, and steadily rose to lieutenant in 1850, commander in 1862, captain in 1866, commodore in 1872, rear admiral in 1878. From October 21, 1862 to February 15, 1865 he was commander on the "Pawnee" in the South Atlantic blockading squadron. In one action the vessel was struck forty-six times, but he succeeded in driving the Confederates from their guns in the wildest confusion. Between 1868 and 1870 he commanded the "Contoocook" and the "Albany," and then filled various positions, as executive officer of the Washington Navy Yard, as governor of the Philadelphia Naval Asylum, as member of the Naval Examining Board and Retiring Board; as superintendent of the Naval Academy, and lastly in command of the Pacific Station, until he was retired January 3, 1888, after an active life of 46 years.

63. **Ann Carter,**[4] daughter of 19 Rev. Thomas Bloomer[3] and Susan [Carter] Balch, was born in 1821, in Fairfax county, Virginia. She married Mr. Ashton, and had two children, Charles and Thomas, who live in Fauquier county, Virginia.

64. **Elizabeth,**[4] daughter of 19 Rev. Thomas Bloomer[3] and Susan [Carter] Balch, was born about 1824, in Virginia, and died during the war in Alabama. She married R. M. Carter. They had three children: Fitzhugh, in the United States army at Fort Henry, near Baltimore; Thomas, a lawyer at San Diego, Cal., and Cassius, in the United States mail service.

65. **Robert M.,**[4] son of 19 Rev. Thomas Bloomer[3] and Susan [Carter] Balch, was born May 7, 1826, in Virginia, and lived in Haywood county, Tennessee. He was a large, fine looking man, with most courtly manners, and was Lieutenant Colonel in the Confederate army, under Gen. N. B. Forrest. After the war he was a lawyer and cotton broker at Memphis. In 1871 he was killed in Crittenden county, Arkansas, by squatters upon lands there which were owned by him and his brother Charles.

66. Charles Carter.[4] son of 19 Rev. Thomas Bloomer[3] and Susan [Carter] Balch, was born in 1828, at Snow Hill, Maryland, and is now living at Lansing, Arkansas. He was with his brother in the Confederate Service.

69. Mary L.,[4] daughter of 19 Rev. Thomas Bloomer[3] and Susan [Carter] Balch, was born in Georgetown, D. C. She lives in Washington, is highly educated, and conducts a school which makes a specialty of preparing candidates for the civil service examinations.

70. Julia R.,[4] daughter of 19 Rev. Thomas Bloomer[3] and Susan [Carter] Balch. She is engaged in conducting a school with her sister Mary.

72. Selina Moore,[4] daughter of 28 Amos Prido[3] and Martha [Leach] Balch, was born October 10, 1808, and died September 14, 1878. She was married August 10, 1824, to Robert Mann, whose brother married 29 Albina Bloomer Balch. He was born June 12, 1805, was in the State Legislature for two terms, and died two days before his wife. They lived near Chester, Illinois, and had seven children : William Balch, b. June 4, 1827, d. March 12, 1853, m., June, 1849, Margaret Webb; Martha Jane, b. Feb. 21, 1829, m., Sept., 1870, Marion Steele, lives at Steelville, Illinois ; Mary Elvira, b. Oct. 25, 1830, d. July 13, 1890, m., Aug. 7, 1857 Harvey Neville; Robert Henry, b. Aug. 26, 1833, d. Sept. 6, 1896, m., Dec. 24, 1857, Susan E. McKay, family at Chester, Illinois ; Albina, b. June 28, 1837, m., Jan., 1859, Dr. Clinton Davis, he d. July 23, 1887 ; John Alexander, b. Nov. 8, 1839, d. Jan. 4, 1893, m., Aug. 9, 1866, Mary E. Holloman ; James Gilbert, b. July 17, 1844, d. May 20, 1852.

73. Stephen Witherspoon,[4] son of 28 Amos Prido[3] and Martha [Leach] Balch, was born December 27, 1806, at Russelville, Kentucky, and died September 19, 1866, at Gardner, Kansas. He married, first, Sophia Sawyer, who died about 1851, and they had eight children.

194* MARY JANE,[5] b. Jan. 1831; m.

195 JOHN DAVID,[5] b. 1833; d. y.

196   CYRUS CALVIN,[5] b. 1835; d. y.
197* MARGARET ELIZA,[5] b. March 5, 1837.
198   MARTHA,[5] b. 1839; d. y.
199   AMANDA,[5] b. 1841; d. y.
200   SAMUEL,[5] b. Oct. 11, 1843; d. Dec. 1861; in army at St. Louis.
201* JONATHAN,[5] b. April 9, 1849.

Stephen W. married second Nancy Harris.

74. Armstead Bluford,[4] son of 23 Amos Prido[3] and Martha [Leach] Balch, was born January 21, 1809, and died March 8, 1837, near Bainbridge, Indiana. He married Vashti Catherwood, who died November 28, 1853. They left one son.

202* ARMSTEAD V.,[5] b. May, 7, 1837.

75. Calvin Whitfield,[4] son of 23 Amos Prido[3] and Martha [Leach] Balch, was born April 25, 1811, at Duck River, Tennessee, and died March 17, 1894, at Edgerton, Kansas. He married first, November 9, 1830, Jane T. McNutt, who was born April 17, 1809, at Rockbridge, Virginia, and died in 1842, in Scott county, Indiana. They had four sons, two of whom were members of the 130th Illinois Infantry Volunteers.

203   JAMES ALEXANDER,[5] b. April 1, 1832; d. March 25, 1868.
204   WILLIAM HAMILTON,[5] b. Sept. 7, 1834; killed in assault on Vicksburg, May 22, 1863.
205   SAMUEL DAVID,[5] b. Sept. 29, 1837; d. from war exposure Aug. 29, 1864.
206   ROBERT STEPHEN,[5] b. April 10, 1840; d. y.

Dr. Calvin W. married second, February 14, 1843, Elizabeth C. McCulley, who was born July 1, 1820, near Natural Bridge, Virginia, and died October 26, 1891, at Edgerton, Kansas. They had ten children, born at Greenville, Illinois.

207* JOSEPH CAMERON,[5] b. May 3, 1845.
208* CHARLES CALVIN,[5] b. Nov. 16, 1846.
209* ELIZABETH JANE,[5] b. Sept. 29, 1848.
210* CLIFFORD JONATHAN,[5] b. April 5, 1850.
211* MARTHA EMELINE,[5] b. Nov. 18, 1852.
212* MARGARET SELINA,[5] b. Feb. 25, 1855.
213   MARY ELVIRA,[5] b. March 13, 1857; m. Wood; lives in Louisburg, Ky.

214* HARVEY AMOS,[5] b. Feb. 20, 1859.
215* HENRY ARMSTEAD,[5] b. Oct. 20, 1862.
216 MINNIE ALICE,[5] b. Feb. 29, 1864; d. Jan. 23, 1865.

Dr. Calvin W. was a successful physician at Greenville, Illinois, until 1864, when he moved with his entire family, two wagons and five horses, to Edgerton, Kansas. They travelled by wagon to St. Louis, and by steamboat, fourteen days, to Kansas. The civil war was then being waged in the country through which they passed, and three-inch oak plank covered the pilot house of the boat to protect the pilot from bullets.

78. Jonathan James Preston,[4] son of 23 Amos Prido[3] and Martha [Leach] Balch, was born January 27, 1816, and is living at Wichita, Kansas, and has a family.

227 STEPHEN,[5] b.

79. Martha Elvira,[4] daughter of 23 Amos Prido[3] and Martha [Leach] Balch, was born September 30, 1821, and died April 11, 1896. She was married November 8, 1838, to Samuel, son of Tobias and Cynthia [Smith] Renner, who was born November 12, 1815, in Greene county, Pennsylvania, and died November 8, 1898. They commenced their married life without capital, settled in Shelby county, Illinois, and by industry and economy bought and improved a large farm, and raised and educated their large family. They are Cumberland Presbyterians. In 1891 they moved into the village of Strasburg. Seven of their twelve children grew up. Martha Elvira, b. July 10, 1841, m. Joseph Rouse; Stephen, b. March 8, 1843, d. Dec. 12, 1861, in Union army; John, b. June 9, 1844, was three years in the Union army; Joseph, b. March 6, 1850; Emeline, b. Feb. 21, 1852, m. Turner; James Calvin, b. Nov. 6, 1853; Mary Elizabeth, b. Sept. 12, 1855, m. Berry Calvin Barker.

80. Monroe Young,[4] son of 23 Amos Prido[3] and Mary [Sawyer] Balch, was born May 7, 1827, and died March 11, 1863, at Moscow, Tennessee, of disease contracted in the Union army. He married, October 11, 1849, Narcissus J. McCord, and they had three sons and two daughters.

81. Sylvester Newton,[4] son of 28 Amos Prido[3] and Mary [Sawyer] Balch, was born August 28, 1829, and died January 1, 1873. He served fifteen months in the Union army. On December 24, 1858, he married Margaret R. Davis, whose brother married 87 Caroline Melissa. They were Presbyterians, and had five children, of whom two grew up.

82. Jane Eliza,[4] daughter of 23 Amos Prido[3] and Mary [Sawyer] Balch, was born May 22, 1831, and married first, March 6, 1851, Johnson Henry, who died in April, 1866. Two of their five children grew up.

Jane Eliza married second John Curlee.

84. Felix Marian,[4] son of 23 Amos Prido[3] and Mary [Sawyer] Balch, was born January 1, 1835, and died November 28, 1876. He married first, January 13, 1854, Jane Stout. Two of their five children grew up.

Felix M. married second, November, 1875, Mary Moore.

85. Maria Theresa,[4] daughter of 23 Amos Prido[3] and Mary [Sawyer] Balch, was born July 22, 1838, and died April 5, 1867. She was married June 3, 1859, to John L. Brands. One of their three children grew up.

86. Rachel Vashti,[4] daughter of 23 Amos Prido[3] and Mary [Sawyer] Balch, was born August 3, 1840, and was married December 27, 1854, to Wilson Stout, who died in January, 1856. They had one child.

Rachael V., in 1858, married, second, William Smith. They are Presbyterians, and live at Ayers, Bond county, Illinois. They have had ten children of whom four boys and three girls grew up.

87. Caroline Melissa,[4] daughter of 23 Amos Prido[3] and Mary [Sawyer] Balch, was born April 5, 1842, and was married April 21, 1859, to James W. Davis, who died September 4, 1873. One son and two daughters of their six children are living.

Caroline M. married second, in September, 1875, **William Roe.** They have one daughter.

88. Charlotte Maletha,[4] daughter of 23 Amos Prido[3] and Mary [Sawyer] Balch, was born July 4, 1844, and was married April 10, 1866, to Henry Sapp. They live at Greenville, Illinois, and have had nine children, of whom three sons and two daughters grew up.

89. Alfred Bolivar,[4] son of 31 John Luther[3] and Melinda N. [White] Balch, was born September 8, 1830, in Sullivan county, Indiana. In the following year his father moved to Coles county, Illinois, and here he grew up with such scant means of education as the new country afforded, and worked on his father's farm. On October 29, 1854, he married Nancy A., daughter of Abram and Elizabeth [Richmond] Bragg. They have had five children, the three eldest born at Camargo, and the other two at Oakley, Illinois.

235 WILLIAM BLOOMER,[5] b. Feb. 26, 1856; d. May 7, 1856.
236 JASPER NEWTON,[5] b. June 8, 1854.
237° JOHN ABRAM,[5] b. March 11, 1860.
238 ALFRED BOLIVAR,[5] b. Oct. 1, 1866; d. Oct. 18, 1868.
239° MARY ELLEN,[5] b. July 4, 1869.

Alfred B. enlisted on November 21, 1861, in Company B, 54th Illinois Infantry as a private and rapidly advanced to the Captaincy of his company. He was captured December 23, 1862, at Union City, Tennessee, by the Confederate command under General Forrest, in which his second cousin 65 Robert M. Balch was a Lieutenant Colonel. He was paroled, and in June, 1863 exchanged. He then joined his regiment in front of Vicksburg, and after the capture of that place, went with General Steele's command, and was at the capture of Little Rock, Arkansas, on Sept. 13, 1863. He was taken prisoner a second time September 14, 1864, by the Confederate forces under General Shelby at Hickory Station, Arkansas, was paroled and on January 1, 1865, exchanged and rejoined his regiment at Little Rock. After going to Kansas, he was twice appointed by the Governor as a delegate to the

Farmers' National Congress. He is engaged in farming and apiculture at Formoso, Kansas.

90. Albina,[4] daughter of 31 John Luther[3] and Melinda N. [White] Balch, was born September 7, 1832, in Pleasant Grove township, Coles county, Illinois, and lives with her sister Martha on the old homestead near Lerna, Illinois. Their sisters Mary Melinda and Angeline Elizabeth also lived with them until their death. They have all been members of the Methodist church, earnest workers in the Sabbath school, and their lives have led along pathways of pleasantness and peace. Martha and Angeline E. received diplomas for work in the Chautauqua courses of Bible study.

91. Alexander Houston,[4] son of 31 John Luther[3] and Melinda N. [White] Balch, was born April 18, 1834, on his father's farm, near Lerna, Illinois, enlisted in the 116th Illinois Volunteers, and died June 1, 1863, in the hospital at Milliken's Bend, near Vicksburg, and was buried in the Soldiers' cemetery. Before the war he was a farmer, and married Harriet Page, of Pratt county, Illinois. They had four children.

240 EMMA M.,[5] b.
241 HENRY ALFRED,[5] b.   ; m. Mary Dobson, Macon County, Ill.
242 LUTHER,[5] b.   ; d. y.
243 EDWARD NELSON,[5] b.; d. y.

94. William,[4] son of 31 John Luther[3] and Melinda N. [White] Balch, was born January 23, 1840, in Randolph county, Illinois, and was married March 11, 1869, to Susan Turpin, who was born at Kesner, Illinois, in 1840, and died December 24, 1892. They had five children.

244 ELLSWORTH TURPIN,[5] b. Dec. 15, 1869.
245 BLOOMER WHITE,[5] b. Feb. 8, 1871.
246 LILLIE MELINDA,[5] b. July 24, 1872.
247 ULLIN SYLVAN,[5] b. Feb. 24, 1876.
248 DONA G.,[5] b. March 6, 1879.

William is a farmer and dealer in live stock at Formoso,

Kansas. He enlisted as a private in company C, First Regiment, Illinois Cavalry, on July 13, 1861. At the nine days' battle of Lexington, Missouri, he carried a dispatch through a cross fire of the enemy and escaped unharmed. His regiment was cut off from water and compelled to surrender, and he enlisted, January 2, 1864, in company B, 54th Illinois Infantry, and was in the fight at Hickory Station, Arkansas, and was again taken prisoner by General Shelby, paroled, exchanged, and rejoined his regiment, and served until the close of the war, and was discharged at Little Rock, October 15, 1865.

97. **Albina Jane,**[4] daughter of 32 'Jonathan Edwards[3] and Elizabeth [White] Balch, was born about 1824, in Sullivan county, Indiana, and married first, Samuel Strain, who died previous to 1870. They had one daughter, 'Alice, who married John Boyd, and ¦had three children—Carl, Frank, and Charles.

Albina J. married second, Graybill, who died and left her his large farm and stock.

Albina J. married third, Mr. Mitchell.

98. **James A.,**[4] son of 32 Jonathan Edwards[3] and Elizabeth [White] Balch, was born about 1826, in Sullivan county, Indiana. He was in the war with the Cayuse Indians in Oregon, in 1854 and 1855, and his health was permanently impaired. He was second lieutenant in the First Oregon Infantry. In 1860 he married Harriet Helm, in Washington Territory. They have three children.

249 FREDERICK HOMAR,[5] b.; a Congregational minister.
250 MARY GERTRUDE,[5] b.
251 HERBERT,[5] b.

100. **Elizabeth,**[4] daughter of 32 Jonathan Edwards[3] and Elizabeth [White] Balch, was born about 1830, and is a school teacher. She married first, W. A. Cheeser, who soon died, and in 1877 she married S. Lee, who died after the births of a son and a daughter.

101. **Evaline,**[4] daughter of 32 Jonathan Edwards[3] and Elizabeth [White] Balch, was born about 1832, and married William Grimes of Indiana. They live in Kansas, and have six children.

102. **Susannah Lavinia,**[4] daughter of 32 Jonathan Edwards[3] and Elizabeth [White] Balch, was born about 1834, and was married in 1863 to John Homer. They have one son, Vernon, b. 1865.

103. **Mary,**[4] daughter of 32 Jonathan Edwards[3] and Elizabeth [White] Balch, was born about 1836, and died in 1876. In 1862 she married L. C. Jones, and had three children—William Riley, Florence Bell, and John.

104. **John Mitchell,**[4] son of 32 Jonathan Edwards[3] and Elizabeth [White] Balch, was born about 1838, and is a missionary Baptist preacher in Arkansas. He married Mary Duisan, in Shelby county, Illinois.

105. **Sarah Caroline,**[4] daughter of 32 Jonathan Edwards[3] and Elizabeth [White] Balch, was born about 1840, and in 1867 married William Leathers, who soon died, leaving one daughter, Isabel Susan, b. 1868.

Sarah C. married second, Isaac Walters. They live in Shelby county, Illinois, and have two children, Mary Jane and Minnie May.

107. **Rufus Colwell,**[4] son of 37 John Bloomer[3] and Sarah [Cook] Balch, was born January 20, 1819, in Bedford county, Tennessee, and is living at Little Rock, Arkansas. He was married in 1841 to Elinor P., daughter of Jane [Bryant] Wootten, in Panola county, Mississippi, where they lived until 1888. Their children were as follows:

258[*] Leonidas Colwell,[5] b. Nov. 20, 1842.
259[*] Jane E.,[5] b. June 8, 1844.
260[*] James C.,[5] b. Sept. 20, 1847; Sept. 6, 1891.
261 Sidney T.,[5] b. Feb. 20, 1850; Oct. 4, 1889; m. Emma Whiplin.
262[*] Annie E.,[5] b. May 11, 1852.

Rufus C. was a farmer, and is a deacon in the Baptist

church. He is a man of proverbial honesty and sturdy mold.
In 1862 he enlisted in the Confederate army as a private, but
rose to the captaincy of cavalry, and served until May, 1865.
He was appointed justice of the peace in 1869, and held the
office for several terms.

109. **Amanda,**[4] daughter of 37 John Bloomer[3] and Sarah
[Cook] Balch, was born in 1822, and died in 1886. She
married Washington B. McGraw, and they had five children.
Winfield, b. 1850; Delia, b. 1853; Brooks, b. 1856; Fannie,
b. 1857; Cora, b. 1859.

110. **Minos Newton,**[4] son of 37 John Bloomer[3] and Sarah [Cook] Balch, was born November 11, 1823, and died
June 7, 1885, at Rufus, Arkansas. He married first, in 1850,
Mary, daughter of Gilbert and Elizabeth Baker, who died in
1853. They had two children.

263[a] MARCELLUS,[5] b. July 27, 1852.
264   MARY E.,[5] b. 1853; d. 1868.

Minos N. married second, in March, 1856, Mary Elander,
daughter of Stanford and Mary [Hargess] Jones. They had
two children born at Tyro, Mississippi, and three born at
Rufus, Arkansas.

265   MARGARET J.,[5] b. May 8, 1879; m. C. M. Ford, Rufus, Ark.
266[a] JOHN STANFORD,[5] b. Oct. 10, 1858.
267   EMILY J.,[5] b. Oct. 12, 1862; m. H. Ford.
268[a] WILLIAM ROSCOE,[5] b. Oct. 2, 1866.
269   MARY C.,[5] b. Aug. 18, 1870; m. April 28, 1888.

Minos N. in 1858 moved to Poinsett county, Arkansas, and
in 1861 to Jackson county. In 1861 he enlisted in the Confederate army, served in the ambulance corps, and was sur-
rendered near Goldsboro, North Carolina, in April, 1865.

111. **John O.,**[4] son of 37 John Bloomer[3] and Sarah [Cook]
Balch, was born April 18, 1826, and died January 15, 1883,
at Rufus, Arkansas. In 1859 he moved to Poinsett county,
Arkansas, and in 1861 to Jackson county. In 1863 he en-
listed in the Confederate army, under General Sterling Price.
He was married September 9, 1847, in De Soto county, Mis-

sissippi, to M. Caroline, daughter of Gilbert and Elizabeth
Baker. She died January 24, 1878. Six of their children
were born at Vicksburg, Mississippi, and four at Rufus, Arkansas.

270   RUFUS G.,[5] b. Nov. 18, 1848; d. Sept. 9, 1866.
271   ROSCOE,[5] b. July 23, 1850; d. Aug. 1, 1868.
272* ALICE,[5] b. July 23, 1852.
273   MARY E.,[5] b. Dec. 12, 1854.
274   GEORGIE ANNA,[5] b. Jan. 16, 1856; d. Dec. 18, 1883.
275* JONAH H.,[5] b. Dec. 22, 1858.
276   JEFFIE D.,[5] b. Jan. 7, 1861; d. Sept. 9, 1866.
277   JOHN M.,[5] b. May 18, 1864; d. Dec. 1, 1883.
278* BAKER F.,[5] b. June 15, 1867.
279   WILLIAM RUSSELL,[5] b. April 11, 1870; teacher at Fisher, Ark.

John C. married second, December 25, 1881, Eliza Smith,
a widow.

112. **Lydia,**[4] daughter of 37 John Bloomer[3] and Sarah
[Cook] Balch, was born April 14, 1827, in Tennessee, and
was married November 25, 1855, to William Wright, a farmer, who was born in Kentucky, and died in Pleasant Grove
township, Illinois. They were Presbyterians, and had four
children : Mary Ellen Brunk, b. Sept. 11, 1856; George
Winfield, b. Dec. 9, 1858 ; Leonidas Balch, b. Oct. 13, 1860 ;
Belle, b. Oct. 19, 1863.

114. **Eliza Tennessee,**[4] daughter of 37 John Bloomer
and Sarah [Cook] Balch, was born January 15, 1830, in Madison county, Mississippi, and married first, Mr. Brown,
who died after they had one child, Sarah, who married T. B.
Rodgers, and lives at Janesville, Illinois.

Eliza T. married second, Mr. Edwards, who died after
they had one child, Mary.

Eliza T. then moved to Illinois, and on August 13, 1871,
married Wily Matthews, and had two daughters, Maud and
Gertrude. The family then moved to Nebraska.

116. **Ann Jane,**[4] daughter of 88 Alfred Moore[3] and Elizabeth [Gammill] Balch, was born June 22, 1820, in Bradford county, Tennessee, and died in March, 1860. She was

married January 27, 1842, to Henry J. M. Reynolds, who was born June 8, 1818, and died April 8, 1870. They lived and died and their children were born in Cumberland county, Illinois. William B., b. Jan. 2, 1844; Alfred M., b. April 7, 1846; Nancy C., b. March 5, 1848; Jane McDonald, b. March 17, 1853; Sarah E., b. June 20, 1855, d. April 12, 1889; George W., b. April 5, 1858, d. y.

120. **George Bell,**[4] son of 38 Alfred Moore[3] and Elizabeth [Gammill] Balch, was born November 1, 1828, in Bedford county, Tennessee, and died September 4, 1886, at Lerna, Illinois, where he was a farmer. He was a ruling elder in the Presbyterian church and a natural poet. On March 19, 1851, he married Margaret S., daughter of Samuel and Nancy [Dryden] Walker, who was born October 1, 1832, in Tennessee. Their children were as follows:

280* SAMUEL WALKER,[5] b. Jan. 28, 1852.
281* ELIZABETH JANE,[5] b. Sept. 18, 1853.
282 ANN MINERVA,[5] b. Aug. 10, 1855; d. Oct. 18, 1886.
283* THOMAS ALEXANDER,[5] } b. Oct. 8, 1858.
284* NANCY McDONALD,[5] }
285* ESTHER REBECCA,[5] b. June 20, 1861.
286* ELLEN DIXON,[5] b. Jan. 31, 1863.
287 MINNIE B.,[5] b. March 30, 1865; Oct. 26, 1881.
289 ELIZA ADALINE,[5] b. June 25, 1868; d. Dec. 9, 1882.
290* ROBERT E.,[5] b. March 26, 1871; lives at Lerna, Ill.
291 MARGARET L.,[5] b. July 3, 1873; d. Oct. 18, 1886.

121. **James Alexander,**[4] son of 38 Alfred Moore[3] and Elizabeth [Gammill] Balch, was born October 20, 1832, in Coles county, Illinois, and died January 4, 1869, on his farm southwest of Lerna. During the civil war he was a captain in the Fifth Illinois Cavalry. He married first, December 13, 1855, Rebecca, daughter of Joseph and Margaret Allison. She died March 31, 1857. They had one child.

292 REBECCA ELIZABETH,[5] b. March 8, 1857; d. June 30, 1863.

Capt. James A. married second, Patience Ann, daughter of Patrick and Elizabeth [Ashmore] Nicholson, and they had five children.

293 PATRICK,[5] b. Oct. 3, 1858; d. Oct. 18, 1859.
294 RHODA JANE,[5] b. March 1, 1860; d. Aug. 21, 1864.
295 MARY ANN,[5] b. June 7, 1861; d. Sept. 30, 1879.
296* SARAH CAROLINE,[5] b. Oct. 14, 1865.
297 EMMA HUNTER,[5] b. July 7, 1867; lives at Mattoon, Ill.

128. David Lawson,[4] son of 40 James Calvin[3] and Eliza Jane [Hazlett] Balch, was born December 7, 1831, in Bradford county, Tennessee, and is a printer at Jackson, Tennessee. He was married September 10, 1857, to Eliza Pamela, daughter of Mark L. and Eliza Andrews, who was born September 10, 1834. They have had six children, born at Franklin, Tennessee.

298* JOHN PARKER,[5] b. Feb. 8, 1859.
299* RICHARD LAWSON,[5] b. May 29, 1860.
300 JAMES CALVIN,[5] b. July 6, 1862; d. July 14, 1862.
301* WILLIAM DEAN,[5] b. Sept. 5, 1863.
302 GEORGE ANDREWS,[5] b. Nov. 8, 1866.
303 MARY ELIZA,[5] b. Aug. 12, 1869; m. James P. Bond.

132. Henry Taylor,[4] son of 40 James Calvin[3] and Anna Elizabeth [Cosby] Balch, was born November 7, 1848, at Athens, Alabama, and is a printer at Nashville, Tennessee. He was married December 8, 1870, to Anna Eliza, daughter of Orville and Lucinda Betts, who was born September 10, 1850, at Nashville. They are Baptists, and their eight children were born at Nashville.

304 GRACIE PORTER,[5] b. Sept. 4, 1871; d. Sept. 8, 1871.
305 CHARLES HENRY,[5] b. Aug. 2, 1872.
306 ALONZO LINDSEY,[5] b. Nov. 2, 1874.
307 WILLIAM NELSON,[5] b. July 5, 1877; d. Jan. 26, 1879.
308 LUCY ENLOE,[5] b. July 9, 1879.
309 MINNEOLA,[5] b. July 2, 1881.
310 JAMES CALVIN,[5] b. May 10, 1884.
311 ARCHIBALD EDWARD,[5] b. Jan. 2, 1891.

138. Levica,[4] daughter of 41 Hezekiah James[3] and Mary [McCord] Balch, was born January 14, 1807, in Logan county, Kentucky, and died at Pleasant Grove township, Illinois, in 1879. She married John W. Rodgers, who was born December 29, 1798, and died May 7, 1864. They

had eight children: Hezekiah James, b. July 12, 1829, d. March 28, 1860; John White, b. Feb. 10, 1831, d. April 13, 1884; Mary Jane, b. 1833; Isaac, b. 1835; Elizabeth, b. 1838, d. April 25, 1858; Theron, b. 1840; Wallace, b. 1842; Eliza, b. 1844.

139. **Wallace Watts,**[4] son of 41 Hezekiah James[3] and Mary [McCord] Balch, was born April 25, 1809, in Giles county, Tennessee, and died June 8, 1886, in Pleasant Grove township, Illinois. He was a Whig, and afterwards a Republican, and owned a large farm near Janesville, Illinois. On December 18, 1834, he married Pamela McCann, who was born in 1813, at Evansville, Indiana, and died March 19, 1886. They were Cumberland Presbyterians, and had eight children.

12   WILLIAM WALLACE,[5] b.   ; d. aged one year.
313   HEZEKIAH JAMES,[5] b.   ; d. aged 12 years.
314• JOHN FRANKLIN,[5] b. Aug. 12, 1838; d. Feb. 16, 1862.
315• WILLIAM WALLACE,[5] b. May 24, 1840.
316• MALISSA ALTHANA,[5] b. Oct. 26, 1843; d. Jan. 8, 1862.
317• THERON EMMET,[5] b. May 9, 1845.
318   LEVICA ANN,[5] b. May, 1848; d. y.
319• MARY ALPHA,[5] b. July 26, 1850.

141. **Hezekiah James Emmet,**[4] son of 41 Hezekiah James[3] and Mary [McCord] Balch, was born September 5, 1819, at Shelbyville, Tennessee, and died April 14, 1885, at Danville, Illinois. He was a physician and surgeon, with a large practice at Westville, Illinois. On April 18, 1843, he married Elizabeth Cassaunder, daughter of Samuel and Elizabeth Elam, of Darwin, Illinois. She was born January 9, 1822, in Butler county, Kentucky, and is living at Terra Haute, Indiana. They had three sons.

320• WALLACE WATTS,[5] b. Jan. 13, 1844; d. Aug. 20, 1844.
321• JAMES HEZEKIAH,[5] b. Nov. 16, 1845.
322• SAMUEL CLAY,[5] b. March 23, 1850.

142. **Julia Maria,**[4] daughter of 43 Theron Eusebius[3] and Alpha [Boyd] Balch, was born February 27, 1812, in Maury county, Tennessee, and died March 31, 1894, at

Pella, Iowa. She married first, July 8, 1828, Alexander Barnett, who died at Campbell, Illinois. They had three children: Hilarion W., b. Sept. 27, 1829, d. y. ; Amazilla C., b. Jan. 22, 1831 ; and Alexander H., b. Jan. 29, 1833 ; d. Dec. 22, 1874.

Julia M. married second, November 19, 1839, Granville D. Neal, and they had seven children : Angeline E., b. Sept. 27, 1840, m. Edmund ; James A., b. March 27, 1842 ; Alpha A. C., b. March 4, 1844 ; Aruna E., b. July 29, 1846, m. Erb ; Mary C., b. Feb. 19, 1848 ; John William, b. Dec. 15, 1850 ; George T. M., b. May 5, 1853.

143. **William Boyd,**[4] son of 48 Theron Eusebius[3] and Alpha [Boyd] Balch, was born September 1, 1813, in Gibson county, Indiana, and died March 20, 1884, in Coles county, Illinois. He was a radical Abolitionist, a Whig, and a Republican, was a great reader until his sight became impaired, and possessed a retentive memory and excellent conversational powers. He owned a large farm near Campbell, Illinois. He was married about 1846 to Mary Ann, daughter of Thomas Craig and Mary Ann Faris. She was born July 14, 1820, in Albion county, Tennessee, and died January 3, 1876. They were Presbyterians, and had seven children, four of whom were school teachers.

323* GEORGE THERON,[5] b. July 9, 1847.
324   MARY ANN DODDS,[5] b. Sept. 22, 1848 ; d. Feb. 12, 1852.
325* THOMAS CRAIG,[5] b. Jan. 19, 1852.
326   ALPHIA JULIA,[5] b. Jan. 29, 1854; d. Feb. 18, 1855.
327* SUSAN MARTHA,[5] b. Dec. 2, 1855.
328* MARY ALPHA,[5] b. April 11, 1858.
329* EMMA ANN,[5] b. Aug. 12, 1863.

144. **John Moorehead,**[4] son of 48 Theron Eusebius[3] and Alpha [Boyd] Balch, was born Feb. 3, 1816, in Bedford county, Tenn., and died February 15, 1888, at Neoga, Illinois, where he was a farmer. He was married December 5, 1839, to his cousin, Elizabeth Amanda, daughter of 45 Ann Kincade [Balch] Campbell. The family are Republicans and Presbyterians. They had five children.

330   THERON AMES,[5] b. Aug. 20, 1841.
331   ZENO CAMPBELL,[5] b. Feb. 8, 1847.
332* WILLIAM TELL,[5] b. Sept. 4, 1850.
333* ALPHA ANN,[5] b. Nov. 9, 1853.
334   MATTIE,[5] b. Nov. 2, 1857.

145. **Emily Clarissa,**[4] daughter of 43 Theron Eusebius[3] and Alpha [Boyd] Balch, was born May 31, 1818, and lives in the state of Washington. She was married in 1838 to Nathaniel Henderson, son of David and Mary Dryden, who was born February 17, 1819, in Bedford county, Tennessee. They have had seven children: Ann, David; Eusebius, b. 1846; Alpha, John, Caroline, Martha.

146. **Martha Jane Kincade,**[4] daughter of 43 Theron Eusebius[3] and Alpha [Boyd] Balch, was born Aug. 7, 1822, in Lawrence county, Ala., and died in June, 1881, at Eureka Springs, Arkansas, and was buried at Mount Horeb, Wisconsin. She was married in August, 1842, to Henderson Nathaniel, son of William and Abbie Dryden, who was born February 20, 1820, in Bedford county, Tennessee. They had seven children, the first born in Coles county, Illinois, and the others at Mount Horeb, Wisconsin. William Theron, b. March 29, 1844; John Alexander, b. Oct. 26, 1848; Jonathan Albert, b. March 22, 1850; Alpha Elizabeth, b. Jan. 16, 1855; Martha Abigail, b.   ; Nathaniel Hezekiah, b. Jan., 1859.

150. **Cornelia Tuston,**[4] daughter of 43 Theron Eusebius[3] and Alpha [Boyd] Balch, was born December 24, 1829, at Paris, Illinois, and died at Mount Horeb, Wisconsin. She married first, Rev. C. P. Newman, and they had two children, who live at Mount Horeb: Silas, b. 1849; Mary, b. 1851.

Cornelia married second, Robert Carden, and they had two children, David and Emily.

151. **George Bell,**[4] son of 43 Theron Eusebius[3] and Alpha [Boyd] Balch, was born March 4, 1832, at Campbell, Illinois, and is a farmer and stock dealer, in partnership with his brother, Hezekiah Theron, near Earlton, Kansas. During

the civil war he was with a regiment of Wisconsin cavalry. In 1869 he married Sarah [Stephens] Noble, a widow of Edward Noble. They have four children.

335 MARTHA,[5] b.
336 EDWARD,[5] b.
337 OBD,[5] b.
338 JAMES GARFIELD,[5] b.

FIFTH GENERATION.
Descendents of James Balch.

155. Elizabeth,[5] daughter of 53 Rev. Lewis P. W.[4] and Anna [Jay] Balch, was born April 20, 1845, and died May 25, 1890. The greater part of her life was spent abroad, where she enjoyed unusual social privileges, obtaining entree, among others, to the Court of Madrid. Besides numerous magazine articles, she wrote a number of acceptable books, among them "Zoreh," "Mustard Leaves," "Old English Homes," and "An Author's Love."

157. Lewis,[5] son of 53 Rev. Lewis P. W.[4] and Anna [Jay] Balch, was born July 7, 1847, and is a physician at Albany, New York. He studied medicine in the office of Dr. Henry Sands, of New York, and in 1870 graduated from the College of Physicians and Surgeons, Columbia College, and became Professor of Surgery in the Albany Medical College. He was secretary of the New York State Board of Health until 1894, when he resigned, and was also health officer for the city of Albany. He married Jane Byrd Swan, who was born September 22, 1847, at Leesburg, Virginia. They have one son.

339 LEWIS,[5] b. May 8, 1872.

158. Alfred Holme,[5] son of 58 Rev. Lewis P. W.[4] and Emily [Wiggin] Balch, was born February 28, 1851, at Chester, Pennsylvania, and is a journalist, living in New York city. For a time he was a chemist for the board of health. He was married March 17, 1887, to Ruth Adelaide [Flanders] Paxton.

159. William Ralston,[5] son of 53 Rev. Lewis P. W.[4] and Emily [Wiggin] Balch, was born December 9, 1852, at Leetown, Virginia, and was married June 21, 1881, to Elizabeth Singerly. They have had one child.

340 ELEANOR,[6] b.   ; d. y.

161. Henry Herbert,[5] son of 53 Rev. Lewis P. W.[4] and Emily [Wiggin] Balch, was born May 7, 1856, at Baltimore, Maryland, and married November 25, 1891, Clarissa Tilghman Fleming, at Washington, D. C. They live at Easton, Maryland, and have two children.

341 HENRY HERBERT,[6] b. Oct. 25, 1892.
342 CLARISSA ANN,[6] b. April 17, 1894.

163. Ernest Berkeley,[5] son of 53 Rev. Lewis P. W.[4] and Emily [Wiggin] Balch, was born January 15, 1860, at Newport, Rhode Island, and lives in New York city. From 1878-79 he was a journalist and from 1880 to 1889 he was engaged in tutoring, and conducted a summer school, known as Camp Chocorua, on an island in Big Asquam lake, New Hampshire. It was a unique institution, a boys' republic, with business customs, banking, courts and laws, in which the boys were taught to govern themselves. Its leading thought was to practically teach the dignity of labor to the sons of the rich. He entered business life, and was connected for two years with the National Cordage Company, and was then occupied for a year in litigation with it, which resulted in its assignment. After this he was with the John Good Cordage Company for two years, and has since been a merchant in trade with Venezuela.

164. Adeline,[5] daughter of 53 Rev. Lewis P. W.[4] and Emily [Wiggin] Balch, was born August 9, 1861, at Newport, Rhode Island, and was married August 31, 1887, to Joseph Howland, son of Rev. Henry Augustus Coit, the first rector of St. Paul's School, and grandson of Rev. Joseph Howland Coit, of Plattsburg, New York. They have one son, Henry Augustus, b. May 26, 1888.

165. **Ellen Mary,**[5] daughter of 53 Rev. Lewis P. W. and Emily [Wiggin] Balch, was born February 25, 1864, at Newport, Rhode Island, where she now lives. She was married August 31, 1887, to Oliver W. Huntington.

167. **Stephen Elliott,**[5] son of 53 Rev. Lewis P. W.[4] and Emily [Wiggin] Balch, was born March 5, 1869, at Montreal, Canada, and is in the auditor's office of the Boston and Albany railroad at Boston, Massachusetts.

178. **William L. H.,**[5] son of 58 Stephen F.[4] and Matilda A. [Boteler] Balch, was born February 3, 1868, and is a merchant at Philadelphia, Pennsylvania. He was married November 9, 1890, to Alice Virginia, daughter of James W. Snyder, of Leetown, West Virginia. She died December 29, 1894. They have two children.

343 MATILDA CATHERINE,[6] b. Dec. 29, 1892.
344 ALICE VIRGINIA,[6] b. Dec. 13, 1894.

183. **Lewis Royal,**[5] son of 58 Stephen F.[4] and Matilda A. [Boteler] Balch, was born August 21, 1877, and is a farmer at Bolington, Virginia. He was married July 10. 1895, to Lena, daughter of Joseph and Martha Fry, of Bolington. They have had one child.

345 JOSEPH ROYAL,[6] b. May 25, 1896; d. May 29, 1896.

194. **Mary Jane,**[5] daughter of 73 Stephen W.[4] and Sophia [Sawyer] Balch, was born in January, 1831, and married, March 5, 1848, Daniel Livingston, of Scotland, who is a farmer. They live at Seward, Nebraska, and have ten children : John Balch, Sophia Catherine, Calvin Whitfield, Samuel Neal, Jonathan Owen, Stephen, Daniel, Margaret Ann, David Alexander, Archy, Flora.

197. **Margaret Eliza,**[5] daughter of 73 Stephen W.[4] and Sophia [Sawyer] Balch, was born March 5, 1837, at Nashville, Illinois, and was married February 28, 1861, to William Smith, who is a retired farmer at Bloomington, Nebraska. They have one child, Mary Willmia, b. Feb. 28, 1874.

201. Jonathan,[5] son of 78 Stephen W.[4] and Sophia [Sawyer] Balch, was born April 9, 1849, in Delaware county, Iowa, and is a teamster at Goddard, Kansas. He married, November 28, 1883, Sophia, daughter of John and Leach Witforth, who was born December 31, 1866, in Prussia, Germany. They have five children.

350 ETTA ELIZABETH,[6] b. Jan. 18, 1886.
351 CHARLES WILLIAMS,[6] b. June 30, 1887.
352 MARY MARGARET,[6] b. Sept. 19, 1889.
353 STEPHEN JOHN,[6] b. Nov. 12, 1891.
354 AMOS PHILIP,[6] b. July 8, 1894.

202. Armstead V.,[5] son of 74 Armstead B.[4] and Vashti [Catherwood] Balch, was born May 7, 1837, at Carpentersville, Indiana, and is a farmer at Bainbridge, Indiana. For four months he was a private in the Union army. He was married November 28, 1867, to Annie, daughter of W. G. and Mariam J. Collins, who was born August 4, 1848, at Sligo, Kentucky. They have had three children.

355 WILLIAM B.,[6] b. Feb. 1, 1869; d. Dec. 3, 1871.
356 JENNIE V.,[6] b. Oct. 19, 1872.
357 ALBERT C.,[6] b. Sept. 13, 1878.

207. Joseph Cameron,[5] son of 75 Calvin Whitfield[4] and Elizabeth C. [McCulley] Balch, was born May 3, 1845, on his father's farm, north of Greenville, Illinois. He arrived with his father in Kansas on April 4, 1864, and joined company K, 13th Militia, Home Guards. He was all through the raid in which General Price was repulsed at Kansas City and Westport, and driven down the line between Kansas and Missouri into Arkansas. In June, 1865, he hired with a freight train to cross the plains to Fort Lyons, on the Arkansas river, and when near Fort Larned became separated with three others, and nearly surrounded by about fifty Indians, but saved their scalps by rapid retreat and the timely arrival of troops from the fort. In 1867 he bought a piece of raw land near Edgerton, Kansas, from a Shawnee Indian, and after cultivating it for 17 years, moved to a farm in

Bronson, on which he is now engaged in apiculture and raising cattle. He was married February 13, 1867, to Mary Ross Erskine, who was born June 18, 1845, in Monroe county, Ohio. They have had seven children, six born at Edgerton, and one at Bronson, Kansas.

358ª WILLIAM CALVIN,⁶ b. Jan. 9, 1868; living at Los Angeles, Cal.
359 JOSEPHINE ALICE,⁶ b. April 19, 1870.
360 ELIZABETH R.,⁶ b. Dec. 22, 1874.
361 JOHN,⁶ b. March 25, 1877; d. May 24, 1877.
362 SAMUEL CORNELIUS,⁶ b. Oct. 3, 1878; d. April 2, 1888.
363 MARY LOUISA,⁶ b. Dec. 18, 1882.
364 ROSE ELLEN,⁶ b. April 18, 1886.

208. Charles Calvin,⁵ son of 75 Calvin Whitfield⁴ and Elizabeth C. [McCulley] Balch, was born November 16, 1846, and lives at Edgerton, Kansas. He was married February 14, 1883, to Mary Emma, daughter of James P. and Elizabeth Newlin. They have two children, born at Norwood, Kansas.

365 CHARLES CLYDE,⁶ b. Oct. 12, 1884.
366 WALLACE MURWOOD,⁶ b. July 2, 1886.

209. Elizabeth Jane,⁵ daughter of 75 Calvin Whitfield⁴ and Elizabeth C. [McCulley] Balch, was born September 29, 1848, and lives at Norwood, Kansas. She was married first, September 19, 1871, to David Whitley Moore, who was born June 26, 1839, in Tazewell county, Virginia, and was a farmer at Norwood, Kansas, where he died March 31, 1885. They had four children : James Edward, b. June 24, 1872 ; Wade Hampton, b. June 14, 1876 ; Mabel Irene, b. Feb. 28, 1878 ; Clifford Ernest, b. Jan. 14, 1885.

Elizabeth J. married second, William Ward Nelson, who was born October 80, 1821, in Indiana, and was a farmer at Centripolis, Kansas, where he died July 30, 1890. They had one child, Nora Balch, b. Oct. 24, 1888.

210. Clifford Jonathan,⁵ son of 75 Calvin Whitfield⁴ and Elizabeth C. [McCulley] Balch, was born April 5, 1850, and is a gold and silver miner at Eureka, Utah. He was married April 8, 1885, at Silver Reef, Utah, to Maggie Ann Hitchings, who was born September 22, 1860, at Pembroke, Wales.

211. **Martha Emeline,**[5] daughter of 75 Calvin Whitfield[4] and Elizabeth C. [McCulley] Balch, was born November 18, 1852, and was married March 23, 1876, to Charles M. Hedrick, who was born in Bland county, Virginia. They live at Kansas City, Kansas, and have four children: **Maggie C.,** b. Feb. 7, 1877 ; **Harold W.,** b. Aug. 4, 1880 ; **Edith May,** b. July 18, 1882 ; **Bessie M.,** b. Aug. 1, 1884.

212. **Margaret Selina,**[5] daughter of 75 Calvin Whitfield[4] and Elizabeth C. [McCulley] Balch, was born February 25, 1855, and was married February 25, 1886, to Edwin George Evans, a farmer, who was born in Wales. They live near Wellsville, Kansas, and have two children: **Elizabeth,** b. April 1, 1889 ; **Charles Frederick,** b. Oct. 21, 1890.

214. **Harvey Amos,**[5] son of 75 Calvin Whitfield[4] and Elizabeth C. [McCulley] Balch, was born February 20, 1859, and is a farmer near Wellsville, Kansas. He was married November 28, 1882, to Elizabeth Ellen Challender, who was born February 27, 1861, in Delaware county, Ohio. They have one child.

367 LOUISA MAY,[5] b. Oct. 3, 1887.

215. **Henry Armstead,**[5] son of 75 Calvin Whitfield[4] and Elizabeth C. [McCulley] Balch, was born October 20, 1862, and is a farmer at Edgerton, Kansas. He was married August 5, 1890, to Mary, daughter of Joseph W. and Emma Seckinger, who was born October 8, 1873, at Kansas City, Missouri. They have three children.

368 CHARLES W.,[5] b. June 7, 1891.
369 ETHEL MAY,[5] b. March 17, 1894.
370 JOHN HENRY,[5] b. Jan. 2, 1896.

237. **John Abram,**[5] son of 89 Alfred Boliver[4] and Nancy A. [Bragg] Balch, was born March 11, 1860, in Douglass county, Illinois, and is a farmer at Montrose, Kansas. He

was married December 24, 1884, to Cleopatra, daughter of
Samuel and Lena [Staver] Simpson. They have six children, born in Jewell county, Kansas.

371 ELVA MAY,[6] b. Nov. 5, 1885.
372 ALTA MALINDA,[6] b. June 11, 1887.
373 WILFRED EARL,[6] b. Oct. 7, 1888.
374 LENA LEOTA,[6] b. Sept. 7, 1890.
375 EDWIN N.,[6] b. Sept. 5, 1893.
376 THERON,[6] b. March 2, 1895.

239. Mary Ellen,[5] son of 89 Alfred Boliver[4] and Nancy
A. [Bragg] Balch, was born July 4, 1869, in Macon county,
Illinois, and was married March 19, 1890, to Marion Frank-
lin, son of Joseph H. and Malinda Thornburg, a farmer in
Jewell county, Kansas. They have three children: Dola
E., b. Feb. 8, 1891; Alfred B., b. Jan. 31, 1893; Nancy A.,
b. Feb. 21, 1896.

258. Leonidas Colwell,[5] son of 107 Rufus Colwell[4]
and Elinor P. [Wootten] Balch, was born November 20,
1842, and was married July 8, 1867, to Elizabeth F., daughter of William and Ruth [Harvey] Walker, of Lawrence
county, Mississippi. She was born October 21, 1840, at
Terry, Mississippi. Their children are as follows:

377* RUFUS WALKER,[6] b. Oct. 3, 1869.
378 HELEN ASHTON,[6] b. Oct. 12, 1871; d. Aug. 6, 1890; m. Oliver.
379 LEONIDAS CHALMER,[6] b. June 5, 1876.
380 ROBERT TAYLOR,[6] b. Aug. 9, 1879.

Leonidas C. enlisted May 8, 1861, as a private in company
E, 12th Mississippi Regiment Infantry, and on May 31, 1862,
at the battle of Seven Pines, Virginia, was severely wounded
in the hip and crippled for life. He then studied law, and in
November, 1870, began practice at Sardis, Mississippi. In
1881 he removed to Little Rock, Arkansas, and there established an extensive practice. In 1886 he was elected to the
General Assembly. He is an unswerving Democrat, and
owns one of the leading stock farms in Arkansas.

259. Jane E.,[5] daughter of 107 Rufus Colwell[4] and

Elinor P. [Wootten] Balch, was born June 8, 1844, and was married in June, 1863, to David Ellis. They live at West Point, Mississippi, and have the following children: Eulalie, b. 1864, m. Emmet Wright, Hot Springs, Miss.; Edward M., b. Dec., 1865, a druggist at West Point; Columbus, b. 1867; Barey, m. Nov. 19, 1896, Isabel Vaccaro, of Memphis, Tenn.; Robert; Walter; Ella, m. Isaac Oliver, West Point; Corinne.

260. James O.,[5] son of 107 Rufus Colwell[4] and Elinor P. [Wootten] Balch, was born September 20, 1847, and died September 4, 1891, at Memphis, Tennessee, where he was a merchant and farmer. He was married in 1880 to Belle Lucas, who was born in 1861, and they had three children.

381 JAMES,[6] b. 1881.
382 ELINOR,[6] b. 1883.
383 ESSIE,[6] b. 1886.

262. Annie E.,[5] son of 107 Rufus Colwell[4] and Elinor P. [Wootten] Balch, was born May 11, 1852, and was married in January, 1879, to Charles Strong, of Alabama. They live at Dublin, Texas, where he is a merchant, and have three children, two born in Mississippi and one in Texas: Octa, b. Dec., 1879; Charles, b. 1884; Annie Laurie, b. 1888.

263. Marcellus,[5] son of 110 Minos N.[4] and Mary E. [Baker] Balch, was born July 27, 1852, in De Soto county, Mississippi, and is a farmer at Rufus, Arkansas. He was married January 22, 1874, to Caroline, daughter of Andrew and Lebelle [Durham] Johnson, who was born April 15, 1856, at Rufus. They have had twelve children, born at Rufus.

384 LUCY,[6] b. June 10, 1875; d. Aug. 1, 1878.
385 RHODA,[6] b. Dec. 18, 1876; d. June 28, 1877.
386 ANDREW,[6] b. June 29, 1878.
387 CHARLES E.,[6] b. July 1, 1880.
388 RUFUS,[6] b. Oct. 6, 1882; d. Sept. 27, 1885.
389 NETTIE,[6] b. Sept. 24, 1884.
390 EFFIE BELLA,[6] b. Feb. 6, 1887; d. Feb. 29, 1892.
391 ELZY B.,[6] b. April 1, 1889.

392 ETHEL,[6] b. June 22, 1891.
393 WILLARD,[6] b. March 16, 1893; d. July 23, 1894.
394 WALKER,[6] b. Jan. 28, 1894.
395 LUCAS,[6] b. Nov. 21, 1896.

266. John Stanford,[5] son of 110 Minos N.[4] and Mary E. [Jones] Balch, was born October 10, 1858, and is a farmer at Rufus, Arkansas. He was married first, December 26, 1878, to Margaret, daughter of James Lorton. She died October 2, 1890. They had five children.

396 LEE O.,[6] b. Jan. 3, 1880.
397 MARY C.,[6] b. July 26, 1881.
398 JAMES M.,[6] b. July 26, 1883.
399 THOMAS H.,[6] b. Aug. 23, 1885.
400 JOHN J.,[6] b. Nov. 2, 1888.

John S. was married second, August 6, 1893, to Sarah Ball. They have two children.

401 ADA,[6] b. April 16, 1894.
402 SUDA,[6] b. Feb. 10, 1896.

268. William Roscoe,[5] son of 110 Minos N.[4] and Mary E. [Jones] Balch, was born October 5, 1866, and was married October 12, 1887, to Mary, daughter of John N. and Mary E. Ball.

272. Alice,[5] daughter of 111 John C.[4] and M. C. [Baker] Balch, was born July 23, 1852, and was married first, December 30, 1869, to James Martin, who died February 21, 1883. They had one daughter, Henrietta, who was born in 1873, and was married April 22, 1896, to William A. Rutherford, and one son, John L., who was born Jan. 16, 1881.

Alice was married second, April 22, 1885, to John M. Cook. They live at Batesville, Arkansas, and have one son, Robert, and one daughter, Marshall.

275. Jonah H.,[5] son of 111 John C.[4] and M. C. [Baker] Balch, was born December 22, 1858, at Tyro, Mississippi, and is a farmer at Cache, Arkansas. He was married July 28, 1878, to Alice, daughter of John Crabtree. They have nine children.

403 BRADFORD H.,⁶ b. Dec. 28, 1880.
404 MARCELLUS G.,⁶ b. Aug. 19, 1882.
405 ELMINA,⁶ b. Dec. 7, 1883.
406 CORENNA,⁶ b. Oct. 16, 1886.
407 FOSTINE,⁶ b. June 25, 1889.
408 MYRTLE MAY,⁶ b. May 5, 1891.
409 GRACE,⁶ b. April 18, 1893.
410 ROELL,⁶ } b. Jan. 28, 1896.
411 IDELL,⁶ }

278. **Baker F.,**⁵ son of 111 John C.⁴ and M. C. [Baker] Balch, was born June 15, 1867, and is a farmer at Rufus, Arkansas. He was married July 1, 1888, to Sarah J., daughter of John N. and Mary E. Ball. They have had three children.

412 SARAH,⁵ b. Sept. 2, 1889.
413 OLIE,⁵ b. Sept. 30, 1891; died Dec. 20, 1891.
414 STANLY,⁵ b. Oct. 29, 1893; d. Dec. 5, 1893.

280. **Samuel Walker,**⁵ son of 120 George Bell⁴ and Margaret S. [Walker] Balch, was born January 28, 1852, at Lerna, Illinois, and was married November 25, 1875, to Malissa Catharine, daughter of Capt. Robert E. Y. and Mary [Vanmeter] Williams. Their children were born in Coles county, Illinois.

415 MARY MARGARET,⁶ b. Oct. 9, 1876; senior at Jacksonville college.
416 CHARLES ADAMS,⁶ b. Dec. 11, 1879; student in Lincoln University.
417 HORACE REED,⁶ b. Sept. 22, 1885.

Rev. Samuel W. farmed and taught school until 1883, and then engaged in mercantile business at Lerna, and studied for the ministry. In September, 1885, he was received into the Illinois Conference, in which he has since successfully preached at the following appointments: Cowden, 1885; Stewardson, 1886; Humbolt, 1888; Homer, 1891; Jacksonville, 1893; Lincoln, 1896.

281. **Elizabeth Jane,**⁵ daughter of 120 George Bell⁴ and Margaret S. [Walker] Balch, was born September 18, 1853, and was married April 21, 1875, to Frank, son of James and Mary McCrory, who is a merchant at Charleston, Illinois. They are Presbyterians, and have had eight

children: Mary, b. March 1, 1876; Lelia, d. y.; Clara, James Balch, Bertha, Esther.

283. **Thomas Alexander,**[5] son of 120 George Bell[4] and Margaret S. [Walker] Balch, was born October 8, 1858, and is a farmer at Lerna, Illinois, a Presbyterian, and a Republican. He was married September 6, 1883, to Louisa America, daughter of William J. and Ellen J. Hughes. They have five children.

418 ELLEN MABEL,[6] b. Oct. 31, 1884.
419 THOMAS MACK,[6] b. Feb. 24, 1887.
420 HARRY HUGHES,[6] b. Dec. 11, 1889.
421 ROBERT MORTON,[6] b. Oct. 31, 1892.
422 WILBUR LELAND,[6] b. May 13, 1896.

284. **Nancy McDonald,**[5] daughter of 120 George Bell[4] and Margaret S. [Walker] Balch, was born October 8, 1858, and was married April 19, 1884, to A. D. Stephenson, who is a farmer at Charleston, Illinois. They are Methodists, and have four children: Florence, b. 1885; Thomas Balch, b. 1887; George, b. 1889; Ralph, b. May 10, 1896.

285. **Esther Rebecca,**[5] daughter of 120 George Bell[4] and Margaret S. [Walker] Balch, was born June 20, 1861, and was married February 22, 1883, to William L., son of Parker and Harriet Clark, a farmer at Surprise, Nebraska. They have five children: Harry Willis, b. Jan., 1884; George Parker, b. Dec., 1886; Millie Fern, b. July, 1889; Margaret Ellen, b. Sept. 5, 1896.

286. **Ellen Dixon,**[5] daughter of 120 George Bell[4] and Margaret S. [Walker] Balch, was born January 31, 1863, and was married August 8, 1888, to John Newton, son of John D. and Eliza Jane Faris, who was born March 20, 1860, in Coles county, and owns a farm near Lerna, Illinois. They are Presbyterians, and have two children: George Balch, b. Dec. 3, 1889; Bertha, b. July 10, 1895.

290. **Robert E.,**[5] son of 120 George Bell[4] and Margaret S. [Walker] Balch, was born March 26, 1871, and is a farmer at Lerna, Illinois. He was married in September,

1891, to Joanna, daughter of Bennett and Nancy [Allison] Nicholson.

296. **Sarah Caroline,**[5] daughter of 121 James Alexander[4] and Patience Ann [Nicholson] Balch, was born October 14, 1865, at Lerna, Illinois, and was married September 1, 1886, to Daniel Webster, son of William and Sarah [Hughs] Ewing. They are Presbyterians, and have had two children : Arthur Balch, b. Sept. 18, 1888; Howard William, b. Jan. 14, 1891, d. March 1, 1891.

298. **John Parker,**[5] son of 128 David Lawson[4] and Eliza P. [Andrews] Balch, was born February 8, 1859, and is a pharmacist at Jackson, Tennessee. He was married March 11, 1883, to Annie, daughter of Robert F. and Euphrasia E. Stribling, who was born August 1, 1863. Their children were born at Jackson.

423 ANNIE FAY,[6] b. Nov. 8, 1884; d. March 15, 1885.
424 DAVID LYELLE,[6] b. Aug. 19, 1889.
425 TERRELL ANDERSON,[6] b. Feb. 24, 1891.

299. **Richard Lawson,**[5] son of 128 David Lawson[4] and Eliza P. [Andrews] Balch, was born May 29, 1860, and is a drygoods salesman, living at Jackson, Tennessee. He was married April 8, 1884, to Mary, daughter of Alfred Anderson and Elizabeth [Rice] Wilbon, who was born May 12, 1864, at Charlotte Court House, Virginia. They have one child, born at Jackson.

426 MARY ELIZA,[6] b. Nov. 5, 1893.

301. **William Dean,**[5] son of 128 David Lawson[4] and Eliza P. [Andrews] Balch, was born September 5, 1863, and was married February 5, 1889, to M. Flora Harris, of Glasgow, Kentucky. They have one child.

427 WILLIAM DEAN,[6] b. June, 1893.

314. **John Franklin,**[5] son of 139 Wallace Watts[4] and Pamela [McCann] Balch, was born August 12, 1838, enlisted in the 8th Illinois Volunteers in the spring of 1861, was in the battles of Bird's Point and Fort Henry, and was killed February 16, 1862, in the charge on Butler's battery,

in the battle of Fort Donelson, and was buried on the battlefield. He married Martha A., daughter of John and Rebecca Gordon, and they had two children, one dying young.

428 FRANCIS,[6] b.

315. William Wallace,[5] son of 139 Wallace Watts[4] and Pamela [McCann] Balch, was born May 24, 1840, near Janesville, Illinois, where he has a farm. He was married November 8, 1866, to Mahala Elizabeth, daughter of Timothy and Sarah Hickle, who was born December 28, 1839, in Delaware county, Ohio. They are Cumberland Presbyterians, and have had seven children.

429 JAMES WALLACE,[6] b. Oct. 1, 1867; d. Nov. 25, 1867.
430 EMMA BERNICE,[6] b. Sept. 10, 1868.
431 TIMOTHY HICKLE,[6] b. May 14, 1871; d. July 10, 1871.
432 SALLIE JANE,[6] b. April 18, 1872; d. Oct. 1, 1872.
433 WILLIAM DAVID,[6] b. Dec. 12, 1873.
434 FLORA ALICE,[6] b. Nov. 16, 1876; d. April 1, 1877.
435 DIASIE ALTHENA,[6] b. Jan. 21, 1879; d. May 21, 1879.

William W. enlisted in September, 1862, in the 5th Illinois Cavalry, served three years, and was, among others, in the battles of Doniphan, Missouri, Pocahontas, Arkansas, Vicksburg, Mechanicsburg, and Jacksonville.

316. Malissa Althana,[5] daughter of 139 Wallace Watts[4] and Pamela [McCann] Balch, was born October 26, 1842, near Janesville, Illinois, where she died January 8, 1862. She married Edwin, son of John and Rebecca Gordon, who was born in Coles county, and they had two children, Alonzo Carlton and Henry Augustine.

317. Theron Emmet,[5] son of 139 Wallace Watts[4] and Pamela [McCann] Balch, was born May 9, 1845, and is a farmer at Georgetown, Illinois. He was in the Union Army during the Civil War. He married Diantha, daughter of George Catlin, of Charleston, Illinois, and they have had eight children, two dying young.

436 FRANKLIN,[6] b. 1867.
437 MINNIE,[6] b. 1869.
438 CATHERINE,[6] b. 1873.

439 FREED,[6] b. 1875.
440 LIBBIE,[6] b. 1877.
441 ALICE,[6] b. 1880.
442 MATT,[6] b.

319. Mary Alpha,[5] daughter of 139 Wallace Watts[4] and Pamela [McCann] Balch, was born July 26, 1850, and was married July 4, 1871, to Grandison, son of Robert and Jane Foote, who was born December 2, 1849, and died March 23, 1890. They lived near Janesville, and had seven children: Bertie Oren, b. Jan. 31, 1872 ; Clarinda Manda, b. July 26, 1874 ; Estella Jesto, b. June 25, 1877 ; Robert Winford W., b. Aug. 26, 1881, d. y. ; Alice Pamela, b. Dec. 13, 1883 ; Hughey, b. Oct. 8, 1885 ; Elsie Jane, b. July 18, 1887, d. Aug. 5, 1888.

321. James Hezekiah,[5] son of 141 Hezekiah J. E.[4] and Elizabeth C. [Elam] Balch, was born November 16, 1845, at Vandalia, Illinois, and was married December 5, 1867, to Mary Isabella, daughter of John and Virena E. [Newlin] Newlin, of Georgetown, Illinois. They live at Terra Haute, Indiana, and have had five children.

443 LIZZIE FLORA,[6] b. Oct. 23, 1868; d. Dec. 18, 1880.
444* JOHN NEWLIN,[6] b. Jan. 30, 1871.
445 MARY ELMA,[6] b. Feb. 15, 1873; d. Dec. 19, 1880.
446 SAMUEL EMMET,[6] b. May 20, 1875.
447 JAMES FRANKLIN,[6] b. July 7, 1878.

322. Samuel Olay,[5] son of 141 Hezekiah J. E.[4] and Elizabeth C. [Elam] Balch, was born March 23, 1850, and was married November 12, 1873, to Mary Etta Hartshorn, of Buckley, Illinois. They had one child.

448 BLANCHE,[6] b. Dec. 30, 1874; d. 1890.

Dr. Samuel C. was a physician in the Medical Board of the Pension Office at Washington, D. C., and is now at Los Angeles, California. He has adopted two orphan girls, whose father was a colonel in the Confederate army.

323. George Theron,[5] son of 143 William Boyd[4] and Mary Ann [Faris] Balch, was born July 9, 1847, at Campbell, Illinois, and was married January 27, 1877, to Nancy Caroline, daughter of Andrew and Evaline Allison, who was

born November 30, 1858, in Coles county. They have four
children.

449 MARY EVELINE,[6] b. March 6, 1881.
450 SUSAN HELEN,[6] b. Feb. 19, 1883.
451 FLORA EMMA,[6] b. Nov. 8, 1885.
452 NELLIE ALLISON,[6] b. Sept. 29, 1895.

George T. is a farmer and school teacher, and owns a
large farm near Lerna, Illinois. He is an elder in the Pleasant Prairie Presbyterian church, and for several years has
been superintendent of the Sunday school.

325. Thomas Craig,[5] son of 143 William Boyd[4] and
Mary Ann [Faris] Balch, was born January 19, 1852, and is
a Methodist minister at Cooper, Cherry county, Nebraska.
He was married May 10, 1876, to Cenora Abigail, daughter
of Richard and Martha Horton. They have five children.

453 EARL,[6] b. Nov. 27, 1878.
454 PAUL,[6] b. June 4, 1881.
455 THOMAS CRAIG,[6] b. April 23, 1885.
456 RUTH,[6]   } twins, b. Aug. 25, 1887.
457 BLANCHE,[6]

Rev. Thomas C. taught school for nine winters. In 1879
he taught near the Kickapoo M. E. church, in Coles county,
Illinois. He and his wife transferred their membership from
the Presbyterian to this church. He was licensed and
preached for a year in Illinois, and for over seven years in
Nebraska, and has had signal success with the lawless ele-
ment of the plains. In 1896 he bought a ranch near Gordon, Nebraska.

327. Susan Martha,[5] daughter of 143 William Boyd[4]
and Mary Ann [Faris] Balch, was born December 2, 1855,
and was married March 19, 1872, to Jacob Phipps, who was
born in Coles county, Illinois, was in the 5th Illinois Cavalry, and died in 1895. Eight children were born on their
farm near Campbell, Illinois: Pelia, Ann, William, Jacob,
Henry, Eva, Alpha.

328. Mary Alpha,[5] daughter of 143 William Boyd[4]
and Mary Ann [Faris] Balch, was born April 11, 1858, and
married Dr. Oscar L. Wilson. They live at Rushville, Ne-

braska, and have had three children, born in Janesville, Illinois: James, Mary, Beatrice.

329. Emma Ann,[5] daughter of 143 William Boyd[4] and Mary Ann [Faris] Balch, was born August 12, 1863, and married Benjamin McNeel. They live at Noxon, Montana, and have had one child, who died young.

332. William Tell,[5] son of 144 John Moorehead[4] and Elizabeth Amanda [Campbell] Balch, was born September 4, 1850, at Campbell, Illinois, and was married April 23, 1879, to Ann, daughter of Austin and Harriet Rice. They live at Croake, Illinois, belong to the United Brethren, and have no children.

333. Alpha Ann,[5] daughter of 144 John Moorehead[4] and Elizabeth Amanda [Campbell] Balch, was born November 9, 1853, and was married to Mark Kelly, of Cumberland county. They are Presbyterians, and have three children.

SIXTH GENERATION.
Descendants of James Balch.

358. William Calvin,[6] son of 207 Joseph Cameron[5] and Mary R. [Erskine] Balch, was born January 9, 1868, and was married October 2, 1893 to Nellie Dana Drake. They live at Los Angeles, California, and have two children.

458 EARL,[7] b. Jan. 6, 1895.
459 NELLIE ETTA,[7] b. 1896.

377. Rufus Walker,[6] son of 258 Leonidas Colwell[5] and Elizabeth F. [Walker] Balch, was born October 3, 1869, in Panola county, Mississippi, and is a lawyer in partnership with his father at Little Rock, Arkansas. He was married July 28, 1892, to Jessie P. Vineyard. They have one child.

460 WALKER COLWELL,[7] b. July 22, 1893.

444. John Newlin,[6] son of 321 James Hezekiah[5] and Mary Isabella [Newlin] Balch, was born January 30, 1871, and was married July 3, 1893, to Carrie Bell, daughter of Isaac and Sarah [Crow] Scott at Crisman, Illinois. They live at Terre Haute, Indiana, and have had one child.

461 HEZEKIAH EMMET,[7] b. Dec. 25, 1894.

Rev. Hezekiah Balch, D. D.

FIRST GENERATION.

1. **Hezekiah Balch,**[1] was born in 1741, on the north side of Deer Creek, in the neighborhood of "Bond's Hope," Maryland, and died at Greenville, Tennessee, in April, 1810. His father is said by tradition to have also been named Hezekiah, and he was probably a cousin of James Balch, of Maryland, the head of the preceding family. He was twice married, first to Hannah Lewis. She possessed a fine intellect and great personal attractions, but in after life was under some mental derangement. They had six children.

    2* DORCAS,[2] b. ; d.
    3* ELIZABETH,[2] b. 1771; d. March 11, 1795.
    4 WASHINGTON,[2] b. ; d.
    5* JOHN TENNANT,[2] b. ; d.
    6 SAMUEL,[2] b. ; d.
    7* ELIJAH WHITFIELD,[2] b. ; d. 1822.

Rev. Hezekiah Balch, D. D., married second in 1808, Ann, daughter of Robert Luckey, of New York State. She was born in Pennsylvania, and died in 1835, aged 72 years, at Jonesborough, Tennessee. They had no children.

Rev. Dr. Balch had dark, lustrous eyes, an erect frame, and commanding presence. Frankness, intrepidity and earnestness characterized his address, but strong convictions and rash impulses led him into many bitter strifes. Between 1758 and 1762 he was a student at Princeton College, but the college records show that he graduated in 1776 in the class with Rev. Hezekiah James Balch. When Orange Presbytery in North Carolina was formed, in 1770, he was ordained as an evangelist. At Greenville, Tennessee, in 1783, he assisted in the regular organization of Mount Bethel church. Under his pastorate Dr. Watts' version of the Psalms was introduced, against violent opposition, but the church took the lead in the valley of the Holston and Tennessee rivers, and was the scene of constant and at times of powerful revival. At this time Dr. Balch, with his predecessor in church and educational work, Dr. Samuel Doak, participated in efforts to organize the chaotic elements of the short-lived state of Franklin.

Greenville College, the first west of the Alleghany mountains, was founded by him, and a charter obtained August 20, 1794. It was located on a large farm three miles south of Greenville, which he had purchased, and he ably presided over it until his death, sixteen years later. He made long tours south and east in the interest of the college, and, while travelling north in 1795, was much impressed with finding that those ministers whose religious sentiments were questioned were of the most assistance in obtaining donations. His spirit of inquiry led him to embrace the views of Dr. Samuel Hopkins, known as Hopkinsianism. Then followed a civil suit to eject him and his adherents from the meeting house, besides which he was called to trial sixteen times before the Presbytery, four times before the Synod, and once before the General Assembly. At this last he made a profound impression, as he contended that his views were the Bible truth. His answer to the charges brought against him was accepted by a clear majority, and he was by obvious implication acquitted. During these trials his scholars, to the number of nearly a hundred, were neglected and obliged to go home. On his return, in the midst of a most tumultuous scene, he retired with a large part of his congregation to a wide-spreading tree and read the papers relating to his trial. Under it he conducted services for several months, until the decision in the civil suit restored the meeting house to them as the ascertained majority.

A lightning stroke, by which he lost his barn, hay and horse, was interpreted by his persecutors as a token of God's anger, but so great was his sense of God's love and adorable sovereignty, that to him the burning of his property was a joyful opportunity for him, by abasing himself in the dust, to exalt his God. At the death of his wife, his words were: " Blessed be God, absolute, unconditional submission to His will is a plaster sufficient for every sore." In his will he gave his soul to his God to be made for Christ's sake, in boundless grace, an eternal vessel of mercy in Heaven, or in righteous judgment for his sins, a vessel of everlasting wrath in hell. Thus did Dr. Balch refuse to make conditions with God, but cordially submitted without reserve for time and for eternity.

An extended biography of Dr. Balch, by his co-worker and successor in Greenville College, Rev. Charles Coffin, D. D., is in Sprague's Annals of the American Pulpit, and other accounts are in Foot's Sketches of North Carolina and the History of the Synod of Tennessee.

SECOND GENERATION.

Descendants of Rev. Hezekiah Balch, D.D.

2. **Dorcas,**[2] daughter of 1 Rev. Dr. Hezekiah[1] and Hannah [Lewis] Balch, was born in North Carolina, and married Mr. Wiley, a merchant in Greenville, Tennessee. They had one son, Samuel Y., who graduated from Princeton in 1838.

3. **Elizabeth,**[2] daughter of 1 Rev. Dr. Hezekiah[1] and Hannah [Lewis] Balch, was born in 1771, in North Carolina, and died March 11, 1795, in East Tennessee. She was married to Rev. Robert Henderson. They had no children.

5. **John Tennant,**[2] son of 1 Rev. Dr. Hezekiah[1] and Hannah [Lewis] Balch, was born at Greenville, and was cast off by his father for dancing. He was a merchant, and was several terms in the Legislature. He married Mrs. Allie [Badger] Dennis. They lived and died at Greenville, and had ten children.

8   ELIZABETH,[3] b. 1808; d.; m. Robert Ray.
9a   JOHN TENNANT,[3] b. Dec. 1, 1809; d. Dec. 12, 1861.

10* HEZEKIAH,[2] b. 1811; d. 1870.
11 PAULINA,[2] b.   ; m. Alexander Jones, lived at Greenville.
12 MATILDA,[2] b.   ; m. T. Thomas.
13* SAMUEL,[2] b. d. 1873 Cooks Mill. Ill.
14 MARIA,[2] b.   ; m. Benson Frazier.
15 ALLIE,[2] b.   ; m. Saddler.
16* ANDREW JACKSON,[2] b.
17 ADELAIDE,[2] b.

7. **Elijah Whitfield,**[2] son of 1 Rev. Dr. Hezekiah[1] and
Hannah [Lewis] Balch, was born at Greenville, Tennessee,
and died in 1822, on the College farm. He was a farmer,
and married Mollie, daughter of George Green. They had
eleven children, born in Greenville.

18 SAMUEL,[2] b.   ; d.
19 ELIZABETH,[2] b.   ; .d.
20* HEZEKIAH B.,[2] b.   ; d.
21 SARAH,[2] b.   ; d.
22* JOHN,[2] b. Sept. 6, 1812.
23 GEORGE WASHINGTON,[2] b. 1814; d.
24 ISABELLA,[2] b. 1816; d.
25 ELIJAH W.,[2] b.   ; d.
26 LUCINDA,[2] b.   ; d.
27 MARIA LEWIS,[2] b.
28 WILLIAM GREEN,[2] b.   ; d.

THIRD GENERATION.
Descendants of Rev. Hezekiah Balch, D.D.

9. **John Tennant,**[3] son of 5 John Tennant[2] and Allie
[Badger] Balch, was born December 1, 1809, and died December 12, 1861, at Mindon, Louisiana. He married Sarah
R., daughter of Nathaniel and Mary V. [Grur] Blackmore,
who was born May 5, 1819, at Fayetteville, Tennessee. They
had ten children.

29* MARY VANCE,[4] b. Sept. 9, 1840.
30* LUCINDA,[4] b. April 5, 1842.
31* JOHN TENNANT,[4] } twins, b. Apr. 28, 1844; } m. J. S. Tult, 4 sons.
32 ALLIE,[4]
33 CATHARINE,[4] b. June 4, 1846; d. April 1, 1867.
34 ANDREW GRUR,[4] b. June 13, 1848; d. April 13, 1851.
35 NATHANIEL B.,[4] b. April 15, 1850; d. Sept. 2, 1851.

36 SAMUEL MILLER,[4] b. June 14, 1852; d. Feb. 28, 1872.
37* LILA S.,[4] b. May 17, 1854.
38 CHARLES HEZEKIAH,[4] born Dec. 7, 1857; d. Jan. 29, 1889.

Rev. John T. studied for the ministry against his father's wishes, and graduated from Greenville College, and in 1836 from Princeton Seminary. He supplied at Tuscumbia, Alabama, Mt. Carmel, Tennessee, Green Lake, Texas, Oak Island and Mindon, Louisiana. He taught Latin to President Andrew Johnson, who, in payment for the instruction, made his clothes.

10. **Hezekiah,**[3] son of 5 John Tennant[2] and Allie [Badger] Balch, was born in 1811, and died in 1870, at Arkadelphia, Arkansas. He was a Methodist minister, married, and left two sons.

13. **Samuel,**[3] son of 5 John Tennant[2] and Allie [Badger] Balch, was born at Greenville, Tennessee, and died in Madison county, Illinois. He married, and left two daughters.

16. **Andrew Jackson,**[3] son of 5 John Tennant[2] and Allie [Badger] Balch, was born at Greenville, Tennessee, and married Miss Volis, of Madison county, Illinois, by whom he had two children.

43 ANNIE,[4] b. ; m. James Montgomery, and lived at Ash Grove, Mo.
44 SAMUEL M.,[4] b. ; lived in Indian Territory.

20. **Hezekiah B.,**[3] son of 7 Elijah Whitfield[2] and Mollie [Green] Balch, was born at Greenville, Tennessee, and was married about 1842 to Ann Christian. They moved to Vicksburg, Mississippi, where their four sons were born.

45 THEODORE H.,[4] b. Feb. 18, 1844; d. Aug. 10, 1861.
46 ARTHUR S.,[4] b. Dec. 25, 1849.
47 WILLIE G.,[4] b. May 21, 1851; d. 1854.
48* ALFRED WILEY,[4] b. Aug. 16, 1852.

22. **John,**[3] son of 7 Elijah Whitfield[2] and Mollie [Green] Balch, was born September 6, 1812, and is a blacksmith at Chireno, Texas. He was married January 12, 1841, to Elizabeth, daughter of Joseph and Bethany Rogers, who was

born August 14, 1826, in Jefferson county, Alabama. Their
eleven children were born in Nacogdoches county, Texas.

49   JOSEPH ELIJAH,[4] b. Sept. 13, 1842; d. March 30, 1863.
50   HANNAH MARIA,[4] b. June 8, 1845.
51   HEZEKIAH B.,[4] b. March 14, 1848.
52   WILLIAM ALFRED,[4] b. July 21, 1850.
53   ROBERT SAMUEL,[4] b. Jan. 5, 1853.
54   MARY ELIZABETH,[4] b. Aug. 7, 1856.
55   JOHN HOUSTON,[4] b. Aug. 2, 1859.
56   GEORGE WASHINGTON,[4] b. Nov. 4, 1861.
57   STEBULUN CARROLL,[4] b. March 22, 1865; d. Sept. 18, 1865.
58   ARTHUR MIDDLETON,[4] b. April 26, 1868; d. Sept. 12, 1871.
59   FANNIE BELLA,[5] b. April 18, 1873.

FOURTH GENERATION.

Descendants of Rev. Hezekiah Balch, D.D.

29. Mary Vance,[4] daughter of 9 Rev. John Tennant[3]
and Sarah [Blackmore] Balch, was born September 9, 1840,
at Mt. Carmel, Tennessee, and was married to George R.
Means. They live at Mexica, Texas, and have six children.

30. Lucinda,[4] daughter of 9 Rev. John Tennant[3] and
Sarah [Blackmore] Balch, was born April 5, 1842, at Norris-
town, Arkansas, and was married first to Edward A. Means,
by whom she had one daughter. Mr. Means died, and she
married, second, James Carroll, by whom she had four children.

31. John Tennant,[4] son of 9 Rev. John Tennant[3] and
Sarah [Blackmore] Balch, was born April 28, 1844, at Nor-
ristown, Arkansas, and served four years in the Confederate
army. In the fall of 1869 he left Bryan, Texas, for New
Orleans, to dispose of some real estate belonging to his
mother in Louisiana. He registered on board the vessel, and
nothing was heard from him afterward. The family were
convinced that he was murdered and thrown overboard. He
was married to Miss Alice Beall, and they had one daughter.

60   KATE,[5] b.   ; m. F. C. Hunnam.

37. **Lila S.,**[4] daughter of 9 Rev. John Tennant[3] and Sarah [Blackmore] Balch, was born May 17, 1854, at Oak Island, Texas, and was married, first, to James McCallum, and had three daughters. She was married, second, to Singleton Trawich, and had two children.

48. **Alfred Wiley,**[4] son of 20 Hezekiah B.[3] and Ann [Christian] Balch, was born August 16, 1852, and is a farmer at Mansfield, Texas. He was married June 19, 1876, to Mary E. Roberts, who was born November 29, 1855 in White County, Tennessee.

WILLIAM BALCH.

FIRST GENERATION.

1. William Balch,[1] of Sparta, Tennessee, is said by two of his grandchildren to have been a brother of Rev. Hezekiah Balch, of Greenville, Tennessee. He lived for a time at Columbus, South Carolina, where he married Rebecca McClelland, after which he moved to Sparta, where he died about 1827. They had nine children.

2* ROBERT McC.,[2] b. Dec. 7, 1797; d. Dec. 11, 1857.
3 REBECCA,[2] b.   ; d.   ; m. Alexander Glenn.
4 MARY,[2] b.   ; d.   ; m. William Glenn.
5* WILLIAM,[2] b. June 10, 1801; d. Aug. 24, 1870.
6 MARGARET,[2] b.   ; d.   ; m. Drury Wammack.
7 JOHN,[2] b.   ; disappeared 1829.
8 SARAH,[2] b.   ; drowned, unm.
9 ELIZABETH,[2] b.   ; d.   ; m. Samuel Williamson.
10* HEZEKIAH,[2] b. 1811; d. July 24, 1873.

SECOND GENERATION.

Descendants of William Balch.

2. Robert McClelland,[2] son of 1 William[1] and Rebecca [McClelland] Balch, was born December 7, 1797, at Columbus, South Carolina, and died December 11, 1857, at Avoca, Alabama, where he was engaged in farming and stock raising. He was married first, March 13, 1822, to Nancy Ann, daughter of Edward and Sarah Helton. She was born June 4, 1803, at Tullahoma, Tennessee, and died July 4, 1841. They had five children.

11 WILLIAM,[3] b. May 6, 1823; d. 1865.
12* EDWARD,[3] b. June 19, 1825; d. April 17, 1882.
13* SARAH,[3] b. May 20, 1831.

14 MARGARET ELIZABETH,[3] b. March 6, 1833; d. July 6, 1877; m. Jack Kirby.
15 ROXY ANN,[3] b. Aug. 21, 1840.

Robert McC. married second, Hannah Wright, by whom he had one daughter.

16* MARTHA ANN,[3] b. May 11, 1844.

5. **William,**[2] son of 1 William[1] and Rebecca [McClelland] Balch, was born June 10, 1801, and died August 24, 1870, at Cad Grove, Texas. For a time he was a farmer at Paduca, Kentucky. In 1828 he moved to Illinois, and the next year returned to Tennessee for his mother and brothers, John and Hezekiah. While on the way John disappeared in the night, and was never afterward heard from. William moved to Texas in 1848. In 1820 he married Phœbe, daughter of Morgan and Sarah Bryant, who was born December 13, 1806, in Tennessee, and died July 24, 1858, at Alvarado, Texas. They had eleven children.

17* SARAH,[3] b. July 15, 1821; d. Feb., 1850.
18* EVAN R.,[3] b. June 21, 1823.
19* REBECCA M.,[3] b. Nov. 19, 1825; d. 1858.
20* JOHN B.,[3] b. March 5, 1827; d. Feb. 13, 1873.
21 WILLIAM M.,[3] b. Nov. 19, 1829; d., s. p. Feb. 22, 1852.
22* ELIZABETH M.,[3] b. July 21, 1833.
23 PHŒBE ANN,[3] b. July 22, 1834; d., s. p. Aug. 25, 1858.
24 JAMES H.,[3] b. April 17, 1837; d. March, 1852.
25 ROBERT F.,[3] b. March 10, 1841; d. Feb. 9, 1849.
26* LUCINDA,[3] b. Aug. 12, 1844.
27* MARY A.,[3] b. Jan. 1, 1848.

William married second, in 1859, Miss Phœbe Farber, and they had four children, born at Alvarado, Texas.

28* JOSEPH A.,[3] b. May 24, 1860.
29 LANISA,[3] b.   ; d. y.
30* SAMUEL BOONE,[3] b. Feb. 24, 1864.
31* MARGARET LOUELLA,[3] b. Oct. 28, 1866.

10. **Hezekiah,**[2] son of 1 William[1] and Rebecca [McClelland] Balch, was born in 1811, and died July 24, 1878, in Madison county, Alabama, where he was engaged in farming, milling, and stock raising. He was married in August,

1840, to Tabitha, daughter of Mecager and Dicy Vaughn.
She was born in 1822, and died June 24, 1874. They had
thirteen children.

    32 WILLIAM M.,[2] b. Dec. 12, 1841.
    33 LOUISA J.,[2] b. 1843.
    34 ROBERT M.,[2] b. Jan. 14, 1844.
    35 JOHN E.,[2] b. 1847; d. 1864.
    36 SARAH R.,[2] b. May 18, 1849; d. July 22, 1869.
    37 JAMES H.,[2] }
    38 TABITHA M.,[2] } twins, b. Dec. 16, 1850.
    39ª SAMUEL WILLIAMSON,[2] b. Dec. 17, 1852.
    40 ANN,[2] b. 1854.
    41 GEORGE A.,[2] b. Feb. 10, 1856.
    42 MARY M.,[2] b. May 22, 1858; d. Nov. 22, 1889.
    43 RUFUS F.,[2] b. Jan. 16, 1861.
    44 MARTHA F.,[2] b. Sept. 1, 1863.

THIRD GENERATION.

Descendants of William Balch.

12. **Edward,**[3] son of 2 Robert McC.[2] and Nancy Ann
[Helton] Balch, was born June 19, 1825, and died April 17,
1882. He married Bella Hillion, and they lived at Avoca,
Alabama, where their children were born.

    45 SARAH ANN,[4] b. March 31, 1847; d. July 7, 1874.
    46 JOHN,[4] b. Oct. 30, 1848.
    47 NANCY E.,[4] b. Feb. 20, 1852.
    48 JAMES,[4] b. Dec. 2, 1854; d. Jan. 14, 1892.
    49 MARY E.,[4] b., Dec. 9, 1856.
    50 MARGARET F.,[4] b. Feb. 15, 1860; d. Nov. 15, 1890.
    51 MARTHA C.,[4] b. Dec. 15, 1868.
    52 MARGARET ELLEN,[4] b. Nov. 24, 1869; d. Dec. 20, 1890.

13. **Sarah,**[3] daughter of 2 Robert McC.[2] and Nancy Ann
[Helton] Balch, was born May 20, 1831, and married J. M.
Briley, a farmer.   They have three children, born at Avoca,
and one at Ora, Alabama: Floral Clementine, b. July 22,
1859 ; Samantha Bell, b. Dec. 30, 1861 ; William B., b. May
26, 1870 ; Sarah A., b. Sept. 21, 1873.

16. **Martha Ann,**[3] daughter of 2 Robert McC.[3] and

Nancy Ann [Helton] Balch, was born May 11, 1844, and
was married February 7, 1868, to J. W., son of Moses and
Martha Ann Crownover, who was born March 7, 1842, was a
farmer and carpenter, and died September 10, 1883. They
had five children : Ella, b. Oct. 17, 1865, d. Oct. 1, 1889 ;
Benjamin, b. April 20, 1868, d. July 3, 1886 ; Thomas B., b.
Oct. 2, 1872, d. April 29, 1876 ; George Walter, b. Aug. 19,
1877 ; Regna, b. Nov. 3, 1880.

17. **Sarah,**[3] daughter of 5 William[2] and Phoebe [Bryant]
Balch, was born July 15, 1821, and died in February, 1850,
at Paducha, Kentucky. She married S. S. Wilson, of New
Jersey, and they had one son, William H., who is a carriage-
maker.

18. **Evan R.,**[3] son of 5 William[2] and Phoebe [Bryant]
Balch, was born June 21, 1823, at Sparta, Tennessee, and is
a farmer and carpenter at Fort Worth, Texas. He was mar-
ried July 1, 1852, to Tasira, daughter of John and Mary
Pyle, who was born December 19, 1829, in Illinois, and died
February 11, 1873. Their two eldest children were born at
Duquoin, Illinois, the fourth at Allenville, Missouri, and the
others in Texas.

53*   JOHN WILLIAM,[4] b. Sept. 22, 1853.
54   JAMES ROBERT,[4] b. June 23, 1855; d. Oct. 24, 1855.
55   MARY JANE,[4] b. Jan. 8, 1857; d. Jan. 27, 1862.
56*   SONORA ELLEN,[4] b. July 27, 1859.
57*   VETURIA ANN,[4] b. Dec. 13, 1861.
58   ELDORADO,[4] b. Jan. 3, 1864; d. March 2, 1865.
59   SARATO NEVADA,[4] b. April 8, 1866.
60   UDENA FAUSTINE,[4] } twins, b. March 13, 1869.
61   UVENA ETHELDA,[4] }

Evan R. was living in Texas at the outbreak of the civil
war, and although a Union man, was drafted and compelled
to serve sixteen months in the Confederate army. He was
not in any battle, and received no pay for his services. In
1848 he went to Texas with his father, but between 1852 and
1855 was in Illinois, and between 1857 and 1860 was in Gentry county, Missouri. Next he lived near Alvarado, Texas,

for ten years, then spent two years in Arkansas, and has since been at Fort Worth.

19. Rebecca M.,[3] daughter of 5 William[2] and Phoebe [Bryant] Balch, was born November 19, 1825, and died in 1853, in Texas. She married H. R. McClure. They lived in Illinois, and had one son, Joseph, b. March 10, 1844, who is married, and lives at Fort Worth, Texas.

20. John B.,[3] son of 5 William[2] and Phoebe [Bryant] Balch, was born March 5, 1827, at Sparta, Tennessee, and died February 13, 1873, at Little Elm, Texas. He went to Texas with his father in 1848, and engaged in farming. On the breaking out of the civil war he at once volunteered in the Confederate army, but his health soon gave out, and he was discharged. In 1850 he married Mary Ann, daughter of John and Delia [Cox] King, who was born at Little Elm. Their children were born at Alvarado, except the youngest, who was born at Little Elm.

62 WILLIAM MORGAN,[4] b. July 10, 1853; d. Nov. 15, 1855.
63 ALEXANDER.[4] b. May 5, 1856; d. March 20, 1890.
64 EVALINE,[4] b. Sept. 6, 1858.
65 JEFFERSON DAVIS,[4] b. June 30, 1861.
66 JOHN PERRY,[4] b. July 20, 1863.
67 GERTRUDE ADELINE,[4] b. Oct. 7, 1865.
68 BEATRICE,[4] b. April 7, 1873.

22. Elizabeth M.,[3] daughter of 5 William[2] and Phoebe [Bryant] Balch, was born July 21, 1833, in Illinois, and lives at Gainsville, Texas. She was married June 10, 1852, to David D., son of James Myers, who was born in 1851, in South Carolina, and is a farmer. They have had six children, born at Alvarado, Texas: William H. H., b. Aug. 22, 1853; Phoebe I., b. June 10, 1855; Mary E., b. April 20, 1857. d. y.; Samuel I., b. July 23, 1858; George W. B., b. Feb. 20, 1861; Malynda E., b. Dec. 4, 1863.

26. Lucinda,[3] daughter of 5 William[2] and Phoebe [Bryant] Balch, was born August 12, 1844, in Illinois, and lived at Sherman, Texas. She was married April 15, 1866, to Joseph S., son of William R. Vestal, of Arkansas. He was born September 6, 1844, and died August 2, 1885. They had seven children, born at Sherman, Texas: William S., b. June 27, 1867, d. Oct. 80, 1870; Imogene, b. April 27, 1869; Leonidas, b. Jan. 10, 1872; Brice, b. April 16, 1875; Mildred, b. April 13, 1877; James, b. Oct. 6, 1879; Claudius F., b. March 6, 1882, d. June 23, 1884.

27. **Mary A.,**[3] daughter of 5 William[2] and Phoebe [Bryant] Balch, was born January 1, 1848, in Illinois, and lives at Crockett, Texas. She was married first, April 22, 1866, to William R., son of William R. and Nancy Vestal, who was born February 8, 1846, in Arkansas, and died October 8, 1873. They had three children: Selman B., b. June 8, 1867; William S., b. June 27, 1870; Allie G., b. July 26, 1873.

She was married second, July 15, 1875, to Christopher C. Teswick, who was born in November, 1888, in South Carolina, and died April 27, 1888. They had three children: Lelah Ida, b. March 17, 1878; Lassa A., b. Nov. 17, 1881; Hugh H., b. Jan. 3, 1884.

28. **Joseph A.,**[3] son of 5 William[2] and Phoebe [Farber] Balch, was born May 24, 1860, at Alvarado, and is a farmer at Denton, Texas. He was married October 25, 1885, to Della, daughter of James and Angeline Cunningham, who was born March 9, 1860, in Coffee county, Tennessee. They have three children.

69 SAMUEL V.,[4] b. Sept. 13, 1886.
70 THOMAS R.,[4] b. July 13, 1888.
71 SORATA P.,[4] b. March 6, 1891.

30. **Samuel Boone,**[3] son of 5 William[2] and Phoebe [Farber] Balch, was born February 24, 1864, at Alvarado, Texas, and is a dealer in live stock at Kansas City, Missouri. He was married January 16, 1893, to Cecelia Evangeline, daughter of Michael and Ellen L. Mulvihill, who was born October 13, 1872, at Kansas City.

31. Margaret Louella,[3] daughter of 5 William[2] and Phoebe [Farber] Balch, was born October 28, 1866, and was married August 29, 1886, to William P., son of William and Mary B. Strain, who was born May 20, 1849, in Bradlee county, Tennessee. Their children were born at Millsap, Texas: Luther Alee, b. July 3, 1887; Bena Dona, b. Dec. 25, 1888; Mary Phoebe, b. Dec. 21, 1890; Milo Balch, b. Dec. 20, 1892.

39. Samuel Williamson,[3] son of 10 Hezekiah[2] and Tabitha [Vaughn] Balch, was born December 17, 1852, near Huntsville, Alabama, and is a farmer, and has a steam mill and gin at Nebo, Alabama. He has served the township as superintendent and trustee for fourteen years, and has been postmaster for seven years. He is justice of the peace, and a deacon in the Baptist church. He was married December 12, 1875, to Martha Ann Parsons, an adopted daughter of James and Ellen Dublin. She was born July 22, 1856, in Madison county, Alabama. They have ten children.

72 HENRY HEZEKIAH,[4] b. Jan. 6, 1877.
73 JOHN THOMAS,[4] b. Aug. 10, 1878.
74 ELLEN,[4] b. Aug. 20, 1880; d. Oct. 21, 1880.
75 JOSEPH AUSTIN,[4] b. Sept. 5, 1881.
76 BURTA LEON,[4] b. Oct. 27, 1883.
77 NOEL LUTHER,[4] b. Feb. 15, 1886; d. June 18, 1888.
78 TABITHA ANN,[4] b. March 29, 1889.
79 BULA OSA,[4] b. Jan. 27, 1891.
80 SAMUEL ALLEN,[4] b. Nov. 22, 1892.
81 ROBERT LESTER,[4] b. May 5, 1895; d. Sept. 28, 1895.

FOURTH GENERATION.
Descendants of William Balch.

53. John William,[4] son of 18 Evan R.[3] and Tasira [Pyle] Balch, was born September 22, 1853, and is a carpenter at Wellington, Texas. He was married July 1, 1877, to Sarah Ann, daughter of John H. and Mary [McSims] Bean, who was born February 1, 1860, in Arkansas. Their children were born at Cedar Hill, Texas.

82 WILLIAM HENBY,[5] b. May 2, 1878.
83 IRENA VIOLA,[5] b. Aug. 7, 1880.
84 RUFUS LYCUREUS,[5] b. Nov. 18, 1882.
85 LEONA BEATRICE,[5] b. Sept. 29, 1885.
86 EVAN OSCAR[5], b. Nov. 16, 1888; d. Oct. 16, 1889.
87 MINNIE ESSIE,[5] b. Dec. 21, 1890.

56. Sonora Ellen,[4] daughter of 18 Evan R.[3] and Tasira [Pyle] Balch, was born July 27, 1859, and was married April 23, 1884, to John A., son of Anderson and Susan Temple, who was born August 8, 1856, at Wheeling, West Virginia. They live at Fort Worth, Texas, and have one child, Aldie Ronald, b. June 19, 1888, at Los Angeles, California.

57. Veturia Ann,[4] daughter of 18 Evan R.[3] and Tasira [Pyle] Balch, was born December 13, 1861, and was married December 3, 1884, to William B., son of William J. and Roxa Parker, who was born April 23, 1854, in Alabama. They live and their children were born at Dunconville, Texas: James McFarlin, b. Nov. 10, 1885 ; Tela Ellen, b. April 6, 1887 ; William Horace, b. Dec. 7, 1890.

UNCONNECTED FAMILIES.

ISRAEL BALCH.

1. Israel Balch[1] was born about 1768, and died in 1833. The only clew to his parentage is a statement by his son that three of his ancestors were English. He is reported to have come from Topsham, Massachusetts, to Keene, New Hampshire, and there married Lucretia Wyman, and had two children, who died in Keene. They then moved to Shrewsbury, Vermont, and bought the farm on which their grandchild, Daniel, now lives. They had five children.

2　LUCRETIA,[2] b.　; d.　; m. Nathaniel Lewis.
3　LORINA,[2] b.　; d.　; m. Starkey.
4　EMILY,[2] b.　; d.　; m. William Phalen.
5　ISRAEL,[2] b.　; d.
6*　ISAAC HARMON,[2] b. 1813; d. July 12, 1879.

6. Isaac Harmon,[2] son of 1 Israel[1] and Lucretia [Wyman] Balch, was born in 1813, and died July 12, 1879, at Shrewsbury, Vermont. He married Harriet Gilman, and seven of their nine children grew up.

7　HARMON,[3] b.　; d.
8　LUCRETIA,[3] b.　; d.
9　NANCY,[3] b.　; d.
10*　DANIEL,[3] b. 1835.
11　HARRIET,[3] b.　; d.
12　EMILY,[3] b.
13*　ISRAEL,[3] b. Aug. 27, 1831.

10. Daniel,[3] son of 6 Isaac Harmon[2] and Harriet [Gilman] Balch, was born in 1835, and lives on his grandfather's farm at Shrewsbury, Vermont. He was married in 1857 to Julia A. Phimley, and they have seven children.

14 HARMON,[4] b.
15 CHAUNCEY,[4] b.
16 WILLIAM,[4] b.
17 GEORGE,[4] b.
18 EDMOND,[4] b.
19 CARRIE,[4] b.
20 DORA,[4] b.

13. Israel,[3] son of 6 Isaac Harmon[2] and Harriet [Gilman] Balch, was born August 27, 1851, and is a dealer in lime at Plymouth Union, Vermont. He was married in 1871 to Stella Daniels, who was born August 15, 1851. They have had three children.

21 WILLIE,[4] b. ; d. y.
22 ANNA,[4] b. Jan. 9, 1874.
23 BURTON,[4] b. June 10, 1875.

WILLIAM D. BALCH.

1. William D. Balch,[1] whose ancestry has not been traced, was born in Northfield, or Gouldsville, Vermont, served in the war, and died Oct. 12, 1862, at New Orleans. He married Zilpha Kinsman, and they had one son and nine daughters, of whom eight grew up, but the names of only two have been ascertained.

2[a] HENRY CLAY,[2] b. May 7, 1844; d. April 7, 1887.
3 SARAH,[2] b ; m., first, Priest; m., second, Sweatt; lives at Salisbury, N. H.

2. Henry Clay,[2] son of 1 William D.[1] and Zilpha [Kinsman] Balch, was born May 7, 1844, at Gouldsville, Vermont, and died April 7, 1887, at Leominster, Mass. He was in a Vermont regiment, and was a manufacturer of horn goods. He was married September 11, 1872, to Altie H., daughter of Luke W. and Matilda Brooks. She was born June 5, 1853, at Townsend, Mass., and lives at Leominster. Their first child was born at East Saginaw, Michigan, the other two at Leominster.

4[a] ALFRED WILLIAM,[3] b. Aug. 27, 1873.
5 LILLIAN MAUD,[3] b. Aug. 7, 1876; m. Sept. 13, 1895. G. V. Kent.
6 IRVING BURTON,[3] b. Jan. 25, 1879.

4. **Alfred William**,[3] son of 2 Henry Clay[2] and Altie H. [Brooks] Balch, was born August 27, 1873, graduated in 1894 from the Massachusetts College of Pharmacy, and is a student at the Harvard Medical School.

JOHN TENNANT BALCH.

1. **John Tennant Balch** was born at Baltimore, Maryland, in 1844, and is a locomotive engineer, living at Atlanta, Georgia. Concerning his ancestry, he has reported indirectly that his line of descent is from James Balch of Mecklenburg, North Carolina, as follows: James[1], Hezekiah[2], John[3], John[4], John Tennant[5]. His father, John[4], was married first to Ruth Blackmore, and had three sons, Andrew, Nathaniel, and John Tennant. John[4] was married second to E. E. Brainard, a school teacher from Massachusetts.

John T. served four years in the Confederate army, and in 1867 was married to Eugema Ireson, of Abbeville, Virginia. They have three children.

2 SEOTA MAY, b   ; m. —— Hudson.
3 MARY ELIZABETH, b   ; m. —— Pelot.
4 CHARLES T., b.   ; was private secretary to Hoke Smith.

DANFORTH BALCH.

1. **Danforth Balch**, whose ancestry has not been traced, crossed the plains in 1847, and took up a donation claim of 348 acres of land on what is now the northwest corner of Portland, Oregon. Here he cleared about 20 acres, lived with his wife Mary Jane, and nine children were born. On October 17, 1859, he died. Then commenced a studied plan of legal robbery and twenty-four years of litigation, through which the minor children were turned out upon the world, without education or property, with the exception of John, who saved about $5,000. The children were as follows:

2 Ann Hamilton, b. 1844; lives in Portland.
3 Hosea, b. 1846; lives in California.
4 John, b. 1854; lived on Sauvies Island, near Portland.
5 Daniel, b. 1855.
6 Celeste, b.
7 Emma, b. 1858; lives at Olympia, Wash.
8 Louis, b.

HENRY BALCH.

1. **Henry Balch**[1] was born June 26, 1828, at Bruton, Somerset county, England, came to the United States in 1848, and settled at Westchester, now a part of New York city, where he now lives. His father's name was Henry. He was married to Margaret Boone, and they have had seven children.

2 Henry,[2] b. July 14, 1855; d. 1893.
3* William,[2] b. Oct. 14, 1859.
4 Bella,[2] b. 1862; m. Jessie Robinson.
5 Robert,[2] b. 1865.
6 Mary,[2] b. 1868; m. William Mallet.
7 Annie,[2] b. 1871; m. George Harrison.
8 Margaret,[2] b. 1872.

3. **William**,[2] son of 1 Henry[1] Margaret [Boone] Balch, was born July 14, 1855, and is a coachman living in New York city. He was married March 10, 1887, to Kate Readon, and they have four children.

9 Josephine,[3] b. Oct. 5, 1888.
10 Margaret,[3] b. July 16, 1891.
11 Henry,[3] b. July 20, 1894.
12 Kate,[3] b. Dec. 11, 1896.

.. WILLIAM HIGGINS BALCH.

1. **William Higgins Balch**[1] was born June 2, 1834, at South Brewham, Somerset county, England, and died December 18, 1889, at Cleveland, Ohio. His father's name was Harry. He was married April 7, 1880, at Cleveland, to

Eliza Maria Lee, who was born at Plymouth, England. Their children were born at West Cleveland.

   2 HARRY LEE,[2] b. Feb. 24, 1881.
   3 FRANK VICTOR,[2] b. Nov. 24, 1883.
   4 RALPH MACY,[2] b. March 5, 1885.

EDWARD T. BALCH.

1. **Edward T. Balch**[1] came to the United States with his father when a child. His grandfather was buried in the family vault in West Ham Abbey, near London, in **1846**. Their estate was then in chancery, and had been for fifty years. He is a physician at Santa Barbara, California.

JOHN BAULCH.

John Baulch came to the United States from England in 1880, and became prominently connected with the New York city fire department. He was commissioned colonel of the 73d New York Volunteers, known as the Second Fire Zouaves, which he assisted in organizing, but owing to the consolidation of the regiment he saw no field service. Two sons were born in the United States: William Baulch, a post trader at Fort Monroe, Virginia; John J. Baulch, a Mason and Knight Templar, and freight agent of the St. Louis Bridge and Tunnel Company.

FREDERICK BAULCH.

Frederick Baulch came to the United States from Stoke, Sub-Hamdon, Somersetshire, England, in 1884, and is a bicycle manufacturer and dealer at Detroit, Michigan. His father, William, was born about 1832, and was drowned in June, 1896. His grandfather, William, was born about 1809, and died in 1894, and his great-grandfather, Simeon, died about 1887, aged over ninety. Five generations were living at one time.

ADDENDA.

PAGE 11.

Abigail Clarke died June 1, 1690.

PAGE 29.

40. **Israel⁴** married Ruth, daughter of Edward and Mary [Haskell] Dodge.

PAGE 47.

Ann Kettell died in 1779.

PAGE 50.

116. **Joshua⁵** married Sarah Tower.

PAGE 55.

Hannah, daughter of Joseph and Hannah [Atkinson] Clement, was born January 29, 1734, and died October 10, 1788.

PAGE 58.

Lydia Twombley died January 18, 1837.

PAGE 62.

GROVE's daughters were: *Frances A.*, d. aged 12. *Laura M.*, b. April 20, 1825, d. Dec. 15, 1896, at Lowell, Mass.; m. Joseph H. Ely, son of James Ely a missionary in the Sandwich Islands. He was born there in 1823 and died in 1874. They had two children, Josephine L., b. April 16, 1858; d. June 3, 1890. Frederick W., b. Dec. 3, 1860; lives at Greenfield, N. H.

PAGE 71.

182. **Jonathan⁶** died January 4, 1812. Abigail Williams was born August 13, 1751.

380 KATHARINE,⁷ d. Dec. 30, 1866; m. Nehemiah Wright Skillings; three daughters: Elizabeth Wright, d. y.; Katharine, d. 1894 in Boston; Anna, b. Dec. 14, 1814, d. Aug. 19, 1894; m. 1835, Dr. Austin Flint.

382ᵃ SAMUEL WILLIAMS,⁷ d. Dec. 1, 1819; see Addenda page 133.

387   ABIGAIL,[7] d. May 2, 1878.
388   ANN,[7] d. April 29, 1884.

PAGE 72.

187. Israel[6] died February 9, 1825. He was married February 2, 1773, to Hannah Kimball. She died in October, 1784.

PAGE 79.

229. Archalaus[6] was a private in Capt. Nathaniel Gage's company of Lexington Alarm militia.

PAGE 91.

Mrs. Betsy [Clay] Balch died July 18, 1858.

PAGE 104.

BETSY H., d. March 4, 1892.

PAGE 105.

NANCY L., d. January, 1893.

PAGE 114.

318. Emily[7] was married May 9, 1826.

PAGE 116.

Delia Persons died October 1, 1896.

PAGE 132.

377. Bezaleel[7].

PAGE 133.

379. Jonathan[7] died September 11, 1803. He was married in 1800, and had two sons.

786 JONATHAN,[8] b. Dec., 1801; died Oct. 12, 1803.
787 THOMAS HASTINGS,[8] b.   ; d. aged 18 months.

382. Samuel Williams[7] was the first merchant from the United States to settle with his family and trade from the empire of Brazil. He lived at Rio Janeiro, where he was minister for the United States. In 1816 he removed to New Orleans, where he died December 1, 1819. He was benevolent, judicious and persevering. He spoke nineteen languages with accuracy, and visited all parts of the world. He was married August 29, 1810, at Rio Janeiro, to Maria Randolph, daughter of William Holmes, of Thoms River, New

Jersey. She was rescued by him from a Brazilian convent, where she was imprisoned for refusing to wed a Spanish nobleman. They had five children.

787a* THOMAS SUMTER,[6] b. Feb. 29, 1812; d. 1884.
787b* MARIA GLORIANA,[5] b. May 20, 1814.
787c* EMILIA ABIGAIL,[5] b. July 1, 1816.
787d* NATILIE CATHARINE,[5] b. 1817.
787e* LOUISA ANNA DAVIDSON,[5] b. Dec., 1819; d. Nov. 20, 1885.

384. David[7] was drowned at sea.

PAGE 135.

393. Polly[7] died October 10, 1848. She was married in August, 1798, to Isaac Winchester, who was born April 19, 1777, and died November 9, 1858. Their children were as follows :

RUTH E., b. Feb. 5, 1800, d. unm. Sept. 26, 1854.
HIRAM, b. May 1, 1804, d. Dec. 27, 1877.
SUSAN A., b. July 28, 1806, d. Feb. 25, 1850; m. Cass. Granddaughter Mrs. P. H. Dreiser, Redlands, Cal.
MARY, b. July 9, 1808, d. April 11, 1841; m. Samuel Tweed, grandson F. Elliot Durfee, Providence, R. I.
LUTHER, b. July 18, 1810. Son Frank B., Providence, R. I.
WILLIAM B., b. Sept. 4, 1811, d. Jan. 12, 1867; granddaughter, Mrs. Osmar Reynolds, Pelham Manor, N. Y.
MERSILVIA, b. Dec. 29, 1813, d. May 10, 1848; m. Preston.
ADELINE, b. Dec. 30, 1815, d. Nov. 28, 1866; m. Henry Potter Knight. Children: *Edward Balch, M. D.*, b. March 27, 1845; *Amelia Sumner*, b. Nov. 18, 1848; *Henry Clifford*, b. Sept. 8, 1853, d. Jan. 3, 1879.
LYDIA A. B., b. Oct. 29, 1818, d. Aug. 10, 1888; m. Edwin D. Elliot; son *William C.*, Providence, R. I.
ISAAC TRASK, b. Feb. 2, 1821, lives at Boston, Mass.
GILMAN K., b. March 11, 1823, lives at Providence, R. I.

PAGE 141.

Catherine [Thomas] Balch died September 24, 1859.

PAGE 154.

985 MARY HARRIS,[5] b. May 7, 1830; d. Dec. 5, 1833.
996 HELEN MARIA,[5] b. May 14, 1833; d. Feb. 14, 1834.

Louisa died January 15, 1894.

PAGE 157.

1002   Albert Battelle,[8] d. March 22, 1897.

PAGE 220.

Lydia Shepard Balch was born in 1784 and died in 1872.

1399   Sophrona,[9] m. Prof. Powers of New York state.

PAGE 339.

Sarah Balch Lawrence died March 10, 1897.

George F. Lawrence died January 16, 1891.

PAGE 355.

1402.   **Benjamin Franklin**[9] died in the fall of 1895.

EXPLANATORY NOTES.

Each person bearing the Balch name is designated by a number. Wherever, in the tabulated lists of children, this number is followed by an asterisk [*] it indicates that the person is more fully described in the next chapter.

The small figures, following the names, indicate the generations removed from the first known settler in America.

The abbreviations are: b., born; d., died; d. y., died young; d. s. p., died without children; m., married; unm., unmarried.

Wherever the genealogy of a female is extended in small type, the names of her children are printed in small capitals; the names of the grandchildren are printed in italics; and the names of great-grandchildren and persons marrying into the family are printed in ordinary type.

Dates are uniformly given throughout this work according to the calendar in vogue at the times they designate, all prior to September 3, 1752, being old style, and all subsequent to September 14, 1752, being new style. Prior to 1752 it was not the custom to begin the new year until the twenty-fifth of March, so that events occurring in January, February and March up to the twenty-fourth were usually dated at the time in the years preceding the ones in which it is now necessary to regard them as having taken place, in order to correctly compute their anniversaries. Wherever such dates are given both years are noted, the first being the year currently written, and the second being the historical year, by which it is now customary to remember the date. The old-style calendar was ten days ahead of the present calendar, prior to March, 1700, and eleven days ahead between March, 1700, and September 3, 1752. To bring an old-style date over to new style, for the purpose of ascertaining its true anniversary, the ten or eleven days' difference should consequently be added.

INDEX.

PERSONS BEARING THE BALCH NAME.

(535)

Numbers refer to pages.

Numbers refer to pages.

Numbers refer to pages.

Numbers refer to pages.

OTHER NAMES THAN BALCH.

Numbers refer to pages.

Numbers refer to pages.

Numbers refer to pages.

Numbers refer to pages.

Numbers refer to pages.

Printed in the USA
CPSIA information can be obtained
at www.ICGtesting.com
LVHW020846140923
PP17886900001B/12